7 seventh edition

CRIME PREVENTION

approaches, practices and evaluations

STEVEN P. LAB
Bowling Green State University

 **LexisNexis®**

 **anderson publishing**
A member of the LexisNexis Group

Crime Prevention, Seventh Edition

Copyright © 1988, 1992, 1997, 2000, 2004, 2007, 2010
Matthew Bender & Company, Inc., a member of the LexisNexis Group
New Providence, NJ

Phone 877-374-2919
Web Site www.lexisnexis.com/anderson/criminaljustice

Library of Congress Cataloging-in-Publication Data

Lab, Steven P.
Crime prevention : approaches, practices, and evaluations / Steven P. Lab. — 7th ed.
    p. cm.
Includes index.
ISBN 978-1-4224-6327-7 (softbound)
1. Crime prevention—United States. 2. Crime prevention—United States—Evaluation. I. Title.

HV7431.L33 2010
364.40973—dc22   2010006984

Cover design by Tin Box Studio, Inc.   EDITOR   Elisabeth Roszmann Ebben
                                              ACQUISITIONS EDITOR   Michael C. Braswell

Last digit is the print number: 10 9 8 7 6 5 4 3 2

TABLE OF CONTENTS

Chapter 1 Crime and the Fear of Crime 1

The Problem of Crime in Society 2
 Official Measures of Crime 2
 Measuring Victimization 6
 Summary 7
The Costs of Crime/Victimization 8
The Fear of Crime 9
 The Discovery of Fear 10
 Defining Fear 10
 Measuring Fear 10
 The Level of Fear 12
 Fear and Crime 13
 Fear and Demographics 14
 Explaining the Divergent Findings 15
  Vicarious Victimization 15
  Perceived Risk and Harm 15
  Incivility 16
  Methodological Factors 17
  Crime and Fear 17
  Benefits of Fear 18
 Fear Summary 18
Summary 18

Chapter 2 Crime Prevention 21

Crime Prevention Through the Ages 22
 Summary 25
Defining Crime Prevention 26
The Crime Prevention Model 27
 Primary Crime Prevention 27
 Secondary Crime Prevention 29
 Tertiary Crime Prevention 29
 Alternate Models and Crime Science 30
Summary 31

Chapter 3 Evaluation and Crime Prevention 33

Types of Evaluation 34
 Impact Evaluation 34

Process Evaluation   36
Cost-Benefit Evaluations   37
Theory and Measurement in Evaluation   38
Theoretical Concerns   38
Measurement Issues   40
Follow-Up Periods   41
Summary   42
The Method for Evaluation   42
Experimental Design   42
Realistic Evaluation   46
Summary   48
An Overview of the Book   48

Section I   **Primary Prevention**   **49**

Chapter 4   The Physical Environment and Crime   51

Crime Prevention Through Environmental Design   52
Access Control   55
Surveillance   55
Activity Support and Motivation Reinforcement   56
Implementation of Environmental Design   56
The Impact of Physical Design   57
The Effects of Individual Factors   58
Lighting   59
Surveillability   60
CCTV   61
Property Identification Programs   63
Alarms   64
Locks, Doors, and Related Access Factors   65
Street Layout and Traffic   65
Summary   66
Physical Design of Neighborhoods   67
A Challenge to Defensible Space   69
Summary   70
Product Design   70
Incivility, Disorder, and Crime   73
Summary   74

Chapter 5   Neighborhood Crime Prevention   79

Types of Neighborhood Crime Prevention Approaches   82
Neighborhood/Block Watch   82
Commmunity Anti-Drug Programs   84
Citizen Patrols   84
Police-Community Involvement   85
Evaluation of Neighborhood Crime Prevention   85
Effects on Community Cohesion   86
Effects on Crime   87

Official Records   87
Victimization Measures   88
Two Examples—Kirkholt and Safer Cities   89
Summary   91
Community Anti-Drug Programs   91
Citizen Patrols   92
Neighborhood Crime Prevention and Fear of Crime   93
Evaluation Issues   95
Citizen Participation and Support   96
Who Participates?   97
Organizing Neighborhood Crime Prevention   99
Summary   102
Chapter Summary   102

Chapter 6   Displacement and Diffusion   105

Crime Displacement   106
Types of Displacement   107
Assumptions   108
Assessing Displacement   110
Displacement: Benign or Malign?   111
Diffusion   112
Offender Choice and Mobility   113
Routine Activities   114
Rational Choice   116
Crime Pattern Theory   118
Summary   121
Evidence of Displacement and Diffusion   121
Displacement Effects   121
Territorial Displacement   122
Temporal Displacement   123
Tactical Displacement   124
Target Displacement   124
Functional Displacement   125
Displacement Summary   125
Diffusion Effects   126
Implications of Displacement and Diffusion   127

Chapter 7   The Mass Media and Crime Prevention   129

The Media and Crime   130
The Level of Reported Crime   130
Media Accounts and Actual Crime   131
Does the Media Cause Crime and Fear?   132
Media and Crime   132
The Media and Fear   134
Summary   135
Mass Media Crime Prevention Activities   135
The McGruff Prevention Campaign   136

Taking a Bite Out of Crime   137
The First Evaluation   137
The Second Evaluation   139
Summary   139
Other Campaigns   139
Crime Newsletters   140
Information Lines   143
Crime-Time Television   145
Publicity and Prevention   146
The Media's Responsibility for Crime Prevention   147
Summary   148

Chapter 8   General Deterrence   149

Deterrence   150
Requirements for Deterrence   151
The Deterrent Effect of Legal Sanctions   152
Cross-Sectional Analyses   153
Severity of Sanctions   153
Certainty of Punishment   154
Combining Severity and Certainty   155
Summary   155
Longitudinal Research   156
Severity of Sanctions   156
Certainty of Apprehension   158
Panel Studies   159
Summary   160
Perceptions and Deterrence   161
Perceived Certainty   162
Perceived Severity   164
Combined Deterrence Factors   164
Summary   166

Section II   Secondary Prevention   167

Chapter 9   Prediction for Secondary Prevention   169

Predicting Future Offending   170
Types of Prediction   172
Clinical Prediction   172
Actuarial Predictions   173
Criminal Career Research   175
Prediction and Crime Prevention   176
Risk Factors and Prediction   176
Family Factors   178
Peer Factors   179
Community Influences on Behavior   179
Psychological/Personality Factors   180
Biological Risk Factors   180
Using Risk Factors as Predictors   181

Predicting Places and Events   182
   Hot Spots for Crime   182
      Repeat Victimization   184
   Summary   189
Implications for Crime Prevention   190

Chapter 10   Situational Crime Prevention   191

The Growth of Situational Prevention   192
The Theoretical Basis   193
The Process of Situational Prevention   194
Situational Typologies   195
   Clarke's 12 Techniques   195
   Expanding the Typology   197
Issues and Concerns with Situational Prevention   200
Situational Prevention Studies   202
   Studies of Crimes against Transit Systems   202
   Motor Vehicle Theft   204
   Theft Offenses   205
   Revictimization   206
   Child Sexual Assault   207
Summary   207

Chapter 11   Partnerships for Crime Prevention   209

Community Policing   210
   Precursors to Community Policing   211
   Defining Community Policing   211
      Community Involvement   213
      Problem Solving   213
      Community Base   214
      Redefined Goals   214
      Summary   214
Problem Identification   215
Partnership Efforts and Assessment   217
   Community Policing   217
   Civil Abatement   218
   "Weed and Seed" Programs   220
   CCP, SACSI, and PSN   221
   Gun Violence   222
   Crime and Disorder Partnerships   223
   Gang Suppression Programs   224
   Problems and Concerns   225
Successful Partnerships   225
Summary   227

Chapter 12   Drugs, Crime, and Crime Prevention   229

The Scope of Drug Use   231
   Self-Reported Drug Use   231

Drug Use Among Offending Populations   233
Summary   235
The Drugs-Crime Connection   235
Interventions and Prevention   238
    Law Enforcement Efforts   238
    Treatment of Drug Users   239
        Maintenance Programs   240
        Therapeutic Communities   241
        Outpatient Drug-Free Programs   242
        Detoxification   242
        Summary and Further Comments   242
    Prevention Programs   243
        Education/Information/Knowledge Programs   244
        Resistance Skills Training   245
        Summary of Prevention Programs   246
Drugs and Crime Prevention   247

Chapter 13   The School and Crime Prevention   249

Theoretical Views   250
Educational Factors and Delinquency   252
    IQ and Delinquency   252
    School Practices and Delinquency   253
    Victimization and Fear in School   254
    Summary   257
School Programs for Delinquency Prevention   257
    Preschool Programs   257
    Elementary and High School Programs   259
        School Atmosphere   259
        Conflict Management/Resolution   261
        Anti-Bullying Efforts   265
        Altering Teaching and Assessment   265
    Alternative Schools   266
    Other Interventions   267
The Future of School/Educational Programs in Crime
Prevention   269

Section III   Tertiary Prevention   **271**

Chapter 14   Specific Deterrence and Incapacitation   273

The Specific Deterrent Effect of Criminal Sanctions   274
    Studies of Imprisonment   275
    Arrest for Domestic Violence   277
    Summary   278
Incapacitation   279
    The Collective Incapacitation of Imprisonment   280
    The Selective Incapacitation of Imprisonment   282
    Electronic Monitoring   284
Future Implications   290

Chapter 15   Rehabilitation   293

The "What Works?" Argument   294
    Subsequent Analyses   295
    Outcome Measures   296
    Levels of Evaluation   297
    Summary   298
Evaluations of Recent Rehabilitation Programs   298
    Cognitive-Behavioral Interventions   299
    Intensive Supervision   300
    Restorative Justice   301
        Victim-Offender Mediation   302
        Family Group Conferencing   303
        Circle Sentencing   303
        The impact of Restorative Justice   304
        Summary   305
    Drug Courts   306
Assessing Rehabilitation and Crime Prevention   309

Chapter 16   Some Closing Thoughts on Crime Prevention and the Future   311

The State of the Evidence   312
Improving Our Knowledge   314
Recognizing the Diversity in Crime Prevention   315
Summary   316

Glossary   317
References   335
Name Index   391
Subject Index   397

To Danielle

Chapter 1

CRIME AND THE FEAR OF CRIME

Key Terms:

fear

fearing subject

functional fear

gatekeepers

incivility

NCVS

panel survey

Part I crimes

Part II crimes

Uniform Crime Reports

vicarious victimization

victimization surveys

Learning Objectives:

After reading this chapter you should be able to:

- Identify and discuss two different measures of crime and victimization

- Discuss the changing crime rates in the U.S.

- Identify shortcomings with the UCR

- Explain how a panel survey works

- Discuss the NCVS and what it shows about victimization

- Provide information on the costs of crime/victimization

- Give a definition of fear and discuss how it manifests itself

- Explain the differences between fear, worry and assessments of crime

- Discuss the levels of fear in society and how fear relates to crime and victimization

- Define vicarious victimization

- Provide reasons for the reported levels of fear

- Define incivility and show how it relates to fear

Crime remains an indisputable fact of life for many, if not most, members of modern society. This is true despite the frequent declarations that crime continues to fall and is reaching levels not seen in years. While the overall level of crime has fallen in recent years, large numbers of citizens are still victimized every year, and for those individuals crime remains a problem. Beyond those who are actually victimized, many individuals are fearful of crime and victimization. That fear has consequences of its own for those who are fearful and for our communities. Crime and fear lead most individuals to turn to the criminal justice system for help. The ability of the criminal justice system to single-handedly alleviate crime and fear in society has been seriously questioned by both proponents and opponents. Despite the claims by some that the reductions in crime since the early 1990s are due to concerted police actions, there is little reason to believe that actions of the criminal justice system are the primary (or sole) cause of the reductions. At the same time, crime and fear still impact the lives of many individuals. Society clearly needs to continue to pursue means of preventing crime and fear.

This first chapter attempts to show how crime and fear have changed over time and remain problems that need to be addressed. It is this information that forms the basis for continued calls for crime prevention actions. After examining the level and change in actual crime in society, this chapter will examine the impact of crime on victims and society. It will also examine the companion issue of fear of crime. Indeed, the "fear of crime" poses a greater, more far reaching problem for society and its members. Demonstrating a need for crime prevention is not difficult to accomplish when you consider the levels of crime and fear in society.

THE PROBLEM OF CRIME IN SOCIETY

The magnitude of the crime problem can be evaluated using both official and victimization measures of crime. The use of official crime statistics, such as the Federal Bureau of Investigation's *Uniform Crime Reports*, provides a view of crime from the standpoint of what the formal criminal justice system must handle. Many critics argue that this provides an inaccurate and incomplete analysis of the true levels of crime in society. These individuals point to the results of victimization surveys as a basis for their argument. While each presents a different absolute level of crime, both tend to reveal similar patterns in criminal activity over time.

Official Measures of Crime

The FBI *Uniform Crime Reports* (UCR) are the most widely used and cited official measures of crime in the United States. The UCR represents the number of criminal offenses known to the police. The reported crime rate reflects only those offenses known as *Part I crimes* (violent crimes: murder, rape, robbery, and assault; property crimes: burglary, larceny, auto theft, and arson). A host of other offenses (i.e. fraud, kidnapping, and drug offenses), known as *Part II crimes*, are not included in the computations and reported crime rates. The resulting crime rates, therefore, reflect only a portion of the offenses with which the formal criminal justice system comes into contact.

Other official crime measures include criminal court filings, conviction records, and jail populations. Each of these alternate measures provides increasingly narrower views of the level of crime because they reflect only cases that have been not been filtered out of the system at an earlier stage of processing. For example, the police control (to a large extent) the number and types of problems that enter the formal justice system. Thus, the police are often referred to as the *gatekeepers* of the criminal justice system. Few offenders or cases enter the criminal justice system without first being processed by the police. The police make the decision to arrest, file reports, and refer the cases to the prosecutor and, subsequently, to the court and correctional arenas. Consequently, any measure of crime based on system processing after the police stage reveals smaller numbers of offenses and offenders than the UCR. The police figures appearing in the UCR are the most inclusive of all official measures. Our interest in the official level of crime in society, therefore, is best indicated by the UCR.

According to the UCR, there were more than 11 million index crimes committed in 2008. Of that number, more than 1.3 million were personal crimes (murder, rape, robbery and aggravated assault) and almost 10 million were property offenses (Federal Bureau of Investigation, 2009). This translates into 3,667 index crimes for every 100,000 people in the United States (also known as the "crime rate"). The corresponding crime rates for personal and property crime are 454.5 and 3,212.5, respectively. Conklin (2003) notes that many individuals compare these figures to those from the mid-1980s and early 1990s and trumpet the great decreases in crime. Even further, these figures are used by various groups to take credit for the decreases: police leaders claim that aggressive police tactics caused the decline, mayors have pointed to wider ranging community policies as the cause, and politicians claim that mandatory sentencing laws caused the changes (Conklin, 2003). While determining the cause of the reductions is important, it is beyond the scope of this book to attempt that task. What is more important is to place the "great reductions" in crime into context.

The trend in violent and property crime since 1961 is shown in Figures 1.1 and 1.2. Figure 1.1 illustrates that the 2008 violent crime rate has fallen almost to the levels in 1975–1977. Thus, it is a true claim that violent crime is lower today than any time in almost 30 years. Similar claims can be made about property crime, although the reference point would be roughly 1969 (see Figure 1.2). Interestingly, all of the levels in these two figures are significantly higher than they were in the 1960s when the President's Commission

Figure 1.1
Change in Violent Crime Rate (per 100,000 population)

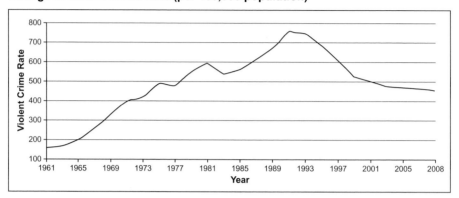

Figure 1.2
Change in Property Crime Rate (per 100,000 population)

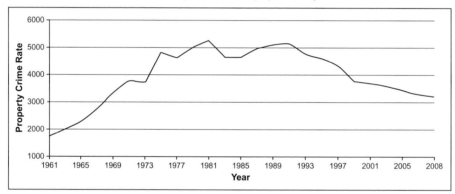

on Law Enforcement and the Administration of Justice lamented the great growth in crime and the need to do something about it.

The crime rates today are significantly higher than what existed throughout the 1960s and the early 1970s. This is especially problematic if you consider the data for violent crimes, which are those crimes that most concern people. Figure 1.1 shows that the violent crime rate in 1961 was 158 offenses for every 100,000 persons. This was less than one-third of the rate in 1977, which is the benchmark against which the recent "reduced rates" are compared. Similarly, the property crime rate in 1961 (1,748) was less than half of the 1973 rate (Figure 1.2). In both cases, the recent figures are still significantly higher than those of 30 to 40 years ago when society was lamenting the high crime it was facing. The property crime rate in 2008 is roughly twice the rate in 1961, while the personal crime rate is roughly three times as high. This suggests that those who point to the great strides made combating crime should be careful not to congratulate themselves too much.

While the UCR shows a large number of crimes are committed in the United States, it still comes under fire from a variety of sources for underreporting the actual level of crime in the country. O'Brien (1985) points out that concerns over the way the data is collected and how the police learn about crime lead many to question the validity of the results. Foremost among the concerns is the question of whether the police records and reports provide an unbiased, complete view of crime in society. Popular wisdom would answer this question with a resounding "No!" Examination of the UCR reveals three major points at which the UCR can be inaccurately adjusted.

First, the UCR is a voluntary system of data collection. It is possible for police departments to adjust their figures in order to enhance the image of their operation and/or their jurisdiction. Police funding is based on service delivery and productivity is often measured by the crime figures they report (O'Brien, 1985). As a result, it may be in the best interests of the department to alter its collection and reporting practices in order to make itself look better. Interestingly, this may be accomplished through both increasing and decreasing the level of crime. For example, an increase in the reported crime rate may be touted as an indication of better police work and improved police effectiveness. This would be especially true if the police had previously announced a "crackdown" on a selected crime and then wished to demonstrate their success. Similarly, a decrease in the level of crime may be pointed to as deterrence brought on by improved police performance.

A second major problem with the UCR involves the ability of individual police officers to adjust the crime rate. Any officer can refrain from making an arrest or a formal report on an incident. Such activity may allow the officer to deflect minor or unimportant events away from an already overburdened criminal justice system. More importantly, however, such discretion factors into a distorted and underrepresented crime rate. Departmental policies may also contribute to this shift in reported crimes. Administrative procedures concerning the handling of crimes may alter the level of reported offenses. McCleary et al. (1982) found that, by requiring all reported cases of burglary to be investigated by detectives, the number of officially recorded burglaries showed an immediate drop. This was attributable to the detectives reclassifying offenses that were not burglaries (i.e. thefts) to their correct UCR categories. Less experienced officers who used to handle these offenses elevated many instances to the burglary category. It is clear that the UCR crime rates are subject to unintentional, as well as intentional, manipulation.

The third criticism of the UCR revolves around the claim that many offenses are not brought to the attention of the police. The police are a reactive force. This means that they primarily respond to calls for service. Despite their patrol function, little crime is encountered directly by the police. They must rely on victims and witnesses to call them for help. The absence of such calls when offenses do occur translates into crimes that are not known to the police and that do not become part of official crime figures. The fact that there is much unreported crime, along with the potential problems of data collection, have prompted many individuals to rely on victimization surveys in order to assess the extent of the crime problem.

Measuring Victimization

Victimization surveys are surveys of the population carried out to measure the level of criminal victimization in society. This form of crime measurement was prompted by the 1967 President's Commission on Law Enforcement and the Administration of Justice, which commissioned surveys to assess the accuracy (or lack thereof) of the UCR. The results of those early surveys suggested that the police data reflected only half of the crime in society (see, for example, Ennis, 1967). Based on those early investigations, victim surveys became a common method for measuring crime by the late 1970s, with the federal government institutionalizing the National Crime Victimization Survey (originally the National Crime Survey) in 1972. These surveys typically inquire about the victimization experiences of a subject and/or his household over a specified period of time (usually the preceding six months or year). Such surveys have been lauded as a more accurate reading of crime in society because they circumvent the problems of official records and they uncover crimes that are not reported to the police.

The *National Crime Victimization Survey* (NCVS) is the best known of the victimization surveys. It is a *panel survey* of households drawn from across the United States, in which a panel of subjects (in this case addresses) are surveyed repeatedly over a specified period. The NCVS contacts the same household every six months for a period of three years, with one sixth of the sample dropping out and being replaced every six months. Interviewers attempt to talk with every household member aged 12 and older. While the NCVS has undergone considerable change in data collection methods in recent years, including the use of computer-aided interviewing and changes in preliminary screen questions, the findings relative to official statistics have remained fairly stable. The success of the NCVS has prompted similar victim surveys in other countries, most notably the British Crime Survey (BCS).

According to the 2008 NCVS, there were over 21 million victimizations in the United States against persons age 12 or older (Rand, 2009). Of that number, almost five million were violent crimes and more than 16 million were property crimes. These raw figures translate into victimization rates of 1,930 violent crimes (per 100,000 population) and 13,470 property crimes (per 100,000 households). These figures, both the raw numbers and the crime rates, are significantly higher than the UCR data. Indeed, the NCVS violent crime rate is roughly four times as high as the UCR violent crime rate. While the NCVS property crime rate is considered for households instead of individuals as in the UCR, the fact that the rate is almost twice as high as the UCR rate is indicative of the fact that property crime is larger than reported in police data. The claims that the UCR underreports crime, therefore, is supported in these figures.

Consistent with UCR figures, the NCVS reveals decreasing victimization levels, with great reductions in violent crime over the past decade. The NCVS estimates that there were 35,646,755 offenses in 1973. This number rose to 41,267,496 in 1981. Since 1981 there has been a relatively steady decline in property victimizations (Rand et al., 1997; Rand, 2009). Conversely, the violent

Table 1.1
Criminal Victimization, 2008 (number and rates per 100,000)

Type of Victimization	Number	Rate
Total Violent Crimes	4,856,510	1,930
Rape/sexual assault	203,530	80
Robbery	551,830	220
Aggravated assault	839,940	330
Simple assault	3,260,920	1,290
Personal Theft	136,710	50
Total Property Crimes	16,319,180	13,470
Household burglary	3,188,620	2,630
Motor vehicle theft	795,160	660
Theft	12,335,400	10,180

Source: Adapted from Rand (2009).

crime rate held fairly steady throughout the 1970s, decreased in the early 1980s, increased from about 1986 until 1994, and has steadily declined since that time (Rand, 2009; Rennison and Rand, 2003). This trend varies somewhat for individual crimes (motor vehicle theft, for example, increased steadily between 1985 and 1991) but the overall trend is consistent with the findings from the UCR.

Victimization studies are not without their critics and shortcomings. Among the many problems inherent in the surveys are the lack of knowledge of what constitutes various crimes on the part of respondents, problems of respondent recall, and issues of question wording. These issues are well documented elsewhere (see O'Brien, 1985) and will not be considered here. The magnitude of the difference between official and victimization figures, however, is too large to be offset solely by the problems of victim surveys. There is little question that victim surveys uncover more crime than official measures.

Summary

Clearly, both official measures of crime and victimization surveys suffer from a variety of shortcomings. The exact nature and level of crime in society is unknown. Official UCR figures reveal a staggering amount of crime. More than doubling those numbers to account for unreported offenses, as victimization figures would suggest, compounds the problem. Even with the recent reductions in crime, the number of offenses is staggering, and the resultant economic and time loss adds to the magnitude of the problem.

The level of crime, whether at its peak or more moderate numbers, exceeds the limits of what the criminal justice system can hope to handle. The system is already overburdened and often simply processes people through the maze of legal requirements while having a questionable impact on the level of crime

(Conklin, 2003). Even if the criminal justice system could claim credit for the recent reductions, there is still a lot of work to do. Compounding the situation is the fact that the bulk of criminal justice system activity (e.g. arrests, convictions, incarceration, and corrections) reflects an after-the-fact approach to crime. The system deals primarily with crimes which have already been committed. There is little, if any, evidence to show that the criminal justice system actually stops crime *before* it occurs.

THE COSTS OF CRIME/VICTIMIZATION

The problem of crime and victimization goes beyond simple counts of the number of offenses. Crime has a number of different impacts on both the victims and society, and in many ways these impacts surpass the size and scope of the UCR and NVCS figures. Economic loss, injuries, the need for medical care and lost time from work are additional measures of crime's impact.

Information on the impact of crime is routinely collected each year by both the UCR and victimization surveys. The most extensive data comes from the NCVS. According to 2006 figures, victims experienced over $18 billion in direct loss from crimes (see Table 1.2). This amounts to an average loss of $731 per victim. Motor vehicle theft results in the highest average loss, followed by robbery and household burglary at roughly $1,200 per offense. The UCR offers similar information on loss from residential burglaries ($2.8 billion), non-residential burglaries ($1.2 billion), larceny ($5.2 billion) and robbery ($472 million). In addition, the UCR estimates that almost $15 billion worth of property was stolen in 2008. What is important to note beyond these dollar figures is that, despite the reductions in the number and rates of crime in recent years, the economic loss per event has steadily increased at a rate greater than inflation.

Beyond measures of monetary loss, the NCVS provides information on the impact of physical injuries and lost time due to victimization. In 2006, almost 28 percent of victims sustained a physical injury, 14 percent required medical care and five percent received hospital care as a result of the offense (Bureau of Justice Statistics, 2008). Almost nine percent of the respondents reported losing time from work, with the related lost income, due to being victimized. Of those who lost time from work due to personal crimes, almost 27 percent missed six or more days while an additional 47 percent missed between one and five days of work.

While the above information paints a serious picture of the impact of crime, the actual impact extends beyond the direct costs to the individual victims reflected in the UCR or the NCVS. Indeed, other offenses have an impact on individual victims, including drunk driving, child abuse, arson, murder and many other offenses. It is also possible to consider the wider societal impact of crime. Anderson (1999) considers a wide range of societal costs, including the production of activities due to crime (e.g. corrections, law enforcement

Table 1.2
Economic Costs to Victims of Crime

NCVS data, 2006	Number of Crimes	Gross Loss (Millions)	Mean Loss	Median Loss
All Crimes	25,183,350	18,410	731	100
Personal Crimes	6,267,610	1,896	303	100
Rape/Sexual Assault	260,940	45	171	350
Robbery	712,610	904	1,269	100
Assault	5,120,840	911	178	100
Purse Snatching	173,220	4	107	70
Pocket Picking	132,110	32	239	87
Property Crimes	18,915,740	16,513	873	100
Household Burglary	3,560,920	4,427	1,243	280
Motor Vehicle Theft	992,260	5,646	5,690	2,500
Theft	14,362,570	6,441	448	100
Percent of Victims sustaining physical injury	27.8%			
Percent of Victims receiving medical care	14.0%			
Percent of Victims receiving hospital care	5.1%			
Percent of Victims losing time from work	8.6%			

UCR data, 2008

Total Value of Property Stolen	$14.8 billion
Estimated Loss from Residential Burglary	$2.8 billion
Estimated Loss from Non-residential Burglary	$1.2 billion
Estimated Loss from Larceny	$5.2 billion
Estimated Loss from Robbery	$471.9 million

Source: Constructed by author from Bureau of Justice Statistics (2008), FBI (2009).

expenditures, safety devices, and security forces), lost time or production due to offenders committing or society addressing crime, the value of lost life and losses due to injuries, and the direct value of the property or loss from an offense. Based on these assumptions, Anderson (1999) estimates the annual cost of crime to U.S. society at $1.7 trillion! While it is possible to question some of the basic assumptions underlying this estimate, there is no question that crime has a huge impact on both the direct victims and on society at large.

THE FEAR OF CRIME

To further compound the problem of the levels of "actual crime" and the economic and physical impact of crime in society, one needs only to examine the perceived levels of crime and the resultant fear held by many members of society. The "fear of crime" presents a view of criminal victimization that, although not necessarily real, forms the basis for daily "inactivity" and anxiety.

Because fear reduction is an important component of many crime prevention programs, it is important to understand the extent of fear and issues related to measuring and understanding fear.

The Discovery of Fear

Fear of crime emerged as a social issue in the mid-1960s and soon became a permanent part of criminological research. Lee (2007) argues that fear was "invented" in the 1960s through a convergence of various factors. Among these were the development of victimization surveys as a part of the 1967 President's Commission on Law Enforcement and the Administration of Justice (and subsequently in other countries), the growth of professional/academic interest in crime and its causes, the use of crime and fear as political capital, and the feminist movement (Lee, 2007). The newly discovered "fear of crime" became an integral part of national and local government policymaking.

Defining Fear

What exactly is fear? Despite the growth of interest in "fear of crime," there remains a lack of consensus on exactly what the term means. Perhaps the most recognized work on this issue is that of Kenneth Ferraro and his associates. Ferraro (1995) defines *fear* as:

> an emotional response of dread or anxiety to crime or symbols that a person associates with crime. This definition of fear implies that some recognition of potential danger, what we may call perceived risk, is necessary to evoke fear (p. 8).

While this definition requires an emotional response, the fear may manifest itself in various ways depending on the person involved and the basis for his or her anxiety. Some individuals fear walking on the streets in their neighborhood while others fear physical attack within their own home. As a result, there may be a shift in physical functioning such as high blood pressure and rapid heartbeat. Alternatively, the individual may similarly alter his or her attitudes about walking alone in certain places or avoiding various activities. To a great extent, the source of the fear for the individual will determine the response to the fear. Regardless of the source of this fear, it is real for the individual.

Measuring Fear

Ferraro (1995) points out that researchers have attempted to measure fear in a variety of ways. Some surveys question respondents about how much they worry about being a victim. Others ask about perceptions of the crime problem in their community. Still other surveys have respondents rate their chances of becoming a victim. These various approaches do not provide the same information.

In an attempt to show the differences between various fear measures, Ferraro and LaGrange (1988) provide a classification scheme that considers the perceptions of the respondent being tapped and the degree to which the method addresses the individual or others (see Figure 1.3). This classification taps *judgments* of risk— how safe the respondent or others are, *values*—how concerned the person is about crime or victimization, and *emotions*—how much the individual is afraid or worried about becoming a victim. Personal fear of crime appears in the lower right hand cell (F). This measure would ask respondents directly about how afraid they are of being the victim of specific crimes, often without reference to any specific place or time. These questions directly tap the "emotions of dread or anxiety" of the individual. At the other extreme (cell A), respondents assess the general safety of other people, quite possibly without even mentioning crime.

Figure 1.3
Classification and Examples of Crime Perceptions

Level of Reference	Level of Perception		
	Cognitive		*Affective*
	Judgments	*Values*	*Emotions*
General	A Risk to others; crime or safety assessments	B Concern about crime to others	C Fear for others' victimization
Personal	D Risk to self; safety of self personal intolerance	E Concern about crime to self;	F Fear for self-victimization

Source: Reprinted from *Journal of Aging Studies*, Vol. 2, Ferraro and LaGrange, "Are Older People Afraid of Crime?" pp. 277–287 (1988) with permission from Elsevier Science.

Interestingly, while discussions of "fear of crime" are common, many researchers utilize measures that reflect risk or assessments of crime levels, rather than the emotional response of the individual (Ferraro, 1995). This diversity is seen in many of the common and large scale surveys. Figure 1.4 presents a sample of "fear" questions used in past surveys and research. Note that the questions vary from asking about perceptions on changes in crime (Harris Poll), to feeling safe outside at night with no mention of crime (NCVS), to rating fear of specific criminal actions (Fear of Crime in America Survey). These differing measures all tap some aspect of the fear definition presented earlier.

Figure 1.4
Common "Fear" Questions

National Crime Victimization Survey:

How safe do you feel or would you feel being out alone in your neighborhood at night?

General Social Survey:

Is there any area right around here— that is, within a mile— where you would be afraid to walk alone at night?

Taking A Bite Out of Crime Campaign Evaluation:

How likely do you think it is that your home will be broken into or burglarized during the next year?

Is having your home burglarized or broken into something that you worry about?

National Opinion Survey on Criminal Justice:

Do you worry very frequently, somewhat frequently, seldom or never about:
- Yourself or someone in your family getting sexually assaulted
- Being attacked while driving your car
- Getting mugged
- Getting beaten up, knifed or shot
- Getting murdered
- Your home being burglarized while someone is at home
- Your home being burglarized while no one is at home

Harris Poll:

In the past year, do you feel the crime rate in your area has been increasing, decreasing, or has it remained the same as it was before?

Fear of Crime in America Survey:

Rate your fear of: (1= not afraid at all; 10= very afraid)
- being approached on the street by a beggar or panhandler
- being raped or sexually assaulted
- being murdered
- being attacked by someone with a weapon
- having your car stolen
- having your property damaged by vandals

The Level of Fear

Trying to delineate the actual level of fear is like trying to hit a moving target. No two studies provide the same results. This may be due largely to the use of varying measures of fear. Despite this fact, it is possible to offer some insight and "ballpark" figures for fear.

Many researchers report that 40 to 50 percent of the population express a fear of crime (Hindelang, 1975; Maguire and Pastore, 1995; Skogan and Maxfield, 1981; Toseland, 1982). Survey results find that roughly 40 percent of the public report that there are areas near their home where they would be afraid to walk alone at night (Gallup, 2006; Pastore and Maguire, 2006). Questions asking about perceived changes in crime in the United States or a respondent's area often result in greater fear levels with 67 percent or more reporting that there is "more" crime than in the past (Gallup, 2006).

Table 1.3 presents data on the level of "worry" about being a victim of specific crimes. Pastore and Maguire (2009) report that approximately 17 percent of respondents worry frequently or occasionally about being murdered, 46 percent worry about having their home burglarized when they are not home, 28 percent worry about a burglary when they are home, 43 percent worry about having their car stolen or broken into, and 29 percent worry about being mugged. Data from the United Kingdom reveal that roughly one-third of respondents indicate they have felt fearful of being victimized in the past year, with half of these indicating that fear one to four times in the past year (Farrall and Gadd, 2004).

Table 1.3
Percent of Respondents Who Frequently or Occasionally Worry About Different Forms of Victimization

	Male	Female	Total
Home being burglarized when not home	45	48	46
Car stolen or burglarized	41	43	43
Being mugged	21	37	29
Home being burglarized when home	22	34	28
Being sexually assaulted	5	31	19
Getting murdered	15	19	17
Being attacked while driving	16	25	21

Source: Maguire and Pastore (2009).

Fear and Crime

One very important fact to keep in mind is that the level of fear exceeds the actual levels of crime. Skogan and Maxfield (1981) illustrate the lack of a connection between crime and fear by showing that, in terms of robbery, approximately 48 percent of the non-victims report feeling somewhat or very unsafe, while 54 percent of the victims report the same fear. The expectation was that victims should express significantly more fear than non-victims. Similarly, both official and victimization measures show that less than 10 percent of the population are victimized, despite fear of 40 percent or more. Perhaps more interesting is the fact that, despite the reductions in crime found in both official and victimization figures, 62 percent of the respondents to a Gallup poll in 2002 believe there was more crime in the U.S. than in the previous year (Pastore and Maguire, 2003).

Another way of looking at fear and crime is to examine the link between fear and past victimization of respondents. Some studies offer empirical support of a positive relationship between victimization and fear of crime (Gomme, 1986; Kale and Kleinman, 1985; Keane, 1995; Kleiman and David, 1983; Lumb et al., 1993; McCoy et al., 1996; Roundtree, 1998; Skogan, 1987; Will and McGrath, 1995). Other studies, however, fail to find any relationship between victimization and fear (Ferraro, 1995; Garofalo, 1979; Gates and Rohe, 1987; Liska et al., 1982; McGarrell et al., 1997; Perkins and Taylor, 1996; Rifai, 1982). Yet another group of researchers argue that the relationship depends on the definitions and measures of fear and/or victimization (Baumer, 1985; Bennett and Flavin, 1994; Ferraro and LaGrange, 1987; Garofalo, 1981; Gomme, 1988).

Fear and Demographics

Besides the diversity in the fear-victimization relationship, the level of fear is not consistent across all demographic groups in the population. It is principally an urban problem and affects the elderly and women to a greater extent than other groups. Greater than 60 percent of those persons living in urban areas express fear of crime. Conversely, only 30 percent of rural residents voice the same fears. A wide range of studies reveal that the elderly and women are the most fearful groups in society (Baumer, 1985; Bennett and Flavin, 1994; Ferraro, 1995; Hindelang et al., 1978; McGarrell et al., 1997; Perkins and Taylor, 1996; Riger et al., 1978; Will and McGrath, 1995). Skogan and Maxfield (1981) note that females are more than three times as fearful as men (22.8% versus 6.4%) on neighborhood streets. Similarly, individuals ages 50–59 are more than twice as fearful (22.2%) as any group of younger persons. The problem is greater for those over age 60, where 40.7 percent feel very unsafe on their neighborhood streets (Skogan and Maxfield, 1981). Other studies suggest that the method of measuring fear affects the age findings. Chiricos et al. (1997), Ferraro (1995), Lumb et al. (1993) and others find that younger respondents are more fearful.

Fear also varies along other demographic lines. Numerous studies report that fearful people tend to be black (Biderman et al., 1967; Chiricos et al., 1997; Lab, 1990; Smith and Lab, 1991; Parker, 1988; Parker and Ray, 1990; Skogan and Maxfield, 1981), lower socioeconomic status (Bennett and Flavin, 1994; Biderman et al., 1967; Gomme, 1986; Greenberg et al., 1985; Riger et al., 1978; Will and McGrath, 1995), and live in large communities (Baumer, 1985; Biderman et al., 1967; Boggs, 1971; Kennedy and Silverman, 1985; Liska et al., 1982; Will and McGrath, 1995). Other studies, however, note the lack of a relationship or a reverse relationship between some of these demographic factors and fear (Gomme, 1986; Gomme, 1988; Kennedy and Krahn, 1984; Kennedy and Silverman, 1985; Lab, 1990; Smith and Lab, 1991; Menard and Covey, 1987; Ortega and Myles, 1987; Toseland, 1982).

Explaining the Divergent Findings

Two basic questions arise from an inspection of past research on fear of crime. First, how do you justify the levels of fear in light of the actual levels and chances of victimization? Second, why do different studies find divergent sets of characteristics among fearful individuals? There is no clear answer to these questions. Instead, there may be many contributing factors.

Vicarious Victimization

One potential explanation involves *vicarious victimization*. Knowing someone who has been the victim of a crime, or simply being told by a friend of a harmful act against a third party, may elicit a sympathetic reaction and empathetic fear of crime. Hough (1995), using 1994 British Crime Survey data, notes that fear is related to measures of vicarious victimization. An even more indirect means of vicarious fear can come from real or dramatic depictions of crime in the media. Primary among these forms would be television. Both fictional police dramas and the reporting of crime and violence in the news inundate the populace with a view that crime is a constant threat to every individual. It is also noteworthy that most depictions are not of everyday "street crimes." Instead, they focus on more heinous and frightening offenses such as murder, rape, and home burglary.

The American Bar Association (1999) speculates that part of the reason for continued high levels of fear despite declining crime may be the increases in television news coverage of murder. Similarly, Williams and Dickinson (1993) note that fear varies in relation to the type of crime news presented in British daily papers. Chiricos and associates (1996), using a random phone survey of adults, report that exposure to both radio and television news is related to higher reported fear, particularly among white female respondents. Just as many theorists argue that criminal behavior can be learned from the media, is there any reason to assume that fearful behavior cannot also be learned?

Perceived Risk and Harm

A second possibility for explaining the inordinate levels of fear centers on the potential harm one encounters if and when victimized (Riger et al., 1978; Skogan and Maxfield, 1981; Warr, 1984). In essence, some individuals may perceive themselves to be at a greater risk of victimization and harm. As noted above, the elderly and women are often found to be the most fearful of crime but are the least victimized. This seeming discrepancy starts to disappear when one considers the potential harm incurred by these groups of people. The elderly are largely on fixed incomes and any loss due to theft, property damage, or medical expenses cannot always be accommodated within their budgets. A minor dollar loss can translate into a major hardship. Similarly, physical injuries to elderly victims can result in lengthy, painful recuperation beyond that needed by younger individuals. The elderly and females also generally face a great physical disadvantage in crime situations. Most offenders are young males who hold an edge in strength and physical prowess. The perceived potential for physical harm is greatly enhanced when the victim and offender represent opposite positions in physical and social power. Using survey data from almost 1,500 elderly respondents in Dade County, Florida, McCoy et al. (1996) find that perceived vulnerability is a strong predictor of fear. Smith and Torstensson (1997) report similar findings in a study of women and elderly in Stockholm, Sweden.

Vulnerability also appears in the form of social isolation (Akers et al., 1987; Bursik and Grasmick, 1993; Kennedy and Silverman, 1985; Riger et al., 1981). Many elderly live alone and have few family members or close friends living nearby. These individuals may feel they have no one to call on for assistance in the aftermath of a crime. They are socially isolated from support networks that are more common among younger members of the population.

A great deal of support for the impact of perceived risk and potential harm is found in Ferraro's (1995) fear study. Ferraro surveyed more than 1,100 respondents from across the United States about their perceived risk, fear of crime, and demographic and neighborhood characteristics. Analyzing perceived risk, he finds that higher risk perceptions are related to higher levels of community crime, signs of incivility and disorder, both direct and indirect victimization, being a female, and being nonwhite. Turning to predicting fear of crime, Ferraro (1995) reports that perceived risk is a significant predictor of general fear, fear of personal crime and fear of property crime, and the strongest predictor of both general and property crime fear. Victimization is <u>not</u> a significant predictor of fear. These results give strong support to the perceived vulnerability argument. Unfortunately, most studies do not measure both perceived vulnerability and fear.

Incivility

A third possible explanation for the lack of a direct victimization-fear connection involves area incivility. *Incivility* refers to physical and social factors involved in disorder and community decline. Physical signs of incivility include the deterioration of buildings, litter, graffiti, vandalism, and abandoned buildings and cars. Among the social signs of incivility are public drunkenness, vagrancy, loitering youths, harassment (such as begging or panhandling), and visible drug sales and use. Both residents and potential offenders may see signs of incivility as indicative of a lack of social cohesion, high transiency, a lack of resources, and/or an uncaring attitude (Lewis and Salem, 1986; Skogan, 1990). Residents may feel a lack of control in the neighborhood that in turn may generate a greater fear of crime.

Several recent studies have analyzed the contribution of incivilities to the level of fear. McGarrell et al. (1997) report that neighborhood disorder/incivility contributes significantly to variation in respondents' fear of crime. Roundtree (1998) finds similar results when analyzing survey data from 5,302 Seattle residents. Residents' perceptions of disorder significantly increased fear of both violent and burglary victimizations. Finally, McCoy et al. (1996) note that dissatisfaction with one's neighborhood (a possible indicator of incivilities) is a key to residents' fear. An alternative view is offered by Ferraro (1995) who claims to find no relationship between incivility and fear. However, neighborhood incivility is the strongest predictor of perceived risk, which may influence levels of fear.

Methodological Factors

Differing methodologies in the studies may also influence the results. As noted earlier, varying "fear" measures can contribute to divergent findings. It is not improbable that the same respondents could provide two different views of fear when asked different questions. For example, survey respondents may give "fearful" responses when asked about walking alone after dark anywhere "within a mile," but few "fear" responses to the likelihood of being raped. Similarly, respondents may feel that crime is a greater problem today than a year ago, but still not worry much about being mugged. The extent of fear also may vary depending on who is answering which questions. Females, for example, worry more about sexual assault than do males. Ferraro (1995) notes that general fear among women is better understood as an extension of the fear of rape. Operationalizing fear in different ways, therefore, produces greatly different results. Variation in fear also may reflect the locale of the study. For example, Chiricos et al. (1997) point out that their results on fear differ from those of Covington and Taylor (1991), despite the similar concerns addressed in the two studies. They speculate that the variation is due to differences between Tallahassee, Florida and Baltimore, Maryland. The setting of the analysis, therefore, can influence the results.

Crime and Fear

Yet another factor influencing the levels of fear involves the actual level of crime. While the fear of crime varies independently from actual victimization and crime, it would be naive to claim that changes in the crime rate have no influence on reported fear. Media reports of increasing crime and spectacular offenses undoubtedly hold some sway over perceptions of safety in the community. Unfortunately, lower crime rates probably do not bring about lower fear as easily. The media does not promote good news to the same extent as bad news. Feelings of fear and worry, once formed, would be difficult to reverse.

Benefits of Fear

Throughout this chapter, fear has been presented primarily as a negative concept. That is, fear is a bad thing that has negative consequences for the individual. Among these negatives are changes in behavior, retreating behind closed doors, not trusting other people, anxiety, and/or depression, to name a few. The logical conclusion to draw is that we need to reduce, and hopefully eliminate, fear. It is possible, however, to view fear as a positive thing.

Jackson and Gray (2009) note that there is such a thing as *functional fear*. In essence, fear can be a good thing, provided the individual uses it as motivation to take precautions. These precautions may range from avoiding certain risky places or times, to utilizing safety devices at home, to pairing up with others for safety when outdoors. A similar proposition is offered by Lee (2007) when he discusses the *fearing subject*. This person is someone who becomes responsible for the safety of himself and his property. Lee (2007) argues that government efforts to publicize and promote fear among the populace is partly calculated to lead individuals to self-protective actions.

Based on these arguments, it would be ill-advised to try to completely eliminate fear. Rather, fear can be healthy for people. The key would be to determine what that "healthy level" is and how to limit a person's fear at that optimal level. Under this approach, eliminating fear would result in people taking unnecessary chances and ignoring risky situations.

Fear Summary

Despite the issues and concerns inherent in measuring fear of crime, one fact remains unchanged. That is, people report being fearful to a much greater extent than they report (either officially or unofficially) being a victim of crime. Because of fear, people respond in a variety of ways. Some individuals will avoid certain places at certain times, or stop going somewhere altogether. Others may install locks and security devices and stay inside their fortress. The public may demand greater police presence. Funds may be expended on self-defense classes, dogs, guns, or other items in an attempt to protect one's self and reduce the feelings of fear. Whatever the response, it is indicative of fear's impact on the individual and society.

SUMMARY

The extent of the crime problem is hard to accurately gauge and is multi-faceted. Attempts to measure the level of crime present a variety of findings and anomalies. While these various counting procedures may not agree on the numerical magnitude of crime and victimization, there is consensus that crime remains a major social problem. Crime may be on the decrease, but it remains far higher today than in the late 1960s when the President's Commission proclaimed that major changes were needed to stem the problem of crime and victimization. Beyond the enumeration of criminal acts, the economic, psychological and time losses due to crime are significant for both the individual victims and society at large. Also problematic is the inordinate levels of fear of crime. Fear far exceeds the actual amount of crime and affects many individuals who never have been, and may never be, crime victims. Crime prevention must be cognizant of both the real and perceived levels of crime and must be prepared to attack crime in all its aspects.

Chapter 2
CRIME PREVENTION

Key Terms:

assize of arms
Chicago Area Project
constable
crime control
crime prevention
crime science
hue and cry
lex talionis
micro-, meso-, and macro-level
   crime prevention
parens patriae

parochial police
primary prevention
secondary prevention
situational crime prevention
social prevention
status offenses
tertiary prevention
thief takers
vigilante movement
watch and ward

Learning Objectives:

After reading this chapter you should be able to:

- Discuss the historic methods used by individuals and communities to respond to and prevent crime

- Provide a definition of crime prevention

- Contrast crime prevention and crime control

- Outline the crime prevention model based on the public health model

- Define primary, secondary and tertiary crime prevention

- Provide examples of prevention activities for each part of the crime prevention model

- Offer examples of other crime prevention models

- Identify the difference between micro-, meso-, and macro-level prevention
- Define and discuss crime science

Crime prevention is not a new idea. Indeed, for as long as people have been victimized there have been attempts to protect oneself and one's family. The term "crime prevention," however, has only recently come to signify a set of ideas for combating crime. Many people suggest that crime prevention today is new and unique, particularly in terms of citizen participation. In reality, many recent activities classified as crime prevention can be seen throughout history. "New" crime prevention ideas and techniques are often little more than reincarnations of past practices or extensions of basic approaches in the (distant) past. It is only in the relatively recent past that the general citizenry has *not* been the primary line of defense against crime and victimization. This chapter will accomplish several things. First, it presents a brief discussion of crime prevention throughout history. Second, a definition for crime prevention will be presented. Third, the chapter presents the general crime prevention model that serves to organize the remainder of the text.

CRIME PREVENTION THROUGH THE AGES

In any discussion it is important to set forth the context from which our ideas and thoughts emerge. Perhaps the best place to start is with an understanding of what has happened in the past. The study of crime prevention is no exception.

The earliest responses to crime were left to the individual and his family. Retribution, revenge and vengeance were the driving forces throughout early history. While such actions would serve to make the victim whole again, it also would eliminate the benefit gained by the offender. It was assumed that potential offenders would see little gain in an offense, thereby *deterring* the individual from taking action. The Code of Hammurabi (approximately 1900 B.C.) outlined retribution by the victim and/or his family as the accepted response to injurious behavior. *Lex talionis*, the principle of "an eye for an eye," was specifically set forth as a driving principle in the Hammurabic law. Such laws and practices provided legitimacy to individual citizen action.

The existence of formal systems of social control is relatively new. Early "policing," such as in the Roman Empire and in France, was concentrated in the cities, conducted by the military, and dealt with issues of the central state and the nobility (i.e. king) (Holden, 1992; Langworthy and Travis, 1994). The general public was left to continue self-help methods.

The Norman conquest of England in 1066 gave rise to an *obligatory* form of avocational citizen policing (Klockars, 1985). Male citizens were required to band together into groups for the purpose of policing each other. If one individual in the group caused harm (to a group or non-group member), the other members were responsible for apprehending and sanctioning the offender. Beyond this obligatory action, a variety of cooperative practices emerged that relied on citizen participation to protect the community and one another. *Watch and ward* rotated the responsibility for keeping watch over the town or area, particularly at night, among the male citizens. Identified threats would cause the watcher to raise the alarm and call for help (*hue and cry*). It was then up to the general citizenry to apprehend and (possibly) punish the offender. Those responding to the call for help were not employees of the state. Rather, they were other common citizens. The "watch and ward" and "hue and cry" ideas were codified in 1285 in the Statutes of Winchester (Klockars, 1985), which also required men to have weapons available for use when called (*assize of arms*), and outlined the role of a *constable*, which was an unpaid position responsible for coordinating the watch and ward system, and overseeing other aspects of the law. It is apparent throughout these actions that crime prevention was a major responsibility of the citizenry.

Similar citizen responsibility was commonplace in the new world colonies and the early United States. The *vigilante movement*, which mirrored early ideas of "hue and cry," was a major component of enforcing law and order in the growing frontier of the young country (Klockars, 1985). Posses of citizens were formed when an offender needed to be apprehended and punished.

The individual, often voluntary, responsibility for crime prevention in England generally persisted until the 1800s. The exceptions to this trend can be seen in the development of paid, private security police for specialized industries or groups (Klockars, 1985; Langworthy and Travis, 1994). The Merchant Police of England, which was established in the sixteenth century to protect the wool industry, is a prime example of an early private police force. The *parochial police*, hired by the wealthy to protect their homes and businesses, is another example.

Entrepreneurial policing appeared with the passage of the Highwayman Act in 1692 England. This law outlined the payment of bounty for the capture of thieves and the recovery of property. The voluntary bounty hunters came to be known as *thief takers* (Klockars, 1985; LaGrange, 1993) who, by the mid 1700s, were organized under the leadership of English magistrates. The thief takers, who were often reformed criminals themselves, were "paid" to protect the public by being able to keep a portion of all recovered property. The evolution of the thief takers from a wholly voluntary activity to a legitimized, organized group under government control was the beginning of a process that ended with the establishment of the Metropolitan Police in London in 1829.

A key to the Metropolitan Police organization was the idea of crime prevention. Sir Robert Peel, who was the driving force behind the Metropolitan

Police Act, and Charles Roman, the commissioner of the new organization, both saw crime prevention as the basic principle underlying police work (LaGrange, 1993). Even earlier attempts at formal policing, such as that in seventeenth century Paris, emphasized crime prevention through methods such as preventive patrol, increased lighting, and street cleaning (Stead, 1983). Formal police forces in the United States, mirroring the movement in England, emerged in the mid-1800s and were restricted primarily to the largest cities in the northeast, leaving citizens to continue their efforts at self-protection.

While much of this discussion has emphasized individual action and self-help, it should not be construed as indicative that protective actions were solely a matter of retribution and revenge. There are numerous examples of alternative approaches that would be considered preventive in nature. Easy examples were the use of walls, moats, drawbridges and other physical design features around cities that protected the community from external invasion. Surveillance, as provided by "watch and ward," allowed the identification of problems before they got out of hand. Yet another early prevention approach was the restriction of weapon ownership as a means of eliminating violent behavior (Holden, 1992).

The advent of the twentieth century witnessed a great deal of change in societal response to deviant behavior. Not only was a formal police force becoming the norm, but other forces were emerging to address crime and deviance. The growth of the scientific study of crime and criminal behavior offered new responses to deviant behavior. The emerging fields of psychology and sociology in the late 1800s and early 1900s were beginning to question the causes of deviant behavior. Rather than carry on the dominant tradition of attributing deviance to the battle between good and evil (God and the devil), researchers were starting to note patterns in where and when offenses occurred and who was involved in the offenses, and to relate these facts to changing social structure and personal relationships. The logical result of this growing study was a movement away from simple responses involving repression, vengeance, retribution, and the like to actions that would attack the assumed causes of deviant behavior. The emerging criminal and juvenile justice systems, therefore, responded by incorporating more prevention oriented functions into their activity.

One prime example of an early "crime prevention" approach was the development of the juvenile court and its efforts to combat the problems of poverty, lack of education, and poor parenting among the lower classes. The preventive nature of the juvenile system can be seen in the *parens patriae* philosophy, which argued that youths needed help and that processing in adult court was geared toward punishment rather than prevention. The expansion of the juvenile court's jurisdiction to cover *status offenses* reflected the belief that curfew violation, smoking, playing in the street, incorrigibility, and other such actions (none of which were proscribed by the criminal code) were indicative of later criminal behavior. Thus, intervening in these status offenses was a means of preventing later crime. The juvenile system, therefore, was clearly an attempt at crime prevention.

Yet another example of early crime preventive action was the Chicago Area Project. Shaw and McKay (1931, 1942) found crime and delinquency concentrating in the central areas of Chicago, where residential transience and an apparent lack of social ties predominated. Shaw and McKay (1942) argued that this constant turnover of residents resulted in an inability of the people to exert any informal social control over the individuals in the area. People were more interested in improving themselves and moving out of these neighborhoods than in improving the area and staying there. Consequently, offenders could act with some degree of impunity in these neighborhoods. The *Chicago Area Project*, founded in 1931, sought to work with the residents to build a sense of pride and community, thereby prompting people to stay and exert control over the actions of people in the area. Recreation for youths, vigilance and community self-renewal, and mediation were the major components of the project (Schlossman and Sedlak, 1983). In essence, the project sought to build ongoing, thriving communities that could control the behavior of both its residents and those who visited the area.

Summary

This short presentation demonstrates that crime prevention is an idea that has been around for as long as there has been crime. While the form has changed and the term "crime prevention" is relatively new, the concern over safety is age old. Throughout most of history, it was the individual's responsibility, either voluntarily or through obligation, to deal with crime and offenders. It has only been in the relatively recent past that society has moved to a system of police, courts, and corrections, which has assumed the primary responsibility for crime. The criminal justice system, however, has been unable to prevent or control crime. Simply increasing the funding for the system has not improved its ability to stop crime. Crime is a societal problem, not just a criminal justice system problem.

Since the late 1960s there has been a growing movement toward bringing the citizenry back as active participants in crime prevention. While many see this type of community action as "new," in reality it is more a movement back to age old traditions of individual responsibility than it is a revolutionary step forward in crime control. Crime prevention must utilize the wide range of ideas and abilities found throughout society. Community planning, architecture, neighborhood action, juvenile advocacy, security planning, education, and technical training, among many other system and non-system activities, all have a potential impact on the levels of crime and fear of crime. The realm of crime prevention is vast and open for expansion.

DEFINING CRIME PREVENTION

The definition of crime prevention varies from study to study and program to program. Ekblom (2005:28) states "Crime prevention is intervention in the causes of criminal and disorderly events to reduce the risks of their occurrence and/or the potential seriousness of their consequences." This definition addresses both crime and its impact on individuals and society. As outlined in the last chapter, the consequences of crime are not inconsequential. While most definitions of crime prevention incorporate the ideas of lessening the actual levels of crime or limiting further increases in crime, few deal with the problem of fear of crime and perceived crime and victimization. This book uses a very simple yet encompassing definition:

> crime prevention entails any action designed to reduce the actual level of crime and/or the perceived fear of crime.

These actions are not restricted to the efforts of the criminal justice system and include activities by individuals and groups, both public and private. Just as there are many causes of crime, there are many potentially valuable approaches to crime prevention.

This definition differs from Ekblom's in that it does not directly address the consequences of crime. The reason for this is twofold. First, if crime and fear are successfully addressed, the consequences are also affected. Second, it is possible to address the consequences of victimization without ever attacking the underlying crime. This can occur in many ways, including payments to victims through victim compensation, the provision of mental health counselors, actions taken to reduce the time lost from participating with the criminal justice process, and any number of other interventions. While these actions are laudable, they do nothing to address the cause of the problems. Therefore, throughout the discussion in this book, the emphasis is on crime and the fear of crime, with the consequences receiving little direct attention.

Crime prevention and crime control are not synonymous. Crime prevention clearly denotes an attempt to eliminate crime either prior to the initial occurrence or before further activity. On the other hand, *crime control* alludes to maintenance of a given or existing level and the management of that amount of behavior. Control also fails to adequately address the problem of fear of crime. Critics of this distinction will fault the author's implicit assumption that society and criminal justice can do something about crime and the fear of crime beyond simple management of an inevitable, inescapable minimal amount of crime. These functionalists would view crime as a social necessity that, regardless of the effort, will always exist. While functionalists may be correct, taking the stance that crime is necessary and all we can do is "control" it leads to a mind-set doomed not to achieve crime "prevention."

THE CRIME PREVENTION MODEL

Crime prevention can be divided into three approaches similar to that found in public health models of disease prevention (see Brantingham and Faust, 1976; Caplan, 1964; Leavell and Clark, 1965; Shah and Roth, 1974). Each of the three areas of prevention—primary, secondary, and tertiary— attack the problem at different stages of development. From the public health viewpoint, primary prevention refers to actions taken to avoid the initial development of the disease or problem. This would include vaccinations and sanitary clean-ups by public health officials. Secondary prevention moves beyond the point of general societal concerns and focuses on individuals and situations that exhibit early signs of disease. Included at this stage are screening tests such as those for tuberculosis or systematically providing examinations to workers who handle toxic materials. Tertiary prevention rests at the point where the disease or problem has already manifested itself. Activities at this stage involve the elimination of the immediate problem and taking steps designed to inhibit a recurrence in the future. The various approaches to crime prevention are directly analogous to this public health model.

Primary Crime Prevention

Primary prevention within the realm of criminal justice "identifies conditions of the physical and social environment that provide opportunities for or precipitate criminal acts" (Brantingham and Faust, 1976). The types of prevention approaches subsumed here take a variety of forms and are located within a wide range of social organizations (see Table 2.1). Included here are environmental design, neighborhood watch, general deterrence, private security, and education about crime and crime prevention. Environmental design includes a wide range of crime prevention techniques aimed at making crime more difficult for the offender, surveillance easier for residents, and feelings of safety more widespread. The use of building plans conducive to visibility, the addition of lights and locks, and the marking of property for ease of identification fall within the realm of environmental design. Neighborhood watches and citizen patrols increase the ability of residents to exert control over their neighborhood and add risk of observation for potential offenders.

Activities of the criminal justice system also fall within the realm of primary prevention. The presence of the police may affect the attractiveness of an area for crime as well as lower the fear of crime. The courts and corrections may influence primary prevention by increasing perceived risk of crime for offenders. Public education concerning the actual levels of crime and the interaction of the criminal justice system and the public may also affect perceptions of crime. In a related way, private security can add to the deterrent efforts of the formal justice agencies.

Table 2.1
Crime Prevention Approaches

PRIMARY PREVENTION:
    Environmental Design—
        Architectural design
        Lighting
        Access control
        Property identification
    Neighborhood Watch—
        Surveillance
        Citizen patrols
    General Deterrence-
        Arrest and conviction
        Sentencing methods
    Public Education-
        Levels of crime
        Fear
        Self-help
    Social Crime Prevention—
        Unemployment
        Poverty
        Employment/Job training
    Private Security

SECONDARY PREVENTION:
    Identification and Prediction—
        Early ID of problem individuals
        Crime area analysis
    Situational Crime Prevention—
        Problem identification
        Situation specific intervention
    Community Policing
    Substance Abuse-
        Prevention and treatment
    Schools and Crime Prevention

TERTIARY PREVENTION:
    Specific Deterrence
    Incapacitation
    Rehabilitation and Treatment

Primary prevention also includes broader social issues related to crime and deviance. Sometimes referred to as *social prevention*, activities aimed at alleviating unemployment, poor education, poverty, and similar social ills may reduce crime and fear by attending to the root causes underlying deviant behavior. These and many other primary prevention behaviors are implemented with the intent of avoiding initial, as well as continued, crime and victimization and may be instrumental at lowering the fear of crime.

Secondary Crime Prevention

Secondary prevention "engages in early identification of potential offenders and seeks to intervene" (Brantingham and Faust, 1976) prior to commission of illegal activity. Implicit in secondary prevention is the ability to correctly identify and predict problem people and situations. Perhaps the most recognizable form of secondary prevention is the idea of situational crime prevention. *Situational crime prevention* seeks to identify existing problems at the micro level and institute interventions that are developed specifically for the given problem. These solutions may involve physical design changes, altering social behaviors, improving surveillance, or any number of other activities. Closely allied to situational prevention is the emergence of community policing. The community policing approach relies heavily on citizen involvement in a problem solving approach to neighborhood concerns.

Many secondary prevention efforts resemble activities listed under primary prevention. The distinction rests on whether the programs are aimed more at keeping problems that lead to criminal activity from arising (primary prevention) or if the efforts are focused on factors that already exist and are fostering deviant behavior (secondary prevention). Secondary prevention may deal with predelinquents or deviant behavior which leads to injurious criminal activity. For example, alcohol and drug use are highly related to other forms of deviance. Targeting drug use as an indicator of criminal propensity is a secondary prevention approach. Schools can play an important role in secondary prevention both in terms of identifying problem youths and in providing a forum for interventions. Clearly, much secondary prevention may rest in the hands of parents, educators, and neighborhood leaders who have daily contact with the individuals and conditions leading to deviance and fear.

Tertiary Crime Prevention

According to Brantingham and Faust (1976), *tertiary prevention* "deals with actual offenders and involves intervention . . . in such a fashion that they will not commit further offenses." The majority of tertiary prevention rests within the workings of the criminal justice system. The activities of arrest, prosecution, incarceration, treatment, and rehabilitation all fall within the realm of tertiary prevention. Non-justice system input to this process includes private enterprise correctional programs, diversionary justice within the community, and some community corrections. Tertiary prevention is often ignored in discussions of crime prevention due to its traditional place in other texts and the great volume of writing on these topics that already exists.

The types of approaches and interventions within each level of crime prevention are certainly not limited to those mentioned. Within each of the three types of prevention there are many variations and novel ways to approach a given crime problem. Indeed, crime prevention techniques are only limited by the imagination of individuals interested in decreasing the levels of crime and fear of crime.

Alternate Models and Crime Science

While this book uses the primary/secondary/tertiary model to organize the discussion of crime prevention, other models exist. One model is a variation on this tripartite view offered by van Dijk and de Waard (1991). Their model adds a second dimension of victim-oriented, community/neighborhood-oriented, and offender-oriented approaches. For example, primary prevention techniques can be divided into actions that target victims, the community, or potential offenders. The authors attempt to refine the public health-based classification system. Crawford (1998) offers another two-dimensional typology that again uses the primary/secondary/tertiary view as a starting point, and adds a distinction between social and situational approaches within each category. Both of these models offer alternative views of crime prevention and ways of conceptualizing crime prevention interventions.

Hunter (2010) adds yet another possible layer to the crime prevention model. Specifically, he sees crime prevention divided into micro, meso, and macro levels, while maintaining the primary, secondary, and tertiary distinctions. *Micro-level* crime prevention targets individuals, small groups, small areas, or small businesses for intervention. These interventions may be very site-specific and target individual vulnerabilities. *Meso-level* prevention looks at larger communities or neighborhoods, or larger groups of individuals or businesses. Examples of this could be entire villages or towns, or possibly a chain of specialty stores. The interventions here will involve larger groups and seek to engender cooperative responses to crime. Finally, *macro-level* crime prevention looks at large communities, society as a whole, or other very large collectives. At this level, responses would involve large-scale social changes, major shifts in educational practices, major new employment opportunities, or legislative changes to address crime and disorder (Hunter, 2010).

An emerging area within the realm of crime prevention is that of *crime science*. Laycock (2005) suggests that crime science is a new discipline, or at the very least a new paradigm, for addressing crime by coupling efforts to prevent crime with the detection of and intervention with offenders. This is in contrast to the existing paradigm within criminal justice where "Crime is seen as fundamentally about offenders rather than situations" (Laycock, 2005:21). The emphasis on offenders means that responses to crime primarily involve the criminal justice system in the apprehension, adjudication and punishment/treatment of offenders. Little or no concern is paid to prevention of crime. Conversely, "[c]rime science ... is the application of the methods of science to crime and disorder" (Laycock, 2005:4).

In essence, crime science attacks crime from a wide range of disciplines using a broad array of tools. Among the disciplines included are those traditionally found in discussions of crime and criminality—sociology, psychology, criminology and criminal justice. Also included, however, are the fields of engineering, biology, physics, architecture, genetics, communications, computer science, education, and many others. Each of these disciplines offers insight to the behavior of individuals, how to control or manipulate the physical and social environment, the development of safety and security devices, or a myriad of other factors that play a role in crime and crime control. A primary goal of crime science is to bring these divergent disciplines together into a functional, coordinated response to crime (Laycock, 2005).

In many ways, crime science fits nicely in the crime prevention model used in this book. An examination of the approaches listed in Table 2.1 shows a wide array of actions and interventions that require the knowledge and expertise from disciplines beyond those typically involved in the criminal justice system. At the same time, the criminal justice system is intimately involved in the detection, apprehension and intervention with offenders, as well as the implementation of new prevention initiatives. Many of the prevention approaches and interventions outlined in this book rely on methods and information drawn from disciplines not traditionally involved in crime or its prevention.

SUMMARY

Crime prevention can take a variety of forms. The model offered in this chapter encompasses diverse prevention methods ranging from physical design of homes and communities, to neighborhood watch, to educating the public, to situationally unique interventions, to drug prevention, to deterrence, incapacitation and rehabilitation. Crime prevention is not limited to the work of the criminal justice system. Instead, it relies on the knowledge and abilities of a very diverse set of individuals and groups who work to apply scientific principles to the understanding and prevention of crime. Beyond just presenting a discussion of different prevention approaches, this book attempts to provide insight to the effectiveness of each approach. Evaluating prevention initiatives, however, is not without its problems. It is to the topic of evaluating crime prevention that we now turn.

Chapter 3

EVALUATION AND CRIME PREVENTION

Key Terms:

context
cost-benefit evaluation
evaluation
external validity
generalizability
gold standard
impact evaluation

internal validity
Maryland Scale of Scientific
    Methods
mechanism
process evaluation
realistic evaluation

Learning Objectives:

After reading this chapter you should be able to:

- Distinguish between impact and process evaluation

- Discuss obstacles to undertaking impact evaluations

- Provide an argument for the value of process evaluations

- Define cost-benefit evaluation and discuss problems with doing them in crime prevention

- Give reasons for why programs and evaluation should be based on sound theory

- Identify measurement problems in evaluating crime prevention programs

- Explain why the appropriate follow-up period is important

- Explain what is meant by the "gold standard" in evaluation

- Discuss the concerns with relying on a single methodological standard for evaluations

- Discuss both threats to internal and external validity, particularly as they impact crime prevention evaluations

- Outline the Maryland Scale of Scientific Methods

- Explain realistic evaluation

The goal of this book is not just to provide information on crime prevention programs and initiatives. Instead, the intent is to offer insight into what works in crime prevention. To accomplish that task, it is necessary to evaluate prevention programs and efforts. Because this text is a survey of the prevention field, it relies on evaluations conducted by other researchers. At first glance it may seem that reporting on evaluations that have already been conducted would be easy and straightforward. Unfortunately, a good deal of debate has occurred over what constitutes "good" evaluation (see, Holcomb and Lab, 2003).

The purpose of this chapter is to discuss the topic of evaluation and lay the groundwork for the evaluation of prevention that appears throughout the chapters. A number of topics will be addressed. First, the different types of evaluations, or as some would argue the different parts of an effective evaluation, are discussed. The second issue to be discussed involves theoretical and measurement problems. The debate about the appropriate methodology for evaluations forms a core topic in the chapter and helps tie together the different threads raised in the earlier sections. The ultimate goal is to lay a foundation for understanding the importance of evaluation in crime prevention.

TYPES OF EVALUATION

In general, *evaluation* refers to investigating the usefulness of some exercise or phenomenon. Evaluation of crime prevention, therefore, refers to investigating the impact of a prevention technique or intervention on the level of subsequent crime, fear or other intended outcome. Making such a determination may require the use of various methodologies. Ekblom and Pease (1995) argue that evaluation research is often viewed as addressing two research goals using diverse methodologies. These goals are generally understanding the implementation of the intervention and the impact of the initiative and are evaluated using two forms of evaluation—process and impact evaluation—respectively. A third form of evaluation—cost-benefit evaluation—is becoming more common.

Impact Evaluation

Impact, or outcome, evaluations focus on what changes (e.g., to the crime rate) occur after the introduction of the policy, intervention, or program. There are many examples of impact evaluations in criminal justice. For example, treatment programs used in correctional settings are evaluated on their effectiveness to reduce recidivism or drug use among offenders. Changes in police patrol practices aimed at reducing the level of drug sales in an area are evaluated in terms of subsequent numbers of sales. In-school interventions that teach students how to respond to problems in a non-aggressive fashion are assessed in terms of the type or amount of future physical confrontations in school. Neighborhood watch programs have been evaluated in terms of their impact on crime levels in the neighborhood and the fear of crime reported by residents. Changes in traffic patterns, walkways, building designs, and the layout of residential complexes have been assessed in terms of changes in crime. Evaluations of newsletters and media efforts to promote preventive activity have looked at the ability of such efforts to not only change citizen behavior but also their victimization levels. These are a few of the many evaluations that can be found throughout the crime prevention literature and discussed in later chapters.

Undertaking impact evaluations in crime prevention poses some interesting problems. One major obstacle is the fact that crime prevention initiatives rarely rely on a single intervention or approach. Rather, crime prevention programs often incorporate a menu of different activities at the same time. For example, neighborhood crime prevention typically includes a watch scheme, property identification, neighborhood cleanup, periodic meetings, and some form of prevention newsletter. The problem for evaluators is identifying which of the many prevention activities is responsible for the observed changes (if any). It is possible that the entire package is necessary to bring about the change, or it is equally plausible that the mix of interventions mitigates any positive impact on crime and fear. It is rare to find that a single prevention activity is undertaken in total isolation from other anti-crime initiatives.

A second set of obstacles for evaluating crime prevention revolves around the fact that the target of the initiatives (and thus the unit of analysis for the evaluation) is a neighborhood or other geographic area. This is not to suggest that implementing a crime prevention program across a neighborhood or community is ill-conceived. Rather, the issue is solely a methodological one, and it is multifaceted. First, neighborhoods cannot be isolated. This means that there are a multitude of other influences on the neighborhood, many of them from the surrounding community or adjacent neighborhoods, that may have an influence on the levels of crime. Second, many interventions are not uniformly applied across an area or adopted by all residents. As a result, it is possible that an intervention appears to have no impact across the area, when in fact those who participate experience a reduction in crime and/or fear. Impact evaluations need to pay special attention to the effectiveness of prevention techniques in cases in which there is not total cooperation or adoption of the intervention. A third concern with impact evaluations of crime prevention programs involves the competing issues of crime displacement and diffusion of benefits. While both of these will be discussed at length later in the book, they refer to the issue of whether the prevention activity influences the level of crime and fear in areas not involved in the initiative. These obstacles to impact evaluations will receive further consideration later in this chapter.

Process Evaluation

Process evaluations consider the implementation of a program or initiative and involve determining the procedures used to implement a specific program. These evaluations also examine the social context within which the program or initiative operates (Ekblom and Pease, 1995). In general, process evaluations offer a detailed descriptive account of the program and its implementation. Process evaluations look at a wide range of variables and topics starting with the initial goals of the initiative and continuing all the way through the current operations (or closing) of the program. Typical factors considered are the mission/goals of the program, the level and quality of program staff, the funding and other resources of the program, obstacles faced in implementing and sustaining the initiative, the degree to which the project was carried out as planned, the level of support for the program, the degree to which the clients complied with the intervention, the quality of the data gathered, and any changes made in the program over time. All of this information is used in assessing the degree to which the intervention was successfully implemented as planned. Advocates of process evaluations point out that the resulting information is pivotal in answering questions about the context of an intervention and what actually took place in the initiative.

Unfortunately, many evaluations only look only at the process. There is often no attempt to undertake an impact evaluation. Thus, it is possible to know what was attempted and how well it was done, but it is impossible to know whether it had any impact on crime and/or fear of crime. Among the more extensive process evaluations in the United States and the United Kingdom are those examining partnership initiatives, including the Comprehensive Communities Programs, the Strategic Approaches to Community Safety Initiative, the Burglary Reduction Initiative and the Crime and Disorder projects. Almost without exception, the U.S. evaluations have been exclusively process oriented (for example, Bureau of Justice Assistance, 1997; Kelling, 1998; Rosenbaum and Kaminska-Costello, 1998). Even where impact evaluations were planned, they were often abandoned before they were funded or completed.

Process evaluations of prevention programs or other initiatives often view success in terms other than reaching the outcome goals of the program. Instead, success is often measured in terms of the number of meetings held, participation by different agencies at the meetings, how long the program has been operating, the number of clients handled, the amount of funds expended, or the development of operational plans. What is missing is the assessment of the program's impact on crime, fear, quality of life, or other intended outcome. From the standpoint of having an impact on crime, process evaluations alone offer no insight.

Given the fact that process evaluations do not answer the key question for many programs (i.e., does it reduce crime), why are they so prevalent? Several reasons are apparent. First, doing a process evaluation can set the stage for an outcome study by indicating whether the intervention or initiative has been implemented correctly and whether the target receives the amount of intervention necessary to bring about the intended change. Second, process evaluations can provide insight into the context within which the intervention operates. Knowing the background of the problem, the operations of the program, what took place, problems that arose, and other factors can provide information on whether the intervention can be used in another place at another time. That is, process evaluations provide insight into the potential generalizability of the intervention. In this sense, therefore, a process evaluation becomes an important part of the overall assessment of the program. Finally, process evaluations have the distinct advantage that they cannot fail. Every process evaluation can tell about what happened, how much took place, how many participated, and other factors. Such information can form the basis of a formidable report showing that an initiative is busy doing a lot of things. Thus, a program can point to numerous accomplishments.

In conjunction with an impact evaluation, process evaluations provide information on the different settings, the implementation of the intervention, and other factors that may have an impact on the results (Tilley, 2002). Process evaluations should accompany an impact evaluation. Process evaluations look at how well the intervention was implemented, was it maintained at the level needed for success, did the experimental group accept the intervention, were there factors that may have kept the program from succeeding, and similar issues. Clearly, there are unique social, physical and situational factors that will affect the ability of a prevention program to have an impact (Ekblom, 2002; Tilley, 2002).

Cost-Benefit Evaluations

The third type of evaluation that deserves mentioning here is that of a cost-benefit evaluation. A *cost-benefit evaluation* (or cost-benefit analysis) seeks to assess whether the costs of an intervention are justified by the benefits or outcomes that accrue from it. Aos (2003) demonstrates that assessing the costs and benefits of a prevention program is an important component of a full evaluation of any program. With limited resources available to it, the criminal justice system (as well as any government or private enterprise) needs to implement programs that can bring about the desired changes for the least cost. Cost-benefit analysis is a form of process evaluation that requires that an impact evaluation be completed at the same time. The reason for this is relatively simple, you cannot determine if the costs are justified if you do not measure the ability of the program to bring about the expected change. Thus, a cost-benefit analysis requires both a process and impact evaluation.

Undertaking a cost-benefit analysis in crime prevention and criminal justice poses some problems not always found in other disciplines. The largest problem involves setting monetary values on factors that are not easily enumerated (Tilley, 2009). For example, placing a value on burglaries that do not occur may be accomplished by taking the average dollar lost from past burglaries and assuming that each prevented burglary is a savings at that dollar figure. How do you place a monetary value, however, on things like reduced fear of crime, trauma from victimization, or psychological/emotional loss due to an assault or homicide? How do you account for time loss that may not be related to days off work? The problem of setting values for many factors is pervasive in social science evaluations. A second problem is making certain that all the of the costs involved in the program (and related to the program operations) are counted. While counting the number of copies made and office hours spent can be completed, it is harder to enumerate the value of lost time spent on other activities, the level of effort expended, and other factors. These problems do not make it impossible to conduct a cost-benefit analysis, although they do make it more challenging.

THEORY AND MEASUREMENT IN EVALUATION

The value of any evaluation, as well as the ability to conduct an evaluation, is largely determined by basic factors related to the underlying theory and the measurement of key concepts. It is not uncommon for evaluations to pay little attention to theory and to uncritically use variables that are not appropriate for answering relevant questions. An additional common evaluation shortfall involves the failure to follow-up on the project. Each of these issues is addressed in turn.

Theoretical Concerns

Crime prevention programs are often implemented, and evaluations are often undertaken, in a theoretical vacuum (Holcomb and Lab, 2003). This means that those implementing and evaluating the intervention pay no attention to the theoretical assumptions underlying the prevention program. Basic questions, such as why should the redesign of the parking deck have an impact on theft from autos, why should a partnership reduce drug use in the community, and why would an educational program reduce aggressive behavior, are often ignored. This is surprising given their centrality to the evaluation of initiatives. It is not be necessary to identify a formal theory for every intervention, but it is necessary to be able to adequately explain why and how the intervention will bring about the desired change.

Despite the argument that evaluations should be guided by the theory underlying the intervention, a great number of successful evaluations are undertaken in a theoretical vacuum. These evaluations may still provide answers to whether or not the program had the intended impact. Why then is the lack of theory a concern for evaluation? One reason is that while these evaluations can tell us if prevention initiatives are successful, they fail to tell us why a program is or is not successful. They also can provide only limited insight to whether the program can be implemented in other places or at other times (Holcomb and Lab, 2003). A second reason for having a solid theoretical basis for the evaluation is that many investigations might not be necessary if the underlying theory for the intervention was examined. There are numerous examples where examination of the underlying theory would have raised questions about the efficacy of the intervention at the outset (Holcomb and Lab, 2003). For example, studies of curfews often fail to recognize that, as they are typically conceived, there is no reason to expect them to have any impact. This is because the underlying argument is that getting youths off the street would make it hard for them to commit offenses. Unfortunately, curfews imposed from late night to early morning (as is typical) will have no impact on the number of crimes during the after school hours when most youths commit their offenses. Clearly, the knowledge of the theory underlying curfews would not only eliminate the need for the evaluation, but also suggest termination of the curfew (Holcomb and Lab, 2003). Basically, evaluations of programs without a theoretical base can be considered as "research in a vacuum." There is no context within which to understand the program, frame the evaluation questions, design the methodological approach, or carry out the evaluation.

If evaluations undertaken with an eye toward theory are preferred, why are so many atheoretical evaluations undertaken? Several reasons are apparent (see Holcomb and Lab, 2003). First, there is an "outcome myopia" that permeates many evaluations. This means that the programs and the evaluators are only interested in whether the program works and not how or why it works. The resulting evaluation simply assumes that a positive outcome is enough to prove the intervention works. While this is a plausible conclusion, it is also possible that other factors are at work and it does not tell anything about why a program does not work when the findings are negative. A second reason for the lack of theory in evaluation is the fact that many program administrators simply "know" that it works. For them, "it is only common sense that it works!" Thus, they are not interested in spending the time, money and/or effort to prove what they already know. There is no reason to explain exactly how a program works or to undertake an evaluation— it simply does. This blind belief in programs is evident in many initiatives that have the ear of politicians who can provide legislative and funding support. A final explanation for the appearance of atheoretical evaluations of crime prevention initiatives is the fact that many programs are the result of grassroots efforts by small groups. These groups are not always interested in evaluations or how the program works, as long as they are happy with it. Evaluations of these programs, therefore, are undertaken by outside researchers who come to the program long after it was initiated. They have few resources to devote to an evaluation and probably have not been collecting data on the project. The result are evaluations that look only at the outcome and ignores the question of why the program should or does work. The evaluator gets in, completes the evaluation, and gets out in relatively short order.

Truly effective evaluations need to be informed by the underlying theoretical rationale for the program under inspection. Just knowing that a program does or does not work is not enough. It is important to understand why an intervention works or does not work. Of equal value is gaining insight to whether a program can be implemented in another place at another time. The underlying theory provides a great deal of information that is lost in evaluations where theory is missing.

Measurement Issues

Measurement of key concepts is a concern in all forms of research, but nowhere is it more evident than in evaluation research. The types of interventions found in crime prevention present some interesting measurement problems. One problem involves measuring the key outcome variables when the intervention is geographically based. While some studies looking at city-wide crime levels can use police data, many crime prevention programs are based on neighborhoods or other small geographic areas that do not coincide with specific police reporting areas. Thus, a great deal of data manipulation is needed if official crime records are to be used. The advent of geographic information systems that allow for the mapping of crime locations has helped to minimize this problem, but only in those locations where this technology is in use.

One possible solution to the problems with using official data is to rely on victim survey data. Indeed, many prevention evaluations incorporate victim surveys along with official crime data. Victim survey data offer a number of advantages, including the ability to collect data for the exact area under consideration, the ability to capture crimes not reported to the police, and the fact that the survey can collect information on fear and personal perceptions that is not found in official records. Unfortunately, victim data is not always available and the collection of that data can be both time consuming and costly. This lack of data is compounded when an evaluation also needs data from a comparison group or area.

The ability of victim surveys to gather data on key concepts such as fear is not without its own problems. As was seen in Chapter 1, operationalizing fear is not straightforward. Fear has been measured in a number of different ways, making it difficult to compare results across studies. It is also problematic if the measure of fear is inappropriate for the type of intervention. For example, asking questions about perceptions of changing crime may not be germane if the intervention involves lighting the neighborhood so residents go out at night. Instead, asking about whether respondents would walk outside at night on their street would fit the prevention technique. The choice of operationalization is greatly contingent on the prevention initiative and the underlying theory. Thus, the need to use theory to inform the prevention program extends naturally to the choice of variables and how they are measured.

Yet another measurement issue involves finding ways to uncover the competing influences in the project that mask the outcomes. An interesting conundrum in crime prevention initiatives is the fact that the programs often try to simultaneously reduce the level of crime while increasing the reporting of crime to the police. A prime example are neighborhood watch programs. These programs typically include a number of initiatives such as property identification, surveillance of neighbors' property, and encouraging the reporting of crime to the police. While the intent is to reduce the level of crime in the neighborhood, it is easy to see how an effective program can appear to have no impact. This would occur if, while the program reduces the actual level of offending in the area, the residents report a larger percentage of the crimes that do occur. The official data, therefore, would appear unchanged even though crime is down. Prevention evaluations need to consider this type of problem and utilize methods (such as pre- and post-project victim surveys) that would uncover this complication.

Follow-Up Periods

An issue closely related to how something is measured is the issue of the appropriate length of time to follow-up the project. The question of follow-up period is actually two sided. First, how long after the implementation of the program or intervention will changes in crime (or other outcome) appear? Second, is there a possibility that over time any initial changes will diminish or disappear? The most common situation is one in which the evaluation considers a relatively short follow-up period, often six months. This occurs because of the immediate desire to know whether the program works and the fact that the costs of an evaluation increase with the follow-up time. A relatively short follow-up time means that any program that requires a lengthy time to have an impact will be seen as ineffective. Alternatively, an initiative with an immediate impact will be declared a success, despite the (unknown) fact that the impact may diminish over time. While there is no rule on the appropriate follow-up time, the evaluation should look to the underlying theory for guidance. The ideal situation would be one where follow-up data is gathered at different intervals, such as three months, six months, 12 months and 18 months. The use of multiple points in time will illuminate both the speed of an intervention's impact (if any) and any evidence that the impact diminishes over time.

Summary

Evaluations that ignore theory (or evaluations of atheoretical programs) and problems with measurement and follow-up are common in studies of crime prevention programs. Much of this is due to the fact that evaluations are often undertaken late in the life of programs when data is more difficult to gather and the program has undergone several changes since its inception. The evaluation also may be undertaken by individuals or groups connected with the intervention and who "know it works," thus adding a potential source of bias. While solutions to these issues are not always easy or cheap, evaluations need to take whatever steps are possible to avoid these problems.

THE METHOD FOR EVALUATION

An inspection of the crime prevention literature reveals great diversity in the methodologies applied in the search for what works in prevention. A great deal of debate about the appropriate methods to use has ensued over the past 10 years. Where one view argues that true experimental design is the preferred approach, the opposite view suggests that the method should be dictated by the questions being asked and the situation within which the intervention exists.

Experimental Design

A great deal of discussion has centered around the claim that only evaluations using (or approximating) a true experimental design are worthy of consideration. Also known as a *randomized control trial* (Tilley, 2009), experimental design has become the gold standard in evaluation. Why is experimental design the preferred approach by many evaluators? From a purely methodological perspective it offers a number of strengths. First, a randomized control trial, which relies on the random assignment of cases into experimental and control groups, increases the likelihood that the two groups being compared are equivalent. Second, there is enough control over the evaluation to make certain that the experimental group receives the treatment or intervention, while the control group does not. There is also the expectation that all other possible factors that could influence the outcome are controlled to the extent that they cannot affect either of the two groups. In essence, the experimental design addresses the various threats to *internal validity*—that is, factors that could cause the results other than the measures that were implemented (see Table 3.1) If the project is able to accomplish these things, any

Table 3.1
Selected Threats to Internal Validity

History	Something taking place independent of the experiment causes the change to take place
Maturation	The aging of the study subjects brings about a change independent of the program or stimulus
Testing	The taking of measurements in the study (such as through surveys, observations, or data collection) causes change to occur in place of or beyond the impact of the stimulus
Instrumentation	Changes in the study measures or study procedure that take place during the project bring about changes
Statistical Regression	Implementing a project that focuses on subjects that are at an extreme end of a measurement (such as low or high crime rate) will naturally regress to a statistical average score over time
Selection	Experimental subjects who are not truly representative of the population of interest will influence the results
Mortality	The incidence of study subjects dropping out during the course of the experiment can bias the results if they are different from those who remain in the project

Source: Adapted by author from Shadish et al. (2002).

changes observed in the experimental group that do not appear in the control group should be attributable to the intervention. The researcher thus feels confident that they "know" the cause of any observed change.

This "gold standard" has a long history in the hard sciences (e.g. biology and chemistry) and is accepted practice. A great deal of attention has been focused on relying on this approach in criminal justice and crime prevention due to the work of Sherman et al. (1997) which was prepared for the U.S. Congress. In that report, the authors opted to rate the existing literature on prevention initiatives according to how closely a study adhered to the standards of a true experimental design (see Berk and Rossi, 1999; Cook and Campbell, 1979). Using the resulting *Maryland Scale of Scientific Methods* (see Table 3.2), Sherman et al. (1997) conclude that bulk of the evidence on prevention activities is that there are relatively few effective programs/ interventions. Subsequent work using this approach has gone so far as to suggest that policy makers should only consider research that meets the gold standard and that research funds should only be expended when an experimental design (or close to it) is possible (Sherman et al., 2002). Unfortunately, applying this standard in crime prevention research (and, more generally, social sciences) is difficult and often not possible.

Table 3.2
Maryland Scale of Scientific Methods

Level 1:	Correlation between a crime prevention program and a measure of crime or crime risk factors at a single point in time.
Level 2:	Temporal sequence between the program and the crime or risk outcome clearly observed, or the presence of a comparison group without demonstrated comparability to the treatment group.
Level 3:	A comparison between two or more comparable units of analysis, one with and one without the program.
Level 4:	Comparison between multiple units with and without the program, controlling for other factors, or using comparison units that evidence only minor differences.
Level 5:	Random assignment and analysis of comparable units to program and comparison groups.

Source: Sherman et al. (1998).

There are various problems with relying exclusively on experimental designs in crime prevention. Foremost among these is the question of whether the results would be applicable in other places, settings, and times—that is, the *generalizability* of the results. This problem involves what are called *threats to external validity*. Table 3.3 lists a variety of threats to external validity. An inspection of this list reveals the wide range of potential problems inherent in trying to replicate the findings of any program evaluation. One major problem is that many interventions target communities and larger collectives, rather than individuals. It is very difficult, if not impossible, to randomly assign communities to experimental and control groups (Ekblom, 2002; Ekblom and Pease, 1995; Laycock, 2002). In the absence of randomization, the best that can be done is to try and identify neighborhoods or communities for the control group which are matched to the experimental areas on as many characteristics as possible. Matching, however, cannot guarantee that the areas are comparable. Even if random assignment is possible or good matching is accomplished, there is no way to isolate the experimental and control communities from all other influences. Most importantly, interventions and initiatives implemented in a community cannot be hidden from sight. People in both the experimental community and the control areas will be able to see what is taking place. This can lead individuals and groups in the control areas to adopt the intervention, or to act in such a way as to impede the intervention in the experimental area. There is simply no way to isolate the experimental community from all outside influences as can be done in a laboratory.

A number of threats to external validity involve issues related to the implementation of an intervention (Tilley, 2009). The individuals/groups involved in an intervention can vary greatly from place to place. This can affect the quality of the intervention or the degree to which a program is fully implemented/delivered as planned (i.e., the dosage). The locations,

Table 3.3
Threats to External Validity

Threat to External Validity	Explanation
Place attributes	Places are never exactly the same, and the details may be important to the effects brought about
Victim attributes	Patterns of victim attributes will vary from one site to another, and the details may be important to the effects brought about
Offender/likely offender attributes	Patterns of offender/likely offender attributes will vary from one site to another, and the details may be important to the effects brought about
Intervenor attributes	Who is involved in delivering the intervention, in terms of leader, front-line worker, or agency will vary from site to site, and the details may be important to the effects brought about
Community/family/peer group attributes	The patterns of social relationships in which offenders and victims are embedded will vary from site to site, and the details may be important to the effects brought about
Intervention attributes	What is done can never be duplicated exactly, and the details may be important to the effects brought about
Non-crime options	Other non-crime behaviors available to those who would otherwise commit an offense will vary from site to site, and the details may be important to the effects brought about
Crime options	Different crime possibilities available to those who would otherwise commit some particular type of offense will vary from site to site, and the details may be important to the effects brought about
Dosage	Intensity of intervention in relation to target people, places of crime problems varies from site to site, and the level may be important to the effects brought about

Source: Tilley (2009). Used by permission.

crime, victims, and offenders are rarely (if ever) exactly the same in different places or times, which may affect the outcome of the intervention. The bottom line is, even if an evaluation shows that a crime prevention intervention is effective in one place, there is no guarantee that it will be just as effective in other places.

The underlying problem for external validity is that, too often, experimental designs fail to consider the *context* within which a program or intervention operates. What this means is that the program may be successful in one location at one time while it is a dismal failure at another location or time. There may be something different about the neighborhoods that is not readily apparent from simple demographic, crime, or social information available about the areas. Simple random assignment or matching cannot eliminate these factors. Instead, there is a need for a thorough process evaluation to accompany the impact analysis.

Another flaw in relying too heavily on experimental design is the fact that it is all too easy to jump to a conclusion that something does or does not work. This may occur when no impact emerges in an analysis— the researcher claims it was a failure and suggests abandoning further use of the intervention. The negative findings, however, may be the result of factors such as poor program implementation, miss specification of the appropriate target or causal mechanism underlying the problem, or resistance by the target (Eck, 2002). In these cases, a well constructed experimental design may find no programmatic impact and declare the intervention a failure, when in fact the intervention can and would work in other settings or if it was properly implemented.

Unfortunately, in many evaluations using rigorous experimental designs, the methodology ends up driving the project rather than allowing the underlying theory to dictate the development of the project or its analysis. You can have a good experimental design and find no impact of a project due to the fact that there was no theoretical reason to expect the intervention to work in the first place. One good example of this appears in evaluations of juvenile curfew laws (discussed earlier in this chapter) where the evaluation design meets the level of scientific rigor outlined by Sherman et al. (1997) but ignores the theoretical flaw underlying the approach. There was really no reason to undertake evaluations just because it met some methodological standard when attention to the theory would have suggested that the intervention would not work.

Realistic Evaluation

Overemphasis on the "correct" methodology (i.e. the gold standard) marginalizes the value of other approaches to building knowledge of crime prevention. Basic knowledge essential to crime prevention has come out of a variety of research endeavors, such as ethnographic and qualitative methodologies. A prime example of this is the knowledge we have on burglars and their choice of targets. Extensive ethnographic research has been completed with different groups of burglars, in different settings, across different countries, and using different approaches, such as from riding around with them in cars to having them rate pictures of homes. These studies (e.g. Bennett, 1986; Bennett and Wright, 1984; Cromwell et al., 1991; Reppetto, 1974; Wright and Decker, 1994) have provided a good deal of insight on the behaviors of burglars that is consistent across the studies (see Chapter 6 for more information). This information is very helpful for understanding what works to prevent residential burglary. Similar research has been completed targeting robbery other property crimes and offenders (e.g. Feeney, 1986; Gill and Matthews, 1994; Shover, 1991; Tunnell, 1992). While these projects do not even approximate the experimental design standards, should we simply ignore the information and abandon this line of inquiry? The answer to this question is "No." Indeed, it is important to recognize that the "gold standard" is not appropriate for all investigations.

Pawson and Tilley (1997) call for a more "realistic" approach to evaluation research. In *realistic evaluation*, rather than relying exclusively on experimental approaches, evaluation needs to observe the phenomenon in its entirety. Two key ideas are central to realistic evaluation– mechanism and context. *Mechanism* refers to understanding "what it is about a program which makes it work" (Pawson and Tilley, 1997:66). In other words, by what process does an intervention impact an outcome measure such as crime or fear of crime? While the most rigorous experimental design can indicate whether a program is responsible for any observed changes, it does not tell *why* the program had an impact on the dependent variable. It is vital to understand the mechanism bringing about the change in order to build basic knowledge and to increase the potential success at transplanting a program from one setting to another (Ekblom 2002).

Beyond just examining the mechanism by which something works, Pawson and Tilley (1997:69) note that "the relationship between causal mechanisms and their effects is not fixed, but contingent." By this, they argue that the *context* in which any intervention is implemented has an impact on its effectiveness. Consequently, the impact of a prevention effort is contingent on the context in which it operates, and subsequently will affect whether the program has a similar impact in different settings (Tilley, 2002). Ekblom and Pease (1995) note that efforts to find a single, best methodological approach to evaluation are short sighted when they ignore the context of the program being studied. Circumstances unique to one setting and context may directly affect the ability of an intervention to achieve its goals. This requires more than a superficial impact evaluation which meets the "gold standard." It is important to combine knowledge of the mechanism by which change is thought to occur with an understanding of the wider context in which specific crime prevention efforts are implemented.

What is needed is recognition that the problem, the theory and the context should determine the appropriate methodology for understanding what works. A single standard is not appropriate for all problems or questions. As Laycock (2002: 234) has so aptly pointed out "'the gold standard' should not be any *particular* methodology, but a process of informed decision-making through which the *appropriate* methodology is chosen."

Summary

Based on the above, this book considers the evidence on crime prevention regardless of the methodology used. What is more important is whether the methodology is sound for the problem and the situation in which it is used. While experimental design informed by good theory and attention to the context of the project is preferred, it is not often available. In those cases, the best knowledge available is discussed and used to inform about what appears to work and not work. Even while recognizing that context is important, there is a clear bias in this book toward emphasizing outcome or impact evaluations. Underlying process evaluation materials and information have been considered throughout the chapters but receive little direct presentation due to space concerns.

AN OVERVIEW OF THE BOOK

The balance of this text attempts to expose the reader to some of the predominant crime prevention issues and techniques of the past 40 years. The discussion is, by necessity, limited and does not deal with all of the prevention programs that have been attempted or evaluated. The goal of the book is to present a sampling of prevention approaches, outline the selected programs and issues, present the research and (primarily impact) evaluations which have been carried out on the programs (if any have been done), and critically examine the prevention effort and the potential of the approach to effect crime and the fear of crime.

Throughout the text, the key criterion for assessing the effectiveness of various crime prevention methods is lower subsequent offending and/or fear of crime. Subsequent offending could be either initial criminal activity (primary prevention) or recidivism (tertiary prevention). Lowered fear of crime could come from any intervention mechanism, especially primary preventive techniques. Although a variety of other outcome measures have been used in assessing crime prevention programs (e.g. program operation, costs, number of clients served), reductions in crime and fear are the ultimate goals. These other outcomes will receive little attention in the following chapters. This does not mean that they are unimportant considerations. Indeed, from a fiscal standpoint it is important to know the costs of programs. However, this does not indicate the ability of the intervention to alter crime or fear of crime.

At the end of many chapters, there is an attempt to summarize what is known about the preventive impact of different interventions. These tables are not all inclusive of the evidence that has been presented in the chapter. Indeed, in many instances, information will appear in the summary tables that has not appeared in the chapter discussions or has only appeared in a very abbreviated fashion. This is due more to space limitations than any relative importance of the topics.

Section I

PRIMARY PREVENTION

The words "crime prevention" typically bring to mind programs that are divorced from the formal criminal justice system and are greatly reliant upon the efforts of the citizenry. Such crime prevention efforts typically fall under the rubric of Primary Prevention. Primary prevention deals with eliminating influences in the physical and social environment that engender deviant behavior. Such programs do not target individuals who are already criminal or prone to criminal behavior, except in a most indirect sense. Instead, primary prevention programs work with general physical and societal factors that provide the opportunity for deviance to occur. The following chapters reflect varying methods aimed at removing or mitigating the criminogenic aspects of society.

Chapter 4 focuses directly on physical design components of crime prevention. Crime Prevention Through Environmental Design (CPTED) has been one of the most widely discussed crime prevention approaches of the past 30 years. The idea behind CPTED is making crime harder to commit and making residents feel more secure in their surroundings. This is accomplished by altering the physical environment. Increased lighting, improved locks, stronger doors, use of surveillance equipment, and other physical changes are intended to bring about greater social cohesion, citizen concern and involvement and, ultimately, reduced crime and fear of crime. Chapter 5 moves to a direct analysis of Neighborhood Crime Prevention. The basic focus is on the mechanisms involved in building neighborhood cohesion and concern through crime prevention activities. Block watch and citizen patrols are key elements of many neighborhood efforts. Chapter 6 investigates competing ideas of displacement and diffusion as a result of crime prevention programming. Typically, reduced levels of crime in crime prevention areas serve as an indicator that crime has been eliminated. There is the potential, however, that the crime is simply displaced along some dimension. In displacement, the overall crime rate remains the same while modifications in the type, timing, or placement of crime occur.

One key element in the discussion of crime prevention is the impact of programs on the fear of crime. Mass media crime prevention techniques, outlined in Chapter 7, represent an attempt to deal directly with the fear of crime, as well as actual crime, across a wide range of societal members. The final chapter in this section focuses on the formal criminal justice system. Deterrence is a cornerstone of formal system processing. General deterrence (as opposed to specific deterrence, which is discussed in Chapter 14) seeks to provide disincentives to persons not yet involved in deviant behavior. This is clearly in the realm of primary prevention. While the earlier chapters examine the impact of crime prevention activities on both crime and fear of crime, the chapter on general deterrence looks only at its effect on actual deviant behavior.

Chapter 4

THE PHYSICAL ENVIRONMENT AND CRIME

Key Terms:

access control
activity support
alley gating
CCTV
CPTED
CRAVED
defensible space
escape
hot products
image
incivility
milieu

motivation reinforcement
natural surveillance
Operation Identification
OTREP
product design
prospect
Reducing Burglary Initiative
refuge
Secure By Design
smart guns
target hardening
territoriality

Learning Objectives:

After reading this chapter you should be able to:

- Define CPTED

- Define defensible space

- List and define Newman's elements of defensible space

- Explain OTREP and its relation to crime

- Discuss four intermediate goals of physical design changes

- List and discuss the core principles of Secure By Design

- Provide insight on the effectiveness of lighting to prevent crime

- Define and discuss the ideas of prospect, refuge and escape as they relate to prevention

- Discuss the evidence on the effectiveness of CCTV

- Explain Operation Identification and its impact

- Demonstrate your knowledge about the impact of street layout on crime prevention

- Discuss neighborhood-wide environmental design programs and their impact on crime and fear

- Discuss Merry's analysis of and conclusions on defensible space

- Explain incivility and its relation to crime and crime prevention

- Discuss the idea of product design and provide examples for crime prevention

- List the MISdeeds of products and their relation to crime

One of the more well-known approaches in primary prevention involves modifying the physical environment. Changing the physical design of a home, business, or neighborhood has the potential of affecting crime in a variety of ways. It is also possible to change the design of different items. Such changes may make it more difficult to carry out a crime. This difficulty can result in lower payoff in relationship to the effort. Another potential impact is that the risk of being seen and caught while committing an offense may be enhanced. Finally, the physical design changes may prompt residents to alter their behavior in ways that make crime more difficult to commit. This chapter introduces and explains various physical design approaches for combating and preventing crime, examines the impact these actions have on crime, and assesses the potential of these approaches.

CRIME PREVENTION THROUGH ENVIRONMENTAL DESIGN

Efforts to alter the physical design of an area or location to impact crime are generally referred to as *Crime Prevention Through Environmental Design* (CPTED). Included in this approach are architectural designs that enhance territoriality and surveillance, target hardening, and the recognition of legitimate users of an area. The basic ideas of CPTED grew out of Oscar Newman's (1972) concept of "defensible space."

Defensible space proposes "a model which inhibits crime by creating a physical expression of a social fabric which defends itself" (Newman, 1972). The idea is that the physical characteristics of an area can influence the behavior of both residents and potential offenders. For residents, the appearance and design of the area can engender a more caring attitude, draw the residents into contact with one another, lead to further improvements and use of the area, and build a stake in the control and elimination of crime. For potential offenders, an area's appearance can suggest that residents use and care for their surroundings, pay attention to what occurs, and intervene if an offense is seen.

Newman (1972) identifies four elements of defensible space—territoriality, natural surveillance, image, and milieu. Each of these factors influences the criminogenic nature of the area (see Table 4.1). *Territoriality* refers to the ability and desire of legitimate users of an area to lay claim to the area. Areal control is based on the establishment of real or perceived boundaries, the recognition of strangers and legitimate users of the area, and a general communal atmosphere among the inhabitants. *Natural surveillance* involves designing an area that allows legitimate users to observe the daily activity of both friends and strangers. This permits residents to observe criminal activity and take action. *Image* refers to building a neighborhood or community that does not appear vulnerable to crime and is not isolated from the surrounding community. Finally, *milieu* suggests that the placement of a community within a larger low-crime, high-surveillance area will inhibit criminal activity. All of the aspects of defensible space seek to present the area as a high risk venture for those seeking to commit crime.

Table 4.1
Elements of Defensible Space

Territoriality-	a sense of ownership over an area which prompts people to take action when something seems amiss
Natural Surveillance-	the ability to observe activity, whether inside or outside, without the aid of special devices (such as closed-circuit television)
Image-	a neighborhood having the appearance that it is not isolated and is cared for, and that residents will take action
Milieu-	the placement of a home, building or community in a larger area characterized by low crime

Source: Newman (1972).

Newman (1972) illustrates the impact of these factors by comparing two public housing projects. The first, a high rise, high crime project, allows strangers easy access through unmonitored, multi-user entrances. In addition, the buildings lack windows and opportunities to observe indoor common areas and outdoor pathways. The size of the project mitigates attempts to recognize legitimate users from strangers due to the great numbers of people in the project. Conversely, the second public housing area consists of low-rise buildings that experience lower crime levels. The project limits the number of families using the same entrances. This enhances the ability of residents to identify strangers. Surveillance is enhanced by entrances that face public thoroughfares. Additionally, the low laying structures make casual observation of outdoor activities through windows more feasible and effective. Newman (1972) argues that defensible space can be accomplished through a variety of physical design actions, including the placement of windows conducive to easy visibility of surrounding areas, the location of entrances that are observable by others, the installation of lights to enhance visibility, and the establishment of common areas that are controllable by residents. All of these features are evident in low-rise housing projects and are either absent or limited in high-rise, high-density projects. Most importantly, these features impact the behavior of both legitimate users and potential offenders (Newman, 1972).

CPTED rests on the assumption that potential offenders are influenced by the costs and benefits inherent in an action. Kaplan et al. (1978) illustrate this with an idea they refer to as *OTREP*. That is, crime **O**pportunity is the result of **T**arget, **R**isk, **E**ffort, and **P**ayoff. The assumption is that offenses can be avoided when there is a high risk of apprehension with little potential payoff. Crime should be reduced as the potential costs outweigh the potential benefits. Manipulating physical design features may be one way to bring about higher costs relative to benefits.

Kushmuk and Whittemore (1981) argue that the effect of physical design changes on crime is indirect and operates through four intermediate goals. These goals are increased access control, surveillance, activity support, and motivation reinforcement. The ability to bring about changes in these intermediate goals should affect the level of crime in the community. Given the importance of these four factors, it is important to have a good understanding of each.

Table 4.2
Intermediate Goals of CPTED

Access Control-	the ability to regulate who comes and goes from an area or building, with the intent of limiting access to legitimate users
Surveillance-	actions which enhance the ability of legitimate users to observe the presence of others and their activities, whether through the use of passive devices (such as the placement of windows) or active measures (such as closed-circuit television)
Activity Support-	functions which assist and enhance interaction between citizens and other legitimate users in the community
Motivation Reinforcement-	enhancing feelings of territoriality and social cohesion through physical design features and building pride in the area

Source: Kushmuk and Whittemore (1981).

Access Control

Access control seeks to allow only those persons who have legitimate business in an area to enter. This reduces the opportunity for crime by increasing the effort needed to enter and exit a building or area for the purpose of committing crime. Many access control strategies are referred to as *target hardening*. That is, they are efforts that make potential criminal targets more difficult to victimize. The use and/or installation of locks, bars on windows, unbreakable glass, intruder alarms, fences, safes, and other devices makes crime more difficult to carry out. Neighborhood designs that could make offending more difficult include limiting the flow of traffic through an area by strangers, changes that limit the number of through-streets, establishing cul-de-sacs and dead-end streets, and enhancing the ability of residents to recognize legitimate users. As well as designing places, it is possible to design products in ways that make them more difficult targets.

Other forms of access control/target hardening take an indirect approach to crime control. The placement of identifying marks on personal property makes stolen goods more difficult to fence and easier to identify and return to victims. The use of warning signs, closed-circuit television cameras and lighting may act as psychological deterrents that increase perceived risk. Indeed, cameras need not be operable, as in many department stores, to serve a target-hardening function.

It is important to note that access control/target hardening measures will not eliminate crime. Any form of access control can be overcome by a clever and persistent criminal. The hope is that the measures will reduce the absolute level of crime in the community. The actual impact of these approaches on crime is discussed later in this chapter.

Surveillance

Surveillance involves any action that increases the chance that offenders will be observed. Newman (1972) suggests placing windows in such a fashion to allow residents to see activity on all sides of their homes. Doors should face the street to allow passersby to view activity taking place inside the entranceways and few families should use the same common entrance so that legitimate users can identify one another. Additionally, pathways in and around the community should leave clear, unobstructed views for residents to see what is awaiting them as they enter and exit their homes (Newman, 1972).

Surveillance can be enhanced in a variety of other ways. The installation of lights should enhance the ability to see what occurs in the area. Outdoor activity and pedestrian traffic increase the number of "eyes on the street." This should have a direct effect on opportunities for crime. The chances of committing a crime and getting away unobserved are diminished as the number of people on the street increases. Underlying these suggestions is the assumption that, if a crime or suspicious individual is seen, the observer will inform the police or take some other action designed to eliminate crime.

Activity Support and Motivation Reinforcement

Kushmuk and Whittemore (1981) present both *activity support* and *motivation reinforcement* as roughly the same thing. Both of these ideas relate to the building of a community atmosphere. The ability to recognize neighbors and identify needs of the community should enhance social cohesion among residents and contribute to a communal atmosphere that works to eliminate crime and other common problems. Activity support and motivation reinforcement may occur indirectly through activities such as street fairs, community days, and other social events. It can also be generated by directly recruiting residents for anti-crime activities or other societal/community issues.

The community atmosphere and caring attitude can be built, in part, through the physical appearance and design of an area (Newman, 1972). In a complimentary fashion, the impact of access control/target hardening and surveillance relies on the behavior of legitimate users. Windows, better lighting, and clear viewing are important only if someone opts to use these features. In addition, residents need the ability to recognize legitimate users from strangers in order to assess whether action is needed. This recognition comes from interaction between legitimate users.

The successful implementation of access control, surveillance, activity support and motivation reinforcement should result in lower crime. Both logical sense and empirical research show that most crime occurs in secret, the offender is seen by few, if any, individuals, and the offender faces little risk of apprehension. One solution to this problem is to increase the effort and risk for the offender.

IMPLEMENTATION OF ENVIRONMENTAL DESIGN

The implementation of environmental design strategies has not always gone smoothly or followed a clear plan. Much of the reason for this is the fact that most efforts have taken place with little or no long-range planning and only intermittent government organization and support. Many of the initial projects, such as in Hartford, Connecticut, and Portland, Oregon, were demonstration projects backed by the government or a private foundation (such as Westinghouse Electric). This does not mean that environmental design has been ignored or has no organizational support.

It is only since the mid-1990s that we have seen major organized movement toward incorporating environmental design into communities in an ongoing fashion. In 1989, the Association of Chief Police Officers (ACPO) in England established the *Secured By Design* (SBD) program. This ongoing initiative emphasizes and promotes the inclusion of safety and security measures in new and existing buildings (ACPO, 2009). The SBD project provides architectural and security assistance to any agency requesting its input. At the present time, there are 14 Design Guides available to assist in building safe and secure homes, facilities and locations (ACPO, 2009). Among these guides are those for new homes, multi-storied dwellings, play areas, and schools. The SBD program includes 6 Core Principles (see Table 4.3), which closely align with the ideas of defensible space, including natural surveillance and access control.

Table 4.3
SBD Core Principles

1.	Integrated Approach
2.	Environmental Quality and Sense of Ownership
3.	Natural Surveillance
4.	Access and Footpaths
5.	Open Space Provision and Management
6.	Lighting

Source: Adapted by author from ACPO (2004).

The passage of the 1998 *Crime and Disorder Act* (CDA) in the United Kingdom is another good example of governmental adoption of environmental design. The CDA mandated the cooperation of many agencies in addressing crime problems. Included in that mandate were plans to rely on architects and planners in efforts to design out crime (Everson and Woodhouse, 2007).

Today there are a wide range of organizations, both national and international, that promote environmental design. Among these are the International CPTED Association, the National Institute of Crime Prevention's CPTED Training web site, and the Designing Out Crime Association (U.K.). There has also been a wide range of projects and evaluations that have been attempted to assess the effectiveness of environmental design changes.

THE IMPACT OF PHYSICAL DESIGN

The impact of defensible space/physical design features on crime and fear can be either direct or indirect. Rubenstein et al. (1980) outline three types of changes or effects that appear in analyses of crime prevention (see Figure 4.1). Type 1 effects are those that measure the direct impact of physical design features (such as locks, lights or fences) on crime. Type 2 effects consider the impact of the physical design on a variety of intervening factors. Possible intervening factors include the attitudes of legitimate users about their community, feelings of territoriality, efforts of community members to combat crime, and an improved community atmosphere. The physical design features bring about changes in these intervening factors prior to effecting crime. Finally, Type 3 measures deal with the direct effect of the intervening factors on crime and the indirect influence of physical design on crime through the intervening factors.

Figure 4.1
Model of Crime Prevention Effects

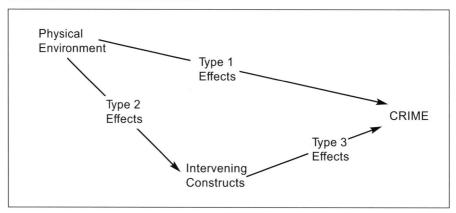

The following discussion of physical design and its influence on crime is divided into several sections. First, the effect of access control/target hardening and surveillance techniques are considered as individual factors. Second, the evaluation moves to studies that examine broad-based uses of defensible space concepts in residential and commercial areas. Finally, altering the physical environment by designing products with prevention in mind is considered.

The Effects of Individual Factors

The ideas of access control/target hardening and surveillance include a wide range of potential interventions for combating crime. Increased street lighting, reduced concealment, installation of locks, use of unbreakable glass, alarms and cameras, marking of property for identification, and security guards are only a few of the available means of prevention. Despite this proliferation of methods, few of these have been subjected to individual evaluation. Most crime prevention programs rely on a range of activities and not just a single approach. Almost without exception, most evaluations look at the direct impact of physical design on crime and/or fear of crime.

Lighting

Efforts to prevent crime by improving the lighting in an areas was a major undertaking in the 1970s and remains a common approach in both the United States and the United Kingdom. Pease (1999) suggests that lighting may impact crime through various mechanisms. For example, lighting may lead to increased outdoor activity and, in turn, greater surveillance. Lighting may also enhance the ability to detect a crime in progress or identify an offender. Advocates often point to the deterrent potential of lights, which may make potential offenders choose less well-lighted areas for their crimes. Lighting should allow potential victims to see their surroundings and may lead them to avoid less well lit locations.

Typical research on the impact of lights contrasts criminal activity in an area that has received new lights with areas that do not receive new or improved lighting. In general, research on lighting has produced inconsistent results, with the greatest differences in outcome appearing between early studies and those done more recently in the United Kingdom. In an early review of 15 relighting projects, Tien et al. (1977) reported a great deal of inconsistency in the results. Seven projects reported decreases in at least some categories of crime, three showed increased crime levels, and seven found no changes in crime attributable to street lighting. The most promising results appeared in assessing its impact on the fear of crime. Of seven programs that measured fear of crime, all but one found that residents and legitimate users "feel safer" as a result of the increased lighting (Tien et al., 1977). Unfortunately, this review of studies considered only 15 of more than 100 projects identified by the authors. This was due to the fact that only 15 analyses relied on methodologically sound evaluation techniques.

More recent studies find a positive impact of lighting. The strongest support for lighting has been offered by Painter and Farrington (1997, 1999a, 1999b) based on a series of analyses conducted in England. Painter and Farrington (1997) report positive effects of lighting in an analysis of experimental and control areas of Dudley. Using victimization survey data, the authors report a 41 percent reduction in crime incidents in the experimental area and only a 15 percent reduction in the control area. In addition, respondents report being more satisfied in the relit areas. A similar analysis of relighting in Stoke-on-Trent also revealed significant reductions in crime in the experimental area as compared to the control area (Painter and Farrington, 1999b). They also report some evidence of reduced fear of crime. The crime and fear results, however, are not as dramatic as that found in Dudley. In both studies, the authors report reduced crime in non-relit areas adjacent to the target experimental neighborhoods. They claim that the impact of lighting is diffused into these other areas.

Farrington and Welsh (2002) attempted to summarize the state of the evidence on lighting by reviewing the existing literature from both the United States and the United Kingdom. For the U.S. studies, crime decreased in only half of the analyses. The results also vary by the type of offense (Farrington and Welsh, 2002). Conversely, all the studies in the United Kingdom show a positive impact of lighting. Once again, the impact varies across type of offense. Farrington and Welsh (2002) conclude that, in general, lighting has a positive impact. They suggest that the differences between the earlier U.S. and more recent U.K. results may be due to two main factors. First, the recent studies tend to be methodologically superior, particularly in terms of the selection of experimental and control sites. Second, the more recent studies rely more on victimization data than police records. Respondent reports may be better measures of what is actually taking place in specific locations.

Despite these promising results, there remain a variety of methodological problems throughout many lighting studies. One of the most problematic relates to the measurement of lighting. Various studies tend to differentiate between "relit" and "unrelit" areas of town without producing evidence of the increased level of illumination or the uniformity of the lighting (Tien et al., 1977). Simply altering the light fixtures does not guarantee an actual change in the amount of illumination. A related problem is the lack of information on many control areas besides the fact that these areas did not receive the new lights (Nair et al., 1993; Tien et al., 1977). Differences in the results could be the result of differences in the areas at the outset. Indeed, the fact that some areas seek out new lighting suggests a basic difference in attitude among residents. A final problem is the fact that most analyses use a short follow-up period which could mask true results (Nair et al., 1993).

Based on the contradictory evidence, how can the popularity of improved lighting schemes be explained? The answer revolves around the issue of fear. Even if relighting does not reduce crime, the ability to see better makes people feel safer. Various studies show reductions in fear following improved lighting. Atkins et al. (1991), for example, report that women and elderly respondents who recognize changes in lighting worry less about crime and feel safer. Painter and Farrington (1997, 1999b) reveal similar findings on improved area satisfaction and reduced fear of crime. Despite the questionable impact on crime and victimization, the findings of lowered "fear of crime" among citizens may be sufficient to continue relighting programs.

Surveillability

Lighting is only one factor that can influence the ability to observe an area. Surveillability also is determined by a wide range of other factors. Fisher and Nasar (1992; Nasar and Fisher, 1993) note the physical design impact on prospect, refuge and escape. *Prospect* refers to the ability of individuals to see an area. Locations that offer greater prospect should engender less fear and victimization than those locations that limit sight lines. *Refuge* deals with the presence or absence of concealment, in which offenders could hide from potential victims. Refuge provides both hiding places and protection for potential offenders. Finally, *escape* addresses the ability of both offenders and victims to escape from an area before and/or after an offense. In essence, physical design features which impact on surveillability should alter both fear and victimization levels.

Fisher and Nasar (1992; Nasar and Fisher, 1993) tested these assumptions using a university site which offered greatly varying degrees of prospect, refuge and escape. Using both surveys and observations, the authors report strong support for their argument. Areas of increased concealment (refuge), blocked prospect, and limited escape elicit greater fear. Crime figures also show greater victimization accompanying blocked prospect and greater concealment (Nasar and Fisher, 1993). The findings are site specific and suggest that analysis needs to focus on the micro-level. That is, while macro-level analyses may suggest that individuals are fearful in a certain area, that fear is actually more targeted at specific places in the area, not the entire area. Interestingly, lighting has no impact on reported fear once the issues of prospect, refuge and escape are considered (Fisher and Nasar, 1992). While limited to a single site on a university campus, these results suggest that a more general view of surveillability is needed than just an analysis of lighting. The research on prospect, refuge and escape provides support for the assumption that people make assessments of their surroundings and respond to the potential danger and fear they interpret in different situations.

Surveillance also can be provided through the use of guards or other individuals hired specifically for that function. Hesseling (1995) demonstrates various forms of "functional surveillance" used in The Netherlands. In one instance surveillance was provided by hiring individuals to ride public transportation in order to reduce violence and fare dodging. Similarly, the employment of caretakers in public housing contributed to reductions in vandalism, graffiti and theft. The use of security guards on city streets to assist the police impacted feelings of safety (Hesseling, 1995). Sorenson (1998) provides similar positive results in an assessment of public housing in three U.S. cities. In general, assigning surveillance responsibilities and providing the means to contact the authorities impacts the level of calls for police service and the level of arrests. Clearly, surveillability has an impact on both crime and fear of crime.

CCTV

Interest and research on closed-circuit television (CCTV) has grown tremendously in recent years, particularly in the United Kingdom. Oc and Tiesdell (1997) noted that over 80 town or city centers in the United Kingdom had CCTV in operation, and an additional 200 CCTV programs operated in other public places. Two years later, Phillips (1999) pointed out that the British government funded more than 550 CCTV programs in the mid- to late-1990s, with funding for additional programs in 1999–2001. This large investment in CCTV has prompted numerous evaluations of the technique.

Brown (1995) and Ditton and Short (1999) report on evaluations of CCTV in five cities. Each evaluation included experimental and control areas as well as outcome measures both pre- and post-installation of CCTV equipment. Brown (1995) notes that the experimental areas experienced reduced levels of burglary, while thefts, vandalism and other offenses declined in individual locations. Results in Airdrie, Scotland, show reductions in overall recorded crime, although there are some increases in recorded drug and motor vehicle offenses (Ditton and Short, 1999). The authors note that the increases may be due to increased detection of offenses through the use of CCTV. Results in Glasgow also show that CCTV impacts crime in the area (Ditton and Short, 1999). Fear also was reduced in areas covered by CCTV (Brown, 1995). Unfortunately, there was also evidence of displacement of crime from areas with CCTV to nearby/surrounding areas (Brown, 1995).

CCTV has also been used in businesses and car parks. Tilley (1993) reports that motor vehicle theft, theft from autos, and vandalism were all reduced in areas monitored with CCTV equipment. Beck and Willis (1999), examining CCTV in fashion clothing stores, report that stores with extensive CCTV systems experience significant reductions in loss after the installation, compared to other stores. They note that the results, however, diminish over time, with the positive results disappearing after six months in the stores with the most extensive CCTV systems (Beck and Willis, 1999).

The impact of CCTV also has been assessed through surveys of the public and offenders. In interviews with shopping center customers in Northampton, England, Tonglet (1998) found that CCTV is a major deterrent to shoplifting. Beck and Willis (1994) reported similar results from a survey of customers and staff of one major retailer. Interviews with burglars in prison or on probation reveal that CCTV is second only to security guards as a deterrent to offending (Butler, 1994). Conversely, Gill and Loveday (2003), interviewing 77 male prisoners with differing offense backgrounds, report that CCTV is seen as an obstacle to overcome but is not considered a deterrent.

Not all evaluations show positive results. Winge and Knutsson (2003), studying the use of CCTV in the Oslo (Norway) central railroad station, report increased detection of crime, increased recorded violent crime, reduced theft from autos, and no change in perceptions about crime in the area. Farrington and associates (2007), looking at both police and victimization data, fail to find any significant positive change in crime in the area covered by CCTV. Waples and Gill (2006) consider the impact of redeployable CCTV, which allows the cameras to be moved from one fixed location to another. Evaluation results show no change in crime or fear for one area, and increased crime in another after deployment of the CCTV initiative (Waples and Gill, 1006). The authors argue that these negative results could be due to various technological problems with the redeployable cameras.

CCTV has been the subject of two major evaluations (Gill and Springs, 2005; Welsh and Farrington, 2002). Both evaluations focused on reviewing studies that utilized strong experimental or quasi-experimental designs, including pre- and post- measures of crime for the experimental and control areas. Welsh and Farrington (2002) reviewed 22 CCTV evaluations from 1978 to 2002. Studies fell into one of three categories: city centers or public housing, public transportation studies, and evaluations in car parks. The examination of 13 studies in city centers or public housing (8 in the U.K. and 5 in the U.S.) revealed mixed outcomes, with five reporting reduced crime levels in the experimental area, three showing increases in crime, and five having no impact (Welsh and Farrington, 2002). Evaluation of individual offenses showed similar discrepancies, although burglary consistently declined under CCTV conditions. CCTV in public transportation revealed two positive evaluations, one negative, and one that had no impact. Of the five programs in car parks, four resulted in reduced crime levels (Welsh and Farrington, 2002). Reanalyzing the data, Welsh and Farrington found a small but positive impact across the pooled 22 studies. Interestingly, all of the positive impacts appeared in the U.K. studies, while no positive findings emerged in the U.S. evaluations. This could be due to the greater familiarity and experience with CCTV in the United Kingdom, both in terms of the technology and in evaluating CCTV initiatives.

In the Gill and Springs (2005) study, crime was reduced in six target areas while it increased in seven areas. However, in only four locations was there a statistically significant change in crime in the experimental areas relative to the control areas, with two changes favoring the experimental area and two favoring the control areas. Reanalyzing the data from the individual evaluations, Gill and Springs (2005) note that CCTV shows no impact on crime. This may be due to increased reporting of crime occurring simultaneously with the change in CCTV. At the same time, fear of crime is reducing in CCTV areas. There is also some evidence of displacement of crime from CCTV areas to other locations (Gill and Springs, 2005).

The evidence from the two studies clearly shows that CCTV has the potential to reduce crime. At the same time, while CCTV holds some promise, it is not a universal cure all for crime problems. Future evaluations need to use appropriate methodologies, including control areas and significant follow-up periods. It is also important to try to disentangle the impact of CCTV from other crime prevention techniques that are in simultaneous use (Farrington and Painter, 2003).

Property Identification Programs

Despite the great proliferation of property identification programs (typically called *Operation Identification*), there is little empirical research on most projects. The basic idea behind these projects is to increase the difficulty for offenders to dispose of marked items. One early review of 99 projects from across the United States reported that, although a majority of the public is aware of the programs, few programs are able to entice more than 10 percent of the population to participate (Heller et al., 1975). Likewise, few programs report significant changes in reported burglary (the targeted offense) and none find an impact on arrests or convictions for burglary (Heller et al., 1975).

One exemplary evaluation of property marking was undertaken in South Wales (Laycock, 1985; 1990). Three physically proximate villages were targeted for the property marking campaign due to their relative isolation from other residential areas. The choice of isolated villages was made in order to reduce the chance that the program would simply displace crime. The program relied on a high degree of publicity, door-to-door contact, and the provision of free equipment and window stickers. Project efforts were successful at engendering participation by 72 percent of the homes. More importantly, the evaluation showed a 40 percent drop in burglary for participating homes with little or no displacement to nonparticipating residences (Laycock, 1985). A follow-up evaluation (Laycock, 1990) revealed greater reductions in burglary in the second year after program implementation. A more thorough examination of monthly burglary data, however, revealed that the year two reductions followed monthly increases in the level of burglary. Further, both the initial and year two reductions in crime followed heavy publicity of the program. Increases in burglary occurred during times of low publicity (Laycock, 1990). This suggests that the results are more related to the media attention and not the property marking.

A recent trend in property identification has been to tag vehicles with ID numbers to combat motor vehicle theft. Rhodes and associates (1997) report that the marking of vehicle parts has a small impact on theft of cars by professional thieves. Various programs seek to make vehicles that are typically not driven at certain times of the day (particularly early mornings) or in certain areas (such as near borders) more recognizable to law enforcement officers through the use of decals and special license plates (Bureau of Justice Assistance, 1998). These identifying marks alert police that the vehicle is out of place and should be stopped. While the programs have not yet been adequately evaluated, these programs are an interesting extension of property marking at home.

Alarms

Alarms represent another possible deterrent to offending. Silent alarms in various Cedar Rapids, Iowa, schools and businesses increased both the numbers of arrests and the clearance rate in buildings with alarms (Cedar Rapids Police Department, 1975). Break-ins at buildings with alarms revealed entry through places not hooked up to the alarms (Cedar Rapids Police Department, 1975). Buck et al. (1993) examined the impact of alarms and other factors on burglary in three Philadelphia suburbs. Alarms proved to be a strong deterrent to household burglary.

Interviews with offenders also reveal the impact of alarms. Reppetto (1974) found that one-third of the offenders checked on the presence or absence of alarms during the planning stages of the offense. Bennett and Wright (1984) asked burglars to evaluate videotape and photos of potential targets. They found that the presence or absence of alarms was a prime consideration in the choice of their targets. Similarly, in interviews with active and incarcerated burglars, Hearnden and Magill (2004) find that 84 percent claim that outside alarms are key factors in their decision-making process.

Locks, Doors, and Related Access Factors

Access control can be improved through the installation of various devices that make entry more difficult. These will not eliminate crime. Rather, a motivated offender will need to work harder and find more effective ways of gaining entrance. The Seattle Law and Justice Planning Office (1975) evaluated the effect of solid case doors, dead bolt locks, pins in sliding glass doors, and construction of short walls aimed at making entry through windows more difficult at four public housing projects. The evaluation found a significant decline in the level of burglary in three of the four target areas. The mode of entry after the improvements were made shifted to the use of open and unlocked windows and doors. This shift was expected due to the increased difficulty posed by the changes (Seattle Law and Justice Planning Office, 1975).

Bennett and Wright's (1984) study of burglars also shows support for the use of target hardening devices. Their subjects list the type of windows and locks as one influence on their decision making. Offenders tend to prefer smaller windows because they are easier to force open. Similarly, the presence of a lock becomes more effective as the difficulty in picking or breaking the lock increases (Bennett and Wright, 1984).

Street Layout and Traffic

The design of streets has been posited as affecting crime through the level of accessibility potential offenders have to an area. Dead-end streets, cul-de-sacs, one-way streets, and street entrances that project a private atmosphere are assumed to cut down on the level of use by strangers and increase the presence of legitimate users. Often this approach is coupled with broader, community planning activities but there have been a few studies aimed specifically at evaluating this method.

Newman and Wayne (1974) compared public and private streets in adjacent areas of St. Louis. A private street is one that is owned and maintained by the residents living on the street, is often a cul-de-sac, and is set apart from the connecting streets by means of landscaping, gates, entranceways, or other similar features. The authors found less crime on private streets and the fear of crime was lower among subjects living on those streets (Newman and Wayne, 1974). They also found more interaction between the residents living on these private streets, which should lead to reduced crime. The lack of comparability between the experimental and control groups, however, suggests that these results be viewed with some caution.

A variety of different types of streets can be compared in evaluating their effect on crime. Bevis and Nutter (1977) look at the relative effect of dead-end, cul-de-sac, "L" type, "T" type, and through traffic streets. These are arranged in order of accessibility with the dead-end street being the least accessible. The authors find a clear relationship existing between the type of street layout and burglary. More accessible streets experience higher rates of burglary (Bevis and Nutter, 1977). Other research (Beavon et al., 1994; White, 1990) shows that property crime increases with increased street accessibility.

Operation Cul-de-Sac in Los Angeles set out to curb gang homicides and assaults in a ten block area by blocking road access in the area. Relying on Part I offense data, Lasley (1998) reports that both homicides and assault fell significantly during the period of the program, and increased after the roadblocks were removed. Donnelly and Kimble (1997) investigate street closures in a 10-square-block area of Dayton characterized by street crime, drugs and prostitution. After a one-year follow-up, overall crime dropped 25 percent and violent crime fell 40 percent, while there is no evidence of displacement to other areas (Donnelly and Kimble, 1997). These projects clearly show the impact of altering traffic flow in high crime areas.

In the United Kingdom, a relatively common attempt to control access is to erect alley gates. *Alley gating* refers to erecting gates on alleys that run behind home and businesses, thereby restricting access to residents or other legitimate users. A key target of this approach is burglary, particularly in areas where the criminals gain access through the rear of the buildings. An evaluation of alley gating in Liverpool reports that roughly 4,000 alley gates had been erected (Home Office, 2001), with a subsequent reduction of 875 burglaries (Bowers et al., 2003). The gates had an impact independent of other crime prevention activities taking place in the target areas. An analysis of alley gating in Cadoxton, South Wales, also reveals clear decreases in burglary after the installation of the gates (Rogers, 2007). Residents in the gated areas also report reduced perceptions of both crime and disorder in the area.

The available evidence illustrates the potential of traffic control as a means of combating crime. Streets and areas that are easily accessible to pedestrian and auto traffic tend to experience higher levels of actual crime and fear of crime. The construction of cul-de-sacs, dead-end streets, alley gates and streets that promote a feeling of ownership will have positive effects for crime prevention.

Summary

As noted earlier, the amount of research aimed at single crime prevention approaches is minimal. Few crime prevention programs are unidimensional in approach. Rather, most plans introduce a variety of techniques to be implemented as parts of a larger prevention package. This makes evaluation of the individual factors problematic and necessitates research focused on entire programs. We now turn to an evaluation of crime prevention efforts that include a range of ideas, including some of those already discussed.

Physical Design of Neighborhoods

Studies of public housing are among the early examinations of area-wide physical design on crime. As noted earlier, Newman (1972) reports that crime varies among public housing with different design features. Various design problems negate attempts to build a sense of community, lay claim to an area (territoriality), present a sense of safety (image), or allow surveillance. Newman and Franck (1980), studying public housing in Newark, St. Louis, and San Francisco, find that accessibility and building size have direct effects on burglary and fear of crime. Building size also affects the use of space and feelings of control over space and indirectly, through control and use of space, on crime and fear. Normoyle and Foley (1988) find that elderly residents in high rise buildings are significantly less fearful than those living in low rise complexes. Additionally, building height is not related to the level of victimization (Normoyle and Foley, 1988). Poyner (1994), reporting on physical design in an English public housing estate, demonstrates that limiting access reduces robbery, but not burglary. The removal of enclosed walkways between buildings effectively limits access, escape and concealment for potential offenders (Poyner, 1994).

Environmental design received one of its biggest tests in the North Asylum Hill area of Hartford, Connecticut. This area received a number of crime prevention efforts including changes in street patterns, landscaping, neighborhood police patrols, and increased citizen organization. The design elements were primarily the creation of cul-de-sacs, the elimination of through streets, creating one-way streets, and the narrowing of street openings— all geared to making the area appear more private and controlled by residents of the area. An initial evaluation revealed great decreases in both burglary and robbery as compared to neighboring South Asylum Hill and the remainder of Hartford (Fowler et al., 1979). Fear of burglary and potential victimization also declined in the area. In addition, there was a corresponding increase in the use of the streets and parks by residents. The evaluation did not show changes in social cohesion or neighborhood commitment (Fowler et al., 1979). A follow-up evaluation three years later (Fowler and Mangione, 1982) supported the findings of reduced vehicular traffic, increased pedestrian usage, and lower levels of fear, but both burglary and robbery had returned to city-wide levels (Fowler and Mangione, 1982). The effect on crime, therefore, was short-lived.

General characteristics of urban neighborhoods provide further insight into the physical design-crime relationship. Greenberg et al. (1982) compare contiguous low and high crime neighborhoods in Atlanta. Low crime areas are characterized by single-family dwellings, few major through streets, few vacant lots, are predominantly residential, and are bounded by other residential areas and factors that prohibit easy access. Uniform building setbacks and private parking, which diminish concealment for offenders, are also part of low crime neighborhoods (Greenberg et al., 1982). These results tend to support the argument that physical features can affect criminal behavior.

The use of physical design changes to combat crime in a commercial area was undertaken in the Union Avenue Corridor (UAC) of Portland, Oregon. The UAC was a commercial strip approximately 3.5 miles long and four blocks wide accommodating businesses ranging from light industry to banks to grocery stores and car dealerships. The surrounding area was middle to low income and predominately black, with a crime rate roughly three times that of the remainder of Portland (Kushmuk and Whittemore, 1981). The crime prevention program included improving street lighting, improving street appearance, changing traffic patterns, providing off-street parking, establishing business and neighborhood groups, and using various promotional events, all with the intent of reducing crime and fear and increasing social cohesion and improving the quality of life.

Kushmuk and Whittemore (1981) note that official measures of crime (robbery and commercial burglary) declined as a result of the prevention activities. Victimization surveys, however, revealed no changes in either the number of offenses or perceptions of victimization. In addition, while the overall fear of crime did not change over the study period, customers were *more* fearful at night and the elderly were *more* fearful, in general, after the crime prevention program. The anticipated changes in crime did not appear. Changes in other outcomes also failed to appear. Neither businessmen nor residents reported any increases in social cohesion or cooperation with the police (Kushmuk and Whittemore, 1981). Residents also did not display any changes in communal activity or support of neighbors. While businessmen reported that their sales had increased since the program's implementation, they felt that the UAC was not in as good a condition as before the program (Kushmuk and Whittemore, 1981). In general, the evaluation showed some changes in crime and other social factors but these movements were not much different from those found in the remainder of Portland.

In 1999, the British government began the *Reducing Burglary Initiative* (RBI) by funding 63 projects across the United Kingdom (Kodz and Pease, 2003). The RBI relies on local communities to identify the causes of the burglary problems in their area and to develop appropriate interventions, many of which are physical design changes, such as target hardening, the installation of alley gates, lighting improvements, fencing and property marking (Kodz and Pease, 2003). Interventions also include neighborhood watch, intensive police crackdowns and other methods (discussed in later chapters). In 40 out of 55 RBI evaluations, the burglary rates fell relative to the control areas (evaluations using comparison areas were not conducted in eight locations). An evaluation of the Fordbridge RBI project, which implemented target hardening, alley gates, electronic entry controls for buildings, and improved street lighting, reports a reduction in burglary of 43 percent for the experimental area (Home Office, 2003a). Similarly, the RBI project in Stirchley, relying on alley gates, fences and property marking (along with a crime prevention newsletter), claims a 53 percent drop in burglary, which is twice the reduction seen in the control area (Home Office, 2003b). These early results on the effectiveness of the RBI suggest that physical design elements are effective at reducing the burglary problem.

Secure By Design (SBD) has also received attention for its impact on crime. As noted earlier, SBD seeks to influence the building of new structures or the redesign of existing sites in ways that will mitigate crime and disorder. In one evaluation of SBD in West Yorkshire, Armitage (2000) notes a significant reduction in crime at the sites that were refurbished following the SBD principles. There was a 26 percent drop in the number of dwelling crimes and roughly half as many residents reported being fearful around their homes. An assessment of environmental design features comparing 25 SBD estates with 25 non-SBD estates also shows the effectiveness of physical design for reducing burglary and general crime (Armitage, 2007). Estates conforming to proper design guidelines are at lower risk for crime than estates not using the design features.

A Challenge to Defensible Space

While it appears that physical design features can impact crime and fear, there is no guarantee that proper design will produce the desired results. Sally Merry (1981) conducted an 18-month participant observation study of a single public housing project that seemed to conform to good defensible space design. The project was composed of low buildings, separate courtyards, few families per entranceway, wide pathways, public space in front of the buildings, and private (fenced) space at the rear of the buildings. Additionally, many of the residents had installed target hardening devices such as locks and window bars. Using a combination of interviews, observation, and official crime figures, Merry (1981) found that the physical design features failed to have any effect on crime or the residents' feelings of safety. Despite the seeming defensibility of the project, Merry (1981) questioned the design features. First, the stairwells and hallways near doors were not easily observable by residents or passersby. Second, many of the outdoor features, such as fences and enclosed trash collectors, actually provided cover for potential offenders. Finally, the layout of the buildings and outdoor areas, although seemingly conducive to territoriality, confused residents and visitors and produced discomfort and disorientation. Clearly, the physical design did not increase interaction between residents and residents rarely intervened in questionable behavior (Merry, 1981). Residents were unable to distinguish strangers from legitimate users, feared future retaliation, and held an uncaring attitude toward those not identified as friends or relatives. Merry attributed these problems to a lack of social cohesion and community identity among the project's residents.

The general failure of the defensible space concept to bring about clear reductions in crime was placed squarely on the inability of the physical environment to effectively create feelings of territoriality and a sense of community concern and action. Merry (1981) noted that "good defensible space design neither guarantees that a space will appear safe nor that it will become a part of a territory which residents defend effectively." An area may be defensible but undefended.

Summary

These various discussions should not be interpreted as indicating that there is no positive effect of defensible space features on crime and fear of crime. An array of studies have found various design features and crime prevention techniques that affect crime and fear. There are, however, a substantial number of studies that produce negative or equivocal results. These contradictory findings may stem from the inability to bring about, or lack of attention paid to, changes in intervening factors, such as social cohesion and feelings of territoriality. The basic premise of Newman's argument is that the physical environment engenders feelings of territoriality and citizen control, which then affect crime. Any failure of physical design, therefore, may be due to an inability of the individual implementation program to bring about these intervening factors.

PRODUCT DESIGN

Physical design for crime prevention is not restricted to homes, businesses or communities. While CPTED and environmental design typically bring to mind the efforts outlined above, it is possible to consider physically designing products in ways that protect them from theft or being used in other offenses. As Clarke and Newman (2005) point out, the targets of crime are everyday objects. It is possible to alter the design of objects to make them less amenable to crime.

Many products lend themselves to crime. These so-called *hot products* which are highly targeted by thieves may be characterized by being *CRAVED*—concealable, removable, available, valuable, enjoyable and disposable (Clarke, 1999). In essence, these are products desired by people because of their construction or makeup and are easily targeted by offenders. For example, electronic devices such as MP3 players and PDAs are easily concealed, expensive, small enough to carry away, and easily disposable. Every "hot product" does not have to fit all the CRAVED factors. Automobiles, for example, are not easily concealable or even disposable, but they are a common theft target.

Ekblom (2008) points out several ways in which products play a role in crime. Presented in terms of a Misdeeds and Security framework, products can be the target of an offense or used within offending behavior (see Table 4.4). In each case, the design of a product either makes the product a viable target for an offense, or the product facilitates some other offense. Following the CRAVED idea, many objects are targeted for their value. Other items may invite vandalism. Yet others can be used in the commission of other crimes, such as altering a document to allow an underage person to purchase alcohol. The key throughout these ideas is the need to recognize the potential problems with products and make appropriate design changes.

Table 4.4
Products and Misdeeds

	Examples
MISappropriated	theft of the product itself
MIStreated	vandalism or destruction of items
MIShandled	returning of stolen goods, use of counterfeit currency, use of fake documents
MISused	use of a product for illegal purposes such as prescription drugs or weapons
MISbehaved with	contamination of products, the ability to set off false alarms without being observed

Source: Constructed by author from Ekblom (2008).

Ekblom (2005) outlines several methods for securing products through design. First, he suggests that it is possible to make products inherently secure. This can be done by making them less attractive or distinctive, and thus less likely to be targeted by offenders. A product can also be designed in such a way that it actually protects other property, such as chairs which can secure purses from theft. Second, product design may incorporate prevention/security devices within the product or its display. Ink tags on clothing or the use of cable locks are examples of this approach. The third approach is to restrict offender access to the target or tools used to target a product (Ekblom, 2005). Other ways of securing products against crime include adding security devices to products (such as security cables or alarms), securing the environment in which the product is located (such as by using safes or access control measures), and employing remote security interventions (such as restricting access to tools needed for crime or controlling the outlets for stolen goods) (Ekblom, 2008). The approach or mechanism to use in protecting products is dictated by both the product itself and the situation in which the product is targeted.

A wide range of products have been the subject of design changes for prevention purposes. The automobile is a prime example of redesign for crime prevention (see Table 4.5). A number of changes have been made in autos to prevent their theft or the theft of items from them (Clarke and Newman, 2005). Ignition locks and steering column locks are universal in new cars, and alarms and locator devices are common, particularly in more expensive autos. Removable radios or radio faces, stronger door locks, and the marking of auto parts with identification numbers all address theft from autos.

Table 4.5

Changes Made at Manufacture to Cars and Crimes Prevented

Crime	Device or Redesign
Unauthorized use and joy-riding	Ignition locks; improved door locks; steering column locks; alarms; immobilizers
Theft of cars or major body parts	As above but also: parts marking; GPS (global positioning system) locators; tamper-proof license plates; microdots
Theft from cars	Stronger door locks; alarms; lockable gas caps; redesigned emblems; security coded radios; removable radios; dispersed audio system
Vandalism	Retractable aerials
Assassination	Armor plating; ram bars
Illegal use of rental car	GPS locators to detect speeding

Source: Clarke and Newman (2005).

Clarke and Newman (2005) offer a number of other examples of product design for prevention purposes. Theft of small items from stores can be made more difficult by putting the item in large packages that are more difficult to conceal. Purse snatching can be prevented by designing them with stronger straps that cannot be cut or broken. Computer hacking has been made more difficult with the introduction of special software. Caller ID has helped to stem telephone harassment (Clarke and Newman, 2005). The design of *smart guns,* which recognize the owner and will only discharge if used by that person is an emerging design technology (Lester, 2001). These and many other examples of product design changes are made for the purpose of preventing different types of crimes.

While the idea of product design for prevention purposes has been gaining attention, relatively few initiatives have been subjected to evaluation (Clarke and Newman, 2005). There are evaluations that often involve weak research designs with no control groups for comparison purposes. Evaluations that have been completed typically suggest that the design changes are effective at bringing about significant reductions in crime (Clarke and Newman, 2005). Stronger evaluation, however, needs to be undertaken.

A number of problems and issues face the movement toward product design for prevention. One primary concern is the fact that most designers are not trained with an eye toward crime prevention, thus making the design process difficult at the outset (Learmont, 2005). Second, the prevention features must be understood by the users/consumers and be simple enough to guarantee that they are employed (Ekblom, 2005; Lester, 2001). Basically, the features need to be user friendly. Third, any changes need to adhere to the aesthetic features of the product. Fourth, there may be both legal and ethical questions to be addressed. The incorporation of electronic tracing devices, for example, raises issues of privacy (Ekblom, 2008; Lester, 2001). Yet another concern with product design involves the issue of increased costs due to the extra features (Ekblom, 2008). It is possible that product redesign can result in costs that are prohibitive. Despite these (and other) concerns, product design for prevention is a growing area of interest that should receive increased attention, particularly for its impact on the level of crime.

INCIVILITY, DISORDER, AND CRIME

A final topic to address is the issue of disorder and incivility. While "crime and disorder" have been addressed throughout this chapter, it is always in terms of action to eliminate these problems. Much of the discussion about physical features deals with the correct design to allow surveillance and feelings of goodwill among legitimate users. It is also important to question the degree to which signs of disorder may actively *promote* criminal activity. This may occur when both signs of physical and social disorder signal that an area or location is not protected and is open to criminal behavior.

Various authors (Hunter, 1978; Skogan, 1990; Taylor and Gottfredson, 1986; Wilson and Kelling, 1982) have presented indicators of physical disorder, including broken windows, abandoned buildings, vacant lots, deteriorating buildings, litter, vandalism, and graffiti. Similarly, they offer social indicators, such as loitering juveniles, public drunkenness, gangs, drug sales and use, harassment (such as begging and panhandling), prostitution, and a lack of interaction among people on the street. Perkins and Taylor (1996), Taylor et al. (1995), and Spelman (1993) suggest that physical disorder can contribute to the growth of social disorder. Examples of such instances would be nonresidential property or abandoned structures interrupting a housing block (Taylor, 1988). The physical layout may inhibit social interaction among residents and allow for social incivilities to arise.

These physical and social indicators are typically referred to as signs of disorder or *incivility*. Incivility in a neighborhood has been proposed as evidence that the residents are not concerned, or at least are less concerned, about what is happening around them than people in areas not characterized by incivility (Lewis and Salem, 1986). Signs of disorder may lead residents to withdraw into their homes and abandon cooperative efforts at improving the neighborhood (Skogan, 1990; Taylor, 1988). This would leave the neighborhood open to potential offenders. The idea of incivilities can be viewed as another part of Newman's "image." For the offender, signs of incivility are indicative of lower risk (Taylor and Gottfredson, 1986). Efforts to minimize disorder and incivility through improvement of the physical and social environment, therefore, should increase perceived risk and decrease crime and fear of crime.

Interestingly, incivility has been accepted almost without question as a cause of crime and fear in society, despite the relative lack of research on the subject. This is somewhat easy to understand when one considers the location of crime and fear in communities. Areas exhibiting physical and social signs of incivility are often the same ones experiencing higher levels of crime and fear. Indeed, a number of studies find that crime and fear are higher in areas displaying signs of disorder (DeFrancis and Titus, 1993; Lynch and Cantor, 1992; Perkins and Taylor, 1996; Skogan, 1990; Spelman, 1993).

The logical assumption to draw from the research on incivility is that efforts to reduce physical and social disorder will effectively reduce crime and fear. Taylor (1997), however, questions the extent to which eliminating signs of disorder, particularly physical signs, will have an impact. He points out that the relationship between disorder and fear is highly contingent on how disorder is measured. Specifically, area disorder measured objectively by independent raters is only marginally related to fear and resident behavior. A strong relationship between disorder and fear (and possibly behavior) appears only when *perceived* incivilities are considered, as subjectively reflected in surveys of residents. Consequently, efforts to reduce physical disorder would have only minimal impact on fear (Taylor, 1997). The challenge is to identify methods of altering the *perceptions* of disorder.

While there may be some disagreement about the actual influence of disorder and incivilities on crime, fear, and citizen behavior, many reasons remain for working to reduce signs of incivility. Perhaps the best reason is that no one should have to live in areas with such problems. Additionally, even minimal effects on crime and fear should be considered a success. Unless research finds that efforts to remove disorder increase crime and fear, there is only an upside to their elimination.

SUMMARY

Examination of the existing evidence on physical design shows some promising results along with a number of instances in which the impact of the techniques is inconsistent. Table 4.6 attempts to provide a general summary of the impact of different physical design techniques across different target areas. A great deal of the support for the results in Table 4.6 does not appear in the earlier discussion. Instead, the table rests on evidence presented here and in other analyses.

Table 4.6
Summary of the Evidence on Physical Design Impact on Crimes

Technique	Homes	Public Housing	Business	School	Workplace	Community
Lighting	B+,T+,V?,F+	B?,R?,T?,V?,F+	B?,R?,T?,V?,F+			B+,R?,T+,V?,F+
CCTV	B?,T?,F+	B?,R?,T?,F+	B?,R?,T+,F+,FR+			B+,R?,T+,F+,V?,GC?
Traffic Patterns/ Street Layout	B+,T,F+					B+,R-,T,V+,F+, GC+
Alarms	B+		B+,R-			
Property ID	B?,T?					
Informal Surveillance	B+,T+,V?	B+,R+,T+,D?	R?	B+,R+,T+,F+		B+,R+,T+,V?,F+,D?
Building Design	B?,F?	B?,R?,T?,F?	B?,R?,T?			B?,R?,T?,F?
Security Screens			R+		V+	
Unbreakable Glass			R+			
Area Improvement	B?,T?,F+	B?,R?,T?,F+	B?,R?,F+			B?,R?,D?,F+
Safes			B+,R+			
Product Design						T+,FR+,AT+

Offenses: B= burglary; R= robbery; T= theft; V= violence/aggression; FR= fraud; F= fear; GC= general crime; AT=auto theft
+ indicates the techniques have been shown to reduce the crime in question
– indicates the techniques have been shown to have no impact on the crime
? indicates that the impact of the technique varies by the project or the context

The left-hand column of the table lists the crime prevention action or technique, while the first row in the table lists the location (home, public housing, businesses, schools, the workplace, or the general community) where evidence on the effectiveness of the technique has been tested. Within the cells of the table are listed the individual crimes that have been examined and an indication of what evaluations, in general have revealed. The top left hand cell, for example, shows that lighting has been found to be effective at reducing burglaries, theft and fear of crime at homes (indicated by a + sign), while the evidence on violence/aggression varies across projects or contexts (indicated by the ? sign). Empty cells reflect the fact that there has been no study of the crime prevention technique's effectiveness in the corresponding location.

An inspection of the table reveals that there are a number of instances in which physical design techniques have been found to be effective. Interestingly, there are also numerous examples in which the evidence is still uncertain, with the results varying across places and situations, and there are several examples in which the techniques have been found to have no impact (for example, traffic patterns have no impact on theft from homes). With so many cases of uncertainly in the findings, how is it possible to have such discrepancies and where does this leave CPTED?

Part of the reason for the discrepancies stems from the nature of social research. First, many of the studies are attempting to investigate the effect of one set of factors on crime. In so doing, the evaluators often fail to consider the vast array of alternative variables that may be contributing to the levels of crime and fear. Second, many studies fail to specify an adequate control group or have no control group. The results of the evaluations, therefore, have no baseline upon which to judge any change or lack of change. The simple use of measures taken prior to and after a change within a single locale or group cannot solve the problem of possible competing influences and factors occurring simultaneously with the intervention of interest. Third, the vast array of study sites makes comparison across studies difficult. It is difficult to compare the various study results in the absence of detailed information on each experimental and control group from each study. The context within which each study is being conducted may greatly influence the results. Evaluations that exhibit positive effects may be taking place in locations that are fundamentally different from those showing negative or no effects. This possibility cannot be assessed from many reports.

The lack of consistent positive results also may be due to the fact that many physical design features contribute to the building of fortresses for protection. Physical design changes, target hardening and access control serve to isolate people from one another. While these efforts may reduce the level of fear of crime, there is a concomitant loss of community. Counter to Newman's assumption that physical design will engender a sense of community, social support, and territoriality, there is little or no evidence that this happens. The heavy orientation toward physical design elements isolates residents into individual fortresses. Crime can be expected to increase where traditional, fortress mentality techniques are employed. As the individual withdraws from the rest of the neighborhood in an attempt to protect himself, the community enters an upward spiral of increased crime, fear, and loss of community.

An alternative is to emphasize crime prevention techniques that prompt the retention, retrieval, and/or enhancement of the community. Neighborhood/ block watch, citizen patrols, community-oriented policing, and similar reactions reflect community-oriented responses to crime and fear. These efforts should reduce crime and fear over time as the community reasserts itself and takes control of the behavior and actions of persons within the community. Rather than assume that alterations in a sense of community, neighborhood cohesion, and similar factors follow physical design changes, a community-oriented model suggests that interventions specifically directed at increasing social interaction, social cohesion, feelings of ownership, territoriality, and reducing fear will be more effective at combating crime and victimization. The next chapter looks at community-oriented crime prevention programs which actively seek to involve the citizens in actions that should engender community/neighborhood cohesion, a sense of control, territoriality, and other factors that will affect both fear and crime. The next chapter focuses on attempts to increase citizen involvement in crime prevention and fill the gap left by simple environmental design approaches.

Chapter 5

NEIGHBORHOOD CRIME PREVENTION

Key Terms:

citizen patrols
Community Anti-Drug programs
Guardian Angels
Kirkholt Burglary Prevention
program
National Night Out
neighborhood watch

parochial control
public control
private control
Safer Cities program
street block
whistle stop

Learning Objectives:

After reading this chapter you should be able to:

- Demonstrate your knowledge of neighborhood watch and the types of activities found in neighborhood watch programs

- Define Community Anti-Drug programs and discuss their impact

- Discuss citizen patrols and their crime prevention capabilities

- Talk about the impact of neighborhood crime prevention on community cohesion

- Provide an overview of the impact of neighborhood crime prevention on crime and fear

- Discuss the Kirkholt Burglary Prevention program and its impact

- Explain the Safer Cities program and its impact

- List problems and issues that hamper the evaluation of neighborhood crime prevention programs

- Talk about who participates in neighborhood crime prevention

- Provide reasons for the divergent findings on who participates in crime prevention

- Discuss research findings on domains of crime prevention

- Outline the five problematic assumptions underlying neighborhood watch

The failure of physical, environmental design changes to always impact crime and fear may be directly attributable to the ability of such activities to live up to the assumptions of the basic theory. Few authors claim that changes in physical design alone will have a major impact on crime. By themselves, locks, lights, windows, and the other physical characteristics can only make offending more difficult and lead to alternative means of committing the crimes. The key element that will reduce and prevent crime is the ability of the physical features to enhance active surveillance, engender community cohesion and promote citizen action against crime.

Crime Prevention through Environmental Design has faltered because of the inability to motivate residents and legitimate users to act against crime. As seen in Chapter 4, the evidence in support of a link between physical design features and intervening factors such as increased social cohesion and use of an area is rarely found in the evaluations. This may be due to the lack of attention paid to these factors. Studies that include intervening elements find little support for the connection between physical design and changes in social cohesion, support, and other intervening constructs. In addition, the conflicting evidence concerning the influence of physical features on crime may be due to conflicting levels of social cohesion, community atmosphere, surveillance, and other intervening variables that are unaccounted for in the studies.

Neighborhood crime prevention seeks to directly influence these intervening constructs and, in turn, affect levels of crime and fear. Neighborhood crime prevention can take a variety of forms that are broader in scope than those discussed in connection with physical design. The possible techniques include neighborhood watch, neighborhood advocacy, citizen patrols, and physical design. Figure 5.1 illustrates the conceptual framework of neighborhood crime prevention.

The wide array of activities demonstrate the fact that crime prevention relies on a number of approaches and cannot be left to one basic set of ideas, such as physical design. The model in Figure 5.1 proposes that intervening changes must occur before the long-term problems are affected. The model shows that some of the design characteristics introduced in the last chapter as initial points of intervention (i.e. property marking and home security) are viewed here as intermediate outcomes of the more general strategies. The most important of these general strategies is citizen involvement. Citizen activity and interest, as we will see, often precedes the other factors, including physical design.

Figure 5.1
Neighborhood-Based Crime Prevention Conceptual Framework

Problems	→	Strategies	→	Intervening Factors	→	Intermediate Outcomes	→	Long-Term Outcomes

• Crime – levels, types
 	
• Fear of crime
 	
• Neighborhood deterioration
 	
• Anomie, lack of cohesion and social control
		• Neighborhood Watch
		
		• Environmental design changes
		
		• Advocacy, police-community cooperation
		
		• Anti-redlining activities
		
		• Focus on youth (employment, recreation, alternatives, etc.)
		
		• Specific activities (escort service, mediation, victim/witness assistance, etc.)
		
		• Education
				• Neighborhood characteristics
				  – Cohesion, sense of community
				  – Size, density
				  – Condition of housing stock
				
				• Law enforcement response
				
				• Past and current crime prevention activities
				
				• Characteristics of organization implementing strategies
						• Increase in citizen involvement, sense of responsibility and control
						
						• Increase in citizen knowledge, change in attitude and behavior
						
						• Strategy-specific outcomes
						  – Increased home security
						  – Cleaner neighborhoods
						  – Increase in property marking
						  – Etc.
						
						• Enhanced police/city agency-community cooperation and interaction
								• Reduction in crime
								  – Reduction in burglary, other specific crimes
								
								• Reduction in fear of crime
								
								• Strengthened neighborhoods
								  – Improved housing stock and general economic base
								  – Increase in cohesion, informal social control

Source: R.F. Cook and J.A. Roehl (1983). *Preventing Crime and Arson: A Review of Community-Based Strategies.* Reston, VA:Institute for Social Analysis.

TYPES OF NEIGHBORHOOD CRIME PREVENTION APPROACHES

A wide variety of neighborhood crime prevention strategies have been proposed and implemented over the years. Since the 1970s, there has been a great proliferation of programs in the United States, United Kingdom, and other countries. While many programs have been instigated and aided by various government agencies or policies, other programs have emerged from the simple realization by citizens that the formal criminal justice system is incapable of solving the crime problem on its own. Regardless of the source of stimulation, neighborhood crime prevention has become a major aspect of crime prevention.

Neighborhood/Block Watch

The basic goal of neighborhood crime prevention is increasing community awareness and problem solving. This can be accomplished through a variety of methods. Foremost among these is bringing neighbors and residents of an area together into *neighborhood watch* groups. These groups, ideally, discuss mutual problems in the neighborhood, work to increase feelings of community, and promote joint action to address their common problems. Neighborhood watch, ideally, is proactive in design. That is, it sets out to identify problems before they occur or, at the very least, as they occur. Neighborhood involvement is meant to recognize and circumvent the problems that lead to an area's decline and accompanying increased crime.

In its most effective form, neighborhood watch should provide informal (and possibly formal) social control in the community. Bursik and Grasmick (1993) note that many neighborhoods are socially disorganized and, consequently, are unable to exert any control over residents or visitors to the area. Building on the early work of Shaw and McKay (1931, 1942), the authors argue that neighborhoods need to draw on resources from a variety of sources in an effort to build social control. Friendships, families, local businesses, churches, schools, and interpersonal networks are examples of local resources upon which neighborhoods can draw and build (Bursik and Grasmick, 1993). Neighborhood watch is one incarnation of social control in a neighborhood.

One way that neighborhood watch contributes to social control is through the heavy use of surveillance. Successful surveillance requires the ability to distinguish legitimate from illegitimate users of an area. The absence of such recognition leaves residents unable to identify someone or something that is out of place. Members of neighborhood organizations become eyes and ears for the police. It is impossible for the legal authorities to be everywhere at the same time. It is the responsibility of ordinary citizens, therefore, to assist in the surveillance function of law enforcement.

The exact number of neighborhood or block watches is not known. Using 1992 national survey data, O'Keefe et al. (1996) report that 31 percent of all respondents belong to some form of neighborhood crime prevention organization. This is an increase from 12 percent in 1991. Dowds and Mayhew (1994), using data from the 1992 British Crime Survey, report that 28 percent of the respondent households participate in neighborhood watch. More recent data for England and Wales suggest that there are more than 140,000 neighborhood watch schemes with more than six million participating households (Crawford, 1998). Internationally, neighborhood watch is more common in New World countries (the United States, the United Kingdom, Canada, Australia, and New Zealand) and Asian countries than other areas (see Table 5.1). Beyond a formal neighborhood watch group, greater numbers of people simply call on neighbors to keep an eye on their home when they are gone (del Frate, 1998). It is important to remember that any numbers on neighborhood watch participation are only approximations. There is no centralized measure of participation in neighborhood watch, so determining involvement is difficult. Exacerbating this problem is the fact that many participants often join for only a short period.

Table 5.1
Cooperative Neighborhood Crime Prevention Participation

Area	Neighborhood Watch	Informal Surveillance
New World	36%	67%
Asia	23	77
Western Europe	18	59
Africa	10	48
Latin America	12	60
Countries in Transition	8	49

Source: del Frate (1998).

The surveillance goal of neighborhood watch is greatly enhanced by instituting various activities. Many neighborhood watch programs include citizen patrols, whistle stop programs, education programs, neighborhood advocacy, neighborhood clean-up, physical design changes, and property identification. These actions often are initiated by the community and not by outside organizations. In a national survey of neighborhood watch programs, Garofalo and McLeod (1988) reported that the most common activity among groups is Operation Identification (appearing in 81% of the programs), followed by security surveys (68%), crime hotlines (38%), and block parenting (27%). Improving street lighting (35%) and physical environmental concerns (38%) are also common activities adopted by neighborhood watch groups. Among the other activities reported by the neighborhood watch groups are escort services, whistle stop, phone chains, court watch, hiring guards, organized surveillance, and victim/witness assistance (Garofalo and McLeod, 1988). The results demonstrate that community groups involve themselves in a wide array of possible crime prevention measures.

Community Anti-Drug Programs

One notable movement in the area of neighborhood anti-crime programs involves the proliferation of *community anti-drug* (CAD) programs. In response to the surge in drug use, particularly cocaine and crack in inner cities during the early 1990s, residents banded together with each other, the police, and various agencies and organizations to attack drug use, drug sales, and related problems (Davis et al., 1993). Many of the neighborhood efforts mirror neighborhood watch programs in their use of surveillance tactics, reporting to the police, working with agencies to clean up the area, providing information to residents, instituting anti-drug programs, and participating in citizen patrols.

While no count of CAD programs is available, it is reasonable to assume that they are prevalent, particularly in larger cities and areas with serious, visible drug problems. For example, in 1991, various community experts nominated 147 anti-drug programs from 20 cities for inclusion in a national evaluation (Davis et al., 1991). The Center for Substance Abuse Prevention's Community Partnership Demonstration Program targeted 252 communities for anti-drug activity (Davis and Lurigio, 1996). Today, the White House Office of National Drug Control Policy oversees the Drug Free Communities Support Program. This program offers funding in support of community coalitions in their efforts to combat drug problems on a variety of levels (Drug Free Communities Support Program, 2009). Included in the community activities is encouraging citizen participation in prevention activity.

Citizen Patrols

Citizen patrols are often a key element of neighborhood watch and represent an active role in surveillance efforts. The sole purpose of patrols is to put more eyes on the street in order to increase the chances of detecting strangers in the area and discovering crimes in progress. Residents are discouraged from physically intervening into any suspicious activity they may find. While most citizen patrols are on foot, mobile patrols can be found in some communities. Participants can be either volunteers or paid individuals. As with block watches, no clear number of citizen patrols is available. The Guardian Angels is one well-known citizen patrol group. Started in 1971, the group is made up primarily of teenagers and young adults, and boasts having 135 chapters in the United States and 12 other countries. It also provides educational materials on safety, an online, Internet safety component, and work with at-risk youth (www.guardianangels.org).

Variations on the citizen patrol theme include Whistle Stop, Radio Watch, and similar projects. These surveillance methods use the simple presence of people on the street. Participants in these programs generally do not serve in any formal capacity or follow any set schedules. Instead, they watch for suspicious persons and activity while partaking in normal daily activity. For example, people in *Whistle Stop* blow a whistle if they see something happening out of the ordinary as they are shopping, working, or simply walking out of doors. *Radio Watch* relies on individuals with two-way radios (such as cab drivers and truckers) or cell phones to report questionable behavior when they see it occurring. Once again, the key is to observe, call the authorities, and not take any further action.

Police-Community Involvement

As will be seen, the police play a major role in many community crime prevention activities and organizations. The police may actually be the initiators and/or leaders of neighborhood watch and other programs. This is largely due to the fact that there is an interdependence between citizens and the police. It is also important to remember that neighborhood organizations are not meant to replace the legal authorities. The intent is to supplement police activities with the eyes, ears, and ideas of community residents. Both the residents and the police, therefore, must share the burden of promoting neighborhood organization and involvement. One way for the police to accomplish this goal is to encourage the populace to take part in controlling crime and calling the police.

Many crime prevention programs rely heavily on police activity. The *National Night Out* program is often coordinated by local police agencies and consists of educational programs, neighborhood organizing, social events, and anti-drug and anti-crime activities (Bureau of Justice Assistance, 1995a). The police can make arrests, provide expertise, coordinate efforts of experts or residents, and/or take other actions needing official sanctions or the force of law. A new direction in policing in recent years has been the idea of Community-Oriented Policing (which will be addressed in Chapter 11). Alterations in police operations, such as the use of foot patrol or store-front stations, are a key in many police-community activities. These actions can bring the police and the public together to enhance the citizen's decision to call the police and become involved in the legal system.

EVALUATION OF NEIGHBORHOOD CRIME PREVENTION

Evaluation of neighborhood crime prevention efforts typically involves two distinct measures of effectiveness. The most logical measure is the impact these activities have on crime and the fear of crime. A second measure of effectiveness is the impact of neighborhood organizing on intervening factors such as social cohesion, a sense of territoriality, and neighborliness. Crime rates and fear of crime change to the extent that these intervening factors are enhanced. The following evaluation of neighborhood crime prevention looks at changes in both the intermediate factors as well as crime and fear of crime.

Effects on Community Cohesion

Studies of neighborhood crime prevention often include an evaluation of the effectiveness of the organization effort. The outcome measures range from simple documentation of existing groups and numbers of participants to some statement about the quality of individual involvement. A few studies rely exclusively upon these process evaluation measures and fail to consider the actual impact on crime and fear. The assumption in these later studies is that changes in intermediary factors inevitably lead to crime prevention.

Several analyses of community crime prevention note the extent of citizen participation in terms of number of neighborhood groups and the number of participants in those groups. Garofalo and McLeod (1988) and O'Keefe and associates (1996) demonstrate widespread participation in various crime prevention activities. Bennett (1990) reports that 64 percent of the residents in one London neighborhood and 44 percent in another claim to participate in neighborhood watch. Crawford (1998) notes that more than six million people participate in neighborhood watch organizations in England and Wales.

While these levels of activity may appear to be admirable, it is unknown how many people regularly attend crime prevention meetings, heed the advice they are given, or do more than simply show up at the meetings. How many people show up at more than the initial organizational meeting? How much impact do a few hundred people have when they are spread out among thousands of groups around the country and how much support do they have in the community at large? These key questions are not clearly answered in most analyses.

Crime prevention programs typically report positive results, such as neighborhood improvements, and assume that these are signs of increased community cohesion and territoriality. One of the problems with this evidence is that many times the improvements are subsidized by funds coming from the government and completed by paid workers from outside the area. While the improvements may be significant, there is little or no evidence that these changes would have been made without the outside intervention. There also is little evidence that these changes were desired by residents of targeted neighborhoods.

Evaluations of neighborhood watch routinely show that watch participants hold very positive attitudes of the police (Brown and Wycoff, 1987; Laycock and Tilley, 1995a; Shernock, 1986; Skogan and Wycoff, 1986; Williams and Pate, 1987, Wolfer, 2001). This finding can be attributed to the increased interaction between citizens and the police that is not oriented around confrontation.

Community watch programs bring citizens and officers together in symbiotic, mutual, problem-solving activity. The police serve neighborhood groups as sources of information on crime and crime prevention techniques. The public, in turn, provides information on suspicious persons, crimes in progress, and relevant crime-solving information. This information is routinely used to argue that neighborhood watch leads to improved community cohesion.

Various studies of neighborhood crime prevention efforts attempt to more directly assess changes in community cohesion and communal support. The results, however, are often mixed. Bennett (1987; 1990), studying neighborhood watch in two areas of London, reports that social cohesion increased in one and decreased in the other. Similarly, an analysis of four organized neighborhoods in Chicago (Rosenbaum et al., 1985) reveals no change in community cohesion for three areas and decreased cohesion in the fourth neighborhood. Lewis et al. (1988) analyzed interviews with residents in five neighborhood watch areas of Chicago both before and after the implementation of increased efforts at organization. Unfortunately, the authors find no change in the frequency of informal discussion between residents or in the number of neighbors known by name, both of which indicate that community cohesion appears to be unaffected by the neighborhood watch programs.

Effects on Crime

The primary interest in neighborhood crime prevention is reduced levels of crime and fear of crime. Community crime prevention techniques are aimed primarily at the property offenses of burglary, larceny, and robbery. Little, if any, impact should be found on crimes of interpersonal violence. The reason for this is that many personal crimes occur between individuals who know one another and within the home. Increased surveillance will not alleviate crimes when the offender and victim are co-residents or legitimate users of the area. Neither would appear out of place nor draw attention to themselves. Only crimes that occur between strangers should experience any great reduction from neighborhood watch activities. The following discussion of effects on crime is divided into three primary areas— studies using official data, analysis of victim survey data, and a discussion of two specific prevention initiatives from Great Britain.

Official Records

Official crime records reveal a positive impact of neighborhood watch programs on crime. Most studies report a lower level of crime (particularly property offenses) in the target communities than control areas and/or decreases compared to pre-program levels. An early comparison of Detroit neighborhoods shows a 58 percent reduction in burglary and 61 percent fewer purse snatchings in the crime prevention community (Figgie International, 1983). Perry (1984), investigating citizen crime prevention in 15 Denver neighborhoods, finds that 11 of the 15 neighborhoods had lower crime rates the year following implementation compared to the year prior to the project. Similarly, Latessa and Travis (1987) note significant drops in burglary, larceny, auto theft, and total crime in an organized area of Cincinnati compared to the rest of the city. The efficacy of the neighborhood efforts is supported by the fact that comparable decreases did not appear for personal crimes (aggravated assault and robbery), which are not the typical target of neighborhood actions.

Many of the projects that are a part of the Reducing Burglary Initiative in the United Kingdom include neighborhood watch, targeted policing, youth programs and other interventions, along with physical design changes in their programs (Kodz and Pease, 2003). In early evaluations in Rochdale and Yew Tree, the programs significantly reduced the burglary levels in the experimental areas relative to the control neighborhoods (Home Office, 2003c, 2003d). Mille and Hough (2004) report an average decrease of 21 percent in burglaries in Reducing Burglary Initiative areas, with decreases in 14 of 16 projects. Similar positive results have been reported elsewhere in the United States and the United Kingdom (Anderton, 1985; Jenkins and Latimer, 1987; Kohfeld et al., 1981; Laycock and Tilley, 1995).

Not all studies using official records reveal uniformly lower levels of crime in crime prevention communities. An evaluation of neighborhood watch programs in London finds no change in crime for organized areas while there were decreases in control neighborhoods (Bennett, 1990). One possible explanation for mixed results would be pre-program differences in the areas or in offending. Neighborhood watch areas with great reductions in crime are often those with high pre-program offense levels (Henig, 1984). The reductions, therefore, could be due to a regression to the more natural crime levels for these areas. Another possibility is varying levels of success at achieving the intervening effects (such as social cohesion).

An important confounding factor in evaluation of neighborhood watch may be changes in the level of reporting to the police. Successful programs should increase the number of calls to the police, which may result in increases in the number of recorded crimes. At the same time, there may be a reduction in crime. This is possible if citizens call the police more often but fewer calls reflect criminal activities. For example, Matthews (1977) reports a nonsignificant decrease in crime but an increased level of calls to the police. Bolkcom (1981) reports a doubling in calls to police accompanied by a decrease in crime. Similarly, a public housing project in Charlotte, North Carolina, reveals increased reports of crime accompanied by a reduced crime rate (Hayes, 1982). The fact that reporting of crime to the police increases is one indication that the neighborhood watch program is successful.

Victimization Measures

The use of victim survey data avoids the confounding influence of changes in reporting crimes to the police. Victim surveys assess the impact of crime prevention programs through personal reports of crime. Studies utilizing victim surveys typically report strong support for neighborhood watch. For example, the Seattle Community Crime Prevention Program, which received exemplary status from the federal government, based its evaluation on victim surveys of crime and reporting of crime to the police. The community crime prevention areas displayed lower burglary rates after program initiation than did corresponding control areas of Seattle (Cirel et al., 1977). At the same time, reporting to the police increased, thus supporting the view that there was a real reduction in crime. Unfortunately, the lower burglary levels persisted for only 12 to 14 months and then increased to the pre-program levels (Cirel et al., 1977). This finding of time-bounded effects suggests that programs need to be periodically reviewed and promoted in order to prolong their effectiveness.

Cook and Roehl's (1983) analysis of Chicago's Northwest Neighborhood Federation also relied on victimization data to evaluate crime prevention efforts. The program included neighborhood watch, a phone chain for passing along information, and property marking. Among the improvements noted by residents was a 12 percent reduction in the level of criminal victimization. Cook and Roehl (1983) also reported a 26 percent increase in the feeling that residents could do something about crime in their neighborhood. A more recent evaluation of neighborhood organizations in Chicago, including the Northwest Federation, revealed mixed findings (Lewis et al., 1988). The Northwest Neighborhood again showed decreased victimization. Conversely, two areas reported increased victimization and the balance of Chicago exhibited virtually no changes in victimization over the same study period.

Despite these positive results, a major study of neighborhood watch in London did not find the same positive results using victimization data (Bennett, 1990). Both household and personal crimes showed increases over the course of the program compared to control areas. In fact, some control areas reported reduced crime for the same period of time. It would appear that the neighborhood watch areas did worse than the other areas.

Two Examples—Kirkholt and Safer Cities

Community crime prevention has received a great deal of attention and support in Great Britain. Two projects, in particular, offer a good deal of insight into the effectiveness of community and neighborhood interventions. These are the *Kirkholt Burglary Prevention project* and the *Safer Cities Program*. Kirkholt is a clearly defined residential area comprised of more than 2,200 dwellings near Manchester and is owned by the local governmental authority. According to the 1984 British Crime Survey, Kirkholt had a burglary rate more than twice that of other high risk areas in England (Forrester et al., 1988). The burglary prevention activities included the removal of pre-payment heating fuel meters in homes, improvements in physical security devices, the use of community teams to conduct security surveys, and the establishment of "cocoon neighborhood watch" (very small groups of homes banded together for surveillance and support). While overall security was an issue, the program specifically targeted repeat burglary victims (Forrester et al., 1988).

Evaluation of Kirkholt took place in two phases and involved extensive interviews with residents, agencies, and other program participants. Results from Phase I, which covered the development of the project and the first seven months of operation, showed a large reduction in burglary from 316 offenses in the pre-program period to 147 offenses after program implementation (Forrester et al., 1988). At the same time, there was a small increase in burglary for the surrounding area. Similarly, the project demonstrated a clear impact on repeat burglary victimization (Forrester et al., 1988; 1990). Potential problems for the Phase I results include the short follow-up period (only seven months) and the fact that the pre-program offense levels were unduly high (Forrester et al., 1990). It is possible that the effect was only short-term or that the reductions reflect a moderation of unreasonably high offense levels that had nowhere to go but down. The Phase II evaluation, however, provided greater support for the project's impact. Overall, the burglary rate fell roughly 75 percent over the life of the project (over four years), while the remainder of the area only saw a decrease of 24 percent (Forrester et al., 1990). Additional support appeared in the fact that repeat victimization was significantly reduced.

Further evidence of the impact of the Kirkholt project can be seen in the levels of program participation. First, Forrester et al. (1990) report that there were 93 "Home Watch" (cocoon neighborhood watch) groups operating, with 20 to 25 households in each. This represented almost all residents in Kirkholt. Second, various local interventions were initiated by the program, including after school projects and work with the Probation Service on programs for offenders. Finally, there was a significant increase in the number of victims who took preventive measures after initiation of the program (Forrester et al., 1990). The evaluations concluded that both physical design features (e.g. the removal of the pre-payment meters) and social efforts (e.g. the cocoon neighborhood watch) were essential elements of the successful project.

In the Safer Cities Program, the British government provided funds for local initiatives aimed at reducing crime and the fear of crime, and the creation of safer cities. Monies were allocated in an attempt to build multi-agency partnerships for fighting social, physical, and economic problems in urban areas (Sutton, 1996; Tilley, 1992). Initial funding was made available to 20 projects in 1988 and was expanded in a second phase in 1993. Each individual program included a coordinator, police participation, various agency representatives, and a steering committee. Each steering committee was supposed to identify and implement preventive actions according to the unique needs of the community. Many of the interventions initiated under the Safer Cities programs included target hardening, property marking, community mobilization, the use of signs and other media, and neighborhood watch activity (Tilley and Webb, 1994).

Evaluations of the Safer Cities initiatives reveal generally positive results. Most locations initiated a wide array of prevention initiatives (Sutton, 1996).

Evidence shows that the level of burglary was reduced (Ekblom et al., 1996b; Mawby, 2001; Tilley and Webb, 1994), apparently as a result of target hardening, neighborhood watch and property identification activities. Additionally, publicity concerning an area's activities was seen as an important part of making an impact for the larger community (Tilley and Webb, 1994). At the same time, however, there is some evidence that burglary may have increased in adjacent areas and locations where the program was not adequately or fully instituted (Ekblom et al., 1996a; 1996b). Clearly, greater impacts on crime were evident in areas where more action was undertaken. Despite these positive results, Sutton (1996) points out that many areas in need of assistance were written off by the steering committees as "lost causes," rather than places to be aggressively targeted. Part of this was due to the fact that some steering committees were much more passive in their activities than others.

Summary

Evaluation of neighborhood crime prevention in both the United States and the United Kingdom shows that preventive actions can impact on the level of crime in the community. This assessment holds true whether the crime rate is measured by official police records or victimization surveys. The level of the change, however, is not equal in all studies and a few studies suggest that crime can become worse in some targeted neighborhoods (e.g. Bennett, 1990; Latessa and Travis, 1987; Lewis et al., 1988; Pate et al., 1987). The key to successful crime prevention activities appears to lie in the level of program implementation. Bowers et al. (2003b) note that the level of *outcome intensity* (that is, the actual implementation of prevention activities), as opposed to the level of planning, preparation, training and other factors (i.e. input intensity), is the most important factor in making changes in crime. The greater the outcome intensity, the greater the reduction in crime. Different background characteristics of the target communities, varying types of available data, and varying evaluation designs also impact on the results.

Community Anti-Drug Programs

Community anti-drug programs (CAD) represent a recent incarnation of community crime prevention initiatives. These programs utilize many of the same forms of intervention, including physical design changes, surveillance, group meetings, phone hotlines for anonymous reporting to the police, and citizen patrols, but also add activities directly targeted at drug problems, such as demanding enforcement of zoning and housing codes in order to eliminate drug houses. Many of these programs grew in the late 1980s and early 1990s in response to the growing drug problem in many cities.

The success of CAD programs should be enhanced by increased levels of social cohesion. While there is some evidence that anti-drug programs have a positive impact on social cohesion, the research results are mixed. Lurigio and Davis (1992), reporting on initiatives in Miami, Seattle, Philadelphia and Baltimore, argue that the programs have significantly increased the social cohesion in three of the four sites. Conversely, Roehl et al. (1995) and Davis et al. (1991) note that actual participation by residents is low (often less than 10%) and many programs operate with only a small core group of dedicated individuals. Results from an analysis of anti-drug initiatives in Chicago's public housing suggests that change may be hard if the residents actively contribute to the problems and the interventions are being driven by outsiders (Popkin et al., 1999).

The more important issue is whether CAD programs are able to reduce the levels of crime and other problems. Using interviews with residents of four CAD programs, Davis et al. (1991) report overall positive results. Residents report fewer drug problems after initiation of the program. The respondents also point to reduced signs of physical decay, increased feelings of empowerment and social control, and greater satisfaction with the area. Similar results are found in analyses of the Community Responses to Drug Abuse program, the Community Partnership Demonstration Programs, and the Chicago Public Housing Authority's Anti-Drug Initiative (Davis and Lurigio, 1996; Popkin et al., 1999; Rosenbaum et al., 1997). The evaluation of the anti-drug programs in Chicago public housing also reveals reduced victimization. Popkin et al. (1995; 1999) point out that residents of target projects report reduced fighting, shootings and drug dealing, both inside and outside the buildings. These positive finding from anti-drug programs may reflect the intensity of resident convictions about drugs and drug-related offenses. Where past crime prevention programs dealt mostly with property crime issues, drug problems come with related gangs, violence, and personal crime problems that might cause greater concern and willingness to act by citizens.

Not all CAD initiatives are embraced by or operated by local residents. Popkin et al. (1995; 1999) note that most of the activities in Chicago's public housing initiative were coordinated and implemented by the police and the housing authority. Citizen participation was difficult to engender. The authors report that the program was successful at implementing drug and weapon sweeps, the hiring of security guards, the institution of new security policies, and reducing offending behavior. Despite the positive results, some residents resented the intrusions and methods used by the housing authority. Indeed, successful legal challenges were mounted in reference to some activities, such as sweeps for weapons. The evaluators suggest that greater involvement by the residents is needed in both the planning and implementation of anti-drug activities (Popkin et al., 1999).

Citizen Patrols

Citizen patrols present the most straightforward attempt by neighborhood residents to increase surveillance. Relatively few studies of citizen patrols exist. One examination of citizen patrol studies shows reduced burglary rates on the order of 20 to 50 percent in patrol areas (Titus, 1984). Latessa and Allen (1980), evaluating paid, citizen foot patrol in Columbus, Ohio, report a great drop in crime in the target areas compared to pre-program figures and control areas. In addition, citizens favor the patrols and their activity (Latessa and Allen, 1980). Similarly, Troyer and Wright (1985), assessing the impact of citizen patrols in a middle-class neighborhood and on a university campus, report that residents strongly favored the patrol and report feeling safer since its initiation. Citizen involvement in patrols undertaken on mass transit facilities in The Netherlands appears to have caused a 33 percent increase in feelings of safety and a clear drop in violence (van Andel, 1989). In general, the research suggests that citizen patrols can be effective at reducing both crime and fear.

The Guardian Angels are one example of citizen patrolling that has gained international attention. Despite the large number of Guardian Angel chapters around the world, few methodologically sound evaluations of the program exist. Pennell et al. (1986), evaluating the Guardian Angels in San Diego, report little impact on the level of crime. Indeed, while violent crime fell by 22 percent in the patrolled areas, the control areas exhibited a drop of 42 percent. Additionally, simple assault increased in the patrolled area. These results are not surprising given the fact that the Angels made only two citizen arrests in the course of 672 patrols over six months (Pennell et al., 1986). Kenney (1986) finds the same lack of change in crime when studying Guardian Angel patrols of the New York City subways.

While the impact on crime may not be great, the Guardian Angels have engendered a great deal of goodwill among the citizens in the areas they patrol. Respondents from several cities report a greater feeling of safety when Guardian Angels are around (Pennell et al., 1986). In addition, the organization is able to keep its own members from becoming involved in criminal activity (Pennell et al., 1986). Other positive findings include the fact that the police believe the Guardian Angels help citizens with a variety of concerns. Early concerns about vigilantism held by the public and police, directed at all citizen patrols and not just the Guardian Angels, have not been realized (Latessa and Allen, 1980; Troyer and Wright, 1985; Yin et al., 1977).

Neighborhood Crime Prevention and Fear of Crime

Besides attempting to eliminate or reduce crime, neighborhood crime prevention programs have the potential to impact fear of crime. Many evaluations investigate changes in fear, often through victim surveys that ask residents about their feelings of safety in the community and their perceived risk of future victimization. Research also tests other dimensions discussed by Ferraro (1995), such as impressions of overall crime in the community, feelings about whether citizens can have an effect on crime and neighborhood problems, and general feelings toward components of the criminal justice system.

Reported reductions in fear of crime can be very dramatic. Figgie International (1983) claims 75 percent fewer subjects respond that they are "very fearful" of crime after neighborhood programming. In another study, 95 percent of the senior citizens who participated in crime prevention reported being less fearful in follow-up surveys (Yagerlener, 1980). Cook and Roehl's (1983) evaluation of the Northwest Neighborhood Federation showed decreases in perceptions of rising crime (22%), decreased fear of burglary (26%), increased feelings that residents could influence crime (26%), and an increase in the belief in neighborhood crime control (26%). Evidence from the Safer Cities program shows reduced fear and reduced worry about crime, especially in areas where crime prevention activities are well known and intensively implemented (Ekblom et al., 1996a; 1996b; Mawby, 2001; Tilley and Webb, 1994). These findings of reduced fear are replicated in a number of other studies (Bennett, 1990; Cohn et al., 1978; Hayes, 1982; Rasmussen et al., 1979).

Efforts at organizing hard to organize areas or implementing prevention with limited community support also demonstrate the fear reducing capabilities of such endeavors. Bennett and Lavrakas (1989) report on concerted efforts to organize 10 high-crime, high-fear inner-city neighborhoods in nine cities. Comparing pre-program to post-program periods, and experimental with non-equivalent control groups, the authors find that fear was significantly reduced in six of the ten neighborhoods. There was no change in three and an increase in one area. Further, overall concern about crime was reduced in five neighborhoods, with no changes in the remaining neighborhoods (Bennett and Lavrakas, 1989). In the analysis of community anti-drug programs in four cities, Davis et al. (1991) report significant reductions in fear, while no changes appear in control areas. Similarly, the Chicago Housing Authority's Anti-Drug Initiative reduced fear, despite the relative lack of resident participation (Popkin et al., 1999). Davis and Lurigio (1996) note that the Community Responses to Drug Abuse program increased resident satisfaction with the area. Finally, Wolfer (2001) reports that elderly respondents who believe there is an active neighborhood watch program nearby are less fearful than those who do not live in a neighborhood watch community.

Not all studies, however, exhibit lower levels of fear nor are the evaluations of fear without problems. Brodie and Sheppard (1977), evaluating crime prevention programs in Denver, uncovered conflicting evidence on fear of crime. While fear of burglary decreased, fear of walking outdoors and feelings of helplessness toward crime increased. Rosenbaum et al. (1986) report increased fear of personal crime, no effect on fear of property crime, and increased perceptions of neighborhood crime. In addition, the programs failed to engender positive attitudes toward the area, had little influence on area deterioration, and did not alter crime prevention efforts of individuals (Rosenbaum et al., 1986). Similarly, the Community Responses to Drug Abuse evaluation reveals no changes in residents' perceptions of crime or fear of crime (Davis and Lurigio, 1996). Other studies also report no change in levels of fear of crime (Bennett, 1987; Latessa and Travis, 1987; Pate et al., 1987).

The failure to find reduced fear in some studies may be due to a variety of problems in the research. First, participation in crime prevention programs and attempts to heighten awareness of crime may engender more, not less, fear and worry. Second, the varying definitions of "fear" makes assessments of program impact difficult. Third, the use of diverse subjects in follow-up surveys (e.g. only those who participate in the crime prevention program, random samples of neighborhoods, or subgroups of the population) makes summarizing the results problematic. Fourth, many programs focus on high crime, high fear areas and prevention efforts face a major challenge for changing attitudes in these locations. Finally, short follow-up times may not be enough to elicit any changes in high crime areas. In general, neighborhood crime prevention appears to successfully reduce fear of crime, particularly where the interventions are appropriately implemented.

Evaluation Issues

Beyond the various problems noted so far in this chapter, there are other issues that hamper the effectiveness and evaluation of neighborhood crime prevention programs. A major concern in any evaluation or discussion of neighborhood watch entails the definition of "neighborhood." Unfortunately, rarely is neighborhood explicitly defined. It is assumed that everyone knows what a neighborhood is and there is no reason to define it. What this means for research and program planning, however, is that everyone involved in the project may be envisioning a (slightly) different area when "neighborhood" is being considered. For example, many cities have areas that can be identified by a name. These names may come from a feature of the area (such as "uptown" or "the park district") or a subdivision name (such as "Shady Acres") or some other identifier. Unfortunately, the simple existence of a name does not mean that the area has set boundaries or that everyone knows the boundaries. Most research takes one of two approaches to handling "neighborhood" in the project. The first is to allow study participants to interpret "neighborhood" on an individual basis. The second is for the researcher to identify the "neighborhood" and gather information on that area, often without consideration of whether the chosen area is meaningful as a "neighborhood" to the people residing in it. In both cases, what may emerge are very different meanings and views about the "neighborhood."

Crime prevention research is particularly susceptible to variations in the definition of neighborhood. Surveys of crime and fear that reference the respondent's neighborhood will invariably be tapping a range of definitions. Crime prevention programs often operate on very different views of the neighborhood. As noted in Chapter 4, large housing complexes (such as Cabrini-Green), the mixed use Union Avenue Corridor in Portland (which was 3.5 miles long), and North Asylum Hill in Hartford have all been considered as neighborhoods. On the opposite extreme, Taylor (1988; 1997) looks at the *streetblock* as the focus for neighborhood control and crime prevention activities. A streetblock consists of the homes on either side of a single block (that is, between two cross-streets). Taylor chooses this bounding based on a belief that it is within this area that social contacts, relationships and interaction are strong. The streetblock may hold more relevance to residents than does the idea of neighborhood. The important point is that "neighborhood" may have many different meanings to different individuals in varied settings. Both research and program implementation need to be mindful of the problems that may arise when "neighborhood" is not defined or when different definitions are being used.

A second concern revolves around the impact of increased surveillance on levels of crime and fear. Neighborhood watch assumes that areas with higher surveillance will experience less crime. Unfortunately, the time order between surveillance and crime is not clear. High crime can (and should) prompt increased surveillance. At the same time, increased surveillance should uncover more crime, especially as measured by police records, due to increased reports of offending. Actual decreases in the amount of crime may not show up due to elevated levels of reporting. The evaluation of crime prevention efforts, therefore, should consider both the changes in citizen reporting practices and official and victimization levels of crime.

Another key problem in evaluating the impact of neighborhood crime prevention is the fact that most interventions are not implemented in isolation from other prevention activities. A consequence of having simultaneous programs and activities is the difficulty of identifying what is working and/or what is causing the problems (Ekblom, 1993; Greenberg et al., 1985). The opposite problem is the expectation that a single intervention will have more than a minimal impact on crime and fear when the causes of the problems are many and varied (Bursik and Grasmick, 1993). A related issue with evaluation research is the failure to adequately assess the program's implementation. Rather than indicate failure, an evaluation showing no or negative impact may reflect the fact that the intervention was not properly implemented, the dosage applied to the problem was not enough, the follow-up time was too short, or there was some other problem (Ekblom, 1993; Laycock and Tilley, 1995; Pawson and Tilley, 2003). Many of these implementation problems arise from the demands for immediate results, competition for resources, or the lack of adequate funding (Ekblom, 1993; Laycock and Tilley, 1995).

CITIZEN PARTICIPATION AND SUPPORT

The results of research on neighborhood crime prevention should be qualified in light of information on citizen participation. Many of the results are presented as generalizable to all neighborhoods. The findings, however, may not be applicable to all subgroups of the population. Indeed, some studies find changes only for program participants. Among the questions that must be answered are: Who participates in community crime prevention efforts? Are these individuals representative of the general population? and Do crime prevention methods affect all persons in the same, or similar, fashion? These inquiries can be addressed through an examination of who participates, and why.

Who Participates?

A demographic analysis of crime prevention participants yields mixed results. Members of community crime prevention and those who take preventive measures more often are males, middle-to-upper income, home owners, more highly educated, white, and live in single family dwellings (Bennett, 1989; Cook and Roehl, 1983; Fisher, 1989; Greenberg et al., 1982; Greenberg et al., 1985; Lavrakas and Herz, 1982; Lavrakas et al., 1981; Luxenberg et al., 1994; Podolefsky and DuBow, 1980; Roehl and Cook, 1984; Shernock, 1986; Skogan, 1988; Skogan, 1989; Skogan and Maxfield, 1981). These characteristics suggest a neighborhood which is demographically homogeneous and stable. The residents have built a stake in the neighborhood and are willing to take action to protect their investment.

These findings do not mean that crime prevention measures cannot and do not appear among other demographic groups. While some studies claim that participants tend to be older (Lab, 1990; Menard and Covey, 1987; Shernock, 1986; Shapland, 1988; Skogan and Maxfield, 1981), others find that most participants are middle-aged (Brown et al., 1984; Greenberg et al., 1985; Lavrakas and Herz, 1982) or younger (Smith and Lab, 1991). Some studies report that females participate more often than males (Bennett, 1989; Lab, 1990; Lavrakas et al., 1981). Similarly, there is a good deal of discrepancy about whether whites or blacks are more likely to be involved in community organizations (Lab, 1990; Lavrakas and Herz, 1982; Lavrakas et al., 1981; Shernock, 1986; Skogan and Maxfield, 1981).

Research indicates that participation in crime prevention groups is related to levels of participation in other groups. Various authors note that people involved in crime prevention efforts tend to be "joiners," who have higher feelings of responsibility toward the community than non-participants. Crime prevention is often a secondary extension of other group activities (Greenberg et al., 1982; Lavrakas and Herz, 1982; Lavrakas et al., 1981). This "joining" phenomenon is reflected in the findings that successful organizations tend to have a strong leader who is able to motivate participation, overcome diversity in opinions, set an agenda, and keep residents interested (Ekblom, 1993; Laycock and Tilley, 1995; Rosenbaum, 1988; Skogan, 1987; Tilley, 1992).

Findings on the relationship between crime/fear and group participation are not as clear. Some evaluations find that higher perceptions of crime, fear, and neighborhood problems are related to crime prevention activity (Bennett, 1989; Lavrakas and Herz, 1982; Menard and Covey, 1987; Pennell, 1978; Skogan, 1987; Skogan, 1989; Skogan and Lurigio, 1992; Skogan and Maxfield, 1981; Taylor et al., 1987). Conversely, others find little or no connection between perceptions of crime, fear of crime, and prevention participation (Baumer and DuBow, 1977; Bennett, 1989; Lab, 1990; Lavrakas and Herz, 1982; Smith and Lab, 1991).

The divergent findings on participation may be due to a number of factors (Lab, 1990). First, different groups of subjects are used in the analyses. Where one study examines the behavior of young urban residents, another may consider middle-aged suburbanites. Yet another may target older rural residents. It is not surprising, therefore, that different results emerge. Second, studies often measure the key variables in different ways. Victimization surveys and police data may tap different dimensions of prevention behavior. Fear measures vary from study to study. Similarly, crime prevention can take a wide variety of forms ranging from citizen patrols to operation identification and neighborhood watch. This diversity in study methodologies may be the cause of the varied results.

Perhaps the greatest problem in comparing studies on crime prevention involves the dubious assumption that all prevention techniques can be subsumed under the single umbrella of "crime prevention." While various authors have attempted to separate crime prevention actions into groups (Conklin, 1975; Furstenburg, 1972; Lavrakas et al., 1981; Pennell, 1978; Skogan, 1981), there have been few attempts to empirically test the proposed groupings. Lavrakas and Lewis (1980), factor analyzing data from four sources, identify two crime prevention dimensions— avoidance and access control. While these items correspond to theoretically proposed groupings, many crime prevention actions did not fit into either group.

Lab (1990), analyzing the 1983 Victim Risk Supplement (VRS) to the National Crime Survey, finds five dimensions of crime prevention behavior and examines crime prevention participation across the different domains. The domains that emerge are surveillance (neighborhood watch type activities), avoidance, target hardening (property marking and alarms), personal security (owning items for protection), and access control (locks and door peepholes). Participation varies across the different types of crime prevention (Lab, 1990). The most consistent result is the failure of victimization to affect participation in any behavior, and that fear of crime has only a minor impact on preventive behavior. A number of demographic factors show a small consistent impact on participatory behavior.

Lab and Hope (1998) replicated these results using 1994 British Crime Survey (BCS) data. The authors uncover five different crime prevention domains (see Table 5.2). These domains include taking evening precautions, neighborhood watch, technological security measures, fortress-type security measures, and self-defense activities. The differences between these results and those of Lab (1990) may be due to three major factors. First, the BCS data set includes a greater array of crime prevention behaviors for analysis. Second, the two studies are based on respondents from different countries. Third, there is a 10-year time gap between the collection of the two data sets. Despite these issues, the fact remains that distinct domains of crime prevention activities are utilized by respondents. Crime prevention is not unidimensional.

Using these domains to analyze citizen participation, Hope and Lab (2001) report clear differences across the various groups of activities in terms of individual demographic characteristics, perceptions of crime and fear, and neighborhood characteristics (see Table 5.3). Some of the greatest differences

Table 5.2
Crime Prevention Domains and Activities

Evening Precautions	Neighborhood Watch	Technological Security	Fortress Security	Self-Defense
Alter Habits	NW Participation	Burglary Alarms	Deadbolt Locks	Carry Weapons
Avoid People	Mark Property	Light Timers	Window Locks	Carry Alarms
Go Out With Others	Watch Neighbors' Homes	Security Surveys	Bars/Grills on Doors and Windows	Self-Defense Classes
Make Special Arrangements	Home Insurance			

Source: Lab and Hope (1998).

in participation across the crime prevention domains are the variations by area characteristics and respondent perceptions, rather than individual demographic characteristics. The results of these two studies suggest that analyses of participation must consider the type of crime prevention being considered. Simply comparing one study to another is prone to comparing different methods and behaviors to one another.

Organizing Neighborhood Crime Prevention

Participation in crime prevention is clearly a problematic issue for program organizers. A number of obstacles inhibit the organization of neighborhoods. First, many individuals live in areas with few opportunities to participate. Second, many programs are initiated because of an existing crime problem. Unfortunately, once the crime problem abates, these programs often fall apart. Programs that persist tend to be multifaceted. When crime and fear begin to subside, these groups turn to other issues and concerns. This type of organization, however, typically appears in more affluent, stable communities.

A third problem involves the inability to organize high crime, inner-city areas that typically need the most help. In most cases, initiatives targeting these areas are unable to prompt more than minimal participation by local residents (Lewis et al., 1988; Pate et al., 1987; Silloway and McPherson, 1985). The reason for this failure may be that people in high-crime areas are more fearful of crime and, in turn, are afraid to join others (often strangers) in a similar position. Individuals who have constructed fortresses in and around their homes are fearful of leaving the fortress, even for the purpose of fighting crime and fear. One exception to these findings is the growth of anti-drug programs in less affluent, high crime, minority neighborhoods (Lurigio and Davis, 1992; Skogan and Lurigio, 1992). As noted earlier, this may be due to the seriousness of the drug problem and related crimes that have emerged in these types of neighborhoods.

Table 5.3
Predictors of Participation in Different Crime Prevention Domains

	Evening Precautions	Neighborhood Watch	Technological Security	Fortress Security	Self-Defense
Demographics:	Younger Female Non-white Married Home owner High education —	Older Female White Married Home owner High education High income	Older Female White Married Home owner High education High income	Older Female — Married Home owner High education High income	Younger Female — Not married Not home owner High education —
Area Factors:	High population High density High % adults High % single adults with children — — —	— — — High % single adults with children Few black households High owner occupation High % council housing	— — High % adults High % single adults with children — High owner occupation High % council housing	— High density High % adults High % single adults with children — High owner occupation —	— — — — — — —
Perceptual Variables:	High assault likelihood High robbery likelihood Robbery victim Unsafe walking alone Unable to defend self Social incivilities — — — — — — — — — —	— — — Unsafe walking alone — — High burglary likelihood Burglary victim High crime area Joiner Goods for theft Detached home Helping neighborhood Satisfied with area Identify strangers — —	— — — — — — High burglary likelihood Burglary victim High crime area — — Detached home — — Unsafe at home alone — —	— — — — — — High burglary likelihood Burglary victim High crime area — — Detached home — — —	High assault likelihood — Robbery victim Unsafe walking alone Abel to defend self Social incivilities — — — Joiner — — — — — Physical incivilities Assault victim

Source: Hope, T. and S.P. Lab (2001), "Variation in Crime Prevention Participation: Evidence from the British Crime Survey," *Crime Prevention and Community Safety: An International Journal* 3:7–22.

Rosenbaum (1987) outlines five problematic assumptions underlying neighborhood watch programs (see Table 5.4). The failure of any of the assumptions would hamper both the organization and maintenance of such programs. We have already seen that neighborhood watch programs are not available to the majority of the population (counter to Assumption 1). Similarly, it has been shown that many people fail to become involved even when the opportunity to do so exists, and participation varies greatly based on demographic, neighborhood, and crime prevention factors (counter to Assumption 2).

Assumption 3 cannot be sustained in light of the research showing a failure to increase group cohesion, reduce fear, or increase participation. Rosenbaum's fourth assumption is violated by the fact that maintaining crime prevention activity is a major problem for most organizations. Most programs flounder once the crime problem subsides. Finally, the assumption that crime prevention is effective at reducing crime and disorder (Assumption 5) finds

Table 5.4
Problematic Assumptions Underlying Neighborhood Watch

Assumption 1

Neighborhood Watch can be easily implemented on a large scale to provide citizens with an opportunity for participation in crime prevention activities.

Assumption 2

If given the opportunity to participate in Neighborhood Watch, most citizens would find the program appealing and would become involved regardless of social, demographic, or neighborhood characteristics.

Assumption 3

If and when citizens get together at Block Watch meetings, the assumption is made that this interaction and discussion will produce a number of immediate effects. These effects include reaching a consensus about problem definition, reducing fear of crime, increasing group cohesion, and increasing participation in both individual and collective crime prevention actions after the meeting.

Assumption 4

Neighborhood Watch organizers (both police and community volunteers) invest in this strategy with the belief that such activities, once initiated, will be sustained.

Assumption 5

A final and vary fundamental assumption underlying Neighborhood Watch is that the collective citizen actions implied by this strategy, if set in motion, would reduce the level of criminal activity and disorder in the neighborhood, thereby setting the stage for a reduction in fear of crime and other neighborhood improvements.

Source: Compiled from Rosenbaum (1987).

only qualified support in past research. Where programs do appear successful, there is some question as to the actual mechanism behind the change. In many instances, it is unclear as to whether the neighborhood program is completely, or integrally, involved in the changes. The failure of neighborhood watch to live up to these five assumptions leads to serious questions about its potential to impact crime and fear.

Summary

In general, it appears that participation is centered more among those who have more (property) at risk, view crime as a problem, and are involved in other social groups. Skogan and Maxfield (1981) note that high crime, heterogeneous, transient areas generate feelings of fear, distrust, suspicion, and anxiety, which tend to isolate people from one another. This isolation mitigates the formation of community crime prevention groups in the neighborhoods which need them the most.

Another explanation is offered by Bursik and Grasmick (1993), who argue that neighborhood social control requires input from private, parochial and public sources (see, Hunter, 1985). *Private control* is based on interpersonal relationships between family members, friends and close associates. *Parochial control* broadens the sources of control to include neighborhood networks and institutions, such as schools, churches or businesses. Finally, *public control* reflects the ability to marshal input, support and resources from public agencies. Bursik and Grasmick (1993) suggest that lower-class, transient, high-crime neighborhoods have the greatest problem developing control at any of these levels. Even if the residents can engender the private and parochial control, their ability to tap into the public dimension is hindered by their economic and political position in society. Skogan (1990) makes a similar argument when pointing out that some communities are unable to mobilize the resources necessary to deal with disorder.

The potential impact of neighborhood watch and community crime prevention is untested in the areas and with the populations where the greatest margin for change exists. It is in high-crime, socially disorganized areas where engendering participation is most challenging, in part because of a vicious cycle between involvement and fear/crime. That is, fear and perceived risk may lead people to retreat into their homes and avoid other people, which in turn mitigates the possibility of group action to address fear and victimization.

CHAPTER SUMMARY

The evidence tends to support the basic idea of neighborhood crime prevention as a means of combating crime and the fear of crime. Table 5.5 summarizes the evidence from neighborhood initiatives. The results generally present neighborhood watch and its component activities as effective methods to reduce crime, victimization and fear of crime. The magnitude of the changes, however, often appear to vary greatly from study to study. Some studies show large absolute reductions in crime. Others present little or no change in target areas accompanied by increased crime in control areas. Still other evaluations, although few in number, find small increases in crime. These varying results are amplified when one considers individual crimes in place of overall crime rates. These discrepant results can be attributed to several factors. Foremost among the causes is the fact that the neighborhood initiative was not successfully implemented. That means that the failure is not in the crime prevention program itself, but it was a failure to mobilize the citizens, fully implement the intervention, or bring the measures to bear on the problem. The failure of some evaluations to find positive results also may be due to the reliance on short-term follow-up, the absence of control groups for comparison, differing operationalizations of key variables (such as crime and fear), and the inability to identify individual effects of different program components.

Table 5.5
Summary of the Evidence on Neighborhood Prevention Programs

Technique	Homes	Public Housing	Community
NW Groups	B⁺,T⁺,F⁺	B?,R?,T?,F⁺	B⁺,R⁺,T⁺,GC?,F⁺
Community Anti-Drug Programs		D⁺,GC⁺	V⁺,D⁺,GC⁺
Citizen Patrols	B?,T?,F⁺	B?,R?,T?,F⁺	B?,R?,T?,GC⁺,F⁺

Offenses: B= burglary; R= robbery; T= theft; V= violence/aggression; FR= fraud; F= fear; GC= general crime
+ indicates the techniques have been shown to reduce the crime in question
− indicates the techniques have been shown to have no impact on the crime
? indicates that the impact of the technique varies by the project or the context

One issue often left unaddressed in crime prevention evaluations is the problem of "crime displacement." Crime displacement refers to the movement of crime, usually to another area, as a result of the crime prevention initiative in the target area. The occurrence of crime displacement represents a shift in crime and not an actual decrease in crime. The extent and impact of displacement is the subject of the next chapter.

Chapter 6
DISPLACEMENT AND DIFFUSION

Key Terms:

benign displacement
cognitive mapping
CRAVED
crime attractors
crime displacement
crime fuse
crime generator
crime pattern theory
diffusion of benefits
distance decay
edges
environmental backcloth
functional displacement
Google Maps

Google Streetview
journey to crime
malign displacement
nodes
paths
perpetrator displacement
Rational Choice theory
Routine Activities perspective
social/crime template
soft determinism
tactical displacement
target displacement
temporal displacement
territorial displacement

Learning Objectives:

After reading this chapter you should be able to:

- List and define six forms of displacement

- Discuss the assumptions underlying displacement

- Provide an explanation of rational choice theory and its relation to displacement

- Distinguish between benign and malign displacement and discuss each

- Explain diffusion of benefits

- Discuss the 10 principles of opportunity and crime

- Explain the routine activities perspective

- Demonstrate your knowledge of offender decision making

- Outline CRAVED and how it influences crime activity

- Outline crime pattern theory and cognitive mapping

- Discuss the impact of modern technology on the construction of cognitive maps

- Discuss the evidence on the extent of each type of displacement

- Provide information on the extent of the diffusion of benefits

Outcome evaluations of crime prevention focus on changes in the level of the targeted crime, fear of crime and/or citizen behavior. The fact that most prevention programs are place specific means that evaluations typically focus only on changes within the target, neighborhood, or community. At the same time, crime prevention programs could have an impact beyond that which is intended. The other changes could be either positive or negative. The crime prevention techniques in one area may unintentionally result in increased crime in another area, on other targets, or at different times. In essence, levels of crime or fear may have simply shifted in response to the prevention efforts. This shift in crime is referred to as crime displacement. The opposite may also occur. Crime prevention efforts targeted at a specific problem in one location may have a positive impact on other locations or crimes. That is, there may be a diffusion of benefits.

Unfortunately, evaluations generally fail to consider the possibility of either displacement or diffusion. This is due to the fact that such assessment is a difficult task. Fortunately, there is a growing recognition of the need to examine displacement and diffusion in evaluations. The purpose of this chapter is to outline the concepts of crime displacement and diffusion, discuss the potential of offenders to shift their crime-related activities, and review the literature on displacement and diffusion.

CRIME DISPLACEMENT

Crime displacement represents change in crime due to the preventive actions of the individual or society. Most discussions of displacement focus on the shift of crime from one place to another (often called crime spillover). The idea is that actions taken to reduce or prevent crime in one set of circumstances simply results in altering the crime. The assumption is that many crime prevention actions simply move the crime around instead of eliminating the overall amount of crime. For example, an increase in police presence in one neighborhood may reduce crime in that area but cause an increase in crime in a contiguous neighborhood. Displacement, however, can take forms other than just the geographical movement of crime.

Types of Displacement

Reppetto (1976) offers five forms of displacement—territorial, temporal, tactical, target and functional. *Territorial* (also referred to as spatial) is the most frequently discussed and represents movement of crime from one location to another. *Temporal displacement*, the movement of offending to another period while remaining in the same area, may manifest itself through a shift in larcenies from the late evening to the early morning. Under *tactical displacement*, the offender utilizes new means to commit the same offense. A shift in burglary from entering through unlocked doors to breaking windows for entry represents a tactical change in the offense. *Target displacement* involves a choice of different victims within the same area. For example, an increase in the use of weapons by store owners may force robbers to choose elderly pedestrians as victims. Reppetto's final form of displacement,

Table 6.1
Forms of Displacement

TERRITORIAL—	movement of crime from one area to another, typically contiguous, area
Example—	a neighborhood watch program is started and the burglars move to another neighborhood
TEMPORAL—	a shift in offending from one time to a different time, such as from day to night
Example—	a citizen patrol is instituted at night, thus prompting burglars to work during the morning hours
TACTICAL—	changing the methods used in the commission of a crime
Example—	the installation of deadbolt locks on doors results in burglars forcing open windows to gain entry
TARGET—	choosing a different victim within the same area
Example—	a neighborhood watch program is started but only half the homes participate, thereby leading offenders to target non-participating homes
FUNCTIONAL—	the offender stops committing one offense and shifts to another
Example—	when burglary becomes more difficult due to target hardening devices the offender decides to commit robbery instead
PERPETRATOR—	one offender ceases activity only to be replaced by another offender
Example—	while crime prevention actions cause an individual to desist from further offending, another individual sees opportunities and begins offending

Functional suggests that offenders change to a new type of offense, such as shifting from larceny to burglary or burglary to robbery. Each of these forms of displacement represents a change in offense behavior on the part of the offender. Barr and Pease (1990) offer a sixth form of displacement— perpetrator. *Perpetrator displacement* occurs when one offender ceases his deviant behavior, only to be replaced by another offender. Crime prevention techniques are a logical cause of any of these types of displacement.

Assumptions

Displacement makes a number of assumptions about both the potential offender and his target. First, displacement assumes that crime is *inelastic*. That is, offenders are driven to commit a certain number of offenses over a given period of time (Reppetto, 1976). If crime is inelastic, it is not eliminated by crime prevention activities. Rather, it is simply moved along one of the displacement dimensions. This idea of inelasticity assumes that the offenders are motivated to commit crime and will seek out opportunities to offend. One key to displacement, therefore, is available opportunities. Felson and Clarke (1998) argue that opportunities are (or can be) limited, thus having an impact on the possibility of displacement.

Second, displacement assumes mobility on the part of the offender (Reppetto, 1976). The mobility can be across time, place, tactic, or any displacement dimension. Not all potential offenders, however, have the same level of mobility (Brantingham and Brantingham, 1984). For example, youthful offenders may not have access to transportation (limiting territorial displacement) or they may be tied to school and curfews (limiting temporal displacement). Race may inhibit individuals from entering areas populated by other racial or ethnic groups. Other offenders may not be psychologically able to shift from one type of crime to another (functional displacement). While such factors may limit displacement, they will not eliminate it for all potential offenders.

Mobility is not determined solely by characteristics of the potential offenders. It may also be limited by features of the surrounding environment (Brantingham and Brantingham, 2003; Brantingham, 2010). This is primarily true in relation to territorial (spatial) displacement, although it is not limited to the spatial domain. The ability of an offender to shift to another location/ time/offense may be limited by the options available to the offender. For example, efforts taken in a small isolated community may not allow for territorial displacement because there are no alternatives for offending nearby. A neighborhood may also be somewhat isolated even within a large city because it has major barriers surrounding it, such as a river on one side and a major interstate highway on another (see Figure 6.1). Individuals who offend in the bounded area of town have limited options for where to move for future offending, while those on the other side of the river have more options.

Figure 6.1
Example of a City with a Geographically Bounded Neighborhood

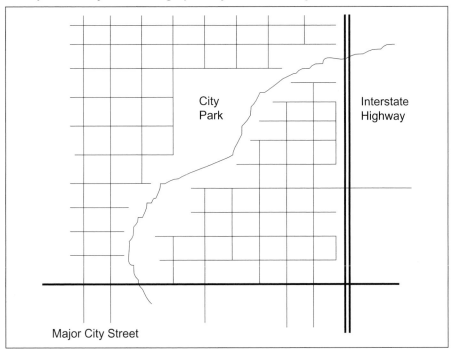

While boundaries do not make displacement impossible, they limit the directions any offenders can take if they are to be displaced (Brantingham and Brantingham, 2003). While mobility may be limited by place, the characteristics of an area may enhance the possibility of offending (Brantingham, 2010). An individual who lives near an area with many targets (such as mixed-use areas with homes, businesses, and entertainment close at hand) may benefit from a wide range of differing opportunities for crime commission. Actions that limit household burglary may simply force the offender to pilfer from stores or rob shoppers in the local commercial strip. In essence, physical location can shut down some opportunities while enhancing others.

A very important third assumption involves the level of volition held by potential offenders. *Rational choice theory* has become a central focus in the study of crime (Clarke and Cornish, 1985; Cornish and Clarke, 1986a). This theory assumes that potential offenders make choices based on various factors in the physical and social environment. Offenders respond to payoff, effort, peer support, risks, and similar factors in making decisions to commit a crime (Cornish and Clarke, 1986b). Displacement views the offender as being a rational individual who is capable of making informed, free-willed choices. He is able to evaluate the costs and benefits inherent in his choice and circumstances, and can make decisions based on those factors.

The ability to make informed choices is required for displacement to occur. The inability to make rational decisions would negate displacement due to crime prevention measures. A seeming contradiction appears between this assumption and the earlier assumption concerning the inelastic nature of offending. The need to commit crime and the ability to choose which crime and where it is to be committed, however, are not exclusive of one another. It is very possible that an offender sees no alternative to crime but is capable of molding his actual criminal behavior around available choices.

A final assumption is that alternative targets and choices are available to the offender. From a crime prevention perspective, this assumption is easy to accept because program implementation is never complete. Some individuals decide not to participate, some targets are not hardened, some actions fail to have an impact, and some ideas are not well suited to a given problem. More importantly, crime prevention programs generally focus only on limited areas or crimes. This results in alternative choices for potential offenders.

Assessing Displacement

While displacement is a possible result of prevention activities, it is rarely directly examined in evaluations. Existing crime prevention research tends to ignore the issue of displacement, or consider displacement only as an after-thought to the research. Claims that displacement does or does not occur are probably ill-advised. Even in studies that include an analysis of displacement at the outset, basic flaws in the investigations limit the ability to make claims about displacement.

Assessments of displacement need to consider a number of factors. First, all of the forms of displacement should be open to examination. Most analyses only consider territorial displacement and totally ignore the other forms. Second, each crime/problem being targeted by the prevention initiative should be examined in detail to answer a number of questions: Who are the likely offenders? When are the offenses taking place? How are the crimes being committed? Where are they occurring? What purpose does the crime serve (i.e., why does it happen)? and similar concerns. The answers to these questions are crucial for both the selection of the crime prevention measures and the potential for displacement. Interestingly, while most crime prevention programs answer these questions when developing the intervention, they are typically ignored when discussions of displacement occur. This is unfortunate because answers to these questions would inform expectations about the type and extent of possible displacement.

Take for example the development of a crime prevention initiative to attack residential burglary. An examination of crime data shows an increase in residential burglary taking place in mid- to late-mornings during the work week. The homes are being entered through unlocked doors or by breaking the locks on doors. Items that are taken tend to be jewelry, silverware, and high end electronics. The police suspect that the offenders are adult professional burglars. Based on this information, a prevention program is initiated that includes the installation of stronger locks, the marking of property, the initiation of increased police patrols during the day, the start of a neighborhood watch group, and mid-day citizen patrols. The same information provides insight to the possible types of displacement that may emerge. To the extent that the offenders are indeed adult professional thieves, it is wise to assume that territorial displacement is a strong possibility. There may also be temporal displacement to nights or afternoons when the patrols are not as prevalent. The offenders may change targets and focus on the homes without the new locks. Any evaluation of the prevention activities should use this insight to build in an assessment of the different forms of displacement. Unfortunately, most crime prevention evaluators look only for territorial displacement to an immediately adjacent neighborhood. No attention is paid to other forms or areas.

Attempts to assess displacement need to explicitly consider the potential offenders, the type of offense, the location, the victims, and other factors involved in the existing criminal activity (Hamilton-Smith, 2002). In depth knowledge of the event and actors will allow the crime prevention planner and evaluator to model the potential for displacement, and build in the appropriate intervention or evaluation methods (Brantingham and Brantingham, 2003; Hamilton-Smith, 2002).

Displacement: Benign or Malign?

The tenor of most discussions of displacement is clearly one of disappointment or dismay at the thought that crime is simply being moved across one of the displacement dimensions. Displacement, however, can be positive. Barr and Pease (1990) divide displacement into two types—"benign" and "malign." *Benign displacement* suggests that changes from displacement may benefit society. For example, the new crime or tactics that are utilized by the offenders may be less serious and offer less danger to the potential victims. Robbery becomes burglary, assault with a deadly weapon becomes simple assault, burglary becomes petty theft, and so on. Displacement may also bring about reduced fear of crime which offsets the problem of actual crime (Barr and Pease, 1990). Conversely, *malign displacement* leads to less desirable outcomes. Efforts aimed at reducing burglary may prompt an increase in robberies and accompanying levels of assault. Another case of malign displacement would be an offender's need to increase the number of crimes in order to offset the reduced payoff garnered from each offense (Gabor, 1990). Such malign displacement may not be tolerable to society.

Barr and Pease (1990) propose that, instead of assuming that all displacement is malign, the main question to be dealt with should be how displacement can "be used to achieve a spread of crime that can be regarded as equitable." Unfortunately, crime is not evenly spread across the social spectrum, which leads to an unequal burden from crime and fear of crime.

Barr and Pease suggest that society, either consciously or unconsciously, has allowed certain areas or neighborhoods to become what they call *crime fuses*. These fuses are places where society allows crime to run relatively unchecked as a safety valve for the rest of society. In the same manner that electrical fuses will carry the dangerous burden and signal a problem by blowing out before the problem spreads to the rest of the system, the crime fuse is an area where crime can operate without bothering the rest of society until it explodes in the area. The solution is then targeted at the point of the problem before it does major harm to the entire community. Displacement may be benign if crime is moved to a "fuse" location. It would not be benign, however, for those living at the crime fuse. A true benign displacement would be one that provides a more even or equal spread of victimization across the community (Barr and Pease, 1990). For Barr and Pease, the question of displacement deals with redistributing crime and victimization in society.

DIFFUSION

Another possible effect of crime prevention programming is the *diffusion of benefits*. Clarke and Weisburd (1994, p. 169) define diffusion of benefits as

> the spread of the beneficial influence of an intervention beyond the places which are directly targeted, the individuals who are the subject of control, the crimes which are the focus of intervention or the time periods in which an intervention is brought.

Rather than shifting the crime, diffusion assumes that prevention efforts will benefit people and places other than those targeted. Diffusion is discussed under a variety of names, including "halo effect" (Scherdin, 1986) and "free bonus effect" (Sherman, 1990).

What accounts for diffusion? Clarke and Weisburd (1994) offer two potential sources for diffusion—deterrence and discouragement. Deterrence can have an impact in various ways. While many prevention efforts are short-lived, the impact on crime often outlasts the period of intervention. Similarly, targeting one location or certain merchandise may result in protecting other targets. In each case, there is an assumption that the chances of being apprehended are heightened and potential offenders are deterred by the risk of being caught. Discouragement works by reducing the payoff and increasing the effort needed to commit a crime (Clarke and Weisburd, 1994).

Both displacement and diffusion have received increased attention in recent years and many evaluations now make claims about apparent displacement or diffusion. Unfortunately, the difficulties inherent in assessing displacement and diffusion mean that these issues are not central to many evaluations. In every case, the degree to which displacement or diffusion occur is related to the degree to which offenders can and do make judgments about offending.

OFFENDER CHOICE AND MOBILITY

Offenders do not commit offenses totally at random. They do not simply walk down the street and attack people, commit robberies, break into homes, or act in other criminal ways with no reason. If offenders did act completely at random, committing crimes with no thought and at any moment, all of our streets would be rife with crimes at any time and nothing anyone could do would have an impact on crime. Thankfully, we know that many places and times are free from crime, and many things can be done to prevent crime. This means that offenders, at least to some degree, make decisions on what to do, when, where, and how. The key for prevention, therefore, is to understand the factors that go into those decisions.

Felson and Clarke (1998) argue that *opportunity* is the cornerstone for all criminal behavior. While opportunity alone is not sufficient for a crime, it is certainly necessary for its commission. In their words, "Individual behavior is a product of an interaction between the person and the setting" (1998:1). Felson and Clarke outline 10 principles of opportunity (see Table 6.2) that attempt to specify how opportunities shape and mold criminal behavior. Many of these principles deal with the variation in opportunities across time, space and circumstances. They also suggest that reductions in opportunity can reduce crime, with little displacement.

Table 6.2
Ten Principles of Opportunity and Crime

1.	Opportunities play a role in causing all crime.
2.	Crime opportunities are highly specific.
3.	Crime opportunities are concentrated in time and place.
4.	Crime opportunities depend on everyday movements.
5.	One crime produces opportunities for another.
6.	Some products offer more tempting crime opportunities.
7.	Social and technological changes produce new crime opportunities.
8.	Opportunities for crime can be reduced.
9.	Reducing opportunities does not usually displace crime.
10.	Focused opportunity reduction can produce wider declines in crime.

Source: Felson and Clarke (1998).

Underlying these 10 principles of opportunity are three primary theoretical orientations—Routine Activities, Rational Choice, and Crime Pattern Theory. Felson and Clarke (1998) see each as a form of opportunity theory. The possibility of displacement and diffusion rely on implicit assumptions about the offenders and decisionmaking that appear in these theoretical perspectives.

Routine Activities

The *routine activities perspective* argues that the normal movement and activities of both potential offenders and victims plays a role in the occurrence of crime. Cohen and Felson (1979) outline three criteria that must exist for crime to occur. There must be (1) a suitable target, (2) a motivated offender, and (3) an absence of guardians. The authors believe that much crime is due to opportunity. That does not mean that offenders do not seek out opportunities. Rather, it implies that the actual choice and commission of an offense is determined by the mutual occurrence of the three conditions.

The routine activities of people have greatly changed over the years. Since World War II many households have moved to two-earner incomes, which leaves many homes unoccupied during the day and, therefore, unguarded (Cohen and Felson, 1979). Increased mobility of the population has led to the establishment of "bedroom communities" which are removed from the watchful eyes of workers and pedestrians. Time spent away from home, either at work or in recreation, opens up opportunities for crime.

Another important change involves the increased availability of suitable targets for crime. The risk of a target is directly related to Clarke's (1999) discussion of hot products, or items that attract attention and are targeted by offenders. Such products meet the tenets of being *CRAVED*. Products that are CRAVED are desired by the offender or others, are visible to potential offenders, and are easier to conceal, transport, and dispose of. What has value today may not be of interest tomorrow. This could be due to the maturation of the offender, the saturation of the item in society, changes in taste, or other factors (Clarke, 1999). The extent to which a target meets the CRAVED criteria will have an impact on the chances of an offense occurring.

Table 6.3
The CRAVED Model for Targets of Theft

C oncealable-	ability of thief to hide items during the crime
R emovable-	size and weight make some items more portable than others
A vailable-	the item must exist and be available to be stolen
V aluable-	items that hold more value will be targeted
E njoyable-	the items must bring enjoyment to the offender
D isposable-	there must be a market for the stolen items

Source: Compiled from Clarke (1999).

The lack of guardianship places a target at greater risk. Eck (1994) proposes triplets of guardianship—*guardians* of targets, *handlers* of offenders, and *managers* of places—which correspond to the elements of routine activities theory. The inner triangle of Figure 6.2 represents the basic components of routine activities—the point at which targets, offenders, and places coincide. The outer triangle indicates the potential guardians or protectors for each of the dimensions. Each type of guardian may be instrumental in determining the level and type of crime that occurs. Guardians, handlers, and managers have the ability to reduce the opportunity for crime by limiting at least one dimension necessary for the commission of an offense.

The guardians are typically the owner of the property, a family member or friend, the police or security, or others who provide surveillance and protection to the target. Guardianship requires more than just the existence of the guardian. It also assumes that the guardian has the physical ability to intervene and the willingness to do so (Reynald, 2009). A handler exerts control over the movement and behavior of the potential offender. These individuals typically include family members and friends of the potential offenders, but may also include social control agents such as probation officers or social service providers. Finally, managers are those who own or are employed by a business (whether public or private) and can take steps to keep offenders from offending or to keep them away from victims or targets. Managers include store clerks, teachers, bartenders, store owners, bouncers, or crowd control personnel.

Most tests of the routine activities hypothesis focus on property crimes, although the chances of personal crime also increase through changes in routine activities. Cohen and Felson (1979) found that the amount of time spent away from home is significantly related to the level of property crime. Similarly, Mustaine and Tewksbury (1998) report that theft is influenced by

Figure 6.2
Routine Activities Triangle

Source: Eck, J.E. (2003). "Police Problems: The Complexity of Problem Theory, Research, and Evaluation." In Knutsson, J. (ed.), *Problem-Oriented Policing: From Innovation to Mainstream*. Monsey, NY: Criminal Justice Press. Reprinted with permission.

activity outside the home, the number of precautions (guardianship) taken, and the types of outside activities in which the victim participates. The same factors related to property crime also apply to enhancing the possibility of physical confrontation between individuals. Personal predatory crimes, such as robbery and sexual assault, are also influenced by routine activities.

Rational Choice

An implicit assumption in routine activities is that offenders make rational choices about when and where to offend. In order for crime prevention activities to have an impact, offenders must be making (somewhat) rational decisions based on their perceptions of needs, risks, payoffs, and other factors. The question of whether offenders choose their targets and, in turn, how they make their choices has been a major source of study. Whether offenders make choices in their offenses can be answered both intuitively and through the literature. On an intuitive level, most people believe that human beings are free-willed. At the same time, however, people recognize that the available choices are limited by time, place, or circumstance. This implies a sort of *soft determinism*. That is, individuals make choices but only within the realm of available opportunities. This is true in all behavior and not just criminal activity. For example, every individual may wish to be comfortable in their daily existence. One person may be independently wealthy, however, while another must work. Further, the choice of work relies upon the physical and mental abilities of the individual, the state of the economy in the area, the competition for jobs, and a host of other factors. The fact that everyone makes choices in life leads to the belief that criminals make similar choices. Additionally, offenders spend the majority of their time participating in normal, socially accepted activities within which they make choices. It would be naive to think that this ability to make choices is removed when criminal behavior is contemplated.

Literature on criminal activity also portrays illegal behavior as guided by choices. Research focused on burglary presents a good illustration of how criminals make choices in their daily activity. Bennett (1986), Bennett and Wright (1984), and Reppetto (1974) find that adjudicated burglars make clear choices in their decision of when and where to commit their crimes. In interviews, burglars note a variety of factors that they consider in their offense planning. Among these factors is the amount of cover available, the level of illumination, the types of locks, doors and windows, the existence of alarms, and the possibility of being observed by neighbors and pedestrians. These findings are supported by various experimental investigations of burglars' choice of target. The existence of inhibiting factors does not result in an absolute prevention of crime. Instead, preventive actions simply present more difficulty and require more planning or consideration. A burglar's assessment of payoff, probability of being caught and punished, and amount of effort required are significantly related to the decision to offend (Piquero and Rengert, 1999). While some offenders abandon a particular target, others view it as a challenge. This indicates that offenders make choices on criminal behavior, just as in non-criminal activity.

Numerous studies provide further evidence that offenders make rational decisions. Studies of both incarcerated and active burglars in England reveal that offenders favor homes with a rear access, cover, isolation from other homes, a lack of nearby surveillance, the absence of alarms and CCTV, and unoccupied homes (Nee and Taylor, 1988; Taylor and Nee, 1988). Research also notes that offenders are attracted by visual signs of wealth, such as well-kept homes and items that could be seen through open windows (Hearnden and Magill, 2004; Nee and Taylor, 1988). Based on interviews with 31 incarcerated burglars, Rengert and Wasilchick (1985) find that offenders commit their crimes when residents are away from their homes—mainly mid-morning and early afternoon. Importantly, burglars typically rely on an established set of "opportunity cues" to identify appropriate targets. Among the cues are closed-up homes without air conditioning in warm months, an absence of cars at home, the entire family leaving together, available concealment, visual signs of wealth, and easy access to the home (Rengert and Wasilchick, 1985).

Wright and Decker (1994), in a large scale study of burglars in St. Louis, uncover a mixture of planning and spontaneity in offending. They report that many burglars have a potential target in mind prior to the actual decision to commit the crime. The offenders are always "half looking" for targets, and use various cues for deciding on appropriate targets, such as signs of valuables, the condition of the property, the type of car in the drive, signs of occupancy, and surveillability.

Bennett (1986) notes that burglars make what appear to be quick, uninformed decisions that, in reality, are rational choices based on prior experience and general knowledge. Indeed, Cromwell et al. (1991), asking burglars to "recreate" their past offenses, report that they make rational choices based on surveillability, occupancy, and accessibility. The reconstructions, however, suggest a more "limited rationality" similar to that proposed by Clarke and Cornish (1985). Offenders tend to point out opportunistic features of various targets and react to situations that arise during normal activity. That is, they "happen upon" vulnerable targets as they go about their daily routine (Cromwell et al., 1991). The offenders appear to respond to a set of internalized cues based on past experience and planning rather than specific detailed planning for each event.

While the foregoing discussion focuses on burglary, choice behavior is not restricted to those offenses. Tunnell (1992) reports on the activity of repeat property offenders, which included burglars, robbers, forgers, and others. He notes that criminal activity is a rational response to situations in which the offender finds himself. Research also suggests that more serious persistent offenders undertake more planning and tend to choose targets where the chances of observation are small (Feeney, 1986; Shover, 1991; Tunnell, 1992). Robbery, auto theft and forgery also show evidence of offender planning and rational decision making (Fleming et al., 1994; Gill and Matthews, 1994;

Lacoste and Tremblay, 2003; Morrison and O'Donnell, 1996; Petrosino and Brensilber, 2003).

Various studies produce a portrait of offenders as rational decision makers who base many of their actions on the costs and benefits they perceive in the contemplated activity. At the same time, the research suggests that offenders do not necessarily construct detailed plans for each and every offense. Rather, the rational choices and preconceived plans may be set into motion when the offender happens upon a situation or target which fits the general description of an appropriate target. Time, place, target, surveillability, and other factors are all considered in a short-hand version of making a rational choice. Indeed, many daily, non-criminal decisions are made more on the subconscious, rather than the conscious, level.

Crime Pattern Theory

Brantingham and Brantingham's (1993b) *crime pattern theory* proposes that crime and criminal behavior fits patterns that can be identified and understood when viewed in terms of where and when they occur. They argue that crime patterns can be understood because of similarities that emerge when you consider

> the specific criminal event, the site, the situation, the activity backcloth, the probable crime templates, the triggering events, and the general factors influencing the readiness or willingness of individuals to commit crimes (Brantingham and Brantingham, 1993b: 284–285).

Two keys to understanding patterns is to understand the environmental backcloth and the social/crime template of the offender. The *environmental backcloth* refers to the social, economic, cultural, and physical conditions within which people operate. While these dimensions are constantly changing, it is possible to discern patterns from them. The *social/crime template* is the idea that people have templates that outline expectations of what will happen at certain times and places given certain behavior by the individual. In essence, the template tells an offender what should occur in a certain place, time or situation. Understanding how people learn about the environment and construct these templates is an important endeavor for understanding the occurrence of crime.

The daily activity of individuals is one source of information used in learning the environmental backcloth and the templates that are used for making decisions. In spatial terms, individuals construct mental images or *cognitive maps* of the environment as they move about the community (Smith and Patterson, 1980). Smith and Patterson (1980) present four factors that are needed to construct and maintain a mental image of an area (see Table 6.4). The first, *recognition*, refers to being able to identify your

Table 6.4
Elements of Cognitive Mapping

Recognition	being able to identify your surroundings
Prediction	being able to identify predict what will take place at a particular location based on recognition of the immediate environment
Evaluation	assessing what behavior is possible and acceptable in a particular area
Action	making a final decision on what to do based on the first three components

Source: Compiled by author from Smith and Patterson (1980).

location and various features in the area. Recognition leads to *prediction*, which involves making connections between the identifiable objects in the area and possible lines of behavior. During *evaluation*, the individual uses the information gathered in the earlier stages and determines which options are acceptable modes of behavior. It is based on the information gained in the first three steps that an individual decides on an appropriate *action*. In essence, cognitive mapping entails the removal of fear and uncertainty for the individual, which allows him to make an informed choice. The more an individual knows about an area, the less fearful he becomes, and the more confident he becomes in making a decision. In essence, a cognitive map is a template used by individuals when contemplating whether to act.

The logical question flowing from the idea of cognitive mapping is how an individual gains recognition of different areas for the purpose of prediction, evaluation, and action. Using the basic ideas of routine activities theory, offenders form cognitive maps through normal daily activity that take an individual into and around various areas. Individuals build on their knowledge as they go to and from work, do their shopping, socialize with others, go to school, or undertake any other daily routine behaviors. Information gleaned from normal activity benefits from the fact that it arouses no suspicion and takes no more time than would normally be used in the legitimate activity alone. Knowledge of potential targets can also be obtained through deliberate, planned inspection and study of various locations. Although this is a possible approach, in itself it may arouse suspicion and future recognition by legitimate users of an area.

The continued growth and sprawl of modern urban communities greatly contributes to the building of larger and more complex cognitive maps. Modern cities and urban areas are conglomerations of smaller, specialized land use areas that provide varying needs and activities for residents. The availability of private and mass transportation allows citizens to live, work, and recreate where they choose. People simply commute between the various locations. These locations can be considered *nodes* of activity (see Figure 6.3)(Brantingham and Brantingham, 1993a, 1996). The transit routes between the nodes are referred to as *paths*. The extent to which an individual utilizes each node and takes various routes (paths) between the nodes helps develop the cognitive map he has

Figure 6.3
Simplified View of a Multinuclei Community with Nodes and Paths

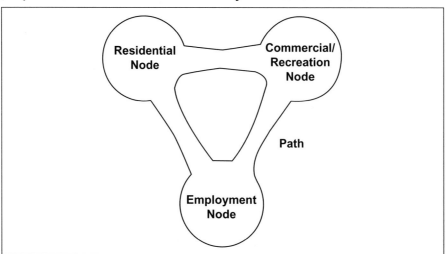

of the nodes, paths and surrounding areas. The further from a node or path one becomes, the less is known about the area, and the chances for action (criminal or legitimate) are diminished. Potential offenders tend to search in the nodes and paths with which they are familiar. Besides the nodes and paths, *edges* of the areas are prime spots for deviant behavior. Edges can be physical, social, or economic (Brantingham, 2010). Physical edges may limit movement of potential offenders and victims. Social and economic edges reflect areas of potential offending due to anonymity between strangers in these locations. These areas are frequented by diverse users, which enhances bringing together potential victims and offenders with limited guardianship (Brantingham, 2010). Greater diversity in people and activity from both sides of the edge enhances the possibility of offenses. (See Brantingham and Brantingham, 1981, 1993a, 1993b, 1996 for more in-depth discussions of these ideas.)

Beyond providing a framework for developing cognitive maps, nodes can serve to promote crime in other ways (Brantingham and Brantingham, 1996). Some nodes may act as *crime generators* by drawing potential victims to the area. They also may be *crime attractors*. These are areas to which potential offenders and others are drawn, such as drug markets, sites of street prostitution, and/or adult clubs and bars. Finally, a node may serve as a *hunting ground* for offenders. That is, offenders recognize that potential victims frequent an area, there is a lack guardians at that location and, consequently, the offender follows the victims to that place.

An emerging possibility for development of cognitive maps and information on potential targets has been made available with the advent of the Internet and its widespread accessibility. Today, a wealth of information, including visual depictions, can be found online. Programs such as Google Maps, Google Streetview, and government property web sites provide varying levels of detail about different addresses and areas. Google Streetview, for example, allows the user to look at an address from the main street, take a 360-degree look around where the observer is positioned, move up and down the street, and zoom in to look at details. While this information reflects only a single point in time, it does provide anyone who wishes to look further into the address and the area. Publicly accessible government documents also provide details of homes and businesses, including room layouts and sizes. All of this information can be used by potential offenders to build mental maps of a target, the surrounding area, and other useful planning materials without ever leaving home and visiting the area. As such, the potential to plan crimes outside the assumptions of routine activities and crime pattern theories is greatly enhanced.

Although discussions of cognitive mapping usually center around territorial or spatial features of behavior, the extension to other dimensions is straightforward. The same process which provides templates of safe areas can provide information on the most suitable targets, tactics, crimes, and times within a given setting. The prediction and evaluation stages of cognitive mapping suggest that each of these decisions is to be considered in the movement to criminal action.

Summary

The research provides strong evidence that crime is not totally opportunistic. Rather, criminal behavior appears to be a rational decision based on situations in which the offender finds himself. While offenders may not spend a great deal of time planning specific offenses, information gained through normal daily activity or interaction with others can guide the "unconscious" decision making of the offender, just like most people make non-criminal daily choices. These facts suggest that both displacement and diffusion are potential responses to prevention behavior.

EVIDENCE OF DISPLACEMENT
AND DIFFUSION

As noted earlier, displacement and diffusion are often referred to in the literature but are rarely the primary focus of study. Rather, they are secondary to many assessments of crime prevention programs and typically receive minor consideration in evaluations. The balance of this chapter attempts to outline evidence on the various forms of displacement, as well as potential diffusion effects.

Displacement Effects

There is little reason to ever expect total displacement of crime, regardless of the type of displacement considered. At the same time, assuming that there will be no displacement may be just as naive. Displacement should be considered as a possible confounding factor in every evaluation. The type and extent of potential displacement to expect needs to be based on the facts about the crime and the prevention initiative.

Territorial Displacement

The most common form of displacement considered in evaluations is territorial displacement. The fact that offenders will travel to commit crimes (known as the *journey to crime*) is well established, and the distance traveled varies by the type of crime, the physical characteristics of the area, and the demographic characteristics of the individual. The distance traveled can be measured in two ways. First is by *Euclidean distance*, which measures in a straight line from the start to the end point. The problem with this approach is that it ignores the fact that physical features (such as buildings, rivers, and highways) make such travel impossible. Instead, people follow roadways, generally selecting those that reduce both distance and travel time. Measures of distance in this way are called *Manhattan distance*.

Beyond how distance is measured, it is important to note that there is a pattern of *distance decay*. This means that the commission of crime decreases as the distance from the offender's home increases. Elfers et al. (2008) argue that this is partly due to the presence of opportunities that exist between the offender's starting point and the intended ending point of travel. While distance decay is the most important factor in distance traveled, opportunities play a role in long distances. Property offenses, which have a greater chance of being planned, tend to have longer travel averages (Pyle, 1974; Rhodes and Conley, 1981; White, 1932). Personal crimes tend to be more spontaneous and occur between family members or friends, thus mitigating long travel distances. Indeed, various studies show that murder, assault, and rape occur within one mile of the offender's home (Amir, 1971; Bullock, 1955; White, 1932). The greater distances associated with property crimes are especially important for the discussion of community crime prevention because these programs usually target property offenses. Distance also tends to increase with the offender's age due to the increased mobility that comes with growing older, leaving school, living on one's own, and ownership of some means of transportation (Nichols, 1980; Phillips, 1980). Additionally, younger individuals probably hold more limited cognitive maps upon which to base offense decisions. Having established the existence of offender mobility, it is reasonable to assume that territorial displacement is a possible consequence of prevention efforts.

Several studies claim evidence of territorial displacement. Fabricant (1979) claims that juvenile arrests cause youthful offenders to move to neighboring locations. Crime prevention programs in Dallas appear to shift some offenders into surrounding suburbs (Dallas Area Criminal Justice Council, 1975). Specifically, changes in Dallas are accompanied by greater increases in six of nine Dallas suburbs. Forrester et al. (1988), investigating the effects of target hardening and social crime prevention measures, claim that the 60 percent decrease in burglary is partially offset by a 25 percent increase in burglary in the surrounding area. Barclay et al. (1996), studying the impact of bicycle patrol on auto theft in one crime hot spot, show large increases in auto theft in two adjacent areas during the project period. The increases also persist after the program ended. Displacement is the best explanation for these findings. Braga et al. (1999), in an analysis of a police crackdown in Jersey City, New Jersey, reports evidence of property crime displacement. In an analysis of CCTV in town centers, Brown (1995) indicates that both robbery and personal theft are displaced to other areas. Territorial displacement is also evident in the Kirkholt and Safer Cities burglary prevention efforts (Ekblom et al., 1996a; Tilley, 1993) and in some of the Burglary Reduction Initiative sites (Bowers and Johnson, 2003; Home Office 2003d).

Not all research finds territorial displacement, even when the project actively searches for it. Ditton and Short (1999), examining the impact of CCTV in two Scottish cities, report no evidence of displacement to areas immediately adjacent to the experimental areas. Armitage et al. (1999) also find no territorial displacement as a result of CCTV installations in three police beats. Evaluating the impact of police enforcement of carrying concealed weapons laws in Kansas City, Sherman and Rogan (1995) uncover no evidence of displacement from target areas to a matched control area. Weisburd and Green (1995) report no displacement resulting from police targeting of drug hot spots in Jersey City. Similarly, Braga et al. (1999) find no shift in calls about robbery, assault, drug offenses, street fights, or disorder incidents from the targeted hot spots to the control areas. Finally, Weisburd et al. (2006), in a study designed specifically to test for territorial displacement, find no such displacement in either prostitution or drug offending. It is evident that territorial displacement appears in some analyses and not in others.

The discrepant results from study to study may be due to the use of different displacement areas in the analyses. Bowers and Johnson (2003) note that the selection of areas into which displacement may occur is critical to the analysis. While most analyses look at an immediately adjacent area, it is not appropriate to assume that the closest neighboring area is the best selection for assessing territorial displacement (Andresen, 2010). It is advisable to identify more than one buffer zone around the target or experimental area and measure changes in zones at different distances from the intervention site (Bowers and Johnson, 2003). In their evaluation of alley gating, Bowers et al. (2003) find no displacement into the areas immediately around the experimental site, but do report displacement to areas further away. One key to uncovering territorial displacement, therefore, may be correctly specifying the potential displacement zone.

Temporal Displacement

Several studies make explicit note about possible offense shifts across time. Two studies claim that, while street lighting reduces the incidence of crime in the relit areas, there is a corresponding increase in daylight crime rates within the same areas (Atlanta, 1975; Wright et al., 1974). This suggests the possibility that the offenses simply moved from night to day. Hesseling (1995) reports finding temporal displacement resulting from increased surveillance in inner city areas. Conversely, in the Barclay et al. (1996) study of auto theft, an explicit attempt to identify temporal changes failed to show any such displacement.

Tactical Displacement

Crime prevention efforts can make the criminal work harder. This is evident through the use of new methods of committing the same crimes on the same targets. One example of this is a shift in burglary from entering through open doors to breaking windows for access. Interviews with burglars indicate that offenders are willing to seek out and utilize different methods when confronted with barriers to committing the crime (Cromwell et al., 1991; Bennett and Wright, 1984; Reppetto, 1974). Crime prevention efforts in Seattle reveal a shift in burglary methods from hardened doors and windows to unlocked entrances (Seattle Law and Planning Office, 1975). Similarly, alley gating has moved the point of entry for burglary from the rear of buildings to the front of homes (Bowers et al., 2003). Allatt (1984) finds that target hardening leads to greater instances of forced locks and broken windows. More recently, Weisburd et al. (2006) report evidence of tactical displacement based on interviews with offenders.

Target Displacement

Target displacement appears in various studies of crime prevention. Gabor (1981) specifically investigates the shift in offending from one set of victims to another set of potential victims. He finds that the Operation Identification program appears to have shifted offending away from program participants to individuals who have not joined the project. This remains true even after controlling for the pre-program victimization rates of the subjects. Offenders also shift from residential areas to commercial establishments as a result of property marking (Gabor, 1981). There is also evidence that offenders target objects that are not as easily marked by the owners. Tilley and Webb (1994) report similar target displacement from property marking efforts. Allatt (1984) finds the unreinforced structures experience higher levels of burglary after the installation of target hardening devices in neighboring buildings. Similarly, Miethe (1991) notes that target hardening devices displace crime to non-hardened targets in the same area of Seattle. Evidence from the Kirkholt burglary project shows that efforts to prevent repeat victimization results in a move to more "new" victims who are not as involved in the program (Forrester et al., 1990). The Reducing Burglary

Initiative in Strichley also reports a shift in burglaries away from homes to non-dwelling structures (Home Office, 2003b).

Functional Displacement

This final form of displacement manifests itself in terms of changes in offenses committed by the offender. The usual way of investigating such displacement is through comparison of different individual crime rates from before and after program implementation. Arthur Young and Co. (1978) report that the crime prevention program at the Cabrini-Green housing project resulted in increased levels of assaults and robbery and decreased numbers of burglaries and thefts. This suggests that the efforts, which deal more with property security, precipitate more personal contact offenses. Allatt (1984) makes similar claims of functional displacement in connection with target hardening efforts in a housing project. Letkemann (1973) shows that bank burglars shift to bank robbery as a response to target hardening undertaken by banks, and Laycock (1984) reveals that efforts to target harden pharmacies results in an increase in the level of pharmacy robberies and other drug offenses. Research on CCTV programs in city centers also shows shifts from motor vehicle theft to theft from motor vehicles (Brown, 1995). Felson et al. (1996) note that improvements in the New York City bus terminal greatly reduced most crime and disorder. There was some evidence, however, of functional displacement to minor property offenses (a form of benign displacement) (Felson et al., 1996).

Displacement Summary

These various studies find that displacement is not an inevitable outcome of prevention initiatives and, when displacement does occur, it is not 100 percent. At the same time, they show that displacement does occur and is a viable concern for discussions of crime prevention. Although the list of studies reporting, or not reporting, each type of displacement is limited, this is probably due to the failure of most evaluations to consider displacement. Interestingly, two reviews that claim to find little evidence of displacement and argue that it should not be a major concern (Eck, 1993; Hesseling, 1994) actually uncover a significant level of various forms of displacement. Both Hesseling's (1994) and Eck's (1993) analyses reveal that roughly half of the studies show evidence of displacement, particularly territorial and target forms. The fact that the authors do not find 100 percent displacement, or displacement in all studies, lead them to conclude it is not a major problem. This is an unrealistic criterion and any evidence of displacement should be a concern to be addressed.

It is very important to note that the level of displacement is typically a small proportion of the total decrease in crime attributed to crime prevention measures. The finding of displacement, therefore, qualifies the impact of the preventive program, but it certainly does not negate the positive results attributable to the intervention. Displacement also can be considered a good sign for crime prevention efforts. These findings show that the crime prevention programs are capable of altering the behavior of the offenders. The offenders are responding to the actions of the legitimate users and are limiting their criminal behavior in relation to the various targets. The problem is that uncovering displacement is very difficult. Indeed, the only way of truly knowing if crime is displaced is to interview offenders and ask them if the crime prevention measure altered their behavior.

Diffusion Effects

Offsetting displacement may be a diffusion of benefits. As noted earlier, diffusion of benefits means that areas, items or individuals not targeted by a crime prevention program also benefit from the intervention. For example, if half of the homes in a neighborhood join block watch, mark their property and take part in surveillance activities, and everyone in the neighborhood experiences reduced victimization and fear, it is probable that the crime prevention of the participants had an impact on the non-participants. This would be a diffusion of benefits. Not unlike displacement, however, measuring diffusion is very difficult.

The typical approach to measuring diffusion would be to examine the change in crime and fear in areas contiguous to the target area. Reductions in the contiguous areas could be due to diffusion effects (Clarke, 1995). At the same time, however, the reductions in both the target and control areas could be a result of general decreases in society. Rather than a diffusion effect, the crime prevention intervention has no impact. Determining whether there is no change or if the changes are due to diffusion would require additional comparison areas (or targets) that would not be expected to experience diffusion due to distance or other circumstances (see Bowers and Johnson, 2003).

Another problem with identifying a diffusion effect would appear when both displacement and diffusion occur at the same time, resulting in no apparent change in the non-treatment area (Weisburd and Green, 1995). In this case, the crime prevention program is successful at reducing crime and/or fear in the target area. At the same time, some of the reduction is the result of displacing offenses to another area, which would normally mean that crime and/or fear in the other area increases. A simultaneous diffusion effect of equal magnitude, however, would offset the increase and show no net change in crime and/or fear.

Despite these concerns with identifying diffusion effects, evaluations are beginning to pay more attention to the possibilities of diffusion in their designs and analyses. Green (1995a), analyzing the impact of a program dealing with neighborhood drug problems, reports a diffusion impact in areas surrounding the targeted sites. The two blocks around the target sites show reductions in deviant behavior, although smaller in magnitude to the experimental sites. Miethe (1991) notes that neighborhood watch efforts in Seattle appear to diffuse to non-participating targets in the same area. Painter and Farrington

(1999), in an analysis of street lighting projects, find decreases in daytime offending for the relit areas, thus suggesting temporal diffusion. Diffusion also is apparent in the Safer Cities program, particularly in areas where the prevention efforts are intensively implemented (Ekblom et al., 1996a; 1996b).

Felson et al. (1996) report that diffusion may actually occur in the opposite direction. That is, changes occurring outside the target area may have an impact on the target, leading to the appearance of program effectiveness. In their study of the New York City bus terminal, Felson and associates note that reductions in crime outside the terminal, dating from prior to the terminal improvements, may be contributing to the crime reductions inside the terminal. In essence, the external changes in robbery and assault may be diffusing into the terminal. (Felson et al. (1996) note that the reductions are greater in the terminal, thus indicating a programmatic impact beyond any possible diffusion.)

While concerns about displacement have existed for some time in the literature, diffusion is a more recent topic. Diffusion should be considered as a counterbalancing force to displacement (Clarke and Weisburd, 1994). Given the fact that both forces could be at work in a project, it is important to design projects that can uncover each of these possible factors. The inability to identify displacement and diffusion would result in an incomplete analysis of program effectiveness.

IMPLICATIONS OF DISPLACEMENT AND DIFFUSION

The possibility of displacement and diffusion are outcomes of crime prevention that should be considered in any program. Studies aptly illustrate that displacement is a plausible outcome of crime prevention programs. At the same time, it would be naive to assume that all crime reduction in an area is due to simple displacement to another place, time, or method, or that programs cannot have a larger impact beyond the immediate target. The amount of displacement is far from 100 percent and typically reflects only a portion of the crime that is prevented in the target area. Diffusion is also a possibility that needs to be considered. Future research needs to pay particular attention to both displacement and diffusion in order to adequately assess their impact on prevention programs.

Chapter 7

THE MASS MEDIA AND CRIME PREVENTION

Key Terms:

anticipatory benefit
crime newsletters
Crime Stoppers
information lines

McGruff
response generalization
Taking a Bite Out of Crime

Learning Objectives:

After reading this chapter you should be able to:

- Talk about media accounts of crime and they relate to actual crime

- Discuss research on whether the media causes crime

- Diagram different ways in which the media/publicity can be used in relation to crime prevention

- Demonstrate your knowledge of the Taking a Bite Out of Crime campaign and its impact

- Discuss the use of crime newsletters and evaluations of their effectiveness

- Explain the use of information lines and their impact

- Provide examples of "crime time television" and discuss the pros and cons of these programs

- Define "anticipatory benefit" and discuss its impact

We have seen that both physical design and neighborhood crime prevention programs have had an impact on crime and fear. At the same time, that impact has been limited in important ways. One shortcoming is that many areas and people are not reached or not involved in the programs. Another potential problem is displacement which may limit the absolute reductions in crime or fear. One response is to utilize programs that reach a wider range of people and engender greater participation. Such efforts would limit the alternatives available to potential offenders. The mass media offers one avenue for creating a more widespread effort.

The impact of the mass media on modern society has been the focus of much research. The great growth of television in the 1950s expanded the potential of the media to influence individual and group behavior. Inspection of the mass media in relation to crime has predominantly looked at the potential of the various information media to create deviant behavior and fear of crime. Relatively little research has focused on the crime preventive and fear reducing capability of the mass media. Programs such as the "Taking a Bite Out of Crime" campaign and Crime Stoppers have used the media as a means of inducing crime prevention activity. Before examining the media and crime prevention, it will be informative to consider the treatment of crime in the media and the effect of the media on deviant behavior and fear.

THE MEDIA AND CRIME

In many respects, one can say that the mass media has an affinity for crime and crime related activity. This is true whether one looks at the coverage of crime in the news or the content of fictional programming on television. Crime accounts for a major portion of the written and broadcast media. A variety of studies have examined the extent of crime in newspapers and on television.

The Level of Reported Crime

One method for analyzing the reporting of crime is to undertake content analyses of newspapers. In one early study, Deutschmann (1959) found that between 10 percent and 15 percent of the stories in selected New York and Ohio newspapers focus on crime. Graber (1980) reports greater attention to crime (22–28% of the stories) in daily newspapers. A wide range of other studies report that crime stories comprise between roughly five percent and 30 percent of newspaper space (Deutschmann, 1959; Otto, 1962; Stempl, 1962; Stott, 1967; Cohen, 1975). Chiricos et al. (1997) claim that newspaper coverage of crime has increased more than 400 percent in recent years. Similar results appear in analysis of U.K. newspapers, where the percent of crime stories has increased from roughly nine percent from 1945–1951, to 21 percent from 1985–1991 (Reiner et al., 2000).

Television news also provides crime information. Graber (1977) notes that roughly 20 percent of the local television news and 10 percent of the national news concerns crime. A follow-up study three years later reveals that 12 to 13 percent of television news is devoted to crime (Graber, 1980). Hofstetter (1976), evaluating the extent of crime stories on national network news, reports that between 16 and 19 percent of the news is devoted to crime. Surette (1998) notes that 10 to 13 percent of national news is crime related, while roughly 20 percent of local news deals with crime. Additional evaluations of network newscasts finds that crime represents 10 percent of the stories (Lowry, 1971) and 13 to 18 percent of the broadcast time (Cirino, 1972).

Another way the media provides crime information is through "entertainment" programs. These can take two different forms. The first is fictional programs. The second can be referred to as "reality programs." The number of fictionalized presentations that involve a crime theme has varied over the years. Dominick (1978) notes that the percent of broadcasting time devoted to crime-related topics has varied from a low of seven percent in 1953 to a high of 39 percent in 1975. Only once since 1966 has the proportion of program time devoted to crime dropped below 20 percent. Surette (1998) claims that 20 to 40 percent of prime-time programs focus on law enforcement and the criminal justice system. The number of reality programs has grown since their advent in the late 1980s. Programs such as "America's Most Wanted" and "Top Cops" continue to thrive in the United States and other countries (Fishman and Cavender, 1998).

Media Accounts and Actual Crime

The correspondence between the media portrayal of crime and the actual extent and types of criminal activity shows a great deal of divergence. Typically, studies report that the media distorts the crime picture by focusing on selected types of crime, overemphasizing the level of crime, and failing to provide accurate or complete information about criminal incidents. A variety of reports show that violent crime is overrepresented in the news media and reality shows (Chermak, 1994; Chermak, 1998; Cirino, 1974; Graber, 1980; Hofstetter, 1976; Hurley and Antunes, 1977; Jones, 1976; Marsh, 1991; Oliver, 1994; Oliver and Armstrong, 1998; Reiner et al., 2000; Sherizan, 1978; Skogan and Maxfield, 1981; Surette, 1992). A similar distortion of the level of violent crime is found in fictional portrayals of crime (Dominick, 1978; Gerbner, 1972; Gerbner et al., 1980; Higgins and Ray, 1978). This overemphasis has the potential to raise the fear of crime in society by presenting violent offenses, especially between strangers on the street, as a common occurrence. Potentially violent confrontations elicit the most fear.

The level of crime and specific information about crime also is distorted in the media. Sherizan (1978), in a study of Chicago newspapers, notes that reported crimes have little in common with actual crime information. Analyzing newspapers from six cities and television news from three, Chermak (1994) reports that roughly half of all crime stories deal with violence, while only 10 percent address property offenses. Further, the seriousness of an offense is significantly related to reporting practices (Chermak, 1998). Research by Lichter et al. (1994) points out that homicides on television occur at a rate more than 1,000 times that found in real life. The media also fails to report on the activity of the criminal justice system or provide much information about the offender and victim (Chermak, 1994; Gordon et al., 1979; Surette, 1992). Skogan and Maxfield (1981) note how the media creates crime images through the skewed presentation of actual crime occurrences. They point out that by drawing together different offenses, committed at different times and places, the media creates an inappropriate image of crime in the community. The media can actually cause an apparent increase in crime by reporting offenses which occur in other communities without clearly noting the location of the offense (Skogan and Maxfield, 1981). The various studies show that the media concentrates on the spectacle of the offense and ignores the potential harm, in terms of increased fear of crime, that may arise from incomplete reporting.

Does the Media Cause Crime and Fear?

One potential problem of media presentations of crime is that viewers receive inaccurate images of crime and the criminal justice system. Several studies note that the public image of crime is influenced by media presentations. Gerbner et al. (1977, 1978, 1979) and Barrile (1980) compare the perception of crime and the criminal justice system held by individuals with differing levels of television exposure. The authors consistently find that respondents answer closer to the "television answer" (the answer that is commonly depicted on television) than to the real world information. The images, therefore, are influenced by media presentations. Perhaps of more interest for us is the ability of the media to cause crime or fear.

Media and Crime

Research has investigated the extent to which the mass media can influence the commission of deviant behavior. One early study of high school students relates the level of violence in the subjects' favorite television programs to their self-reported aggressive behavior (Hartnagel et al., 1975). The study finds a weak positive association between the level of media violence and reported violent behavior. More importantly, the students' perception of violence in the programs is related to violent behavior. A similar study of television viewing by youths (Belson, 1978) compares the violent behavior of two groups of boys—those with high exposure to media violence and those with low exposure. Belson (1978) reports that individuals with higher exposure commit more serious violent offenses. This relationship holds true for films that portray violent interpersonal relations, unnecessary violence, realistic violence, and violence presented as acceptable. Sports violence, cartoon, science fiction, and slapstick violence do not elicit the same response in viewers (Belson, 1978).

Two studies by Phillips (1982; 1983) investigate the effect of fictionalized suicides and prize fights on personal violence. One study examines the number of suicides that follow fictionalized suicides on soap operas. Controlling for holidays, non-fictional suicides presented in the media, and season of the year, Phillips (1982) finds that the U.S. suicide rate and attempted suicides significantly increase after soap opera suicides. These increases are true especially for urban females who are most similar to characters presented in daily soap operas. Phillips' second study (1983) reports a significant increase in homicide three to four days after heavyweight prize fights. This finding persists when controlling for day of week, holidays, and season. Indeed, the effect is greater for the more publicized fights. The homicide victims after a fight generally hold the same demographic characteristics as the fight's loser (Phillips, 1983).

Reviewing studies of television violence, Andison (1977) finds that 25 of 67 studies show a moderate positive relationship between viewing violence and subsequent aggression. An additional 27 analyses report a weak positive relationship. Examination of the studies in chronological order reveals increasingly stronger relationships between media presentations and violence. There also appears to be a larger effect on adults. This is possibly due to accumulated exposure over longer time spans (Andison, 1977). Andison's findings rely heavily on laboratory studies that utilize various forms of aggression such as electric shock and self-reported feelings of aggression. The generalizability of these findings to situations outside of the sterile, laboratory environment can be seriously questioned and Andison (1977) notes that the more realistic field studies find weaker, but still positive, relationships between television and aggression.

Research also has focused on pornography as a cause of violence, particularly sexual violence against women. The U.S. Attorney General's Commission on Pornography (1986) concludes that there is a direct link between viewing pornography and aggression. The primary support for their conclusion comes from experimental laboratory studies on the connection between various forms of pornography and subsequent violence. While such experiments provide the ability to control for many outside influences and, arguably, allow for a closer examination of causality (Huesmann and Malamuth, 1986), there are serious flaws in the methodology that require caution in interpreting the results (Lab, 1987). First, many studies anger subjects prior to their screening a pornographic stimulus. After the viewing, not unexpectedly, the subject aggressively retaliates against the earlier aggressor. The researchers argue that it is the exposure to pornography that brings about the aggression and conveniently ignore the fact of the prior provocation. Second, the method of aggression in laboratory studies (such as overinflated blood pressure cuffs, electric shocks, noxious noise, and derogatory evaluations of tasks) are not equivalent to rape, assault, or other forms of violence outside the laboratory setting. Third, the sterile laboratory setting does not provide the same conditions under which the subjects would be viewing pornography and committing aggressive acts in the real world. Finally, the study subjects are typically undergraduate students who are not representative of the general population (Lab, 1987).

Where laboratory research claims a relatively strong media-behavior link, field and natural experiments provide more tentative conclusions (Lab, 1987). In a review of research on media violence, Geen and Thomas (1986) note that field experiments and natural studies show greatly equivocal results. While some studies report a strong media-violence connection, others show no media impact on behavior. Despite the fact that field results are more generalizable, proponents of a media-aggression link tend to place more emphasis on laboratory experiments in which they have more control over different variables (see, for example, Geen and Thomas, 1986; Huesmann and Malamuth, 1986).

Another problem with media studies involves the time order of the assumed causal relationships. The studies present the results in such a way that exposure to the media causes aggressive behavior. In many analyses, it is equally plausible that people who are already aggressive or are naturally prone to aggression simply choose to view more aggression. Their aggressive nature may be temporally prior to their choice of media exposure. In addition, the impact of the media presentation is probably mediated by the extent of exposure, predisposition of the viewer, social support for aggression, past rewards or punishments for aggression, the environment, and other factors (Huesmann and Malamuth, 1986).

This brief review presents at least qualified support for a connection between media presentations and viewer behavior. Most studies find weak to moderate relationships between actual behavior and television accounts of crime and aggression. There also exists a strong theoretical tradition of modeling, learning, arousal, and cognitive cuing which supports a connection between the mass media and aggression. At the very least, excessive exposure to media violence can influence some viewers to be more aggressive (Huesmann and Malamuth, 1986). The preponderance of data and positive research findings suggest that the media does have some influence on behavior (Surette, 1992).

The Media and Fear

Besides causing deviant behavior, media presentations may also increase people's fear. Several authors note that crime news increases fear (Ditton and Duffy, 1983; Gunter, 1987; Sherizan, 1978; van Dijk, 1978). Heath (1984) and Liska and Baccaglini (1990) report that local crime stories, particularly those dealing with sensational events, tend to raise the level of fear among readers. Examining 10 British daily newspapers and their relationship to fear, Williams and Dickinson (1993) find that fear varies with the saliency of the crime reports. That is, stories that place the offense in a framework familiar to the reader have a greater impact than those more removed from the reader's experiences.

Newspapers are not the only media form found to influence fear. High levels of television viewing also have been found to raise fear (Gerbner et al., 1979; Doob and Macdonald, 1979). Chiricos et al. (1996) report on the impact of various media forms on fear in Tallahassee, Florida. Analysis shows that television and radio news is related to fear, while written news has no relationship with fear levels. Further, the media-fear relationship is qualified by demographic factors, with television news being linked to higher fear among victims, women, white, lower income, and middle-aged respondents. Combining the effects of demographic factors, the news effect is limited primarily to white females (Chiricos et al., 1996). These results support Garofalo's (1981) argument that the fear-media relationship is qualified by the introduction of demographic factors, not unlike the findings of different fear levels displayed by different respondents when the media is not considered. In Great Britain, *Crimewatch U.K.,* a counterpart to *America's Most Wanted,* increased fear in one-third of its viewers (Dobash et al., 1998).

Summary

The preceding discussions show that the media does influence both criminal behavior and fear. Exposure to the media is a daily fact of life for almost every citizen. There is a clear ability for the media to influence the images of crime held by the populace. More importantly, the media appears to be a factor in molding behavior. In the same way that the media may contribute to aggressive behavior and fear, it is possible that exposure to the mass media could bring about more realistic images of crime and prompt people to adopt crime prevention techniques.

MASS MEDIA CRIME PREVENTION ACTIVITIES

Crime prevention through the mass media can take a variety of forms and has the potential to impact in different ways. Bowers and Johnson (2005) show that the media (publicity) can be used for several purposes: increasing the risk to offenders, increasing the perceived risk to offenders, encouraging safety practices by the public, and reassuring the public (see Figure 7.1). Successful use of the media may result in reduced crime and fear of crime. Examples of the use of media in crime prevention are the McGruff campaigns, crime newsletters, information lines such as Crime Stoppers, and the recent growth of "reality television" programs. Each of these attempts to provide varying amounts of crime education, fear reduction, and crime prevention activity that, hopefully, will translate into lower levels of actual crime.

Figure 7.1
Uses of Media/Publicity in Crime Prevention

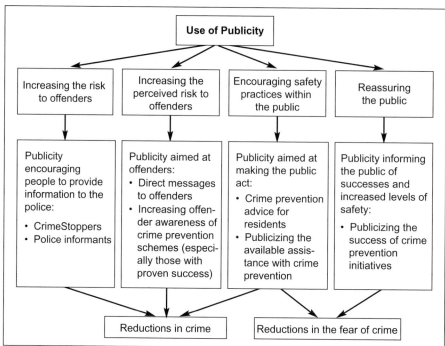

Source: Bowers, K.J. and S.D. Johnson (2005). "Using Publicity for Preventive Purposes." In Tilley, N. (ed.), *Handbook of Crime Prevention and Community Safety*. Portland, OR: Willan Publishing. Reprinted with permission.

The McGruff Prevention Campaign

Perhaps the most well-known media crime prevention campaign was instituted in the late 1970s by the Crime Prevention Coalition of America and the Advertising Council. These organizations joined forces to launch the "Taking a Bite Out of Crime" program, featuring McGruff the crime dog. In 1982, the National Crime Prevention Council (NCPC) was formed to manage the ongoing McGruff Project. The program operates today with the same four basic objectives it had in the beginning. First, it attempts to alter the public's feelings about crime and the criminal justice system. This is clearly an educational component aimed at instilling a realistic view of crime and the role of the legal system in stopping crime. Second, the program attempts to generate feelings of citizen responsibility for crime and crime prevention. Third, it tries to enhance citizen cooperation with the criminal justice system for fighting crime. The final goal is to enhance already existing crime prevention efforts.

Public service announcements provide the means of realizing these objectives. Many of the announcements feature a cartoon character known as *"McGruff"* (a dog in a trench coat) who presents simulated crimes and notes the proper actions viewers should take when confronted with similar situations.

A number of different themes or issues have appeared in the television, radio, and print announcements. Home security/neighborhood watch, crime prevention for a safer community, child/teen protection and involvement, children's drug abuse prevention, and violence prevention have been major topics over the years. The current campaigns are listed in Figure 7.2 and include cyberbullying, identity theft, and fraud against seniors. The emphasis throughout the campaign is on individual and community ability to take action.

Figure 7.2
Current McGruff Campaigns

Cyberbullying
Bullying Prevention
Identity Theft
Internet Safety
Neighborhood Involvement
Senior Fraud

Source: Compiled from NCPC (2009).

Taking a Bite Out of Crime

The *Taking a Bite Out of Crime* media campaign is the most recognizable component of the work of the NCPC today. According to the NCPC (2009), more than three-quarters of all youths in the United States recognize McGruff and more than 4,000 law enforcement agencies use McGruff in their activities. The "Taking a Bite Out of Crime" campaign has relied on a significant amount of monetary support and personnel time from various sources. The NCPC (2009) notes that more than $1.4 billion worth of advertising time and space has been donated for the program. This does not include production costs or costs of booklets, posters, and other program-related items that have been made available since the program started in 1979. Two large-scale evaluations have been completed on the program.

The First Evaluation

A two-pronged evaluation of this campaign was conducted from 1979 to 1981 (O'Keefe and Mendelsohn, 1984). The first part of the evaluation consisted of surveying 1,200 adults from across the country. The second phase involved a panel survey of adults in Buffalo, Detroit, and Milwaukee. The panel survey took measurements three months prior to the introduction of the campaign and again after more than a year and a half of campaign exposure. Among the issues investigated were the level of exposure to the public service announcements and the impact of the campaign on subsequent attitudes and crime prevention behaviors. The evaluation did not include any measures of actual crime. Self-reported victimization and attitudes served as the dependent variables.

The national survey found that roughly 50 percent of the respondents saw the campaign announcements (O'Keefe and Mendelsohn, 1984). Unfortunately, only three percent of this figure were able to recall the advertisements without some prompting by the interviewers. The vast majority (78%) saw the advertisements on television. Comparison across demographic groups revealed fairly even exposure in the population. The lone exception to this finding was the low number of older respondents (33%) who expressed a familiarity with the McGruff materials. O'Keefe and Mendelsohn (1984) speculated that this could be partly attributable to the fact that the materials typically appear later at night when the advertising time is not as profitable and older respondents are less likely to be watching the television.

The national survey also probed the extent of knowledge retained from the messages and the self-reported behavior of respondents as a result of the information. Almost 90 percent of the respondents were able to describe specific suggestions made and 22 percent said they learned something new (O'Keefe and Mendelsohn, 1984). The evaluators also found that better than 50 percent of the survey subjects felt more responsible for crime prevention because of the advertisements and a full 25 percent reported taking precautions suggested in the announcements. Regrettably, 22 percent of those surveyed reported feeling *more* fearful of criminal victimization. They attributed this feeling directly to the McGruff campaign materials. This increase in fear was opposite to program expectations and directly contradicted the efforts to present scenarios that would not elicit increased fear.

The panel survey component of the evaluation presented more in-depth results. Similar to the national findings, the panel survey revealed wide exposure to the campaign materials (O'Keefe and Mendelsohn, 1984). Interestingly, the level of interest in the materials was higher for those already concerned with crime and crime prevention activities. Exposure to the advertisements had no impact on perceptions of neighborhood crime, perceived changes in the crime rate, or a sense of safety at night. Only minor, and contradictory, changes were found in relation to individual crimes.

Exposure to the public service announcements resulted in changes in crime prevention activities. Specific activities suggested by the announcements (e.g. neighborhood watches, use of lights and locks, reporting suspicious persons to the police) increased after exposure to the materials. Preventive measures not dealt with in the messages (e.g. indoor lighting, stopping mail and paper deliveries, installing alarms) were not affected, as expected. The adoption of the crime prevention measures was not uniform across the panel subjects. While men's attitudes about crime prevention changed more than women's, women and upper income respondents tended to gravitate more to cooperative crime prevention activities (O'Keefe and Mendelsohn, 1984). Lower income respondents chose individual alternatives like increased lighting and more outdoor activities.

The Second Evaluation

A second evaluation was conducted in 1992 and involved interviewing a national sample of adults, as well as law enforcement and media representatives. Compared to the earlier evaluation, 80 percent of the citizen respondents reported having seen the announcements, an increase of 30 percent (O'Keefe et al., 1996). Exposure was greatest among younger respondents, males (by 6% over females), those with at least a high school education, and victims. The impact of the announcements was uniformly in the expected direction. Respondents reported feeling more competent about crime prevention participation, taking more action, and becoming more concerned about crime (O'Keefe et al., 1996). Interestingly, the evaluation did not uncover demographic differences between those learning from the announcements and those reporting no impact.

Similar positive results appear in the media and law enforcement responses. More than two-thirds of the media respondents reported using the materials in the past, with 75 percent of the television stations having aired announcements during the past year (O'Keefe et al., 1996). Both the media and law enforcement respondents noted that the materials were valuable in both crime and drug prevention efforts. Of particular note was the introduction of *"WE PREVENT"* announcements in the early 1990s which asked viewers to call a toll free telephone number and request information on how to deal with problems such as random violence. Media respondents rated these announcements high in terms of quality, appropriateness and interest compared to other public service materials (O'Keefe et al., 1996).

Summary

In general, the "Taking A Bite Out of Crime" campaign facilitates attitudinal changes in the groups that traditionally are the least vulnerable to crime and those already interested in crime prevention issues. This mirrors the findings of who joins neighborhood watch and other crime prevention programs. O'Keefe and Mendelsohn (1984) also note that behavioral changes do not always correspond to attitudinal adjustments. That is, many individuals try out various crime prevention measures without reporting any attitudinal shifts about crime or fear. Based on both evaluations, O'Keefe et al. (1996) suggest that the program keep its main themes and continue to find ways to reach vulnerable groups in society. In addition, the campaign should attempt to identify distinct needs of different audience groups and target announcements to their situations.

Other Campaigns

One media campaign in England that attempted to educate individuals about auto theft and juvenile vandalism met with varied results (Riley, 1980; Riley and Mayhew, 1980). The attempt to deal with vandalism had no effect on parental attitudes or the crime rates in the target area. Auto thefts, on the other hand, declined in the experimental area relative to a control location. A burglary awareness/education program in Jerusalem utilizing radio, public lectures, and various forms of literature was recalled by more than 50 percent of the surveyed public and 46 percent altered their behavior or took precautions in accordance with the campaign's suggestions (Geva and Israel, 1982). Participants also reported higher feelings of safety compared to non-participants or pre-exposure levels. The actual level of burglary dropped by 32 percent in the target area compared to a 22 percent increase in the rest of Jerusalem and a six percent rise in the control area (Geva and Israel, 1982). A media campaign aimed at auto theft in Australia using television, newspapers, magazines, and letters reached only 28 percent of the public but was able to increase the preventive behavior of those exposed to the campaign (Wortley et al., 1998). These studies illustrate that media campaigns have the potential to change both the levels of fear and actual amounts of crime. Other evaluations show that the message reaches the public, but relatively few individuals report undertaking the suggested prevention activities (Kuttschreuter and Wiegman, 1998; Sacco and Silverman, 1981; van Dijk and Steinmetz, 1981).

The inconsistent and weak results in the various program evaluations suggest that the programs may need to be better targeted. Sacco and Trotman (1990) note that the impact of a mass media crime prevention campaign is related to the saliency of the program for the viewer. Individuals who recognize crime as a problem are more likely to be influenced by the program and report changes in attitude and behavior. While widespread exposure of a program is a plus, crime prevention campaigns need to reach the intended or most vulnerable audiences (see also O'Keefe at al., 1996). The generic nature of large scale approaches may also hamper their effectiveness. Sacco and Trotman (1990) suggest that programs need to set modest, realistic goals that focus on specific attitudes and behaviors. Viewers are more likely to take precautions that are presented in the media than to strike out on their own to find the proper forms of crime prevention behavior (O'Keefe and Mendelsohn, 1984). While most crime prevention programs present fictionalized or very general accounts of crime in order to minimize any impact on fear, this also reduces the saliency of the program. Finally, Sacco and Trotman (1990) point out that crime prevention programs require assistance for individuals who lack resources and power to follow the specific prevention techniques. More specific media campaigns, such as area newsletters and crime stoppers programs, may engender increased citizen participation in crime prevention activities.

Crime Newsletters

Providing more salient information to the public can be accomplished through the distribution of *crime newsletters*. Unlike widely distributed mass media campaigns, which are limited in terms of their time frame and the level of specificity, newsletters can be targeted to a much more limited audience and tailored to the needs of those individuals. Newsletters also can provide information on a wide range of related topics, including the level of crime in an area and prevention techniques for the public (see Table 7.1). In addition, they may provide detailed, in-depth discussions of both crime and potential crime prevention measures. Totally different newsletters need not be prepared for each neighborhood or targeted group. Instead, a single newsletter dealing with general crime and crime prevention information can be developed for wide distribution. Salience can be enhanced through the insertion of separate fact sheets and information sent to different areas and individuals.

Crime newsletters have been utilized in a large number of locations but have received extensive evaluation only in Evanston, Illinois (Lavrakas, 1986; Lavrakas et al., 1983), Houston (Brown and Wycoff, 1987; Lavrakas, 1986), and Newark (Lavrakas, 1986; Williams and Pate, 1987). The format of the newsletters in these three cities is basically the same. Each includes various articles on crime prevention and comments on crime problems. In addition, crime information specific to different locations is included in the letters. The crime information includes such items as the level and types of crime committed in the area, rough location of offenses, and relevant information about offenders and victims. This allows the reader to assess the particulars about the crimes and apply that information to his or her own situation.

The newsletters have the potential to influence citizen behavior in a number of ways. First, the newsletters are an educational tool. They can present more realistic versions of the actual crime rate and, perhaps, bring down the fear of crime. The opposite effect, however, is also possible. Fear of crime could increase due to the distribution of crime news. In turn, this could restrict, rather than increase, citizen behavior. A second possibility is they can raise the level of concern about crime among the citizenry. Hopefully, any increase in concern will result in a third outcome—increased citizen crime prevention activities.

The evaluation of the newsletters in the three cities followed roughly the same procedures (Brown and Wycoff, 1987; Lavrakas, 1986; Williams and Pate, 1987). Each evaluation randomly assigned homes to one of three conditions. One set of homes received the newsletter containing crime specific information. A second sample of homes received newsletters without the

Table 7.1
Newsletter Content Areas

Self-protection Techniques
Ways to Report Crime
Locations of Police or Protection Resources
Dangerous Areas
Offender Addresses
Area Crime Problems

Source: Compiled from Barthe (2010).

crime information. These subjects saw only the articles and crime prevention information. The remaining sample of homes acted as a control group and did not get any newsletter. Despite the similarity in content and evaluation design, the evaluation results differ across the three cities.

The most consistent finding is that individuals who report receiving the newsletters hold favorable assessments of them. This is true for both the newsletters with and without the specific crime information (Lavrakas, 1986). There is a slight tendency for those receiving the version containing crime data to view the letters as more interesting.

There is less consistency in the impact on fear of crime, concern for crime prevention, and precautions taken as a result of the newsletters. In Evanston, the newsletters increase the recipient's knowledge of the crime problem but have no effect on the fear of crime (Lavrakas et al., 1983; Lavrakas, 1986). The Houston evaluation shows increased fear of property victimization among respondents receiving crime information in the letters (Brown and Wycoff, 1987; Lavrakas, 1986) and the Newark evaluation fails to uncover any changes in fear of crime or perceptions of change in the crime problem (Lavrakas, 1986; Williams and Pate, 1987). In terms of crime prevention activity, Evanston respondents who receive letters containing crime information take more crime prevention precautions than those individuals not receiving the letters or those receiving letters without crime data (Lavrakas et al., 1983; Lavrakas, 1986). Houston respondents report similar levels of crime prevention activity across all study groups, although those receiving the newsletter feel more competent to avoid victimization than do non-receivers (Lavrakas, 1986). Finally, Newark residents who do not receive the newsletter report taking more crime prevention precautions than those who receive either version of the newsletter. The newsletter does result in greater feelings of self-protection among those viewing the materials (Lavrakas, 1986).

The inconsistent findings in the evaluations may be attributable to differences in the study sites. Lavrakas (1986) points out that the more effective campaign in Evanston relied on hand distribution of the newsletter. Mailing of the newsletter in the other cities may adversely affect the perceived importance of the materials. The newsletters may be relegated to the status of junk mail delivered by postal workers. A second difference between the cities concerns the educational level of the recipients. More Evanston respondents report graduation from high school and participation in higher education than do those in either of the other locations (Lavrakas, 1986). This factor may influence the actual level of readership of the newsletters and the amount of impact the printed documents have on the viewer. Third, Lavrakas (1986) notes that the Evanston evaluation relies on interviews with the head of the household while both the Houston and Newark studies survey any adult member of the household. It is reasonable to assume that the head of a household makes most decisions on the institution of household crime prevention activity. Failure to target the head of the house, therefore, may fail to uncover any precautions that are taken. One final problem may be the choice of information and format for the various newsletters. Both Houston and Newark borrowed the basic newsletter framework from Evanston. It is possible that the similarity of presentation, given the dissimilarity of cities, is partially at fault for the discrepant results.

Newsletters have the potential to affect fear of crime, perceptions of crime and victimization, and crime prevention behavior. The failure of the three newsletter evaluations presented here to reveal consistent impacts does not relegate the newsletter approach to failure. The problems noted above suggest that more caution needs to be taken in the choice of format, presentation, and evaluation of a newsletter. The consistent findings of public interest and acceptance of the information should be enough to assure its continuation.

Information Lines

The idea behind *information lines* is twofold. First, and foremost, is the solicitation of information about specific crimes from the public. The second aspect is the public presentation of crime information involving citizens in crime prevention. Perhaps the most widely known program of this type is Crime Stoppers. *Crime Stoppers*, and variations on this program, generally operates by offering rewards to citizens for information about crimes. Often, unsolved offenses are presented to the public through the mass media along with a plea by law enforcement officials for information regarding the crime. The informant is usually guaranteed anonymity for the information through the use of code names or numbers and reward money comes from public donations. Crime Stoppers started in Albuquerque, New Mexico, in 1976 and today there are 1,175 programs around the world (Crime Stoppers International, 2009). Programs are found in 20 countries, including the United States, Canada, the Caribbean, Europe, Australia, the Pacific, South Korea, India, and South Africa. While most programs are community based, there are chapters found at various schools and colleges. Programs typically offer rewards of up to $1,000 for information leading to the arrest of a suspect. Crime Stoppers programs are a tool to bring the public, media, and the criminal justice system into a cooperative crime prevention effort.

Crime Stoppers International (2009) claims that more than 1.2 million cases have been cleared since 1976 (see Table 7.2). More than 811,000 arrests

Table 7.2
Crime Stoppers Facts and Figures, 2009

	United States	**International**
Number of Cases Cleared	848,919	1,263,200
Number of Arrests Made	511,101	811,088
Amount of Awards Paid	$77 M+	$94 M+
Value of Property Recovered	$1.0 B+	$1.9 B+
Value of Drugs Seized	$2.8 B+	$7.1 B+
Total $ Recovered	$3.9 B+	$9.0 B+

Source: www.c-s-i.org/stats.php; www.crimestopusa.com

have been made, with more than $94 million in rewards paid. In addition, the authorities have recovered more than $1.9 billion in stolen property and seized more than $7 billion in drugs as a result of the Crime Stoppers program (Crime Stoppers International, 2009). Money for the rewards is typically donated by businesses or solicited through fundraising, and the advertisements themselves are usually donated by the media.

Several evaluations of Crime Stoppers have been conducted. Rosenbaum et al. (1989) report on a national evaluation of Crime Stoppers in the United States. The evaluation included a telephone survey of 602 Crime Stoppers programs and surveys of police coordinators, Crime Stoppers boards of directors and mass media executives. The surveys show that programs typically share resources with one another and receive high praise from the administrators, media personnel, and police coordinators. Many media respondents indicate that, while they are not currently participating in the program, they would be happy to do so if they were approached. Unfortunately, these programs are difficult to evaluate in terms of any reduction in fear of crime or lower crime and victimization (Rosenbaum et al., 1989).

Gresham et al. (2001) report on an evaluation of Crime Stoppers in the United Kingdom. The researchers interviewed key stakeholders, conducted observations of program operations, tracked phone calls, and reviewed program documents. In 2000, more than 500,000 calls were received by Crime Stoppers, but only 12 percent of those provided usable information (i.e. actionable calls), and only 5,423 arrests were made (Gresham et al., 2001). The bulk of the actionable calls reflected drug and motor vehicle offenses. Interestingly, only one-fifth of the actionable calls were in direct response to specific media presentations. The rest of the calls dealt with offenses or crimes not presented in the media. Also of note, Gresham et al. (2001) found that most rewards went unclaimed. More than £3.7 million (over $7 million) worth of stolen property was recovered and more than £34 million (over $65 million) in drugs were seized (Gresham et al., 2001). As in the United States, there is strong support for Crime Stoppers from the police, media and public.

The Crime Stoppers program in Australia has had similar success. Most of the targeted crimes presented on television are violent crimes (84%) and almost 140,000 calls were received in 2002 (Challinger, 2003). Unfortunately, less than two percent of the calls resulted in an arrest. Despite that fact, almost 600,000 (U.S.) worth of stolen property was recovered and over $5 million (U.S.) in drugs were seized (Challinger, 2003). Support for the program rivals that found in United States and United Kingdom assessments.

Despite the positive results reported in the evaluations, there is no indication that programs like Crime Stoppers have reduced crime or the fear of crime. It is possible that fear could actually increase through the media presentation of unsolved, and often heinous, crimes. Reduced crime could only be effected through the greater risks of apprehension as a result of the program. There also are concerns that Crime Stoppers programs may engender negative results. Among the potential problems are the pretrial publicity that is necessary, questions about the validity of paid testimony, the problem of anonymous testimony, and the possibility of false accusations (Rosenbaum et al., 1989). Indeed, the U.S. national evaluation estimates that most tips come from criminals (25%) or fringe players (41%) rather than from common citizens (35%) (Rosenbaum et al., 1989). Another problem is that advertised rewards have the potential to overburden law enforcement with meaningless calls and confusion (Kelley, 1997). Despite the potential problems, Crime Stoppers programs are a valuable tool in the gathering of crime-related information and providing crime information to a wide range of citizens.

Crime-Time Television

One trend in the mass media since the mid-1980s has been the focus on previously unsolved crimes in prime-time network programming. Among these are programs such as *America's Most Wanted*, *Unsolved Mysteries*, and *Top Cops* in the United States (Nelson, 1989) and *Crimewatch U.K.* in the United Kingdom (Dobash et al., 1998). These shows typically re-enact serious crimes for which no offender has been apprehended. The dramatizations often use the actual law enforcement personnel and citizens involved in the case. After the presentation of a case, viewers are prompted to call a toll-free telephone number to report any information they may have about the case or the whereabouts of the suspect.

The impact of these shows has received increased attention in recent years. Kelley (1997) notes that of the 1,133 subjects showcased on *America's Most Wanted*, 441 have been found and taken into custody subsequent to the airing of the program. It is uncertain, however, the degree to which the program can be considered directly responsible for most of these apprehensions. Nelson (1989) points out that these programs encourage citizen cooperation with the police. Donovan (1998) notes that "America's Most Wanted" received an average of 3,000 calls per show in 1994, but few contributed valuable information. A similar Dutch program claims a clearance rate of 25 to 30 percent for broadcast crimes (Brants, 1998). While most calls may not result in useful information, the fact that calls are being made can be considered a significant achievement of the programs. One producer views the program as the catalyst for a "nationwide neighborhood watch association" (Nelson, 1989).

On the other hand, these programs hold the potential for causing trouble. First, mass media presentations can potentially bias court cases and lead to appeals based on excessive pretrial publicity and the inability to seat an unbiased jury. Indeed, one such motion has been made in the case of motorcycle gang members accused of murdering an individual after one program re-enacted the event and asked viewers for more information. Second, depictions of crimes where the offender has not been apprehended may lead other individuals to copy the offenses.

Third, Winkel (1987) notes that viewers may generalize from the response being promoted in the program (such as simply calling for help) to other possible responses not featured in the program (such as carrying weapons and taking direct action). Such a *response generalization* would be an unintended consequence of the program. Vigilante behavior is one possible generalization of efforts to increase citizen involvement. Indeed, citizen action in the apprehension of the Los Angeles hillside strangler and the Bernard Goetz case in New York are examples of citizens having taken actions that were not promoted by the programs aimed at increasing citizen involvement and cooperation. While not all citizens will generalize beyond the message provided in the media, there is clear evidence that such actions do grow out of media presentations (Winkel, 1987). The popularity of "crime-time" programs will ensure that they continue to appear on television for the immediate future. The extent to which they will have an impact on crime, fear of crime, and citizen participation needs to be examined further.

Publicity and Prevention

While this chapter has focused primarily on large mass media efforts, smaller scale and targeted publicity about prevention programs and initiatives can have an impact on the success of crime prevention efforts. That impact may actually occur prior to or separate from the actual prevention initiative. That is, the publicity may reduce crime in and of itself. The assumption underlying this possibility is that the publicity impacts the offender's perceptions of risk and payoff, rather than changing the behavior of victims (Johnson and Bowers, 2003).

Smith et al. (2002) suggest that changes in crime that predate the actual implementation of a crime prevention program are a form of *anticipatory benefit*. In one sense, this could be a form of diffusion of benefits that arises most probably from the fact that offenders, victims, and others know about a forthcoming prevention activity and begin to respond prior to the activation of the intervention. Publicity about an impending intervention may be the impetus for the anticipatory benefits. That publicity can be intentional, as in situations where public announcements are made about a project, or it may be more informal through networking that takes place during the planning and early implementation stages for an intervention. Smith et al. (2002) present findings in support of their hypothesis based on an analysis of 52 studies in which there was evidence of pre-initiative crime reductions.

Several studies reveal evidence of anticipatory benefits stemming from publicity. Barclay et al.'s (1996) analysis of activities aimed at reducing crimes in parking lots shows reductions in crime that began after publicity started but before the actual intervention took place. Similarly, both Brown's (1995) and Armitage et al.'s (1999) studies of CCTV present evidence of downward trends in crime prior to the actual installation of the cameras but after the program was announced. Johnson and Bowers (2003) present the strongest argument for the impact of publicity to bring about anticipatory benefits. In an analysis of 21 Reducing Burglary Initiative sites, the authors assessed the timing of reductions in burglary against the initiation of publicity and the actual prevention activities. Their results show that there is a significant reduction in burglary preceding the actual program implementation. In addition the declines correspond to the advent of the publicity on the forthcoming efforts (Johnson and Bowers, 2003). Based on these results, the authors argue that publicity has an independent impact on crime and that programs could possibly bring down crime by publicizing a prevention program, even if the program never takes place (Bowers and Johnson, 2003; Johnson and Bowers, 2003)! At the very least, publicity should be considered as a part of any prevention initiative.

THE MEDIA'S RESPONSIBILITY FOR CRIME PREVENTION

Throughout this chapter we have discussed the potential of the media for enhancing crime prevention activity. One recent analysis, however, suggests that the media must assume some of the blame for the continued failure of policies to deal with crime. Lavrakas (1997) argues that the media fails to critically assess claims regarding the efficacy of crime control policies. In particular, politicians are able to promote interventions and crime policy without being held accountable for their rhetorical arguments. The author argues that the media has a responsibility to do more than simply report what legislators say. Instead, the media should be critically questioning those positions and challenging politicians to provide proof for their arguments (Lavrakas, 1997).

Lavrakas (1997) demonstrates his argument through an analysis of 1994 anti-crime legislation. Analyzing stories in the *New York Times*, Lavrakas points out that the media often focuses on the disagreement between legislators about crime policy, but rarely deals with the substantive merit of the various measures being debated. In essence, the media does a poor job at handling political posturing and tends to accept gross comments about "worthlessness" in relation to programs without demanding that the source prove that claim.

Why does the media do such a poor job? First, Lavrakas (1997) suggests that the news media is typically not educated about criminal justice and crime policy. Few journalists receive any real education about the criminal justice system or crime prevention. Second, the media does not hold politicians accountable for their actions or rhetoric. Consequently, politicians will not change their posturing and the public will not receive the information it needs to make informed decisions. What the public receives is a sanitized version of what is taking place through "sound bites" or catchy phrases. Lavrakas calls for educating the media (and politicians) about crime prevention, as well as demanding that more research be conducted on prevention initiatives. He argues that crime prevention will continue to suffer until the media starts to hold policymakers accountable for their actions.

SUMMARY

The use of the media is a relatively new approach in crime prevention. Research on the exposure of the public to media information and the findings that media portrayals of aggression may affect levels of viewer aggression suggests that the same tools could influence crime preventive behavior. Analysis of media crime prevention campaigns shows that media presentations can affect fear of crime, feelings of self-confidence in avoiding victimization, and the adoption of crime prevention precautions. Unfortunately, the level and extent of these changes is not uniform across the evaluations. It appears that the choice of presentation format and the modes of evaluation are key elements in uncovering positive effects. Any modification in actual crime is extremely difficult to uncover. This is primarily due to the focus on perceptions of fear and crime and not on crime itself. Changes in the level of actual crime must rely on the successful modification of these other factors. Once the fear of crime and the level of crime prevention efforts are changed, then the ultimate goal of reduced crime can start to appear.

Chapter 8
GENERAL DETERRENCE

Key Terms:

brutalization effect
celerity
certainty
cross-sectional study
deterrence
experiential effect

general deterrence
hedonistic
longitudinal study
panel design
severity
specific deterrence

Learning Objectives:

After reading this chapter you should be able to:

- Define deterrence

- Identify and define the two types of deterrence

- List and define the requirements for a deterrent effect

- Discuss the findings of cross-sectional analyses of deterrence

- Relate the results of longitudinal investigations of deterrence

- Explain the brutalization effect of the death penalty

- Demonstrate your knowledge of panel designs and results of research using them

- Discuss the problems with making claims that executions reduce the homicide rate

- Discuss the research on perceptions and deterrence

- Define and discuss what is meant by the experiential effect

- Provide a summary on the ability to deter people from committing crime

Any discussion of primary prevention would not be complete without a look at the deterrent effects of punishment. Recall that primary prevention attempts to eliminate or reduce the level of deviant behavior prior to its occurrence. The bulk of the discussion so far has focused on the crime prevention activities of the general public. Most people today believe that official agencies of social control are, or should be, responsible for eliminating crime. Indeed, the actions of criminal justice agencies are aimed at the elimination of crime through deterrence.

One of the leading writers on the subject defines *deterrence* as "influencing by fear" (Andenaes, 1975). According to this writer, potential offenders decide to refrain from committing criminal acts due to a fear of apprehension and punishment. The likelihood of deterrence increases as the risk of punishment increases. An actual experience of punishment does not have to occur before an individual can be deterred. Instead, Andenaes (1975) assumes that the threat of punishment would be enough if the proper circumstances exist. The idea of "threat" and interest in diverting initial or future activity prompts Andenaes to refer to deterrence as "general prevention." It is prevention of the potential offense by use of fear. Deterrence is a major form of crime prevention and has served as a cornerstone of criminal justice. To ignore deterrence in a discussion of crime prevention would indicate a lack of understanding of the role of deterrence. On the other hand, deterrence has forged a place of its own in criminology. It is not necessary, therefore, to devote a large space to deterrence in this text. This chapter will present the underlying ideas of deterrence and briefly examine the research on one type of deterrence— general deterrence. More in depth discussions of deterrence will be left for other writers.

DETERRENCE

Deterrence can be broken down into two distinct types— specific and general. *Specific deterrence* refers to efforts that keep the individual offender from violating the law again in the future. The hope is that the experience of punishment will deter the individual who has been punished from future illegal activity. The offender who is incarcerated for burglary is expected to be deterred by the experience from committing any further acts of burglary once he is released from the institution. The punishment is not expected affect anyone other than the targeted individual. In a strict sense, the deterrent action also should only have an impact on the same criminal act. One would not expect that other deviant acts, such as rape or assault, to be affected by punishment for burglary. Property crimes like larceny may see a change due to the punishment of burglary, but not to the same extent as for burglary.

General deterrence, on the other hand, aims to have an impact on more than the single offender. The apprehension and punishment of one person hopefully serves as an example to other offenders and potential law violators. In this instance, the incarceration of a single burglar should deter other individuals from committing burglary. As with specific deterrence, general deterrence should have its greatest impact on similar criminal acts.

Both types of deterrence assume a rational offender. Any deterrent effect rests upon the ability of an offender to make choices of whether or not to violate society's behavioral standards. Accordingly, the inability to make rational decisions would mitigate any effect of deterrence. Rationality also assumes that potential offenders are *hedonistic* (i.e., man seeks pleasure and avoids pain). Punishment is assumed to be painful to the individual and the outcome of criminal activity represents the pleasure component. Deterrence seeks to offset any pleasure received in the crime by introducing an equal or slightly higher level of pain. Such an action should result in an elimination of further law violation. General deterrence, resting heavily on the assumption of a rational individual, suggests that the pain experienced by one person will be seen as potential pain by persons contemplating a similar act.

This chapter looks only at general deterrence for two major reasons. First, the emphasis of this chapter is on primary prevention. Primary prevention deals with prevention before an act has occurred by making changes and taking actions that avoid the commission of a criminal act. General deterrence looks at the effect of punishing one individual on the future behavior of other persons. This means changing the behavior of societal members prior to their commission of criminal acts. General deterrence clearly fits the criteria of prevention before initial criminal action. Second, specific deterrence focuses on the activity of an individual who has already violated the law and seeks to prevent such an individual from committing future criminal acts. This emphasis on the relationship between clear cases of criminality and future activity falls within the realm of tertiary prevention. Additionally, specific deterrence is often confused with incapacitation. The inhibition of offending as a result of complete control over an individual is not synonymous with specific deterrence. As noted earlier, specific deterrence deals with activity after imposition of punishment, not during punishment. The relationship between incapacitation and specific deterrence will be explored in Chapter 14.

Requirements for Deterrence

The deterrent effect of punishment relies on the existence of three factors. These are the severity, certainty, and celerity of the punishment. *Severity* involves making certain that punishments provide enough pain to offset the pleasure received from the criminal act. The basic assumption behind this idea is that the individual chooses his behavior after weighing the benefits of the crime against the potential costs incurred if he is caught. From this perspective, crime is the result of an analysis that presents more pleasure from the illegal activity than pain. Severity seeks to eliminate the positive, pleasurable outcome of the activity and replace it with negative, unwanted pain. The point at which the pain outweighs the pleasure determines the level at which the punishment is set.

Certainty deals with the chances of being caught and punished for one's behavior. The imposition of pain necessitates the identification, apprehension, conviction, and sentencing of the offender. The level of severity would have no impact on the decision making of an individual if that individual sees no chance of being subjected to the punishment. For general deterrence, the absence of enforcement of a law suggests to other potential offenders that the system either does not care about the questionable behavior or that the system is incapable of imposing its will and the punishment.

The third component of successful deterrence is celerity. *Celerity* refers to the swiftness of the societal response. The assumption underlying celerity is that a punishment that is temporally far removed from the action will not have the same impact as a punishment occurring soon after the action. The ability of the individual to equate the delayed pain from the punishment to the earlier pleasure derived from the offense is greatly diminished over time. For example, a child who disobeys his mother at 10:00 A.M. and is told "Wait until your father gets home" will most likely fail to equate the discipline imposed by the father at 5:00 P.M. to the behavior occurring seven hours earlier. The time frame for adults might be greatly expanded beyond a single day or week, but the principle remains the same. The pleasure received from the deviant act has long since dissipated when the pain is applied long after the activity. The more closely the pain follows the pleasure, the greater the chance that the individual will equate the two events.

Deterrence relies on the existence of all three of these components. The absence of any one can seriously impede the deterrent effect of the punishment. Despite the close interrelationship between these factors, most research on deterrence has focused on only one factor at a time. The other two are taken as a given or ignored entirely. Research almost totally ignores celerity (perhaps because of the legal requirements placed on case scheduling) and deals mainly with severity and certainty. The following discussion of deterrence research is organized along two dimensions. The first part deals with studies of the deterrent effect of the law. Studies on the death penalty dominate this discussion due to its traditional place in deterrence research. Studies in this section will be further broken down into cross-sectional and longitudinal analyses. The second approach looks at studies based on the perceptual nature of deterrence. That is, what do individuals perceive about the possibilities for apprehension and punishment? Various researchers believe that the failure of deterrence is due to the lack of knowledge or misperceptions about the deterrent aspects of the law.

The Deterrent Effect of Legal Sanctions

Studies on deterrence take one of two general forms—cross-sectional and longitudinal. *Cross-sectional studies* simply compare differences between different individuals, groups, states, or other aggregate. *Longitudinal analyses* look for changes over time, primarily due to shifts in law or criminal justice system activity. Panel designs have received increased attention in recent years, particularly in studies of the death penalty. Each of these types of analysis are considered in this section.

Cross-Sectional Analyses

One important source of deterrence research focuses on the impact of the death penalty across jurisdictions. The underlying assumption in this research is the belief that, given the severity of the penalty, the death sentence should have a great deterrent effect. While death penalty studies are well-known, these studies deal only with an extreme form of punishment and generally ignore the issues of certainty and celerity. Consequently, it is important to look a variety of punishments and actions.

Severity of Sanctions

Cross-sectional studies of the death penalty typically examine the differences in homicide between areas that have and those that do not have the death penalty. Most studies use states as the units of analysis. For example, these studies frequently compare the homicide rate in a state that has the death penalty to the homicide rate in a contiguous state which does not have the death penalty. The assumption is that, if the death penalty has a deterrent effect, the state with the penalty will have a lower homicide rate.

Ehrlich (1977), one of the leading advocates for the deterrent effect of the death penalty, claims a strong connection between the penalty and lower homicide rates. Comparing death penalty to non-death penalty states, Ehrlich reports that more than 20 homicides are deterred for every execution. The author notes that, not only does the death penalty deter, the length of imprisonment also lowers the homicide rate (Ehrlich, 1977).

The work of Ehrlich has been severely criticized on methodological grounds. The most common criticism involves the choice of variables that the author includes in his analysis. For example, simply designating states as death penalty and non-death penalty does not reveal whether there are unknown differences other than the penalty between the states (McGahey, 1980). States are certainly not similar on all counts just because they do or do not use the death penalty. Other unknown factors may be the cause of the difference in homicide rates instead of the assumed effect of the death penalty. Another related criticism of cross-sectional studies (in general) is the use of states as the level of analysis. States are not necessarily homogeneous within themselves. That is, there may be a great deal of diversity within the state. In addition, jurisdictional boundaries of states do not totally eliminate the possible diffusion effect of the death penalty sanction from one place to another. Persons residing in one state may be influenced by the use or existence of the death sentence in a neighboring state. Clearly, the populace may not know about the law or may be affected by an execution regardless of where the penalty is imposed.

Attempting to address the problem of jurisdictional boundaries, Archer et al. (1983) examine the deterrent effect of the death penalty in a cross-national study. The use of nations should minimize the likelihood of vicarious deterrence from one country to another. The authors look at "de jure," or the existence of death penalty statutes, instead of "de facto" death penalties, which refer to the actual use of the sentence. Archer et al. (1983) find little support for the deterrent argument. The existence of the death penalty is related to lower homicide rates in some countries and higher levels of homicide in other countries. This finding holds true for various follow-up time periods. The largest problem with this study is its failure to consider other confounding influences on the homicide rates. That is, the inconsistent results may be due to other differences between the nations and not to a varying impact of death penalty laws. A second problem may involve the focus on severity to the exclusion of the other deterrent factors. The simple existence of a law says nothing about the actual use, or certainty, of that law being applied.

Certainty of Punishment

A few studies have examined the effect of certainty of punishment, but typically do not address the death penalty. These studies do not directly measure the severity of the sanction. Tittle and Rowe (1974) look at the certainty of arrest and its effect on the crime rate. Using data for Florida, the authors note that certainty of arrest has no effect when the probability of arrest (the arrest rate) is very low. Certainty only plays a part when the arrest rate reaches and exceeds 30 percent. Geerken and Gove (1977) look at the certainty of arrest for other types of offenses. Property offenses, which have a higher likelihood of being planned and therefore should be deterred, are negatively related to the arrest clearance rate. There is almost no relationship between more spontaneous personal crimes and arrest. Forst (1977) also finds that states with higher conviction rates have lower levels of homicide. The relationship is confounded, however, by the influence of other social variables such as the racial and economic make-up of the states. Finally, Yu and Liska (1993) report that arrest certainty is strongly related to deterrence, with the impact being race specific. That is, the black and white crime rates are related to the black and white arrest rates, respectively, and the relationship is stronger for blacks. These studies appear to show that while there is a connection between the certainty of arrest and punishment and lower crime rates, the nature of the relationship is not totally clear.

More recent studies have looked at the certainty of punishment using data drawn at the individual level. Rather than using statistics on different aggregates, these studies compare data from different demographic groups. Fraser and Norman (1989), for example, compare the deterrent impact of system involvement for chronic and first-time offenders. Chronic offenders are those with four or more prior felony adjudications. Both groups are examined at the end of their juvenile careers (age 17). The authors expect that the one time offenders hold a higher fear of apprehension and punishment. Interestingly, the two groups of juveniles report similar levels of fear of apprehension (Fraser and Norman, 1989). Differences in the level of offending are attributed to non-deterrence factors such as school involvement and peer influences. A similar analysis of high school students in Toronto reveals an equally minor deterrent effect (Keane et al., 1989). In this study, past contact with the police for marijuana use has little, if any, impact on reports of current use. This is especially true of male respondents. Females, however, report some deterrent effects from police contact (Keane et al., 1989). Again, other factors than deterrence are important in the commission of deviant acts.

Combining Severity and Certainty

Various studies have combined the analysis of severity and certainty. One early study (Gibbs, 1968) reports that the homicide rate is negatively related to severity and certainty of punishment. Gibbs bases his analysis on differences between states in the number and length of prison sentences for homicide. Tittle (1969), conducting a similar analysis for all FBI Part I offenses and including controls for various demographic variables, finds a negative relationship between severity and homicide but not for the other offenses. The remaining Part I crimes are affected only by the certainty of the punishment (Tittle, 1969). Passell (1975) reports finding an effect of both severity and certainty. Looking at legal and demographic variables for states, he finds that the conviction rate (certainty) and the prison sentence (severity) are both negatively associated with state homicide rates. Finally, Sampson (1986) assesses certainty through local arrest rates and severity by the risk of jail and imprisonment in 171 U.S. cities. Controlling for various demographic factors, both certainty and severity have an impact on robbery but have little effect on homicide (Sampson, 1986).

Summary

The finding of statistically significant relationships in the cross-sectional deterrence research has not been without criticism. Chiricos and Waldo (1970) dispute the findings of deterrent effects in certainty and severity of punishment. Their analysis of state homicide statistics over two decades uncovers varying levels of significance for different time periods and different times. They attribute these discrepancies to the methodology used in the studies (Chiricos and Waldo, 1970). Logan (1972) suggests that the factors of severity and certainty act against one another. He notes that increases in the severity of punishment may lead criminal justice personnel to be more selective in who they subject to the punishment. Likewise, an increase in certainty could result in alteration of the charges or public outcries for changes in the law. Either way, certainty and severity are modified to accommodate alterations in the other factor.

Longitudinal Research

The more widely noted form of deterrence research entails longitudinal analysis. Longitudinal studies look at the introduction of a change on the outcome variable. One example of this is the examination of homicide rates prior to and after the imposition of the death penalty. The advantages of the longitudinal approach are many. First, the same jurisdiction is being considered at both points in time, thereby negating the problem faced in cross-sectional studies of biased results due to differences between the multiple areas under study. Second, the use of a single jurisdiction enhances the ability to identify alternative causes. The researcher is able to isolate both the point in time that the intervention occurs and when changes in the dependent variable occur. A third advantage of longitudinal analysis is that the observer can see when the changes occur, evaluate the time lag between the intervention and the change, and examine whether the effect is short- or long-term. That is, do the changes in the dependent variable diminish over time and return to the pre-intervention level? These advantages, among others, make longitudinal analysis the preferred technique.

Severity of Sanctions

Ehrlich (1975) provides one early and controversial longitudinal study. While examining the relationship between homicide and probabilities of apprehension, conviction, and execution, Ehrlich claims that each execution deters seven to eight homicides. This result persists when controlling for a number of demographic variables, including age of the population and socio-economic indicators (Ehrlich, 1975). The results of this study have been used as the basis of arguments in favor of the death penalty in front of the U.S. Supreme Court.

The results of this study came under immediate fire. Critics point to the choice of data and operationalization of the variables as the most problematic issues in Ehrlich's study. Passell and Taylor (1977), in a reassessment of Ehrlich's results, report that the deterrent finding holds true only for the years 1963–1969. Removal of these years and examination of 1933–1962 shows no significant deterrent effect. The inclusion of the 1960s is an important point of contention. It was during this time that the homicide rate was increasing, while use of the death penalty was decreasing or being removed from statutes. As a result, the finding of a deterrent relationship was inevitable. Passell and Taylor (1977) and Bowers and Pierce (1975) also demonstrate that altering the methodological technique eliminates much of the significance of Ehrlich's results.

Despite the shortcomings of Ehrlich's work, the deterrent effect of the death penalty received much subsequent attention. Phillips (1980) evaluates the effects of executions on homicides using weekly crime data. Comparing the weeks immediately prior to executions to the weeks right after the event, the author finds that the imposition of the death penalty results in a short-term reduction in homicide. The savings in life, however, is eliminated by an increase in homicides over subsequent weeks (Phillips, 1980). The executions appear to delay, instead of eliminate, homicide. A similar study (McFarland, 1983) supports Phillips' results. McFarland (1983) looks at the deterrent effect of four executions in the United States—Gary Gilmore in 1977, John Spenkelink in 1979, Jesse Bishop in 1979, and Steven Judy in 1981. Using weekly homicide rates, McFarland finds that none of the executions had a deterrent effect on weekly homicide rates. An initial finding of reduced homicides following the Gilmore execution is eliminated when controls for bad weather in the east and south during the week after the event are introduced (McFarland, 1983). These studies look at the short-term effect of executions and may fail to pick up any long-term impacts.

Several analyses look at longer periods. Decker and Kohfeld (1984) examine the long-term effect of the death penalty on homicides in Illinois. Using homicide and demographic data for 1933–1980, their analysis reveals that executions have an insignificant negative effect on homicide. Social factors, meanwhile, have a stronger relationship to the level of homicide (Decker and Kohfeld, 1984). Similarly, Sorenson et al. (1999) report on the impact of executions over a 14-year period in Texas. Monthly homicide rates are unrelated to the number of executions. Instead, various demographic measures are better predictors of the homicide rate (Sorenson et al., 1999). Bailey (1998) examines the impact of the first execution in Oklahoma on homicides over the subsequent 68 weeks. In general, he finds little evidence of a deterrent effect from the execution. Katz and colleagues (2003), examining annual state-level data from 1950–1990, report that the death penalty has little, if any, impact on homicide rates. One strong explanation for the lack of a deterrent effect is the small number of executions that take place relative to the number of people convicted and those sentenced to death. There is also a great deal of variation over time in homicide rates, making it difficult to impart any changes in homicide to the rare executions (Donohue and Wolfers, 2005; Katz et al., 2003). Donohue and Wolfers (2005) note that the uncertainty of executions makes it difficult to assume that the death penalty would have much of an impact. With rare exceptions, the studies looking exclusively at the severity of the sanction fail to find a deterrent impact in the death penalty.

An alternative possible impact of executions is an increase in subsequent offending. Not surprisingly, most studies do not find a positive relationship between executions and homicide. This finding does appear, however, in an analysis of executions in New York between 1907–1963 (Bowers and Pierce, 1980). Bowers and Pierce claim that there are two more homicides in the month immediately following an execution and one more in the second month after an execution than would be normally expected. It appears that the use of the death penalty causes an absolute increase of three homicides after the execution. Bowers and Pierce (1980) refer to this as the *brutalization effect* of the death penalty. Cochran et al. (1994) and Cochran and Chamblin (2000) report a brutalization effect as a result of executions. Bailey (1998) notes that the evidence for brutalization appears in stranger killings and persists after controlling for other predictors.

Longitudinal studies of deterrence have not been confined to the death penalty. Sanctions for drunk driving also may have a deterrent effect. Ross (1982) reviews the effects of drunk driving laws in different countries. Increases in the severity of sanctions for drunk driving appear to have little, if any, impact on the level of drunk driving. The author notes that changes in the level of severity are often undermined by criminal justice system workers who fail to cite offenders or file different charges (Ross, 1982). One analysis of changes in drunk-driving laws shows a similar lack of a deterrent effect (West et al., 1989). In July 1982, Arizona altered its statutes to mandate a 24-hour jail sentence, license suspension, and a minimum $250 fine for a first drunk-driving offense. Using monthly statistics from 1976 to 1984, West et al. (1989) note that there was a temporary decrease in fatalities and no impact on DWI citations. More importantly, the minor observed changes that did occur appear to be due to media coverage and not the legislated changes. Other analyses of drunk driving legislation confound changes in severity of sanction with the introduction of certainty.

Certainty of Apprehension

Certainty of apprehension and punishment can be studied in a variety of ways. One method involves altering the law. For example, the British Road Safety Act established that a blood alcohol level above .08 percent constitutes an offense (Ross, 1982). There is no question of the guilt of an individual meeting this criteria. Accompanying such certainty levels are increases in the severity of punishments. Severity, however, is secondary to the evaluation of certainty in most studies. Ross (1982) reports that most alterations in the definition of legal drunkenness result in reduced levels of traffic casualties. The effect is short-lived, however, with the numbers of accidents returning to the pre-intervention levels. This appears to hold true across the various jurisdictions examined. Phillips et al. (1984), reexamining the impact of the British Road Safety Act, find that the law has minimal impact on the number of traffic casualties. The number of miles driven and the incidence of rainfall are better explanatory variables. Interestingly, attempts to further increase the certainty of apprehension through the use of intensive police "blitzes" appears to have a positive deterrent effect (Ross, 1982). This holds true at least for the duration of the blitz.

The activity of the police may also provide a deterrent effect. Bursik et al. (1990) evaluate the effect of arrest patterns on neighborhood robbery. The authors examine calls for police service over 100 weeks in five Oklahoma City neighborhoods. An inspection of the data reveals that on-site arrests have no deterrent impact on the number of robberies. Two potential problems in assessing the impact of the police actions involves the low number of robberies and the low on-site arrest rate. Both of these factors may cover an actual impact of arrest (Bursik et al., 1990). D'Alessio and Stolzenberg (1998), using data from Orange County, Florida, report that, as the number of arrests increase, the level of criminal activity the following day significantly declines. The authors claim that police activity is a strong deterrent on future behavior.

Another way of analyzing the impact of police actions is to look at police crackdowns. Sherman's (1990) review of police efforts to crack down on various types of offenses (drunk driving, prostitution, drug sales) find a brief, immediate deterrent impact on the target offense. While the deterrent effect decayed over time, there is evidence of a lingering deterrent impact after the end of some crackdowns (Sherman, 1990). Sherman and Weisburd (1995), reporting on intensive patrol at crime hot spots, find that patrol has a significant deterrent effect on calls for service and crime/disorder. Efforts to interrupt gang violence in Boston through intensive police and criminal justice system intervention also resulted in reduced offending (Kennedy, 2008). Similar analyses of police crackdowns in England also uncover a deterrent effect on crime (Tilley, 2004).

Panel Studies

Several recent analyses have relied on panel data as a means of avoiding problems with both cross-sectional and longitudinal approaches. A *panel design* follows a number of separate units (such as states, counties or individuals) over a period of time. In many respects it is a combination of cross-sectional and longitudinal approaches in a single study. Shepherd (2005) notes that both cross-sectional and longitudinal designs suffer from serious problems. Simple longitudinal designs result in aggregating disparate observations into a single group. The results from one state, for example, may be offset by those from another state, thus masking the results from each individual state. Cross-sectional designs cannot account for changes over time and often miss key differences between study units within the same cross-section. Typical longitudinal and cross-sectional studies also have few observations, both across time and in terms of units (e.g. states) (Shepherd, 2005). Many of the recent panel studies of the death penalty utilize county-level data over a long period of time.

Most of the recent panel analyses claim strong support for a deterrent effect of the death penalty. Dezhbakhsh et al. (2003) investigate the deterrent effect of capital punishment using county-level data for 1977–1996. This data allows them to consider economic, demographic and jurisdictional variations across the counties. Using a complex statistical model, the authors claim that each execution deters 18 homicides (Dezhbakhsh et al., 2003). Shepherd (2004) conducts a similar analysis using state-level panel data and considers both sentences to death row and actual executions as potential deterrents. The author claims that each death row sentence deters 4.5 murders, while each execution results in three fewer homicides. Shepherd (2004) also notes that death sentences that are carried out with greater celerity also reduce the number of homicides.

A final study to be considered here uncovers important qualifiers on the deterrent impact of the death penalty. Shepherd (2005) undertakes a similar panel analysis to those already discussed using county-level data and controls for economic, demographic and jurisdictional factors. While the overall finding is that each execution results in 4.5 fewer murders, the results vary significantly across states. Indeed, the death penalty is a deterrent in six states, while it has a brutalization effect in 13 states. Attempting to identify the reason for this difference between states, Shepherd (2005) considers the number of executions carried out it the different states. She finds that there is a threshold number of executions that must be reached in order for the death penalty to have a deterrent impact. Her analysis shows that there needs to be at least nine executions for capital punishment to be a deterrent to homicide (Shepherd, 2005). States conducting fewer executions will see an increase in homicides (the brutalization effect).

Unfortunately, several methodological concerns with the work of Dezhbakhsh et al. (2003), Shepherd (2004) and others, claiming a strong deterrent effect of the death penalty, call their conclusions into question. As previously mentioned, the wide variation in year-to-year homicide rates makes it difficult to attribute any change in homicide to criminal justice system activity. The few executions, coupled with fluctuating homicide rates, makes it difficult, if not impossible, to detect any impact of executions (Donohue and Wolfers, 2005). Many of the measures of criminal justice system operations included in the analyses are also subject to great variation and measurement error (Fagan et al., 2006), thus affecting the overall results (Tonry, 2008). Donohue and Wolfers (2005) also note that Dezhbakhsh et al.'s (2003) data show increases in many violent personal offenses (including rape and assault) at the same time that it presents questionable changes in homicide. The general consensus is that executions have limited, if any, impact on homicide (see, for example, Fagan et al., 2006; Donohue and Wolfers, 2005; Katz et al., 2003; Pratt et al., 2008).

Summary

The research points to a few general findings. First and foremost, the research presents contradictory results on the deterrent effect of sentences, particularly the death penalty. There is little or no evidence that severity has an individual deterrent effect. Conversely, certainty of apprehension and punishment seems to have some impact on the level of offending. One problem with this latter statement is the fact that many of the studies that look at certainty also are dealing with crimes that have a fairly severe penalty attached. Clearly, increasing the certainty of apprehension and punishment for homicide is accompanied by either the death penalty or substantial lengths of imprisonment. The occurrence of one factor results in the second. Why, then, do studies that look at both severity and certainty only find an effect related to certainty? The answer may revolve around the perceived risk of apprehension and punishment.

PERCEPTIONS AND DETERRENCE

The ability of punishment to deter offenders rests upon various assumptions about the knowledge held by potential violators regarding the law and the criminal justice system. The existence of a law or the actual imposition of a sanction will only affect individuals who perceive risks to themselves. Individuals ignorant of the law cannot be expected to refrain from the proscribed behavior simply due to the law's existence. The lack of knowledge about the chances for arrest and the penalty incurred for breaking the law also may result in a lack of deterrence. For example, simple knowledge that shoplifting is a crime may not be enough to deter. The potential offender may believe that the chances of apprehension are slim and that the penalty for violation is probation (an acceptable alternative for the individual). In either of these cases the chances for deterrence are not great. This lack of deterrent effect is due to the differing perceptions about the law and the criminal justice system held by potential offenders.

Various studies find that offenders, as well as the general population, are often unaware of the legal codes and changes in the law. Andenaes (1975), in a review of studies on public perceptions of law and criminal sanctions, notes that the general public has little knowledge about penalties for offenses. Additionally, offenders find out about sanctions only after becoming involved in the system. He points out that, even if an individual has knowledge about penalties, a move to another state will often result in changes in the law and sanctions. Indeed, statutory changes within a state usually go unnoticed by the populace (Andenaes, 1975). It also must be noted that legal statutes can only give information about possible sanctions. Statutes do not necessarily alter the chances of apprehension or the actual imposition of the maximum penalty possible. Indeed, research demonstrates that the criminal justice system adjusts to accommodate changes in the law through such means as charge and plea bargaining (Tonry, 2008). A variety of other studies also note that the public has little knowledge about the law and changes in statutes (Berger et al., 1990; Tonry, 2008; Williams and Hawkins, 1986; Zimring and Hawkins, 1973). It is important, therefore, to examine the role of perception in the study of general deterrence.

Perceived Certainty

The deterrence literature provides evidence that increased perception of risk is related to reduced deviant behavior. Erickson and associates (1977), surveying 1,700 high school students, find that the level of perceived certainty of arrest or incarceration is inversely related to the level of self-reported delinquency. That is, juveniles who envision higher chances of being arrested or incarcerated for a given offense are less likely to engage in that form of deviant behavior. Erickson et al. (1977) also point out that the social condemnation of an offense may influence the level of offending to the same extent as the perceptions of apprehension and punishment. It may be that the level of social condemnation helps to establish these perceptions of system reaction. Nagin (1998), reviewing the deterrence literature, claims that the research shows a clear impact of perceived risk on reduced chances for committing crime.

Other studies find little impact on perceptions. Jensen et al. (1978), studying 5000 high school students, and Piliavin and associates (1986), examining 17–20 year old dropouts, find little, if any, relationship between perceived certainty of apprehension and self-reported involvement. Indeed, Piliavin et al. (1986) report that the opportunity to commit a crime is more influential than the perception of risk or sanctions. Foglia (1997), testing the influence of perceptions on high school students from low-income, high-crime areas, shows that perceived certainty is not related to self-reported delinquency. The author suggests that the results may be attributable to income and residential status of the respondents.

One of the problems with research on perceived certainty of punishment is the time order of the perception and actual involvement with the criminal justice system. Researchers have questioned whether the perception of apprehension deters crime or whether the actual apprehension of an individual raises the perception of risk (Bishop, 1984a; Bishop, 1984b; Jensen and Stitt, 1982; Paternoster et al., 1982; Paternoster et al., 1985; Saltzman et al., 1982). This latter possibility is termed the *experiential effect*. The problem with most research on perceived certainty of apprehension and punishment is that the analyses measure a person's perceptions and relate that to past deviant behavior. Problematically, a finding of low perceived risk along with past participation in criminal activity may indicate that the lack of past apprehension engenders the current view of low risk (an experiential effect). The perception comes causally after the behavior. The critics of this research point to the need to relate current perceptions to future deviant activity. This then would indicate a deterrent and not an experiential effect.

A number of studies have investigated the relative merits of deterrence and experiential effects. Jensen and Stitt (1982) report on the results of a self-report survey of past behavior, intended future behavior, and perceived risk. They find that the perceived risk of apprehension is significantly related to intentions to violate the law in the future. Individuals who see little risk of apprehension indicate a higher likelihood of violating the law than do other individuals. In addition, they report that perceived risk is a better indicator of future intentions than past deviant behavior (Jensen and Stitt, 1982). The problem with this study is the use of intended behavior in place of actual measures of activity. It is possible that the intentions will never come to fruition.

One solution to the problems of looking at the relation between perceptions and behavior is the use of longitudinal data. Such an approach can measure the perceptions at an earlier point in time and return to measure the actual behavior of the subjects at a later date. Bishop (1984a; 1984b) evaluates the impact of perceptions on future behavior (deterrence effect) and the impact of behavior on future perceptions (experiential effect). She finds that high levels of perceived risk of apprehension result in lower levels of future behavior. This supports the deterrence argument. The effect of past delinquent behavior, however, has a larger effect on subsequent perceptions than the perceptions have on the behavior. This means that the experiential effect is greater than the deterrent outcome (Bishop, 1984a). Three other studies based on self-reports of college freshmen also find that the experiential effect is stronger than the deterrent effect (Paternoster et al., 1982; Paternoster et al., 1985; Saltzman et al., 1982). Paternoster et al. (1985) note that inexperienced individuals who initially hold high perceptions of risk modify their perceptions after they begin to partake in the activity without being arrested. The experience with the behavior, devoid of apprehension, changes the perceptions. This is the experiential effect at work.

Stafford and Warr (1993) reconceptualized experience, both direct and vicarious, as a key element of deterrence. Direct and indirect experiences with punishment and punishment avoidance influence the level of deterrence. In essence, experiences impact on the individual's perceptions. Rather than view experiences as separate from deterrence, they are a vital part of the deterrent effect. Paternoster and Piquero (1995) claim that the "experiential" effect actually molds deterrence factors. Similarly, Jacobs (1996) argues that individuals use experience and situational cues to alter their behavior in order to avoid apprehension and punishment.

The evaluations of perception do not find an absence of deterrence. Rather, they find that deterrence is not as important as the experience of the individual. Each study reports at least a moderate deterrent effect from perceived risk of apprehension. The level of certainty of apprehension, however, is diluted by the absence of past apprehension. At the same time, experience can be conceptualized as a key component of deterrence. These studies also look only at the perception of certainty of apprehension and punishment. Although certainty appears to be the most important of the deterrent criteria, based on the research reported earlier in this chapter, perceptions of severity and celerity, as individual factors and in relation to certainty, need to be investigated.

Perceived Severity

The perception of severity of punishment has not received as much attention as certainty of apprehension. The studies reviewed by Andenaes (1975) look at the knowledge of sanctions and perceptions of severity but do not relate these factors to the deterrence of future behavior. Meier and Johnson (1977) look at self-reports of deviant behavior and reasons given for not offending. Focusing on adult marijuana use, they examine a variety of independent measures including legal variables (e.g., statutory knowledge, perceived severity), social support (i.e. friend's use), attitudes toward drug use, and various demographic factors. They find that as the perceived severity of the sanction increases the level of marijuana use decreases. A measure of certainty of apprehension shows no relation to the dependent variable. Severity, along with the combined legal factors, however, hold minimal influence compared to the contribution of social background characteristics and social support factors (Meier and Johnson, 1977). A replication of this study (Williams, 1983) reports the same basic findings, further questioning the importance of severity in deterrence.

Williams and Hawkins (1989) investigate the impact of arrest and perceived consequences of arrest on wife assault. Included in the study are measures of perceived legal sanctions, chances of going to jail, damage to interpersonal attachments, stigma from arrest, and putting conventional activities (such as one's job) at risk. Surveying married and cohabiting U.S. males, the authors report that the perception of stigma and social disapproval are the greatest concerns of the respondents. The possibility of going to jail and being sanctioned by the legal system are less of a deterrent than the social factors (Williams and Hawkins, 1989). All of these studies may suffer from the competing issues of experiential and deterrent effects discussed earlier.

Combined Deterrence Factors

A few studies attempt to gauge perceptions of certainty, severity, and/or celerity within the same analysis. One study (Tittle, 1977) reports that the level of approval for a behavior outweighs the deterrent aspects of perceived certainty or severity of punishment. Similarly, Hollinger and Clark (1983) find that perceived severity and certainty have a deterrent influence. The level of employee theft diminishes as perceptions of risk increase and the individual sees harsher sanctions as a possible outcome. Pestello (1984) presents the results of a study that considers all three deterrent factors—certainty, severity, and celerity. The author surveyed high school students about their school misbehavior and the perceptions of each of the deterrent elements as they relate to school discipline. The results show that perceived severity and celerity of punishment increases the fear of consequences for behavior that, in turn, reduces the possibility of misbehavior (Pestello, 1984). This is one of the few studies that reports a significant effect of severity on behavior. One potential reason for this is the focus on school misbehavior instead of criminal or delinquent behavior. Unfortunately, each of these studies suffers from the problem of time order in their analyses. The measures of perception are taken at the same time as the measures of behavior, which raises the possibility of the experiential effect.

Two researchers have attempted to isolate the deterrent effects from the possible confounding influences of experiences by using panel studies to evaluate perceptions. Paternoster (1989a; 1989b), surveying high school students, notes that perceived severity and perceived certainty of punishment have only a minor influence on marijuana use, liquor use, petty theft, and vandalism. Decisions to offend or reoffend are based primarily on extralegal factors such as moral beliefs about the behavior, and peer associations and influences (Paternoster, 1989a). A minor deterrent effect appears only in relationship to perceived certainty of marijuana and liquor use among prior non-offenders (Paternoster, 1989b). Concentrating on drinking and driving behavior, Green (1989a; 1989b) also finds that perceived certainty and perceived severity have little impact. The most important influences on drunk-driving behavior are informal, extra-legal factors such as moral commitment, social approval, and demographic differences (Green, 1989a; 1989b). Piquero and Paternoster (1998) similarly find that experience is more influential than deterrence in relation to drinking and driving. These studies add to the argument that perceptions of certainty and severity have little influence on actual behavior.

Klepper and Nagin (1989) provide one of the strongest arguments in favor of perceived certainty and severity as deterrents. The authors report that the perceived probability of detection and prosecution, as well as perceived severity of punishment, are strong deterrents for tax noncompliance. Interestingly, the impact of perceived certainty and severity is not negated by the introduction of demographic factors. The strength of the findings are surprising given past deterrence research. Klepper and Nagin (1989) argue that their findings are unique due to the fact that tax noncompliance is an affirmative action that must be consciously considered. That is, every individual must clearly choose to violate the tax law in light of both costs and incentives for the action. Additionally, they use a very homogeneous sample composed of 163 graduate students in business with a 100 percent response rate. Finally, they provide the respondents with very specific scenarios that alter the level of tax noncompliance. These factors are superior to many other studies that deal with heterogeneous samples and vague questions about actions that the individual may never have to consider taking.

Despite this last study, the overall research on perceptions reports similar findings to the results presented in earlier parts of this chapter. Certainty of apprehension appears to hold the most potential for improving the possibility of deterrence. Both severity and celerity tend to hold little or no impact in deterring behavior. The confounding of deterrent with experiential effects makes clear interpretation of the findings difficult. It does appear, however, that experience plays a larger role in determining perceptions than perceptions have on future behavior. Perceptions do seem to have some deterrent impact for individuals.

SUMMARY

The deterrence literature fails to find any strong compelling arguments that the law and sanctions have any major impact on the level of offending. The most clear cut finding seems to indicate that increased certainty of apprehension and punishment results in reduced offending. Severity appears to have little influence on behavior, except as shown in recent panel analyses of the death penalty. The failure of severity to have much impact may be due to the lack of knowledge that individuals have about the actual sanctions and the chances of being caught and receiving the punishment. An analysis of the perceptual literature, however, fails to clarify the impact of deterrence. The research findings reflect the fact that perceptions are based on past experiences much more than future activities are based on present perceptions. Again, certainty seems to hold the most power.

The finding that certainty of apprehension and punishment is the most important factor suggests that any deterrent effect must rest on efforts by the criminal justice system and society to increase the level of risk for offenders. At the same time, changes that increase perceptions of risk, whether through experience, avoidance or something else, also contribute to deterrence. This risk can come from the crime prevention techniques discussed earlier in the book. Failure to increase the risk of apprehension and punishment does not mean that the crime rate will rise. Rather, it indicates that the sanctioning power of the criminal justice system alone is not enough to keep motivated individuals from offending.

Section II

SECONDARY PREVENTION

The orientation of secondary prevention focuses activity on individuals, places, and situations that have a high potential for deviance. Secondary prevention is concerned with intervening in those situations and with those persons who display a tendency toward criminal behavior. Similar to primary prevention, the emphasis is still on preventing crime prior to its initial occurrence. Once a criminal act has occurred, any intervention that takes place falls under the realm of tertiary prevention. Perhaps the core concern for secondary prevention, therefore, is the prediction of future criminal activity.

The problem of making predictions is taken up in Chapter 9. Typically, prediction is assumed to focus on the behavior of individuals. Two major methods for making predictions of future dangerousness are *clinical* and *actuarial*. These approaches generally fail to make adequate judgments and often result in large numbers of false predictions. The use of criminal careers in prediction offers other insight, particularly because past criminal behavior is closely related to future transgressions. Besides trying to make accurate predictions, it may be possible to identify risk factors for future behavior. In this case the idea is to uncover factors that are strongly related to later criminality. A third approach is to try to identify locations or situations where deviance is more likely. Consequently the focus shifts from people to places, times, and circumstances. Each of these approaches to prediction is considered.

The remaining chapters look at specific interventions. Chapter 10 focuses on situational crime prevention. Situational prevention techniques target specific problems, places, persons, or times. Problem identification and program planning are cornerstones to the situational approach. The impact of these interventions are more focused than typically found in primary prevention, although many of the same ideas will be used, particularly physical design changes. Chapter 11 shifts our focus to the role of the police and partnerships in crime prevention activity. Community policing and partnerships are relatively new ideas and seek to build cooperative alliances among the police, other agencies, and citizens. Local problems and potential solutions will be identified through the interaction among all interested parties. Similarly, the preventive actions will depend on a variety of people. The police act as "community managers" in the situational orientation and are key actors in any partnership.

Chapter 12 looks at the question of drug use and its relationship to crime. While drug use and trafficking have become major concerns again in recent years, we know little about the causal relationship between drug use and crime. What is known is that there is a strong correlation between drug use and deviant activity. Targeting drug users, therefore, is one method of identifying individuals at risk of committing other offenses. The chapter looks at the extent of drug use, the connection between drug use and crime, and the treatment/ prevention programs aimed at curbing drug use.

Another possible source of intervention, aimed primarily at youths, is the schools. Schools are in a prime position to identify and intervene with juveniles heading toward criminal activity. Chapter 13 examines the role schools play in engendering deviant lifestyles as well as the secondary preventive efforts that schools can provide. The emphasis of secondary prevention on the future behavior of potential deviants leads to discussions of juveniles and delinquent activity. Most intervention with adults occurs after the commission of a criminal act and, thus, falls under tertiary prevention, which is discussed later.

Chapter 9

PREDICTION FOR SECONDARY PREVENTION

Key Terms:

actuarial prediction
adolescent-limited offending
authority conflict
boost explanation
clinical prediction
covert behavior
CRAVED
ecological fallacy
event dependency
false negative predictions
false positive predictions

flag explanation
hot products
hot spots
life-course-persistent offending
near repeat
overt behavior
prospective mapping
repeat victimization
risk factors
risk heterogeneity
virtual repeats

Learning Objectives:

After reading this chapter you should be able to:

- Identify key factors in making predictions about future behavior in criminal justice

- Distinguish between false positive and false negative predictions

- Compare and contrast clinical and actuarial prediction

- Discuss criminal career research and its use for prediction

- Identify different categories of risk factors for crime and provide examples of factors within each category

- Define life-course-persistent and adolescent-limited offending

- Identify three pathways to delinquent behavior

- Demonstrate your knowledge of hot spots, hot products, and prospective mapping
- Define repeat victimization and discuss its extent
- List and discuss different types of repeat victimization
- Compare and contrast risk heterogeneity and event dependency explanations for repeat victimization
- Provide arguments for why targeting repeat victimization makes sense for crime prevention

Secondary prevention techniques rest heavily on the idea of identification and prediction. Rather than intervene with entire communities or neighborhoods, or establish programs to reach the general public, secondary prevention techniques rely on efforts to identify potential offenders, places, or situations that have a higher likelihood for criminal activity. One primary problem for secondary prevention, therefore, is proper identification and prediction. Predicting who will and who will not become deviant, where and when crime will occur, who will be a victim, what items will be targeted by offenders, and related topics is often a difficult or involved effort. This chapter briefly explores the problem of prediction and identification for prevention purposes. The discussion is divided into three general areas. These are predicting offending behavior, analysis of risk factors for deviance, and identifying places, times, and individual victimization.

PREDICTING FUTURE OFFENDING

Making predictions about future behavior, whether deviant or conventional, involves making a number of initial decisions. Perhaps the first issue is the determination of what is being predicted. In criminal justice, predicting recidivism is perhaps the most common endeavor. Impact evaluations of interventions, whether punitive or rehabilitative, typically look at various measures of subsequent offending. Rearrest, reconviction, reincarceration, seriousness of future activity, and revocation of probation or parole are common measures of recidivism. Prediction of recidivistic activity, however, does not address the central concern of secondary prevention, which would be predictions of initial deviant acts by individuals. This is often expressed in terms of predicting potential dangerousness. Potential dangerousness is an important consideration in the activity of criminal justice professionals and nowhere is this more evident than in the juvenile justice system, which is premised upon potential future involvement in adult criminal activity. Secondary prevention hopes to keep the potential offender from ever realizing that potential.

Prediction also requires choosing the proper variables for use in the analyses. Some variables or indicators will predict future behavior better than others. The challenge is to identify the best predictors. The choice of predictor variables often reflects the orientation of the researcher making the prediction. Psychologically trained evaluators typically rely on information gathered by means of clinical interviews and psychological tests covering an individual's personality, interpersonal relationships, and life experiences. More sociologically oriented classifiers look to age, ethnicity, socioeconomic status, group affiliation, family background, and other demographic factors. Past deviant behavior and contact with formal systems of control are typically important for all researchers. Seldom are all of the variables used in the same study. It is the selective choice of variables that may invalidate or limit the applicability of the predictions.

A final important consideration in predicting future behavior is the degree of accuracy in the predictions. When we make a prediction and it proves to be accurate, we are not concerned. On the other hand, making wrong predictions can have dire consequences. Error in prediction takes two forms—false positive and false negative predictions. Each of these has a different impact on the individual being evaluated and/or society. In terms of criminal/deviant behavior, *false positive predictions* are those in which an individual is predicted to do something in the future (e.g., recidivate, offend, act dangerously) but is not found to act in that fashion after follow-up. Conversely, *false negative predictions* declare that the person is not a future threat but the individual does engage in the negative behavior at a later time.

Table 9.1
Potential Outcomes of Prediction

True Positive Prediction	something is predicted to occur and it does (a successful prediction)
False Positive Prediction	something is predicted to occur but it does not (a failed prediction)
True Negative Prediction	something is predicted not to occur and it does not (a successful prediction)
False Negative Prediction	something is predicted not to occur but it does occur (a failed prediction)

The problems inherent in false predictions should be quite evident. "Potential" offenders or recidivists often are subjected to interventions or harsher and/or more prolonged treatment or punishment because of that potential. A false prediction means that the individual is unduly denied his or her freedom based on an inaccurate finding. On the other hand, false negative predictions may result in ignoring individuals, or the early or outright release of individuals who will cause further harm to society. Mistakes of this kind subject society to unnecessary harm. Given the complexity of human behavior, it is unreasonable to suggest that prediction methods will ever be able to completely eliminate the incidence of false positive and false negative predictions. The issue, therefore, is limiting the number of false predictions.

Types of Prediction

Prediction generally falls into one of two categories—clinical prediction and actuarial prediction. Clinical predictions have predominated in criminal justice, particularly in terms of sentencing and treating individuals. Actuarial prediction has been a more recent choice given the availability of large amounts of data and problems with clinical techniques. A specialized actuarial approach uses criminal career information to predict future deviance. Each of these is discussed below.

Clinical Prediction

Clinical predictions are based on a rater's evaluation of an individual, usually after interviews and direct examination of the subject and his or her records. The training and disposition of the individual rater often determines what variables and factors are important in arriving at a decision. The rater can use various psychological tests, demographic information about the individual, family and individual background information, or interviews of the subject in making a determination. There are no firm rules for which items must be used, when they should be used, which are the most important, or whether more than one type of information is used. In most cases, the individual rater has total discretion.

Research on the clinical prediction of violence reveals a great tendency for false determinations, both positive and negative. Monahan (1981), summarizing some of the more well-known clinical studies, finds remarkably consistent results, despite variation in what is being predicted, follow-up periods, and predictive items used in the studies. In all nine studies he reviews, the percent of false positive predictions exceeds 50 percent and in six of the nine analyses it is more than 80 percent. These false positive predictions are disturbing, particularly in cases in which extended follow-up periods are considered. Longer follow-up should reduce the evidence of false positive predictions. For individuals predicted to commit an act of violence or aggression, few actually do so. Conversely, the false negative predictions are very small. Despite this, the combined level of false positives and false negatives is unacceptable. These results seriously damage any claim of predictive efficacy of clinical diagnosis.

A number of factors may explain the poor clinical predictions. First, the determination of subsequent offending or dangerousness may be too strict. Many analyses require actual injury to another person or reincarceration during the follow-up period. An offender, however, may not be severely sanctioned even though harm is committed by the individual. Second, the variables being used to determine future behavior may not be predictive of the type of behavior under consideration. This is a clear possibility given the level of disagreement found among individuals who normally conduct clinical evaluations. Ziskin (1970) notes that agreement between two psychiatrists cannot be found more than about 50 to 60 percent of the time. A final set of problems relates to the adequacy of the information on which evaluators make their judgments. Many clinical interviews are of short duration, which allow only minimal observation. Predictions based on limited observations may produce predictions based on incomplete or distorted information. These factors, among others (see Ennis and Litwack, 1974; Pfohl, 1978; Scheff, 1966; Scheff, 1967), may account for the great levels of false predictions found in clinical studies.

Actuarial Predictions

Actuarial prediction refers to making predictions based on known parameters in the data. The best example of actuarial prediction is the setting of rates by the insurance industry. The cost of life insurance is based on the known mortality rates for the population group to which the applicant belongs. Males have shorter life spans, on the average, than females. This results in shorter periods in which to pay into the insurance account. In turn, the premiums for insurance are slightly higher for males. The prediction is based solely on known, statistical factors. Similarly, car insurance rates are determined by past accident levels and claims. Young males are involved in more accidents, which leads to higher insurance premiums for all young males.

The key to actuarial prediction is the identification of the appropriate predictive items. Factors typically used in criminal justice include age, race, sex, socioeconomic status, educational status, IQ, criminal history, the immediate offense, family background, and psychological test results. As in the clinical studies, actuarial evaluations greatly vary in their choice of items and techniques.

Burgess (1928) introduced a simple form of actuarial prediction in which individuals were scored as either 0 or 1 based on the presence or absence of certain predictive factors. The U.S. Parole Commission's Salient Factor Score was a prime example of this technique (Gottfredson et al., 1975). The original Salient Factor Score included seven items predictive of past success on parole (see Table 9.2). One point was awarded for each item characterizing an individual. Prisoners who accumulated higher numbers of points were viewed as better risks and subsequently awarded parole release. Greenwood (1982), using a Burgess-type method with self-report data from incarcerated adult offenders, claimed to be able to predict who was a high-rate and who was a low-rate offender. Unfortunately, flaws in the methodology limited the applicability of the results and the scale made a large number of false predictions (Decker and Salert, 1986).

Table 9.2
Example of Salient Factor Score Items

1.	No prior convictions
2.	No prior incarcerations
3.	A first commitment at age 18 or later
4.	A commitment offense that does not include auto theft
5.	No prior parole revocations
6.	No drug dependence
7.	At least a high school education
8.	Having been employed at least six months in the prior two years before incarceration
9.	A place to live with relatives and/or family upon release

Source: D.M. Gottfredson et al. (1975)."Making Paroling Policy Explicit." *Crime and Delinquency* 21:34–44.

A wide variety of techniques have been used to construct actuarial prediction scales. The methods vary from the simple additive procedures of Burgess (1928) to more sophisticated techniques, including multiple regression, predictive attribute analysis, association analysis. The results of these different approaches, however, do not uncover any single best method (Farrington, 1985; Gottfredson and Gottfredson, 1985; Wilbanks, 1985). Similar results emerge when using each and there is often little predictive power in any of the methods. Wilbanks (1985) reports between 25 and 33 percent false predictions for different methods. Similarly, Farrington (1985) finds that an average of 45 to 50 percent of the predictions are false positive predictions, regardless of the method used, with false negative predictions comprising about 10 to 15 percent of the negative estimates.

A number of observations can be made about actuarial prediction based on the foregoing discussion. First, the level of error is smaller than that found in clinical studies (Meehl, 1954; Wilbanks, 1985). Second, the use of different predictive techniques does not appear to alter the results. The level of error remains about the same across methods, although different individuals are misclassified in the various approaches. Finally, on the negative side, actuarial prediction consistently attempts to predict individual behavior based on group data. This is a totally inappropriate use of the data and is referred to as the *ecological fallacy*. It is not possible (barring very specific circumstances) to impute the behavior of a single person from the activity of a larger group (Stouthamer-Loeber and Loeber, 1989). Instead, the results of an actuarial approach suggest that, given a group of people with certain characteristics, including a certain percentage of offending individuals, the same percentage of persons from an identical group would be expected to act in the same fashion. It is not possible, however, to identify which individuals will make up that offending percentage. Clearly, the inevitable result of both clinical and actuarial prediction is some degree of false prediction.

Criminal Career Research

One strong predictor of future criminal behavior is past offending (see, for example, Blumstein et al., 1985; Chaiken and Chaiken, 1982; Farrington, 1983; Gottfredson and Gottfredson, 1986; Peterson et al., 1981; Stouthamer-Loeber and Loeber, 1989). This fact has led many researchers to examine criminal careers as a means of improving the prediction of criminal behavior. In these analyses, past criminal behavior is used to predict future offending. Criminal career research uses known patterns of deviant behavior to establish the probability of offending for similar subjects.

One approach to studying criminal careers involves the inspection of behavior for *career specialization*. This is especially appropriate for a discussion of secondary prevention because findings of specialization could be used to tailor an intervention strategy aimed at individual problem groups. Unfortunately, studies of specialization typically find that individuals partake in a wide range of activity over the span of their lives (see, for example, Erickson, 1979; Petersilia et al., 1978). Specialization appears primarily among individuals committing 10 or more offenses (Farrington et al., 1988) and with some adults committing drug offenses, burglary, robbery, and fraud (Blumstein et al., 1988; Kempf, 1986, 1987; Stander et al., 1989). It is important to note that, while the degree of specialization among some adults is greater than expected by chance, diversity in offending is much more common.

Another approach to criminal career research involves investigating patterns of activity. This research looks for changes in offending over time. It may be possible to predict, based on patterns, which individuals will continue their behavior and which will cease. In perhaps the most well-known study of patterns in offending, Wolfgang et al. (1972) look at change in behavior from one point in time to another for a sample of 3,475 Philadelphia boys. The authors find tremendous crossover between offenses and this diversity persists throughout the careers of the subjects. At no point in the careers do clear patterns or movement to specific types of offending take place (see also Rojek and Erickson, 1982). A major shortcoming of this study is that it only looks at subsequent offenses based on the one, immediately preceding, offense. It is not known whether knowledge of multiple past offenses would improve the prediction of later offenses. Lab (1984a) attempts to address this shortcoming by inspecting changes through the past 10 offenses for three birth cohorts of juveniles. While he uncovers no clear patterns of offending, the results show that most offending is confined to status and victimless offenses, and only six percent of the subjects ever commit a major property or personal offense. Only three percent ever have contact for two or more major offenses (Lab, 1984a). Interestingly, these studies report a high level of desistance, with two-thirds to three-quarters of the juveniles ceasing offending before a fourth offense and prior to becoming an adult.

The failure of research to uncover clear patterns in criminal careers does not mean that useful information is absent in the studies. An important finding from the research is that youthful offenders who continue on to adult careers are those who commit more frequent and more serious offenses as juveniles (Kempf, 1988; Shannon, 1982). Unfortunately, the finding that delinquent behavior predicts later misconduct does not mean it is impossible to make accurate predictions of which individuals will continue offending. Knowledge of conviction as a juvenile only improves prediction of adult behavior by 20 percent (Shannon, 1983). Instead, past deviant activity should be considered as a risk factor (see discussion later in this chapter).

In summary, studies of criminal careers typically fall short of their goal. There is a lack of specialization in offending and an absence of patterns in deviant behavior. Perhaps the one fact that most researchers agree on is that chronic offenders (typically defined as having five or more police contacts) tend to continue committing crime. Indeed, chronic juvenile offenders are more likely to become serious adult offenders. The usefulness of this information, however, is limited because one cannot predict who will have a serious criminal career until the career has already been established.

Prediction and Crime Prevention

Prediction remains an integral part of many activities in the criminal justice system. Decisions made at all levels of the system involve prediction, although rarely is "prediction" a conscious part of the decision. Choices by police officers to arrest, by prosecutors to press charges, by judges to sentence, and by parole commissions to release offenders all involve predicting the likelihood of future deviant behavior. Unfortunately, prediction is often inaccurate. The usefulness of traditional clinical, actuarial, and even criminal career techniques for prediction in crime prevention is suspect.

RISK FACTORS AND PREDICTION

A more recent trend in identifying who will commit offenses (i.e., prediction) involves the identification of risk factors related to deviant behavior. Most discussions of risk factors do not make the assumption that individuals who exhibit these traits will inevitably become criminal or act in some inappropriate fashion. Rather, the risk factors are indicators of who may become deviant in the future. There is usually no attempt to make predictions about specific individuals. The risk factors are only indicators or flags that can signal the need for increased attention or possible assistance for individuals.

The identification of potential risk factors is not a new idea. Indeed, the idea of working with youths at risk of becoming delinquents or later adult criminals is a cornerstone of the juvenile justice system. The very premise of the juvenile court is to work with troubled at-risk youths. Implicit in this task is the idea of identifying the factors underlying the juvenile's behavior and working to alter those conditions. Likewise, most criminological theory is based on the idea of identifying the best predictors of criminal activity in order to develop appropriate interventions. While not typically referred to as risk factors, the variables that are found to be related to delinquency and criminality are risk factors. A good deal of research in recent years has shifted to an explicit focus on identifying risk factors.

Risk factors can be broken down into various categories. Typical groupings found in the literature are family, peer, community, psychological/personality, and biological risk factors (see Table 9.3). While different authors may classify individual risk factors slightly differently, these categories are generally representative of those used in the literature. The information presented below is not intended as an exhaustive list of risk factors. Rather, the intent is to offer some insight into some of the more recognized variables that have been discussed in the literature.

Table 9.3
Common Risk Factors Found in the Research

Family
  parental criminality
  poor parental supervision
  harsh discipline
  inconsistent discipline
  abuse/maltreatment
  family bonding/relationships
  broken homes
  family size
  socioeconomic status
  family conflict
  family functioning

Peers
  gang membership
  peer deviance/criminality
  sibling criminality

Community
  economic deprivation/poverty
  disorder/incivilities
  availability of firearms/drugs
  socioeconomic status
  gang activity
  area crime/violence
  community disorganization

Table 9.3 *Cont'd.*

School
    suspension/expulsion
    truancy
    school attitude
    academic failure
    school quality
    dropping out

Psychological/Personality
    hyperactivity
    impulsivity
    inability to concentrate
    learning disabilities
    low IQ
    anxiety
    aggressiveness

Biological
    prenatal complications
    perinatal complications
    low birth weight
    drug use during pregnancy
    poor nutrition
    neurotransmitter problems
    low at rest heart rate
    neurological injuries

Family Factors

A wide range of family situations and factors influence both the immediate care of an individual as well as later behavior. One factor often promoted in the literature is the relation between parental criminality and the behavior of the offspring. Farrington (1989) claims that having a parent arrested is related to later offending by male offspring. This relationship appears in a variety of other studies (e.g. Farrington, 1996; Farrington and Loeber, 1998; McCord, 1977; West and Farrington, 1973). A related risk factor deals with poor parental supervision and inconsistent and harsh discipline. In one early study, McCord (1979) found a strong relationship between youthful offending and the type of parental discipline and supervision. Capaldi and Patterson (1996), Hawkins et al. (1995), Loeber and Stouthamer-Loeber (1986), Wells and Rankin (1988) and others report that violence and aggression are more prevalent for youths from homes exercising harsh and inconsistent discipline.

Another factor often pointed to as a predictor of later deviant behavior is being the recipient of or witness to abuse and maltreatment. In perhaps the most recognized study on this topic, Widom (1989) finds that both physical abuse and neglect predict later participation in criminal activity. Data from the

Rochester Youth Study uncover similar findings (Smith and Thornberry, 1995). While these results support commonly held beliefs about the impact of abuse on later behavior, there is evidence in these same studies that the impact varies by type of abuse (such as between physical abuse and neglect) and inclusion of other factors (such as age, race, sex, etc.). These facts, however, do not eliminate the general finding that maltreatment is related to later deviance.

Other family factors that are considered in the literature include family relations or bonding (Catalano and Hawkins, 1996; Farrington and Loeber, 1998; Gorman-Smith et al., 1996; Hirschi, 1969), family size (Capaldi and Patterson, 1996; Farrington and Loeber, 1998), and broken homes (Farrington and Loeber, 1998). The most important observation to make based on this varied literature is that family functioning is an important contributor to the present and future behavior of youths. The identification of family risk factors offers an opportunity to develop appropriate interventions.

Peer Factors

The influence of peers is generally viewed as one of the most important factors involved in adolescent behavior (Elliott, 1994; Elliott and Menard, 1996; Lipsey and Derzon, 1998; Thornberry et al., 1995). Of particular importance to adolescence is the presence and/or participation in youth gangs. Participation in gangs is related to higher levels of offending (Esbensen and Huizinga, 1993; Thornberry et al., 1993; Thornberry, 1998) as well as initiation into deviant activity (Elliott and Menard, 1996). Data from the Cambridge Youth Study suggests that the antisocial behavior of siblings is also a potential predictor of delinquent activity (Farrington, 1989).

Community Influences on Behavior

Another potential source of risk is the community within which an individual is raised and lives. Studies of community influences are long-standing in criminology, with some of the earliest analyses being the work of Shaw and McKay (1942) and their contemporaries in Chicago. That early work forms the basis of many recent analyses that look to community problems, such as economic deprivation, disorder/incivility, poor neighborhood integration and similar factors, as contributors to individual deviance (see, for example, Bursik and Grasmick, 1993; Sampson and Lauritsen, 1994; Shannon, 1991; Skogan, 1990). Other community influences related to levels of delinquency and criminality include the availability of firearms (Block and Block, 1993; Lizotte et al., 1994; Sheley and Wright, 1995), low socioeconomic status (Elliott et al., 1989; Farrington, 1989; Lipsey and Derzon, 1998; Smith and Jarjoura, 1988), and level of gang activity (see above). Each of these community factors contributes to the level of risk.

Another set of community factors that contribute to risk involves schools. While schools are a part of the community, they may contribute uniquely to risk. Poor academic performance and school failure are common factors related to current and later deviance. Hirschi (1969) points out that schools and academic participation are key factors in delinquent behavior. Various studies show that dropping out of school and low academic achievement are strong correlates of delinquency (Farrington, 1989; Gold and Mann, 1972; Thornberry et al., 1985; West and Farrington, 1973). In a recent study, Maguin and Loeber (1996) argue that problems and failure at school are significantly related to the extent and seriousness of delinquency. While a relationship between school factors and delinquency clearly exists, the exact causal mechanism between the various factors is not as easily identified. This issue will receive more attention in Chapter 13.

Psychological/Personality Factors

An array of psychological and personality variables have been identified as risk factors for aggressive behavior. Brennan et al. (1993) note that hyperactivity among preteens is significantly related to violent behavior during the young adult years. Similar results appear in research comparing hyperactive boys with their non-hyperactive siblings (Loney et al., 1983). Impulsivity and problems with concentration also are related to higher levels of adolescent deviance (Farrington, 1989; Farrington and Loeber, 1998; Loney et al., 1983). Other factors often related to deviant behavior include learning disabilities, low IQ, and similar issues that may inhibit an individual's success in school and elsewhere (see, for example, Denno, 1990; Lipsey and Derzon, 1998; Loeber et al., 1993; Loeber et al., 1995; Maguin and Loeber, 1996).

Biological Risk Factors

Biological risk factors are identified in a number of studies, although they do not receive the same degree of attention as other groups of factors. The major reason for this state of affairs is the fact that criminology is dominated by social scientists who focus their attention on other variables. Among the possible biologically based risk factors are prenatal and perinatal complications (Brewer et al., 1995; Farrington, 1996; Kandel and Mednick, 1991; Reiss and Roth, 1993). Included here are low birth weights, complications with pregnancy, drug use while pregnant, and poor nutrition. Neurotransmitters, such as serotonin, are other biological risk factors possibly related to deviant behavior (Moffitt et al., 1997). Neurotransmitters are bodily chemicals that transmit messages in the brain. Yet another biological factor related to violent delinquent behavior is a low resting heart rate (Farrington, 1997; Raine, 1993).

The evidence for the impact of many of these factors on later behavior is relatively weak (see, for example, Denno, 1990), although there is some evidence of a relationship in various studies.

Using Risk Factors as Predictors

Many researchers attempt to use risk factors as predictors of later deviance. Lipsey and Derzon (1998) conducted a meta-analysis to specify risk factors from two different age groups—ages six to 11 and ages 12 to 14—on violent and serious behavior among individuals ages 15 to 25. They report that the key predictors from the six-to-11 age group are general offending and substance use, socioeconomic status of the family, having antisocial parents, and being male. From the 12-to-14 age group, the best predictors are general offending, violence and aggression, and having antisocial peers. Overall, offending, substance use, and antisocial peers are the strongest risk factors for later deviant behavior (Lipsey and Derzon, 1998). A very important qualifier in their study, however, is the fact that there is a high level of false positive predictions using these risk factors. That is, use of the risk factors to predict behavior will err by predicting many individuals will be deviant when, in fact, they will not.

A second analysis attempts to show differences between risk factors for two types of offending. These are *life-course-persistent* and *adolescence-limited* offending. In simple terms, Howell and Hawkins (1998) are attempting to identify risks of continuing deviant behavior over the long term (i.e., life-course persistent), as opposed to offending mainly in adolescence (i.e., adolescence-limited). Among the risk factors for life-course-persistent offending are poor social environments, social cognitive difficulties, poor academic abilities, poor family management, and neuropsychological problems. Conversely, adolescence-limited offending risk factors include prior antisocial behavior, poor parent-child relations, antisocial peers, and poor academic performance (Howell and Hawkins, 1998). Based on this information, the authors offer various suggestions for interventions aimed at the key risk factors. Data from the Pittsburgh Youth Study also illuminate the use of risk factors to attack deviant behavior. Kelly et al. (1997) and Browning and Loeber (1999) identify three pathways to delinquent behavior. The first, *authority conflict*, reflects early stubbornness, which leads to later defiance and avoidance of authority. Related problems include running away, truancy, and ungovernability. *Covert behavior* typically begins with minor acts of lying and theft, moves on to property crimes (such as vandalism and property destruction) and then moderately serious delinquency (such as joyriding and more serious theft), and eventually culminates in serious property delinquency, including burglary and auto theft. The final pathway of *overt behavior* commences with aggressive activity (bullying and teasing) and leads to fighting and violent activity (Kelly et al., 1997). It is important to note that these pathways are neither mutually exclusive nor exhaustive. That is, some youths will exhibit activity in all three and others may not be limited to these avenues. The authors show that many of the Pittsburgh youths fall into one of these patterns. The research also notes various risk factors, especially learning disorders, prior violence, problem behavior at home, and impulsivity (Browning and Loeber, 1999; Kelly et al., 1997).

The results of these studies suggest that risk factors are useful tools in identifying potential problem individuals. What is rarely identified is the accuracy of predictions that rely on these risk factors. Explicit attempts to assess accuracy do not always provide promising results (Lipsey and Derzon, 1998). Most analyses identify risk factors based on prior correlational analyses and fail to test the adequacy of any predictions based on those findings.

Risk factors should be used as indicators of possible future problem behavior. They should not be viewed as good predictors of behavior. Indeed, many individuals, particularly youths, may exhibit many of the risk factors but fail to ever act in socially inappropriate ways. Because many risk factors are indicative of conditions or situations that are not optimal for normal functioning, they should be considered as a signal that some intervention is needed for the best interests of the individual. Should the interventions also reduce the level of subsequent offending, this would be an added bonus. Perhaps more appropriately for crime prevention, individuals who are already exhibiting antisocial behavior should be examined for signs of risk factors, and action should be taken to correct or ameliorate the problem.

PREDICTING PLACES AND EVENTS

Prediction for secondary prevention does not have to be limited to predicting which individuals in which situations will turn to delinquency or criminality. It is also possible to consider predicting the where and when of offending/victimization. This activity is not a new or unique idea. Indeed, it is common for police agencies to distribute their resources differentially across their jurisdiction and at different times of the day. Further, classic research on crime examined the timing of events, albeit crudely, according to season of the year (see Lab and Hirschel, 1988, for a discussion). Today, researchers are employing new and developing technologies and data sources for identifying the "where" and "when" of offending. The following discussion will look at prediction in terms of Hot Spot analysis, Repeat Victimization, and related topics.

Hot Spots for Crime

It has long been common practice for the police to identify locations and times that are more prone to criminal activity. Neighborhood bars, for example, experience more aggression and violence than lounges in nice restaurants. Similarly, assault is more prevalent in the evening than during the mid-morning. Knowing even these two basic facts shows that many problems cluster in both time and place. The challenge, therefore, is to identify these clusters and use that information as a starting point for implementing appropriate interventions.

Perhaps the most recognizable example of this activity involves "hot spot" research. Sherman (1995:36) defines *hot spots* as "small places in which the occurrence of crime is so frequent that it is highly predictable, at least over a one-year period." Analyzing calls for police service in Minneapolis, Sherman et al. (1989) find that 50 percent of all calls for service came from only three percent of the locations. All domestic disturbance calls appear at the same nine percent of the places, all assaults are at seven percent of the locations, all burglaries occur at 11 percent of the places, and all robbery, sexual misconduct, and auto theft calls appear at five percent of the possible locations. Similarly, Spelman (1995) notes that 10 percent of the locations in Boston account for 30 percent of police calls for service.

Attempts to identify hot spots are also useful in pointing out what types of crimes and locations coincide. Block and Block (1995), using mapping techniques to examine crime data for three Chicago communities, report that hot spots often surround elevated transit stops and major intersections. These are locations where potential victims can be located and offenders have options for escape. Looking at auto theft in Philadelphia, Rengert (1997) identifies hot spots but notes that the locations of the hot spots change according to different times of the day and night. Tourist attractions and educational institutions may be hot spots for auto theft during the day, while entertainment venues, bars, and other adult night spots become greater target areas in the evenings and at night (Rengert, 1997). Clearly, hot spots can be anywhere—businesses, schools, abandoned buildings, vacant lots, housing complexes or intersections—or anytime—evenings, late night, weekends, holidays, or vacation months.

An important qualifier when considering hot spots should be stability over time. That is, is the identified crime concentration a temporary situation, or does the hot spot persist over a period of time? The answer to this question is critical for whether the hot spot can be targeted for intervention. If it is a transitory condition, any intervention may take place after the hot spot has dissipated. Any prevention initiative would need to shift as well (Johnson et al., 2008). Unfortunately, it is not uncommon for the question of temporal variation to go unaddressed. Townsley and Pease (2002) argue that relying on hot spots identified with limited temporal data may lead to targeting anomalous crime concentrations that will disappear as the crime settles back to its normal level (i.e., a regression artifact). Perhaps more importantly, Johnson et al. (2005; 2008) claim that the movement of crime, even over short periods, limits the value of identifying hot spots using traditional methods. The authors suggest the use of *prospective mapping*, or the creation of maps that predict future crime locations based on knowledge of recent events. This is based on findings that show a burglary at one location results in heightened chances of victimization at nearby locations (Johnson and Bowers, 2004). Prospective mapping alleviates the problem of targeting hot spots when they move around.

A finding that crime concentrates in certain locations or at certain times suggests that the targeting of hot spots may be an effective starting point for crime prevention. The identification of a hot spot should prompt analyses to uncover what factors make a location a good spot for crime (Spelman, 1995) and offer insight into preventive responses. One set of tools that is becoming a central component to police planning is computer mapping programs. Software, such as the Spatial and Temporal Analysis of Crime program (STAC) and Drug Market Analysis Program (DMAP), are commonplace in policing (Rich, 1995). Mapping and hot spot research can supply information not only on crime but also on information about the neighborhood, site, or time at which an activity is taking place.

An interesting new approach to hot spots is the idea of *hot products*. Clarke (1999) discusses hot products as items that attract attention and are targeted by thieves. Further, such items may help explain the existence and distribution of hot spots. Hot products are those that fit Felson and Clarke's (1998) idea of *VIVA*: **V**alue, **I**nertia, **V**isibility and **A**ccessibility. *Value* is determined by potential offenders and not necessarily the monetary cost of the item. What has value today may not be of interest tomorrow. This could be due to the maturation of the offender, the saturation of the item in society, changes in taste, or other factors. *Inertia* deals with the weight and portability of the item. Further, a target can only be at risk if it is *Visible* to potential offenders. Finally, the target must be *Accessible* to offenders (Felson and Clarke, 1998). The extent to which a target meets these criteria will have an impact on the chances of an offense occurring.

Clarke (1999) expands on the idea of VIVA by proposing CRAVED (**C**oncealable, **R**emovable, **A**vailable, **E**njoyable, and **D**isposable), which further explains the existence of hot spots. Clarke argues that identifying and acknowledging the influence of "hot products" leads to a number of potential prevention measures. Physical design ideas, such as electronic tagging, location transmitters, bar coding, and similar methods of identifying property are prime examples of ways to address hot products. It is also possible to develop other actions specifically aimed at hot products.

Repeat Victimization

Yet another recent topic in the literature involves identifying repeat victimization and focusing efforts to prevent future transgressions. *Repeat victimization* can be considered in terms of both people or places being victimized at least a second time within some period of time subsequent to an initial victimization event. Farrell (2005) offers six types of repeat victimization (see Table 9.4). These types are analogous to the variation found in forms of displacement offered in Chapter 6. For example, target repeat victimization considers the same person or place being victimized at least a second time. Target repeat is the one most commonly referenced in discussions of repeat victimization. No matter which type is being considered, the assumption is that evidence of recurring victimization can be used for directing preventive actions.

Table 9.4
Typology of Repeat Victimization

Repeat Type	Characteristics	Examples
Target	Crime against the same target	Crime against the same person, building, household, vehicle, or other target, however defined
Tactical (virtual)	Crimes requiring the same skill, or modus operandi, to commit. Often the same type of target	Particular type of locks picked (on different types of property); Web sites with particular types of security are repeatedly targeted; theft of same model of car; burglary of property with same layout
Temporal	An offending spree—temporal proximity is the defining characteristic	Multiple burglaries of different properties in the same night; theft of car, then a robbery and getaway
Spatial (near)	Crime in nearby location due to proximity and characteristics	High-crime areas; hot spots
Crime type	The same target victimized by different types of crime	The same target is burglarized, assaulted, robbed at different times
Offender	Victimization of same target by different offenders	A property appears attractive to different offenders; any easy or rewarding target

Source: Farrell, G. (2005). "Progress and Prospects in the Prevention of Repeat Victimization." In Tilley, N. (ed.), *Handbook of Crime Prevention and Community Safety*. Portland, OR: Willan Publishing. Reprinted with permission.

A variety of recent studies note that repeat victimization is not an uncommon event. Polvi et al. (1990) are credited with introducing the idea of repeat victimization. In their analysis, the risk of being a repeat burglary victim is 12 times higher than expected and this risk is more pronounced immediately after an initial burglary. This heightened risk persists for roughly three months and then levels off to normal expected levels. Other writers rely on major victimization surveys, such as the National Crime Victimization Survey (NCVS), the British Crime Survey (BCS), or the International Crime Victim Survey (ICVS) to demonstrate the existence of repeat victimization.

Ellingworth et al. (1995), using BCS data from 1982 through 1992, point out that roughly one-quarter to one-third of all property crime is committed against people victimized five or more times within a one-year period. This means that almost two-thirds of victims are repeat victims. Similarly, roughly 50 percent of personal crimes appear as repeat victimizations (Ellingworth et al., 1995). Using data from the 2000 ICVS, Farrell et al. (2005) find that roughly 40 percent of the crimes are repeat offenses. The level of repeat victimization ranges from a high of 43 percent for sexual crimes to a low of nine percent for car theft. More than one-third of assaults and threats are also repeats (Farrell et al., 2005).

One problem with identifying repeat victimization involves the impact of short time frames within which repeats can occur. Ellingworth et al. (1995) note that most levels of repeat victimization in the BCS are probably under-reports because they rely on repeats only within a one-year time frame, which minimizes the potential for repeats before or after the survey boundaries. The problem of short time frames for repeat victimization is very evident when considering the NCVS. The NCVS reveals significantly lower repeat victimization compared to the ICVS for every category of victimization, including sexual offenses (51% repeats in the ICVS; 23% in the NCVS), assaults and threats (46% ICVS; 26% NCVS), and burglary (40% ICVS; 18% NCVS) (Farrell et al., 2005). The reason for this is the six-month time frame used by the NCVS and the 12-month time frame in the ICVS. Kleemans (2001) notes that nine percent of repeat burglaries occur within one month, 30 percent occur within six months, and almost half occur within one year. Thus, the time frame under consideration makes a difference for the finding of repeat victimization.

Beyond documenting the extent of repeat victimization, research also provides information on the time frame of repeats. Pease (1998) notes that a great deal of revictimization tends to occur within a short period after the first victimization. Similar results appear in Bowers et al.'s (1998) examination of repeat victimization of non-residential locations and Johnson et al.'s (1997) burglary study. In both analyses, the risk of repeats remains higher within relatively short periods after the initial victimization. Weisel (2005) demonstrates that the time frame for many repeats remains short for a range of offenses (see Table 9.5). For example, 15 percent of domestic violence repeats

Table 9.5
Time Frame for Repeat Victimization

Offense	Proportion of Repeats by Time Period	Where
Domestic violence	15% within 24 hours 25% within five weeks	Merseyside, England
Bank robbery	33% within three months	England
Residential burglary	25% within a week 51% within a month	Tallahassee, Florida
	11% within one week 33% within one month	Merseyside, England
Non-residential burglary	17% within one week 43% within one month	Merseyside, England
Property crime at schools	70% within a month	Merseyside, England

Source: Weisel (2005).

take place within one day and 35 percent occur within five weeks (Lloyd et al., 1994). Similarly, 25 percent of repeat burglaries occur within one week and 51 percent occur within one month (Robinson, 1998). The information on the time frame of repeats can be useful for the timing of prevention initiatives.

Explanations for repeat victimization can generally be divided into two categories—risk heterogeneity and state dependence (Farrell et al., 1995). *Risk heterogeneity*, or a *flag* explanation (Gill and Pease, 1998), suggests that the prior victimization or some other factor identifies the victim or location as an appropriate target for further victimization. As such, subsequent victimizations may be committed by different offenders who are attracted to the target by its apparent vulnerability or some other characteristic. Farrell et al. (1995) use the example of repeated fights at a bar as an indication of risk heterogeneity, where people looking for fights or interested in risky situations are attracted to establishments with a reputation for conflict. Those locations and/or the employees of those bars are then at a higher risk for repeat victimization.

Event dependency, or *boost* explanations (Gill and Pease, 1998), refers to situations in which (usually) the same offender commits another offense based on the past experiences with that victim or location. Successful past offending leads to another attempt against the same target. It is possible under this situation that a new offender commits a follow-up offense as a result of information shared between offenders. In this case, specific information about the target based on a past offense is the key to subsequent actions.

Farrell et al. (1995) point out that both risk heterogeneity and event dependency assume that potential offenders are rational (Rational Choice Theory) and that their experiences (Routine Activities) offer information on the risk, effort, and payoff to be expected from different courses of action. Both arguments find support in Gill and Pease's (1998) study of incarcerated robbers. Their subjects indicate that repeat victimizations are related to information from past offenses (theirs or others) and planning. Bowers and Johnson (2004) uncover support for the event dependency explanation in a study of residential burglary.

The identification and documentation of repeat victimization holds a great deal of potential for preventing crime. Laycock and Farrell (2003) provide a number of reasons for targeting repeat victimization. They point out that targeting repeat victimization allows the police to better allocate manpower and resources where they have the greatest chance to have an impact. In a similar fashion, targeting repeat victimization often means targeting hot spots and hot products. A focus on repeat victimization also means implementing crime prevention in high-crime areas, thus having an impact on both the specific target and potential nearby targets (Laycock and Farrell, 2003). The authors also note that targeting repeat victimization should result in less displacement than initiatives that are more unfocused. Another advantage is that repeat victimization may involve more prolific and serious offenders, thus prevention efforts have a greater likelihood of addressing persistent offenders (Laycock and Farrell, 2003).

Targeting past victims and locations also provides good information on how to intervene. Ratcliffe and McCullagh (1999), for example, note that the analysis of past offenses can provide information on the mode of entry, time of offending, property targeted, and other factors that can form the basis for preventive actions. Importantly, there is greater similarity in repeats committed soon after the initial act, but the similarity declines over time. Based on these facts, Spelman (1995) notes that short-term, immediate responses targeted at victims should have a greater impact than either long-term interventions or prevention aimed at broader groups or neighborhoods. Clarke et al. (2001) suggest that studies of repeat victimization can also provide insight into the decision-making process of the offenders. Evidence from an analysis of repeat burglary supports the idea that burglars repeat their offense after a period of time in order to steal the items that have been purchased to replace the goods taken in the first offense (Clarke et al., 2001).

Existing research suggests that targeting repeat victimization can effectively reduce crime. The Kirkholt Burglary Prevention Program, for example, targeted repeat victimization and worked with current victims as means of reducing further burglaries. Results suggest that this effort successfully reduced further offending (Pease, 1998). Farrell and Pease (2006), reviewing 11 studies from the United States, the United Kingdom, and Australia, note that both repeat burglary and overall burglary are reduced by focusing prevention efforts on repeat offending. Table 9.6 offers a list of effective and ineffective methods for addressing repeat victimization.

Despite the increased interest in repeat victimization and evidence of the effectiveness of targeting repeat victimization, there are issues that require more attention. First, while evidence shows that there is a good deal of repeat victimization, not all criminal acts are followed by another one against the same location or individual. Identifying which acts will result in a repeat victimization prior to the subsequent act is an elusive task. The existing research offers an after-the-fact analysis of the extent of repeat victimization. It is possible,

Table 9.6
Effective and Ineffective Factors for Preventing Repeat Victimization

Effective Factors

- Specific tactics tailored to the crime
- Use of multiple tactics
- Strong intervention implementation
- Focus on high-crime-rate situations

Ineffective Factors

- Use of inappropriate or weak prevention programs
- Poor implementation
- Replicating prevention initiatives from other times/places without consideration of the current context
- Attacking crime where the rate of repeat victimization is low

Source: Compiled from Farrell and Pease (2006).

therefore, that targeting prevention activities at past victims may result in a great deal of unnecessary effort. On the other hand, such targeting should be more effective than interventions aimed at the general public, many of whom would never become a victim in the first place.

A second issue deals with *virtual repeats* (Pease, 1998). A virtual repeat involves a follow-up victimization of a similar person, place, or item. For example, a series of robberies at different locations of a single company (such as a fast food store) or theft of the same brand of car could be considered repeat victimization if the subsequent offenses are committed due to the similarity in the situations (such as similar store layout or similar auto amenities). Pease (1998) suggests that these should be considered repeat victimizations. As such, they offer different issues for directing crime prevention activities. Johnson and Bowers (2002; 2004) illustrate this issue when they consider burglaries that take place at neighboring homes as a type of repeat victimization, which they call a near repeat. Their argument is that a local burglary elevates the risk of burglary, at least in the near term, for other proximate homes.

Other unanswered questions involve whether repeats should be considered in terms of people or places being victimized, how many victimizations are required before it is considered a repeat (especially in terms of common commercial thefts such as shoplifting), whether attempted offenses should be counted as repeats, and whether similar (but not identical) offenses should be used as a sign of repeat victimization (Pease, 1998). An interesting, but as yet understudied, topic is the issue of repeat perpetrators (Everson and Pease, 2001). This complement to the idea of repeat victims may offer additional insight into the choice of crime prevention interventions. While no clear answers are available for these questions/issues, the potential for using repeat victimization within crime prevention remains strong.

Summary

Hot spot research, repeat victimization, and related topics represent innovative approaches to narrowing the individuals or situations that will be targeted by crime prevention activities. Farrell (2005) illustrates the overlap of several concepts found in this chapter and suggests that the effectiveness of preventive efforts will be most enhanced by targeting the intersection of the different domains (see Figure 9.1). Clearly, the idea of allocating resources by time and place is common in policing. It should be no more difficult to borrow that idea and apply it to general preventive efforts used by the criminal justice system or any other group or agency. Both hot spot and repeat victimization analyses, among others, offer insight into the "where" and "when" issues of instituting crime prevention.

Figure 9.1
Intersection of Domains for Crime Prevention Efficiency

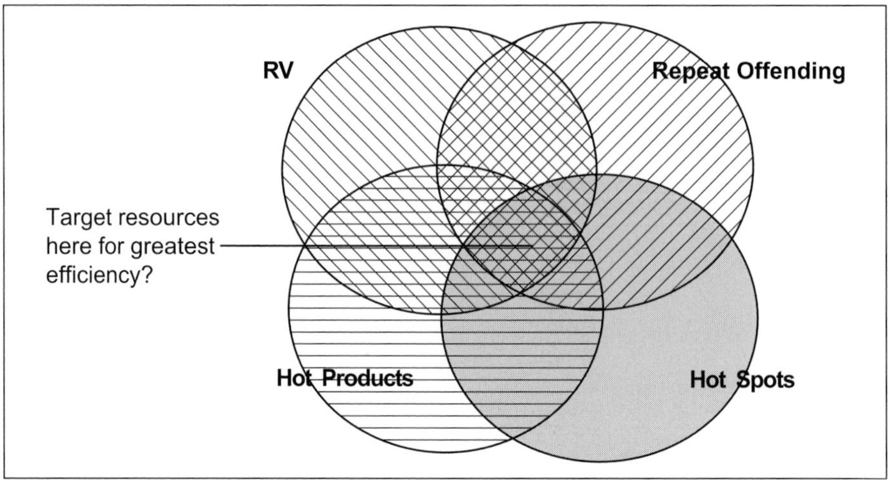

Source: Farrell, G. (2005). "Progress and Prospects in the Prevention of Repeat Victimization." In Tilley, N. (ed.), *Handbook of Crime Prevention and Community Safety*. Portland, OR: Willan Publishing. Reprinted with permission.

IMPLICATIONS FOR CRIME PREVENTION

Prediction is an important part of crime prevention—particularly secondary prevention. This is true especially for attempting to intervene with individuals and situations where a high propensity for criminal and deviant behavior exists. The identification of persons who are headed for future juvenile or adult criminality would allow the introduction of appropriate crime prevention techniques prior to the deviant activity. Unfortunately, the prediction of future behavior of individuals typically results in large numbers of false predictions. Research on criminal careers also has failed to adequately identify high-risk individuals prior to the establishment of a career. More recent research on risk factors uncovers a number of variables related to later deviant behavior. It may be possible to use identified risk factors as a basis for focused, preventive interventions.

Another approach to prediction is to turn attention away from predicting individual behavior and toward prediction of places, times, and targets of offending. This approach suggests that it may be fruitful to orient prevention activities from the perspective of the victim, rather than the potential offender. Any technique that assists in the delineation of potential victims or targets would offer insight into the "where" and "when" of prevention efforts. The geographic and temporal identification of hot spots, the identification of hot products, and the use of information on repeat victimization are approaches with potential use in secondary crime prevention. These approaches need to receive increased attention and continued refinement in order to make the information more useful for prevention.

Chapter 10

SITUATIONAL CRIME PREVENTION

Key Terms:

crime pattern theory

immobilizers

lifestyle perspective

permissibility

pressures

prompts

provocations

rational choice theory

routine activities theory

situational prevention

Learning Objectives:

After reading this chapter you should be able to:

- Define situational prevention

- Identify and discuss the theoretical bases for situational prevention

- Explain the changes in the situational typology over time

- Provide criticisms directed at situational prevention and give responses to those criticisms

- Offer several examples of situational prevention in action, including the evaluation evidence on those techniques

- Demonstrate how situational techniques can be used with personal crimes

The targeting of crime prevention efforts is nowhere more evident than under the rubric of situational crime prevention. Many of the prevention techniques discussed under primary prevention form the basis of interventions discussed in this chapter. Instead of attempting to make sweeping changes in an entire community or neighborhood, situational prevention is aimed at specific problems, places, persons, or times. The situational approach assumes that a greater degree of problem identification and planning will take place prior to program implementation and that the impact will be more focused. The identification of places and individuals at risk of victimization, especially focusing on repeat victimization, are central to a great deal of situational prevention. This chapter outlines the growth of situational crime prevention since the early 1980s, discusses the various traditional rationales upon which it is based, and provides examples of situational techniques in action.

THE GROWTH OF SITUATIONAL PREVENTION

The root ideas for situational crime prevention can be traced largely to the crime prevention work of the British Home Office in the 1970s (Clarke, 1983). In pursuit of interventions that could successfully address different crime problems, the Home Office undertook a wide array of projects aimed at reducing factors specific to different crimes, places, and situations. Clarke (1995) points out that much of this work grew out of the recognition that crime often reflects the risk, effort, and payoff as assessed by the offender. In essence, offenders make choices about which opportunities are the most profitable, and act in accordance with that assessment.

Clarke (1983:225) offers the following definition of *situational prevention*:

> situational crime prevention can be characterized as comprising measures (1) directed at highly specific forms of crime (2) that involve the management, design, or manipulation of the immediate environment in as systematic and permanent a way as possible (3) so as to reduce the opportunities for crime and increase the risks as perceived by a wide range of offenders.

Implicit in this definition are a number of assumptions about the offender and crime commission that appear in various theories and theoretical perspectives. The key part of the definition is the third caveat—"reduce the opportunities" and "increase the risks as perceived ... by offenders." Situational prevention rests on the idea that it is possible to make changes in the environment that will make offending less attractive to potential offenders. This assumes that offenders do not simply act on impulse, and they have control over whether they take action or not. There is a clear belief that offenders make choices. Cusson (1993) argues that crime is deterred because the offender perceives risk in a given situation. As a result, offenders seek out or respond to places, times, and potential victims that offer the least risk.

THE THEORETICAL BASIS

Rational choice, routine activities, and lifestyles perspectives are important considerations for situational prevention. Each set of ideas provides insight into the ability of offenders to respond to crime opportunities. While it is common for discussions of these perspectives to focus on potential offenders, the potential victim is also an important part of the equation.

The cornerstone of situational crime prevention is the belief that offenders respond to opportunities and make choices in offending. *Rational choice theory* posits that individuals make decisions on whether to commit an offense based on an array of inputs, including the effort involved, the potential payoff, the degree of peer support for the action, the risk of apprehension and punishment, and the needs of the individual (Clarke and Cornish, 1985; Cornish and Clarke, 1986a, 1986b). This does not mean that every offender makes a totally free-willed choice to commit a crime. Rather, what it suggests is that individuals do not simply commit an offense every time an opportunity presents itself. Potential offenders make a calculated decision about crime that is mediated by factors such as those noted above.

Research on burglars serves as a good example of the issues involved in rational choice. Bennett (1986) and Wright and Decker (1994) point out that burglars often commit their crimes in order to fulfill other needs and desires. These may be immediate needs, such as cash for drug purchases or to meet expectations of one's peers, or longer term desires for property or status. In attempting to satisfy these drives, the offender may consider a wide range of targets and methods. Among the physical and social factors that affect a burglar's decision may be the level of concealment, the amount of light, the presence of locks, evidence of valuable property, surveillability from other places, and the presence of other people (Bennett, 1986; Bennett and Wright, 1984; Cromwell et al., 1991; Nee and Taylor, 1988; Rengert and Wasilchick, 1985; Wright and Decker, 1994). It is important to note that throughout these discussions there is at least a tacit recognition of the limited nature of the offender's choices. Indeed, many of the choices may be made with little or no conscious decision making by the individual at the time of the offense (Wright and Decker, 1994). While it may appear that rational choice is not taking place, the decisions may have been fashioned through a variety of past experiences, activities, and inputs. This same process should not only apply to burglary, but also other offenses.

One source of the information upon which an offender bases decisions, whether consciously or subconsciously, is his daily routines. *Routine activities theory* argues that the daily activity of individuals results in the convergence of motivated offenders with suitable targets in the absence of guardians (Cohen and Felson, 1979). This convergence provides opportunities for crime to occur. Cohen and Felson (1979) demonstrate the importance of routine activities by showing that increases in the number of unoccupied homes during the day and the greater availability of portable valuables during the 1960s help to explain increases in residential burglary. Increasing mobility in society serves to bring targets and offenders together with greater frequency than ever before. Both the opportunity and choices for offending are enhanced.

Where routine activities deals with both the offender and the victim, the *lifestyle perspective* specifically focuses on the activity of the victim as a contributing factor in criminal acts. Hindelang et al. (1978) suggest that an individual's lifestyle and behavioral choices help determine whether he/she will be victimized. For example, frequenting a bar in which violent fights are common increases the risk you will be involved in such a confrontation. Similarly, working in a convenience store located in a high-crime neighborhood enhances the possibility of being a robbery victim. In both situations the individual's lifestyle has an impact on the potential of becoming a victim or a repeat victim.

It is possible to broaden the lifestyle ideas to consider both victimization risk and opportunity provision. That is, one's lifestyle has the potential to offer opportunities to commit crime, as well as become a victim. A lifestyle that offers little structure, such as a job where you are unsupervised and are greatly mobile, may place you in situations where targets are identifiable and guardians are absent. Consequently, the individual has the choice of either committing a crime or refraining from doing so. The combination of lifestyle and routine activities ideas is a natural extension of both perspectives and offers a broader view of potential choice parameters.

The rational choice, routine activities, and lifestyles theories/perspectives fit nicely with *crime pattern theory*. This theory argues that criminal behavior fits patterns that can be understood in terms of when and where crime occurs (Brantingham and Brantingham, 1993b). It is through daily activities that individuals develop templates about the social and physical environment within which they operate. This information is important for identifying both targets as well as threats for potential offenders. Likewise, studying the behavior of offenders and analysis of past offending provides insight into the crimes and potential prevention mechanisms.

This brief review of rational choice, routine activities, lifestyle, and crime pattern theories/perspectives illustrates many of the issues underlying situational crime prevention ideas. In each case, deviant activity can be seen as a result of converging factors that influence opportunities for and the decision to commit crime. Actions that limit those choices, therefore, hold the potential to reduce crime and fear of crime.

THE PROCESS OF SITUATIONAL PREVENTION

Besides drawing on a number of relatively new theoretical approaches, situational prevention also distinguishes itself by approaching problems in a very systematic fashion. Essentially four steps are involved: (1) study the problem, (2) identify possible responses, (3) implement the intervention, and (4) evaluate and adjust the intervention. Situational prevention starts with a specific, identifiable crime problem. That problem is then subjected to study, drawing on as wide an array of information and perspectives as possible. This stage offers an important distinction from many other crime control efforts that rely on traditional police and criminal justice system responses to solve problems. Under situational prevention, formal social control agents are only one source of input. Based on the findings of the analysis, an intervention is identified and implemented. At this point the prevention process continues with an evaluation of the program impact, with the intent of making changes in the response, if necessary. Situational prevention, therefore, is a dynamic process of problem identification, response identification, program implementation, and evaluation and adjustment.

SITUATIONAL TYPOLOGIES

The growth of situational crime prevention can be seen in the ongoing development of a situational typology. In one of the earliest presentations on situational prevention, Clarke (1983) provided a simple three-pronged approach to interventions:

- surveillance

- target hardening

- environmental management

Surveillance included many of the ideas discussed in earlier chapters, including the concepts of natural surveillance, formal surveillance, and surveillance by employees (see Clarke and Mayhew, 1980). Target hardening included interventions such as locks, unbreakable glass, safes, and other security devices. Environmental management referred to making changes that reduce the opportunity for crime. Two examples provided by Clarke (1983) were paying employees by checks rather than in cash, thereby making robbery less lucrative for offenders, and the introduction of airline baggage and passenger screening for the detection of weapons and bombs, thus reducing the number of skyjackings.

Clarke's 12 Techniques

As one would expect, the original three categories quickly became too simplistic and confining as the number of situational crime prevention interventions grew. In 1992, Clarke offered an expanded classification of situational techniques that reflected three very general orientations: "increasing the effort," "increasing the risk," and "reducing the rewards." Within each of these categories, Clarke (1992) outlined four subgroups of prevention approaches, yielding a total of 12 situational prevention techniques. Table 10.1 provides an abbreviated version of Clarke's 1992 typology.

Table 10.1
Clarke's 1992 Situational Prevention Techniques

Increasing the Effort
1.   Target Hardening
2.   Access Control
3.   Deflecting Offenders
4.   Controlling Facilitators
Increasing the Risk
5.   Entry/Exit Screening
6.   Formal Surveillance
7.   Surveillance by Employees
8.   Natural Surveillance
Reducing the Rewards
9.   Target Removal
10. Identifying Property
11. Removing Inducements
12. Rule Setting

Source: Adapted from R.V. Clarke (1992). *Situational Crime Prevention: Successful Case Studies*. Albany, NY: Harrow and Heston.

Many of the techniques are self-explanatory or rest on ideas introduced earlier in this book. Under "Increasing the Effort" are target hardening, access control, deflecting offenders, and controlling facilitators. "Deflecting offenders" involves actions that offer alternatives to undesirable behavior. Examples would include providing a board upon which graffiti can be painted, or providing a meeting place for youths away from open businesses or public thoroughfares (Clarke, 1992). The idea of "controlling facilitators" deals with limiting or eliminating situations or items that contribute to crime, such as guns, alcohol, or public phones (which may be used for drug sales). Methods for "Increasing the Risk" rest mainly on formal or informal surveillance efforts. "Entry/exit screening" is a form of surveillance that allows the detection of potential offenders. The screening of passengers at airports and placing electronic sensors in merchandise to prevent its theft are two examples of entry/exit screening. The final category of "Reducing the Rewards" includes target removal, identifying property, removing inducements, and rule setting. "Target removal" reflects actions such as limiting the cash kept in the checkout register and requiring exact fare on buses. In both cases, the potential payoff from a robbery or theft is limited. Similarly, "removing inducements" means eliminating attractive targets such as a sports car parked on a public street or the wearing of popular sports team jackets to school. Finally, Clarke (1992) offers "rule setting" as a means of setting a standard of conduct for employees and the public, and placing people on notice that their behavior is being monitored for compliance.

Throughout these techniques, Clarke attempts to show the breadth of possibilities for crime prevention. He notes that relying on prevention activities that rest solely on making changes in hardware is too simplistic and short-sighted (Clarke, 1992). Instead, prevention needs to consider broader social bases for interventions, which situational prevention techniques offer. Any examination of Clarke's 12-stage typology can easily lead to interventions that are dominated by physical changes in the environment. Based on Clarke's (1983) definition, which proposes the "management, design, or manipulation of the immediate environment," a physical interpretation is not surprising. A closer look, however, that considers opportunity and the "choice" dimension of situational prevention, argues for a broader interpretation of situational interventions.

Expanding the Typology

Clarke and Homel (1997) responded to concerns and limitations in the original 12-cell typology by proposing an expanded list of 16 situational techniques. The expansion sought to address two key issues (Clarke and Homel, 1997). First, research suggested that the 12 categories were neither exhaustive nor mutually exclusive. Several of the original groupings could be divided to enhance internal consistency of the ideas (Clarke and Homel, 1997). One example of this adjustment was dividing the original "controlling facilitators" into the categories of "controlling facilitators" and "controlling disinhibitors." The former maintained the original concern with guns and other items that make crime easier, the latter addressed factors that reduce the social and psychological barriers to crime commission, such as the use of alcohol and drugs (Clarke and Homel, 1997).

Second, the original 12 categories failed to include techniques that focused on the social and psychological contexts of offending (Clarke and Homel, 1997). In response, the authors added categories that addressed guilt, shame, and embarrassment ("Inducing Guilt or Shame"), which may arise as a result of participating in deviant activity. Guilt and similar feelings may emerge because of the incongruence individuals see between their actions and the moral code they hold or the view of significant others in their lives (Clarke and Homel, 1997). This expanded typology shifted situational prevention away from the heavy emphasis on physical changes toward a greater reliance on psychological and social factors. For example, each of the original categories was relabeled to reflect the offender's perceptions—"Increasing *Perceived* Effort," "Increasing *Perceived* Risks," and "Reducing *Anticipated* Rewards." In each case the new title allowed for both an actual change in effort, risk, or reward *and* altered *perceptions* (Clarke and Homel, 1997). It is possible that a situational technique has little *physical* impact, but a major psychological impact. Despite these changes, Wortley (1996) argued that the typology was still not complete. In particular, the area of "inducing guilt or shame" was not exhaustive. He posited that guilt and shame are not the same thing and that these concepts need to be separated.

Wortley (2001) also argued that the matrix of situational prevention over-emphasized elements that can control or inhibit offending, while ignoring the factors that precipitate or lead to crime. He offered four categories of precipitators: prompts, pressures, permissibility, and provocation. *Prompts* involve events or situations that may support the opportunity for crime, such as open doors or others committing crime. *Pressures*, on the other hand, are more direct stimuli that lead to action. Deviant peers, going along with the crowd, or following orders to do something wrong are good examples of such pressures. *Permissibility* reflects situations or beliefs that place criminal behavior into an acceptable light. The belief that everyone breaks the law or that the victim had it coming makes the action more acceptable and permissible. Finally, *provocations* are factors that make an individual uncomfortable, frustrated, irritable, or otherwise aroused to the point of taking some form of action, of which crime is one possibility (Wortley, 2001).

Wortley's (1996, 2001) discussions of guilt, shame, and precipitating factors took the view that the social and psychological dimensions of both prevention and crime causation were under-developed in Clarke and Homel's (1997) typology. Clarke and Homel (1997), however, rejected Wortley's (1996) initial suggestions because broadening situational prevention to include efforts to change the "general disposition to offend" was too broad for a "situational" approach. Similarly, Cornish and Clarke (2003) pointed out that a basic assumption underlying situational prevention is that there are always individuals who are willing to offend. A motivated offender is a given. Cornish and Clarke (2003) noted that Wortley's (1996; 2001) arguments take the opposite position that offenders are not always motivated. Instead, there are factors that will provide the needed motivation for criminal activity. Attempting to address Wortley's (2001) concerns, Cornish and Clarke (2003) offered a new situational typology that includes cues that may motivate individuals to offend.

The typology appearing in Table 10.2 attempts to incorporate elements of precipitation into the general situational crime prevention framework. The original ideas of taking actions to alter the real and perceived effort, risks, and rewards from criminal behaviors are maintained, with expanded techniques under each heading. The techniques addressing guilt and shame are also maintained primarily under the heading of "Remove Excuses." Wortley's (2001) ideas of reducing permissibility also appear under the removing excuses category. Methods to address the precipitating factors of prompts, pressures, and provocations appear under the "Reducing Provocations" heading. Cornish and Clarke (2003) note that the addition of motivational factors to the more traditional opportunity factors in the matrix allows the techniques to address the behavior of various individuals with different levels of motivation to commit crime.

The situational typology serves various purposes. Perhaps the most beneficial aspect is to place the great array of situational crime prevention activities and programs into a theoretical framework. Many specific interventions, such as the installation of locks and lights, take place with little understanding of the underlying rationale for why they should work. While there are implicit

Table 10.2
Twenty-Five Techniques of Situational Prevention

Increase the Effort	Increase the Risks	Reduce the Rewards	Reduce Provocations	Remove Excuses
1. Target harden: • Steering column locks and immobilisers • Anti-robbery screens • Tamper-proof packaging	6. Extend guardianship: • Take routine precautions: go out in groups at night, leave signs of occupancy, carry phone • "Cocoon" neighborhood watch	11. Conceal targets: • Off-street parking • Gender-neutral phone directories • Unmarked bullion trucks	16. Reduce frustrations and stress: • Efficient queues and police service • Expanded seating • Soothing music/muted lights	21. Set rules: • Rental agreements • Harassment codes • Hotel registration
2. Control access to facilities: • Entry phones • Electronic card access • Baggage screening	7. Assist natural surveillance: • Improved street lighting • Defensible space design • Support whistleblowers	12. Remove targets: • Removable car radio • Women's refuges • Pre-paid cards for pay phones	17. Avoid disputes: • Separate enclosures for rival soccer fans • Reduce crowding in pubs • Fixed cab fares	22. Post instructions: • "No Parking" • "Private Property" • "Extinguish camp fires"
3. Screen exits: • Ticket needed for exit • Export documents • Electronic merchandise tags	8. Reduce anonymity: • Taxi driver IDs • "How's my driving?" decals • School uniforms	13. Identify Property: • Property marking • Vehicle licensing and parts marking • Cattle branding	18. Reduce emotional arousal: • Controls on violent pornography • Enforce good behavior on soccer field • Prohibit racial slurs	23. Alert conscience: • Roadside speed display boards • Signatures for customs declarations • "Shoplifting is stealing"
4. Deflect offenders: • Street closures • Separate bathrooms for women • Disperse pubs	9. Utilize place managers: • CCTV for double-deck buses • Two clerks for convenience stores • Reward vigilance	14. Disrupt markets: • Monitor pawn shops • Controls on classified ads • License street vendors	19. Neutralize peer pressure: • "Idiots drink and drive" • "It's OK to say No" • Disperse troublemakers at school	24. Assist compliance: • Easy library checkout • Public lavatories • Litter bins
5. Control tools/weapons: • "Smart" guns • Disabling stolen cell phones • Restrict spray paint sales to juveniles	10. Strengthen formal surveillance: • Red light cameras • Burglar alarms • Security guards	15. Deny benefits: • Ink merchandise tags • Graffiti cleaning • Speed bumps	20. Discourage imitation: • Rapid repair of vandalism • V-chips in TVs • Censor details of modus operandi	25. Control drugs and alcohol: • Breathalyzers in pubs • Server intervention • Alcohol-free events

Source: D.B. Cornish and R.V. Clarke (2003). "Opportunities, Precipitators, and Criminal Decisions: A Reply to Wortley's Critique of Situational Crime Prevention." In M.J. Smith and D.B. Cornish (eds.), *Theory for Practice in Situational Crime Prevention.* Monsey, NY: Criminal Justice Press. Reprinted with permission.

theoretical arguments in many of the programs, understanding why a program does or does not work requires more explicit recognition of the mechanisms at work. The situational typology helps to organize those discussions. In a complementary fashion, the cataloging of the diverse prevention efforts into a classification system helps to identify the potential causal factors at work. That is, the underlying theories gain support when it is possible to demonstrate their applicability and usefulness. The rational choice, routine activities, and lifestyle perspectives all contribute to the development of the situational techniques and benefit from the alignment of different studies into a coherent typology. The recent addition of techniques for addressing precipitating factors broadens the theoretical traditions and causal mechanisms under consideration in prevention initiatives. On a very practical note, a classification scheme such as this serves as a simple reference tool for those attempting to implement prevention programs.

ISSUES AND CONCERNS WITH SITUATIONAL PREVENTION

As with any topic, there are a number of concerns and unresolved issues. One set of issues relates to the adequacy of the typology. Clarke (1992), Clarke and Homel (1997) and Cornish and Clarke (2003) all present specific interventions that deal with effort, risk, reward, and other topics. Unfortunately, the authors fail to point out that the general categorizations are not mutually exclusive. That is, various interventions may influence more than one factor (both objectively and subjectively). A technique that increases risk also may increase the effort. For example, the presence of security guards or closed-circuit television increases the risk of being caught. These actions, however, also increase the effort needed to successfully complete an offense. At the same time, successfully completing a crime despite high risk and effort could lead to greater (psychic) rewards (or monetary gain if the presence of protection reflected greater value). The fact that the categories are not mutually exclusive does not negate the usefulness of the classification scheme. Rather, it suggests that the underlying mechanisms are more complex than they first appear in the typology.

On the other hand, Clarke, Homel, Cornish, and others point out that the typologies are incomplete and in need of further explication. The authors view the typology as a dynamic undertaking that will require modification as research and theory emerge. The very fact that the typology has evolved from 12 to 25 general techniques over roughly a 10-year period attests to the dynamic nature of the undertaking. Indeed, an attempt to finalize a typology could be viewed as limiting its usefulness.

Clarke (2005) lists seven common misconceptions about situational crime prevention and offers rebuttals to each (see Table 10.3). Critics often note that situational prevention addresses symptoms rather than the causes

Table 10.3
Seven Misconceptions of Situational Crime Prevention

Criticism	Rebuttal
1. It is simplistic and atheoretical crime pattern and rational choice.	It is based on three crime opportunity theories: routine activities, It also draws on social psychology
2. It has not been shown to work; it displaces crime and often makes it worse	Many dozens of case studies show that it can reduce crime, usually with little displacement
3. It diverts attention from the root causes of crime	It benefits society by achieving immediate reductions in crime
4. It is a conservative, managerial approach to crime	It promises no more than it can deliver. It requires that solutions be economic and socially acceptable
5. It promotes a selfish, exclusionary society	It provides as much protection to the poor as to the rich
6. It promotes Big Brother and restricts personal freedoms	The democratic process protects society from these dangers. People are willing to endure inconvenience and small infringements of liberty when these protect them from crime
7. It blames the victim	It empowers victims by providing them with information about crime risks and how to avoid them

Source: Clarke, R.V. (2005). "Seven Misconceptions of Situational Crime Prevention." In Tilley, N. (ed.), *Handbook of Crime Prevention and Community Safety.* Portland, OR: Willan Publishing. Reprinted with permission.

of crime (Clarke, 1995; Crawford, 1998; Kleinig, 2000) and this may result in temporary, short-lived solutions to immediate problems. These situational interventions fail to consider more basic social and cultural problems, such as poor education, unemployment, and discrimination. Clarke (2005) argues that, despite this fact, situational crime prevention provides clear benefits to society, and does not preclude simultaneous efforts to address causes of crime. A second major criticism is that situational crime prevention is atheoretical and overly simplistic. Such arguments fail to note the rich and developing theoretical arguments (e.g., routine activities and crime pattern) that direct a great deal of prevention activity.

Critics also argue that some situational techniques may be overly intrusive and border on "Big Brother" watching everyone's activities (Clarke, 1995; Crawford, 1998; von Hirsch, 2000). The use of CCTV, electronic tagging, and other surveillance measures allow greater oversight and control of people. Interestingly, the use of technology for crime prevention has found widespread acceptance among the general public. Examples of this are the use of CCTV and x-ray technology at airports. Some critics argue that there is little evidence that situational prevention techniques are effective at preventing crime. These claims ignore the fact that many programs have successfully reduced crime, and that displacement is never 100 percent. Crawford (1998) and others (see von Hirsch et al., 2000) also suggest that situational interventions may work against already marginalized groups and can build barriers between citizens and the community. Situational techniques, however, can be used to protect both the rich and the poor, and may include activities that bring citizens together in cooperative endeavors.

An additional failure of situational prevention is that it does not explicitly address the issue of fear of crime. By focusing on the perceptions of potential offenders, situational techniques are geared mainly toward the reduction of criminal activity, and evaluations typically ignore the issue of fear. Any impact on fear would appear mainly to the extent that fear is directly related to the level of crime. This does not mean that some situational techniques would not affect fear. As interventions are implemented, particularly by residents and other legitimate users, fear may be reduced. Unfortunately, this possible outcome is rarely addressed.

SITUATIONAL PREVENTION STUDIES

The balance of this chapter offers a brief overview of studies examining the impact of various situational crime prevention techniques. For most of the discussion, the emphasis is on the impact of various prevention techniques. In some cases the examples highlight suggestions for situational prevention for specific crime problems. It is not possible to provide example studies for each of the 16 techniques offered by Clarke and Homel (1997). Instead, the studies reviewed here should provide the reader with some insight into the types of initiatives that have been undertaken and the breadth of the problems to which situational techniques have been applied. A broader array of studies can be found in other forums (see, for example, Clarke, 1992, 1993, 1996).

Studies of Crimes against Transit Systems

Public transportation has been the target of various offenses. Among these are fare avoidance and vandalism. The failure to pay fares is common across different forms of public transportation and a single response is not possible due to the diversity in types of transit system (bus, train, etc.) and the means by which offenders evade payments. An assessment of fare evasion on the British Columbia transit system began with a fare evasion audit in order to assess the extent and location of the problem (DesChamps et al., 1991). The audit identified various methods of fare evasion, which formed the basis for a redesign of ticket machines and passes, promotions encouraging the purchase of transit passes, and focused investigations of counterfeit fare media (DesChamps et al., 1991). An evaluation of the intervention revealed significant drops in the level of fare evasion.

Actions taken to address fare evasion in the London underground transit system, the New York subway system, and the Dutch transit system also have proven effective at reducing the problem. The London system instituted a new ticketing system and installed automatic gates at select underground stations. Comparing post-intervention to pre-intervention ticket sales, Clarke (1993) reports reductions in fare evasion of almost two-thirds. The New York subway system introduced new ticketing systems, along with physical barriers and increased staff control of entrances (Weidner, 1996). Evaluating the impact by comparing the number of arrests and summonses after the changes to those before, Weidner (1996) reports a small but clear decline in the target station, with increases in neighboring stations. In an evaluation of the Dutch transit systems, Van Andel (1989) found that fare evasion on buses often occurred due to the ability of riders to enter and exit the buses through a rear door, thus avoiding the driver. In response, the system introduced monitors on the buses and a change in procedure that required passengers to enter the bus near the driver and prove payment (van Andel, 1989). As in the other evaluations, fare evasion significantly fell from the pre-intervention levels.

Public transportation systems also suffer an undue level of vandalism. In one of the most widely cited studies, Sloan-Howitt and Kelling (1990) reported on the efforts to eliminate graffiti from New York subway trains. Numerous attempts to thwart graffiti artists, through such efforts as using graffiti-proof paint and securing rail yards, failed to have an impact. In a true situational approach, an assessment of why graffiti artists insisted on using the trains found that what was important to the artists was for their work to "get up" and for people to see it (Sloan-Howitt and Kelling, 1990). The logical solution to the problem, therefore, was to devise a means whereby no one would ever see the work, thus depriving the artist of his audience. Consequently, the subway system instituted a policy of cleaning up each train car. Once cleaned, it was not allowed in service (and was immediately taken out of service) if it was ever vandalized by graffiti. This eliminated the ability of the artists to "get up" on the trains and eventually stopped further graffiti vandalism (Sloan-Howitt and Kelling, 1990).

Poyner (1988) reports on a different approach to curbing vandalism on double-decker buses in one area of England. An analysis of the problem found that offenders tended to be school-aged boys and vandalism occurred on buses with only a driver. The lack of surveillance was addressed by installing video cameras on several buses, although only two buses had functioning cameras. An important companion to the hardware introduction was heavy publicity and an educational program aimed at youths. The project resulted in a significant drop in repair costs (by roughly two-thirds) for the entire fleet of 80 buses (Poyner, 1988). Surveillance also was found to be a factor in reduced vandalism in the Dutch transportation study (van Andel, 1989).

Another examination of vandalism appears in Felson et al.'s (1996) study of problems at the New York Port Authority's bus terminal. In order to address issues such as vagrancy, drug problems, and other illegal activities, the terminal improved maintenance and cleaning, eliminated blind corners and niches (i.e., hiding places), improved lighting and signs, renovated restrooms, increased surveillability, trained police in problem solving, and improved the businesses in the terminal. While the myriad of interventions makes it difficult to assess the specific cause of any change, Felson et al. (1996) report that maintenance problems were reduced, users' ratings of cleanliness improved, and signs of drug and alcohol use declined (among other changes).

Motor Vehicle Theft

Motor vehicle theft is a continuing problem that has generated a variety of different proposed solutions. Mayhew et al. (1976) and Webb (1994) examined the impact of steering column locks on the level of motor vehicle theft in England, Wales, and West Germany. Both analyses show that increasing the difficulty of motor vehicle theft led to reductions in the level of theft. Since the mid-1990s, increased use of automobile immobilizers has been undertaken to avert auto theft. *Immobilizers* are electronic devices that, in the absence of the key, prevent the car from operating (Brown, 2004). These devices have been required in all new cars in the European Union since 1995. Analysis of immobilizers in the United Kingdom reveals clear reductions in auto theft (Brown, 2004). Efforts to address motorcycle theft have often involved legislating the use of helmets (Mayhew et al., 1989). The need for helmets should reduce opportunistic theft because most offenders do not have a helmet available to them, thus making them easily recognizable to others. Evaluations in England, The Netherlands, and (the former) West Germany all find reduced motorcycle theft after the initiation of helmet laws (Mayhew et al., 1989).

Other efforts to limit auto theft have included changing the design of parking decks and parking areas, increasing use of security cameras, and introducing patrols. Poyner (1991) reports on prevention efforts in two different parking areas—a parking deck in town and a university parking lot. For the parking deck, it was determined that physical changes aimed at restricting access to the vehicles was the key to prevention, along with improved lighting and increased presence of legitimate users. The evaluation showed significant reductions in auto thefts after program implementation, as compared to two other area parking lots. The university project implemented improved lighting, closed-circuit television monitoring, and changes eliminating obstructions to observation. The lot receiving closed-circuit equipment showed the greatest drop in auto thefts, and there was some evidence that a nearby lot also benefited through decreased thefts (a possible diffusion effect) (Poyner, 1991). A study of the impact of bicycle patrols on auto theft in Vancouver uncovered a large drop in thefts during the month of patrol operation, as well as after the patrol was discontinued (Barclay et al., 1996).

There is evidence that interventions to reduce auto theft have caused some displacement. One form of displacement is to older cars that have not been outfitted with steering column locks or immobilizers (Brown, 2004; Mayhew et al., 1976; Webb, 1994). Brown (2004) also noted evidence of tactical displacement (movement to stealing keys) due to the introduction of immobilizers. Displacement has also appeared in increased thefts of motorcycles and mopeds (Mayhew et al., 1976; Webb, 1994). The bicycle patrol in Vancouver uncovered large increases in auto thefts for adjacent areas during the month of the intervention (Barclay et al, 1996). It would appear that displacement is evident in some evaluations of efforts to prevent auto theft.

Theft Offenses

Situational techniques have been used in relation to a wide array of theft offenses, including theft of library materials, shoplifting, thefts from shopping bags, robbery, theft of phone services, and identity theft. Each form of crime poses unique problems and can be addressed in various ways.

The impact of electronic tagging of property has been demonstrated in a number of studies. In one study, Scherdin (1986) addressed the problem of thefts from a university library. The author found that the tagging of books resulted in both a significant decrease in lost books and an increase in the number of items processed through circulation. Perhaps of greater impact was the simultaneous reduction in lost audiovisual materials that could not be tagged (Scherdin, 1986). This suggests a diffusion of benefits from the books to other library holdings. Electronic tagging has also become more prominent in retail establishments. Farrington et al. (1993) report that electronic tagging significantly reduced the level of shoplifting. Similarly, Handford (1994) indicates that computer stores using electronic tagging experience low theft levels relative to national data for comparable stores.

The marketplace also offers targets other than the stores themselves. Shoppers may be victimized through pick-pocketing or robbery. Poyner and Webb (1992) report on efforts to eliminate thefts from shopping bags in a crowded marketplace. An analysis of the problem suggested that an important contributing factor was the congestion caused by narrow aisles. The solution, therefore, was to widen the aisles, thereby relieving the congestion and increasing the surveillance opportunities. Their evaluation of the changes showed great reductions in the level of thefts after the redesign efforts (Poyner and Webb, 1992). Holt and Spencer (2005) report on efforts to reduce robberies at ATM locations. Based on interviews with convicted street robbers, the authors worked with banks to make ATMs safer by demarcating safe zones around the cash dispensers. This approach established a psychological barrier between potential victims and offenders. Holt and Spencer (2005) note a significant reduction in robberies at the marked ATMs compared to the control ATMs, which were unchanged.

Long-distance telephone services have also been the target of theft. One location where this took place on a large scale was the New York City bus terminal (Bichler and Clarke, 1996). Offenders would watch legitimate users enter phone card numbers when making calls and then fraudulently use that number to make other calls or "sell" phone time to other individuals. In addition, the offenders essentially controlled entire phone banks in the bus terminal from which they conducted their business. The response to the problem was multifaceted and included the elimination of some pay phones, electronically restricting some phones to local calls, the relocation of phones to areas that could be better controlled and monitored, and the closing off of phones at certain times. The evaluation of the efforts revealed large reductions in the number of fraudulent calls (Bichler and Clarke, 1996; Felson et al., 1996).

Identity theft is a major problem in modern society, particularly given the Internet and other technologies that allow for impersonal commerce to take place. Berg (2008) demonstrates a variety of situational techniques that should be effective at combating identity theft. Among the suggestions are employing antivirus programs to block the theft of personal information from a computer, data encryption to make stolen information and computers useless, physical security of computers, banning the use of portable devices (e.g., memory sticks) that can capture data from computers, and stronger methods to validate the identification of an individual attempting to make a purchase (Berg, 2008). The impact of situational prevention techniques on identity theft and related fraud is evident in the analysis of changes to debit and credit card procedures. Levi (2008) reports huge reductions in losses after the introduction of computer chips to cards and the use of PINs (personal identification numbers). Other effective interventions are the use of fraud alerts (e.g., calls to card owners when unusual activity is noted on an account) and more in-depth identity checks when an individual applies for credit or forms of identity (e.g., passports) (Levi, 2008).

Revictimization

Situational prevention has great potential in relation to targeting previous victims and offense sites. One place where this was undertaken was the Kirkholt Housing estates near Manchester, England (Forrester et al., 1988; 1990). A major thrust of the program was to target burglary victims to prevent further offenses. Among the prevention actions were improved physical security of homes, property identification, and "cocoon" Neighborhood Watch (small numbers of homes per group). A key element of the project was the removal of pre-payment fuel meters in burglarized homes. Evaluations of these efforts revealed significant reductions in repeat burglaries after program implementation. The absence of the pre-payment meters may have been the most important of the prevention measures. Anderson and Pease (1997) report on another attempt at targeting repeat victimization in Huddersfield, England. Victims received a graduated response based on the number of prior victimizations. Possible responses included the installation of alarms, security surveys, consultation with police, and cocoon Neighborhood Watch. Inspection of offense figures over a 25-month period shows reduced repeat victimization in the target area and an overall burglary decline of 70 percent (Anderson and Pease, 1997).

Child Sexual Assault

Typical discussions of situational crime prevention involve property offenses and largely avoid interpersonal crimes. While it is possible to argue that personal crimes are more likely to be spontaneous and less likely to be planned than property crimes, this does not mean that situational techniques cannot be used with personal offenses. Tremblay (2006) notes that the Internet has greatly enhanced the ability of pedophiles to interact, attract victims, and gain social support for their behavior. As such, it is possible to use situational techniques to increase the effort and risks of pursuing victims online. Wortley and Smallbone (2006) argue that it is possible to attack child sexual abuse by attacking the opportunity dimension of offending. They suggest that it is possible to increase the effort by making it difficult for offenders to enter areas where children are found or by enhancing the screening of potential employees in businesses that cater to youths. It is also possible to reduce facilitators by limiting access to pornography or contact with other offenders. Increasing risks and reducing permissibility are also avenues to explore with child sexual assault. Wortley and Smallbone's (2006) discussion of situational techniques with child sexual assault is illustrative of the possibilities for using situational prevention to combat personal offenses.

SUMMARY

Several observations can be drawn from studies of situational prevention. First, there is an emphasis on property crimes, which is to be expected given the theoretical bases underlying the approach. This does not mean, however, that it cannot be applied to personal offenses. Second, a wide array of interventions appears in the literature and this diversity is evident both across different crime problems and within the same offenses. What this suggests is that the prevention initiatives truly are "situational" in nature and cannot simply be applied to the same crime that appears in different places at different times. Third, research successfully demonstrates the effectiveness of programs that target effort, risk, and reward. We have not discussed guilt and shame techniques, primarily because these ideas are in need of further empirical testing. Fourth, in many analyses there is evidence of either displacement or diffusion, despite the fact that many of the research designs do not specifically test for them. It is important to note that displacement is never 100 percent. Finally, the focused nature of situational prevention efforts may help maximize the success of the programs. Programs that attempt to make modest changes in specific problems at specific times and places should be more successful than multifaceted programs aiming for large-scale changes.

Situational crime prevention offers an approach that seeks to target specific problems with individualized interventions. As such, these techniques epitomize the ideas of secondary prevention. This does not mean that we are looking at entirely new forms of interventions. Indeed, many of the actions discussed in the later part of this chapter are the same ideas we discussed under primary prevention. The success of situational approaches has moved these ideas into the forefront of many crime prevention discussions and will continue to receive a great deal of attention in the future. The next chapter addresses a topic that also seeks to identify specific problems and implement targeted interventions—partnerships.

Chapter 11

PARTNERSHIPS FOR CRIME PREVENTION

Key Terms:

CAPS
civil abatement
community policing
Operation Ceasefire
order maintenance
problem solving

Project Safe Neighborhoods
pulling levers
SACSI
SARA
Weed and Seed

Learning Objectives:

After reading this chapter you should be able to:

- Debate the meaning of "community policing" by discussing different definitions and key features of it

- List and define the features of community policing

- Tell what SARA stands for and discuss its component parts

- Provide examples of community policing programs and talk about their effectiveness

- Discuss civil abatement approaches and their impact

- Talk about project Weed and Seed, including how it is supposed to work and what evaluations show

- Demonstrate your knowledge of SACSI and PSN

- Discuss Operation Ceasefire and its replications

- Give an overview of Crime and Disorder partnerships in the United Kingdom

- List and discuss the keys to successful partnerships

The inability of the police to handle the crime problem alone and the recognition that crime and disorder cannot be dealt with solely through the arrest and prosecution of offenders has led to the development of alternative responses and methods. Partnership initiatives are at the forefront of these activities. While many of the ideas and interventions found in partnerships are similar to those found in general citizen crime prevention, the onus for action is on the police and social service agencies to work in cooperation with one another and the general public. These endeavors often seek to target specific problems. The underlying philosophy is to encourage interaction and cooperation between police officers, residents, community groups, and other agencies to solve problems. Rosenbaum (2002:180) notes that:

> the value of partnerships in theory lies in their responsiveness to the etiology of complex problems, their ability to encourage interagency cooperation both inside and outside the criminal justice system, their ability to attack problems from multiple sources of influence and to target multiple causal mechanisms ...

In many respects, partnerships mirror ideas found in situational prevention. A key assumption is that there are factors underlying the crime and disorder problems in the community. The typical police response to the problems, that being arrest and prosecution, does little to address the causes of the problems. Arrest and prosecution deal mainly with the overt symptoms. These new approaches seek to identify problems and potential solutions, as well as implement interventions. As such, partnerships fall squarely in the realm of secondary prevention. They target high-risk situations.

In the United States, the most recognized partnership effort is community policing (although community policing is not always called a partnership). Because of its high profile, community policing receives a great deal of attention in this chapter. After discussing the problems of defining community policing and identifying how community policing should work, the chapter turns to evaluating the effectiveness of community policing programs and partnership initiatives.

COMMUNITY POLICING

Understanding community policing requires some knowledge of the more traditional view of what the police are and what they should do. For most people, the formal police role is to answer calls about crime, undertake investigations, make arrests and assist in the prosecution of offenders. Fighting crime (and crime prevention) is primarily the responsibility of the police. Consequently, the police are often judged by the level of crime in the community. Arrests are the benchmark by which the public judges police effectiveness.

The police also are called on to provide *order-maintenance* functions that do not deal with an immediate criminal action. Order-maintenance functions include responding to disabled autos, escorting funerals and parades, dealing with barking dogs, responding to false alarms and noise complaints, and delivering messages. Various studies show that these activities consume the majority of police time, with the police spending roughly 20 percent of their time on actual law enforcement efforts (Kelling, 1978; Lab, 1984b; Walker, 1983; Wilson, 1968). While critics argue that the police should not be involved in order-maintenance activities, Hoover (1992) argues that order maintenance is a key part of traditional policing and serves to keep society functioning in an orderly fashion. As such, order maintenance enhances the law enforcement efforts of the police.

Precursors to Community Policing

Trying to respond to all of the desires of the citizenry is not an easy task and is one possible reason for the inability of the police to control serious crime. Criticism of the police and the apparent failure of past police practices to stem the crime problem have led to the introduction of different strategies. One approach was the revival of foot patrol. Research shows that foot patrol has had a mixed impact on crime (Bowers and Hirsch, 1987; Esbensen, 1987; Police Foundation, 1981; Trojanowicz, 1983), although it appears to reduce the level of citizens' fear and improve attitudes toward the police (Brown and Wycoff, 1987; Police Foundation, 1981; Trojanowicz, 1983). The police are also a key ingredient of both the establishment and maintenance of Neighborhood Watch and citizen crime prevention initiatives. Underlying these activities has been the recognition that the police cannot solve crime on their own or address the increased calls for assistance by the public. The police need to build better relations with citizens and increase the involvement of citizens in crime prevention and crime policy.

Some police initiatives appear at first glance to be nothing more than traditional policing but are actually indicative of community policing efforts. A prime example of this is police sweeps or intensive patrol operations that target specific problems in localized areas. Sherman (1990), for example, points out that a massive police crackdown in one area of New York effectively reduced drug crimes, robbery, and homicide, although the impact did not persist long after the effort ended. Similarly, a police crackdown on a drug market in Lynn, Massachusetts, was successful at reducing drug-related crimes in the area (Kleiman and Smith, 1990). In these cases the police simply used their traditional powers of arrest, albeit in a concerted effort, to impact on the crime problem. The localized character of the interventions is a key element in community policing initiatives.

Defining Community Policing

The fact that elements of community policing appear in past practices demonstrates that community policing is not a totally new idea. The term "community policing," however, is a relatively new one. In addition, there has been a shift in the basic orientation of everyday police activity emerging under the rubric of "community policing." This shift is from the traditional view of "crime fighting" through arrests to a view that fighting crime involves a broader set of interventions.

Arriving at a single definition of community policing has proved to be an elusive goal. While a single definition has not emerged, the various definitions found in Table 11.1 tap the essential elements offered by most writers. Most of these definitions reflect the fact that community policing is more of a philosophy of policing, rather than a clearly definable method (see, for example, Greene and Mastrofski, 1988; Trojanowicz and Bucqueroux, 1989; Walker, 1999). Beyond the fact of this philosophical shift, the various definitions of community policing generally include several essential features. These are

Table 11.1
Definitions of Community Policing

> **Weisel and Eck (1994:51):**
>
> a diverse set of practices united by the general idea that the police and the public need to become better partners in order to control crime, disorder, and a host of other problems.
>
> **Wilkinson and Rosenbaum (1994:110):**
>
> "Community Policing" represents a fundamental change in the basic role of the police officer, including changes in his or her *skills*, *motivations*, and *opportunity* to engage in problem-solving activities and to develop new partnerships with key elements of the community.
>
> **Oliver (1998:51):**
>
> A systemic approach to policing with the paradigm of instilling and fostering a sense of community, within a geographical neighborhood, to improve the quality of life. It achieves this through the decentralization of the police and the implementation of a synthesis of three key components: (1) the redistribution of traditional police resources; (2) the interaction of police and all community members to reduce crime and the fear of crime through indigenous proactive programs; and (3) a concerted effort to resolve the cause of crime, rather than the symptoms.
>
> **Office of Community Oriented Policing Services (2006):**
>
> Community policing focuses on crime and social disorder through the delivery of police services that includes aspects of traditional law enforcement, as well as prevention, problem-solving, community engagement, and partnerships. The community policing model balances reactive responses to calls for service with proactive problem-solving centered on the causes of crime and disorder. Community policing requires police and citizens to join together as partners in the course of both identifying and effectively addressing these issues.

community involvement, problem solving, a community base, and redefined goals for the police.

Community Involvement

First, community policing requires cooperation between the police and other members of the community. The community members may be individual citizens, citizen groups, business associations, legislative bodies, and other local agencies (such as health departments, building inspectors, and community development offices). Community involvement does not stop at the point of calling the police when something occurs. Instead, citizens must be involved in identifying and solving all sorts of community problems—not just criminal acts.

Problem Solving

The emphasis on *problem solving* is perhaps the most important element of community policing. Rather than simply dealing with the crime that occurs through investigation and arrest, community policing challenges officers to identify the underlying causes and contributors to the crime, and seek out solutions to those problems. Community policing, therefore, sees crime as a symptom of more basic concerns. The police can either deal with the symptom or try to address the ultimate cause. While law enforcement should do both, the community policing orientation shifts the primary attention to the underlying problems.

This orientation also appears under the name *problem-oriented policing*. Problem-oriented policing means approaching issues and problems differently based on the uniqueness of each situation. This is a drastic shift from the traditional view that the police should use the criminal code to respond to calls for service. If the code prohibits the activity, the police can (and should) make an arrest and set the criminal justice system in motion. At best, this response will eliminate further criminal behavior through either its deterrent or incapacitative effect. Events that are not proscribed in the criminal code can be ignored. The problem-oriented approach argues that invoking the criminal code is only one avenue for dealing with societal issues. Instead, different problems require alternative solutions or interventions. The police, therefore, need to identify and pursue solutions to the root problem.

The difference between problem-oriented policing and community policing is not always clear or great. One potential differentiating element is the explicit reliance on the community in community policing. This is not an absolute difference, because many "problem-oriented" approaches also rely on community involvement. At the same time, police sweeps and intensive patrol can be considered problem-oriented responses that do not need or require citizen participation. Second, Hoover (1992) suggests that problem-oriented and community policing differ in the duration of the police intervention. Problem-oriented policing involves sustained order maintenance focusing on specific problems and needs over a limited period. Conversely, community policing sets up the police as *community managers* who are involved in wide-ranging community issues over an extended period (Hoover, 1992). This distinction highlights the central role of the community in community policing.

Community Base

Critical to community policing is the decentralization of the police operation. Community policing typically means assigning officers to a specific neighborhood. This may be done in a variety of ways, including the establishment of neighborhood stations, storefront offices, foot patrol, and others. The assignments are long term, with the expectation that the officers will intimately get to know the community, its problems, and its citizens. Community policing assumes that the failure of the police to identify problems and relate to citizens, among others, is due to the distance that central stations and patrol cars place between officers and citizens. The daily interaction with the community should alert the officer to the problems and needs of the residents. The expected result is increased goodwill on the part of residents and an increased desire by citizens to assist and involve themselves with the police.

Redefined Goals

The fourth major element of community policing involves altering the goals of policing. In one sense, this is closely allied to the idea of identifying and attacking the root causes of problems. At the same time, however, this could mean a great shift in how the police are judged. Most departments are judged, both by themselves and the citizenry, in terms of the number of arrests made. Community policing initiatives, to the extent that they deal with underlying causes and involve officers in non-arrest activities, require that the department and officers be held to different standards. In addition to arrests, community policing programs can be judged by reduced crime, the elimination of problem properties, increased feelings of safety, less neighborhood disorder, community cohesion, and many other outcomes. It is important to note that community policing should emphasize the ends, rather than the means to the ends. That is, instead of focusing on how things get done, the primary concern is the elimination of the root problem.

Summary

Other key features of community policing offered in the literature include a less rigid organizational structure, a focus on disorder, different training for officers, collaboration, de-emphasizing calls for service or arrests, and recognizing the complexity of criminal behavior (Carter, 1995; Eck and Rosenbaum, 1994; Hope, 1994; Walker, 1999; Watson et al., 1998; Wilkinson and Rosenbaum, 1994). Many of these ideas are implicit in the four major themes listed above. It is important to note that all of these ideas must work in unison. Just having one component, such as community offices, is not enough. Community policing requires fundamental changes in philosophy, strategy, and programming (Cordner, 1995).

It is also possible to identify what community policing is not. Community policing is not police-community relations. While community policing should build better rapport and relations between the police and the public, that effort is not enough to qualify as community policing. Another common misconception is that moving police officers to foot patrol, storefront offices, or other methods of decentralization is the same as community policing. Unfortunately, unless there is a corresponding change in the other elements of community policing, these efforts only change the location of traditional policing. Community policing also is not simply targeting a problem or location using traditional police techniques. These efforts may be new for the police organization, but they do not involve other societal members in the problem solving. Indeed, many traditional police activities can masquerade as community policing by shifting officers and using new names. It is important, however, to make more fundamental changes in the organization's operations.

PROBLEM IDENTIFICATION

Perhaps the central task of any partnership is the identification of problems and their solutions. Eck and Spelman (1989) offer a four-step process for problem solving. These steps are scanning, analysis, response, and assessment (*SARA*). *Scanning* involves the identification of the problems, issues, and concerns in the community. This information may arise from the observations officers make as they work in the community, from residents or businesses who bring problems to the officers, from other agencies (such as schools or hospitals) in the community, or from the systematic study of data and information on the area. One primary method used in scanning involves computer-generated analyses of when and where crime occurs. The analysis of crime "hot spots" (Sherman, 1995) or the generation of crime maps represents two such attempts. Other efforts may involve the analysis of calls for service, systematic observation of the community, or surveying citizens or community groups. In every case, the police should be working in partnership with others to identify problems that need to be addressed.

The second stage is the *analysis* of the problem. It is particularly important that more than just the police are involved in this activity. An array of individuals and agencies should participate in the analysis. For example, if drug dealing is centered in a house, apartment, or public housing building, the police, landlords, housing authority personnel, the health department, and/or the city attorney need to be involved in the problem analysis. If the drug activity centers around youths, it may be advisable to include the schools, probation office, or youth groups in the process. The intent is to bring together a diversity of expertise and insight. This diversity will bring different information and viewpoints and assist in understanding what factors are involved in the problem.

It is from this cooperative interaction that different *responses* will emerge. Who is involved in implementing the response will vary greatly. In some cases the police may have little day-to-day involvement in the intervention because the identified response requires expertise and abilities that the police do not have. An example of this would be the use of civil litigation against owners of property where drug use is allowed to continue. While the police can deliver summonses, much of the work will be conducted by lawyers for the jurisdiction and other departments that can help to shut down the building (such as a health department).

The final, but essential, step is *assessment*. Eck and Spelman (1989) note that this entire process can succeed only if the interventions are evaluated for their effectiveness. This evaluation, however, is not meant simply as a means of gauging success. Rather, its importance is found in the feedback it provides to the process and to improving (or altering) the intervention. A graphic depiction of the process can be seen in Figure 11.1.

Figure 11.1
A Problem-Solving Process

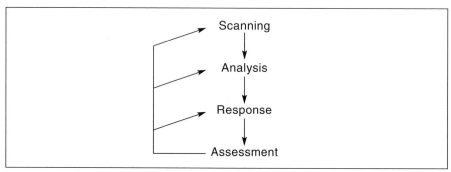

Source: J.E. Eck and W. Spelman (1997). "Who Ya Gonna Call? The Police as Problem-Busters." *Crime and Delinquency* 33:53–70.

Variations on the SARA process or other systematic problem-solving processes that involve the community are essential for community policing partnering. No matter what technique or approach is used, the effort revolves around dealing with the causes of the problems, not the symptoms. Consequently, assessment of the intervention requires looking at more than just reduced crime, increased arrests, or other outcomes typically relied on by the police.

PARTNERSHIP EFFORTS AND ASSESSMENT

The move toward partnership programs continues to grow throughout the United States, Canada, the United Kingdom, and many other countries. Under the heading of community policing, Wycoff (1995) reported that approximately 800 law enforcement agencies in 1993 had implemented community policing in the United States. As of 2001, more than 10,000 law enforcement agencies reported more than 113,000 community police officers on duty in the United States (Zhao et al., 2002). Partnerships, however, appear under a variety of headings and involve police in a wide range of capacities. These partnerships vary greatly, largely due to the emphasis on identifying interventions that address a specific problem. The following pages discuss various partnership initiatives.

Community Policing

While community policing can take a wide array of forms in different communities, it is often discussed as a unitary program. Despite the great amount of money and effort put into promoting community policing, many police departments do little to actually include the public and other agencies in problem-solving activities. This does not mean that some police departments are not attempting to build true partnerships through community policing. The *Chicago Alternative Police Strategy* (CAPS) is a good example of successfully implementing a community-oriented policing approach. Chicago opted to move its entire police force into community policing. The Chicago Alternative Police Strategy (CAPS) began in five of the city's 25 police beats in 1993 with the support of the police administration and the mayor (Hartnett and Skogan, 1999). Key aspects of the program include assigning officers to permanent neighborhood beats, the involvement of residents in the identification of problems and potential solutions, and reliance on other agencies (both public and private) to address identified issues. Citizen interaction is the cornerstone of the program and the police initiate beat meetings to meet neighborhood residents and engender meaningful interaction between the officers and citizens. These meetings identify a wide range of local problems, including gangs, drugs, graffiti, burglary, and physical and social disorder (Skogan and Hartnett, 1997).

As expected under community policing, CAPS responses varied from neighborhood to neighborhood. Improved police enforcement appears throughout the project and often focuses on drug problems. Efforts to clean up problem locations and generally improve the physical conditions of neighborhoods represent a major initiative in the program. The ability to improve the areas is directly related to the ability to mobilize other city services that are suited to those efforts. Mobilizing residents to provide surveillance, work with one another, call the police, and take other actions also appear throughout the project. These actions have successfully reduced the signs of physical decay, had an impact on the extent of visible gang and drug activity, reduced area crime rates, and improved resident's attitudes and assessments of the police and the city (Skogan and Hartnett, 1997). Unfortunately, this one good example is an exceptional case amid many others in which community policing is little more than a means to hire more officers and build good public relations.

One of the reasons for this state of affairs is the fact that community policing programs rarely undergo any form of rigorous evaluation. At best, evaluations tend to be process evaluations that look at the number of community policing officers hired and put on the street, or the assignment of officers to "community" or neighborhood offices or beats, thus making them community police officers. Most evaluations fail to assess the degree of problem solving taking place, the number and breadth of community members or agencies involved in the problem identification and problem solving, or the changes in crime, fear, or disorder related to the problem-solving efforts. The outcome is clearly inconsequential to the claim that community policing is being undertaken.

Evidence does exist that the police can build cooperative partnerships with citizens and other agencies, but when outcome evaluations are completed, the results are typically modest. Some studies show reductions in crime, while others do not. Zhao and his colleagues (2002, 2003) analyzed the impact of community policing on arrests and crime. Based on city-level data, they report that agencies receiving community policing funds make a significantly greater number of arrests (Zhao et al., 2003) and those cities experience significantly lower levels of violent and property crimes (Zhao et al., 2002). What these analyses do not reveal is the actual community policing activities and the types of partnering efforts that bring about these changes. It does suggest, however, that community policing creates positive change.

Civil Abatement

An interesting partnership for dealing with problems, particularly drug issues, involves the use of *civil abatement* procedures. This approach seeks to involve landlords, citizens, health departments, zoning boards, and city/county attorneys in the application of civil (and sometimes criminal) codes. The advent of these efforts can be traced to work in Portland, Oregon, in 1987 (Davis and Lurigio, 1998). In terms of drug crimes, these efforts seek to eliminate the use of locations for drug sales or drug use. Property owners can be fined, buildings can be confiscated or boarded up, tenants can be evicted, or structures can be demolished as a result of abatement procedures. Abatement attempts to reduce crime by altering the opportunities for the actions (Mazerolle and Roehl, 1998).

Oakland's Beat Health program focuses on drug problems and related issues of physical and social disorder in neighborhoods. A key aspect of the program is the use of SMART teams (Specialized Multi-Agency Response Team), which rely on the cooperation of police, citizens, and other groups to solve problems. Civil court remedies are a cornerstone of the project, although police enforcement and patrol are important components. In a series of reports, Mazerolle and her colleagues (Green, 1995b; Mazerolle and Roehl, 1999; Mazerolle et al., 1998) demonstrate the effectiveness of the program. One hundred target sites, divided evenly into experimental and control groups, formed the basis of the evaluation. At experimental sites, landlords were contacted by police and received assistance (from the police and other agencies) in dealing with problem tenants, including evicting intransigent individuals. Civil proceedings could be brought against both the landlords and the tenants. Data from calls for police service, interviews, and observations over more than three years reveals significant declines in signs of physical and social disorder, decreased drug sellers, and increased levels of civil behavior (Green, 1995b; Mazerolle and Roehl, 1999; Mazerolle et al., 1998). Control areas showed increased problems or little change in key outcomes. A comparable program in St. Louis reveals successes at building citizen and agency cooperation, reducing signs of disorder, and reducing calls for service to the police (Hope, 1994).

San Diego has instituted a similar drug enforcement program. The Drug Abatement Response Team (DART) works to compel landlords to take action against properties and tenants involved in drug offending (Eck, 1998; Eck and Wartell, 1998; Eck and Wartell, 1999). Based on the assumption that drug offenses flourish where there is a lack of oversight and management of properties, the program seeks to force owners to take responsibility for their property. To test this assumption, researchers divided problem properties into three groups. The key experimental group received a letter outlining the problems at the property and potential actions that could be taken (including civil action), followed by meetings with the police and other interested parties. A second group of property owners received the letter with only suggested responses. No follow-up meetings or assistance took place. The control group received no DART action. Evaluation results showed greatest improvement at the full DART intervention sites. Evictions were more evident in the treatment group, as were lowered levels of crime and drug problems (Eck, 1998; Eck and Wartell, 1998; Eck and Wartell, 1999). The results are greatest in the immediately following months, but persist across the 30-month follow-up period.

These results show that civil abatement projects can be successful at building coalitions of citizens and agencies that are effective at curbing the target problem. At the same time, however, civil abatement can be a long, cumbersome process, particularly if the property owner opts to fight the procedures through the courts. Smith and Davis (1998) note that, while many landlords comply with abatement, there are significant costs associated with legal procedures, lost rental income, salaries for security guards, and other interventions. Consequently, landlords often oppose the programs and perceive of themselves as victims in the process. Hope (1994) notes that use of civil litigation may be most effective as a persuasive tool to bring about quicker responses, such as the sale of the property to a more responsible owner.

"Weed and Seed" Programs

"Weed and Seed" is a federally sponsored project initiated in 1991 to revitalize communities through a process of "weeding" out existing problems and "seeding" areas with programs and initiatives that inhibit the return of the problems. Many of these programs target areas with heavy drug problems. The weeding portion of the program relies primarily on police enforcement activities and subsequent prosecution of offenders (Conley and McGillis, 1996; Dunworth and Mills, 1999). Seeding can take a variety of forms, depending on the needs of the community. Typical efforts may be demolition of abandoned property, physical improvement of the area, the building of businesses, developing educational and employment services and opportunities, and the establishment of community organizations. The seed portion of the program is often initiated by police agencies but requires the involvement of diverse agencies and groups with expertise beyond that of typical law enforcement agencies. As of 1999, Weed and Seed had been implemented in 200 sites throughout the United States with funding of roughly $49 million (Dunworth and Mills, 1999).

An early evaluation of Weed and Seed pointed out that the programs often did only half of the job. Tien and Rich (1994), evaluating the program in three areas of Hartford, Connecticut, reported successful police efforts to weed out various problems in the neighborhoods. Unfortunately, the seeding efforts failed to materialize. Instead, there was a great deal of evidence that the project failed to gain a consensus among the participating agencies on what to do and how to do it (Tien and Rich, 1994). The authors also noted that there was a lack of funds to carry out the seeding part of the program. Kennedy (1996) noted similar findings when looking at other locations. Most efforts focused on cleaning up neighborhoods (weeding), rather than on improving education, employment, health, and economics in the communities (seeding).

A national evaluation of the program offers more positive results. Focusing on eight sites, the evaluation reports evidence of reduced crime problems in several sites (Dunworth and Mills, 1999; Dunworth et al., 1999). Among the positive results are: drug crimes down in four sites, personal crime down in three locations, improved resident perceptions in five areas, improved perceptions of the police, and increased feelings that the areas are getting better. In almost every case, the Weed and Seed locations fared better than the control areas studied. These results, however, are not overwhelmingly positive. There are clear indications of marginal or no changes on many dimensions.

The authors point to several factors that may explain the failure to find uniform positive results. First, the seeding aspects of the program are the most difficult to achieve and require a great deal of effort and planning. Locations that have been most successful at gaining agreement and participation in the seeding activities appear to fare better than other areas (Dunworth and Mills, 1999). Second, many locations need prolonged weeding. The failure to continue enforcement efforts during and after seeding may allow crime problems to return. Third, the failure to adequately prosecute individuals arrested in the weeding stage may result in the offenders returning to the same area (Dunworth et al., 1999). Finally, it may be necessary to target the Weed and Seed efforts at smaller geographic areas that are more easily mobilized and changed (Dunworth and Mills, 1999). While these factors may not explain all of the failures and successes, they offer insight into what appear to be more successful practices.

The Weed and Seed approach makes a great deal of sense and has the potential to have a significant impact on communities. Clearly, what is needed is a great commitment from the varied agencies to work in a true partnership, which is essential to a successful program (Tien and Rich, 1994). One way to accomplish this may be through the development of detailed seeding interventions before any aspect of the program begins (including weeding activities) (Dunworth and Mills, 1999). This would eliminate the problem of getting partway into the project without knowing exactly where you are going. It is also important that the program attempt to build the interventions from the bottom up. That is, rather than trying to bring a program into an area from the outside, the program should work with the local constituencies to identify and implement the intervention (Dunworth et al., 1999).

CCP, SACSI, and PSN

Three major U.S. initiatives for partnership building are the *Comprehensive Communities Program* (CCP), the *Strategic Approaches to Community Safety Initiative* (SACSI), and *Project Safe Neighborhoods* (PSN). Each of these projects has similar features. CCP was initiated in 1994 as a partnership-building initiative to fight crime and improve the quality of life in communities (Bureau of Justice Assistance, 2001). Fifteen communities have participated in the project. The major key to CCP is to use a problem-solving approach that includes a wide array of community individuals, agencies, and groups. Of particular interest is to bring the individuals and groups most affected by crime into the project. The SACSI project was initiated in five sites in 1998 to fight primarily violent personal crimes. The lead agency in the SACSI sites is the local U.S. Attorney's Office, which attempts to build a partnership consisting mainly of other criminal justice agencies. In addition, each partnership includes a local research team whose task is to analyze the problem in the community, participate in selecting the appropriate response, and evaluate the operations of the SACSI team. Local, state, and federal law enforcement agencies; probation and parole offices; local, state, and federal attorneys; and social service agencies form the primary core of participants.

The most recent federal effort at establishing partnerships to fight crime is the PSN project. Started in 2000, PSN can be considered an outgrowth of SACSI and it focuses primarily on reducing firearms violence (PSN, 2003). The project has five core components: partnerships, strategic plans, training, outreach, and accountability. Like SACSI, the project, led by the U.S. Attorney in each judicial district, attempts to bring together law enforcement and other criminal justice agencies in order to focus on identifying problems and initiating solutions. Each district is expected to have plans that fit the unique situation in the area. The public is involved mainly through an educational outreach plan. In all three of these initiatives (CCP, SACSI and PSN), the partnerships are primarily made up of official criminal justice personnel.

The evaluations that have been done on these projects are mainly process evaluations. The materials available on the CCP spend a great deal of time describing the activities of the partnerships in each site, with special attention paid to the coalition-building activities (see Bureau of Justice Assistance, 2001; Kelling et al., 1999). Few of the sites provide outcome measures on changes in crime, and those that do generally fail to provide data for comparable control areas (Bureau of Justice Assistance, 2001). It is not possible, therefore, to know whether the results are due to the CCP initiative or some other cause. Similarly, most material available on the SACSI project is restricted to process evaluations, which show that partnerships can be successfully established, although a concerted effort is often needed to sustain them. One analysis of SACSI in St. Louis (Decker et al., 2005) did look at reduction in the target behavior (gun crime) and notes that homicides decreased after the initiation of the project. An evaluation of SACSI in New Haven presents promising results. The New Haven project, TimeZup, involved a range of participants, including local law enforcement, the U.S. Attorney's office, the State Attorney's office, probation, parole, corrections, and social services (Hartstone and Richetelli, 2005). The authors note decreased levels of violent gun crimes, calls for service, and numbers of guns seized. Other positive results included reduced fear of crime and increased confidence in the police (Hartstone and Richetelli, 2005). Several case studies on PSN projects have been completed but each represents a process evaluation (Bynum and Decker, 2006; Decker and McDevitt, 2006; Klofas and Hipple, 2006; McDevitt et al., 2006).

Gun Violence

Several partnerships have addressed gun violence, particularly among juveniles and gang members. Perhaps the most well-known of these is Boston's *Operation Ceasefire*. Begun in 1996, the project had several key features. Perhaps the most important feature was the creation of an interagency working partnership. The task for the group was to assess the nature of the gun problem and the dynamics of youth violence in Boston, and to identify and implement an effective intervention (Kennedy et al., 2001). The outcome of the planning was a set of interventions aimed primarily at gangs and gang members. Utilizing the manpower and resources of the police, probation, parole, and district attorney's office, the project used a strict enforcement policy for all individuals and groups involved directly or indirectly in gun violence. Dubbed "*pulling levers*," the project would take any and all actions possible against violators. That meant that any gun violence would result in the immediate arrest and full prosecution of violators. Probation and parole violators were vigorously prosecuted for any violation of the conditions of their release. Gangs and gang members were notified of the project and the potential consequences of their actions (Kennedy et al., 2001). Social service agencies and federal agencies (such as Immigration and Naturalization, which was used to deport non-citizen offenders) were also included in the project.

An evaluation of Operation Ceasefire shows overwhelming positive results. Braga et al. (2001) report a 63 percent drop in monthly juvenile homicides after initiation of the project. Similarly, calls to the police about shots being fired decreased by 32 percent and there was a corresponding drop of 25 percent in assaults with guns (Braga et al., 2001). While it is not possible to claim that the drop in firearm offenses is due solely to Operation Ceasefire, there is reason to believe that the project was a major contributor to the declines.

Two replications of Operation Ceasefire appeared in Los Angeles and Atlanta. In Los Angeles, among the groups participating in the partnership were the local police departments, probation, parole, various prosecutors' offices, community centers, job training programs, churches, and school groups (Tita et al., 2005). Many of the interventions mirror those from Boston, both enforcement and prevention. Tita et al. (2005) note that violent crime fell as a result of the enforcement tactics, while a small change was found in gun and gang crime. Prevention measures had little impact. The Atlanta project focused on juvenile firearms violence and relied on similar partners to those in the other programs. Both prevention and enforcement tactics appear in the project (Kellermann et al., 2006). The results, however, fail to show support for the program. Decreases in homicide cannot be attributed to the intervention (Kellermann et al., 2006). These three projects provide mixed evidence on the effectiveness of partnerships.

Crime and Disorder Partnerships

The passage of the U.K. Crime and Disorder Act in 1998 mandated the establishment of community partnerships to combat crime and related problems. These partnerships are meant to include the local police and a variety of community constituencies, including housing authorities, victims, health professionals, probation officers, and others. Newburn (2002) notes that the goal is to address "multi-dimensional problems with multi-dimensional responses." Crime is not the only problem to be tackled, thus the need for wide participation by varied groups other than law enforcement. More than £925 million have been spent funding partnerships between 1999 and 2005 (Ellis et al., 2007).

A key component of the Crime and Disorder Act is that each partnership is to carry out a crime audit (data collected for planning and evaluation purposes) every three years, based on data for the prior three years. Information should come from a variety of sources, such as police statistics, victimization surveys, probation data, education, and environmental health. The police are required to consult with the partnership and use the data to form prevention strategies and evaluate those strategies (Walklate, 1999). Several authors point out that some attempts to form partnerships have met with less than full success, the police are often the major contributor to the process, and the exact role of the participants is often poorly outlined (see, for example, Hughes, 2002; Phillips, 2002; Tierney, 2001). Hughes (2002) points out that many partnerships target crimes that are easier to address (such as burglary) while ignoring more difficult crimes and social problems that are harder to change. A good deal of the published work about the Crime and Disorder Act examines the politics surrounding the Act and the development of crime audits (see Crawford, 2001; Gilling, 2005; Hughes et al., 2002). The National Audit Office (2004) notes large reductions in reported crimes since the initiation of partnerships, however it is not clear the extent to which the partnerships caused the reductions. Consequently, it is unclear to what extent these new partnerships are having a significant impact on crime and disorder.

Gang Suppression Programs

In the mid-1990s, the Office of Juvenile Justice and Delinquency Prevention (OJJDP) initiated the *Community-Wide Approach to Gang Prevention, Intervention, and Suppression Program*. The program aimed to initiate a comprehensive set of strategies including suppression, opportunities provision, and social interventions. OJJDP funded program implementation and evaluation in five cities (Bloomington-Normal, IL; Mesa, AZ; Riverside, CA; Tucson, AZ; and San Antonio, TX). Each of the programs drew on the expertise of law enforcement, schools, employment organizations, and other social service agencies.

Several factors emerge across the evaluations. First, several cities struggled with building programs that included grassroots community organizations. Most of the participants remained official criminal justice agencies and other social service providers (Spergel et al., 2001; 2002; 2004a; 2004b). Second, suppression remains the primary response in at least three cities (Spergel et al., 2001; 2002; 2003; 2004b). Finally, the more successful programs offered a wider array of activities that could be considered opportunities provision and social interventions, such as counseling, referrals, and job training.

The program's impact on gang membership and crime is also mixed. The evaluations of the Bloomington-Normal, Mesa, and Riverside programs report reduced offending and reduced arrests among youths in the experimental neighborhoods (Spergel et al., 2001; 2002; 2003). While the Bloomington-Normal program appears to have reduced the level of gang participation (Spergel et al., 2001), there was no apparent impact in Riverside, Tucson, or San Antonio (Spergel et al., 2003; 2004a; 2004b). Despite the mixed results of the programs, the evidence suggests that a successfully implemented program that targets a wider array of interventions than just suppression activities has the ability to positively affect the level of gang crime and gang membership.

Problems and Concerns

Many studies that show the potential positive impact of partnerships also demonstrate some stumbling blocks and weaknesses. Implementation is often a problem due to the change in philosophy being imposed on police officers (Bennett, 1994; Eck and Rosenbaum, 1994; Rosenbaum, 2002; Sadd and Grinc, 1994). Crawford (2001) notes that clear power differentials exist between the participants, which makes cooperation difficult and the participants cautious about their roles. There are also differences in the level and type of resources that the various partners can contribute, thus raising the possibility that those with greater expertise and more resources have more input into the selection of problems and their solutions (Crawford, 2001; Tilley, 2005). Some critics point to problems that reflect traditional views of police roles. For example, some critics claim that community policing initiatives result in delayed response time and the need for additional officers in order to do both the traditional law enforcement and community policing jobs (Skolnick and Bayley, 1988; Wycoff, 1995). Rosenbaum (2002) also notes that some people are concerned that partnerships are dysfunctional and tend to act too slowly. Critics also claim that partnerships tend not to be truly representative of the community, thus defeating the intended purpose of having community input (Rosenbaum, 2002).

Many of these issues and concerns may be due to the newness of the ideas. Participants who are involved tend to develop a positive attitude toward partnership efforts (Rosenbaum, 2002; Skogan, 1995). The lack of an extensive track record for partnerships, and the fact that relatively few outcome evaluations have been completed also makes it difficult to sell the idea. Partnerships are difficult to study and what information is available tends to be exclusively process evaluations.

SUCCESSFUL PARTNERSHIPS

The research on partnerships illuminate several keys to building successful partnerships (see Table 11.2). One of the most important factors is identifying and recruiting strong leaders and managers (Brown, 2006; Hedderman and

Williams, 2001; Homel et al., 2004; Scott, 2006). These individuals are essential for maintaining focus for the partnership and promoting enthusiasm over time. The failure to adequately identify the target problem and the appropriate intervention is a common problem. Building agreement is no an easy task (Homel et al., 2004; Kelling, 2005). Researching the problem to truly understand its extent and causes greatly assists in building agreement, as well as subsequent activities (Kelling, 2005; Scott, 2006). Once the problem and intervention are identified, it is necessary to recruit qualified staff for implementing the project (Homel et al., 2004; Hedderman and Williams, 2001; Scott, 2006). Training and education of the various participants in partnerships is essential to both the effectiveness of the efforts and their acceptance (Sadd and Grinc, 1996; Skogan, 1995; Skolnick and Bayley, 1988). Members of the partnership need to be educated about community outreach, coalition building, and problem identification.

Table 11.2
Features of Successful Partnerships

1.	Identify strong leaders and managers
2.	Agree on the problem and intervention
3.	Recruit qualified staff
4.	Research the problem
5.	Build grass roots support
6.	Identify adequate funding and resources
7.	Provide good oversight of project implementation
8.	Evaluate the efforts

Successfully proceeding with the intervention requires a number of other actions. Foremost among them is building grass roots support in the community (Scott, 2006). Interventions have a better chance of success if the public cooperates rather than fights the efforts. Many partnership initiatives become unilateral activities by the police, or are poorly coordinated and implemented (Buerger, 1994; Moore, 1994; Sadd and Grinc, 1994, 1996; Skogan, 1995, 1996). Community support also contributes to identifying and securing adequate resources and funding (Homel et al., 2004; Scott, 2006; Tilley, 2005). Without resources, projects cannot function. Once a project is operating there is a need for good project oversight (Brown, 2006; Hedderman and Williams, 2001; Homel et al., 2004). A final key to success is including a meaningful process and impact evaluation (Scott, 2006). This evaluation should be conducted by researchers or agencies not involved in the program delivery (Homel et al., 2004).

SUMMARY

A major argument underlying partnerships entails the fact that crime and community problems are beyond the ability of the criminal justice system to solve by itself. The police and other criminal justice agencies need to partner with social service agencies, community groups, and the citizenry if they are to have an impact on the underlying causes of crime. These collaborations have the potential to bring a wide array of new and innovative ways of looking at problems, as well as proposing solutions to those problems. They also bring different skills, abilities, and resources that can be used to implement the proposed solutions. Unfortunately, up to this point there have been relatively few good outcome evaluations conducted on community policing and partnership initiatives. What has been produced are extensive process evaluations that point out the issues and concerns with building and operating a coalition. The next step is to evaluate whether they have a significant impact on crime and fear.

Chapter 12

DRUGS, CRIME, AND CRIME PREVENTION

Key Terms:

ADAM program
D.A.R.E.
detoxification
methadone maintenance
Monitoring the Future
National Survey on Drug Use and
   Health

National Youth Survey
Psychopharmacological
Reciprocal
resistance skills training
spurious
systemic violence
therapeutic communities

Learning Objectives:

After reading this chapter you should be able to:

- Provide insight to the extent of drug use in society and among offending populations

- Demonstrate your knowledge of key sources of data on drug use

- Diagram the possible relationships between drug use and crime, and discuss the evidence on each

- Tell what a psychopharmacological explanation of the drugs-crime relationship is

- Identify different forms of drug treatment

- Discuss NIDA's principles of effective treatment

- Talk about maintenance programs and their impact on drug use

- Explain what a therapeutic community is and the extent of its effect

- Define "detoxification" and relate its ability to affect drug use

- Discuss NIDA's principles of effective prevention

- Discuss D.A.R.E.: what it is and what impact it has had

- Explain the purpose behind education/information/knowledge programs and their impact on drug use

The relationship between drug use and crime is a persistent concern in society. Since the mid-1970s, violent crime stemming from the drug trade has been a regular feature on the evening news and in the print media. Graphic depictions of drug crimes pique the interest of both the public and the criminal justice system. The federal government responds to this concern by continuing its "war" on drugs. Efforts to reduce the supply of drugs are the primary means of attack in this war. This emphasis on supply reduction targets the drugs at various points—arrests of the street-level dealer, identifying and prosecuting the drug "kingpin," and drug interdiction at the borders to the country. Less emphasis is placed (at least at the federal level) on the treatment of substance abusers or the prevention of initial use.

The issue of drug use is best addressed within the framework of secondary prevention. For many individuals, drug use itself is not a concern. Those who use drugs do so voluntarily. They purchase the drug and use it themselves. At no point do they forcibly make another individual use drugs. In this respect, drug use is a victimless crime. Both the offender and the victim are the same individual. Most individuals do not know of anyone who uses illicit drugs on a daily basis, or at least are not aware that someone they know is a daily user. Consequently, actual drug use is not a concern. Societal concern arises from problems and issues related to drug use. For example, crimes committed to provide funds for drugs become a problem affecting more than the consensual user. There is now a clear victim. Similarly, society often bears the costs related to caring for a user's family or handling addicted individuals. There is also evidence of pressure on youths to participate in drug use. Such pressure may force an impressionable individual into use and other related problems. The drug problem, therefore, includes more than just the individual choice to use a drug.

Drug use is one means of predicting or identifying potential problems in society. Targeting those involved in drug use may serve to alleviate the problems (crime and otherwise) that stem from drug use. As with many interventions, those tied to drug issues do not fall exclusively in the realm of secondary prevention. Efforts to work with current users are themselves tertiary in nature. Other methods aimed at preventing initial use may be construed as primary prevention, especially if implemented on a broad scale. The fact that the actual concern in dealing with drugs lies with the related crime and societal problems, however, means that drug issues are most properly dealt with in terms of secondary prevention.

In discussions of the drug problem, there are a number of unresolved issues. The first deals with the actual level of drug use/abuse in society and changes in drug use over time. Second, implicit in the concern about drug use is the assumption of a clear drug-crime connection. The common belief is that drug use causes other criminal behavior. A third issue involves the effectiveness of different interventions. What impact do law enforcement, treatment, and other preventive approaches have on the level of drug use and related crime? Answers to this question may suggest the proper means of dealing with drug use in the future.

THE SCOPE OF DRUG USE

The extent of drug use is somewhat difficult to gauge due to the difficulties of measuring private behavior. Unlike most other crimes, drug use has no victim independent of the offender—they are one and the same. Available data relies on self-reports of drug use in the general population or on information on known offenders. A discussion of both of these sources is presented below in order to gain some understanding about the drug problem.

Self-Reported Drug Use

Perhaps the most-well known survey of drug use is the *Monitoring the Future* (MTF) Project carried out by Johnston and associates. This project consists of surveying representative high school students (8th, 10th, and 12th graders), college students, and young adults (Johnston et al., 2009). Young adults refers to high school graduates within 10 years of leaving school. While the survey probes a variety of factors, the most important set of information deals with the level and type of drug use. Table 12.1 presents information on lifetime, annual, and past-month drug use for high school seniors, college students, and young adults in 2008. It can be seen that drug use varies by type of drug.

Looking at the data for all age groups in 2008, the most prevalent drug is alcohol. This is true for all three time frames—lifetime, annual, and past month. Alcohol is used by at least 70 percent of the individuals over their lifetime, with one-half to two-thirds claiming alcohol use during the past month. Marijuana is the next most prominent drug for all age groups over all time periods. The remainder of the drugs are used by very few respondents. This is particularly pronounced in the "past-month" category, where less than four percent of any age group admits to use of any drug. While lifetime use is higher (as expected in light of the longer time frame) it is frequent use that should be of greatest interest, thus the focus on the past-month category.

Another source of information on drug use is the *National Survey on Drug Use and Health* which is conducted by the Substance Abuse and Mental Health Services Administration (SAMHSA). This survey covers a representative sample of U.S. respondents age 12 and older. Table 12.2 provides data for

Table 12.1
Lifetime, Past Year, and Last 30 Day Drug Use by 12th Graders, College Students and Young Adults, 2008 (percentages)

Drug	Lifetime			Past Year			Last 30 Days		
	12th Grader	College Student	Young Adult	12th Grader	College Student	Young Adult	12th Grader	College Student	Young Adult
Any Illicit Drug	47.4	49.5	59.3	36.6	35.2	33.8	22.3	18.9	19.3
Marijuana	42.6	46.8	55.9	37.3	32.3	28.6	19.4	17.0	16.0
Hallucinogens	8.7	8.5	14.8	5.9	5.1	3.8	2.2	1.7	0.9
Cocaine	7.2	7.2	14.8	14.4	4.4	6.0	1.9	1.2	1.9
Crack	2.8	1.4	4.3	1.6	0.5	0.9	0.8	0.1	0.4
Heroin	1.3	0.7	1.9	0.7	0.3	0.5	0.4	–	0.1
Amphetamines	10.5	9.1	14.6	6.8	5.7	5.3	2.9	2.8	2.2
Methamphetamine	2.8	1.9	6.3	1.2	0.5	1.0	0.6	0.0	0.3
Barbiturates	8.5	6.4	10.6	5.8	3.7	4.7	2.8	1.4	1.9
Alcohol	71.9	85.3	88.4	65.5	82.1	83.6	43.1	69.0	68.9

Source: compiled from Johnston et al. (2009).

Table 12.2
Drug Use by Different Adult Age Groups, 2008 (percentages)

Drug	Ever Used				Past Year				Past Month			
	18–20	21–25	26–34	35+	18–20	21–25	26–34	35+	18–20	21–25	26–34	35+
Any Illicit Drug	51.6	59.9	58.2	47.5	36.3	31.5	19.8	8.1	21.5	18.4	11.2	4.7
Marijuana	45.1	53.9	51.3	40.6	30.9	25.3	14.9	5.2	18.7	15.0	8.8	3.2
Cocaine	10.9	16.7	16.7	16.7	5.8	5.4	4.0	1.1	1.6	1.5	1.5	0.4
Crack	1.8	3.4	4.8	3.7	0.7	0.6	0.7	0.4	0.2	0.2	0.3	0.1
Heroin	1.1	1.6	1.9	1.7	0.4	0.5	0.3	0.1	0.2	0.2	0.1	0.1
Hallucinogens	14.2	20.1	22.2	13.6	8.2	5.2	1.7	0.2	2.3	1.3	0.6	0.0
Stimulants	7.8	12.3	11.2	8.4	3.6	3.2	1.6	0.4	1.0	1.1	0.7	0.1
Methamphetamine	2.7	6.0	7.2	5.3	0.8	0.9	0.6	0.2	0.1	0.3	0.1	0.1

Source: compiled from SAMHSA (2008).

four adult age groups. As in the MTF, marijuana is the most commonly used drug across all age groups and time frames. Hallucinogens and cocaine are the next most commonly used drugs, although the percent claiming use drops significantly when considering the last year or last month time periods. For most drugs, few individuals report use in any time category.

The figures in Tables 12.1 and 12.2 are interesting for several reasons. First, drugs that are of the most concern to society are used by very few individuals. Cocaine, crack, heroin, and the other drugs are not the most prevalent drugs in use. Alcohol, a legal drug for adults, is the most commonly used substance. Second, data based on drug use in the past year and last 30 days show the same depressed level of illicit drug use among all groups of respondents. Lifetime and past-year use should not be used as an indicator of a drug "problem" because such use may simply reflect ordinary experimentation (Stephens, 1987). The low figures in the tables suggest mainly experimental use of illicit drugs. Third, the use of most drugs has generally remained stable with some temporary increases in the mid-1990s (trend data not shown). These self-report data suggest that the drug problem (at least in terms of illicit drugs) is relatively minor, although the recent increases need to be carefully monitored.

The self-report figures must be considered cautiously due to some inherent deficiencies. With the MTF data there is a question of generalizability. The data are not representative of the entire population. The fact that the high school and college subjects are (or were) attending school ignores the fact that many youths drop out of high school or do not go to college. Dropping out is especially great among inner-city youths, where the drug trade appears to be most concentrated. Johnston et al. (1989) point out that roughly 15 to 20 percent of high school students drop out and are not included in the survey each year, and that dropouts tend to use drugs more often than non-dropouts. In a study of runaway/homeless youths, Fors and Rojek (1991) find that these individuals report two to seven times the level of substance use/abuse than do school youths. These facts suggest that the MTF data underreport the level of drug use.

Self-report figures, such as those presented here, suggest that the drug problem is not as serious as usually presented. Clearly, the use of illicit drugs is not running rampant in society. Few individuals use illicit drugs with even the grossest measure of regularity (within 30 days). Figures for daily use fall to almost zero for illicit drugs. This is not to suggest that drugs are not a problem. Those who drop out appear to use drugs at a much higher rate than high school graduates. Similarly, criminal offenders may be more involved in drugs than non-offenders. The extent to which drugs are used by offenders can be examined through other sources of information.

Drug Use Among Offending Populations

It is commonly assumed that many offenders are regular users of illicit drugs and that drug use is intricately related to the commission of crime.

Support for such a contention comes from various studies of offenders. The simple number of arrests and convictions for drug offenses provides evidence in support of this claim. Belenko (1990) reports that the number of drug arrests increased 52 percent from 1980 to 1987, while the total number of arrests rose only 11 percent. Similarly, drug convictions in U.S. District Courts rose by 134 percent compared to only 27 percent for all other cases (Belenko, 1990).

The now defunct *Arrestee Drug Abuse Monitoring* (ADAM) program provided more in-depth information on drug use by offenders in 35 cities. This program was an expansion of the *Drug Use Forecasting* (DUF) program sponsored by the National Institute of Justice, which began in 1987. The DUF program was a means of ascertaining the extent of drug use by arrested subjects. Arrestees voluntarily agreed to be interviewed and gave a urine sample for testing. The urinalysis tested for 10 different drugs (cocaine, opiates, marijuana, PCP, methadone, benzodiazepine (Valium), methaqualone, propoxyphene (Darvon), barbiturates, and amphetamines). All information was anonymous. The data provided information on the type of drug use, changes in use over time (data is collected quarterly), the age, race, and sex distribution of users, and arrest charges related to different drugs (National Institute of Justice, 1990).

ADAM results for 2000 (the last year for which information is available) showed that drug use is very common among arrestees. Urinalysis reveals that better than 50 percent of all male arrestees and roughly 40 percent or more female arrestees test positive for recent drug use of any type (24 to 48 hours for all drugs except marijuana, which has a 30-day test period). Cocaine and marijuana are the most prevalent drugs according to test results. Drug use also varies from city to city and between males and females and across racial/ethnic groups (National Institute of Justice, 2003). Data from the British ADAM program shows that 69 percent of arrestees test positive for drug use and 58 percent report alcohol use (Holloway and Bennett, 2004).

Drug use figures are also available for inmates of correctional institutions. James (2004) notes that roughly 25 percent of the jail inmates are sentenced for drug offenses. Additionally, 66 percent of the prisoners in local jails report regular alcohol use and 68 percent report regular drug use. One-third of the inmates claim using alcohol and 29 percent claim using drugs at the time of their offense (James, 2004). Sickmund and Snyder (2006) report that roughly 10 percent of the youths in residential facilities are there due to drug-related offenses.

These figures, based on offending populations, provide a more serious picture of drug use than those from surveys of the general population. As with the other data, there are potential problems to keep in mind. First, this information reflects only the individuals who are caught by the system. It is possible that the use of drugs increases the risk of apprehension for these offenders. Those not apprehended may not use drugs, or at least not at the same level. Second, the ADAM data reflect drug use in 35 major urban areas. Consequently, the results are only generalizable to other comparable large cities. Drug use probably differs between large and small communities, just as crime differs.

Summary

The data on drug use, both from self-reports of the general population and from offending groups, provide valuable information. The general population data suggest that illicit drug use is not as widespread as the media portrays. Most drug use appears to be experimental or occasional in nature. The data on offenders point out that drug use is common among those who are apprehended for crimes. While not necessarily representative of all offenders, those who are caught make up a large group of individuals. The results, therefore, should not be dismissed simply due to low clearance rates or lack of representativeness. Drug use may be considered a risk factor in other criminal behavior. That is, the use of drugs may be a predictor of other deviant activity. This fact receives further support when considering the relationship between drug use and crime, which is taken up next.

THE DRUGS-CRIME CONNECTION

The connection between drug use and crime has received a great deal of attention. A simple inspection of data reveals a strong correlation between drugs and crime. Situations in which many of the offenders test positive for drug use provide a strong basis for claiming a causal relationship. Simple correlations, however, are not enough to establish clear evidence of causation.

The relationship between drug use and crime has been hypothesized to take a variety of forms. White (1990) outlines four possible models for the relationship (see Figure 12.1). First, drug use causes criminal activity. Second, criminal activity causes drug use. Third, there is a reciprocal relationship in which both drug use and criminal activity cause one another. Finally, the relationship between the two is spurious with other factors (possibly the same ones) causing drug use and crime. Various studies have attempted to untangle which causal sequence is correct.

Figure 12.1
Possible Relationships Between Drug Use and Crime

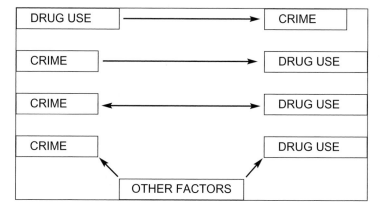

The first model attempts to show that drugs cause the user to commit other crimes. Crime may be the result of a psychopharmacological reaction, economic need, or simple participation in the drug trade (Goldstein, 1989). The *psychopharmacological* explanation suggests that various drugs have a direct impact on the user, both physically and psychologically, which impels the individual to act in such a way that society deems unacceptable. The intent of the individual may not be to commit a crime. The drug simply determines the action, which may or may not be criminal. The *economics* of drug use can also lead to deviance. The increasing need for money to secure drugs can lead to property crimes. Various studies show that drug users are often involved in property offenses (Anglin and Speckart, 1988; Chaiken and Chaiken, 1982; Collins et al., 1985; Harrison and Gfroerer, 1992; Johnson et al., 1985; Johnson et al., 1988; National Institute of Justice, 1990). Participation in drug use also may lead to systemic violence (Goldstein, 1989). *Systemic violence* refers to violence resulting from competition among drug dealers, retaliation for poor drug quality or high prices, robbery of drug dealers or users, and other factors related to the drug trade. Using New York City data, Goldstein et al. (1992) report that 74 percent of all drug-related homicides are due to systemic factors of the drug trade. To the extent that crime fits one of these categories, the first model finds qualified support. Of the three potential arguments, the psychopharmacological explanation is the most difficult to prove and has been criticized for ignoring evidence that much drug use actually reduces physical action and violent tendencies, and only appears in interaction with specific dispositions and social/cultural settings (McBride and Schwartz, 1990). The economic and systemic arguments require attention to the temporal order in the drugs-crime relationship.

Studies claiming support for drug use causing crime typically rely on studies of drug addicts or high-rate users of drugs. Ball and associates (1983), studying 354 heroin addicts, note that their crime rate is four to six times higher when they are actively using drugs. Similarly, Collins et al. (1985) report that daily heroin/cocaine users tend to commit property offenses at a substantially higher rate than weekly users or non-users. Drug use, especially involving expensive drugs and drug habits, necessitates the commission of "income-generating crimes" in order to maintain the pattern of use (Collins et al., 1985). Anglin and Hser (1987) and Anglin and Speckart (1988) note that arrests and self-reported crimes increase at the onset of first narcotics use and first daily use, and decrease at last daily use. Use also declines during treatment and increases when subjects leave treatment (Anglin and Hser, 1987; Anglin and Speckart, 1988). Huizinga et al. (1994) note that changes in substance abuse precede changes in the levels of other delinquent activity.

The second possibility is that involvement in crime causes drug use. Numerous studies suggest that involvement in criminal behavior precedes drug use. Using longitudinal data on almost 2,000 high school graduates in the Youth in Transition project, Johnston and associates (1978) report that general delinquency predates most drug use. The authors argue that youths turn to drug use as an extension of other deviant behavior. Data from the *National Youth Survey* (NYS), an ongoing longitudinal panel study, reveal essentially the same result. Information on delinquency, drug use, and demographic factors for the first six waves of data collection (1976–1983) shows a general progression in behavior starting with minor delinquency and leading to alcohol use, index offenses, marijuana use, and polydrug use, in that order (Huizinga et al., 1989). Except for the early appearance of alcohol, illicit drug use temporally follows delinquent/criminal behavior. Indeed, the authors note that minor delinquency precedes polydrug use 99 to 100 percent of the time (Huizinga et al., 1989). Chaiken and Chaiken (1990), examining data from the NYS, a survey of prison inmates, and a sample of New York City drug addicts, note that delinquency predates drug use at least 50 percent of the time. The same pattern of drug use following delinquency is reported by Inciardi et al. (1993) in a study of serious inner-city delinquents. Other authors (Anglin and Hser, 1987; Anglin and Speckart, 1988; Elliott and Ageton, 1981; Elliott et al., 1989; Hunt, 1990; Johnson et al., 1985) also note that drug use follows crime. The typical explanation for this finding is that drug use is simply another form of deviant behavior, and involvement with delinquency/criminality provides resources and contacts necessary for entering into drug use.

Given the studies reporting a different sequencing in the drugs-crime relationship, it is plausible to argue that the actual relationship is *reciprocal*. That is, criminal activity leads to drug use and drug use leads to criminal activity. Support for a reciprocal relationship can be found in many studies. Nurco et al. (1988) note that addiction increases crime by "previous offenders." Studies of drug addicts typically relate that arrests "increase" after drug use or intensified use, leading to the conclusion that the subjects committed offenses prior to that point in time (Anglin and Hser, 1987; Anglin and Speckart, 1988; Collins et al., 1985). Hunt (1990) points out that, while prostitution increases with drug use, a substantial number of female drug users participated in prostitution and other offenses prior to drug use. Finally, Van Kammen and Loeber's (1994) analysis of data for Pittsburgh youths shows that property offending predicts the onset of drug use, although drug use escalates the commission of personal crime. It would appear that, regardless of which came first, drug use and crime may contribute to each other. Drug use leads to crime and crime leads to drug use.

The argument that seems to be gaining the strongest support is the claim that the relationship between drug use and delinquency is spurious. This simply means that, while use and crime exist at the same time and vary in a similar fashion, neither is the ultimate cause of the other. Rather, they are caused by either the same common factors or by different factors. Huba and Bentler (1983) and Kandel et al. (1986) claim that there is no causal relationship between drug use and crime. Rather, these two sets of behavior are caused by other similar factors. White and associates (1987), using self-report data for almost 900 youths, point out that there are common causes of delinquency and drug use. Foremost among these factors are peer and school influences. The same analysis of the

NYS data, which points out a sequence of behavior beginning with minor offending and ending with polydrug use (Huizinga et al., 1989), concludes that the actual cause of the behaviors probably lies with a common set of spurious influences. Other research leads to the same conclusion (Collins, 1989; Elliott et al., 1979; Elliott et al., 1985; Fagan and Weis, 1990; Hawkins and Weis, 1985; Kandel et al., 1986; Loeber, 1988; White, 1990).

The fact that drug use is related to criminal activity cannot be disputed. The causal relationship, however, is unclear. The inability to definitively identify a causal sequencing does not render the relationship useless to crime prevention. A strong correlation between the two behaviors means that drug use can be used as a predictor of other criminal behavior (Elliott and Huizinga, 1984; Kandel et al., 1986; Newcomb and Bentler, 1988). The research cited above also suggests that each behavior contributes to the other, thereby providing insight for intervention and treatment. It may be possible to attack crime by attacking drug use. Certainly, targeting drug users for intervention means dealing with those who are at higher risk of participating in other criminal activities. Intervening with drug users will also reduce crime to the extent to which drug use does contribute to criminal activity.

INTERVENTIONS AND PREVENTION

Interventions aimed at limiting drug use and related crime take a variety of forms. Most of the approaches fall under three general areas—law enforcement, treatment, and prevention. The great number and diversity of possible responses to the drug-crime problem cannot be adequately discussed in the space available. Indeed, some of the proposed solutions do not fit in the present discussion. The following discussion, therefore, is somewhat selective. Among the topics not covered here (or covered in abbreviated fashion) are efforts at drug interdiction and foreign policy issues, targeting organized crime, drug testing, decriminalization, and legalization. While each of these topics is worthy of discussion, they are beyond the scope of the present work.

Law Enforcement Efforts

The current "drug war" is primarily an effort that uses law enforcement techniques as the primary weapon against drug use. This is evident in the federal government's budgetary priority favoring law enforcement over treatment or prevention programs. Underlying law enforcement actions is the assumption that drug use and related crime can be limited or eliminated by supply reduction. Taking drugs off the street will make it more difficult for users to locate the drugs and, if the drugs can be found, the price will be driven so high that many potential users will simply abstain. In essence, these approaches assume that the demand for drugs is a factor of the supply.

Police crackdowns on drug availability are common responses. New York City's Operation Pressure Point involved saturating the Alphabet City area on the Lower East Side of Manhattan with police officers and resources. Drug buyers could shop around different dealers, often in plain view, in order to secure the best price and quality in the area (Zimmer, 1987). The police operation was credited with thousands of arrests, the elimination of the drug supermarket, and significant reductions in robbery, burglary, and homicide (Kleiman, 1988). Unfortunately, the program led some dealers and buyers to find new means for doing business (i.e., displacement) and the program lasted only as long as the police maintained their heightened presence (Johnson et al., 1990; Kleiman and Smith, 1990). Similar results appeared in an evaluation of a police crackdown in Lynn, Massachusetts.

The fact that gangs are becoming more involved in drug use and sales (Fagan, 1989) has led various jurisdictions to jointly target gangs and drugs. Los Angeles's Community Resources Against Street Hoodlums (CRASH) program is a prime example of police targeting of gang behavior. These efforts, however, have yet to show an impact on the drug problem or other gang behavior, including gang homicides (Kleiman and Smith, 1990). As noted in the last chapter, the police also have been intimately involved in abatement programs that target drug locations.

The size and scope of the drug problem appear to be more than basic police enforcement can handle. Attacking the retail level of the drug chain may result in many arrests but will probably have little impact beyond overburdening the already overcrowded criminal justice system (Belenko, 1990). Similarly, assumptions that law enforcement efforts will significantly reduce the supply of drugs for any long period are ill-conceived. There is a need for an accompanying reduction in the demand for drugs.

Treatment of Drug Users

Drug treatment can take a wide variety of forms and may involve greatly divergent approaches. Research on treatment programs has provided some insights regarding what is most effective. The National Institute on Drug Abuse (NIDA) offers a list of 13 principles of effective treatment (see Figure 12.2). These principles address the general issues that can be applied across different programs in ways that respond to the unique needs of the clients.

Most interventions can be grouped into one of four general types. These are maintenance programs, therapeutic communities, outpatient drug-free programs, and detoxification. While each of these groupings promotes a different major emphasis, many similarities and common features appear across the programs. For example, counseling and therapy of one sort or another appear in virtually all of the programs. A recent innovation has been the establishment of drug courts. Each of these will be briefly examined below.

Figure 12.2
NIDA's 13 Principles of Effective Treatment for Drug Abuse

1.	No single program is appropriate for all individuals
2.	Treatment needs to be readily available
3.	Effective treatment attends to multiple needs of the individual
4.	Treatment and service plans must be assessed continuously and modified as necessary
5.	Remaining in treatment for an adequate period of time is critical for effectiveness
6.	Counseling (individual and/or group) and other behavioral therapies are critical components
7.	Medications are an important element of treatment for many patients
8.	Addicted or drug-abusing individuals with coexisting mental disorders should have both disorders treated in an integrated way
9.	Medical detoxification is merely the first stage of addiction treatment and by itself does little to change long-term use
10.	Treatment does not need to be voluntary to be effective
11.	Possible drug use during treatment must be monitored continuously
12.	Treatment programs should provide assessment of HIV/AIDS and other infectious diseases, and counseling to help patients modify or change behaviors
13.	Recovery from drug addition is a long-term process and frequently requires multiple episodes of treatment

Source: National Institute on Drug Abuse (1999).

Maintenance Programs

Maintenance most often appears in the form of *methadone maintenance.* These are outpatient programs that involve the provision of methadone to heroin/opiate addicts. Methadone is an oral substitute for heroin, which needs to be taken only once in a 24-hour period. Over time, those on maintenance will no longer experience the highs and lows of addiction to other drugs. Methadone patients ideally achieve a state whereby they do not suffer withdrawal pains and are able to function normally on a daily basis (Stephens, 1987). A primary assumption underlying these programs is that the patient is unable to function without some form of drug use and that methadone is an acceptable substitute for other, more damaging drugs.

Most methadone maintenance programs include a variety of components. Periodic urinalysis is used to check that patients are not using other drugs while receiving methadone. Counseling, both individual and group, along with guidelines for behavior and sanctions for violations, is common (Anglin and

Hser, 1990). Some programs attempt to slowly detoxify their patients. That is, they attempt to reduce the methadone dosage and wean the subjects from the need for any drug use. The level of these various components, however, varies greatly from program to program (Ball et al., 1986).

Evaluations of the effectiveness of methadone maintenance programs show generally positive results. Various researchers (Anglin and McGlothlin, 1984; Ball et al., 1987; Hser et al., 1988) report that methadone patients use fewer illicit drugs, commit fewer crimes, and are arrested less often than when not on the program. Additionally, the termination of methadone maintenance shows a return to pre-program levels of drug use and criminal activity (Anglin et al., 1989; McGlothlin and Anglin, 1981). It would appear from these results that maintenance is a feasible approach to the drug-crime problem. The programs, however, are not without critics. Stephens (1987) points out that these programs are applicable only to narcotics and ignore the much larger numbers of other drug users. Additionally, the patients are often non-productive and on welfare. They do not necessarily re-enter the job market and become productive societal members. Anglin and Hser (1990) further point out that the research typically fails to use adequate control groups. The results, therefore, are subject to much criticism.

Therapeutic Communities

Therapeutic communities emphasize providing a supportive, highly structured atmosphere within which individuals can be helped to alter their personality and develop social relationships conducive to conforming behavior (Anglin and Hser, 1990). These residential programs operate as surrogate families for clients. In many cases, therapeutic communities are run by current or past clients. The daily routine is often very structured and includes intensive group sessions. Programs may also include education, vocational training, or mandatory employment. Examples of therapeutic communities are Synanon, Daytop Village, and Phoenix House. The research on therapeutic communities consistently show lowered drug use and criminal activity (Anglin and Hser, 1990; Coombs, 1981; DeLeon, 1984; DeLeon and Rosenthal, 1989).

Two recent studies have assessed therapeutic community-based programs. Swartz et al. (1996) evaluate the Integrated Multi-Phasic Program Assessment and Comprehensive Treatment (IMPACT) program. This program deals primarily with single, unemployed, minority males with long criminal histories. The program results indicate that recidivism is tied to the length of treatment, with longer treatment resulting in lower recidivism. Inciardi (1996) reports on the KEY program, which is a prison-based therapeutic community in Delaware. Both six- and 18-month follow-up data show that many more program clients remain drug- and arrest-free than do control group clients (Inciardi, 1996). These studies bolster the claims of program success.

Outpatient Drug-Free Programs

Outpatient programs often resemble therapeutic communities in most respects except for the residential component. Individual and group counseling is the cornerstone of these programs and may involve professionals or simply other group members. Social skills training, vocational programming, social interaction, referral to other sources of assistance, and possibly short-term drug maintenance are also common components (Anglin and Hser, 1990). Alcoholics Anonymous and Narcotics Anonymous are well known examples of this type of program. The impact of these programs is highly questionable. The primary concern with most evaluations is the fact that clients can drop out at any time. These outpatient programs are more likely to suffer from client mortality than are other interventions (Anglin and Hser, 1990). Hubbard and associates (1984) note that the programs have a marginal impact on crime due to their open nature. Evaluations based only on those individuals who remain in treatment may result in artificially high success rates. The actual success based on all clients who enter the program, whether they complete or not, would be less impressive.

Detoxification

Detoxification refers to the use of drugs in an effort to remove an individual from an addiction to another illicit drug. As opposed to maintenance programs, detoxification uses drugs in a short-term program of controlled withdrawal. The basic idea is to wean the client from the addiction with the minimal amount of discomfort and pain. These types of programs can be found in many hospitals and facilities throughout the country, and target a wide range of drugs from alcohol to heroin. Detoxification may be accompanied with counseling, referral, or other services. Anglin and Hser (1990) point out that while short-term follow-up shows that detoxification is successful at eliminating drug use, detoxification has not been adequately evaluated over the long-term. Bellis (1981) notes that detoxification is used by some addicts to reduce the need for massive amounts of a drug in order to get high. The detoxification simply allows the addict to start the cycle of addiction over again by achieving a high with smaller amounts of the drug.

Summary and Further Comments

It is generally accepted that most forms of treatment are effective at reducing the use of and need for drugs (Visher, 1990). Indeed, Simpson and Sells (1981), studying data from the Drug Abuse Reporting Program (DARP), report that all four types of treatment (maintenance, therapeutic communities, out-patient, and detoxification) achieve lower drug use, lower criminal behavior, and improved employment status from four to six years after treatment. These results are significantly different than for a non-treatment control group. Research also suggests that, while forced treatment has less impact than voluntary treatment (Anglin, 1988; DeLong, 1972; Maddux, 1988), it does reduce the daily use of drugs and criminal activity (Anglin and McGlothlin, 1984). Thus, the new drug courts should be able to affect drug use and related criminal behavior. The impact of court-ordered programs may be attributable to the longer time spent in treatment which is typical of these programs (Visher, 1990). At the very least, the impact of enforced treatment provides further support to the claim that treatment has a positive impact on use and crime.

Prevention Programs

Prevention programs that aim to keep individuals from initially using drugs (primary prevention) usually target juveniles. It is during adolescence that most people experiment with and enter into patterns of drug use. Prevention modalities cover a range of issues and approaches, including the dissemination of factual information about drugs and their consequences, the building of self-esteem, taking responsibility for making choices, and learning how to handle peer pressure. Most often, prevention programs incorporate more than one approach. In a similar fashion to treatment programs, NIDA outlines 16 principles for effective prevention programs (see Figure 12.3). The following discussion is divided into the two most prominently promoted and evaluated prevention techniques. These are the information/education/knowledge programs and the resistance skills techniques.

Figure 12.3
NIDA's 16 Principles of Effective Prevention for Drug Abuse

1.	Prevention programs should enhance protective factors and reverse or reduce risk factors
2.	Prevention programs should address all forms of drug abuse, alone or in combination, including underage use of legal drugs; the use of illegal drugs; and the inappropriate use of legally obtained substances, prescription medications, or over-the-counter drugs
3.	Prevention programs should address the type of drug abuse problem in the local community, target modifiable risk factors, and strengthen identified protective factors
4.	Prevention programs should be tailored to address risks specific to population or audience characteristics, such as age, gender and ethnicity
5.	Family-based prevention programs should enhance family bonding and relationships and include parenting skills; practice in developing, discussing and enforcing family policies on substance abuse; and training in drug education and information

6. Prevention programs can be designed to intervene as early as preschool to address risk factors for drug abuse, such as aggressive behavior, poor social skills and academic difficulties

7. Prevention programs for elementary school children should target improving academic and social-emotional learning to address risk factors for drug abuse

8. Prevention programs for middle or junior high and high school students should increase academic and social competence

9. Prevention programs aimed at general populations at key transition points, such as the transition to middle school, can produce beneficial effects even among high-risk families and children

10. Community prevention program that combine two or more effective programs can be more effective than a single program alone

11. Community prevention programs reaching populations in multiple settings are most effective when they present consistent, community-wide messages in each setting

12. When communities adapt programs to match their needs, community norms, or differing cultural requirements, they should retain core elements of the original research-based intervention

13. Prevention programs should be long-term with repeated interventions to reinforce the original prevention goals

14. Prevention programs should include teacher training on good classroom management practices such as rewarding appropriate student behavior

15. Prevention programs are most effective when they employ interactive techniques, such as peer discussion and parent role-playing, that allow for active involvement in learning about drug abuse and reinforcing skills

16. Research-based prevention programs can be cost-effective

Source: National Institute on Drug Abuse (2004).

Education/Information/Knowledge Programs

Education/information/knowledge programs focus their efforts on providing subjects with factual information about drugs, drug use, and the consequences of drug use. Such programs attempt to teach subjects about the different drugs, how they work, and their effects on the user. Information may also include data on the extent of drug use and what happens if an individual is caught and processed in the criminal justice system. The basic assumption is that such knowledge will allow the individual to make an informed choice about drug use. Proponents assume that, armed with these facts, most individuals will opt to avoid drugs.

Evaluations provide mixed results concerning these programs. Botvin (1990) points out that these programs are effective at increasing subjects' knowledge about drugs. Schaps et al. (1986) also claim that drug education reduces the use of alcohol and marijuana by females but has no impact on comparable males. The change in use, however, is short-lived and no effect is noted one year after the program ended. Tobler (1986), analyzing results from 143 drug prevention programs for youths, notes that information (knowledge) techniques have no impact on behavior. Other authors (Abadinsky, 1989; Botvin, 1990; Botvin and Dusenbury, 1989; Eiser and Eiser, 1988; Hanson, 1980; Kinder et al., 1980; Swadi and Zeitlin, 1987; Weisheit, 1983) report similar negative results and even suggest that the knowledge leads many youths to experiment with drugs in order to "find out for themselves" about drugs. The programs appear to pique the curiosity of some youths and prompt an increased, rather than decreased, use of drugs.

Resistance Skills Training

Resistance skills training comes under a variety of names with the most well-known being the "Just Say No" campaign and the *Drug Abuse Resistance Education* (D.A.R.E.) program. While many individuals view this as too simplistic an approach, *resistance skills training* involves a set of ideas dealing with recognizing problematic situations and issues, dealing with peer pressure, recognizing pressure from media presentations, knowing proper responses to temptations, building self-esteem and assertiveness, and knowing how and when to take a stand. The implicit assumption in this type of prevention is that drug use is largely a function of situation and peer involvement. Youths need to learn how to recognize peer pressure and how to make proper decisions in the face of that pressure. These programs may also provide factual information about drugs within the larger discussion of resisting temptations to participate in drug use. A key part of any information presented deals with the actual levels of use in society, emphasizing the fact that most individuals do not use illicit drugs. This provides youths with data that say they are in the majority if they resist drugs.

Research on the impact of resistance skills training is mixed. Botvin and associates have conducted a series of studies on the impact of Life Skills Training (LST) on subsequent tobacco, alcohol, and marijuana use (Botvin and Eng, 1980, 1982; Botvin et al., 1980; Botvin et al., 1983; Botvin et al., 1984). The reports show that the LST program is successful at reducing the number of youths who smoke, drink, and use marijuana. The program appears to be most effective at reducing the use of tobacco (Botvin and Dusenbury, 1989). The longevity of the impact may be somewhat at issue with the longest follow-up being only two years. Other studies have reported similar positive results, especially for tobacco use (Botvin, 1990; Luepker et al., 1983; McAlister et al., 1980; Telch et al., 1982).

Perhaps the most recognized intervention is D.A.R.E. Begun in Los Angeles in 1983, DARE targets elementary school youths through a police officer-taught curriculum. In recent years DARE has expanded to junior and senior high schools, as well as implementing a parent program. An estimated 22,000 police officers in 7,000 communities have taught D.A.R.E. to more than 25 million elementary school students since the program's inception (Bureau of Justice Assistance, 1995b). Various methodologically rigorous evaluations fail to find any significant impact of D.A.R.E. on drug use behavior. Ringwalt et al. (1991), Clayton et al. (1991) and Rosenbaum et al. (1994), looking at schools from different jurisdictions, all report no impact on substance use. In a recent evaluation, D.A.R.E. participants and control youths were tracked for more than a six-year period to assess the impact of the program. Rosenbaum and Hanson (1998) conducted surveys twice a year in order to consider the influence of D.A.R.E., other programs, dropping out, and other factors that could alter the results. The authors report that D.A.R.E. had little impact on attitudes, beliefs, or social skills directly addressed by the program. More importantly, D.A.R.E. had no significant impact on any measure of drug use. For suburban subjects, there was some evidence of *higher* drug use among D.A.R.E. participants (Rosenbaum and Hanson, 1998). Wysong et al. (1994) also found no impact in a similar longitudinal analysis.

Given the negative results, how do you explain the popularity and persistence of D.A.R.E.? There are several possible explanations. First, D.A.R.E. has a strong national organization behind it. Second, the program is minimally intrusive into the lives of the youths, primarily due to its presentation in schools. Third, the ability to bring police and juveniles together in a non-threatening situation has a great deal of appeal. Finally, the program may contribute to a more positive school environment.

Other resistance skills programs also show few positive results. Kim's (1988) analysis of the Here's Looking At You (HLAY) alcohol education program, which includes resistance education, finds no difference in the use of alcohol by experimental and control youths. Except for attitude changes, the program has little impact on the experimental subjects (Kim, 1988). The potential of resistance skills training to have an impact on the use of more serious drugs has been questioned by other researchers. Newcomb and Bentler (1988), for example, claim that these approaches are effective only with experimentation and minor drug use. Tobler (1986), however, reports that "peer programs" (the "Just Say No" approach) are effective at reducing the use of all types of drugs. This finding should not be surprising given the fact that most individuals start off using minor drugs, such as alcohol, tobacco, and marijuana, before moving on to more serious substances. Success at mitigating the use of these minor drugs should snowball into lower levels of more serious drug use.

Summary of Prevention Programs

The evidence on prevention programs suggests that the impact is often minimal. Resistance skills training presents mixed results. Programs that emphasize providing factual information about drugs also fail to have much impact. In fact, these efforts may cause an increased curiosity on the part of adolescents and subsequent experimentation and use of illicit drugs. Other programs that stress self-esteem, self-awareness, and interpersonal growth in the absence of specific strategies for dealing with drugs (typically referred to as affective education programs) also demonstrate minimal influence on drug use (Botvin, 1990; Schaps et al., 1986; Tobler, 1986). While there appears to be hope for the prevention of drug use, most of the programs need to be evaluated with longer follow-up periods and better research designs, particularly using adequate comparison groups.

DRUGS AND CRIME PREVENTION

The relationship between drug use and criminal activity is a complex one. The extent to which drug use causes crime or crime causes drug use is not clear. There is certainly a strong correlation between the two activities. This suggests that knowledge of one can be used to attack the other. From the standpoint of secondary crime prevention, drug use can be used as a predictor of individuals at a higher risk of committing other criminal acts. While not every user of drugs commits other offenses, the evidence shows that those who regularly use illicit drugs and/or use a large amount of drugs are more disposed to criminal behavior. At the very least, drug use can identify individuals for further intervention.

To the extent to which drug use is a cause or contributor to criminal activity, drug prevention and treatment programs may be effective at limiting or eliminating other crime. The treatment and prevention proposals and programs discussed in this chapter show that effective strategies do exist. Most need further analysis over longer periods in order to definitively outline their impact and potential. In a strict sense, the treatment programs outlined above are tertiary prevention programs—they deal with individuals who have already entered into drug use. Likewise, the prevention programs fall into the realm of primary prevention due to their implementation in schools and the targeting of all youths. If the emphasis is simply on targeting the drug use with no concern for related problems, these efforts belong under the headings of primary and tertiary prevention.

The emphasis of the present discussion, however, is on the role drug use plays in contributing to and/or causing other criminal acts. This brings the topic squarely into the realm of secondary crime prevention. Arguments about the victimless status of drug use, possession, and other drug crimes are automatically beyond the concerns of secondary prevention. The criminal status of drug use does not affect its place as a tool in secondary prevention. Consequently, other arguments, such as those over legalization and decriminalization, are not germane to the discussion. These topics are left for other authors to consider.

Chapter 13

THE SCHOOL AND CRIME PREVENTION

Key Terms:

alternative schools
bullying
feeble-minded
G.R.E.A.T.
Head Start
meta-analysis

PATHS
peer mediation
Perry Preschool program
Project PATHE
Reducing Conflict Creatively Program
tracking

Learning Objectives:

After reading this chapter you should be able to:

- Provide insight into the role of schools and education in causing crime and delinquency

- Define "tracking" and demonstrate how it relates to delinquency

- Discuss the relationship between IQ and delinquency

- Talk about the extent of victimization at school and responses to that problem

- Identify different preschool programs and discuss their impact on crime and delinquency

- Demonstrate your knowledge of Project PATHE and its impact

- Explain how altering the school atmosphere can change behavior

- Identify at least four school programs that address conflict management/resolution

- Discuss the PATHS program and its effectiveness

- Talk about the G.R.E.A.T. program, including what it is and what evaluations of it show

- Discuss bullying prevention programs and their impact

- Explain what alternative schools are and related information on the degree to which they have an impact on delinquency

The school has come to be seen as a prime actor in the development and prevention of delinquent behavior. This ascendance to prominence is reflected in a number of theories of deviant behavior, research focusing on the correlates and causes of behavior, government and private reports linking schools and education to delinquency, and the advent of delinquency intervention programs intimately tied to schools and education. Teachers and others in the schools have a great deal of contact with society's youth and are in a position to identify problems as they emerge. The ability to use school problems and concerns to predict possible problems later in life places school personnel in the midst of secondary prevention. Although not criminal, school problems are used as indicators of possible future delinquent or criminal activity both in and out of school. Schools are also prime locations for implementing secondary prevention programs. Many interventions often deal with predelinquent youths and youths having problems in school.

The relationship between school and delinquency is not always easy to understand. Many of the associations are indirect and must be understood within the context of the educational mission and the form of society. Consequently, prevention programs may not always seem to be aimed at delinquency. Rather, the interventions are geared toward the specific problematic factors found in the schools. The present chapter will attempt to develop the role of schools as an agent of secondary prevention through a three-step process. First, it is necessary to discuss the theoretical support for the role schools play in delinquency. Second, the specific aspects of the educational process that are important for discussing delinquency must be examined. Finally, the chapter will examine programs that have been established to intervene in the harmful aspects of school, with special attention paid to programs demonstrating an impact on subsequent delinquency and in-school misbehavior.

THEORETICAL VIEWS

Many theorists emphasize the importance of schools in developing behavior. Cohen (1955), Cloward and Ohlin (1960), and Merton (1968) point to blocked attainment and feelings of failure as a source of deviant behavior. Each of these theorists claims that an individual faced with little or no chance of success in legitimate endeavors will turn to deviant avenues for sources of success and support. For juveniles who have not yet entered the adult world, the school becomes the setting for gauging success and failure. For example, a juvenile who is faced with failing grades while his friends are successful at their studies may be labeled as a failure by those same friends and/or teachers. The lack of success may push a youth to seek out others having the same difficulties. In an attempt to regain some feeling of status and success, failing youths may turn to deviance and acting-out behaviors.

The actual causal process relating schools and delinquency can take a variety of forms. Hirschi (1969) claims that diminished academic ability results in poor academic achievement. Failure in school can foster dislike for school attendance, a lack of concern for societally proscribed behavior, and eventual movement into delinquent behavior. An expanded, more detailed causal process (Gold, 1978) proposes that incompetence as a student leads to failed aspirations and success expectations that, in turn, results in being excluded from more successful students and student activities. This exclusion invariably lowers a youth's self-image and feelings of worth, resulting in associating with other marginal youths or deviant behavior as a means of salvaging a positive self-image. Gold (1978) refers to this choice of deviance as an *ego defense*, which acts to counterbalance the negative feedback experienced in the school setting. While only examples, these processes are indicative of how schools and the educational process can influence behavior.

These causal chains rest on the assumption that youths value scholastic achievement. Negative evaluations in the educational setting would then hold the potential for lowering the juvenile's self-esteem. Support for this proposition is found in many studies. One of the more influential studies of the educational system in the United States found that parents of all social classes are very interested in their children's scholastic success (Coleman, 1966). Vinter and Sarri (1965) report that this emphasis on educational success extends to the youths themselves. Two studies show that minority and poor students place a higher value on education than do other students (Coleman, 1966; Reiss and Rhodes, 1959). Despite this near-universal desire to achieve in school, lower class and minority students invariably make up the group that most often fails. In addition, those who fail in school typically exhibit misbehavior and delinquency both in and out of school.

Any number of studies can be pointed to in support of the school failure-delinquency relationship. Polk and Hafferty (1966) note that students who do poorly in school and are not committed to scholastic achievement admit to higher levels of deviant behavior. Hirschi (1969), studying approximately 4,000 boys, finds that youths with low commitment to school and educational achievement display higher levels of self-reported delinquency. Thornberry et al. (1985) show that students who drop out of school exhibit higher levels of delinquency and adult criminal behavior than do high school graduates. Jarjoura (1993) specifies the dropout effect by demonstrating that the dropout-delinquency relationship only holds when the reason for dropping out is related to school problems. Studies by Gold and Mann (1972), West and Farrington (1973), and Jerse and Fakouri (1978) report that delinquents generally achieve lower grades than non-delinquents. A wide variety of other studies, using both self-report and official measures of deviance and various measures of academic achievement, support the academic achievement-delinquency relationship (Empey and Lubbeck, 1971; Kelly and Balch, 1971; Kelly and Pink, 1975; Phillips and Kelly, 1979; Polk and Schafer, 1972; Polk et al., 1974; President's Commission on Law Enforcement and the Administration of Justice, 1967).

EDUCATIONAL FACTORS AND DELINQUENCY

The relationship between educational achievement and delinquency is not a simple one. Various intervening variables enter into the formula. The basic causal processes outlined earlier provide reasonable starting points for identifying the specific aspects of school and education that lead a juvenile to deviant activity. Most of these explanations involve student success and achievement. The ability of a student to achieve can be affected by factors independent of the school. The ability of the student prior to entering school can affect academic success. One possible measure of ability is the IQ test. Another set of influences on achievement may be the format and workings of the school itself. Factors such as tracking, in-school indicators of success, and the quality of the teachers and resources can all affect student outcomes. An important additional factor may be the extent of victimization in the school. The victimization of an individual may drive the student away from school. Victimization problems in schools can result in a preoccupation with crime and safety, rather than obtaining a meaningful education. The following paragraphs attempt to outline the impact of various factors on student success.

IQ and Delinquency

The role of intelligence in the etiology of deviant behavior has been a matter of debate for many years. The early IQ tests were used to screen entrants to the United States in order to keep the mentally deficient out of the country. The so-called *feeble-minded* (those with low IQs) were viewed as a threat to the moral and intellectual life of the nation. It was assumed that these individuals would disproportionately contribute to the level of delinquency and criminal activity.

These early fears have found much support in later research. Hirschi and Hindelang (1977), in a review of the major research in the area, establish that IQ is an important correlate of delinquency. A variety of studies substantiate that low IQ is positively correlated to higher levels of official delinquency (Reiss and Rhodes, 1961; Short and Strodbeck, 1965; Wolfgang et al., 1972) and self-reported measures of delinquency (Hirschi and Hindelang, 1977; Weis, 1973; West, 1973). The major question unanswered in most of these analyses is whether IQ is a direct causal factor or simply lays the groundwork for other factors to intervene. Hirschi and Hindelang (1977) claim that IQ is not a direct causal factor. Instead, low IQ leads to a number of other events that, in turn, facilitate the acquisition of delinquent behavior. Among the intervening factors suggested by these authors is school achievement, academic performance, and attitude toward school. The introduction of these factors into the IQ-delinquency relationship as control variables tends to eliminate the relationship (Hirschi and Hindelang, 1977; West, 1973; Wolfgang et al., 1972). The influence of IQ, therefore, appears only in those instances when IQ affects other school variables.

School Practices and Delinquency

Achievement in school emerges as the key element in the relationship between school and delinquency. The failure to succeed in school leads to frustration, withdrawal from the institution, and an increased potential for deviant behavior. A variety of school practices can operate against success and school attachment and lead to delinquency. Among these practices is tracking, poor instruction, irrelevant instruction, and methods of evaluation.

Tracking refers to the process of assigning students to different classes or groups based on the perceived needs of the student. The most common form of tracking appears in high school where students find themselves placed into "college preparatory" or "vocational" groups. The former indicates an expectation of going to and succeeding in college. The latter signifies a belief that college is beyond the abilities of the student. Schafer et al. (1971) show that students in the vocational track, regardless of their social class, prior grades, or IQ score, respond with lower grades. In addition, these students typically participate in fewer activities and are more likely to drop out of school, misbehave, and commit delinquent acts. The reasons for the lower achievement lay in the expectation, by both teachers and students, that lower track students will not succeed, are not in the educational mainstream, and are not worth as much as college-bound students (Kelly and Pink, 1982; Schafer et al., 1971).

Many students also are faced with poor and/or irrelevant instruction. Views that lower-class and minority students are not college material often result in the assignment of less competent teachers to schools and classes serving these youths (Schafer and Polk, 1967; Schafer et al., 1971). In addition, these schools typically receive less financial support. As a result, the students develop a sense of failure, a lack of self-esteem, and may become dissatisfied and bitter toward the system. The practice of segregating some youths and implicitly labeling them as second class (particularly if they are in special classes within a larger school) can result in a self-fulfilling prophesy. They are expected to do worse and thus they live up (down?) to this expectation.

The irrelevance of instruction for some students grows out of the types of materials they are being taught, especially in the vocational education tracks

(Wertleib, 1982). Schools are seldom able to keep up with the rapid changes and modifications in jobs and the workforce. The materials being taught in the school are outmoded before the youth has the opportunity to use the information. Vast changes in production and technology have established jobs for which many youths are unqualified and have eliminated jobs that previously employed hundreds or thousands of people. Instruction becomes more irrelevant when students cannot find employment upon leaving school. These factors make the instruction irrelevant and obsolete (Papagiannis et al., 1983). Students often are trained in very specific tasks that they cannot use outside of the school. At the same time, they are not prepared to enter college, undertake further instruction, or secure other jobs.

The emphasis on testing invariably leads to feelings of failure. For the "A" student, grades are a reward for hard work and indicate positive achievement. The movement toward proficiency tests (mandated for promotion and graduation in many states) often results in resentment on the part of those students who do not pass the tests. The failing student may be held back or placed into special classes that segregate and label him. Slow and failing youths may be excluded from many of the extracurricular activities that can help make school a fun, enjoyable experience. Failing students may be humiliated in front of other students, may not be expected to achieve, and are often considered second-class citizens within an institution they are forced to attend (Schafer and Polk, 1967).

Victimization and Fear in School

One result of these and other school practices is the attempt by some students to gain recognition and status through alternative, albeit unacceptable, behavior. School misbehavior leads to further alienation, exclusion from the mainstream of the student body, and further acting out. It also leads to an atmosphere in which education becomes secondary to security.

For the offending youth, school misbehavior can be seen as accomplishing three things (Gold, 1978). First, the behavior is aimed at the source of the problem—the school. Second, the youth's peers are present in school to view the activity and the offender is able to "show off" or bring attention to him- or herself. Finally, the misbehavior is a declaration that the youth will not sit idly by while the school continuously belittles him. Continued sanctions and acting out may lead to delinquent behavior outside of the school setting.

Misbehavior also has an impact on others in the school, either directly as the target of an offense or indirectly through vicarious victimization and a shift in emphasis from learning to survival. The problem of crime in school has been described as "a serious national problem" (G. Gottfredson and D. Gottfredson, 1985). The U.S. Department of Justice routinely collects data on crime and victimization in schools. Figures from 2007 (Table 13.1) show that a total of 1,510,900 crimes were committed against students at school (DeVoe et al., 2009). This represents 57 offenses for every 1,000 students. While theft offenses comprise more than half of the crimes, more than 684,000 offenses are violent crimes. Another way of looking at crime at school is to look at the percent of students reporting victimization at school. One striking item in this data is the relative stability of victimization across the grade levels. In light of media accounts of violent acts in schools (especially homicides), it is important to note that a good deal of in-school violence appears as threats and minor acts, including pushing and shoving (Anderson, 1998; Lockwood, 1997), rather than serious violence. Indeed, few homicides occur in school, with only 30 during the 2006-2007 school year—the highest since 33 during 1998-1999 (Dinkes et al., 2009)

Table 13.1
Student Victimization at School by Selected Characteristics, 2007[a]

Student Characteristics	Total	Theft	Violent[b]	Serious Violent[c]
Total N	1,510,900	862,800	684,100	118,300
Rate per 1,000 students	57	31	26	4
Total percent	4.3%	3.0%	1.6%	0.4%
Gender (percents)				
Male	4.5	3.0	1.7	0.5
Female	4.0	3.0	1.4	0.2
Race/Ethnicity (percents)				
White	4.3	3.1	1.5	0.2
Black	4.3	3.0	1.6	—
Hispanic	3.6	2.2	1.4	0.8
Asian	3.6	3.2	—	—
Other	8.1	4.5	4.5	—
Grade (percents)				
6th	4.1	2.7	1.5	—
7th	4.7	2.7	2.4	0.4
8th	4.4	2.5	2.1	—
9th	5.3	4.6	1.2	—
10th	4.4	3.6	1.2	—
11th	4.0	2.6	1.5	0.6
12th	2.7	1.9	0.8	—

[a] Data for students aged 12 to 18.
[b] Violent crimes include rape, sexual assault, robbery, aggravated assault and simple assault.
[c] Serious violent crimes include the violent crimes except for simple assault.

Source: Dinkes et al (2009). *Indicators of School Crime and Safety, 2009.* Washington, DC: Bureau of Justice Statistics

Beyond actual victimization, students fear of victimization can be debilitating and lead to negative behaviors. Table 13.2 presents data on the levels of fear and avoidance behavior due to fear among students age 12–18 over a six-month period (Dinkes et al., 2009). More than seven percent of all students report fear of being attacked at school. While less than one percent report staying home from school altogether due to fear, this still translates into more than 200,000 students. Almost six percent avoid specific places in school due to fear, including hallways, restrooms, and the cafeteria. Lab and Clark (1996), studying junior and senior high schools in one large Midwestern county, found that more than 11 percent of the students fear being attacked at school. Additionally, 16 percent rate their school as "unsafe" or "very unsafe." Other studies also show that a small but significant number of youth (10% or more) either stay home or avoid certain places/events at school due to fear of assault or theft (Kaufman et al., 1998; Lab and Clark, 1996; Lab and Whitehead, 1994; Metropolitan Life, 1993; Metropolitan Life, 1994; Ringwalt et al., 1992).

Table 13.2
Students Avoiding School or Activities Due to Fear of Attack or Harm, 2007

	Percent	N
Total	7.2	1,908,505
Stayed home from school	0.8	212,056
Avoided school activities	1.8	477,126
Avoided class	0.7	185,549
Places avoided		
Entrances	1.5	397,605
Hallways/stairways	2.6	689,182
Cafeterias	1.9	503,633
Restrooms	2.6	689,182
Other places	1.5	397,605

Source: Compiled from Dinkes et al. (2009).

A second student response to crime and fear is to carry weapons to school for protection. Dinkes et al. (2009) report that 18 percent of youths carried a weapon in the past month, with six percent claiming to carry them at school. Lab and Clark (1996) report that 24 percent of junior and senior high school students have carried a weapon to school for protection at least once over a six-month period. Studies focusing on inner-city schools report even higher levels of weapons in school (Sheley et al., 1995).

Students are not the only individuals victimized at schools. Teachers and staff are also subject to crime and subsequent feelings of fear. During the 2007–2008 school year, almost 290,000 teachers (7.5%) reported being threatened with injury by a student during school (Dinkes et al., 2009). Another 154,000 teachers (4.0%) were actually the victim of physical attack by a student at school (see Table 13.3).

Table 13.3
Teacher Reports of Victimization at School, 2007-2008

	N	%
Threat of injury	289,600	7.5
Physically attacked	154,400	4.0

Source: Compiled from Dinkes et al. (2009).

Summary

The level of misbehavior, victimization, fear, and safety measures in schools is a concern for various reasons. First, these concerns detract from the primary mission of educating youths. Time spent on crime and disruption means less time spent in getting an education. Similarly, avoiding school means the youths are missing out on important classroom time. Second, many of the responses to victimization and fear are more inappropriate than appropriate. Certainly, the presence of weapons offers the possibility of more serious confrontations and problems, not to mention the illegality of bringing weapons to school. The failure to address these problems will simply add to the other deleterious aspects of schools.

SCHOOL PROGRAMS
FOR DELINQUENCY PREVENTION

A wide range of programs and educational strategies have emerged to address delinquency both in and outside of schools. Among the suggested educational changes are the provision of relevant instruction, the use of flexible groupings that allow movement in and out of ability levels, the development of meaningful and useful instruction, the use of teaching materials relevant for students of different backgrounds, the use of alternative grading strategies, and the institution of disciplinary measures that do not alienate or segregate students from the mainstream of the school (Schafer and Polk, 1967). Sadly, many of the suggested changes have not been instituted or have received only cursory attention in widely scattered locales. This indicates that the impact of such changes on education in general, and delinquency in particular, is still unknown. At the same time, several programs and strategies have received significant attention.

Preschool Programs

One suggestion for attacking school problems involves early preparation of children for school. Preschool programs are viewed as a means of establishing a level of competence that avoids early placement into differential ability tracts, building a positive attitude toward school, and providing basic social skills to youths who are not prepared to enter school. The advent of preschool as a technique in fighting school problems and delinquency can be found in the 1967 President's Commission on Law Enforcement and the Administration of Justice.

Perhaps the best-known preschool program is the *Head Start* program. Head Start proposes that disadvantaged youths are not prepared to enter school without some form of early intervention targeted at social and intellectual skills (Gottfredson, 1987). Advocates of preschool programs point out that early school failure typically persists into the later years (Schweinhart and Weikart, 1989). Head Start is meant to provide youths with positive early experiences and, in turn, successful long-term academic careers. The extent to which Head Start has succeeded in achieving its goals is questionable. Gottfredson (1987) notes that the program is typically not well-implemented and that any gains made in the program fade over a year or two. Head Start has not been evaluated in terms of its effect on later delinquency or criminality.

The most extensively studied preschool program is the *Perry Preschool* (High/Scope) program. The program, begun in 1962, seeks to provide students with a positive introduction to education. This is accomplished by involving the children in the planning of activities, a low child-teacher ratio, and enhanced reinforcement of student achievement. Perhaps the most critical feature of the program is the frequent home visits with parents. Berrueta-Clement et al. (1984) claim that the program sets in process a sequence of events that leads from program participation to higher academic performance to enhanced educational commitment and scholastic achievement to prosocial behavior. Unlike most preschool programs, the Perry program includes an evaluation component consisting of randomly assigning youths to either the program or a non-preschool control group. All study subjects are from low-income black families, typified by low parental education, unemployment, and single-parent households. All children were tracked throughout school and were periodically surveyed through age 19, with follow-up evaluations undertaken through age 40 (see Berrueta-Clement et al., 1984, for a more thorough discussion of the program methodology).

Evaluation of the Perry Preschool program presents some impressive claims. The program appears to significantly increase measures of academic performance, reduce the need for special education and remedial work, prompt more positive attitudes toward school, enhance the high school graduation rate, and result in lower unemployment after graduation from high school (Berrueta-Clement et al., 1984). The program also claims that fewer experimental students are arrested as either adults or juveniles than are control students. Schweinhart (1987) points out that the experimental group reports fewer serious offenses at both ages 15 and 19. Results through age 27 reveal that about one-half as many program participants are arrested compared to control group subjects. The frequency of their offenses is also about one-fourth of that for control youths (Schweinhart et al., 1993). Schweinhart and Xiang (2003), reporting on data through age 40, find significantly fewer lifetime and adult arrests among experimental subjects, with fewer arrests for violent crimes, property crimes, and drug offenses.

Other preschool projects also report positive effects on experimental subjects. The Consortium for Longitudinal Studies (Lazar et al., 1982) and reviews of various preschool programs (Berrueta-Clement et al., 1984; Gottfredson, 1987) present data showing improved academic performance and less need for special education in the future. Unfortunately, unlike the Perry Preschool program, these studies typically show that the results are short-term and fade within the first two years of elementary school. Most studies also either fail to address the program's impact on delinquency or fail to find any strong positive effects.

Many programs that suggest positive results typically focus on academic achievement rather than delinquency or criminality. The generalizability of the results is also limited due to the heavy study of lower-class, minority youths (Schweinhart and Weikart, 1989). No systematic study has been undertaken on more representative population groups.

Elementary and High School Programs

Programs dealing with academic performance and school misbehavior can be found throughout the educational system. Unfortunately, most of these efforts fail to address the impact of the programs on subsequent delinquency and crime. Many researchers simply assume that changes in achievement, self-esteem, and other school-based outcomes will, in turn, affect delinquency (Gottfredson, 1987). Most programs that specifically address the question of delinquency are those that appear in junior and senior high schools. The reason for this is simple—in general, youths do not come to the attention of the juvenile justice system until they reach these grades. Prior to that time, misbehavior is handled in the home or is simply ignored.

School Atmosphere

Altering the general school environment is one suggestion for addressing misconduct in schools. Opening up participation in decision making (to both students and staff) allows everyone to take ownership of both the solutions and the successes of controlling problems. Denise Gottfredson (1986a; 1986b) reports on the effectiveness of *Project PATHE* (Positive Action Through Holistic Education) in Charleston, South Carolina. This project takes a broad-based approach to the school environment by bringing teachers, administrators, students, parents, and agencies together in making decisions about education and the school. Underlying this approach is the idea that the various parties must see a stake in education and believe that education is important. The parties will care more about education if they have some say in the educational process. Project PATHE isolates a variety of factors including school pride, career-oriented programs, student team learning, and individual services as targets for change.

Project PATHE was initiated in five middle schools and two high schools from 1980 to 1983. Pre- and post-program measures, as well as data from two non-equivalent comparison schools were used in an evaluation of the program. groups. The results offered mixed support. Experimental schools report higher test scores and graduation rates than the control schools (D. Gottfredson, 1986a). Attendance at school, however, did not seem to be affected by the program. Delinquency measures showed the greatest degree of disparity across and within schools. At the school level, there was some improvement in overall delinquency in the high school but no significant change for the middle schools. The control schools also showed no change over the study period. Changes in individual types of delinquency appeared in various schools. For example, drug use was reduced in one school but not in others. Some teachers reported lower levels of victimization in individual schools.

These results suggest that, while the program has no overall effect on the schools as a group, improvements can be found in individual schools (D. Gottfredson, 1986b). The qualified success of Project PATHE may be due to alterations in the school system and study design after the onset of the project. Changes in the school administration, the closing and consolidating of some schools, and the inability of some programs to be adequately implemented during the study suggest that the project would produce better results in a more stable setting (D. Gottfredson, 1986b).

Lab and Clark (1996) also investigated the idea of altering the school environment through cooperative decision making. Evaluating 44 junior and senior high schools, the authors note that order and control in a school is engendered most effectively by bringing students, staff, and administrators together. The traditional methods of administratively imposing strict control and harsh discipline on students is not productive (Lab and Clark, 1996). The authors also find that schools with lower victimization and problem behaviors are those that work to develop a "normative" approach to discipline and control. This means that schools in which there is more agreement on discipline and control measures experience fewer problems than schools in which there is little agreement (Lab and Clark, 1996). Schools should strive, therefore, to build consensus through inclusion in the decision-making process.

The Charlotte School Safety Program attempts to address the issue of school safety by developing a cooperative problem-solving process that involves students, school staff, and police (Kenney and Watson, 1998). The program emphasizes changing the school environment using techniques similar to those found in community-oriented policing. Problem identification and problem solving are key elements of the intervention and an attempt is made to integrate these activities into the normal classroom curriculum. It is important to change the attitudes of the students and to turn the student body into an agent for positive change in the school (Kenney and Watson, 1998). The program was tested in the eleventh grade social studies classes of a single Charlotte high school during the 1994–1995 school year. The problem-solving activities were addressed one to two days each week within small groups of six to 10 students.

An evaluation of the Charlotte program indicates positive changes in the target school compared to a matched control school. The evaluation used surveys of students at both schools, interviews with school staff, observations within the school, and inspections of student problem-solving worksheets. The first evidence of success is the ability of the students to identify and agree on problems in the school, and their ability to suggest and implement changes in school procedures. Kenney and Watson (1998) also note significant reductions in student's fear of crime at school, reduced fighting, fewer threats against teachers, lower numbers of suspensions for violence, and fewer calls for police assistance. Little change in these items was evident at the control school. Teachers also report fewer class disruptions and improved relations between students and faculty (Kenney and Watson, 1998). The greatest concern with the evaluation is its reliance on a single school and work with only those students in eleventh grade social studies. In general, the results of research on changing the school environment suggests the efforts bring about positive changes in the schools.

Conflict Management/Resolution

Teaching students how to handle conflict and make proper choices when faced with difficult situations (such as peer pressure to use drugs or commit a crime) is a popular intervention that takes a variety of forms. Conflict management/resolution is a common program in schools. These programs appear under a variety of names, including dispute resolution, dispute mediation, conflict resolution, conflict management, and others. The basic goal of these programs is to avoid and/or resolve conflicts before they escalate into serious problems (such as physical confrontations). School programs typically include a strong teaching component in which kids learn that conflict is natural and that it can be managed through various processes (Ohio Commission, 1993). A key component in many programs is *peer mediation*, in which students are trained to assist one another in resolving disputes in such a way that all parties to the dispute accept the resolution. Many elements of school-based programs can be found in community mediation and dispute resolution programs (see Garofalo and Connelly, 1980a, 1980b for a discussion of these programs). The growth of programs in the community and the generally positive evaluations of those programs (see, for example, Bridenback et al. 1980; Coates and Gehm, 1989;

Reichel and Seyfrit, 1984; Roehl and Cook, 1982) have contributed to the establishment of school-based programs.

One exemplary program is the *Promoting Alternative Thinking Strategies* (PATHS). PATHS is intended to be a five-year-long curriculum offered in elementary schools, focusing on five specific topics. Those topics are: self control, understanding emotions, building a positive self-image, relationships, and interpersonal problem solving (Greenberg and Kusche, 1998). The curriculum is intended to reduce both behavioral and emotional problems, while building self control and problem-solving abilities. PATHS has undergone several evaluations utilizing experimental and control groups of regular students, as well as special needs students. Using follow-up period of up to two years, the results consistently reveal improved problem-solving ability, increased planning activity, reduced self-reported conduct problems, and reduced teacher reports of conduct problems (Greenberg and Kusche, 1996; 1997; Greenberg et al., 1995). Interestingly, all of these positive results are based on a single year of program exposure, as opposed to the intended five-year program. Greenberg and Kusche (1998) suggest that PATHS can be adopted for use with different populations and for implementation outside the school setting.

The *Resolving Conflict Creatively Program* (RCCP) in New York City included student mediation as a core component of the intervention. This program includes programming in the elementary, secondary, and special education curriculum, as well as a separate parent program (DeJong, 1993). The elementary curriculum consists of 12 lessons dealing with issues of communication, cooperation, feelings, diversity, peacemaking, and resolving conflicts. The entire curriculum (in primary and secondary schools) consists of 51 lessons and includes a heavy reliance on peer mediation and parental involvement. DeJong (1993) reports that students successfully learn the lessons, are involved in fewer fights, and believe that they can handle problems better as a result of the program. The impact of the program increases with the number of lessons and the quality of the teacher training (Samples and Aber, 1998).

Similarly, the *Responding in Peaceful and Positive Ways* (RIPP) program targets sixth graders and includes lessons on appropriate responses to conflict situations and how students can avoid violence (Farrell and Meyer, 1997). Evaluations of the program show fewer discipline problems, fewer suspensions from school, and less fighting by students participating in the program. The State of Ohio initiated a number of demonstration projects in schools aimed at providing students with problem-solving skills and instituting peer mediation programs in the schools. Based on the first three years of the program, participating schools report reduced suspensions and increased successful mediations. Students also report a greater willingness to stop fights and talk out disputes as a result of the program (Ohio Commission, 1993). Unfortunately, this program has not undergone a rigorous evaluation.

The *Gang Resistance Education and Training* (G.R.E.A.T.) Program is a well-known program targeting gangs and gang behavior. Not unlike the Drug Abuse Resistance Education (D.A.R.E.) program, G.R.E.A.T. is taught by local police officers in middle schools. The original curriculum, consisting of nine lessons, was expanded to 13 one-hour lessons and is presented in middle schools (see Figure 13.1). The goal of the program is to "prevent youth crime, violence and gang involvement" (BJA, 2005). The thrust of the program is to provide youths with the necessary skills for identifying high-risk situations and resisting the pressure/allure of taking part in gangs and gang activity. Beyond targeting just ganging, program curricula are geared toward increasing self-esteem, changing attitudes, and eliminating participation in violent behavior. A key component of G.R.E.A.T. is to teach non-violent conflict resolution techniques to the youths.

Figure 13.1
G.R.E.A.T. Middle School Curriculum

1. Welcome To G.R.E.A.T.
   - Program Introduction
   - Relationship Between Gangs, Violence, Drugs, and Crime
2. What's the Real Deal?
   - Message Analysis
   - Facts and Fiction About Gangs and Violence
3. It's About Us
   - Community
   - Roles and Responsibilities
   - What You Can Do About Gangs
4. Where Do We Go From Here?
   - Setting Realistic and Achievable Goals
5. Decisions, Decisions, Decisions
   - G.R.E.A.T. Decision-Making Model
   - Impact of Decisions on Goals
   - Decision-Making Practice
6. Do You Hear What I Am Saying?
   - Effective Communication
   - Verbal vs. Nonverbal
7. Walk In Someone Else's Shoes
   - Active Listening
   - Identification of Different Emotions
   - Empathy for Others
8. Say It Like You Mean It
   - Body Language
   - Tone of Voice
   - Refusal-Skills Practice

Figure 13.1. *(Cont'd)*

---

  9.   Getting Along Without Going Along
       • Influences and Peer Pressure
       • Refusal-Skills Practice

  10.   Keeping Your Cool
       • G.R.E.A.T. Anger Management Tips
       • Practice Cooling Off

  11.   Keeping It Together
       • Recognizing Anger in Others
       • Tips for Calming Others

  12.   Working It Out
       • Consequences for Fighting
       • G.R.E.A.T. Tips for Conflict Resolution
       • Conflict Resolution Practice
       • Where to Go for Help

  13.   Looking Back
       • Program Review
       • "Making My School a G.R.E.A.T. Place" Project Review

---

Source: Bureau of Justice Assistance (2005).

The G.R.E.A.T. program has undergone extensive evaluation. Utilizing both cross-sectional and longitudinal data, Esbensen and Osgood (1999) reported promising findings. Based on survey results from 5,935 eighth grade students in 11 school districts, students who completed the G.R.E.A.T. curriculum report lower delinquency rates, more prosocial attitudes about the police and schools, and higher self-esteem (Esbensen and Osgood, 1999). The longitudinal evaluation finds less victimization, less risk-taking behavior, improved attitudes toward the police, increased numbers of prosocial peers, and more negative views about gangs among those youths receiving the G.R.E.A.T. lessons (Esbensen et al., 2004). Unfortunately, the evaluation failed to find any impact on the more important target of the project—reduced gang participation. While this is disappointing, the promising results led the sponsors of the G.R.E.A.T. program to undertake a revision of the curriculum that resulted in the current 13-lesson scheme. The new curriculum is currently undergoing evaluation.

The growth of conflict management/resolution programs in schools remains an important effort in many places, despite that fact that many programs have not undergone rigorous evaluations and many studies suggest that the approach may not have a great impact (Bynum, 1996). The reason for this may be the fact that many programs do not reach a large enough portion of the student body and the programs are not very well integrated into other school activities. School-based conflict management programs are still relatively new and need to undergo further evaluation.

Anti-Bullying Efforts

Bullying prevention is identified as an exemplary program for attacking violence by youths (Elliott, 2000). The most notable of these efforts is that of Olweus and his colleagues (1994; 1995; Olweus and Limber, 2000). *Bullying* behavior includes both physical and verbal aggression that is repeated over time and is meant to intentionally harm the victim (Olweus and Limber, 2000). Studies in Norwegian, Swedish, and U.S. schools find that at least 15 percent of the students report being either bullied or being the offender (Melton et al., 1998, Olweus, 1993).

Developed in Norway, the model anti-bullying program is aimed at the entire school and relies on active student, teacher, and parent participation. The program attempts to raise awareness about the problem of bullying, establish rules and regulations governing the behavior and responses to offending, train staff on how to integrate discussions on bullying into the curriculum, require meetings between parents and teachers, and hold meetings between bullies and their victims. The program also works with the families of offenders to address the problems outside of school. Based on survey data gathered before the onset of the program and periodically over a two-year follow-up period, Olweus (1994; 1995) reports significant reductions in bullying, classroom disruption, and general delinquency. Replicating the program in England, Whitney et al. (1994) report similar positive results, particularly for students in younger grades. This suggests that the intervention should be targeted at young students before bullying behavior becomes ingrained in individuals. Finally, Melton et al. (1998), testing the program in South Carolina grade schools, find significant reductions in bullying, as well as vandalism, general delinquency, and school misbehavior.

Based on these results, anti-bullying programs appear promising as a means to prevent both the initial aggression and subsequent offending and antisocial behavior. Olweus and Limber (2000), however, offer several cautions related to implementing the program. First, the program is better suited to elementary schools than junior or senior high schools. This suggests that earlier intervention is preferable over later projects. Second, the program requires significant time and effort on behalf of teachers and parents. Third, significant training of teachers and parents is required for the successful implementation of the program. Finally, schools need to actively include non-teaching staff, parents, and students in the daily operation of the intervention.

Altering Teaching and Assessment

Educational practices such as tracking or the use of alternative schools (see discussion below) may isolate youths having problems from the mainstream of the educational system and result in even more problems. Another option may be to alter the teaching practices in the classroom in an attempt to improve the chances for all youths. The Seattle Social Development Project is a good example of such a program. This project introduces special instructional techniques into the mainstream classroom as a means of strengthening the educational experiences of low achievers. The program consists of mastering materials before moving on to new topics, individualized progression rather than comparison to other youths, small group learning, frequent positive reinforcement for good work, and strong classroom management. Initial results show only minimal changes in academic achievement and self-report delinquency, although positive results appear for some classrooms and individual subject areas (Hawkins et al., 1988). More recent analyses, which consider a lengthy follow-up period, show generally positive results. Hawkins and his colleagues report increased academic achievement, lower levels of delinquency and violence through age 18, and lower teacher ratings of aggression (Hawkins et al., 1998). These findings suggest that efforts to tailor teaching needs and classroom practices to accommodate students' needs can have a positive impact on both academic achievement and social behavior.

Alternative Schools

Many school programs are targeted at specific groups of youths, rather than at the entire school. Such programs may seek to remove those having problems from the school or may set up individual classrooms or programs within the school. *Alternative schools* represent a major attempt to dispel the negative experiences of many problem youths. The basic idea behind alternative schools is the provision of a positive learning atmosphere, which increases feelings of success within an atmosphere of warmth and acceptance (Gold, 1978). The process involves recognizing the needs of the individual student and meeting those needs through interventions such as one-on-one instruction, unstructured grading practices, instruction tailored to the interests of the student, the development of close relationships between students and teachers, the involvement of the students in the instruction process, and advancement based on individual progress.

Although alternative education programs have become commonplace, few evaluations of these schools look at their effect on delinquent behavior, especially acts committed outside of the school. Denise Gottfredson (1987) reports on the effectiveness of 17 school-based delinquency prevention programs in 15 high-crime communities. Most of the interventions entail alternative schools or classrooms within mainstream schools. The programming within the schools includes personalized instruction, student participation in decision making, the use of behavior modification techniques, informal control, and peer assistance. Overall, the results show reduced delinquency, improved school safety, reduced in-school victimizations, enhanced attachment to school, and reductions in interactions with delinquent peers (D. Gottfredson, 1987). While not all of the projects show the same degree of success, the pattern across the studies suggests that alternative educational practices can make a difference. The results must be tempered somewhat due to the lack of adequate comparison groups and the subsequent possibility of alternative factors that may be influencing the results. The consistency of the results, however, suggests that these problems may be minor.

Cox (1999) considers the impact of an alternative school program for middle school students (grades 6–8). Youths attend the program for one semester and then return to their regular school. While at the alternative school, students participate in activities aimed at improving their academic performance and self-esteem, as well as lowering their delinquent behavior. The program evaluation compared students randomly assigned to the alternative school and a control group. The results show an immediate impact on self-esteem and grades. Unfortunately, there is no change in self-reported delinquency, and the positive changes disappear after the subjects return to their regular school. Cox (1999) speculates that a one-semester program may not be long enough to ensure long-term change. Students may need prolonged exposure to the alternative school format.

One meta-analysis suggests that alternative schools have little, if any, impact on delinquency. In a *meta-analysis*, the data from different studies is reanalyzed in order to make direct comparisons between the results. Cox et al. (1995) analyzed the results from 57 studies conducted from 1966 to 1993. The authors uncover some evidence that alternative school programs increase school performance, improve attitudes toward school, and other similar outcomes. Unfortunately, they are unable to find any significant improvement in client delinquency. Compounding these results is the fact that the most methodologically rigorous studies show the least impact. Gold and Mann (1983) also caution that alternative school settings may isolate youths from the mainstream students and that this may cause other problems, particularly with later reintegration to regular schools. It would appear, therefore, that further study and experimentation with alternative schools is needed before making strong claims for its impact on subsequent delinquent behavior.

Other Interventions

A wide range of other interventions are being used to alter youthful behavior, both in schools and in the community. The U.S. Department of Education has initiated two programs in recent years aimed at dealing with crime and other problem issues for youths. These are the Safe and Drug Free Schools program and the Safe Schools/Healthy Children initiative. While driven by legislative mandates, the two programs incorporate a wide range of different interventions. Much of the diversity rests on the decisions of the different school districts, who they include in the planning of programs (e.g., parents, police, etc.), and what programs they decide to implement.

The programs have provided a great deal of funding and had a major impact on programming in schools. Along with other agencies (including the U.S. Office of Juvenile Justice and Delinquency Prevention), the Department of Education has undertaken various evaluations under these programs. Unfortunately, the research has been focused primarily in two areas—measuring the extent of victimization and fear in schools, and process evaluations of the implementation of programs. Relatively little comprehensive outcome evaluation has been conducted.

Truancy reduction programs have received increased attention in recent years in many jurisdictions. Many of these efforts involve a combination of picking up truant youths and returning them to school (or taking them into custody) and holding parents accountable for their truant children. Two underlying issues drive most of these efforts. First, removing truants from the street eliminates any offenses those youths might have committed while out of school. The school provides supervision, thereby reducing the level of crime during the school day. Second, reducing truancy should lead to increased educational attainment and higher graduation rates. This should lead to greater chances of (meaningful) employment and fewer chances of turning to crime in the future. Clearly, the arguments underlying such initiatives make sense and easily lead to anti-truancy initiatives. The impact of such programs on crime (both current and long-term), however, is unknown. Most truancy reduction programs rely on process evaluations, which count the number of youths handled and the methods used to dispose of the cases.

Another recent movement has been to establish after-school programs for youths. As with other programs, these efforts have multifaceted goals. Perhaps the most common argument underlying these initiatives is that keeping youths busy and supervised after school mitigates the possibility of them getting into trouble. Indeed, there is clear evidence that youthful offending peaks in the late afternoon and early evening, particularly on school days, with roughly 20 percent of all juvenile violent crime occurring on school days between 3:00 and 7:00 (OJJDP, 1999). Therefore, projects that can keep juveniles busy after school hold the potential of reducing the level of crime in the community. This same argument underlies the calls for midnight basketball leagues and other initiatives that occupy unsupervised free time. A secondary argument used to support many after-school programs reflects the belief that educationally based programs can increase the academic achievement of participating youths. Interestingly, despite the great interest in these kinds of interventions, almost no evaluation has been conducted. Most of the existing literature focuses on what these programs look like and how to initiate one, rather than on whether they are successful at achieving their intended mission. This holds true for both crime and educational outcomes.

A great deal of additional research is needed on these programs. While concerted efforts have gone into developing these interventions and implementing the projects, relatively little time and effort has gone into assessing the impact of the projects on delinquency and youthful misconduct. Most of the evaluations are simple process studies that tell how the program was initiated, who was involved, how many meetings took place, and how much money was spent. What is needed now is to know how much delinquency was averted and to what extent the schools are safer places.

THE FUTURE OF SCHOOL/EDUCATIONAL PROGRAMS IN CRIME PREVENTION

There is little doubt that schools hold a key position in the growth and development of youth. Schools deal with virtually every child for a major portion of his or her formative years. The trend in society has been to delay the entry of people into the societal mainstream and prolong the period known as adolescence. As a result, schools have had to assume more and more responsibility for the socialization of children. Increased responsibility for handling adolescents may prove to be a mixed blessing. Schools have so far failed to adequately respond to juvenile misbehavior displayed both in and out of school. To fault the schools, however, without considering the position that has been thrust upon them is not warranted. The schools have not been prepared or expected to lead the fight against delinquent activity. The criticism that they have failed in handling delinquency ignores this fact, and the additional fact that they have not been given the resources to adequately do their multi-faceted job. Despite these facts, the school is a logical point for intervention.

The programs that have been initiated and evaluated provide some hope that future deviant behavior can be prevented. There are clear indications that some educational interventions are effective at reducing recidivism (see Table 13.4). Perhaps the highest hurdle to be considered in the evaluations is the relatively short time span that many of these programs have been in operation. Educational programs aimed at stemming misbehavior should be allowed sufficient time to operate prior to declaring them effective or ineffective. Just as society does not expect that an individual can be educated in a short time span, neither should it expect that short-term programs can reverse trends that have been growing for many decades. For example, the stigma of tracking cannot be overcome in the span of a single year in alternative classes. Positive outcomes from intervention programs should be used as a guide for expanding and altering the overall educational system. A companion problem is the fact that many educational programs and interventions have not undergone outcome evaluations. The Safe and Drug Free Schools program, the Safe Schools/Healthy Children initiatives, truancy reduction efforts, and most after-school programs have been the subject of process evaluations with little attention paid to their impact on crime and delinquency. A great deal of attention should be paid to evaluating these efforts.

Table 13.4
Summary of the Evidence of School/Education Programs on Crimes

Technique	School	Community
Anti-bullying Programs	V+,GC+	V+,GC+
Preschools		V+,D+,GC+
School Atmosphere	D?,F+	
Mediation/Dispute Resolution	T−,V+,F?	F?
Alternative Schools	GC?	
Offenses: T = theft; D = drug crimes; V = violence/aggression; F = fear; GC = general crime/delinquency + indicates the techniques have been shown to reduce the crime in question − indicates the techniques have been shown to have no major impact on crime ? indicates that the impact of the technique varies by the project or the context		

The educational system should continue to serve as a focal point for modifying behavior and preventing deviant activity. Teachers and educators are in an ideal position to observe juvenile behavior, providing assistance, and alerting others to potential problems. The failure to incorporate the school and education system in crime prevention is to ignore a tool that has a great potential for success. The fact that schools and the criminal justice system can work together can be seen in various programs that have established cooperative arrangements between these institutions (Lindsey and Kurtz, 1987; Rubel, 1989). This does not mean that the solution to crime has been found. It does suggest that one of the most important ingredients in crime prevention has been underused.

Section III

TERTIARY PREVENTION

The following chapters are devoted to a brief overview of Tertiary Prevention methods. Tertiary Crime Prevention deals with the elimination of recidivistic behavior on the part of offenders. The emphasis is on actions taken to keep the confirmed offender from further harming society. Although the identification of individuals for insertion into prevention measures is straightforward (i.e., past deviant behavior), prediction is still an important component of many tertiary prevention approaches. Prediction at this stage of prevention focuses on predicting recidivism and not initial offending.

For the most part, tertiary prevention rests within the confines of the formal justice system. Chapter 14 explores the impact of specific deterrence and incapacitation on the level of crime and recidivism. Specific deterrence involves the imposition of sanctions upon the individual in the hopes that these actions will keep that specific individual from further engaging in crime once the punishment has ceased. Perhaps the clearest example of this approach is the setting of different imprisonment periods for different crimes and individuals with the aim of deterring offending once the individual is released. Incapacitation typically looks at the reduction in crime attributable to the confinement period itself. Physical control over a person's behavior makes the commission of criminal actions in larger society an impossibility. Incapacitation can also be accomplished using emerging technology through electronic monitoring. Specific deterrence and incapacitation are related features of imprisoning offenders. The effects of these actions on recidivism and the overall crime rate, as well as the costs of these approaches, are discussed.

Chapter 15 looks at the alternative goal of criminal justice intervention with offenders—rehabilitation. The rehabilitative ideal dominated the correctional end of the formal justice system throughout most of the twentieth century. This domination, however, has often been rhetorical and not in practice. Nevertheless, a wide array of rehabilitative practices have been introduced. The most common comment made about rehabilitation, however, is that "nothing works." This view has stirred controversy since its declaration in the mid-1970s and forms a basis for the chapter. Despite the discouraging results, rehabilitation continues to be a major focus of system effort. Numerous innovative approaches have emerged in recent years which advance the idea of rehabilitation. Two of these, restorative justice and drug courts, are considered in this chapter.

Each of the following discussions is limited in scope and depth. The areas of deterrence, incapacitation, and rehabilitation each have voluminous literature devoted to them. It is not the aim of the chapters to explore the many nuances and issues raised in these areas. Instead, the chapters are intended to summarize the available materials as to their impact on crime and recidivism.

Chapter 14

SPECIFIC DETERRENCE AND INCAPACITATION

Key Terms:

active (continuous signaling)
   system
Big Brother
collective incapacitation
electronic monitoring
incapacitation

Minneapolis Domestic Violence
   experiment
net-widening
passive (programmed contact)
   system
specific deterrence

Learning Objectives:

After reading this chapter you should be able to:

- Show the difference between specific deterrence and incapacitation

- Discuss the effectiveness of imprisonment to have a specific deterrent effect

- Outline the Minneapolis Domestic Violence experiment, cite its findings, and discuss the results of its replication studies

- Compare and contrast collective and selective incapacitation

- List and define assumptions underlying incapacitation

- Present information on the findings from studies of collective incapacitation of imprisonment

- Discuss the costs of achieving a collective incapacitation effect

- Outline findings on selective incapacitation or imprisonment

- Point out problems with selective incapacitation

- Compare and contrast active and passive electronic monitoring systems

- List and discuss potential advantages of EM

- Provide information on the effectiveness of EM to reduce recidivism and have other effects

- Discuss problems and concerns with the use of EM

Specific deterrence and incapacitation are two prominent methods for preventing convicted offenders from committing further crimes. Both methods seek to prevent crime through intervention with individuals who have already harmed society and shown a disposition toward deviant activity. The prevention of crime through these approaches revolves around punishment of the offender. The form of punishment most considered in evaluations of specific deterrence and incapacitation is incarceration. Despite the similarity in the punishment, the actual process by which specific deterrence and incapacitation brings about crime prevention is very different.

Specific deterrence is aimed at the individual offender and his or her future behavior. Chapter 8 discussed the general deterrent effect of punishment. At that time the emphasis was on the ability of the criminal law and its sanctions, whether de jure or de facto, to deter individuals who have not yet violated the criminal law but have the potential for so doing in the future. The emphasis shifts in specific deterrence from the non-offender to the criminal. Concern also shifts to the actual imposition of the law and its sanctions. *Specific deterrence* seeks to prevent the offender from further deviant actions through the imposition of punishments that will negate any pleasure or advantage gained by participation in criminal activity.

Incapacitation also seeks to prevent future crime on the part of the offender. The method by which this occurs is the simple control of the individual, which prohibits the physical possibility of future criminal activity. For example, if the person is locked up and under total physical control, it is a physical impossibility for the individual to commit a crime in society. The most commonly discussed form of incapacitation is incarceration. There is no assumption on the part of incapacitation that the individual will be deterred from committing further crimes once released from the institution. The only consideration is the number of offenses that can be prevented by keeping the offender locked up for a specified period. An alternative form of incapacitation is electronic monitoring of offenders.

THE SPECIFIC DETERRENT EFFECT
OF CRIMINAL SANCTIONS

Relatively little research has been devoted to the study of specific deterrence. Interest in deterrence has focused on the impact of laws and sanctions on the general population and not just the individuals who are subjected to the actions of the criminal justice system. Intuitively, specific deterrence should be a logical outcome of system intervention. Among the goals of bringing an offender to justice is the prevention of future criminal activity by that individual. Punishments are different for different offenses due to the type of offense and the assumptions regarding the hedonistic value of the offense and the punishment. The sanction is meant to offset the amount of pleasure received through the crime. By so doing, the individual will see no advantage or gain in future transgressions. As in general deterrence, the individual is assumed to be a rational person making decisions based on a cost-benefit analysis.

Although many types of punishment are imposed by the criminal justice system, incarceration is assumed to have the greatest potential for deterring the individual from future criminal acts. This does not mean that fines, probation, community service orders, cease and desist orders, and other penalties have no deterrent value. These other forms of punishment, however, leave the individual his or her freedom and generally represent more lenient attitudes toward the behavior in question. The hope is that they will have some deterrent capability because they are reserved for more minor offenses. Incarceration is used in cases in which the offense is more heinous or the individual is a repeat offender for whom more mild punishments have not had the desired impact. The expected deterrent effect of punishment, regardless of the type, however, is not uniformly found in the research.

Studies of Imprisonment

Many evaluations of specific deterrence look to the effect of imprisonment on subsequent offending. The easiest form of evaluation considers the recidivism rate of individuals who have spent some time in an institution. This approach presents a bleak picture for specific deterrence. In one early analysis, Glaser (1964) reported that approximately one-third of prison releases are eventually reincarcerated. This figure represents subjects who were not deterred from further offending by their punishment. While this finding is somewhat disturbing, the specific deterrent effect of imprisonment is probably even worse. This is due to the fact that Glaser considers only reincarceration, and many offenses do not result in a prison sentence. Consequently, many individuals who commit further acts of deviance and do not return to prison are not included in Glaser's (1964) recidivism results. The actual level of further offending could be substantially higher. Gibbs (1975) notes that more than 50 percent of all prison releases are believed to recidivate. Indeed, a study of 641 offenders released from prison in North Carolina finds that 80 percent of the subjects are rearrested within three years (Witte, 1980).

The simple use of aggregate recidivism data can be misleading. One common mistake is the lumping together of serious with less serious offenders or offenders with differing offense careers. Recidivism is typically higher for individuals who have longer offense histories and those receiving harsher sentences (Gibbs, 1975). Consequently, the failure to randomly assign individuals to different punishments or to consider comparable groups of prisoners makes the interpretation of aggregate recidivism figures highly suspect. Such results, however, are commonly cited as representative of recidivism rates for institutionalized groups.

An alternative method for analyzing specific deterrence considers the effect of length of imprisonment on parole outcome. This approach usually compares the recidivism rate for parolees who serve differing amounts of time in an institution. The major problem with this form of analysis is that longer periods of imprisonment are related to more serious offenses, longer offense histories, behavior in the institution, and a variety of other factors. An analysis of recidivism while on parole must control for these influences and isolate the impact of time served on recidivism.

One study of parole outcome looks at almost 15,000 burglars paroled in 1968 and 1969. Babst et al. (1972) examine the recidivism rate for 22 groups of burglars categorized by drug use, alcohol use, prior record, and age at release for the study subjects. Comparing similar groups of subjects with varying lengths of institutional stay reveals no consistent relationship between the time served and parole outcome after one year. The few instances in which a difference is accountable to length of stay appears in subgroups that contain few individuals (Babst et al., 1972).

Beck and Hoffman (1976) and Gottfredson et al. (1977) also examine the impact of sentence length on parole outcome. In the first study, the authors divide subjects into five groups based on their risk of recidivating while on parole. Using a two-year follow-up, the authors report that, in general, there is more recidivism as the length of time served in prison increases (Beck and Hoffman, 1976). Significantly, individuals who are given a fairly good prognosis for success on parole tend to do worse as the amount of time spent in prison increases. Gottfredson et al. (1977), dividing their subjects into nine separate categories based on various discriminating factors, reveal that the time served in prison has no impact on recidivism for four categories of parolees, while three groups of subjects show higher recidivism as the time served increases to 49 months. Conversely, time served has a positive impact for those who spend 50 months or more in prison (Gottfredson et al., 1977). The results of these studies strongly suggest that the length of imprisonment has a differential effect for different risk subjects.

One major problem with the studies above is the inability to randomly assign parolees to varying lengths of time served and then compare the parole outcome figures. Berecochea and Jaman (1981), however, are able to randomly vary the time served, with one group serving six additional months in prison. Looking at 12- and 24-month follow-up figures, the authors find no statistically significant differences in the likelihood of return or returns for new complaints. They conclude that the severity of punishment is unrelated to recidivism (Berecochea and Jaman, 1981). The major problem with this study is that the six-month difference in length of imprisonment may not be sufficient for a specific deterrent effect to become viable.

Finally, Weisburd et al. (1995) examine the specific deterrent effect of imprisonment on white-collar criminals. The authors use data from various jurisdictions and follow up incarcerated offenders over a 10-year period. Contrary to expectations, there is no evidence that imprisonment deters the subjects from further offending (Weisburd et al., 1995). Indeed, there is evidence that those in prison recidivate at a slightly higher rate than those in the control group. The authors speculate that, for white-collar criminals, the prison experience adds little to the impact of arrest, prosecution, and conviction. Thus, the non-prison controls have been equally deterred without the need for imprisonment.

These studies of length of imprisonment and deterrence suffer from one major problem. In no instance is there a control for the types of treatment received by the subjects. Controls are introduced for age, offense, substance use, and other common variables, but at no time is the rehabilitative program experienced by the inmates considered. This is a potentially damaging concern. The emphasis of many correctional institutions and programs, especially during the periods covered by these studies, was on the rehabilitation of the offender. The failure to consider the differential provision and/or use of these programs may alter the study results. Most of the analyses do not even address this question.

Arrest for Domestic Violence

Several studies of specific deterrence examine the differential impact of police decisions on subsequent spouse abuse. The *Minneapolis Domestic Violence Experiment* (Sherman and Berk, 1984) investigates the deterrent effect of arrest, separation, and police counseling in misdemeanor spouse abuse situations. Officers were instructed to randomly apply the different responses (randomization determined by the researchers) in all cases of spouse abuse. The only exceptions to this process include cases in which the police officer is threatened, there is a demand for arrest by one party, or there is an injury as a result of the offense. The study looks at 314 cases taking place over a 17-month period. A six-month follow-up period reveals that arrests result in lower recidivism levels using both official and self-report measures of subsequent behavior (Sherman and Berk, 1984), suggesting a strong specific deterrent effect. Despite these results, a number of problems are inherent in the study (Binder and Meeker, 1988). First, officers were not always able or willing to impose the sanction dictated by the experimental procedure. Second, few officers actually participated in the study. The officers were self-selected and a few of these provided the vast majority of the cases for study. Third, the self-report follow-up was completed on less than one-half of the cases. Finally, it is possible that many of the subjects chose not to file official reports or reply to self-reports concerning subsequent instances of spouse abuse. The extent and impact of these problems is unknown.

Replications of the Minneapolis study fail to confirm the original results. Dunford (1990) reports that arrests in Omaha, Nebraska, have no greater impact on future activity than does separating or counseling the parties involved in the dispute. The finding holds using both official and self-report data for subsequent assaultive situations. Interestingly, issuing warrants for suspects who left before the police arrived results in fewer subsequent arrests compared to those not arrested by warrant. Dunford (1990) suggests that this positive impact may be due to the fact that those who fled prior to the arrival of the police had more to lose from an arrest, thus an arrest or formal system involvement would be a deterrent. A second replication in Charlotte, North Carolina (Hirschel et al., 1991, 1992), uncovers results similar to those in Omaha. In a city-wide experiment, the researchers reveal that arrest is no better at deterring subsequent behavior than issuing citations or advising and separating the disputants. The results persist in both official and self-report data. Both of these evaluations pay particular attention to the shortcomings of the Sherman and Berk (1984) study and appear to have avoided the same problems. Consequently, the results of the original study need to be viewed with skepticism.

Where the prior studies considered the impact of arrest, other analyses consider the impact of prosecution on subsequent domestic violence. Thistlethwaite et al. (1998), studying misdemeanor domestic assault in Hamilton County, Ohio, report that offenders receiving more severe punishments tend to recidivate less often. Time on probation or in jail, however, is not related to future domestic violence (Thistlethwaite et al., 1998). Conversely, Davis et al. (1998) claim that the outcome of prosecution (i.e., cases declined, dismissed, or not convicted) is not related to recidivism in Milwaukee County data. Clearly, the factors related to deterring repeat domestic violence remain unknown.

Summary

These studies of specific deterrence do not present clear results. A variety of analyses present findings contradicting a deterrent effect of harsh punishment. These studies find that recidivism increases as the length of time served in prison or the harshness of the sanction increases. Shorter periods of imprisonment and milder sanctions appear to result in lower recidivism. This may suggest that the offender responds to benevolent actions on the part of the sanctioning bodies. It would also indicate that harsher punishments are imposed on more problematic and serious offenders. Other studies, however, show that punishment does deter future behavior or reveals inconsistent results.

Problems within the study designs appear to be the major reasons for the varying findings. The inability to randomly assign punishments or choose subjects represents one stumbling block. A second failure of the evaluations involves the decision of researchers to ignore relevant factors such as the use or type of treatment applied to the subjects. Indeed, many studies of specific deterrence grew out of interest about the rehabilitative effect of imprisonment and various programs. Few of the evaluations presented above address the possible confounding influence of any rehabilitative program that may have existed. There does not appear to be any strong movement to continue study of specific deterrence, as evidenced by the rarity of evaluations. The present state of knowledge does not provide strong support for the argument.

INCAPACITATION

While imprisonment may not deter an individual from committing deviant acts again in the future, it does keep the subject from committing crimes against society while in the institution. Simply put, incapacitation provides control over the individual, thus precluding behavior that is harmful to society. Incapacitation does not imply anything about the individual's behavior once released from incarceration or control. Incapacitation can take two different forms—collective and selective. *Collective incapacitation* refers to the imposition of sentences upon everyone exhibiting the same behavior with no concern for the potential of the individual. For example, all burglars receive the same sentence. No consideration is given to the potential of the different individuals who commit the offense. The end result is punishment aimed at all similar offenders with the intent of eliminating subsequent offenses. The basis of collective incapacitation is the legal finding of a past offense.

Under *selective incapacitation* the emphasis is on identifying high-risk offenders and subjecting only that group to intervention. All offenders found guilty of the same crime are not punished equally. Those who are judged to be greater threats to society may receive longer, harsher terms of imprisonment. Others judged to be of little threat are subjected to minimal time in prison or sentenced to an alternate punishment. The intent is to maximize the incapacitation effect without subjecting all offenders to long prison terms or control.

The evaluation of incapacitation effects rests on a number of assumptions concerning criminal activity. The most basic assumption is that individuals commit some base rate of offenses every year. Using this figure, it is possible to estimate the number of offenses that are averted through the incapacitation of an individual. For example, if it is assumed that an individual commits 10 crimes per year, the incapacitative effect of a one-year prison sentence is a reduction of crime by 10 offenses for every person so incarcerated. This finding must be qualified, however, by other considerations.

It is also assumed that there is a constant rate of offending over time and an individual's criminal career is not simply put on hold while incapacitated. Instead, the number of years served in prison, for example, is subtracted from the overall number of years offending. The inability to make this assumption would result in no incapacitative effect because the time served would simply postpone and not eliminate the level of offending. A further assumption is that an incapacitated individual is not replaced by another offender. The simple replacement of one individual by another would again result in no net change in offending. Replacement could take two forms. First, the incapacitation of an individual who commits crimes as part of a group may result in the continuation of crime by the remaining group members. Second, crimes committed in the context of an ongoing business interest, such as organized crime, may result in the business finding a replacement for the incapacitated subject.

These assumptions have varying effects on the evaluation of collective and selective incapacitation. The following discussion focuses on the incapacitative effect of two interventions—imprisonment and electronic monitoring (EM).

The Collective Incapacitation of Imprisonment

The evidence on collective incapacitation from imprisonment offers results ranging from small to large changes in the level of crime. Clarke (1974), using the Philadelphia cohort data (Wolfgang et al., 1972), estimates that incarcerating boys prior to age 18 reduces index offenses by five percent for white youths and 15 percent for non-whites. Adjusting the figures to reflect the contribution of juvenile activity to the overall crime rate (i.e., approximately 28 percent of the yearly index crimes), Clarke (1974) notes that incapacitating juveniles will only result in a modest one to four percent decrease in the index crime rate. Greenberg (1975), using official records to estimate the criminal careers of adult offenders, claims that doubling the amount of time spent in prison would only decrease crime by 0.6 percent to 4.0 percent. Conversely, reducing the prison population by 50 percent would only increase the number of crimes by 1.2 percent to 8.0 percent. (Greenberg, 1975). Finally, Peterson and Braiker (1980), using self-report data on the level of offending prior to incarceration and estimates of the average individual crime rate, find that incarceration reduces the level of burglary by only six percent and auto theft by seven percent (Peterson and Braiker, 1980). They claim a much larger incapacitation effect for armed robbery, where 22 percent of the offenses are averted through the imprisonment of offenders.

Each of the studies presented above assumes a constant crime rate across all offenders. The actual level of offending, however, probably varies greatly from individual to individual. Marsh and Singer (1972) attempt to consider individual differences in the level of offending by dividing their target population of robbers into six subgroups, each with different offense rates. Examination of the effect of a one-year increase in incarceration for each subgroup reveals an incapacitation effect ranging from 35 to 48 percent (Marsh and Singer, 1972). This is a great departure from the figures uncovered in the studies using constant, aggregate crime rates.

Differences in criminal justice system policies also may result in varying incapacitation effects. Shinnar and Shinnar (1975) claim that small variations in the estimated crime rate, given constant system response, can result in vast differences in incapacitation. Similarly, minor changes in system policy can alter the incapacitative effect of imprisonment (Shinnar and Shinnar, 1975). The potential for incapacitation is present in simply altering the criminal justice system response to crime.

Evidence for improving incapacitation through modifying system response is found in various studies. Using data for Denver, Colorado, Petersilia and Greenwood (1978) estimate a 31 percent decrease in violent crimes and a 42 percent decrease in burglaries would have occurred if a five year mandatory sentence had been imposed on individuals for prior felony offenses. Withholding the mandatory sentence until a second felony conviction would have reduced the incapacitative effect to 16 percent for violent offenses and 15 percent for burglaries. Van Dine et al. (1979), looking at data for Columbus, Ohio, claim that a five-year mandatory sentence for felony offenders would have resulted in a 17.4 percent decrease in violent index crimes. Imposing the mandatory sentence only after a second offense would reduce the number of offenses by only 6.0 percent. Cohen (1983), investigating five-year mandatory sentences, reports that the use of such punishments for prisoners with prior records would reduce index crimes by Washington, D.C. arrestees by 13.7 percent. Similar to the other studies, mandatory sentences after a second offense have a more modest effect on the number of crimes (3.8% reduction in offenses) (Cohen, 1983).

The differences in studies of collective incapacitation may be due to different estimates used in the analyses. Unfortunately, the proposed reductions in crime are often quite modest. Despite the questionable impact of collective incapacitation programs, jurisdictions persist in implementing such programs, albeit under the rubric of *three-strikes* laws. The modest impact of collective incapacitation is further confounded by the costs of such strategies.

The costs of incapacitation can be examined in terms of the number of people who need to be incarcerated and the dollar costs of accommodating this population. Cohen (1978) estimates the level of increased incarceration necessary to achieve a 10 percent reduction in index crime, a reduction of 100 index crimes, and a 10 percent reduction in violent crimes. Estimates for various states are found in Table 14.1. The table shows that small reductions in crime require large increases in the percent of people sentenced to prison. For example, a 10 percent reduction in the California index crime rate requires a corresponding 157.2 percent increase in the prison population. The smallest change related to a decrease in index crimes appears in Mississippi, where it is still necessary to increase the incarcerated population by 33.7 percent. It is clear that incapacitation exacts a high cost in terms of the number of offenders who need to be incarcerated.

Incapacitation also involves an increased monetary burden for society. Walker (1985) presents a number of estimates related to an incapacitation strategy. Using conservative figures related to the number of people who must be incarcerated (based on Van Dine et al., 1979), Walker (1985) notes that, nationally, a 25 percent incapacitation effect necessitates the incarceration of 1,200,000 new prisoners. Each of these new prisoners will require bed space and upkeep, and these costs can be considerable. Greenwood et al. (1994) point out that new prisons (in the early 1990s) cost approximately $97,000 per bed to build and an annual operating cost of more than $20,000 per prisoner. Based on Walker's projected increase in needed beds, the construction costs alone would require about $125 billion. The yearly operating cost would be an additional $24 billion. Using data on California's three-strikes law, Greenwood et al. (1994) estimate that an additional $5.5 billion per year would be needed in California to incarcerate all qualifying offenders.

Table 14.1
Level of Change Needed in Imprisonment Necessary for Incapacitation

State	Percent Increase in Prison Population Needed to Achieve:		
	10% Decrease in Index Crimes	**Reduction of 100 Index Crimes**	**10% Decrease in Violent Crime**
California	157.2	36.1	22.8
New York	263.5	67.2	57.0
Massachusetts	310.5	103.4	26.6
Ohio	82.5	34.7	12.0
Kentucky	86.1	44.8	16.0
New Hampshire	118.0	98.9	8.4
Mississippi	33.7	39.1	13.0
North Dakota	122.0	144.2	19.6

Source: Adapted from J. Cohen (1978). "The Incapacitative Effect of Imprisonment: A Critical Review of the Literature." In A Blumstein et al. (eds.), *Deterrence and Incapacitation: Estimating the Effects of Criminal Sanctions on Crime Rates*. Washington, DC: National Academy Press.

It would appear that the costs, both in terms of numbers of persons in prison and the dollars needed to accomplish this feat, outweigh the benefits accrued from the effort. A possible solution to this would be the incapacitation of only the individuals who are a clear threat to society. Such selective incapacitation may eliminate the need to increase the prison population in order to bring about lower levels of crime.

The Selective Incapacitation of Imprisonment

Selective incapacitation differs from collective efforts by imposing punishment on a select few individuals. The emphasis is on the identification of offenders who are high risk. High risk refers to the chances for future criminal activity. The individuals who are more likely to display antisocial behavior in the future, and thus pose a risk to society, are subjected to longer periods of incarceration. Advocates of selective incapacitation point to the lower cost of incarcerating only a portion of all offenders along with a presumed savings in the number of future offenses.

The idea of selective incapacitation received its greatest boost from a Rand Corporation report written by Peter Greenwood (1982). In an attempt to identify a group of individuals who should be incapacitated, Greenwood surveyed almost 2,200 prison inmates in California, Texas, and Michigan who were serving time for burglary or robbery. Examining self-report records and official documents concerning past behavior, arrests, convictions, and incarcerations, the author composed a seven-item scale that purportedly distinguishes between high-, medium-, and low-rate offenders (see Figure 14.1). Greenwood (1982) applied this scale to the Texas and California prisoners to test for the incapacitative effect of the scale.

Greenwood (1982) suggests that by reducing the time served by low- and medium-risk inmates and increasing the terms for high-risk offenders, it is possible to reduce robbery by 15 percent while lowering the California prison population by five percent. He compares this to a collective incapacitation approach that would require a 25 percent increase in the prison population to achieve the same 15 percent reduction in robberies. On the other hand, a 15 percent decrease in burglary requires a seven percent increase in the number of prisoners in California, even using a selective incapacitation approach (Greenwood, 1982). Figures for Texas are not as encouraging, with a 10 percent decrease in robbery requiring a 30 percent increase in the prison roles. A similar reduction in burglary requires a 15 percent rise in the prison population. The differences between California and Texas are due to the much lower offense rates in Texas, which affect the estimates. Despite the contradictory results, advocates of selective incapacitation often point to the 15 percent robbery reduction accomplished through an overall decrease of five percent in the prison population (Greenwood, 1982).

Figure 14.1
Greenwood's Selective Incapacitation Prediction Scale

1.	Prior conviction for the same offense
2.	Incarcerated for more than 50 percent of the preceding two years
3.	Conviction before the age of 16
4.	Served time in a juvenile facility
5.	Drug use in the preceding two years
6.	Drug use as a juvenile
7.	Employed less than 50 percent of the preceding two years

Source: P.W. Greenwood (1982). *Selective Incapacitation*. Santa Monica, CA: RAND.

Greenwood's (1982) figures have been severely criticized by other researchers. Visher (1986; 1987) points out that there are serious problems with the data, including the inability of some inmates to accurately recall past events and time periods, and problems with estimating the level of offending prior to incarceration. Large differences between California, Texas, and Michigan offense rates complicate the analysis (Visher, 1986). Reanalyzing the data, Visher (1986) reports lower estimates of the number of crimes committed and subsequently lower estimates of incapacitation. She finds a selective incapacitative effect of only five to 10 percent in California and increased crime in both Texas and Michigan. These new estimates seriously question the efficacy of selective incapacitation.

A number of other problems permeate the issue of selective incapacitation. The foremost concern rests on the ability to predict future behavior. As discussed in Chapter 9, the ability to predict behavior is poor at best. Second, incapacitation assumes that the rate of offending remains constant over time. If an offender's career would end during the time served in prison, the value of incarceration is lost. Third, estimates of incapacitation typically assume constant levels of arrest, conviction, and incarceration rates across low-, medium-, and high-rate offenders. This assumption is very questionable. High-rate offenders face a greater chance of detection and subsequent system action, simply because of the increased chances for him or her to be caught. Fourth, prison inmates may not be representative of the entire criminal population and results based on studies of inmates have questionable generalizability. Finally, there is a serious question concerning society's right to punish an individual for potential dangerousness and not just actual behavior. Implicit in selective incapacitation is the imposition of a longer sentence in order to avoid what might happen if an individual is released. Given the poor ability to accurately predict future behavior, this approach subjects many individuals to unnecessary punishment. In summary, although selective incapacitation holds much intuitive appeal, there does not seem to be a solid empirical basis for invoking the process at this time.

Electronic Monitoring

Incapacitation can also be achieved without the use of incarceration. The advent of electronic monitoring (EM) introduced a new avenue to incapacitation. Home confinement using electronic monitoring has prospered largely due to the growth and problems encountered by the prison system in the United States. The physical infrastructure of institutional corrections in the United States has not grown at the same pace as the prison population. In 1995, the number of prisoners in state facilities exceeded the design capacity by 62 percent (Bureau of Justice Statistics, 1997). Many jurisdictions are under court orders to reduce the size of their jail or prison populations. The initial response to these challenges has been the call for additional prisons. The public, however, is reluctant to pay the costs for new bed space, despite their calls for getting tough on offenders.

The response to overcrowding, legal challenges, rising crime, and public sentiment has been the development of various alternatives to incarceration.

Electronic monitoring (EM) is one possible solution to the call for increased supervision and protection of society when offenders are released into the community. The idea of keeping track of individuals using an electronic device dates back to Schwitzgebel and associates (1964) who described an EM system and discussed its potential uses. Jack Love, a New Mexico judge, took the idea of monitoring offenders from a 1977 comic strip in which Spiderman was tracked by means of a wrist transmitter and commissioned the development of a tracking device. The device, often called a "GOSSlink" after its inventor Michael Goss, was first used in 1983 on a small group of offenders in New Mexico (Niederberger and Wagner, 1985). The primary aim of the EM system was to monitor compliance with curfews and home confinement (Vaughn, 1989). Interest in this novel technique quickly prompted the development of similar devices by various companies and the adoption or testing of the technology in jurisdictions across the country.

Electronic monitoring has developed into two primary systems or types—active and passive. *Active, or continuous signaling, systems* keep track of the offender on a continuous basis. This system consists of a transmitter, receiver, and a central computer. The transmitter is a small, tamper-proof device, often smaller than a package of cigarettes, which is typically strapped to the offender's ankle. A constant signal is emitted by the transmitter and is picked up by a receiver attached to the home phone. When the offender is within range of the receiver (typically around 200 feet) the receiver registers the offender's presence. The receiver notifies the central computer of a violation if the offender should move out of range. A probation officer or other individual typically checks on the violation in order to confirm the information and take appropriate action. The computer system can be programmed to allow the offender to go to work, attend school, or participate in other activities. The system simply logs the times the offender leaves and returns home. A continuous computer printout of the offender's activity can be evaluated at any time.

The *passive system* consists of similar equipment, but requires periodic activation of the system. This system is also referred to as a *programmed contact system*. A passive system randomly calls the offender's home to certify the presence of the individual. When called, the offender must place the transmitter/encoder into a verifier/receiver. The individual may also be required to answer questions that are used in a voice verification. This system registers the absence of the offender if the phone is not answered, if the phone is persistently busy, or if the offender fails to properly use the equipment. As with the active equipment, the system can be programmed for certain days and hours in order to accommodate allowable absences. Indeed, passive systems are often set up with a graduated schedule of contacts in which the system checks on offenders more often in the early weeks and gradually reduces the number of contacts as time passes without violations (Gable, 1986; Maxfield and Baumer, 1990).

The most recent innovation has been a coupling of these systems with *global positioning system* (GPS) technology (Lilly, 2006). GPS technology uses satellites to locate a person or monitor his or her movements. This can be done on either a continuous basis or intermittently. One major advantage of this technology is there is no need for a home monitoring device or the use of any telephone lines. GPS technology has been used for many years for locating stolen vehicles. Adding GPS to EM programs makes it more difficult for offenders to abscond.

Proponents of electronic monitoring point to a variety of advantages stemming from its use. First, EM can possibly alleviate the overcrowding of correctional institutions. Second, the use of electronic monitors enhances the ability to supervise offenders in the community and can incapacitate offenders better than simple probation or parole. Third, the system reduces the costs of monitoring offenders in the community. Fourth, EM provides an "intermediate" level of punishment for offenders who do not need to be sentenced to an institution, yet may need more than simple probation. Fifth, advocates see EM as a more humane method for dealing with offenders as compared to incarceration. Finally, electronic monitors assist reintegration into society by allowing offenders to remain in the community, maintain family and friendship ties, and support the family. The discussion that follows focuses primarily on issues of recidivism.

The adoption of EM has steadily increased since its initial use in New Mexico in 1983. In 1986, there were 10 known manufacturers of EM equipment and only 10 jurisdictions in the United States using the technology (Friel et al., 1987; Schmidt, 1986). The number of EM programs has increased greatly since that time. The use of EM technology has spread beyond the United States to more than 17 countries, including Canada, the United Kingdom, Australia, New Zealand, Germany, Argentina, Israel and Taiwan (Stacey, 2006). In the United States, it is estimated that more than 125,000 offenders are on EM each day (Stacey, 2006). Haverkamp et al. (2004) provide estimates for yearly caseloads on EM for various European countries (see Table 14.2), with approximately 20,000 in England and 3,000 in Sweden.

EM is not intended to be used with all offenders. The fact that the beginnings of EM and home confinement are rooted in the problem of jail and prison overcrowding points to the idea that these alternatives are meant for

Table 14.2
Estimates of EM Use in Europe, 2004

Country	Yearly EM Number
England	20,000
Sweden	3,000
Belgium	2,100
The Netherlands	390
France	255
Portugal	39

Source: Adapted from Haverkamp et al. (2004).

offenders who would normally be confined in an institution. Most programs require that potential clients come from pools of offenders ordered to jail, prison, pretrial detention, or those who cannot raise bail (Charles, 1989; Ford and Schmidt, 1985; Maxfield and Baumer, 1990; Vaughn, 1989). Excluding offenders from EM who would normally be set free with minimal or no supervision avoids the problem of using the new program as a means of intervening with an entire new set of clients. EM programs do not wish to be seen as a form of *net-widening* (i.e., bringing more people under the umbrella of social control). Programs also tend to target less serious offenders or offenders deemed inappropriate for incarceration (such as DUI offenders), although serious offenders are targeted by some programs (Friel et al., 1987; Maxfield and Baumer, 1990; Padgett et al., 2006).

The degree to which offenders on EM violate the conditions of their release or recidivate while on home confinement is a prime consideration in the evaluation of the programs. In general, evaluations show favorable results in terms of both technical violations and further offending. Evaluation of one post-conviction program in Kenton County, Kentucky, reveals that roughly eight percent of the offenders placed on EM commit some technical violation resulting in their removal from the program (Ball et al., 1988; Lilly et al., 1987). More importantly, slightly more than five percent of the offenders commit new crimes. This recidivistic behavior, however, is significantly less than that of a pre-program control group of offenders (20% recidivism). Evaluation of a Palm Beach County, Florida, program reveals similar positive results with less than 10 percent recidivism (Ball et al., 1988; Palm Beach County Sheriff's Department, 1987). Unfortunately, the Palm Beach program provides no figures for comparable offenders handled under alternative or traditional methods. This lack of a control group leaves in doubt the actual impact of the program. A recent evaluation of EM in Florida notes that those in the program commit fewer technical violations and have lower recidivism levels, despite the fact that those on EM are higher-risk clients (Padgett et al., 2006). Evaluation of post-conviction EM in Canada also suggests lower recidivism, although the results vary by program and are confounded by the risk levels of the clients (Bonta et al., 2000). An evaluation in the United Kingdom reports lower recidivism for those on EM compared to control subjects (Dodgson et al., 2001; Mortimer, 2001).

EM is also used as a form of pretrial supervision for individuals who cannot post bond or who would otherwise be released. Cooprider and Kerby (1990), reporting on a pretrial program in Lake County, Illinois, note that those released on EM have a higher violation rate than those released on recognizance (19% compared to 13%), although the violations are for technical problems and not new offenses. A second evaluation of EM reports a higher violation rate for pretrial releasees than post-conviction offenders (27% compared to 19%) (Maxfield and Baumer, 1990). Violations could include new charges, absconding, and technical violations. Maxfield and Baumer (1990) and Baumer et al. (1993) suggest that greater violations by pretrial subjects may be due to the fact that a wider array of clients and problems are involved at pretrial than at post-conviction. Those on post-conviction release also have a greater degree of certainty concerning the future, whereas pretrial subjects are awaiting word of the future. In general, studies dealing with pretrial use of EM present generally favorable results with relatively low levels of violations.

Electronic monitoring programs for juveniles report similar failure rates as those presented above. Vaughn (1989), gathering data from nine juvenile programs in the United States, indicates that the failure rates range from 4.5 percent to 30 percent. As in other studies, most of the failure appears in the form of technical violations and not additional criminal or delinquent behavior. Data on 845 youths reveal only five new offenses known by the program and only 18 cases in which the youths ran away while on the system (Vaughn, 1989). The preponderance of technical violations is borne out in a recent national survey of EM programs (Schmidt, 1989). Relatively few failures can be attributed to new offenses.

An interesting variation in the use of EM involves the enforcement of domestic violence protection orders. Erez et al. (2004) report on a program in which defendants are ordered to wear the ankle bracelet but the base monitoring unit is placed in the home of the victim. When a defendant nears the victim's home, the EM system registers his presence and an alert is sent to the authorities and the victim. Victims can also carry a monitor when away from home to protect against the defendant (Erez et al., 2004). An analysis of more than 600 cases in which the EM was used shows few violations, with most involving simple "drivebys" and no attempt to actually contact the victim (Erez et al., 2004).

EM with GPS monitoring is also used with paroled sex offenders in New Jersey. The New Jersey State Parole Board (NJPB) notes that the technology has been employed with 225 dangerous sex offenders. The use of GPS offers a variety of advantages, most notably the ability to place an offender at an offense location during the commission of a crime. This enhances the ability to clear a case and greatly improves the odds of getting a conviction. Based on data for the first year of operation, only one of 225 parolees under GPS surveillance committed a new sex crime, with an additional 19 committing a technical violation (NJBP, 2007). This is significantly lower that the U.S. recidivism rate for sex offenders.

The goal of reducing overcrowding also has not been realized. The fact that most programs deal with a relatively small number of individuals at any point in time means that there is little if any relief for overcrowded jails and prisons. The continued growth of the prison/jail population, despite the growth of EM, is adequate evidence showing that EM has had no impact on overcrowding. Changing the analysis to an examination of the number of days spent outside of an institution, however, provides more positive results. Offenders in Kenton County spent 1,712 days of incarceration at home. The Palm Beach County offenders completed 10,716 incarceration days in the community (Ball et al., 1988). Where the number of offenders is not large, each day outside the institution represents an improvement in the crowding situation.

Despite the great growth and support for EM, a number of problem areas and concerns are advanced by various writers. One area of concern relates to operational issues faced by agencies using the technology. Vaughn (1989) notes that EM is a labor-intensive system that operates 24 hours a day. This round-the-clock monitoring is not the norm for many probation and parole departments (Friel and Vaughn, 1986). Constant monitoring and response to violations increases the personnel costs to the administrative agency, especially if the agency is traditionally oriented to daytime operations. In addition, many offenders spend only a short time on the system before being granted outright release or moving on to other programs. This great turnover means that the screening process, data entry, program hook-up, and other tasks must be undertaken on a continuing basis with new clients. It is conceivable that new staff will be needed for the sole purpose of operating the EM system, thus increasing the personnel costs to the host agency (Vaughn, 1989).

Second, critics of electronic monitoring point out the potential of the technology to simply extend the reach of the criminal justice system. They note that most innovations aimed at reducing the size and scope of intervention actually result in more persons under some form of social control (i.e., net-widening). Because electronic monitoring does not eliminate or limit the existing institutional space, it is possible that the technology will increase the number of individuals under daily supervision of the criminal or juvenile justice systems. While few studies attempt to evaluate the degree of net-widening that may be taking place, Ball et al. (1988), Lilly et al. (1987), and Maxfield and Baumer (1990) provide preliminary evidence that net-widening is not occurring to any great degree.

Another concern is that the use of EM may place the public at greater risk. EM programs cannot guarantee that the offenders will not or cannot commit additional offenses while in the community. There is nothing to physically keep an offender from offending or absconding. There are times, such as when an offender is supposed to be at school or work, when he is not being monitored. Any mistake by the equipment at detecting a violation also leaves society at risk.

Finally, EM is viewed by many as an Orwellian means of controlling the population. The government is taking on the image of Big Brother—always watching us in order to correct our behavior whenever we step out of line. The extent of that ability is apparent in the fact that there are offenders under 24-hour surveillance using GPS technology. EM can extend state intervention into our homes and daily activities. The fact that EM requires the compliance of the entire family exacerbates this feeling of control. Many individuals object to such interventions on the basis of the sanctity of the home and the fear of an overreaching government. While the technology and monitoring may be legal, there is the larger social question of where to draw the line of governmental intervention in the community.

The use of electronic devices to monitor offenders has quickly found a place in the daily operations of the criminal justice system. Since the early 1980s, EM has grown from the plot of a comic strip to programs in every state and other countries. The growth can be attributed to the overcrowding of prisons, the development of the technology, the desire to do something with offenders, and the acceptance of the idea by criminal justice system personnel and the public.

This review suggests that EM is a viable method for handling both adults and juveniles at post-conviction and pretrial stages of intervention. The low violation rates and the dominance of technical violations favor the use of electronic monitoring. One major problem with the evaluations is the failure of most studies to randomly assign subjects to EM and non-EM status. Programs typically select their clients based on criteria that are geared toward the most promising individuals, thus leading to success in evaluations (Bonta et al., 2000). A second qualifier involves the fact that many studies do not have adequate, or any, control groups with which to compare EM clients. Despite these shortcomings, EM appears to be a permanent component of criminal justice supervision.

FUTURE IMPLICATIONS

The research on specific deterrence and incapacitation presents a mixed picture. Studies of specific deterrence present contradictory results concerning the deterrent effects of punishment. While society calls for stronger sanctions, it may be that these interventions play an aggravating role in deviant behavior. The offender may view harsh punishment as a breaking point with conventional society and an opportunity to turn to further deviant activity. The act of putting an individual behind bars may be more criminogenic than deterrent. The uncertain knowledge about individual hedonistic values makes the selection and imposition of punishment for deterrence a difficult, if not impossible, task. The lack of attention paid to specific deterrence and the inability to separate rehabilitation from punishment in research impedes the evaluation of this approach.

Incapacitation, whether collective or selective, has great intuitive appeal for society. The idea of punishing an individual for the harm he caused is an accepted method for dealing with deviant behavior. Extending that period of punishment in order to keep an individual from committing another offense is an easily acceptable modification. The costs of such a policy, however, may be high. The number of persons who must be housed in order to achieve even a small decrease in crime is staggering even using the most conservative figures. Translating these bodies into dollars leads to budgets that the public has not been willing to accept. As with specific deterrence, the research literature holds little promise for an acceptable incapacitation strategy at this time.

Another possible alternative is incapacitating offenders in the community through the use of electronic monitoring. EM offers a cost-effective means for releasing offenders into the community while providing a degree of control over them. The evaluation research suggests that the level of both technical violations and new offending is relatively low. Despite problems and concerns with EM programs, they appear to be a viable alternative to incapacitation through incarceration.

Chapter 15

REHABILITATION

Key Terms:

aggregate level evaluation
Circle Sentencing
Cognitive Thinking Skills
drug courts
Family Group Conferencing
individual-level evaluation

Intensive Supervision Probation
Multi-Systemic Therapy
restorative justice
risk, need, and responsivity
tautological
Victim-Offender Mediation

Learning Objectives:

After reading this chapter you should be able to:

- Give arguments on both sides of the "nothing works" controversy

- List and discuss different outcome measures used in treatment research

- Compare and contrast aggregate and individual-level evaluation

- Provide examples of cognitive behavioral interventions, relate their approach, and tell how effective they are

- Explain what ISP programs are and what impact they have had

- Define restorative justice and name three different types

- Outline Victim-Offender Mediation

- Explain how Family Group Conferencing works

- Discuss Circle Sentencing

- Relate the impact of restorative justice in terms of participant satisfaction and recidivism

- Explain how drug courts are expected to influence their clients
- Briefly discuss the common elements of drug court programs
- List advantages of drug courts
- Identify problems/issues with drug court programs

Throughout most of the twentieth century, the major method of achieving tertiary prevention was the rehabilitation of offenders. Various forms of rehabilitation dominated the handling of criminals, and a complete listing and brief explanation of all of the various treatment programs set up to deal with deviant behavior would fill many volumes. Despite the move toward increased punitiveness since the 1970s, rehabilitation has remained a driving interest in the correctional field. Given this, one would assume that there is clear evidence of successful intervention. The state of the evidence, however, is not as clear. This chapter examines the debate on the rehabilitation controversy, discusses the problems inherent in the research and debate, and considers a few promising rehabilitation approaches. Space and time constraints prohibit all but a brief examination of specific intervention approaches. Many other texts have been written and devoted exclusively to the examination of rehabilitation.

THE "WHAT WORKS?" ARGUMENT

No one truly interested in the study of rehabilitation can be unaware of the eulogy placed on treatment that "with few and isolated exceptions, the rehabilitative efforts that have been reported so far have had no appreciable effect on recidivism" (Martinson, 1974). With this single statement, the very basis of correctional intervention was shaken. The foundation for this assessment was an examination of literature on rehabilitation appearing between 1945 and 1967 (Lipton et al., 1975). The authors considered 231 studies in which there was a treatment evaluation with a control group, an outcome measure attributable to the treatment, sufficient information about the intervention and evaluation for making a judgment, a sufficiently large sample size to make inferences, and, in general, a sound research methodology. The authors examined a wide range of intervention techniques, including counseling, educational and vocational training, medical treatment, psychological therapy, probation, parole, and community programs. As already noted, the effect of these various programs on recidivism was negligible (Martinson, 1974). Other outcome variables, such as adjustment to prison, attitude adjustment, and educational improvement, show some positive effects on offenders. These changes, however, are relatively unimportant given the major goal of preventing further criminal behavior.

Subsequent Analyses

The finding of little or no effect of rehabilitation on recidivism appears in a variety of other reports since the work of Martinson (1974) and Lipton et al. (1975). Wright and Dixon (1977), reviewing 96 studies from 1965–1974, report that treatment has little impact on recidivism. The authors further note that most of the evaluations employ poor research design, fail to use random assignment, and do not present adequate information for subsequent analysis. Another examination of 18 rehabilitation programs in New York City comparing both pre- and post-program levels of deviance and program participants with a control group arrives at the same conclusion (Fishman, 1977). Fishman reports higher recidivism for participants under age 18, no difference for those ages 19 and 20, lower recidivism for young adult participants (ages 21–39), and no difference for subjects age 40 and over. Comparison of recidivism rates for the various projects does not uncover any significant differences among the rehabilitative techniques.

A reanalysis of the Lipton et al. (1975) findings undertaken by the National Academy of Sciences concludes that the original authors "were reasonably accurate and fair in their appraisal of the rehabilitation literature" (Sechrest et al., 1979). The only major point of departure in the reanalysis involves the feeling that the earlier analysis *overstates the effectiveness* of the reviewed programs. Sechrest et al. (1979) claim that the earlier report falls short in its criticism of the studies. The original review appears to have overlooked a variety of critical problems within the research reports, particularly concerning the methodological shortcomings and the results of the evaluations. More recent reviews of the literature also fail to find strong support for rehabilitation. Gensheimer et al. (1986) report that, of 44 studies spanning 1967–1983, there is no evidence of a rehabilitative effect accruing from the interventions. Finally, Lab and Whitehead (1988), presenting data from 55 research reports from 1975–1984, reveal 33 comparisons with no difference or worse recidivism by experimentals and only 15 with positive results. Based on these literature reviews, which span a variety of decades and rehabilitative strategies, it is possible to conclude that rehabilitation is not very effective at reducing recidivism.

Not all researchers, however, are ready to sound the death knell for rehabilitation. One leading proponent of rehabilitation (Palmer, 1975), claims that Martinson (1974) ignores a variety of positive findings in his analysis. Palmer (1975) notes that certain programs have positive effects on certain individuals under certain conditions. The emphasis should not be on finding a single cure-all for the entire range of offenders (Palmer, 1975). Indeed, Martinson (1979) agrees that there are instances in which rehabilitation does have a positive impact on an individual's behavior. Nevertheless, the overall finding that most programs report little or no success with the majority of subjects still holds true (Martinson, 1979). Support for the belief that some programs work with some select individuals also can be found in recent reviews by Graziano and Mooney (1984),

Garrett (1985), and Mayer et al. (1986). While the evidence shows some reduced recidivism, the greatest changes appear in other outcome measures (e.g., psychological adjustment, academic improvement, institutional adjustment). The data also suggest that more rigorous studies find less of an impact on recidivism than evaluations that are not as concerned with the research methodology.

Andrews et al. (1990) argue that treatment has a definite positive impact on recidivism. The authors suggest that treatment that pays attention to the principles of *risk, need, and responsivity* (basically matching the correct subjects with the correct intervention) can have a significant impact on recidivism (Andrews et al., 1990). They purportedly prove their point through a reanalysis of the Whitehead and Lab (1989) data and an analysis of adult data. Lab and Whitehead (1990), however, argue that Andrews and associates fail to define their terms in such a way that their argument can be tested, and they fail to follow their own criteria in classifying subjects and studies. More importantly, their presentation is *tautological*. That is, they use a circular argument in which they use the existing literature to identify risk, need, and responsivity and then use that same literature as data to prove the correctness of their position (Lab and Whitehead, 1990; Logan and Gaes, 1993). Anyone can prove something that already exists.

In a series of papers, Lipsey (1990; 1999; Lipsey and Wilson, 1993; 1998) reports on perhaps the most extensive evaluations of the rehabilitation literature. Throughout the analyses, the author finds positive effects from rehabilitative treatment. For example, Lipsey and Wilson (1998) report an overall six percent difference in recidivism between experimental and control subjects across 200 studies. It is important to note, however, that there is a great deal of heterogeneity across the studies, with different types of treatment having different effects. Treatments that focus on interpersonal skills, cognitive-behavioral interventions, multimodal approaches and community-based programs typically have a greater impact than other interventions (Lipsey and Wilson, 1998; Losel, 1995). Lipsey (1990) argues that research on the impact of rehabilitation needs to consider the type of treatment, the setting in which it is delivered, the method of evaluation, and other factors when assessing the evidence. Lowenkamp et al. (2006) note that interventions with stronger program integrity (that is, strong program implementation, good offender assessment, etc.) are more effective at reducing recidivism than those that have weak integrity.

There is no uniform opinion regarding the effectiveness of rehabilitation. This state of disarray can be attributed to underlying conceptual differences between the opponents in the debate. Major points of divergence are the choice of outcome measure and the level of evaluation. Each of these factors can alter the results of evaluations and reviews.

Outcome Measures

The traditional measure of success in rehabilitation has been the elimination of deviant behavior. Usually this means lowering recidivism. Measuring recidivism, however, can be very difficult. Recidivism has been defined in many ways—ranging from reincarceration (a very strict criterion) to simple referral of the individual to any source of help (a very lax definition). Each of the definitions is problematic. For example, reincarceration is a relatively rare event for some types of offenders and, therefore, the levels of recidivism may be quite low. Alternatively, recidivism measured as simple contact with the police can greatly inflate the outcome. The varied choice of recidivism measure is a major problem in attempts to review and consolidate the results of different reports.

Perhaps the most common outcome measures in the rehabilitation literature are those that do not look to recidivism or deviant behavior. These measures include educational and vocational achievement, changes in self-esteem, attitudinal shifts, psychological adjustment, community adjustment, and costs of intervention. Many proponents of rehabilitative efficacy point to improvements in these dimensions as proof of program effectiveness. Unfortunately, while many of these outcomes are found in the literature, changes in these dimensions often appear during the in-program period and fail to persist long after release from the program. The alternative outcome measures, however, should remain secondary concerns to the prevention of criminal activity. The major problem for rehabilitation is future deviant behavior. Unless a clear connection can be found between the alternative outcomes and lower recidivism, these outcomes should remain secondary in the evaluation of rehabilitation programs. Indeed, the emphasis of tertiary crime prevention is on subsequent levels of recidivism.

Levels of Evaluation

The debate between critics and proponents of rehabilitation often rests on the appropriate level of evaluation to be employed in the analysis. Studies that report negative findings for rehabilitation usually rely on aggregate evaluation. *Aggregate-level evaluation* looks for changes across large groups of subjects. Changes in rates of offending or recidivism are the common metric by which programs are to be judged. A small or nonexistent change in the overall rate of crime is indicative of a failed intervention. In essence, aggregate evaluation searches for quantitative changes in behavior. The reviews cited earlier, which indicated minimal impact (e.g., Gensheimer et al., 1986; Lab and Whitehead, 1988; Lipton et al., 1975; Martinson, 1974; Sechrest et al., 1979; Whitehead and Lab, 1989; Wright and Dixon, 1977) all rely heavily on the failure of rehabilitation to shift recidivism rates.

Proponents of rehabilitation favor *individual-level evaluations*. The individual level focuses on qualitative changes rather than quantitative shifts in offending. These qualitative movements may appear as simple adjustments in the type of offending. For example, an offender may shift from robbery, which involves a physical confrontation, to property offenses, such as burglary or larceny. This would affect the rate for specific offenses but do little for the overall crime rate. Individual-level analysis also is able to focus on other, non-crime-related measures of change. Attitudinal shifts, psychological adjustment, ability to relate to others, and increased life skills are examples of alternate outcomes that can be found when looking at individual progress. Virtually any program can point to at least a few successes when the criteria for success is movement along one of these qualitative dimensions. It is this individual level of evaluation that prompts Palmer (1975; 1983), Martinson (1979), Garrett (1985), and others to claim that some rehabilitation works for some clients.

Summary

There is still a great deal of debate on the impact of rehabilitation on recidivism, although most reviews claim to find at least some positive support for rehabilitation. Strong claims of success typically rely on alternative outcome measures. Evaluations that do not use random assignment of study subjects or follow strict methodological techniques tend to show better results (Garrett, 1985; Mayer et al., 1986), as do evaluations of demonstration projects where there is a great deal of control over the intervention and its implementation (see, for example, Lipsey et al., 2001). Perhaps the key to developing effective interventions is matching the appropriate subjects to the proper treatment. Andrews et al. (1990) incorporate this in their discussion of risk, need and responsivity. Unfortunately, the ability to make such selections remains an elusive problem. The majority of programs do not know which clients are best served by their treatment, nor do they know how to identify the proper subjects once they are aware of differential program impact. As a result, tertiary crime prevention can be achieved only in a limited way.

EVALUATIONS OF REHABILITATION PROGRAMS

Rehabilitation efforts persist despite the many criticisms of rehabilitation. A variety of intervention programs continue to be tried and some present encouraging results. Several programs attempt to adhere to the basic premises of risk, need, and responsivity as proposed by Andrews et al. (1990). Other programs are the outgrowth of existing correctional programs, such as Intensive Supervision Probation (an enhanced form of probation). The following presentations are not meant to be all-inclusive nor representative of all types of intervention. It should briefly acquaint the reader with a few interesting approaches of the recent past.

Cognitive-Behavioral Interventions

The results of meta-analyses of treatment programs and the debate about the effectiveness of correctional treatment have led to several suggestions about appropriate treatment. Cullen and Gendreau (2000) outline several general principles that appear to underlie effective programs. First, interventions should target known predictors of deviant behavior and recidivism. Second, interventions should be behavioral and address the cognitive processes that lead to antisocial activity. Such interventions would seek to alter the decision-making processes of individuals, help offenders to identify prosocial responses to challenges, and develop skills and techniques for avoiding problem behavior. Third, successful programs will target high-risk offenders in community settings using well-trained staff and interventions matched to the needs of offenders. Cullen and Gendreau (2000) claim that interventions that follow these guidelines will achieve positive results. Various programs exist that follow the suggestions of Cullen and Gendreau (2000). Multi-Systemic Therapy and the Cognitive Thinking Skills Program are two examples. The idea that behavior is affected by a wide array of social and environmental factors underlies *Multi-Systemic Therapy* (MST) (Cullen and Gendreau, 2000). MST is a community-based intervention that attempts to address family, peer, school, community, and other influences that may prompt or lead to deviant behavior. The actual intervention will vary based on the needs of the individual, and it is dynamic and changes according to the needs and progress of the client. Each client receives intensive services, in the community, from a team of therapists who are held accountable for the successes or failures of the program (Cullen and Gendreau, 2000). Evaluations of MST reveal reduced delinquency and improvements in risk-related behaviors (Borduin et al., 1995; Brown et al., 1999).

The *Cognitive Thinking Skills Program* (CTSP) is also a multi-modal intervention that utilizes a range of techniques targeting cognitive-behavioral problems (Gaes et al., 1999). The CTSP focuses on identifying cognitive deficits and inappropriate decision making by individuals. Typical problems are impulsive behavior, egocentric activity, selfishness, and an inability to express oneself (Gaes et al., 1999). Highly trained program staff offer 70 hours of skills training to clients. CTSP has been adopted across Canada, as well as in several U.S. states and the United Kingdom. Gaes et al. (1999), reviewing evidence on CTSP, report that fewer treatment subjects recidivate than non-treatment control clients. While the differences tend to be statistically significant, many of the differences are small. The most positive findings emerge from CTSP implementation in community settings (Gaes et al., 1999).

The increased use of cognitive-behavioral interventions prompted Lipsey et al. (2001) to undertake a meta-analytic review of the existing studies. The authors considered only evaluations that included experimental or quasi-experimental designs with a focus on recidivism. This decision results in only

14 studies of primarily male, white juveniles or young adult clients. The results show that all but one project reports lower recidivism among experimental youths, although in only three of the 13 positive findings is the difference between experimental and control groups statistically significant (Lipsey et al., 2001). Despite this fact, the authors point out that the global mean difference (i.e., the results across all studies) is statistically significant, indicating that the results are greatly influenced by a minority of the evaluations. Of particular importance is the finding that the best results appear in demonstration projects in which the intervention is set up specifically for testing and evaluation, and there is reason to believe that the program is better implemented and delivered (Lipsey, 1999; Lipsey et al., 2001). The better results also appear in studies of juveniles treated in the community.

Intensive Supervision

Many proponents of rehabilitation point to the intensive supervision of probationers and parolees as a tool in reducing subsequent deviant activity. Advocates also claim that these programs are less costly, reduce prison over-crowding, protect society, and rehabilitate offenders (Clear and Hardyman, 1990; Tonry, 1990; Tonry and Lynch, 1996). Indeed, many more offenders are placed on probation or parole every year than are incarcerated. The impact of probation and parole, whether intensive or otherwise, on recidivism is not clear. Much of the debate centers on the level of supervision provided to the client. The assumption is that more positive results accrue from closer supervision.

Intensive supervision (ISP) programs exist in every state. Typical features of ISP are team supervision, a high number of contacts between the client and officer, curfew and/or house arrest, restitution, employment or school atten-dance, drug testing, community service, counseling, and treatment (Byrne, 1990; Petersilia and Turner, 1993).

The New Jersey ISP program is a good example of such interventions. The program deals with relatively low-risk, non-violent offenders who have spent a short time in prison. The average caseload for the probation officer is 16, with the expectation that the officer will have almost daily contact with each client (either in person or by phone) (Pearson, 1985). The number of contacts are lessened as the client is found to be reliable and no infractions are detected. Evaluation of the New Jersey program shows that ISP clients have a lower recidivism rate (measured as new arrests) than individuals who remain in prison (Pearson, 1988; Pearson and Harper, 1990). Despite this claim, 44 percent of the ISP clients are returned to prison. The lower recidivism rate may be due to the fact that ISP clients are not randomly selected. The subse-quent recidivism figures, therefore, may be indicative of the lack of compara-bility between the ISP and prison groups (Pearson, 1988). Indeed, the fact that ISP deals with less serious offenders can artificially inflate the success of the program (Clear and Hardyman, 1990).

Evaluations of other ISP programs present varying results. Erwin (1990), using data on 2,322 clients in Georgia, notes that the ISP clients commit less serious subsequent offenses. Unfortunately, there is no difference in reincarceration rates in three and five year follow-ups for ISP clients and individuals who served their time in prison (Erwin, 1990). These results are even more discouraging in light of the fact that the program actually targets low-risk offenders (Morris and Tonry, 1990). Three California ISP programs report no difference in subsequent arrests or incarceration for randomly assigned subjects (Petersilia and Turner, 1990). At the same time, the study reports more violence by ISP clients, possibly due to the random assignment used in conjunction with serious offenders. Evaluations across sites in the United States also fail to find any strong impact on recidivism (see Gowdy, 1993; Petersilia and Turner, 1993; Turner et al., 1992). As expected from intensive monitoring, most studies report relatively high rates of technical violations (Erwin, 1990; Gowdy, 1993; Pearson, 1988; Pearson and Harper, 1990; Petersilia and Turner, 1990, 1993; Turner et al., 1992). Latessa and Allen (2003), reviewing ISP evaluations, report that ISP clients recidivate less than control subjects (i.e., at least 5% lower recidivism) in four studies, recidivate more in six analyses, and perform comparably to controls in six other evaluations.

In addition to reductions in recidivism, advocates of ISP argue that reduced prison overcrowding and lower costs will result from the program. In terms of overcrowding, there is no evidence that ISP has had any appreciable impact on the number of incarcerated individuals (Tonry, 1990). Indeed, given the high revocation rate due to technical violations and the relatively small numbers of persons placed in ISP programs, there can be little effect on prison populations. Cost savings are also difficult to demonstrate. New Jersey figures suggest cost savings of roughly $7,000 per client compared to incarceration (Pearson, 1988) and Georgia claims a $6,000 per client savings (Erwin, 1990). These figures, however, do not consider the impact of any net-widening that may take place or the fact that ISP is more costly than regular probation supervision (Gowdy, 1993; Petersilia and Turner, 1993; Turner et al., 1992).

Research on intensive supervision suggests varied effects. Results differ somewhat by type of offender, measures of recidivism, evaluation of cost, and impact on system overcrowding. There appears to be limited evidence of a positive effect of intensive supervision. The fact that the public accepts ISP as a viable program, perhaps due to the perceived safety from increased surveillance, may explain the continued interest in the program.

Restorative Justice

An emerging and growing approach for addressing criminal acts is restorative justice. As opposed to retributive justice, which focuses on the lawbreaker and the imposition of sanctions for the purposes of deterrence, vengeance and/or punishment, *restorative justice* seeks to repair the harm that was done to both the victim and the community. At the same time, there is an underlying assumption that the offender can benefit or be "repaired" by participating in the restorative process. This is accomplished by bringing together a range of interested parties in a non-confrontational setting, including the victim and the offender, as well as family members or friends, criminal justice system personnel, and members of the general community. The participants, as a group, seek to understand the actions that led to the criminal or antisocial behavior, reveal the feelings and concerns of all parties, negotiate or mediate a solution agreeable to everyone, and assist in implementing that solution (Bazemore and Maloney, 1994). Kurki (2000:266) notes that "restorative justice is about relationships—how relationships are harmed by crime and how they can be rebuilt to promote recovery and healing for people affected by crime."

While the term "restorative justice" is relatively new, elements of restorative justice have been around for a long time. Braithwaite (1999:2) notes that "[r]estorative justice has been the dominant model of criminal justice throughout most of human history for all the world's peoples." Weitekamp (1999) points out that many of the restorative justice practices being used today can be traced directly to historical traditions that have survived in indigenous cultures. Of particular note are the practices of Aboriginal tribes, Inuits, and Native American and Native Canadian Indian tribes.

Restorative justice takes a variety of different forms, although they all attend to the same basic tenets. Indeed, "restorative justice" is often referred to as "transformative justice," "social justice," "balanced and restorative justice," "peacemaking," or other terms. Braithwaite (2002) notes that many of these terms and programs have been incorporated into the more general idea of restorative justice. Most discussions of restorative justice outline three primary types of programs—Victim-Offender Mediation, Family Group Conferencing, and Circle Sentencing.

Victim-Offender Mediation

Victim-Offender Mediation, also referred to as Victim-Offender Reconciliation Programs (VORP), is a direct outgrowth of the dispute resolution/dispute mediation programs of the early 1970s (Umbreit, 1999). *Victim-Offender Mediation* (VOM) is typically a post-conviction process (although pre-conviction programs exist) in which the victim and the offender are brought together to discuss a wide range of issues. A trained mediator also attends these meetings. Participation in VOM is voluntary for the victim, but the offender may be required by the court to participate as a part of the court process (Umbreit, 1999). VOM programs may be a part of the formal criminal justice system, or may be run by other agencies that are not directly connected to the system.

The most important concern addressed in the VOM meetings is to identify for the offender the types and level of harm suffered by the victim as a result of the crime. At the same time, the offender is given the chance to explain why he committed the act and the circumstances that may underlie his behavior. The focus of the meetings is on repairing the harm done to the victim, helping the victim heal (both physically and emotionally), restoring the community to the pre-crime state, and reintegrating the offender into society (Umbreit et al., 2003). Both parties are considered equal participants in the process and given time to express themselves and their feelings about the crime. The outcome of these meetings should be a mutually agreeable resolution. Among the potential tangible outcomes for the victim may be the offender making monetary restitution or providing service to repair the harm done. Perhaps of equal importance are changes in understanding by both parties about each other, and changes in behavior and attitude on the part of the offender.

Family Group Conferencing

Family Group Conferencing (FGC) is based on practices of the Maori in New Zealand. The greatest difference between FGC and VOM is the inclusion of family members, close friends, and other support groups of the victim and offender in the conferences. There is also the possibility of including criminal justice system personnel, including social workers, police officers, and an offender's attorney (Van Ness and Strong, 2002). This expansion of participants is very important, in that the families and support persons are expected to take some responsibility in monitoring the offender and making certain that any agreements are carried out after the conference (Kurki, 2000).

FGC first appeared in 1989 in New Zealand with an exclusive focus on juveniles ages 14 to 17 (Kurki, 2000). While most conferences deal with minor juvenile misbehavior, they can include serious offenses and repeat offenders. Similar to VOM, the emphasis in FGC is on engendering discussion among the parties about what took place, why it occurred, and the most appropriate steps to take to address the harm. Unlike VOM, the conferences do not include a formal mediator. Rather, FGC includes a facilitator who attempts to keep the discussions moving in a positive direction until an agreement can be reached among all parties. Conferences can be held either pretrial or post-trial, and have become a part of police and pretrial diversion programs in both the United States (McGarrell et al., 2000) and Australia (Moore and O'Connell, 1994).

Circle Sentencing

The third type of restorative justice program to be discussed is Circle Sentencing. *Circle Sentencing* is based on North American Indian processes, which invite all interested parties to participate in determining the appropriate sanctions for offenders (Van Ness and Strong, 2002). Included in the circles are all of those typically found in FGCs, as well as other community members who wish to be included. These circles are also referred to as "peacemaking circles" (Bazemore and Umbreit, 2001). Most cases handled by sentencing circles involve minor offenses, although some programs will consider more serious crimes (Stuart, 1996). A major difference between Circle Sentencing and the other forms of restorative justice is that this approach is regularly used with both adults and juveniles (Kurki, 2000).

Every participant in the sentencing circle is given the opportunity to speak, express his or her feelings about the crime, and offer opinions and rationales about the outcome of the discussion. The fact that the circles include (potentially) a wide array of participants means that a great deal of planning and preparation is needed before the actual meeting (Kurki, 2000). The intended outcome of the circle is consensus on a plan of action, which may include explicit sentencing recommendations to the trial judge and/or a range of community-based interventions (Van Ness and Strong, 2002). The recommendations of the circles can include recommendations for jail or prison time (Stuart, 1996). The decision of the circle is often binding on the offender (and may be specifically incorporated into the official court record) and a failure to adhere to the decision may result in further criminal justice system processing or being returned to the circle (Van Ness and Strong, 2002).

The Impact of Restorative Justice

Restorative justice programs are intended to have a number of different possible outcomes, including repairing the harm done to the victim and rehabilitating the offender. Assessing the impact of the interventions, however, is difficult. Many evaluations focus on victim and offender satisfaction with the process, and the level of compliance or completion of the agreed-upon settlement. Less common are analyses of the impact of the programs on subsequent offending by the offender. In addition, very little research has been conducted on Circle Sentencing, thus most of the comments in this section refer to VOM and FGC.

With very few exceptions, both victims and offenders express satisfaction with the restorative process in which they have participated (Braithwaite, 1999). This is true of VOM, FGC, and Circle Sentencing. Evaluations of VOM typically reveal that between 75 and 100 percent of the participants express satisfaction with the mediation (Kurki, 2000). Similarly high levels of satisfaction arise from FGCs (Bazemore and Umbreit, 2001; Moore and O'Connell, 1994; Umbreit et al., 2003). The level of satisfaction is also reflected in feelings by participants that the process is fair (McGarrell et al., 2000; Umbreit, 1999; Umbreit and Coates, 1993; Umbreit et al., 2003).

A companion to satisfaction is the ability of the meetings to achieve consensus on a solution and whether the parties carry through with the agreement. Again, there is evidence that most meetings culminate in an agreement and most parties comply with the settlement (Braithwaite, 1999; Kurki, 2000; Schiff, 1999; Umbreit and Coates, 1993). Restitution is a common component of many agreements and evaluations reveal that 90 percent or more of the offenders in FGC comply with the ordered restitution (Wachtel, 1995). McGarrell et al. (2000) note that participants in a conferencing program completed the program at a significantly higher rate than normal diversion clients.

This information on satisfaction and compliance must be tempered somewhat by the fact that participation in the programs is voluntary. This is especially true for victims, although offenders can also opt out of the process in many places. The fact that the program is voluntary may mean that only individuals who are more amenable to the process to begin with are included in the programs. There may be a built-in bias in favor of positive results. Umbreit et al. (2003), for example, point out that only 40 to 60 percent of the victims and offenders who are asked to participate in VOM agree to do so. Similarly, McCold and Wachtel (1998) report that almost six out of 10 FGC cases never materialize due to a refusal to participate.

While reductions in the level of subsequent offending is the crime prevention goal one would desire from restorative justice programs, there is relatively little research on offender recidivism found in the restorative justice literature. Most evaluations of recidivism have appeared in relation to VOM programs. Umbreit and Coates (1993), comparing youths who participated in VOM to those undergoing typical juvenile justice processing in three states, report significantly less recidivism on behalf of the VOM sample. In their analysis of restorative justice conferences for youths in Indianapolis, McGarrell et al. (2000) report a 40 percent reduction in recidivism for the program youth when compared to those undergoing normal system processing. Umbreit et al. (2001) provide evidence that youths completing VOM projects in two Oregon counties reduce their offending by at least 68 percent in the year after program participation compared to the year before the intervention. Finally, Nugent et al. (1999) note that both the level of reoffending and the seriousness of subsequent offenses is lower for youths who enter and complete VOM programs. Despite these positive results, a great deal of additional research is needed on the impact of restorative justice programs, especially in relation to FGC and Circle Sentencing programs, and programs focusing on adults. There also remains a need to identify and understand the conditions under which different restorative justice programs work and do not work (Braithwaite, 2002).

Summary

The increasing interest in restorative justice in recent years has led to the growth of programs around the world. Despite the growing popularity with restorative justice approaches, there are a number of problems and concerns that require attention. One problem is that these programs may be too ambitious in their attempt to solve very complex societal problems (Kurki, 2000). A second concern is that there is an underlying level of coercion in most programs and many programs do not allow (or at least frown upon) the presence of defense attorneys, thus raising the issue of an accused's constitutional rights and procedural safeguards (Feld, 1999; Levrant et al., 1999). A third problem involves how the "community" is defined and who is allowed to represent the community (Kurki, 2000). This can be a very important concern because the participants help mold the outcome and the expectations for the solution. Fourth, there is still a lack of good evaluation of the preventive efficacy of the interventions. Finally, Feld (1999) notes that there is a distinct imbalance of power in most restorative justice programs. This is especially problematic when juvenile offenders must face not only the victim but also the victim's support groups, members of the criminal justice system, and potentially strangers from the general community.

Drug Courts

Specialized courts for addressing specific forms of offenders and offenses are becoming common throughout the United States. Drug courts are perhaps the most recognizable and widespread (although it can be argued that the juvenile court system is itself a specialized court). The tremendous increase in drug crimes in the late 1980s and early 1990s, coupled with the get-tough approach to crime and mandatory sentencing laws, helped contribute to overcrowded court dockets and overcrowding in the correctional system. In an attempt to address these problems in 1989, Dade County, Florida, decided to establish a separate court for processing drug offenders. Today, every state hosts at least one drug court. The Office of National Drug Control Policy (2009) reports that there are more than 2,140 drug courts in operation and almost 300 more are in the planning stages. Of the existing drug courts, roughly 1,200 are adult courts, 455 are for juveniles, 30 are focused on families, and the rest target other groups (Huddleston et al., 2008). These courts supervise more than 70,000 clients at any one time (Huddleston et al., 2008). The great growth in drug courts is partly attributable to the passage of the Violent Crime Control and Law Enforcement Act of 1994, which authorized federal funding for drug court programs.

The underlying philosophy for drug courts is to use the court's authority to prompt participation in and successful completion of treatment aimed at reducing drug use and related criminal behavior. The courts represent a coalition of prosecutors, police, probation officers, judges, treatment professionals, social service agencies, and other community groups working together to get the offenders off drugs and keep them off drugs (Drug Courts Program Office, 2000). The court can use its coercive powers to force offenders into the program and to maintain abstinence from drugs. The court accomplishes this task by offering to dismiss criminal charges or to withhold sentencing of offenders if they agree to enter and complete the drug court program. Drug courts operate both at the pre-adjudication stage of criminal justice processing, or at post-adjudication by suspending sentences pending successful completion of a drug court program.

The actual drug court process varies from location to location, although there is a set of common core elements that are found throughout most programs. Among the common elements is frequent appearances before the court, regular drug testing, treatment assessment, participation in at least one treatment program, and aftercare. The court appearances typically follow a graduated pattern with more appearances in the early weeks of the program and fewer appearances as the client demonstrates progress. Initial appearances could be as often as twice a week or as seldom as two to three times a month. These appearances serve as a time for the judge to offer praise and support, warn the offender to do better, or threaten the offender with sanctions if his behavior and progress do not improve (Gottfredson et al., 2003). Regular drug testing is a critical second component of drug court intervention. The knowledge that they will be tested on a regular basis for an extended period provides an added level of accountability to the entire process.

The third common element, treatment assessment, may actually take place before acceptance into the drug court program. The assessment serves to identify the needs of the individual offender and to match up the offender with the appropriate interventions. Common treatment programs may include detoxification, methadone maintenance, support groups, counseling, and other activities directly related to the drug problem. Treatment can also take the form of educational programming, vocational training, employment assistance, housing assistance, and similar help with everyday living experiences (Drug Courts Program Office, 1998). The mandated treatment typically lasts for at least one year, although the specifics of the treatment regimen may change over that period. The final major component is an aftercare plan for the individual. Rather than simply releasing the individual from the drug court and treatment program, most programs offer some form of follow-up assistance ranging from further treatment to support groups.

Advocates of drug courts point to a number of program advantages. One consideration is the ability to free up valuable time in regular court dockets and to alleviate the overcrowding in correctional institutions. Both of these problems have been exacerbated by the growth in the number of drug offenders. Based on available drug court statistics, more than 100,000 offenders have been handled by the drug courts. This means that this number of offenders has not been incarcerated in the already overcrowded jails and prisons, and a significant number have not been subjected to normal court processing (this is true only of pre-adjudication programs). Unfortunately, it is difficult to document the degree to which the drug courts have had either impact. There is always the potential of the program to cause net-widening. That is, the new program opens up new space in the system to handle new clients.

A second advantage is the provision of treatment to the offender. While most correctional institutions offer the opportunity for some type of treatment, their primary concern with housing a large number of individuals in a secure setting often means that treatment is not always available or appropriate. The drug courts, however, are premised upon the need to match the offenders with appropriate treatment. Individuals who do not meet the criteria necessary for the treatment program or who are identified as not amenable to the treatment may be excluded (see, for example, Gottfredson et al., 2003). The offenders who are admitted to the drug court program are guaranteed of some type of treatment.

A final major advantage is keeping the offender in the community. This is less costly than incarceration. In addition, the offender is not cut off from the family and community support groups and mechanisms that are crucial for long-term success after the program. Family ties are not severed and employment can be maintained while the person is participating in a drug court program in the community.

Evaluations of the effectiveness of drug court programs present a mixed picture. Various analyses report that drug court participants recidivate at a significantly lower level than comparison groups (Brewster, 2001; Goldkamp and Weiland, 1993; Gottfredson et al., 2003; Harrell, 1998; Listwan et al., 2003; Spohn et al., 2001). Other analyses find no difference between treatment and comparison groups or higher recidivism for drug court clients (Belenko et al., 1994; Granfield et al., 1998; Miethe et al., 2000). Evaluations typically look at rearrest and/or reconviction for either drug offenses, any crimes, or both.

The divergence in results is probably due to problems and unresolved issues in most of the analyses. One major problem is that many studies compare drug court program graduates to individuals who fail to finish the program. This situation sets up a comparison of two unequal groups—those who are successes and those who are failures. It should not be surprising to find that those who complete the program recidivate less because they are successes to begin with, while those who did not complete are failures at the outset of the evaluation and would be expected to also commit more offenses. The problem of non-equivalent control and treatment groups does not appear only in this situation. Many evaluations note at the outset of the project that the groups are not equivalent.

A second concern is that many evaluations only measure recidivism during program participation (GAO, 1997). This process raises two potential problems. One problem is that it is common to count technical violations of program rules as a form of recidivism. Persons not in the program, therefore, are not subject to these forms of recidivism. A second problem is that, even if technical violations are ignored, the heightened surveillance that is a part of drug court programs raises the probability that violation is identified and action is taken against the individual.

A third concern with the evaluation results is that the studies typically ignore the large number of offenders who are terminated from the program, either by choice or because of failure to follow the rules. This is a different problem from that offered above because in this case the studies compare only those who complete the program to a control group. The level of program termination can be quite large, with several analyses noting that one-third or more of the drug court clients are terminated from, or are not active in, the program (see, for example, GAO, 1997; Gottfredson et al., 2003). What these studies may be doing is comparing only the best, most promising clients to the control group, while the control group includes individuals who would have dropped out of the program had they been selected for the program. The groups are not truly comparable in this situation. Ignoring the dropouts is also problematic because they may be indicative of programmatic failure. The program, therefore, needs to assess the reasons for the failure (was it the program, the client, or something else) and make needed changes.

Despite the fact that evaluations have not been able to declare drug courts an unqualified success, this approach continues to grow and attract attention. The number of drug courts is growing every year and the idea is expanding to include juvenile drug courts and other specialty courts. The driving forces behind the movement are a combination of federal and state funding, vociferous support from drug court advocates, savings over incarcerating offenders, and an acceptance that combining treatment with the sanctioning power of the court is the best way to proceed. What is needed is extensive evaluation of the drug court movement that attends to the concerns raised above.

ASSESSING REHABILITATION AND CRIME PREVENTION

The results of the various summaries and programs presented here leave one wondering about the use of rehabilitation as a tool of crime prevention. Even though many specific rehabilitation programs are, by necessity, omitted from the present discussion, the array of reviews and programs that are discussed show minimal impact on recidivism. This finding prompts many researchers to give up on rehabilitation as a viable form of crime prevention. It is important to note, however, that select interventions show promising results. Among those promising programs are cognitive-behavioral therapies and multi-dimensional interventions, both of which match offenders and treatments in intensive programming, particularly in the community.

The greatest support for rehabilitation programs can be found in studies that use alternate outcome measures. There is clear evidence that rehabilitation can improve an individual's outlook and self-esteem. Various programs have been successful at increasing the educational and vocational achievement of clients. Psychological adjustment has been improved by some interventions. These and other outcomes, however, do not address the central concern of tertiary crime prevention. Tertiary prevention is focused on the elimination or lowering of subsequent levels of delinquent/criminal behavior. It is here that evaluations of rehabilitation have had limited success.

Proponents of rehabilitation point to these alternate forms of success along with the great cost savings of many programs as a rationale for continued work with offenders. Indeed, few studies show a deleterious impact from rehabilitation. The clients simply do no better than if they had been handled through conventional processing and incarceration. Any cost savings of rehabilitation over traditional handling without any risk to society may be reason enough to continue experimenting with various interventions. Also, the failure of past programs should inform us about possible effective programs. Evidence that this is occurring can be seen in the many attempts to match the proper client to the proper intervention.

Interestingly, many of the most recent rehabilitation efforts, such as ISP, restorative justice, and drug courts, rely on the community as either the source of or setting for interventions. Intensive supervision works with clients outside the residential setting. Restorative justice includes a wide array of community members and groups in the interventions. Drug courts seek rehabilitation in the community setting. The reason for this is the recognition and belief that the community influence and atmosphere are important aspects of rehabilitation and crime prevention. The ideas of identifying and using community resources are no different from that found in both primary and secondary crime prevention. While these rehabilitative efforts have not engendered great reductions in recidivism, they do suggest that these are fruitful directions for tertiary prevention to pursue.

Chapter 16

SOME CLOSING THOUGHTS ON CRIME PREVENTION AND THE FUTURE

Learning Objectives:

After reading this chapter you should be able to:

- Provide an overview of the evidence on crime prevention
- Identify problems of evaluation that need to be addressed in future analyses

Crime prevention encompasses a wide diversity of ideas and approaches. Indeed, no two individuals will necessarily see or define crime prevention in exactly the same way. It is not unlike the old parable where several blind men are led to an elephant and asked to explain what it is in front of them. The individual touching the trunk will define it differently than those persons touching a leg or the tail. While it may be easier for sighted people to provide a more complete description, it is still probable that each individual will emphasize or concentrate on different aspects of the elephant. Discussions of crime prevention often provide that same type of variation in explanations. Both the person relating the information and the individual hearing it may be envisioning slightly different things. While neither is inherently right or wrong, they are not exactly the same.

Throughout this book, an attempt has been made to offer a variety of perspectives on crime prevention. In essence, I have tried to touch the elephant at a variety of different places and relate the important facts about each. At the same time, there has been a conscious effort to relate the varied parts to one another in order to try to show how the parts can make up a more meaningful whole. Each of the individual chapters can, for the most part, stand on its own. Each relates some facet of crime prevention. Taking them together, however, should offer a more complete view of crime prevention in its many possible incarnations. I am equally convinced that I have missed a leg or an ear, here or there. In the balance of this brief concluding chapter, I will attempt to offer some summary comments about crime prevention, and point out areas or ideas that I have omitted or given only cursory attention.

THE STATE OF THE EVIDENCE

There should be no doubt that crime prevention works. Effective interventions have been offered throughout the chapters. The extent of crime prevention's impact, however, varies across time and place, as well as from one approach to another. Indeed, not every program has the same impact in every situation. Crime may be reduced in one place while there is no impact on the fear of crime. Transplanting that same program to another location may result in the opposite outcome—crime stays the same but fear is reduced. No single approach to crime prevention has proven to be applicable in all situations. Indeed, most interventions appear to work in limited settings with different types of offenders and problems. The greatest challenge, therefore, is to identify the causal mechanisms at work so that effective programs can be replicated in other places and other times.

Traditionally, actions that fall under primary prevention have been the ones most people think of when they hear of crime prevention. Physical security devices and neighborhood prevention programs dominate many discussions. There is little doubt that changes in the physical design of a building or an area can alter the form and extent of crime. At the very least, these actions make crime more difficult for the potential offender to successfully complete. Citizens also report feeling safer as a result of such design changes. Neighborhood watch and other cooperative citizen programs also show promise at changing crime and citizens' perceptions. The major stumbling block is getting fearful citizens out of their homes and into these prevention groups. Programs and initiatives still struggle with engendering citizen participation after more than 30 years of concentrated efforts to build such grassroots organizations.

Even when primary prevention efforts do take hold, there are many unanswered questions that need to be addressed. Foremost among those questions is how much of the impact on crime is the result of overall reductions and how much is simply displaced? While not all crime is displaced, there is ample evidence to suggest that displacement is a real possibility in most analyses. One important challenge, therefore, is to further investigate the mechanisms that cause displacement and identify measures that can mitigate the extent of its occurrence.

The shift toward situational prevention is evidence of an admission that prevention initiatives need to be targeted at smaller, more well-defined problems and that the interventions need to be cooperative ventures between different individuals and groups. Many times the activities under situational prevention are the same as those found in primary prevention programs. Situational prevention and community policing are perhaps the most recognizable ideas under what constitutes secondary prevention. At the same time, other efforts and interventions, such as those taking place in schools to deal with problem youths, also qualify as secondary techniques. What draws these diverse ideas together is the explicit attempt to deal with individuals, groups, or places that have a high potential to cause later trouble. There is clear evidence that careful consideration of a problem can lead to effective solutions. Among the key problems here are the difficulties in predicting the future, problems with engendering support from other individuals and groups, and convincing people that the criminal justice system cannot do the job by itself. While much secondary prevention relies on the police and the system to initiate activities, the solutions often fall outside the training and abilities of system personnel. The community must be involved.

Despite the growth of prevention activities that focus on citizen and community involvement, the formal system of justice remains an important player in the prevention of crime. No one has yet called for eliminating the criminal justice system in favor of informal community action. Indeed, the criminal justice system is important in dealing with the people and situations in which a crime has already occurred. Specific deterrence, incapacitation, and rehabilitation are functions for which the system retains primary responsibility. At the same time that society turns these activities over to formal social control agencies, it is clear that the community has a role to play in tertiary prevention. The move to keep offenders in the community, whether through intensive supervision, electronic surveillance, or drug courts, is growing. Efforts to punish and rehabilitate offenders are also including the community more and more. Where tertiary prevention remains a part of the formal system of justice, there is evidence that a broader base for interventions is emerging.

In general, crime prevention encompasses a broad range of ideas and activities. More importantly, many of the efforts have been successful at reducing crime and fear of crime. Unfortunately, uncovering the exact mechanism at work is not always evident and continuing work is needed in these areas.

IMPROVING OUR KNOWLEDGE

While there is clear evidence that many crime prevention initiatives successfully reduce crime and fear, there is parallel data that show minimal impact of the same efforts at other places or times. The key issue, therefore, becomes unraveling the mechanism at work in the differing assessments. In general, more attention needs to be paid to the evaluation component of the prevention programs. First, many programs have not been subjected to any evaluation beyond simple description of the process used in establishing the intervention and the success of that process in terms of the number of meetings held and the level of attendance. This type of evaluation tells nothing about the impact on crime and fear of crime, although the programs are often touted as successful because of the organizing efforts. A second evaluation problem is the lack of appropriate control or comparison groups in the research. Where reductions in criminal behavior do appear, the studies often fail to adequately assess the changes in relation to an area or group which is not the subject of the intervention. Thus, it is difficult, if not impossible, to make an informed judgment on the success or failure of the project. The reason for this failure is often tied to the fact that many evaluations are afterthoughts to the project. The evaluation is added after the project is initiated, thus making it more difficult to undertake a strong research design. It is impossible at that point to undertake an experimental design, and difficult to set up a strong quasi-experimental design.

The problem of evaluation is further complicated by the introduction of many actions at the same time. For example, physical design changes, neighborhood watch, citizen patrols, Operation Identification, and media campaigns often overlap. It becomes impossible to evaluate which, if any, intervention has a positive (or negative) impact on crime. The default assumed by most observers when positive results emerge (i.e., reduced crime and reduced fear) is that the entire package is a success. Unfortunately, it may be that a single component is driving the results and there is no need to implement the large-scale, perhaps costly, package of initiatives. Knowing what aspect of the project worked best is an important piece of information. Conversely, finding that a package of initiatives has little or no impact may lead the evaluators to conclude overall failure when the more appropriate assessment might be that the individual efforts are working against one another. For example, the installation of home security devices may serve to drive people into their fortress at the same time that block watch is trying to bring the residents together. An evaluation may show no impact on crime and suggest that the project is a failure. An assessment that can disentangle the two initiatives, however, may show that the block watch organizing has a positive impact, while the physical security impedes positive change. Research needs to focus on disentangling the impact of simultaneous prevention efforts.

A fourth evaluation issue is to recognize that every crime prevention technique cannot be expected to have an equal or positive impact in all possible situations. Some techniques are better suited for certain problems and places than others. This is one of the central tenets of situational prevention and community policing efforts. Evaluations need to carefully assess the match between techniques and the location and timing of their implementation. This concern is not only evident in primary and secondary prevention efforts, but is also pivotal for tertiary crime prevention, particularly in relation to rehabilitation and treatment efforts. Research shows that certain programs have a positive impact on certain individuals, given the proper conditions. The major problem is in predicting potential offenders and identifying those who are amenable to different interventions. Many positive results of crime prevention interventions may be directly attributable to utilizing the proper approach in individual circumstances.

A final concern for evaluation deals with the time frame in which a technique is expected to make a difference. Many interventions are evaluated shortly after implementation. The expectation is that the program should have an immediate impact of crime, fear, and other factors. In reality, however, many changes take time to appear. This may be due to several factors. First, an intervention that appears to be in full operation may require a longer period to make changes in long-standing community or individual behaviors. Second, change may be gradual and the initiation of positive outcomes may not be identifiable in an evaluation undertaken immediately after the project. A third possibility is that a short-term evaluation finds a significant change in crime and/or fear. Unfortunately, long-term evaluation may uncover a diminishing impact, perhaps back to pre-program levels. In each of these cases, the evaluation must be cognizant of the potential confounding introduced by short follow-up periods.

RECOGNIZING THE DIVERSITY IN CRIME PREVENTION

One goal of the book has been to demonstrate the diversity of crime prevention techniques. At the same time, it is important to recognize that the topics and literature covered in the chapters is somewhat selective. There are many topics that have not been addressed, and most of those that do appear in these pages could receive a great deal more attention. There is simply no way to comprehensively cover all the different permutations that make up crime prevention in a single book. The following paragraphs are meant to alert the reader to some of the other topics that fall under the rubric of crime prevention.

One key topic that has not been addressed is the politics of crime prevention. Crawford (1998) and Gilling (1997) both address the political forces that have directed crime prevention initiatives, particularly in the United Kingdom. They argue that many prevention programs follow the prevailing political sentiment in the countries. Thus, Neighborhood Watch will be promoted at one point, physical design will dominate at another time, and an emphasis on working with offenders may emerge at yet a different point. Large societal changes, such as social prevention, will require the right political climate to emerge before any significant alterations appear. These arguments may be more salient in the United Kingdom and other countries where the national government has more influence over policy than in the United States, but this perspective is somewhat applicable in the United States when one considers that the federal government does set funding and research priorities. A clear example of this is the fact that community policing is a "favored child" in Washington, D.C., at this point. Another example may be that most communities have some area that serves, in Barr and Pease's (1990) words, as a "crime fuse." The choice of that area, whether conscious or unconscious, is tied to political considerations. Perhaps the most important issue to remember is that crime prevention, in whatever form, does not exist in a vacuum. The political nature of crime prevention is one area that could receive more attention.

A wide range of other topics have received minimal or no attention in this book. Some of those include possible discussions of juvenile diversion, gun control, interventions with gangs, three-strikes laws, shaming of offenders, and private police and private security. The book has also avoided technical discussions of security devices, such as the relative value of different locks, doors, or alarms. These topics, along with many others, could be included in discussions of crime prevention. Indeed, there are other materials that focus on many of these areas. Many topics are emerging at a rate faster than most people can keep up with the information. Improved technology is a prime example of these changes. These issues are fodder for other discussions.

SUMMARY

The ideas and topics addressed in this book are among the many possible prevention approaches that are used and are emerging to address the persistent problems of crime and fear in society. Such efforts will continue to grow. The effectiveness of these ideas rests on quality evaluation and a willingness to adapt and change. Only through research and modifications can the programs evolve into effective interventions. Evaluation of crime prevention techniques will remain a pivotal issue in dealing with crime and fear of crime throughout the future.

GLOSSARY

Access control—idea of only allowing people who have legitimate business in an area to enter; reduces the opportunity for crime by increasing the effort needed to enter and exit a building or area for the purpose of committing crime

Active (continuous signaling) system—a form of electronic monitoring of offenders that keeps track of the offender on a continuous basis; system consists of a transmitter, receiver, and a central computer

Activity support—actions taken to build a community atmosphere; efforts that enhance the ability to recognize neighbors and identify needs of the community; enhance social cohesion among residents and contribute to a communal atmosphere, which works to eliminate crime and other common problems; includes efforts such as street fairs, community days, and other social events

Actuarial prediction—predictions based on known parameters in the data; example is the setting of life or auto insurance rates

ADAM program—Arrestee Drug Abuse Monitoring; a means of ascertaining the extent of drug use by arrested subjects; arrestees voluntarily agree to be interviewed and give a urine sample for testing

Adolescence-limited offending—offending that takes place mainly in adolescence

Aggregate-level evaluation—looking for changes across large groups of subjects; changes in rates of offending or recidivism

Alley gating—erecting gates on alleys that run behind homes and businesses, thereby restricting access to residents or other legitimate users

Alternative schools—individual classrooms or programs within a school, set up to dispel the negative experiences of many problem youths; the provision of a positive learning atmosphere, which increases feelings of success within an atmosphere of warmth and acceptance

Anticipatory benefit—changes in crime that predate the actual implementation of a crime prevention program; most probably from the fact that offenders, victims, and others know about a forthcoming prevention activity and begin to respond prior to the activation of the intervention

Assize of Arms—required men to have weapons available for use when called on to protect the community

Authority conflict—offending pathway that begins with early stubbornness and leads to later defiance and avoidance of authority; running away, truancy, and ungovernability

Benign displacement—the argument that changes from displacement may benefit society

Big Brother—term used to refer to the ability of the government to monitor the behavior of the citizenry

Boost explanation—also known as event dependency; situations in which (usually) the same offender commits another offense based on the past experiences with that victim or location

Brutalization effect—the argument that the use of the death penalty causes an increase in subsequent homicides

Bullying—behavior that includes both physical and verbal aggression that is repeated over time and is meant to intentionally harm the victim

CAPS—Chicago Alternative Police Strategy; program that includes assigning officers to permanent neighborhood beats, the involvement of residents in the identification of problems and potential solutions, and reliance on other agencies (both public and private) to address identified issues

Celerity—requirement for deterrence; refers to the swiftness of societal response to an offense

Certainty—requirement for deterrence; deals with the chances of being caught and punished for one's behavior

Chicago Area Project—founded in 1931, sought to work with the residents to build a sense of pride and community, thereby prompting people to stay and exert control over the actions of people in the area

Chicago School—sociological school of thought that promoted the idea that changes in the organization and social processes of a community can have a direct effect on crime and disorder

Circle Sentencing—also referred to as peacemaking circles; all interested parties are invited to participate in determining the appropriate sanctions for offenders; includes families, friends, agency representatives, and members of the general community; intended outcome of the circle is consensus on a plan of action that may include explicit sentencing recommendations to the trial judge and/or a range of community-based interventions

Citizen patrols—often a key element of Neighborhood Watch; purpose is to put more eyes on the street in order to increase the chances of detecting strangers in the area and discovering crimes in progress; residents are discouraged from physically intervening into any suspicious activity

Civil abatement—the use of civil codes to attack crime problems; most notable is the involvement of landlords, citizens, health departments, zoning boards, and city/county attorneys in addressing drug problems

Clinical predictions—predictions based on a rater's evaluation of an individual, usually after interviews and direct examination of the subject and his or her records

Closed-Circuit Television (CCTV)—systems that allow the active or passive surveillance of activity

Cognitive maps—mental images of the environment

Cognitive Thinking Skills Program—a multi-modal intervention that utilizes a range of techniques targeting cognitive-behavioral problems; focuses on identifying cognitive deficits and inappropriate decision making by individuals

Collective incapacitation—the imposition of sentences on everyone exhibiting the same behavior with no concern for the potential of the individual

Community anti-drug (CAD) programs—residents banding together with each other, the police, and various agencies and organizations to attack drug use, drug sales, and related problems

Community policing—a new philosophy of policing rather than a clearly definable method; generally includes community involvement, problem solving, a community base, and redefined goals for the police

Constable—an unpaid position responsible for coordinating the watch and ward system and overseeing other aspects of the law

Context—the idea that "the relationship between causal mechanisms and their effects is not fixed, but contingent" (Pawson & Tilley, 1997); the impact of prevention efforts is contingent on the context in which they operate, and subsequently will affect whether the program has a similar impact in different settings

Cost-benefit evaluation—also known as cost-benefit analysis; seeks to assess whether the costs of an intervention are justified by the benefits or outcomes that accrue from it

Covert behavior—offending pathway that typically begins with minor acts of lying and theft, moves on to property crimes and then moderately serious delinquency, and eventually culminates in serious property delinquency

CRAVED—concealable, removable, available, valuable, enjoyable, and disposable

Crime attractors—areas to which potential offenders and others are drawn, such as drug markets, sites of street prostitution, and/or adult clubs and bars

Crime control—maintenance of a given or existing level and the management of that amount of behavior; also fails to adequately address the problem of fear of crime

Crime displacement—the shift of crime due to the preventive actions of the individual or society; six types—territorial, temporal, tactical, target, functional, and perpetrator

Crime fuses—places where society allows crime to run relatively unchecked as a safety valve for the rest of society

Crime generators—locations that draw potential victims to the area

Crime newsletters—printed materials targeted to a limited audience and tailored to the needs of those individuals; provide detailed, in-depth discussions of both crime and potential crime prevention measures

Crime pattern theory—proposes that crime and criminal behavior fit patterns that can be identified and understood when viewed in terms of where and when they occur; crime patterns can be understood because of similarities that emerge when you consider "the specific criminal event, the site, the situation, the activity backcloth, the probable crime templates, the triggering events, and the general factors influencing the readiness or willingness of individuals to commit crimes" (Brantingham & Brantingham, 1993b:284–285)

Crime prevention—any action designed to reduce the actual level of crime and/or the perceived fear of crime

Crime Prevention Through Environmental Design (CPTED)—in general, efforts to alter the physical design to affect crime

Crime science—a new discipline, or at the very least a new paradigm, for addressing crime by coupling efforts to prevent crime with the detection of and intervention with offenders; "the application of the methods of science to crime and disorder" (Laycock, 2005)

CrimeStoppers—the most widely known information line program; generally operates by offering rewards to citizens for information about crimes

Cross-sectional study—compares differences among different individuals, groups, states, or other aggregate

D.A.R.E.—Drug Abuse Resistance Education; in-school program taught by law enforcement officers, emphasizing resistance skills training

Defensible space—proposes "a model which inhibits crime by creating a physical expression of a social fabric which defends itself" (Newman, 1972)

Deterrence—"influencing by fear" (Andenaes, 1975)

Detoxification—the use of drugs in an effort to remove an individual from an addiction to another illicit drug; basic idea is to wean the client from the addiction with the minimal amount of discomfort and pain

Developmental criminology—focus on the relationship between infant and early childhood experiences and circumstances, and the extent to which these predict future violent or deviant behavior

Diffusion of benefits—"the spread of the beneficial influence of an intervention beyond the places which are directly targeted, the individuals who are the subject of control, the crimes which are the focus of intervention or the time periods in which an intervention is brought" (Clarke & Weisburd, 1994: 169)

Distance decay—the commission of crime decreases as the distance from the offender's home increases

Drug courts—one form of emerging specialty courts; use the court's authority to prompt participation in and successful completion of treatment aimed at reducing drug use and related criminal behavior; courts represent a coalition of prosecutors, police, probation, judges, treatment professionals, social service agencies, and other community groups

Ecological fallacy—the attempt to predict individual behavior based on group data; imputing the behavior of a single person from the activity of a larger group

Edges—areas on the periphery of nodes and paths that are prime spots for deviant behavior; edges, both physical and perceptual, experience greater diversity in people and activity

Electronic monitoring—a form of home confinement in which individuals can be tracked by placing an electronic device on them

Environmental backcloth—the social, economic, cultural, and physical conditions within which people operate

Escape—the ability of both offenders and victims to escape from an area before and/or after an offense

Experiential effect—the idea that the actual apprehension of an individual raises the perception of risk

Evaluation—refers to investigating the usefulness of some exercise or phenomena; evaluation of crime prevention refers to investigating the impact of a prevention technique or intervention on the level of subsequent crime, fear, or other intended outcome

Event dependency—also known as a boost explanation; situations in which (usually) the same offender commits another offense based on the past experiences with that victim or location; successful past offending leads to another attempt against the same target

False negative predictions—predictions that declare that the person is not a future threat but the individual does engage in the negative behavior at a later time

False positive predictions—predictions in which an individual is predicted to do something in the future (e.g. recidivate, offend, act dangerously) but is not found to act in that fashion after follow-up

Family Group Conferencing—similar to Victim-Offender Mediation but includes family members, close friends, and other support groups of the victim and offender in the conferences; may also include criminal justice system personnel, including social workers, police officers, and an offender's attorney

Fear—"an emotional response of dread or anxiety to crime or symbols that a person associates with crime. This definition of fear implies that some recognition of potential danger, what we may call perceived risk, is necessary to evoke fear" (Ferraro, 1995:8)

Fearing subject—someone who becomes responsible for the safety of himself and his property

Feeble-minded—term used in the early 1900s to denote those with low IQs

Flag explanation—also called risk heterogeneity; a prior victimization or some other factor identifies the victim or location as an appropriate target for further victimization

Functional displacement—when offenders change to a new type of offense, such as shifting from larceny to burglary or burglary to robbery

Functional fear—fear as a good thing provided the individual uses it as motivation to take precautions

Gatekeepers—term often used to describe the police because they control (to a large extent) the number and types of problems that enter the formal justice system; few offenders or cases enter the criminal justice system without first being processed by the police

General deterrence—aims to have an impact on more than the single offender; the apprehension and punishment of a single individual serves as an example to other offenders and potential law violators

Gold standard—term that has come to be used to refer to true experimental design in evaluation

G.R.E.A.T.—Gang Resistance Education and Training; taught by local police officers in middle schools; goal of the program is to "prevent youth crime, violence and gang involvement" (BJA, 2005); provide youths with the necessary skills for identifying high-risk situations and resisting the pressure/allure of taking part in gangs and gang activity; program curricula are geared toward increasing self-esteem, changing attitudes, and eliminating participation in violent behavior

Guardian Angels—one example of citizen patrolling that has gained international attention; mainly found in large urban areas; mainly consisting of young individuals

Head Start—best-known preschool program; proposes that disadvantaged youths are not prepared to enter school without some form of early intervention targeted at social and intellectual skills

Hedonistic—man seeks pleasure and avoids pain

Hot products—items that attract attention and are targeted by thieves

Hot spots—"small places in which the occurrence of crime is so frequent that it is highly predictable, at least over a one-year period" (Sherman, 1995:36)

Hue and cry—identified threats would cause those watching over the town to raise the alarm and call for help

Hunting ground—nodes where offenders recognize that potential victims frequent the area, there is a lack of guardians and, consequently, the offender follows victims to that place

Image—refers to building a neighborhood or community that does not appear vulnerable to crime and is not isolated from the surrounding community

Immobilizers—electronic devices that, in the absence of the key, prevent a car from operating

Impact evaluation—focus on what changes (e.g., to the crime rate) occur after the introduction of the policy, intervention, or program

Incapacitation—method to prevent future crime on the part of the offender by imposing control over the individual that prohibits the physical possibility of future criminal activity

Incivility—refers to various factors involved in disorder and community decline; two general categories of incivility outlined in the literature are physical and social; physical signs of incivility include the deterioration of buildings, litter, graffiti, vandalism, and abandoned buildings and cars; social signs of incivility include public drunkenness, vagrancy, groups of loitering youths, harassment (such as begging or panhandling), and visible drug sales and use

Individual-level evaluation—focus on qualitative changes rather than quantitative shifts; may appear as simple adjustments in the type of offending

Information lines—programs with a dedicated telephone line for the solicitation of information about specific crimes from the public; involving citizens in crime prevention

Intensive supervision Probation (ISP)—probation using team supervision, a high number of contacts between the client and officer, curfew and/or house arrest, restitution, employment, or school attendance, drug testing, community service, counseling, and treatment **Journey to crime**—the fact that offenders will travel to commit crimes

Kirkholt Burglary Prevention program—major anti-burglary initiative in the United Kingdom; relied on partnership

Lex talionis—the principle of "an eye for an eye"; retribution

Life-course-persistent offending—offending that continues over the long term, including when a juvenile and an adult

Lifestyle perspective—grows out of research on victimization and specifically focuses on the activity of the victim as a contributing factor in criminal acts; an individual's lifestyle and behavioral choices help determine whether he or she will be victimized

Longitudinal study—look for changes over time, primarily due to shifts in law or criminal justice system activity

Macro-level crime prevention—looks at large communities, society as a whole, or other very large collectives

Malign displacement—idea that efforts aimed at reducing crime may prompt an increase in offending or more serious crime

Maryland Scale of Scientific Methods—rating method for determining how closely a study adheres to the standards of a true experimental design

McGruff—part of the "Take a Bite Out of Crime" campaign; a cartoon dog in a trench coat who presents simulated crimes and notes the proper actions viewers should take when confronted with similar situations

Mechanism—refers to understanding "what it is about a program which makes it work" (Pawson & Tilley, 1997:66)

Meso-level crime prevention—in larger communities or neighborhoods, or larger groups of individuals or businesses

Meta-analysis—the reanalysis of data from different studies in order to make direct comparisons between the results

Methadone maintenance—outpatient programs that involve the provision of methadone to heroin/opiate addicts; primary assumption is that the patient is unable to function without some form of drug use and that methadone is an acceptable substitute for other, more damaging drugs

Micro-level crime prevention—targets individuals, small groups, small areas, or small businesses for intervention

Milieu—idea that placement of a community within a larger, low-crime, high-surveillance area will inhibit criminal activity

Minneapolis Domestic Violence experiment—project to investigate the deterrent effect of arrest, separation, and police counseling in misdemeanor spouse abuse situations

Monitoring the Future (MTF) Project—annual survey of representative high school students (8th, 10th, and 12th graders), college students, and young adults; probes a variety of factors; the most important set of information deals with the level and type of drug use

Motivation reinforcement—actions taken to build a community atmosphere; efforts that enhance the ability to recognize neighbors and identify needs of the community; enhance social cohesion among residents and contribute to a communal atmosphere, which works to eliminate crime and other common problems; includes efforts such as street fairs, community days, and other social events

Multi-Systemic Therapy (MST)—a community-based intervention that attempts to address family, peer, school, community, and other influences that may prompt or lead to deviant behavior; involves parental and family interventions, social-cognitive strategies, and academic skills services to address a range of related risk factors and behavioral problems

National Crime Victimization Survey (NCVS)—the best known of the victimization surveys

National Survey on Drug Use and Health—survey conducted by the Substance Abuse and Mental Health Services Administration (SAMHSA) measuring drug use by a representative sample of U.S. respondents age 12 and older

National Night Out—program coordinated by local police agencies; consists of educational programs, neighborhood organizing, social events, and anti-drug and anti-crime activities

National Youth Survey (NYS)—an ongoing, longitudinal panel study of youths; collects information on delinquency, drug use, and demographic factors

Natural surveillance—involves designing an area that allows legitimate users to observe the daily activities of both friends and strangers; permits residents to observe criminal activity and take action

Near repeat—offenses that take place at neighboring locations; a type of repeat victimization

Neighborhood Watch—bringing together neighbors and residents of an area in order to promote crime prevention activity

Net-widening—bringing more people under the umbrella of social control

Nodes—locations of activity: such as home, work, school, and shopping

Operation Ceasefire—partnership in Boston to address gun violence, particularly among juveniles and gang members; creation of an interagency working partnership to assess the nature of the gun problem and the dynamics of youth violence, and to identify and implement an effective intervention

Operation Identification—property marking to increase the difficulty for offenders to dispose of marked items

Order maintenance—police functions that do not deal with an immediate criminal action; includes responding to disabled autos, escorting funerals and parades, dealing with barking dogs, responding to false alarms and noise complaints, and delivering messages

OTREP—Opportunity is the result of Target, Risk, Effort, and Payoff; assumption that offenses can be avoided when there is a high risk of apprehension with little potential payoff

Overt behavior—offending pathway that commences with aggressive activity (bullying and teasing) and leads to fighting and violent activity

Panel design—research design that follows a number of separate units (such as states, counties, or individuals) over a given period

Panel survey—survey in which a group of subjects is surveyed repeatedly over a specified period; the NCVS surveys the same households every six months over a three-year period

Parens patriae—philosophy underlying the juvenile court that argues that youths needed help rather than processing in adult court, which is geared to punishment rather than prevention

Parochial control—sources of control from neighborhood networks and institutions, such as schools, churches, or businesses

Parochial police—police hired by the wealthy to protect their homes and businesses

Part I crimes—part of the Uniform Crime Reports; also known as the Index crimes; includes the violent crimes of murder, rape, robbery, and assault, and property crimes of burglary, larceny, auto theft, and arson

Part II crimes—part of the Uniform Crime Reports; all offenses not included in the Part I category

Passive (program contact) system—form of electronic monitoring that requires periodic activation of the system; the system randomly calls the offender's home to certify the presence of the individual

PATHS—Promoting Alternative Thinking Strategies; a five-year-long curriculum offered in elementary schools focusing on self-control, understanding emotions, building a positive self-image, relationships, and interpersonal problem solving; intended to reduce both behavioral and emotional problems, while building self-control and problem-solving abilities

Paths—transit routes between nodes

Peer mediation—program in which students are trained to assist one another in resolving disputes in such a way that all parties to the dispute accept the resolution

Permissibility—situations or beliefs that place criminal behavior into an acceptable light; for example, the belief that everyone breaks the law or that the victim had it coming

Perpetrator displacement—occurs when one offender ceases his deviant behavior, only to be replaced by another offender

Perry Preschool program—also known as the High/Scope program; most extensively studied preschool program; seeks to provide students with a positive introduction to education by involving the children in the planning of activities, a low child-teacher ratio, and enhanced reinforcement of student achievement

Pressures—direct stimuli that lead to action; deviant peers, going along with the crowd, or following orders to do something wrong

Primary prevention—"identifies conditions of the physical and social environment that provide opportunities for or precipitate criminal acts" (Brantingham & Faust, 1976)

Private control—control based on interpersonal relationships between family members, friends, and close associates

Problem-oriented policing—approaching issues and problems differently based on the uniqueness of each situation

Problem solving—perhaps the most important element of community policing; dealing with crime by identifying the underlying causes and contributors to crime and seeking out solutions to those problems

Process evaluations—consider the implementation of a program or initiative and involves determining the procedures used to implement a specific program

Project PATHE—Positive Action Through Holistic Education; a broad-based approach to the school environment that brings teachers, administrators, students, parents, and agencies together in making decisions about education and the school

Project Safe Neighborhoods (PSN)—an outgrowth of SACSI; focuses primarily on reducing firearms violence through partnerships, strategic plans, training, outreach, and accountability

Prompts—events or situations that may support the opportunity for crime, such as open doors or others committing crime

Prospect—the ability of individuals to see an area; areas that offer greater prospect should engender less fear and victimization than locations that limit sight lines

Prospective mapping—the creation of maps that predict future crime locations based on knowledge of recent events

Provocations—factors that make an individual uncomfortable, frustrated, irritable, or otherwise aroused to the point of taking some form of action, of which crime is one possibility

Psychopharmacological—explanation suggesting that various drugs have a direct impact on the user, both physically and psychologically, which impels the individual to act in a way that society deems unacceptable

Public control—the ability to marshal input, support, and resources from public agencies

Pulling levers—term used to signify a strict enforcement policy for all individuals and groups involved directly or indirectly in a crime problem; coined in Operation Ceasefire

Radio Watch—individuals with two-way radios (such as cab drivers and truckers) report questionable behavior when they see it occurring

randomized control trial—a true experimental design

Rational choice theory—assumes that potential offenders make choices based on various factors in the physical and social environment; offenders respond to payoff, effort, peer support, risks, and similar factors in making decisions to commit a crime

Realistic evaluation—evaluation that considers the phenomenon in its entirety rather than relying exclusively on experimental approaches; two key ideas central to realistic evaluation are mechanism and context

Reciprocal—in relation to crime, means that criminal activity leads to drug use and drug use leads to criminal activity

Reducing Burglary Initiative (RBI)—U.K. program that relies on local communities to identify the causes of the burglary problems in their area and to develop appropriate interventions; includes a wide range of interventions, many of which are physical design changes, such as target hardening, the installation of alley gates, lighting improvements, fencing, and property marking

Refuge—the presence or absence of concealment, in which offenders could hide from potential victims; provides both hiding places and protection for potential offenders

Repeat victimization—people or places being victimized at least a second time within a certain period of time subsequent to an initial victimization event

Resistance skills training—a set of ideas dealing with recognizing problematic situations and issues, dealing with peer pressure, recognizing pressure from media presentations, knowing proper responses to temptations, building self-esteem and assertiveness, and knowing how and when to take a stand

Resolving Conflict Creatively Program (RCCP)—school program including student mediation as a core component; elementary curriculum consists of 12 lessons dealing with issues of communication, cooperation, feelings, diversity, peacemaking, and resolving conflicts

Response generalization—generalizing from the response being promoted in a program (such as simply calling for help) to other possible responses not featured in the program (such as carrying weapons and taking direct action)

Restorative justice—approach that seeks to repair the harm that was done to both the victim and the community, and to "repair" the offender; accomplished by bringing together a range of interested parties in a nonconfrontational setting, including the victim and the offender, as well as family members or friends, criminal justice system personnel, and members of the general community

Risk factors—individual or environmental conditions that have been found to be associated with an increased likelihood of antisocial behavior, such as crime or violence

Risk heterogeneity—also called a flag explanation; a prior victimization or some other factor identifies the victim or location as an appropriate target for further victimization

Risk, need, and responsivity—according to advocates of rehabilitation, the three factors that are essential to meet for successful interventions; basically matching the correct subjects with the correct intervention

Routine activities perspective—argues that the normal movement and activities of both potential offenders and victims plays a role in the occurrence of crime; crime requires (1) a suitable target, (2) a motivated offender, and (3) an absence of guardians

SACSI—Strategic Approaches to Community Safety Initiative; lead by local U.S. Attorney's Offices; attempts to build a partnership consisting mainly of other criminal justice agencies to attack crime problems

Safer Cities Program—program under which the British government provided funds for local initiatives aimed at reducing crime and the fear of crime, and the creation of safer cities; key was building multi-agency partnerships for fighting social, physical, and economic problems in urban areas

SARA—problem-solving approach that includes Scanning, Analysis, Response, and Assessment

Seattle Social Development Project—a comprehensive developmental crime prevention strategy; program creates a template for communities and researchers to work together to evaluate particular risk factors in a specific context and match interventions that have been successful at addressing those risk factors while strengthening protective factors

Secondary prevention—"engages in early identification of potential offenders and seeks to intervene" (Brantingham & Faust, 1976)

Secured By Design (SBD)—an ongoing program in England that emphasizes and promotes the inclusion of safety and security measures in new and existing buildings

Selective incapacitation—emphasis on identifying the high-risk offenders and subjecting only that group to intervention

Severity—requirement for deterrence; involves making certain that punishments provide enough pain to offset the pleasure received from the criminal act

Situational prevention—"characterized as comprising measures (1) directed at highly specific forms of crime (2) that involve the management, design, or manipulation of the immediate environment in as systematic and permanent a way as possible (3) so as to reduce the opportunities for crime and increase the risks as perceived by a wide range of offenders seeks to identify existing problems at the micro level and institute interventions which are developed specifically for the given problem" (Clarke, 1983:225)

Smart guns—guns that recognize the owner and will only discharge if used by that person

Social/crime template—the idea that people have templates that outline expectations of what will happen at certain times and places given certain behavior by the individual; a template tells an offender what should occur in a certain place, time, or situation

Soft determinism—individuals make choices but only within the realm of available alternatives presented to them

Specific deterrence—efforts that keep the individual offender from violating the law again in the future

Spurious—means that neither factor is the ultimate cause of the other; rather, both are caused by either the same common factors or by different factors

Status offenses—offenses that are only illegal if committed by individuals of a certain status; typically used with juveniles and outlines behavior such as curfew violation, smoking, playing in the street, and incorrigibility

Streetblock—consists of the homes on either side of a single block (that is, between two cross-streets)

Surveillance—any action that increases the chance that offenders will be observed by residents

Systemic violence—refers to violence resulting from competition between drug dealers, retaliation for poor drug quality or high prices, robbery of drug dealers or users, and other factors related to the drug trade

Tactical displacement—utilizing new means to commit the same offense

"Take a Bite Out of Crime"—public information media campaign; objectives of altering the public's feelings about crime and the criminal justice system, generating feelings of citizen responsibility and cooperation with the criminal justice system, and enhancing already existing crime prevention efforts

Target displacement—choosing different victims within the same area

Target hardening—efforts that make potential criminal targets more difficult to victimize, such as the installation of locks, bars on windows, unbreakable glass, intruder alarms, fences, safes, and other devices

Tautological—a circular argument

Temporal displacement—the movement of offending to another time period while remaining in the same area; may manifest itself through a shift in larcenies from the late evening to the early morning

Territorial displacement—also referred to as spatial; represents movement of crime from one location to another

Territoriality—refers to the ability and desire of legitimate users of an area to lay claim to the area

Tertiary prevention—"deals with actual offenders and involves intervention … in such a fashion that they will not commit further offenses" (Brantingham & Faust, 1976)

Therapeutic communities—residential communities that emphasize providing a supportive, highly structured atmosphere within which individuals can be helped to alter their personality and develop social relationships conducive to conforming behavior; operate as surrogate families for clients

Thief takers—voluntary bounty hunters; organized under the leadership of English magistrates; typically, reformed criminals "paid" to protect the public by being able to keep a portion of all recovered property

Threats to external validity—factors that would limit the generalizability of the results to other places, settings, and times

Threats to internal validity—factors that could cause the results other than the measures that were implemented

Tracking—the process of assigning students to different classes or groups based on the perceived needs of the student; common forms of tracking appear in high school, where students find themselves placed into "college preparatory" or "vocational" groups

True negative prediction—something is predicted not to occur and it does not (a successful prediction)

True positive prediction—something is predicted to occur and it does (a successful prediction)

Uniform Crime Reports (UCR)—the most widely used and cited official measures of crime in the United States; collected by the Federal Bureau of Investigation; reflects the number of criminal offenses known to the police

VIVA—the risk of a target is directly related to Value, Inertia, Visibility and Access

Vicarious victimization—a sympathetic reaction or empathetic fear of crime due to knowing someone who has been the victim of a crime or simply being told of a harmful act against a third party

Victim-Offender Mediation—typically a post-conviction process in which the victim and the offender are brought together with a mediator to discuss a wide range of issues; most important concern addressed in the meetings is to identify for the offender the types and level of harm suffered by the victim as a result of the crime; focus of the meeting is on repairing the harm done to the victim, helping the victim heal (both physically and emotionally), restoring the community to the pre-crime state, and reintegrating the offender into society

Victimization surveys—surveys of the population carried out to measure the level of criminal victimization in society

Vigilante movement—mirrored early ideas of "hue and cry"; a major component of enforcing law and order in the growing frontier of the young country in which posses of citizens were formed when an offender needed to be apprehended and punished

Virtual repeats—a follow-up victimization of a similar person, place, or item after the initial action; for example, a series of robberies at different locations of a single company (such as a fast-food store) or theft of the same brand of car

Watch and ward—a system whereby the responsibility for keeping watch over the town or area, particularly at night, was rotated among the male citizens

Weed and Seed—a federally sponsored project initiated in 1991 to revitalize communities through a process of "weeding" out existing problems and "seeding" areas with programs and initiatives that inhibit the return of the problems

Whistle Stop—residents blow a whistle if they see something happening out of the ordinary as they are shopping, working, or simply walking out of doors

REFERENCES

Abadinsky, H. (1989). *Drug Abuse*: An Introduction. Chicago: Nelson Hall.

Akers, R.L., A.J. LaGreca, C. Sellers, and J. Cochran (1987). "Fear of crime and victimization among the elderly in different types of communities." *Criminology* 25:487–506.

Allatt, P. (1984). "Residential security: containment and displacement of burglary." *Howard Journal* 23:99–116.

American Bar Association (1999). *The State of Criminal Justice. Center for Media and Public Relations*. Available at: http://www.abanet.org/media/factbooks/cj17.html.

Amir, M. (1971). *Patterns of Forcible Rape*. Chicago, IL: University of Chicago Press.

Andenaes, J. (1975). "General prevention revisited: research and policy implications." *Journal of Criminal Law and Criminology* 66:338–365.

Anderson, D. and K. Pease (1997). "Biting back: Preventing repeat burglary and car crime in Huddersfield." In R.V. Clarke (ed.), *Situational Crime Prevention: Successful Case Studies*, Second Edition. Guilderland, NY: Harrow and Heston.

Anderson, D.A. (1999). "The aggregate burden of crime." *Journal of Law and Economics* 42:611–642.

Anderson, D.C. (1998). "Curriculum, culture, and community: The challenge of school violence." In Tonry, M. and M.H. Moore (eds.), *Youth Violence*. Chicago: University of Chicago Press.

Anderton, K.J. (1985). *The Effectiveness of Home Watch Schemes in Cheshire*. Chester, Eng.: Cheshire Constabulary.

Andison, F.S. (1977). "TV violence and viewer aggression: a culmination of study results, 1956–1976." *Public Opinion Quarterly* 41:314–331.

Andresen, M. (2010). "Displacement." In Fisher, B.S. and S.P. Lab (eds.), *Encyclopedia of Victimology and Crime Prevention*. Thousand Oaks, CA: Sage.

Andrews, D.A., I. Zinger, R.D. Hoge, J. Bonta, P. Gendreau, and F.T. Cullen (1990). "Does correctional treatment work?: A clinically relevant and psychologically informed meta-analysis." *Criminology* 28:369–404.

Anglin, M.D. (1988). "The efficacy of civil commitment in treating narcotics addiction." *Journal of Drug Issues* 18:527–546.

_____ and Y. Hser (1987). "Addicted women and crime." *Criminology* 25:359–397.

_____ (1990). "Treatment of drug abuse." In Tonry, M. and J.Q. Wilson, (eds.), *Drugs and Crime*. Chicago: University of Chicago Press.

Anglin, M.D. and W.H. McGlothlin (1984). "Outcome of narcotic addict treatment in California." In Times, F.M. and J.P. Ludford (eds.), *Drug Abuse Treatment Evaluation: Strategies, Progress and Prospects*. Washington, DC: National Institute on Drug Abuse.

Anglin, M.D. and G. Speckart (1988). "Narcotics use and crime: A multisample, multimethod analysis." *Criminology* 26:197–233.

Anglin, M.D., G.R. Speckart, M.W. Booth and T.M. Ryan (1989). "Consequences and costs of shutting off methadone." *Addictive Behaviors* 14:307–326.

Aos, S. (2003). "Cost and benefits of criminal justice and prevention programs." In Kury, H, and J. Obergfell-Fuchs (eds.), *Crime Prevention: New Approaches*. Mainz, Germany: Weisser Ring.

Archer, D., R. Gartner and M. Beittel (1983). "Homicide and the death penalty: a cross-sectional test of a deterrence hypothesis." *Journal of Criminal Law and Criminology* 74:991–1013.

Armitage, R. (2000). An Evaluation of Secured By Design Housing within West Yorkshire. Briefing Note 7/00. London, ENG: Home Office.

_____ (2007). "Sustainability versus safety: Confusion, conflict and contradiction in designing out crime." In Farrell, G., K.J. Bowers, S.D. Johnson and M. Townsley (eds.), *Imagination for Crime Prevention: Essays in Honour of Ken Pease*. Cullompton, Devon, ENG: Willan Pub.

_____, G. Smythe, and K. Pease (1999). "Burnley CCTV evaluation." In K. Painter and N. Tilley (eds.), *Surveillance of Public Space: CCTV, Street Lighting and Crime Prevention*. Monsey, NY: Criminal Justice Press.

Arthur Young and Co. (1978). *Second Year Report for the Cabrini-Green High Impact Project*. Chicago, IL: Chicago City Department of Development and Housing.

Association of Chief Police Officers (2004). *Secured By Design Principles*. Available at: http://www.securedbydesign.com.

_____ (2009). *Secured By Design*. Available at: http://www.securedbydesign.com

Atkins, S., S. Husain, and A. Storey (1991). *The Influence of Street Lighting on Crime and the Fear of Crime*. London: Home Office.

Babst, D.V., M. Koval, and M.G. Neithercutt (1972). "Relationship of time served to parole outcome for different classifications of burglars based on males paroled in fifty jurisdictions in 1968 and 1969." *Journal of Research in Crime and Delinquency* 9:99–116.

Bailey, W.C. (1998). "Deterrence, brutalization, and the death penalty: Another examination of Oklahoma's return to capital punishment." *Criminology* 36:711–734.

Ball, J.C., E. Corty, S.P. Petroski, H. Bond, and A. Tommasello (1986). "Medical services provided to 2,394 patients at methadone programs in three states." *Journal of Substance Abuse Treatment* 3:203–209.

Ball, J.C., E. Corty, R. Bond, and A. Tommasello (1987). "The reduction of intravenous heroin use, non-opiate abuse and crime during methadone maintenance treatment- Further findings." Paper presented at the Annual Meeting of the Committee on Problems on Drug Dependency, Philadelphia.

Ball, J.C., J.W. Shaffer, and D.N. Nurco (1983). "The day-to-day criminality of heroin addicts in Baltimore: A study in the continuity of offense rates." *Drug and Alcohol Dependence* 12:119–142.

Ball, R.A., C.R. Huff, and J.R. Lilly (1988). *House Arrest and Correctional Policy: Doing Time at Home*. Newbury Park, CA: Sage.

Barclay, P., J. Buckley, P.J. Brantingham, P.L. Brantingham, and T. Whinn-Yates (1996). "Preventing auto theft in suburban Vancouver commuter lots: Effects of a bike patrol." In Clarke, R.V. (ed.), *Preventing Mass Transit Crime*. Monsey, NY: Criminal Justice Press.

Barr, R. and K. Pease (1990). "Crime placement, displacement, and deflection." In M. Tonry and N. Morris (eds.), *Crime and Justice*, vol. 12. Chicago, IL: University of Chicago Press.

Barrile, L.G. (1980). "Television and Attitudes about Crime". Ph.D. dissertation, Boston College.

Barthe, E. (2010) "Crime newsletters." In Fisher, B.S. and S.P. Lab (eds.), *Encyclopedia of Victimology and Crime Prevention*. Thousand Oaks, CA: Sage.

Baumer, T.L. (1985). "Testing a general model of fear of crime: Data from a national survey." *Journal of Research in Crime and Delinquency* 22:239–255.

_____ and F. DuBow (1977). "Fear of crime in the polls: what they do and do not tell us." paper presented at the American Association of Public Opinion Research Meeting.

Baumer, T.L., M.G. Maxfield, and R.I. Mendelsohn (1993). "A comparative analysis of three electronically monitored home detention programs." *Justice Quarterly* 10:121–142.

Bazemore, G. and D. Maloney (1994). "Rehabilitating community service: Toward restorative service in a balanced justice system." *Federal Probation* 58:24–35.

Bazemore, G. and M.S. Umbreit (2001). "A Comparison of Four Restorative Conferencing Models". *Juvenile Justice Bulletin*. Washington, DC: Office of Juvenile Justice and Delinquency Prevention.

Beavon, D.J.K., P.L. Brantingham, and P.J. Brantingham (1994). "The influence of street networks on the patterning of property offenses." In Clarke, R.V. (ed.), *Crime Prevention Studies*, vol. 2. Monsey, NY: Criminal Justice Press.

Beck, A. and A. Willis (1994). "Customer and staff perceptions of the role of closed-circuit television in retail security." In Gill, M. (ed.), *Crime at Work: Studies in Security and Crime Prevention*. Leicester, UK: Perpetuity Press.

_____ (1999). "Context-specific measures of CCTV effectiveness in the retail sector." In K. Painter and N. Tilley (eds.), *Surveillance of Public Space: CCTV, Street Lighting and Crime Prevention*. Monsey, NY: Criminal Justice Press.

Beck, J.L. and P. B. Hoffman (1976). "Time served and release performance: a research note." *Journal of Research in Crime and Delinquency* 13:127–132.

Belenko, S. (1990). "The impact of drug offenders on the criminal justice system." In Weisheit, R. (ed.), *Drugs, Crime and the Criminal Justice System*. Cincinnati, OH: Anderson Publishing Co.

_____, J.A. Fagan and T. Dumanovsky (1994). "The effects of legal sanctions on recidivism in special drug courts." *Justice System Journal* 17:53–80.

Belson, W.A. (1978). *Television Violence and the Adolescent Boy*. Westmead, UK: Saxon House.

Bellis, D.J. (1981). *Heroin and Politicians: The Failure of Public Policy to Control Addiction in America*. Westport, CT: Greenwood.

Bennett, R.R. and J.M. Flavin (1994). "Determinants of fear of crime: The effect of cultural setting." *Justice Quarterly* 11:357–382.

Bennett, S.F. and P.J. Lavrakas (1989). "Community-based crime prevention: An assessment of the Eisenhower Foundation's neighborhood program." *Crime and Delinquency* 35:345–364.

Bennett, T. (1986). "Situational crime prevention from the offender's perspective." In K. Heal and G. Laycock (eds.), *Situational Crime Prevention: From Theory into Practice*. London: Her Majesty's Stationery Office.

_____ (1987). *An Evaluation of Two Neighborhood Watch Schemes in London*. Cambridge: Institute of Criminology.

_____ (1989). "Factors related to participation in neighbourhood watch schemes." *British Journal of Criminology* 29:207–218.

_____ (1990). *Evaluating Neighborhood Watch*. Aldershot: Gower.

_____ (1994). "Community policing on the ground: Developments in Britain." In Rosenbaum, D.P. (ed.), *The Challenge of Community Policing: Testing the Promises*. Thousand Oaks, CA: Sage.

_____ and R. Wright (1984). *Burglars on Burglary*. Brookfield, Vt.: Gower.

Berecochea, J.E. and D.R. Jaman (1981). *Time Served in Prison and Parole Outcome: An Experimental Study. Report No. 2*. Sacramento: California Department of Corrections.

Berg, A. (2008) "Preventing identity theft through information technology." In McNally, M.M. and G.R. Newman (eds.), *Perspectives on Identity Theft*. Monsey, NY: Criminal Justice Press.

Berger, D.E., J.R. Snortum, R.J. Homel, R. Hauge, and W. Loxley (1990). "Deterrence and prevention of alcohol-impaired driving in Australia, the United States, and Norway." *Justice Quarterly* 7:453–466.

Berk, R.A. and P.H. Rossi (1995). *Thinking About Program Evaluation*, Second Edition. Thousand Oaks, CA: Sage.

Berrueta-Clement, J.R., L.J. Schweinhart, W.S. Barnett, A.S. Epstein, and D.P. Weikart (1984). *Changed Lives: The Effects of the Perry Preschool Program on Youths Through Age 19*. Ypsilanti, MI: High/Scope Press.

Bevis, C. and J.B. Nutter (1977). *Changing Street Layouts to Reduce Residential Burglary*. St. Paul, Minn.: Governor's Commission on Crime Prevention and Control.

Bichler, G. and R.V. Clarke (1996). "Eliminating pay phone toll fraud at the port authority bus terminal in Manhattan." In Clarke, R.V. (ed.), *Preventing Mass Transit Crime*. Monsey, NY: Criminal Justice Press.

Biderman, A.D., L.A. Johnson, J. McIntyre, and A.W. Weir (1967). *Report on Victimization and Attitudes Toward Law Enforcement*. Washington, DC: U.S. Government Printing Office.

Binder, A. and J.W. Meeker (1988). "Experiments as reforms." *Journal of Criminal Justice* 16:347–358.

Bishop, D.M. (1984a). "Deterrence: a panel analysis." *Justice Quarterly* 1:311–328.

_____ (1984b). "Legal and extralegal barriers to delinquency: a panel analysis." *Criminology* 22:403–319.

Block, R.L. and C.R. Block (1993). "Street Gang Crime in Chicago." *Research in Brief*. Washington, DC: National Institute of Justice.

____(1995). "Space, place and crime: Hot spot areas and hot places of liquor-related crime." In Eck, J.E. and D. Weisburd (eds.), *Crime and Place*. Monsey, NY: Criminal Justice Press.

Blumstein, A., J. Cohen and D.P. Farrington (1988). "Criminal career research: Its value for criminology." *Criminology* 26:1–36.

Blumstein, A., D.P. Farrington, and S. Moitra (1985). "Delinquency careers: Innocents, desisters, and persisters." In Tonry, M. and N. Morris (eds.), *Crime and Justice*, vol. 6. Chicago, IL: University of Chicago Press.

Boggs, S.L. (1971). "Formal and informal crime control: An exploratory study of urban, suburban and rural orientations." *Sociological Quarterly* 12:319–327.

Bolkcom, C.A. (1981). *Rock Island Anti-Crime Block Club Organizing*. Washington, DC: National Criminal Justice Reference Service.

Bonta, J., S. Wallace-Capretta, and J. Rooney (2000). "A quasi-experimental evaluation of an intensive rehabilitation supervision program." *Criminal Justice and Behavior* 27:312–329.

Borduin, C.M., B.J. Mann, L.T. Cone, S.W. Henggeler, B.R. Fucci, D.M. Blaske, and R.A. Williams (1995). "Multi-systemic treatment of serious juvenile offenders: Long-term prevention of criminality and violence." *Journal of Consulting and Clinical Psychology* 63:569–578.

Botvin, G.J. (1990). "Substance abuse prevention: Theory, practice and effectiveness." In Tonry, M. and J.Q. Wilson (eds.), *Drugs and Crime*. Chicago: University of Chicago Press.

____, E. Baker, N. Renick, A.D. Filazzola, and E.M. Botvin (1984). "A cognitive-behavioral approach to substance abuse prevention." *Addictive Behaviors* 9:137–147.

Botvin, G.J. and L. Dusenbury (1989). "Substance abuse prevention and the promotion of competence." In Bond, L.A. and B.E. Compas (eds.), *Primary Prevention and Promotion in the Schools*. Newbury Park, CA: Sage.

Botvin, G.J. and A. Eng (1980). "A comprehensive school-based smoking prevention program." *Journal of School Health* 50:209–213.

____(1982). "The efficacy of a multicomponent approach to the prevention of cigarette smoking." *Preventive Medicine* 11:199–211.

Botvin, G.J., A. Eng, and C.L. Williams (1980). "Preventing the onset of cigarette smoking through life skills training." *Journal of Preventive Medicine* 9:135–143.

Botvin, G.J., N. Renick, and E. Baker (1983). "The effects of scheduling format and booster sessions on a broad spectrum psychological approach to smoking prevention." *Journal of Behavioral Medicine* 6:359–379.

Bowers, K.J., A. Hirschfield, and S.D. Johnson (1998). "Victimization revisited: A case study of non-residential repeat burglary on Merseyside." *British Journal of Criminology* 38:429–452.

Bowers, K.J. and S.D. Johnson (2003). "Measuring the geographical displacement and diffusion of benefit effects of crime prevention activity." *Journal of Quantitative Criminology* 19:275–301.

____(2004). "Who commits near repeats?: A test of the boost explanation." *Western Criminology Review* 5(3):12–24.

____(2005). "Using publicity for preventive purposes." In Tilley, N. (ed.), *Handbook of Crime Prevention and Community Safety*. Portland, OR: Willan Publishing.

Bowers, K.J., S.D. Johnson, and A.F.G. Hirschfield (2003a). *Pushing Back the Boundaries: New Techniques for Assessing the Impact of Burglary Schemes*. Home Office Online Report 24/03. London, UK: Home Office.

Bowers, K.J., S.D. Johnson, and A.F.G. Hirschfield (2004). "The measurement of crime prevention intensity and its impact on levels of crime." *British Journal of Criminology* 44:419–440.

Bowers, W.J. and J.H. Hirsch (1987). "The impact of foot patrol staffing on crime and disorder in Boston: An unmet promise." *American Journal of Police* 6:17–44.

Bowers, W.J. and G.L. Pierce (1980). "The illusion of deterrence in Isaac Ehrlich's research on capital punishment." *Yale Law Journal* 85:187–208.

Braga, A.A., D.M. Kennedy, A.M. Piehl, and E.J. Waring (2001). "Measuring the impact of operation ceasefire." In *National Institute of Justice, Reducing Gun Violence: The Boston Gun Project's Operation Ceasefire*. Washington, DC: National Institute of Justice.

Braga, A.A., D.L. Weisburd, E.J. Waring, L.G. Mazerolle, W. Spelman, and F. Gajewski (1999). "Problem-oriented policing in violent crime places: A randomized controlled experiment." *Criminology* 37:541–580.

Braithwaite, J. (1999). "Restorative justice: Assessing optimistic and pessimistic accounts." In M. Tonry (ed.), *Crime and Justice: A Review of Research*. Vol. 25. Chicago: University of Chicago Press.

_____(2002). *Restorative Justice and Responsive Regulation*. New York: Oxford University Press.

Brantingham, P.L. (2010). "Crime pattern theory." In Fisher, B.S. and S.P. Lab (eds.), *Encyclopedia of Victimology and Crime Prevention*. Thousand Oaks, CA: Sage.

Brantingham, P.L. and P.J. Brantingham (1981). "Notes on the geometry of crime." In Brantingham, P.J. and P.L. Brantingham (eds.), *Environmental Criminology*. Beverly Hills: Sage.

_____(1984). "Burglar mobility and crime prevention planning." In Clarke, R. and T. Hope (eds.), *Coping with Burglary*. Boston: Kluwer-Nijhoff.

_____(1993a). "Nodes, paths and edges: Considerations on the complexity of crime and the physical environment." *Journal of Environmental Psychology* 13:3–28.

_____(1993b). "Environment, routine, and situation: Toward a pattern theory of crime." In Clarke, R.V. and M. Felson (eds.), *Routine Activities and Rational Choice*. New Brunswick, NJ: Transaction Pub.

_____(1996). "Environmental criminology and violent choices." Paper presented at the American Society of Criminology Annual Meeting, Chicago.

_____(2003). "Anticipating the displacement of crime using the principles of environmental criminology." In M.J. Smith and D.B. Cornish (eds.), *Theory for Practice in Situational Crime Prevention*. Monsey, NY: Criminal Justice Press.

Brantingham, P.J. and F.L. Faust (1976). "A conceptual model of crime prevention." *Crime and Delinquency* 22:284–296.

Brants, C. (1998). "Crime fighting by television in The Netherlands." In Fishman, M. and G. Cavender (eds.), *Entertaining Crime: Reality Television Programs*. New York: Aldine de Gruyter.

Brennan, P.A., B.R. Mednick, and S.A. Mednick (1993). "Parental psychopathology, congenital factors, and violence." In Hodgins, S. (ed.), *Mental Disorder and Crime*. Newbury Park, CA: Sage.

Brewer, D.D., J.D. Hawkins, R.F. Catalano, and H.J. Neckerman (1995). "Preventing serious, violent, and chronic offending: A review of evaluations of selected strategies in childhood, adolescence, and the community." In Howell, J.C., B. Krisberg, J.D. Hawkins and J. Wilson (eds.), *Sourcebook on Serious, Violent, and Chronic Juvenile Offenders*. Thousand Oaks, CA: Sage.

Brewster, M.P. (2001). "An evaluation of the Chester County (PA). drug court program." *Journal of Drug Issues* 31:171–206.

Bridenback, M.L., P.L. Imhoff, and J.P. Blanchard (1980). *The Use of Mediation/Arbitration in the Juvenile Justice Process: A Study of Three Programs*. Tallahassee, FL: Office of the State Courts Administrator.

Brodie, D.Q. and D.I. Sheppard (1977). "Neighbors Against Crime Together: A Project Evaluation." Paper presented at the National Conference on Criminal Justice Evaluation.

Brown, B. (1995). *CCTV in Town Centres: Three Case Studies*. London, UK: Home Office Police Research Group.

Brown, E.J., T.J. Flanagan, and M. McLeod (1984). *Sourcebook of Criminal Justice Statistics*. Washington, DC: U.S. Government Printing Office.

Brown, L.P. and M.A. Wycoff (1987). "Policing Houston: reducing fear and improving service." *Crime and Delinquency* 33:71–89.

Brown, R. (2004). "The effectiveness of electronic immobilization: Changing patterns of temporary and permanent vehicle theft." In Maxfield, M.G. and R.V. Clarke (eds.), *Understanding and Preventing Car Theft*. Monsey, NY: Criminal Justice Press.

_____ (2006). "The role of project management in implementing community safety initiatives." In Knutsson, J. and R.V. Clarke (eds.), *Putting Theory to Work: Implementing Situational Prevention and Problem-Oriented Policing*. Monsey, NY: Criminal Justice Press.

Brown, T.L., S.W. Henggeler, S.K. Schoenwald, M.J. Brondino, and S.G. Pickerel (1999). "Multisystemic treatment of substance abusing and dependent juvenile delinquents: Effects on school attendance at posttreatment and 6-month follow-up." *Children's Services: Social Policy, Research and Practice* 2:81–93.

Browning, K. and R. Loeber (1999). "Highlights of Findings from the Pittsburgh Youth Study." *OJJDP Fact Sheet, No. 95*. Washington, DC: Office of Juvenile Justice and Delinquency Prevention.

Buck, A.J., S. Hakim, and G.F. Rengert (1993). "Burglar alarms and the choice behavior of burglars: A suburban phenomenon." *Journal of Criminal Justice* 21:497–508.

Buerger, M.E. (1994). "The limits of community." In Rosenbaum, D.P. (ed.), *The Challenge of Community Policing: Testing the Promises*. Thousand Oaks, CA: Sage.

Bullock, H.A. (1955). "Urban homicide in theory and fact." *Journal of Criminal Law, Criminology and Police Science* 45:565–575.

Bureau of Justice Assistance (1995a). *National Night Out: A Community-Police Partnership Program*. Washington, DC: U.S. Department of Justice.

_____ (1995b). *Drug Abuse Resistance Education (DARE)*. Washington, DC: U.S. Department of Justice.

_____ (1997). *Comprehensive Communities Program: Promising Approaches*. Washington, DC: Bureau of Justice Assistance.

____(1998). *The Watch Your Car Program*. Washington, DC: U.S. Department of Justice.

____(2001). *Comprehensive Communities Program: Program Account*. Washington, DC: U.S. Department of Justice.

Bureau of Justice Statistics (1997). *Correctional Populations in the United States, 1995*. Washington, DC: Department of Justice.

____(2008). *Criminal Victimization in the United States, 2006, Statistical Tables*. Washington, DC: Bureau of Justice Statistics.

Burgess, E.W. (1928). "Factors influencing success or failure on parole." In Bruce, A.A., A.J. Harno, E.W. Burgess and L. Landesco (eds.), *The Workings of the Indeterminate-sentence Law and the Parole System in Illinois*. Springfield, Ill.: Ill. State Board of Parole.

Bursik, R.J. and H.G. Grasmick (1993). *Neighborhoods and Crime: The Dimensions of Effective Community Control*. New York: Lexington.

Bursik, R.J., H.G. Grasmick, and M.B. Chamlin (1990). "The effect of longitudinal arrest patterns on the development of robbery trends at the neighborhood level." *Criminology* 28:431–450.

Butler, G. (1994). "Commercial burglary: Offenders' perspectives." In Gill, M. (ed.), *Crime at Work: Studies in Security and Crime Prevention*. Leicester, ENG: Perpetuity Press.

Bynum, T. (1996). "Reducing school violence in Detroit." Paper presented at the National Institute of Justice Crime Prevention Conference. Washington, DC.

____and S.H. Decker (2006). *Project Safe Neighborhoods: Strategic Interventions. Chronic Violent Offenders Lists: Case Study 4*. Washington, DC: National Institute of Justice.

Byrne, J.M. (1990). "The future of intensive supervision and the new intermediate sanctions." *Crime and Delinquency* 36:6–41.

Capaldi, D.M. and G.R. Patterson (1996). "Can violent offenders be distinguished from frequent offenders? Prediction from childhood to adolescence." *Journal of Research in Crime and Delinquency* 33:206–231.

Caplan, G. (1964). *Principles of Preventive Psychiatry*. New York: Basic Books.

Carter, D.L. (1995). "Community policing and D.A.R.E.: A practitioner's perspective." *BJA Bulletin* (June). Washington, DC: U.S. Department of Justice.

Catalano, R.F. and J.D. Hawkins (1996). "The social development model: A theory of antisocial behavior." In Hawkins, J.D. (ed.), *Delinquency and Crime: Current Theories*. New York: Cambridge University Press.

Catalano, S.M. (2006). *Criminal Victimization, 2005*. Washington, DC: Bureau of Justice Statistics.

Cedar Rapids Police Department (1975). *Installation, Testing, and Evaluation of a Large-scale Burglar Alarm System for a Municipal Police Department—A Second Phase Completion Report*. Cedar Rapids, Iowa: Cedar Rapids Police Department.

Chaiken, J.M. and M.R. Chaiken (1982). *Varieties of Criminal Behavior*. Santa Monica, CA: Rand.

____(1990). "Drugs and predatory crime." In Tonry, M. and J.Q. Wilson (eds.), *Drugs and Crime*. Chicago, IL: University of Chicago Press.

Challinger, D. (2003). *Crime Stoppers: Evaluating Victoria's Program.* Canberra, AUS: Australian Institute of Criminology.

Charles, M.T. (1989). "The development of a juvenile electronic monitoring program." *Federal Probation* 53(2):3–12.

Chermak, S.M. (1994). "Body count news: How crime is presented in the news media." *Justice Quarterly* 11:561–582.

_____(1998). "Predicting crime story salience: The effects of crime, victim, and defendant characteristics." *Journal of Criminal Justice* 26:61–70.

Chiricos, T.G., S. Eschholz, and M. Gertz (1996). "Crime news and fear: Toward an identification of audience effects." Paper presented at the American Society of Criminology Annual Meeting.

Chiricos, T.G., M. Hogan, and M. Gertz (1997). "Racial composition of neighborhood and fear of crime." *Criminology* 35:301–324.

Chiricos, T.G. and G.P. Waldo (1970). "Punishment and crime: an examination of some empirical evidence." *Social Problems* 18:200–217.

Cirel, P., P. Evans, D. McGillis, and D. Whitcomb (1977). *Community Crime Prevention Program, Seattle, Washington: An Exemplary Project.* Washington, DC: National Institute of Justice.

Cirino, R. (1972). *Don't Blame the People.* New York: Vantage Books.

_____(1974). *Power to Persuade.* New York: Bantam Books.

Clarke, R.V. (1983). "Situational crime prevention: Its theoretical basis and practical scope." In Tonry, M. and N. Morris (eds.), *Crime and Justice*, vol. 4. Chicago: University of Chicago Press.

_____(1992). *Situational Crime Prevention: Successful Case Studies.* Albany, NY: Harrow and Heston.

_____(1993). "Fare evasion and automatic ticket collection on the London underground." In Clarke, R.V. (ed.), *Crime Prevention Studies*, vol. 1. Monsey, NY: Criminal Justice Press.

_____(1995). "Situational crime prevention." In Tonry, M. and D.P. Farrington (eds.), *Building a Safer Society: Strategic Approaches to Crime Prevention.* Chicago: University of Chicago Press.

_____(1996). *Preventing Mass Transit Crime.* Monsey, NY: Criminal Justice Press.

_____(1999). *Hot Products: Understanding, Anticipating and Reducing Demand for Stolen Goods.* London, UK: Home Office Policing and Reducing Crime Unit.

_____(2005). "Seven misconceptions of situational crime prevention." In Tilley, N. (ed.), *Handbook of Crime Prevention and Community Safety.* Portland, OR: Willan Publishing.

_____and D. Cornish (1985). "Modeling offenders' decisions: A framework for policy and research." In Tonry, M. and N. Morris (eds.), *Crime and Justice*, vol. 4. Chicago, IL: University of Chicago Press.

Clarke, R.V. and R. Homel (1997). "A revised classification of situational crime prevention techniques." In Lab, S.P. (ed.), *Crime Prevention at a Crossroads.* Cincinnati: Anderson Publishing Co.

Clarke, R.V. and P.M. Mayhew (1980). *Designing Out Crime.* London: HMSO.

Clarke, R.V. and G.R. Newman (2005). "Introduction." In Clarke, R.V. and G.R. Newman (eds.), *Designing Out Crime from Products and Systems*. Monsey, NY: Criminal Justice Press.

____ (2005). "Modifying criminogenic products: What role for governments?." In Clarke, R.V. and G.R. Newman (eds.), *Designing Out Crime from Products and Systems*. Monsey, NY: Criminal Justice Press.

Clarke, R.V., E. Perkins, and D.J. Smith, Jr. (2001). "Explaining repeat residential burglaries: An analysis of property stolen." In G. Farrell and K. Pease (eds.), *Repeat Victimization*. Monsey, NY: Criminal Justice Press.

Clarke, R.V. and D. Weisburd (1994). "Diffusion of crime control benefits: Observations on the reverse of displacement." In Clarke, R.V. (ed.), *Crime Prevention Studies*, vol. 2. Monsey, NY: Criminal Justice Press.

Clarke, S. (1974). "Getting em out of circulation: does incarceration of juvenile offenders reduce crime?" *Journal of Criminal Law and Criminology* 65:528–535.

Clayton, R.R., A. Cattarello, and K.P. Walden (1991). "Sensation seeking as a potential mediating variable for school-based prevention interventions: A Two year follow-up of DARE." *Journal of Health Communications* 3:229–239.

Clear, T.R. and P.L. Hardyman (1990). "The new intensive supervision movement." *Crime and Delinquency* 36:42–60.

Cloward, R. and L. Ohlin (1960). *Delinquency and Opportunity: A Theory of Delinquent Gangs*. New York, NY: The Free Press.

Coates, R.B. and J. Gehm (1989). "An empirical assessment." In Wright, M. and B. Galaway (eds.), *Mediation and Criminal Justice: Victims, Offenders and Community*. Newbury Park, CA: Sage.

Cochran, J.K. and M.B. Chamlin (2000). "Deterrence and brutalization: The dual effects of executions." *Justice Quarterly* 17:685–706.

Cochran, J.K., M.B. Chamlin, and M. Seth (1994). "Deterrence or brutalization?: An impact assessment of Oklahoma's return to capital punishment." *Criminology* 32:107–134.

Cohen, A.L. (1955). *Delinquent Boys: The Culture of the Gang*. Glencoe, IL: The Free Press.

Cohen, J. (1978). "The incapacitative effect of imprisonment: a critical review of the literature." In Blumstein, A., J. Cohen and D. Nagin (eds.), *Deterrence and Incapacitation: Estimating the Effects of Criminal Sanctions on Crime Rates*. Washington, DC: National Academy Press.

____ (1983). "Incapacitation as a strategy for crime control: possibilities and pitfalls." In Tonry, M. and N. Morris (eds.), *Crime and Justice*. Vol.5. Chicago, IL: University of Chicago Press.

Cohen, L.E. and M. Felson (1979). "Social change and crime rate trends: a routine activities approach." *American Sociological Review* 44:588–608.

Cohen, S. (1975). "The evidence so far." *Journal of Communication* 25:14–24.

Cohn, E.S., L. Kidder, and J. Harvey (1978). "Crime prevention vs. victimization: the psychology of two different reactions." *Victimology* 3:285–296.

Coleman, J.S. (1966). *Equality of Educational Opportunity*. Washington, DC: U.S. Government Printing Office.

Collins, J.J. (1989). "Alcohol and interpersonal violence: Less than meets the eye." In Weiner, N.A. and M.E. Wolfgang (eds.), *Pathways to Criminal Violence*. Newbury Park, CA: Sage.

Collins, J.J., R.L. Hubbard, and J.V. Rachal (1985). "Expensive drug use and illegal income: A test of explanatory hypotheses." *Criminology* 23:743–764.

Conklin, J.E. (1975). *The Impact of Crime*. New York: Macmillan.

____(2003). *Why Crime Rates Fell*. Boston: Allyn and Bacon.

Conley, C. and D. McGillis (1996). "The federal role in revitalizing communities and preventing and controlling crime and violence." *NIJ Journal* 231:24–30.

Coombs, R.H. (1981). "Back on the streets: Therapeutic communities' impact upon drug abusers." *American Journal of Alcohol Abuse* 8:185–201.

Cook, R.F. and J.A. Roehl (1983). *Preventing Crime and Arson: A Review of Community-Based Strategies*. Reston, VA: Institute for Social Analysis.

Cook, T.D. and D.T. Campbell (1979). *Quasi-experimentation: Design and Analysis Issues for Field Settings*. Chicago, IL: Rand McNally College Pub.

Cooprider, K.W. and J. Kerby (1990). "A practical application of electronic monitoring at the pretrial stage." *Federal Probation* 54:28–35.

Cordner, G.W. (1995). "Community policing: Elements and effects." *Police Forum* 5(3):1–8.

Cornish, D.B. and R.V. Clarke (1986a). *The Reasoning Criminal*. New York: Springer-Verlag.

____(1986b). "Situational prevention, crime displacement and rational choice theory." In Heal, K. and G. Laycock (eds.), *Situational Crime Prevention: From Theory into Practice*. London: Her Majesty's Stationery Office.

____(2003). "Opportunities, precipitators and criminal decisions: A reply to Wortley's critique of situational crime prevention." In M.J. Smith and D.B. Cornish (eds.), *Theory for Practice in Situational Crime Prevention*. Monsey, NY: Criminal Justice Press.

Covington, J. and R.B. Taylor (1991). "Fear of crime in urban residential neighborhoods: Implications of between- and within-neighborhood sources for current models." *Sociological Quarterly* 32:231–249.

Cox, S.M. (1999). "An assessment of an alternative education program for at-risk delinquent youth." *Journal of Research in Crime and Delinquency* 36:323–336.

____, W.S. Davidson, and T.S. Bynum (1995). "A meta-analytic assessment of delinquency-related outcomes of alternative education programs." *Crime and Delinquency* 41:219–234.

Crawford, A. (1998). *Crime Prevention and Community Safety: Politics, Policies and Practices*. London: ENG: Longman.

____(2001). "Joined-up but fragmented: Contradiction, ambiguity and ambivalence at the heart of New Labour's 'Third Way'". In R. Matthews and J. Pitts (eds.), *Crime, Disorder and Community Safety*. New York: Routledge.

Crime Stoppers International (2009). Http://www.c-s-i-org/stats.php.

Crime Stoppers, U.S.A. (2009). Http://www.crimestopusa.com.

Cromwell, P.F., J.N. Olson, and D.W. Avary (1991). *Breaking and Entering: An Ethnographic Analysis of Burglary*. Newbury Park, CA: Sage.

Cullen, F.T. and P. Gendreau (2000). "Assessing correctional rehabilitation: Policy, practice and prospects." In J. Horney (ed.), *Policies, Processes, and Decisions of the Criminal Justice System. Criminal Justice 2000*. Washington, DC: National Institute of Justice.

Currie, E. (1998). *Crime and Punishment in America*. New York: Metropolitan Books.

Cusson, M. (1993). "A strategic analysis of crime: Criminal tactics as responses to precriminal situations." In Clarke, R.V. and M. Felson (eds.), *Routine Activity and Rational Choice*. New Brunswick, NJ: Transaction.

D'Alessio, S.J. and L. Stolzenberg (1998). "Crime, arrests, and pretrial jail incarceration: An examination of the deterrence thesis." *Criminology* 36:735–762.

Dallas Area Criminal Justice Council (1975). *Geographic Crime Displacement in the Dallas Area*. Dallas, TX: author.

Davis, R.C. and A.J. Lurigio (1996). *Fighting Back: Neighborhood Antidrug Strategies*. Thousand Oaks, CA: Sage.

_____(1998). "Civil abatement as a tool for controlling drug dealing in rental properties." *Security Journal* 11:45–50.

Davis, R.C., A.J. Lurigio, and D.P. Rosenbaum (1993). *Drugs and the Community: Involving Community Residents in Combating the Sale of Illegal Drugs*. Springfield, IL: Charles C Thomas.

Davis, R.C., B.E. Smith, A.J. Lurigio, and W.G. Skogan (1991). *Community Response to Crack: Grassroots Anti-Drug Programs*. Washington, DC: National Institute of Justice.

Davis, R.C., B.E. Smith, and L.B. Nickles (1998). "The deterrent effect of prosecuting domestic violence misdemeanors." *Crime and Delinquency* 44:434–442.

Decker, S.H., G.D. Curry, S. Catalano, A. Watkins, and L. Green (2005). *Strategic Approaches to Community Safety Initiative (SACSI). in St. Louis*. Washington, DC: National Institute of Justice.

Decker, S.H. and C.W. Kohfeld (1984). "A deterrence study of the death penalty in Illinois, 1933–1980." *Journal of Criminal Justice* 12:367–378.

Decker, S.H. and J. McDevitt (2006). *Project Safe Neighborhoods: Strategic Interventions. Gun Prosecution Case Screening: Case Study 1*. Washington, DC: National Institute of Justice.

Decker, S.H. and B. Salert (1986). "Predicting the career criminal: An empirical test of the Greenwood scale." *Journal of Criminal Law and Criminology* 77:215–236.

DeJong, W. (1993). "Building the peace: The resolving conflict creatively program (RCCP)." *NIJ Program Focus*. Washington, DC: Department of Justice.

DeLeon, G. (1984). "Program-based evaluation research in therapeutic communities." In Tims, F.M. and J.P. Ludford (eds.), *Drug Abuse Treatment Evaluation: Strategies, Progress and Prospects*. Washington, DC: National Institute on Drug Abuse.

_____and M.S. Rosenthal (1989). "Treatment in residential therapeutic communities." In Kleber, H. (ed.), *Treatment of Psychiatric Disorders: A Task Force Report of the American Psychiatric Association*, vol. 2. Washington, DC: American Psychiatric Association.

del Frate, A.A. (1998). *Preventing Crime: Citizens' Experiences Across the World. UNICRI Issues and Reports No. 9*. New York: United Nations.

DeLong, J.V. (1972). "Treatment and rehabilitation." *Dealing with Drug Abuse: A Report to the Ford Foundation*. New York, NY: Praeger.

Denno, D.W. (1990). *Biology and Violence: From Birth to Adulthood*. Cambridge: Cambridge University Press.

DesChamps, S., P.L. Brantingham, and P.J. Brantingham (1991). "The British Columbia transit fare evasion audit: A description of a situational prevention process." *Security Journal* 2:211–218.

Deutshmann, P.J. (1959). *News-Page Content of Twelve Metropolitan Dailies*. Cincinnati: Scripps-Howard Research Center.

Dezhbakhsh, H., P.H. Rubin, and J.M. Shepherd (2003). "Does capital punishment have a deterrent effect?: New evidence from postmoratorium panel data." *American Law and Economics Review* 52:344–376.

Dinkes, R., J. Kemp, K. Baum and T.D. Snyder (2009). *Indicators of School Crime and Safety: 2009*. Washington, DC: U.S. Department of Education and U.S. Department of Justice. Accessed 12-13-09 from http://nces.ed.gov/pubs2010/2010012.pdf.

Ditton, J. and J. Duffy (1983). "Bias in the newspaper reporting of crime news." *British Journal of Criminology* 23:159–165.

Ditton, J. and E. Short (1999). "Yes, it works, no, it doesn't: Comparing the effects of open-street CCTV in two adjacent Scottish town centres." In K. Painter and N. Tilley (eds.), *Surveillance of Public Space: CCTV, Street Lighting and Crime Prevention*. Monsey, NY: Criminal Justice Press.

Dobash, R.E., P. Schlesinger, R. Dobash, and C.K. Weaver (1998). " 'Crimewatch UK': Women's interpretation of televised violence." In Fishman, M. and G. Cavender (eds.), *Entertaining Crime: Television Reality Programs*. New York: Aldine de Gruyter.

Dodgson, K., P. Goodwin, P. Howard, S. Llewellyn-Thomas, E. Mortimer, N. Russell, and M. Weiner (2001). *Electronic Monitoring of Released Prisoners: An Evaluation of the Home Detention Curfew Scheme*. Home Office Research Study 222. London, ENG: Home Office.

Dominick, J.R. (1978). "Crime and law enforcement in the mass media." In Winick, C. (ed.), *Deviance and Mass Media*. Beverly Hills: Sage.

Donnelly, P. and C. Kimble (1997). "Community organizing, environmental change, and neighborhood crime." *Crime and Delinquency* 43:493–511.

Donohue, J.J. and J. Wolfers (2005) "Uses and abuses of empirical evidence in the death penalty debate." *Stanford Law Review* 58:791–846.

Donovan, P. (1998). "Armed with the power of television: Reality crime programming and the reconstruction of law and order in the United States." In Fishman, M. and G. Cavender (eds.), *Entertaining Crime: Reality Television Programs*. New York: Aldine de Gruyter.

Doob, A.N. and G.E. Macdonald (1979). "Television viewing and fear of victimization: is the relationship causal?" *Journal of Personality and Social Psychology* 37:170–179.

Dowds, L. and P. Mayhew (1994). "Participation in Neighbourhood Watch: Findings from the 1992 British Crime Survey". *Research Findings No. 11*. London, UK: Home Office Research and Statistics Department.

Drug Courts Program Office (1998). *Looking at a Decade of Drug Courts*. Washington, DC: U.S. Department of Justice.

_____(2000). *About the Drug Courts Program Office*. Washington, DC: U.S. Department of Justice.

Drug Free Communities Support Program (2009) Overview. Accessed 11-2-09 from http://www.oncp.gov/dfc/overview.html.

Dunford, F.W. (1990). "System initiated warrants for suspects of misdemeanor domestic assault: A pilot study." *Justice Quarterly* 7:631–654.

Dunworth, T. and G. Mills (1999). "National Evaluation of Weed and Seed." *NIJ Research in Brief*. Washington, DC: National Institute of Justice.

Dunworth, T., G. Mills, G. Cordner and J. Green (1999). *National Evaluation of Weed and Seed: Cross-site Analysis*. Washington, DC: National Institute of Justice.

Eck, J.E. (1993). "The threat of crime displacement." *Criminal Justice Abstracts* 25:527–546.

_____(1994). "Drug Markets and Drug Places: A Case-control Study of the Spatial Structure of Illicit Drug Dealing." Doctoral dissertation, College Park, MD: University of Maryland.

_____(1998). "Preventing crime by controlling drug dealing on private rental property." *Security Journal* 11:37–43.

_____(2002). "Learning from experience in problem-oriented policing and situational prevention: The positive functions of weak evaluations and the negative functions of strong ones." In N. Tilley (ed.), *Analysis for Crime Prevention*. Monsey, NY: Criminal Justice Press.

_____(2003). "Police problems: The complexity of problem theory, research and evaluation." In Knutsson, J. (ed.), *Problem-Oriented Policing: From Innovation to Mainstream*. Monsey, NY: Criminal Justice Press.

_____and D.P. Rosenbaum (1994). "The new police order: Effectiveness, equity, and efficiency in community policing." In Rosenbaum, D.P. (ed.), *The Challenge of Community Policing: Testing the Promises*. Thousand Oaks, CA: Sage.

_____(1989). "A problem-oriented approach to police service delivery." In Kenney, D. (ed.), *Police and Policing: Contemporary Issues*. New York: Praeger.

Eck, J.E. and J. Wartell (1998). "Improving the management of rental properties with drug problems: A randomized experiment." In Mazerolle, L.G. and J. Roehl (eds.), *Civil Remedies and Crime Prevention*. Monsey, NY: Criminal Justice Press.

_____(1999). "Reducing Crime and Drug Dealing by Improving Place Management: A Randomized Experiment." *NIJ Research Preview*. Washington, DC: National Institute of Justice.

Ehrlich, I. (1975). "The deterrent effects of capital punishment: a question of life and death." *American Economic Review* 65:397–417.

_____(1977). "Capital punishment and deterrence: some further thoughts and additional evidence." *Journal of Political Economy* 85:741–788.

Eiser, C. and J.R. Eiser (1988). *Drug Education in Schools*. New York: Springer-Verlag.

Ekblom, P. (1993). "Scoping and scoring: Linking measures of action to measures of outcome in a multi-scheme, multi-site crime prevention programme." In Zahm, D. and P. Cromwell (eds.), *Proceedings of the International Seminar on Environmental Criminology and Crime Analysis*. Coral Gables, FL: Florida Criminal Justice Executive Institute.

_____(2002). "From the source to the mainstream is uphill: The challenge of transferring knowledge of crime prevention through replication, innovation and anticipation". In N. Tilley (ed.), *Analysis for Crime Prevention*. Monsey, NY: Criminal Justice Press.

_____(2005). "Designing products against crime." In Tilley, N. (ed.), *Handbook of Crime Prevention and Community Safety*. Portland, OR: Willan Publishing.

____(2008). "Designing products against crime." In Wortley, R. and L. Mazerolle (eds.), *Environmental Criminology and Crime Analysis*. Cullompton, Devon, ENG: Willan Pub.

____, H. Law and M. Sutton (1996a). *Safer Cities and Domestic Burglary*. London, UK: Home Office Research and Statistics Directorate.

____(1996b). *Domestic Burglary Schemes in the Safer Cities Programme. Research Findings No. 42*. London, UK: Home Office Research and Statistics Directorate.

Ekblom, P. and K. Pease (1995). "Evaluating crime prevention." In M. Tonry and N. Morris (eds.), *Crime and Justice: A Review of Research*, Vol. 19. Chicago: University of Chicago Press.

Elfers, H., D. Reynald, M. Averdijk, W. Bernasco and R. Block (2008). "Modelling crime flow between neighbourhoods in terms of distance and of intervening opportunities." *Crime Prevention and Community Safety* 10:85–96.

Ellingworth, D., G. Farrell, and K. Pease (1995). "A victim is a victim is a victim? Chronic victimization in four sweeps of the British Crime Survey." *British Journal of Criminology* 35:360–365.

Elliott, D.S. (1994). "Serious, violent offenders: Onset, developmental course, and termination." *Criminology* 32:1–21.

____(2000). "Editor's introduction." In D. Olweus and S. Limber (eds.), *Bullying Prevention Program. Blueprints for Violence Prevention*. Boulder, CO: Institute of Behavioral Science.

____and S.S. Ageton (1981). *The Epidemiology of Delinquent Behavior and Drug Use among American Adolescents, 1976–1978*. Boulder, CO: Behavioral Research Institute.

Elliott, D.S., S.S. Ageton, and R.J. Canter (1979). "An integrated theoretical perspective on delinquent behavior." *Journal of Research in Crime and Delinquency* 16:3–27.

Elliott, D.S. and D.H. Huizinga (1984). *The Relationship between Delinquent Behavior and ADM Problems*. Boulder, CO: Behavioral Research Institute.

Elliott, D.S., D.H. Huizinga, and S.S. Ageton (1985). *Explaining Delinquency and Drug Use*. Beverly Hills, CA: Sage.

Elliott, D.S., D.H. Huizinga, and S. Menard (1989). *Multiple Problem Youth: Delinquency, Substance Use and Mental Health Problems*. New York: Springer-Verlag.

Elliott, D.S. and S. Menard (1996). "Delinquent friends and delinquent behavior: Temporal and developmental patterns." In Hawkins, J.D. (ed.), *Delinquency and Crime: Current Theories*. Cambridge: Cambridge University Press.

Ellis, E., J. Fortune and G. Peters (2007) "Partnership problems: Analysis and re-design." *Crime Prevention and Community Safety* 9:34–51.

Empey, L.T. and S.G. Lubbeck (1971). *Explaining Delinquency*. Lexington, MA: Lexington Books.

Ennis, B.J. and T.R. Litwack (1974). "Psychiatry and the presumption of expertise: flipping coins in the courtroom." *California Law Review* 62:693–752.

Ennis, P.H. (1967). *Criminal Victimization in the U.S.: A Report of a National Survey. President's Commission on Law Enforcement and the Administration of Justice. Field Surveys II*. Wash., DC: U.S. Government Printing Office.

Erez, E., P. Ibarra and N.A. Lurie (2004). "Electronic monitoring of domestic violence cases—A study of two bilateral programs." *Federal Probation* 68(1). Accessed 12/1/09 from http://www.uscourts.gov/fedprob/June_2004/monitoring.html.

Erickson, M.L. (1979). "Some empirical questions concerning the current revolution in juvenile justice." In Empey, L.T. (ed.), *The Future of Childhood and Juvenile Justice*. Charlottesville, VA: University of Virginia Press.

_____, J.P. Gibbs and G.F. Jensen (1977). "The deterrence doctrine and the perceived certainty of legal punishments." *American Sociological Review* 42:305–317.

Erwin, B.E. (1990). "Old and new tools for the modern probation officer." *Crime and Delinquency* 36:61–74.

Esbensen, F. (1987). "Foot patrols: Of what value?" *American Journal of Police* 6:45–65.

_____ and D. Huizinga (1993). "Gangs, drugs and delinquency in a survey of urban youth." *Criminology* 31:565–589.

Esbensen, F. and D.W. Osgood (1999). "Gang Resistance Education and Training (G.R.E.A.T.): Results from the national evaluation." *Journal of Research in Crime and Delinquency* 36:194–225.

Esbensen, F., D. Peterson, T.J. Taylor, A. Freng, and D.W. Osgood (2004). "Gang prevention: A case study of a primary prevention program." In F. Esbensen, S.G. Tibbetts and L. Gaines (eds.), *American Youth Gangs at the Millennium*. Long Grove, IL: Waveland Press.

Everson, S. and K. Pease (2001). "Crime against the same person and place: Detection opportunity and offender targeting." In G. Farrell and K. Pease (eds.), *Repeat Victimization*. Monsey, NY: Criminal Justice Press.

Everson, S. and P.F. Woodhouse (2007). "Designing out crime: Has section 17 of the UK's Crime and Disorder Act 1998 been effective?" In Farrell, G., K.J. Bowers, S.D. Johnson and M. Townsley (eds.), *Imagination for Crime Prevention: Essays in Honour of Ken Pease*. Cullompton, Devon, UK: Willan Pub.

Fabricant, R. (1979). "The distribution of criminal offenses in an urban environment: a spatial analysis of criminal spillovers and of juvenile offenders." *American Journal of Economics and Society* 38:31–47.

Fagan, J. (1989). "The social organization of drug use and drug dealing among urban gangs." *Criminology* 27:633–670.

_____ and J.G. Weis (1990). *Drug Use and Delinquency among Inner City Youth*. New York: Springer-Verlag.

Fagan, J., F.E. Zimring and A. Geller (2006) "Capital punishment and capital market: Market share and the deterrent effects of the death penalty." *Texas Law Review* 84:1803–1867.

Farrall, S. and D. Gadd (2004). "The frequency of the fear of crime." *British Journal of Criminology* 44:127–132.

Farrell, A.D. and A.L. Meyer (1997). "The effectiveness of a school-based curriculum for reducing violence among urban sixth-grade students." *American Journal of Public Health* 87:979–988.

Farrell, G. (2005). "Progress and prospects in the prevention of repeat victimization." In Tilley, N. (ed.), *Handbook of Crime Prevention and Community Safety*. Portland, OR: Willan Publishing.

_____ and K. Pease (2006). "Preventing repeat residential burglary victimization." In Welsh, B.C. and D.P. Farrington (eds.), *Preventing Crime: What Works for Children, Offenders, Victims and Places*. New York: Springer.

Farrell, G., C. Phillips, and K. Pease (1995). "Like taking candy: Why does repeat victimization occur?" *British Journal of Criminology* 33:384–399.

Farrell, G., A. Tseloni, and K. Pease (2005). "Repeat victimization in the ICVS and the NCVS." *Crime Prevention and Community Safety* 7(3):7–18.

Farrington, D.P. (1983). "Offending from 10 to 25 years of age." In Van Dusen, K.T. and S.A. Mednick (eds.), *Prospective Studies of Crime and Delinquency*. Boston: Kluwer-Nijhoff.

____(1985). "Predicting self-reported and official delinquency." In Farrington, D.P. and R. Tarling (eds.), *Prediction in Criminology*. Albany, N.Y.: SUNY Press.

____(1989). "Early predictors of adolescent aggression and adult violence." *Violence and Victims* 4:79–100.

____(1996). "The explanation and prevention of youthful offending." In Hawkins, J.D. (ed.), *Delinquency and Crime: Current Theories*. Cambridge, UK: Cambridge University Press.

____(1997). "The relationship between low resting heart rate and violence." In Raine, A., P.A. Brennan, D.P. Farrington and S.A. Mednick (eds.), *Biosocial Bases of Violence*. New York, NY: Plenum.

____, T.H. Bennett and B.C. Welsh (2007). "The Cambridge evaluation of the effects of CCTV on crime." In Farrell, G., K.J. Bowers, S.D. Johnson and M. Townsley (eds.), *Imagination for Crime Prevention: Essays in Honour of Ken Pease*. Cullompton, Devon, ENG: Willan Pub.

Farrington, D.P., S. Bowen, A. Buckle, T. Burns-Howell, J. Burrows, and M. Speed (1993). "An experiment on the prevention of shoplifting." In Clarke, R.V. (ed.), *Crime Prevention Studies*, vol. 1. Monsey, NY: Criminal Justice Press.

Farrington, D.P. and R. Loeber (1998). "Transatlantic replicability of risk factors in the development of delinquency." In Cohen, P., C. Slomkowski and L.N. Robbins (eds.), *Where and When: Geographic and Generational Influences on Psychopathology*. Mahwah, NJ: Erlbaum.

Farrington, D.P. and K.A. Painter (2003). "How toe evaluate the impact of CCTV on crime." *Crime Prevention and Community Safety* 5(3):7–16.

Farrington, D.P., H.N. Snyder, and T.A. Flinnegan (1988). "Specialization in juvenile court careers." *Criminology* 26:461–488.

Farrington, D.P. and B.C. Welsh (2002). *Effects of Improved Street Lighting on Crime: A Systematic Review*. London, UK: Home Office.

Federal Bureau of Investigation (2005). *Crime in the United States, 2004*. Washington, DC: Department of Justice. Available at: http://www.fbi.gov/ucr.

____(2006). *Crime in the United States, 2005*. Washington, DC: Department of Justice. Available at: http://www.fbi.gov/ucr.

____(2009). *Crime in the United States, 2008*. Washington, DC: Department of Justice. Available at: htpp://www.fbi.giv/ucr.

Feeney, F. (1986). "Robbers as decision makers." In Cornish, D.B. and R.V. Clarke (eds.), *The Reasoning Criminal: Rational Choice Perspectives on Offending*. New York: Springer-Verlag.

Feld, B.C. (1999). "Rehabilitation, retribution and restorative justice: Alternative conceptions of juvenile justice." In G. Bazemore and L. Walgrave (eds.), *Restorative Juvenile Justice: Repairing the Harm of Youth Crime*. Monsey, NY: Criminal Justice Press.

Felson, M., M.E. Belanger, G.M. Bichler, C.D. Bruzinske, G.S. Campbell, C.L. Fried, K.C. Grofik, I.S. Mazur, A.B. O'Regan, P.J. Sweeney, A.L. Ullman, and L.M. Williams (1996). "Redesigning hell: Preventing crime and disorder at the port authority bus terminal." In Clarke, R.V. (ed.), *Preventing Mass Transit Crime*. Monsey, NY: Criminal Justice Press.

Felson, M. and R.V. Clarke (1998). *Opportunity Makes the Thief: Practical Theory for Crime Prevention*. London, ENG: Home Office Police and Reducing Crime Unit.

Ferraro, K.F. (1995). *Fear of Crime: Interpreting Victimization Risk*. Albany, NY: SUNY Press.

_____ and R.L. LaGrange (1987). "The measurement of fear of crime." *Sociological Inquiry* 57:70–101.

_____ (1988). "Are older people afraid of crime?" *Journal of Aging Studies* 2:277–287.

Fisher, B.S. (1989). "The 'community hypothesis' revisited: The effects of participation after controlling for self-selection bias." Paper presented at the American Society of Criminology Annual Meeting, Washington.

_____ and J.L. Nasar (1992). "Fear of crime in relation to three exterior site features: Prospect, refuge, and escape." *Environment and Behavior* 24:35–65.

Fishman, M. and G. Cavender (1998). *Entertaining Crime: Television Reality Programs*. New York: Aldine de Gruyter.

Fishman, R. (1977). "An evaluation of criminal recidivism in projects providing rehabilitation and diversion services in New York City." *Journal of Criminal Law and Criminology* 68:283–305.

Fleming, Z., P. Brantingham, and P. Brantingham (1994). "Exploring auto theft in British Columbia." In Clarke, R.V. (ed.), *Crime Prevention Studies*, vol. 3. Monsey, NY: Criminal Justice Press.

Foglia, W.D. (1997). "Perceptual deterrence and the mediating effect of internalized norms among inner-city teenagers." *Journal of Research in Crime and Delinquency* 34:414–442.

Ford, D. and A. Schmidt (1985). *Electronic Monitored Home Confinement. National Institute of Justice Research in Action*. Washington, DC: National Institute of Justice.

Forrester, D.H., M.R. Chatterton, and K. Pease (1988). "The Kirkholt Burglary Prevention Demonstration Project." *Home Office Crime Prevention Paper no. 13*. London, UK: Her Majesty's Stationery Office.

Forrester, D.H., S. Frenz, M. O'Connell, and K. Pease (1990). *The Kirkholt Burglary Prevention Project: Phase II*. London, ENG: Home Office.

Fors, S.W. and D.G. Rojek (1991). "A comparison of drug involvement between runaways and school youths." *Journal of Drug Education* 21:13–25.

Forst, B.E. (1977). "The deterrent effect of capital punishment: a cross-state analysis of the 1960s." *Minnesota Law Review* 61:743–767.

Fowler, F. and T.W. Mangione (1982). *Neighborhood Crime, Fear and Social Control: A Second Look at the Hartford Program*. Washington, DC: National Institute of Justice.

Fowler, F., M.E. McCalla, and T.W. Mangione (1979). *Reducing Residential Crime and Fear: The Hartford Neighborhood Crime Prevention Program*. Washington, DC: National Institute of Law Enforcement and Criminal Justice.

Fraser, M. and M. Norman (1989). "Chronic juvenile delinquency and the 'suppression effect': An exploratory study." *Journal of Offender Counseling, Services and Rehabilitation* 13:55–73.

Friel, C.M. and J.B. Vaughn (1986). "A consumer's guide to the electronic monitoring of probationers." *Federal Probation* 50(3):3–14.

_____ and R. del Carmen (1987). *Electronic Monitoring and Correctional Policy: The Technology and Its Application*. Washington, DC: National Institute of Justice.

Furstenburg, F.F. (1972). "Fear of crime and its effects on citizen behavior." In A. Biderman (ed.), *Crime and Justice: A Symposium*. New York, NY: Nailburg.

Gable, R.K. (1986). "Application of personal telemonitoring to current problems in corrections." *Journal of Criminal Justice* 14:167–176.

Gabor, T. (1981). "The crime displacement hypothesis: An empirical examination." *Crime and Delinquency* 27:390–404.

_____ (1990). "Crime displacement and situational prevention: Toward the development of some principles." *Canadian Journal of Criminology* 32:41–73.

Gaes, G.G., T.J. Flanagan, L.T. Motiuk, and L. Stewart (1999). "Adult correctional treatment." In M. Tonry and J. Petersilia (eds.), *Prisons*. Chicago: University of Chicago Press.

Gallup (2006). The Gallup Poll [Online]. Washington, DC: The Gallup Organization. Available at: http://poll.gallup.com.

Garofalo, J.(1979). "Victimization and the fear of crime." *Journal of Research in Crime and Delinquency* 16:80–97.

_____ (1981). "Crime and the mass media: a selective review of research." *Journal of Research in Crime and Delinquency* 18:319–350.

Garofalo, J. and K.J. Connelly (1980a). "Dispute resolution centers, part I: major features and processes." *Criminal Justice Abstracts* 12:416–436.

_____ (1980b). "Dispute resolution centers, part II: outcomes, issues, and future directions." *Criminal Justice Abstracts* 12:576–611.

Garofalo, J. and M. McLeod (1988). "Improving the Use and Effectiveness of Neighborhood Watch Programs." *NIJ Research in Action*. Washington, DC: National Institute of Justice.

_____ (1989). "The structure and operations of neighborhood watch programs in the United States." *Crime and Delinquency* 35:326–344.

Garrett, C.J. (1985). "Effects of residential treatment on adjudicated delinquents: a meta-analysis." *Journal of Research in Crime and Delinquency* 22:287–308.

Gates, L.B. and W.M. Rohe (1987). "Fear and reactions to crime: A revised model." *Urban Affairs Quarterly* 22:425–453.

Geen, R.G. and S.L. Thomas (1986). "The immediate effects of media violence on behavior." *Journal of Social Issues* 42:7–27.

Geerken, M.R. and W.R. Gove (1977). "Deterrence, overload, and incapacitation: an empirical evaluation." *Social Forces* 56:424–447.

General Accounting Office (1997). *Drug Courts: Overview of Growth, Characteristics, and Results*. Washington, DC: U.S. Government Printing Office.

Gensheimer, L.K., J.P. Mayer, R. Gottschalk, and W.S. Davidson (1986). "Diverting youth from the juvenile justice system: a meta-analysis of intervention efficacy." In Apter, S.J. and A.P. Goldstein (eds.), *Youth Violence: Programs and Prospects*. New York, NY: Pergamon.

Gerbner, G. (1972). "Violence in television drama: trends and symbolic functions." In Comstock, G.A. and E.A. Rubinstein (eds.), *Television and Social Behavior*. vol. 1. Washington, DC: U.S. Government Printing Office.

_____, L. Gross, M.F. Eleey, M. Jackson-Beeck, S. Jeffries-Fox, and N. Signorielle (1977). "TV violence no. 8: the highlights." *Journal of Communication* 27:171–180.

Gerbner, G., L. Gross, M. Jackson-Beeck, S. Jeffries-Fox, and N. Signorielle (1978). "Cultural indicators: violence profile no. 9." *Journal of Communication* 28:176–207.

Gerbner, G., L. Gross, N. Signorielle, and M. Morgan (1980). "Television violence, victimization, and power." *American Behavioral Scientist* 23:705–716.

Gerbner, G., L. Gross, N. Signorielle, M. Morgan, and M. Jackson-Beeck (1979). "The demonstration of power: violence profile no. 10." *Journal of Communication* 29:177–196.

Geva, R. and I. Israel (1982). "Anti-burglary campaign in Jerusalem: pilot project update." *Police Chief* 49:44–46.

Gibbs, J.P. (1968). "Crime, punishment, and deterrence." *Social Science Quarterly* 48:515–530.

Gill, M. and K. Loveday (2003). "What do offenders think about CCTV?" *Crime Prevention and Community Safety: An International Journal* 5(3):17–26.

Gill, M. and R. Matthews (1994). "Robbers on robbery: Offenders' perspectives." In Gill, M. (ed.), *Crime at Work: Studies in Security and Crime Prevention*. Leicester, ENG: Perpetuity Press.

Gill, M. and K. Pease (1998). "Repeat robbers: Are they different?" In Gill, M. (ed.), *Crime at Work: Increasing the Risk for Offenders*. Leicester, UK: Perpetuity Press.

Gill, M. and A. Spriggs (2005). *Assessing the Impact of CCTV*. London, UK: Home Office.

Gilling, D. (1997). *Crime Prevention: Theory, Policy and Politics*. London, UK: UCL Press.

_____ (2005). "Partnerships and crime prevention." In Tilley, N. (ed.), *Handbook of Crime Prevention and Community Safety*. Portland, OR: Willan Publishing.

Glaser, D. (1964). *The Effectiveness of a Prison and Parole System*. Indianapolis, IN: Bobbs-Merrill.

Gold, M. (1978). "Scholastic experiences, self-esteem, and delinquent behavior: a theory for alternative schools." *Crime and Delinquency* 24:290–308.

_____ and D. Mann (1972). "Delinquency as defense." *American Journal of Orthopsychiatry* 42:463–477.

_____ (1983). "Alternative schools for troublesome youths." *Urban Review* 14:305–316.

Goldkamp, J.S. and D. Weiland (1993). "Assessing the impact of Dade County's felony drug court." *NIJ Research in Brief*. Washington, DC: U.S. Department of Justice.

Goldstein, P.J. (1989). "Drugs and violent crime." In Weiner, N.A. and M.E. Wolfgang (eds.), *Pathways to Criminal Violence*. Newbury Park, CA: Sage.

_____, H.H. Brownstein, and P.J. Ryan (1992). "Drug-related homicide in New York: 1984 and 1988." *Crime and Delinquency* 38:459–476.

Gomme, I.M. (1986). "Fear of crime among Canadians: A multi-variate analysis." *Journal of Criminal Justice* 14:249–258.

_____ (1988). "The role of experience in the production of fear of crime: A text of a causal model." *Canadian Journal of Criminology* 30:67–76.

Gordon, M.T., J. Reiss, and T. Taylor (1979). *Crime in the Newspapers and Fear in the Neighborhoods: Some Unintended Consequences*. Evanston, IL: Center for Urban Affairs, Northwestern University.

Gorman-Smith, D., P.H. Tolan, A. Zelli, and L.R. Huesmann (1996). "The relation of family functioning to violence among inner-city minority youths." *Journal of Family Psychology* 10:115–129.

Gottfredson, D.C. (1986a). "An empirical test of school-based environmental and individual interventions to reduce the risk of delinquent behavior." *Criminology* 24:705–731.

_____(1986b). *An Assessment of a Delinquency Prevention Demonstration with both Individual and Environmental Interventions*. Baltimore: Johns Hopkins University.

_____(1987). "Examining the potential of delinquency prevention through alternative education." *Today's Delinquent* 6:87–100.

_____, S.S. Najaka, and B. Kearley (2003). "Effectiveness of drug treatment courts: Evidence from a randomized trial." *Criminology and Public Policy* 2:171–198.

Gottfredson, D.M., P.B. Hoffman, M.H. Sigler, and L.T. Wilkins (1975). "Making paroling policy explicit." *Crime and Delinquency* 21:34–44.

Gottfredson, D.M., M.R. Gottfredson, and J. Garofalo (1977). "Time served in prison and parole outcomes among parolee risk categories." *Journal of Criminal Justice* 5:1–12.

Gottfredson, G.D. and D.C. Gottfredson (1985). *Victimization in Schools*. New York: Plenum.

Gottfredson, S.D. and D.M. Gottfredson (1985). "Screening for risk among parolees: policy, practice, and method." In Farrington, D.P. and R. Tarling (eds.), *Prediction in Criminology*. Albany, NY: SUNY Press.

_____(1986). "Accuracy of prediction models." In Blumstein, A., J. Cohen, J.A. Roth and C.A. Visher (eds.), *Criminal Careers and 'Career Criminals'*. Vol. 2. Washington, DC: National Academy Press.

Gowdy, V.B. (1993). "Intermediate sanctions." *NIJ Research in Brief*. Washington, DC: U.S. Department of Justice.

Graber, D. (1977). "Ideological components in the perceptions of crime and crime news." Paper presented to the Meeting of the Society for Study of Social Problems.

_____(1980). *Crime News and the Public*. New York, NY: Praeger.

Granfield, R., C. Eby, and T. Brewster (1998). "An examination of the Denver drug court: The impact of a treatment-oriented drug-offender system." *Law and Policy* 20:183–202.

Graziano, A.M. and K. Mooney (1984). *Children and Behavior Therapy*. New York, NY.: Aldine.

Green, D.E. (1989a). "Past behavior as a measure of actual future behavior: An unresolved issue in perceptual deterrence research." *Journal of Criminal Law and Criminology* 80:781–804.

_____(1989b). "Measures of illegal behavior in individual-level deterrence research." *Journal of Research in Crime and Delinquency* 26:253–275.

Green, L. (1995a). "Cleaning up drug hot spots in Oakland, California: The displacement and diffusion effect." *Justice Quarterly* 12:737–754.

_____(1995b). "Policing places with drug problems: The multi-agency response team approach." In Eck, J.E. and D. Weisburd (eds.), *Crime and Place*. Monsey, NY: Criminal Justice Press.

Greenberg, D. (1975). "The incapacitative effect of imprisonment: some estimates." *Law and Society Review* 9:541–580.

Greenberg, M.T. and C. Kusche (1996). *The PATHS Project: Preventive Intervention for Children: Final Report.* Washington, DC: National Institute of Mental Health.

Greenberg, M.T. and C. Kusche (1997). "Improving children's emotion regulation and social competence: The effects of the PATHS curriculum." Paper presented at the Society for Research in Child Development Meeting, Washington, DC.

Greenberg, M.T. and C. Kusche (1998). *Promoting Alternative Thinking Strategies (PATHS). Blueprints for Violence Prevention.* Boulder, CO: Institute of Behavioral Science.

Greenberg, M.T., C. Kusche, E.T. Cook, and J.P. Quamma (1995). "Promoting emotional competence in school-aged children: The effects of the PATHS curriculum." *Development and Psychopathology* 7:117–136.

Greenberg, S.W., W.M. Rohe, and J.R. Williams (1982). *Safe and Secure Neighborhoods: Physical Characteristics and Informal Territorial Control in High and Low Crime Neighborhoods.* Washington, DC: National Institute of Justice.

_____(1985). *Informal Citizen Action and Crime Prevention at the Neighborhood Level: Synthesis and Assessment of the Research.* Washington, DC: National Institute of Justice.

Greene, J.R. and S.D. Mastrofski (1988). *Community Policing: Rhetoric or Reality?* New York, NY: Praeger.

Greenwood, P.W. (1982). *Selective Incapacitation.* Santa Monica, CA: Rand Corp.

Greenwood, P., C.P. Rydell, A.F. Abrahmse, J.P. Caukins, J. Chiesa, K.E. Model, and S.P. Klein (1994). *Three Strikes and You're Out: Estimated Benefits and Costs of California's New Mandatory Sentencing Law.* Santa Monica, CA: Rand.

Gresham, P., J. Stockdael, I. Bartholomew, and K. Bullock (2001). *An Evaluation of the Impact of Crimestoppers. Briefing Note 10/01.* London, UK: Home Office.

Gunter, B. (1987). *Television and the Fear of Crime.* London, UK: Libby.

Hamilton-Smith, N. (2002). "Anticipated consequences: Developing a strategy for the targeted measurement of displacement and diffusion of benefits." In N. Tilley (ed.), *Evaluation for Crime Prevention.* Monsey, NY: Criminal Justice Press.

Handford, M. (1994). "Electronic tagging in action: A case study in retailing." In Gill, M. (ed.), *Crime at Work: Studies in Security and Crime Prevention.* Leicester, UK: Perpetuity Press.

Hanson, D.J. (1980). "Drug education: Does it work?" In Scarpitti, F.S. and S.K. Datesman (eds.), *Drugs and the Youth Culture.* Beverly Hills, CA: Sage.

Harrell, A. (1998). "Drug Courts and the Role of Graduated Sanctions." *NIJ Research Preview.* Washington, DC: National Institute of Justice.

Harris Poll (n.d.). New York, NY: Harris Interactive.

Harrison, L. and J. Gfroerer (1992). "The intersection of drug use and criminal behavior: Results from the national household survey on drug abuse." *Crime and Delinquency* 38:422–443.

Hartnagel, T.F., T.J. Teevan, and J.J. McIntyre (1975). "Television violence and violent behavior." *Social Forces* 54:341–351.

Hartnett, S.M. and W.G. Skogan (1999). "Community policing: Chicago's experience." *National Institute of Justice Journal* (April):3–11.

Hartstone, E.C. and D.M. Richetelli (2005). *Final Assessment of the Strategic Approaches to Community Safety Initiative in New Haven*. Washington, DC: National Institute of Justice.

Haverkamp, R., M. Mayer and R. Levy (2004). "Electronic monitoring in Europe." *European Journal of Crime, Criminal Law and Criminal Justice* 12:36–45.

Hawkins, J.D., M.W. Arthur, and R.F. Catalano (1995). "Preventing substance abuse." In Tonry, M. and D.P. Farrington (eds.), *Building a Safer Society: Strategic Approaches to Crime Prevention*. Chicago, IL: University of Chicago Press.

Hawkins, J.D., H.J. Doueck, and D.M. Lishner (1988). "Changing teaching practices in mainstream classrooms to improve bonding and behavior of low achievers." *American Educational Research Journal* 25:31–50.

Hawkins, J.D., D.P. Farrington, and R.F. Catalano (1998). "Reducing violence through the schools." In Elliott, D.S., B.A. Hamburg and K.R. Williams (eds.), *Violence in American Schools*. Cambridge, UK: Cambridge University Press.

Hawkins, J.D. and J.G. Weis (1985). "The social development model: An integrated approach to delinquency prevention." *Journal of Primary Prevention* 6:73–97.

Hayes, J.G. (1982). *The Impact of Citizen Involvement in Preventing Crime in Public Housing*. Charlotte, NC: Charlotte Housing Authority.

Hearnden, I. and C. Magill (2004) *Decision-making by House Burglars: Offenders' Perspectives*. London, UK; Home Office.

Heath, L. (1984). "Impact of newspaper crime reports on fear of crime: Multimethodological investigations." *Journal of Personal and Social Psychology* 47:263–276.

Hedderman, A. and C. Williams (2001). "Making Partnerships Work: Emerging Findings from the Reducing Burglary Initiative." *Home Office Briefing Note 1/01*. London, UK: Home Office.

Heller, N.B., W.W. Stenzel, A.D. Gill, R.A. Kolde, and S.R. Shimerman (1975). *Operation Identification Projects: Assessment of Effectiveness*. Washington, DC: Law Enforcement Assistance Administration.

Henig, J.R. (1984). *Citizens Against Crime: An Assessment of the Neighborhood Watch Program in Washington, D.C.* Washington, DC: George Washington University, Center for Washington Area Studies.

Hesseling, R.B.P. (1994). "Displacement: A review of the empirical literature." In Clarke, R.V. (ed.), *Crime Prevention Studies*, vol. 3. Monsey, NY: Criminal Justice Press.

_____(1995). "Functional surveillance in The Netherlands: Exemplary projects." *Security Journal* 6:21–25.

Higgins, P.B. and M.W. Ray (1978). *Television's Action Arsenal: Weapon Use in Prime Time*. Washington, DC: U.S. Conference of Mayors.

Hindelang, M. (1975). *Public Opinion Regarding Crime, Criminal Justice, and Related Topics*. Washington, DC: Department of Justice.

_____, M.R. Gottfredson, and J. Garofalo (1978). *Victims of Personal Crime: An Empirical Foundation for a Theory of Personal Victimization*. Cambridge, MA: Ballinger.

Hirschel, J.D., I.W. Hutchinson, C.W. Dean, J.J. Kelly, and C.E. Pesackis (1991). *Charlotte Spouse Assault Replication Project: Final Report*. Charlotte, NC: University of North Carolina at Charlotte.

Hirschel, J.D., I.W. Hutchinson, and C.W. Dean (1992). "The failure of arrest to deter spouse abuse." *Journal of Research in Crime and Delinquency* 29:7–33.

Hirschi, T. (1969). *Causes of Delinquency*. Berkeley: University of California Press.

_____and M. Hindelang (1977). "Intelligence and delinquency: a revisionist review." *American Sociological Review* 42:571–587.

Hofstetter, C.R. (1976). *Bias in the News*. Columbus, OH: Ohio State University Press.

Holcomb, J.E. and S.P. Lab (2003). "Evaluation: Building knowledge for crime prevention." In H. Kury and J. Obergfell-Fuchs (eds.), *Crime Prevention: New Approaches*. Mainz, GER: Weisser Ring.

Holden, R.N. (1992). *Law Enforcement: An Introduction*. Englewood Cliffs, NJ: Prentice-Hall.

Hollinger, R.C. and J.P. Clark (1983). "Deterrence in the workplace: perceived certainty, perceived severity of employee theft." *Social Forces* 62:398–419.

Holloway, K. and T. Bennett (2004). "The Results of the First Two Years of the NEW-ADAM Programme". *Home Office Online Report 19/04*. London, UK: Home Office.

Holt, T. and J. Spencer (2005). "A little yellow box: The targeting of automatic teller machines as a strategy in reducing street robbery." *Crime Prevention and Community Safety* 7(2):15–28.

Home Office (2001). *Installing Alley-gates: Practical Lessons from Burglary Prevention Projects*. Briefing Note 2/01. London: Home Office.

_____(2003a). *Reducing Burglary Initiative Project Summary—Fordbridge, Solihull. Supplement 2 to Findings #204*. London, UK: Home Office.

_____(2003b). *Reducing Burglary Initiative Project Summary—Stirchley, Birmingham. Supplement 4 to Findings #204*. London, UK: Home Office.

_____(2003c). *Reducing Burglary Initiative Project Summary—Rochdale. Supplement 1 to Findings #204*. London, UK: Home Office.

_____(2003d). *Reducing Burglary Initiative Project Summary—Yew Tree, Sandwell. Supplement 3 to Findings #204*. London, UK: Home Office.

Homel, P., S. Nutley, B. Webb, and N. Tilley (2004). *Investing to Deliver: Reviewing the Implementation of the UK Crime Reduction Program*. London, UK: Home Office.

Hoover, L.T. (1992). "Police mission: An era of debate." In Hoover, L.T. (ed.), *Police Management: Issues and Perspectives*. Washington, DC: Police Executive Research Forum.

Hope, T. (1994). "Problem-oriented policing and drug market locations: Three case studies." In Clarke, R.V. (ed.), *Crime Prevention Studies*, vol. 2. Monsey, NY: Criminal Justice Press.

_____and S.P. Lab (2001). "Variation in crime prevention participation: Evidence from the British Crime Survey." *Crime Prevention and Community Safety: An International Journal* 3(1):7–22.

Hough, M. (1995). *Anxiety About Crime: Findings from the 1994 British Crime Survey*. London, UK: Home Office.

Howell, J.C. and J.D. Hawkins (1998). "Prevention of youth violence." In Tonry, M. and M.H. Moore (eds.), *Youth Violence*. Chicago, IL: University of Chicago Press.

Hser, Y., M.D. Anglin, and C. Chou (1988). "Evaluation of drug abuse treatment: A repeated measure design assessing methadone maintenance." *Evaluation Review* 12:547–570.

Huba, G.J. and P.M. Bentler (1983). "Causal models of the development of law abidance and its relationship to psycho-social factors and drug use." In Laufer, W.S. and J.M. Day (eds.), *Personality Theory, Moral Development and Criminal Behavior*. Lexington: D.C. Heath.

Hubbard, R.L., J.V. Rachal, S.G. Craddock, and E.R. Cavanaugh (1984). "Treatment outcome prospective study (TOPS): Client characteristics and behaviors before, during and after treatment." In Tims, F.M. and J.P. Ludford (eds.), *Drug Abuse Treatment Evaluation: Strategies, Progress and Prospects*. Washington, DC: National Institute on Drug Abuse.

Huddleston, C.W., D.B. Marlow and R. Casebolt (2008). *Painting the Current Picture: A National Report Card on Drug Courts and Other Problem-solving Court Programs in the United States*. Washington, DC: Bureau of Justice Assistance. Accessed 12-1-09 from http://www.ndci.gov/sites/default/files/ndci/pcpII1_web[1].pdf

Huesmann, L.R. and N.M. Malamuth (1986). "Media violence and antisocial behavior: An overview." *Journal of Social Issues* 42:1–6.

Huizinga, D.H., R. Loeber, and T. Thornberry (1994). *Urban Delinquency and Substance Abuse: Initial Findings: Research Summary*. Washington, DC: Office of Juvenile Justice and Delinquency Prevention.

Huizinga, D.H., S. Menard, and D.S. Elliott (1989). "Delinquency and drug use: Temporal and developmental patterns." *Justice Quarterly* 6:419–456.

Hughes, G. (2002). "Crime and Disorder reduction partnerships: The future of community safety?" In G. Hughes, E. McLaughlin, and J. Muncie (eds.), *Crime Prevention and Community Safety: New Directions*. Thousand Oaks, CA: Sage.

_____, E. McLaughlin and J. Muncie (2002). *Crime Prevention and Community Safety: New Directions*. Thousand Oaks, CA: Sage.

Hunt, D.E. (1990). "Drugs and consensual crimes: Drug dealing and prostitution." In Tonry, M. and J.Q. Wilson (eds.), *Drugs and Crime*. Chicago: University of Chicago Press.

Hunter, A. (1978). "Symbols of incivility: Social disorder and fear of crime in urban neighborhoods." Paper presented at the American Society of Criminology Annual Meeting, Dallas.

_____(1985). "Private, parochial and public school orders: The problem of crime and incivility in urban communities." In Suttles, G.D. and M.N. Zald (eds.), *The Challenge of Social Control: Citizenship and Institution Building in Modern Society*. Norwood, NJ: Ablex Pub.

Hunter, R. (2010). "Crime prevention: Micro, meso, and macro levels." In Fisher, B.S. and S.P. Lab (eds.), *Encyclopedia of Victimology and Crime Prevention*. Thousand Oaks, CA: Sage.

Hurley, P. and G.E. Antunes (1977). "The representation of criminal events in Houston's two daily newspapers." *Journalism Quarterly* 54:756–760.

Inciardi, J.A. (1996). "A corrections-based continuum of effective drug abuse treatment." *NIJ Research Preview*. Washington, DC: U.S. Department of Justice.

_____, R. Horowitz, and A.E. Pottieger (1993). *Street Kids, Street Drugs, Street Crime: An Examination of Drug Use and Serious Delinquency in Miami*. Belmont, CA: Wadsworth.

Jackson, J. and E. Gray (2009). "Functional fear and public insecurities about crime." *British Journal of Criminology* 49:1–22.

Jacobs, B.A. (1996). "Crack dealers and restrictive deterrence: Identifying narcs." *Criminology* 34:409–432.

James, D.J. (2004). *Profile of Jail Inmates, 2002.* Washington, DC: Bureau of Justice Statistics.

Jarjoura, G.R. (1993). "Does dropping out of school enhance delinquent involvement?: Results from a large-scale national probability sample." *Criminology* 31:149–172.

Jenkins, A.D. and I. Latimer (1987). *Evaluation of Merseyside Home Watch.* Liverpool: Merseyside Police.

Jensen, G.F., M.L. Erickson, and J.P. Gibbs (1978). "Perceived risk of punishment and self-reported delinquency." *Social Forces* 57:57–78.

Jensen, G.F. and B.G. Stitt (1982). "Words and misdeeds: hypothetical choices versus past behavior as measures of deviance." In Hagan, J.(ed.), *Deterrence Reconsidered: Methodological Innovations.* Beverly Hills, CA: Sage.

Jerse, F.W. and M.E. Fakouri (1978). "Juvenile delinquency and academic deficiency." *Contemporary Education* 49:108–109.

Johnson, B.D., K. Anderson, and E.D. Wish (1988). "A day in the life of 105 drug addicts and abusers: Crimes committed and how the money was spent." *Sociology and Social Research* 72:185–191.

Johnson, B.D., P.J. Goldstein, E. Prebel, J. Schmeidler, D.S. Lipton, B. Sprunt, and T. Miller (1985). *Taking Care of Business: The Economics of Crime by Heroin Abusers.* Lexington, MA: Lexington Books.

Johnson, B.D., T. Williams, K.A. Dei, and H. Sanabria (1990). "Drug abuse in the inner city: Impact on hard-drug users and the community." In Tonry, M. and J.Q. Wilson (eds.), *Drugs and Crime.* Chicago, IL: University of Chicago Press.

Johnson, S.D. and K.J. Bowers (2002). "Domestic burglary repeats and space-time clusters: The dimensions of risk." *European Journal of Criminology* (forthcoming).

_____ (2003). "Opportunity is in the eye of the beholder: The role of publicity in crime prevention." *Criminology and Public Policy* 2:497–524.

_____ (2004). "The burglary as a clue to the future: The beginnings of prospective hot-spotting." *The European Journal of Criminology* 1:237–255.

Johnson, S.D., K. Bowers, and A. Hirschfield (1997). "New insight into the spatial and temporal distribution of repeat victimization." *British Journal of Criminology* 37:224–241.

Johnson, S.D., K.J. Bowers, and K. Pease (2005). "Predicting the future or summarizing the past?: Crime mapping as anticipation." In Smith, M.J. and N. Tilley (eds.), *Crime Science: New Approaches to Preventing and Detecting Crime.* Portland, OR: Willan Publishing.

Johnson, S.D., S.P. Lab and K.J. Bowers (2008). "Stable and fluid hotspots of crime: Differentiation and identification." *Built Environment* 34:32–45.

Johnston, L.D., P.M. O'Malley, and L.K. Eveland (1978). "Drugs and delinquency: A search for causal connections." In Kandel, D.B. (ed.), *Longitudinal Research on Drug Use: Empirical Findings and Methodological Issues.* Washington, DC: Hemisphere Pub.

Johnston, L.D., P.M. O'Malley, and J.G. Bachman (1989). *Drug Use, Drinking, and Smoking: National Survey Results from High School, College, and Young Adult Populations.* Washington, DC: U.S. Government Printing Office.

Johnston, L.D., P.M. O'Malley, J.G. Bachman, and J.E. Schulenberg (2009). *Monitoring the Future: National Survey Results on Drug Use, 1975–2008*. Washington, DC: National Institutes of Health.

Jones, E.T. (1976). "The press as metropolitan monitor." *Public Opinion Quarterly* 40:239–244.

Kale, B.L. and P. Kleinman (1985). "Fear, crime, community organization, and limitations on daily routines." *Urban Affairs Quarterly* 20:400–408.

Kandel, D.B., O. Smicha-Fagan, and M. Davies (1986). "Risk factors for delinquency and illicit drug use from adolescence to young adulthood." *Journal of Drug Issues* 16:67–90.

Kandel, E. and S.A. Mednick (1991). "Perinatal complications predict violent offending." *Criminology* 29:519–529.

Kaplan, H.M., K.C. O'Kane, P.J. Lavrakas, and E.J. Pesce (1978). *Crime Prevention Through Environmental Design: Final Report on Commercial Demonstration; Portland, Orego*n. Arlington, VA: Westinghouse Electric Corp.

Katz, L. S.D. Levitt and W. Shustorovich (2003). "Prison conditions, capital punishment, and deterrence." *American Law and Economics Review* 5:318–343.

Kaufman, P., X. Chen, S.P. Choy, K.A. Chandler, C.D. Chapman, M.R. Rand, and C. Ringel (1998). *Indicators of School Crime and Safety, 1998*. Washington, DC: Office of Educational Research and Improvement and Office of Justice Programs.

Keane, C. (1995). "Victimization and fear: Assessing the role of offender and offence." *Canadian Journal of Criminology* 37:431–455.

_____, A.R. Gillis, and J. Hagan (1989). "Deterrence and amplification of juvenile delinquency by police contact." *British Journal of Criminology* 29:336–352.

Kellermann, A.L., D. Fuqua-Whitley, and C.S. Parramore (2006). *Reducing Gun Violence: Community Problem Solving in Atlanta*. Washington, DC: National Institute of Justice.

Kelley, J. (1997). "Police lines often clogged with false, unreliable clues." *USA Today* (Jan. 31):1–2.

Kelling, G.L. (1978). "Police field services and crime: The presumed effects of a capacity." *Crime and Delinquency* 24:173–184.

_____(1998). *Columbia's Comprehensive Communities Program: A Case Study*. Washington, DC: BOTEC Analysis Corporation.

_____(2005). "Community crime reduction: Activating formal and informal control." In Tilley, N. (ed.), *Handbook of Crime Prevention and Community Safety*. Portland, OR: Willan Publishing.

_____, S.K. Costello, M.R. Hochberg, A.M. Rocheleau, D.P. Rosenbaum, J.A. Roth, W.G. Skogan, and W.H. Sousa (1999). *Cross-Site Analysis of the Bureau of Justice Assistance Comprehensive Communities Program*. Washington, DC: National Institute of Justice.

Kelly, B.T., R. Loeber, K. Keenan, and M. DeLamatre (1997). "Developmental Pathways in Boys' Disruptive and Delinquent Behavior." *Juvenile Justice Bulletin*. Washington, DC: Office of Juvenile Justice and Delinquency Prevention.

Kelly, D.H. and R. Balch (1971). "Social origins and school failure: a re-examination of Cohen's theory of working class delinquency." *Pacific Sociological Review* 14:413–430.

Kelly, D.H. and W.T. Pink (1975). "Status origins, youth rebellion, and delinquency; a reexamination of the class issue." *Journal of Youth and Adolescence* 4:339–347.

Kelly, J. (1997). "Police lines often clogged with false, unreliable clues." *USA Today* (Jan. 31):1–2.

Kempf, K. (1986). "Offense specialization: Does it exist?" In Cornish, D.B. and R.V. Clarke (eds.), *The Reasoning Criminal: Rational Choice Perspectives on Offending*. New York: Springer-Verlag.

____(1987). "Specialization and the criminal career." *Criminology* 25:399–420.

____(1988). "Crime severity and criminal career progression." *Journal of Criminal Law and Criminology* 79:524–540.

Kennedy, D. (2008). *Deterrence and Crime Prevention*. London: Routledge.

Kennedy, D.M. (1996). "Neighborhood revitalization: Lessons from Savannah and Baltimore." *NIJ Journal* 231:13–17.

Kennedy, D.M., A.A. Braga, and A.M. Piehl (2001). "Developing and implementing operation ceasefire." In *National Institute of Justice, Reducing Gun Violence: The Boston Gun Project's Operation Ceasefire*. Washington, DC: National Institute of Justice.

Kennedy, L.W. and H. Krahn (1984). "Rural-urban origin and fear of crime: The case for 'rural baggage'." *Rural Sociology* 49:247–260.

Kennedy, L.W. and R.A. Silverman (1985). "Perception of social diversity and fear of crime." *Environment and Behavior* 17:275–295.

Kenney, D.J. (1986). "Crime on the subways: Measuring the effectiveness of the Guardian Angels." *Justice Quarterly* 3:481–498.

____and T.S. Watson (1998). *Crime in the Schools: Reducing Fear and Disorder with Student Problem Solving*. Washington, DC: Police Executive Research Forum.

Kim, S. (1988). "A short- and long-term evaluation of Here's Looking At You alcohol education program." *Journal of Drug Education* 18:235–242.

Kinder, B.N., N.E. Pape, and S. Walfish (1980). "Drug and alcohol education programs: A review of outcome studies." *International Journal of the Addictions* 15:1035–1054.

Kleemans, E.R. (2001). "Repeat burglary victimisation: Results of empirical research in the Netherlands." In G. Farrell and K. Pease (eds.), *Repeat Victimization*. Monsey, NY: Criminal Justice Press.

Kleiman, M.A.R. (1988). "Crackdowns: The effects of intensive enforcement on retail heroin dealing." In Chaiken, M. (ed.), *Street Level Drug Enforcement: Examining the Issues*. Washington, DC: National Institute of Justice.

Kleiman, M.A.R. and K.D. Smith (1990). "State and local drug enforcement: In search of a strategy." In Tonry, M. and J.Q. Wilson (eds.), *Drugs and Crime*. Chicago, IL: University of Chicago Press.

Kleinman, P. and D. David (1983). "Victimization and perception of crime in a ghetto community." *Criminology* 11:307–343.

Kleinig, J. (2000). "The burdens of situational crime prevention: An ethical commentary." In A. von Hirsch, D. Garland and A. Wakefield (eds.), *Ethical and Social Perspectives on Situational Crime Prevention*. Oxford, UK: Hart Pub.

Klepper, S. and D.S. Nagin (1989). "The deterrent effect of perceived certainty and severity of punishment revisited." *Criminology* 27:721–746.

Klockars, C.B. (1985). *The Idea of Police*. Beverly Hills, CA: Sage.

Klofas, J. and N.K. Hipple (2006). *Project Safe Neighborhoods: Strategic Interventions. Crime Incident Reviews: Case Study 3*. Washington, DC: National Institute of Justice.

Knudten, R.D., M.S. Knudten, A.C. Meade, and W.G. Doerner (1977). "Victims and witnesses: their experiences with crime and the criminal justice system." *Monograph*. Washington, DC: National Institute of Law Enforcement and Criminal Justice.

Kodz, J. and K. Pease (2003). *Reducing Burglary Initiative: Early Findings on Burglary Reduction. Findings #204*. London, UK: Home Office.

Kohfeld, C.W., B. Salert, and S. Schoenberg (1981). "Neighborhood associations and urban crime." *Community Action* (Nov/Dec):37–44.

Koper, C.S. (1995). "Just enough police presence: Reducing crime and disorderly behavior by optimizing patrol time in crime hot spots." *Justice Quarterly* 12:649–672.

Kurki, L. (2000). "Restorative and community justice in the United States." In M. Tonry (ed.), *Crime and Justice: A Review of Research*. Vol. 27. Chicago: University of Chicago Press.

Kushmuk, J. and S.L. Whittemore (1981). *A Reevaluation of the Crime Prevention Through Environmental Design Program in Portland, Oregon*. Washington, DC: National Institute of Justice.

Kuttschreuter, M. and O. Wiegman (1998). "Crime prevention and the attitude toward the criminal justice system: The effects of a multimedia campaign." *Journal of Criminal Justice* 26:441–452.

Lab, S.P. (1984a). "Patterns in juvenile misbehavior." *Crime and Delinquency* 30:293–308.

_____(1984b). "Police productivity: The other eighty percent." *Journal of Police Science and Administration* 12:297–302.

_____(1987). "Pornography and aggression: A response to the U.S. Attorney General's commission." *Criminal Justice Abstracts* 19:301–321.

_____(1990). "Citizen crime prevention: Domains and participation." *Justice Quarterly* 7:467–492.

_____and R.D. Clark (1996). *Discipline, Control and School Crime: Identifying Effective Intervention Strategies. Final Report*. Washington, DC: National Institute of Justice.

Lab, S.P. and J.D. Hirschel (1988). "Climatological conditions and crime: The forecast is …?" *Justice Quarterly* 5:281–300.

Lab, S.P. and T. Hope (1998). "Assessing the impact of area context on crime prevention behavior." Paper presented to the Environmental Criminology and Crime Analysis Conference, Barcelona, Spain.

Lab, S.P. and J.T. Whitehead (1988). "An analysis of juvenile correctional treatment." *Crime and Delinquency* 34:60–85.

_____(1990). "From 'nothing works' to 'the appropriate works': The latest stop on the search for the secular grail." *Criminology* 28:405–418.

_____(1994). "Avoidance behavior as a response to in-school victimization." *Journal of Security Administration* 17(2):32–45.

Lacoste, J. and P. Tremblay (2003). "Crime and innovation: A script analysis of patterns in check forgery." In M.J. Smith and D.B. Cornish (eds.), *Theory for Practice in Situational Crime Prevention*. Monsey, NY: Criminal Justice Press.

LaGrange, R.L. (1993). *Policing American Society*. Chicago: Nelson-Hall.

Langworthy, R.H. and L.F. Travis III (1994). *Policing in America: A Balance of Forces*. New York, NY: Macmillan.

Lasley, J. (1998). "'Designing Out' Gang Homicides and Street Assaults." *NIJ Research in Brief*. Washington, DC: National Institute of Justice.

Latessa, E.J. and H.E. Allen (1980). "Using citizens to prevent crime: An example of deterrence and community involvement." *Journal of Police Science and Administration* 8:69–74.

____(2003). *Corrections in the Community*, Third Edition. Cincinnati: Anderson Publishing Co.

Latessa, E.J. and L.F. Travis (1987). "Citizen crime prevention: Problems and perspectives in reducing crime." *Journal of Security Administration* 10:38–50.

Lavrakas, P.J. (1986). "Evaluating police-community anticrime newsletters: the Evanston, Houston, and Newark field studies." In Rosenbaum, D.P. (ed.), *Community Crime Prevention: Does It Work?* Beverly Hills, CA: Sage.

____(1997). "Politicians, journalists, and the rhetoric of the "crime prevention" public policy debate." In Lab, S.P. (ed.), *Crime Prevention at a Crossroads*. Cincinnati: Anderson.

____and E.J. Herz (1982). "Citizen participation in neighborhood crime prevention." *Criminology* 20:479–498.

Lavrakas, P.J. and D.A. Lewis (1980). "The conceptualization and measurement of citizens' crime prevention behaviors." *Journal of Research in Crime and Delinquency* 17:254–272.

Lavrakas, P.J., J. Normoyle, W.G. Skogan, E.J. Herz, G. Salem, and D. Lewis (1981). *Factors Related to Citizen Involvement in Personal, Household, and Neighborhood Anti-Crime Measures: Executive Summary*. Washington, DC: National Institute of Justice.

Lavrakas, P.J., D.P. Rosenbaum, and F. Kamiski (1983). "Transmitting information about crime and crime prevention to citizens: the Evanston newsletter quasi-experiment." *Journal of Police Science and Administration* 11:463–473.

Laycock, G. (1984). *Reducing Burglary: A Study of Chemist's Shops*. London, UK: Home Office.

____(1985). *Property Marking: A Deterrent to Domestic Burglary? Crime Prevention Planning Unit: Paper 3*. London: Home Office.

____(1990). "Operation identification: How much of a solution?" Paper presented at the American Society of Criminology Annual Meeting, Baltimore.

____(2002). Methodological issues in working with policy advisers and practitioners. In N. Tilley (ed.), *Analysis for Crime Prevention*. Monsey, NY: Criminal Justice Press.

____(2005). "Defining crime science." In Smith, M.J. and N. Tilley (eds.), *Crime Science: New Approaches to Preventing and Detecting Crime*. Portland, OR: Willan Publishing.

____and G. Farrell (2003). "Repeat victimization: Lessons for implementing problem-oriented policing." In Knutsson, J. (ed.), *Problem-Oriented Policing: From Innovation to Mainstream*. Monsey, NY: Criminal Justice Press.

Laycock, G. and N. Tilley (1995). "Implementing crime prevention." In Tonry, M. and D.P. Farrington (eds.), *Building a Safer Society: Strategic Approaches to Crime Prevention*. Chicago, IL: University of Chicago Press.

____(1995a). *Policing and Neighbourhood Watch: Strategic Issues*. London, UK: Home Office Police Research Group.

Lazar, I., R. Darlington, H. Murray, J. Royce, and A. Snipper (1982). "Lasting Effects of Early Education: A Report from the Consortium for Longitudinal Studies." *Monographs of the Society for Research in Child Development,* no. 47.

Learmont, S. (2005). "Promoting design against crime." In Clarke, R.V. and G.R. Newman (eds.), *Designing Out Crime from Products and Systems.* Monsey, NY: Criminal Justice Press.

Leavell, H.R. and E.G. Clarke (1965). *Preventive Medicine for the Doctor in His Community: An Epidemiological Approach,* Third Edition. New York, NY: McGraw-Hill.

Lee, M. (2007). Inventing Fear of Crime: Criminology and the Politics of Anxiety. Cullompton, Devon, ENG: Willan Pub.

Lester, A. (2001). *Crime Reduction through Product Design.* Canberra, AUS: Australian Institute of Criminology.

Letkemann, P. (1973). *Crime as Work.* Englewood Cliffs, NJ: Prentice-Hall.

Levi, M. (2008). "Combating identity and other forms of payment fraud in the UK: An analytical history." In McNally, M.M. and G.R. Newman (eds.), *Perspectives on Identity Theft.* Monsey, NY: Criminal Justice Press.

Levrant, S., F.T. Cullen, B. Fulton, and J.F. Wozniak (1999). "Reconsidering restorative justice: The corruption of benevolence revisited?" *Crime and Delinquency* 45:3–27.

Lewis, D.A., J.A. Grant, and D.P. Rosenbaum (1988). *The Social Construction of Reform.* Evanston, IL: Northwestern University Press.

Lewis, D.A. and G. Salem (1986). *Fear of Crime: Incivility and the Production of a Social Problem.* New Brunswick: Transaction.

Lichter, S.R., L.S. Lichter, and S. Rothman (1994). *Prime Time: How TV Portrays American Culture.* Washington, DC: Regnery.

Lilly, J.R. (2006). "Issues beyond empirical EM reports." *Criminology and Public Policy* 5:93–102.

____, R.A. Ball, and J. Wright (1987). "Home incarceration with electronic monitoring in Kenton County, Kentucky: An evaluation." In McCarthy, B.R. (ed.), *Intermediate Punishments: Intensive Supervision, Home Confinement and Electronic Surveillance.* Monsey, NY: Criminal Justice Press.

Lindsey, E.W. and P.D. Kurtz (1987). "Evaluation of a school-juvenile court team approach to delinquency prevention." *Children and Youth Services Review* 9:101–115.

Lipsey, M.W. (1990). "Juvenile delinquency treatment: A meta-analytic inquiry into the variability of effects." Paper presented at the American Society of Criminology Annual Meeting, Denver.

____ (1999). "Can rehabilitative programs reduce the recidivism of juvenile offenders? An inquiry into the effectiveness of practical programs." *Virginia Journal of Social Policy and Law* 6:611–641.

____, G.L. Chapman, and N.A. Landenberger (2001). "Cognitive-behavioral programs for offenders." *Annals of the American Academy of Political and Social Sciences* 578:144–157.

Lipsey, M.W. and J.H. Derzon (1998). "Predictors of violent or serious delinquency in adolescence and early adulthood: A synthesis of longitudinal research." In Loeber, R. and

D.P. Farrington (eds.), *Serious and Violent Juvenile Offenders: Risk Factors and Successful Interventions*. Thousand Oaks, CA: Sage.

Lipsey, M.W. and D.B. Wilson (1993). "The efficacy of psychological, educational, and behavioral treatment." *American Psychologist* 48:1181–1209.

Lipsey, M.W. and D.B. Wilson (1998). "Effective interventions for serious juvenile offenders: A synthesis of research." In R. Loeber and D.P. Farrington (eds.), *Serious and Violent Juvenile Offenders: Risk Factors and Successful Interventions*. Thousand Oaks, CA: Sage.

Lipton, D., R. Martinson, and J. Wilks (1975). *The Effectiveness of Correctional Treatment: A Survey of Treatment Evaluation Studies*. New York, NY: Praeger.

Liska, A.E. and W. Baccaglini (1990). "Feeling safe by comparison: Crime in the newspapers." *Social Problems* 37:360–374.

Liska, A.E., J.L. Lawrence, and A. Sanchirico (1982). "Fear of crime as a social fact." *Social Forces* 60:760–770.

Listwan, S.J., J.L. Sundt, A.M. Holsinger, and E.J. Latessa (2003). "The effects of drug court programming on recidivism: The Cincinnati experience." *Crime and Delinquency* 49:389–411.

Lizotte, A.J., J.M. Tesoriero, T.P. Thornberry, and M.D. Krohn (1994). "Patterns of adolescent firearms ownership and use." *Justice Quarterly* 11:51–73.

Lloyd, S., G. Farrell and K. Pease (1994). *Preventing Repeated Domestic Violence: A Demonstration Project on Merseyside. Home Office Crime Prevention Unit Paper #49*. London, UK: Home Office.

Lockwood, D. (1997). "Violence Among Middle School and High School Students: Analysis and Implications for Prevention". *NIJ Research in Brief*. Washington, DC: National Institute of Justice.

Loeber, R. (1988). "Natural histories of conduct problems, delinquency and related substance abuse." In Lahey, B.B. and A.E. Kazdin (eds.), *Advances in Clinical Child Psychology*, vol. 11. New York: Plenum Press.

____, S.M. Green, K. Keenan, and B.B. Lahey (1995). "Which boys will fare worse? Early predictors or the onset of conduct disorder in a six-year longitudinal study." *Journal of the American Academy of Child and Adolescent Psychiatry* 34:499–509.

Loeber, R. and M. Stouthamer-Loeber (1986). "Family factors as correlates and predictors of juvenile conduct problems and delinquency." In Tonry, M. and N. Morris (eds.), *Crime and Justice: An Annual Review of Research*, Vol. 7. Chicago: University of Chicago Press.

Loeber, R., P. Wung, K. Keenan, B. Giroux, M. Stouthamer-Loeber, W.B. VanKammen, and B. Maughan (1993). "Developmental pathways in disruptive child behavior." *Development and Psychopathology* 5:103–133.

Logan, C.H. (1972). "General deterrence effects of imprisonment." *Social Forces* 51:63–72.

____ and G.G. Gaes (1993). "Meta-analysis and the rehabilitation of punishment." *Justice Quarterly* 10:245–264.

Loney, J., M.A. Whaley-Klahn, T. Kosier, and J. Conboy (1983). "Hyperactive boys and their brothers at 21: Predictors of aggressive and antisocial outcomes." In Van Dusen, K.T. and S.A. Mednick (eds.), *Prospective Studies of Crime and Delinquency*. Boston: Kluwer-Nijhof.

Losel, F. (1995). "The efficacy of correctional treatment: A review and synthesis of meta-evaluations." In J. McGuire (ed.), *What Works: Reducing Reoffending*. West Sussex, UK: John Wiley and Sons.

Lowenkamp, C.T., E.J. Latessa, and P. Smith (2006). "Does correctional program quality really matter?: The impact of adhering to the principles of effective intervention." *Criminology and Public Policy* 5:575–594.

Lowry, D. (1971). "Greshaw's law and network TV news selection." *Journal of Broadcasting* 15:397–408.

Luepker, R.V., C.A. Johnson, D.M. Murray, and T.F. Pechacek (1983). "Prevention of cigarette smoking: Three year follow-up of educational programs for youth." *Journal of Behavioral Medicine* 6:53–61.

Lumb, R.C., R.D. Hunter, and D.J. McLain (1993). "Fear reduction in the Charlotte Housing Authority." In Zahm, D. and P. Cromwell (eds.), *Proceedings of the International Seminar on Environmental Criminology and Crime Analysis*. Coral Gables, FL: Florida Criminal Justice Executive Institute.

Lurigio, A.J. and R.C. Davis (1992). "Taking the war on drugs to the streets: The perceptual impact of four neighborhood drug programs." *Crime and Delinquency* 38:522–538.

Luxenburg, J., F.T. Cullen, R.H. Langworthy, and R. Kopache (1994). "Firearms and Fido: Ownership of injurious means of protection." *Journal of Criminal Justice* 22:159–170.

Lynch, J. and D. Cantor (1992). "Ecological and behavioral influences on property victimization at home: Implications for opportunity theory." *Journal of Research in Crime and Delinquency* 29:335–362.

Maddux, J.F. (1988). "Clinical experience with civil commitment." In Leukefeld, C.G. and F.M. Tims (eds.), *Compulsory Treatment of Drug Abuse: Research and Clinical Practice*. Washington, DC: National Institute on Drug Abuse.

Maguin, E. and R. Loeber (1996). "Academic performance and delinquency." In Tonry, M. and N. Morris (eds.), *Crime and Justice*, Vol. 20. Chicago, IL: University of Chicago Press.

Maguire, K. and A.L. Pastore (1995). *Sourcebook of Criminal Justice Statistics, 1994*. Washington, DC: Bureau of Justice Statistics.

Marsh, H.L. (1991). "A comparative analysis of crime coverage in newspapers in the United States and other countries from 1960–1989: A review of the literature." *Journal of Criminal Justice* 19:67–80.

Marsh, M. and M. Singer (1972). *Soft Statistics and Hard Questions*. Croton-on-Hudson, NY: Hudson Institute.

Martinson, R. (1974). "What works? Questions and answers about prison reform." *The Public Interest* 35:22–54.

_____ (1979). "New findings; new views: a note of citation regarding sentencing reform." *Hofstra Law Review* 7:243–258.

Matthews, K.E. (1977). "Community crime prevention program, July 1, 1973 to August 31, 1976." Paper presented at the National Conference on Criminal Justice Evaluation.

Mawby, R.I. (2001). *Burglary*. Portland, OR: Willan Publishing.

Maxfield, M.G. and T.L. Baumer (1990). "Home detention with electronic monitoring: Comparing pretrial and postconviction programs." *Crime and Delinquency* 36:521–536.

Mayer, J.P., L.K. Gensheimer, W.S. Davidson, and R. Gottschalk (1986). "Social learning treatment within juvenile justice: a meta-analysis of impact in the natural environment." In Apter, S.J. and A.P. Goldstein (eds.), *Youth and Violence: Problems and Prospects*. New York, NY: Pergamon.

Mayhew, P., R.V. Clarke, A. Sturman, and J.M. Hough (1976). *Crime as Opportunity*. London, UK: HMSO.

Mayhew, P., R.V. Clarke, and D. Elliot (1989). "Motorcycle theft, helmet legislation and displacement." *Howard Journal* 28:1–8.

Mazerolle, L.G. and J.A. Roehl (1998). "Civil remedies and crime prevention: An introduction." In Mazerolle, L.G. and R. Roehl (eds.), *Civil Remedies and Crime Prevention*. Monsey, NY: Criminal Justice Press.

_____(1999). "Controlling Drug and Disorder Problems: Oakland's Beat Health Program." *NIJ Research in Brief*. Washington, DC: National Institute of Justice.

Mazerolle, L.G., J. Roehl, and C. Kadleck (1998). "Controlling social disorder using civil remedies: Results from a randomized field experiment in Oakland, California." In Mazerolle, L.G. and J. Roehl (eds.), *Civil Remedies and Crime Prevention*. Monsey, NY: Criminal Justice Press.

McAlister, A., C.L. Perry, J. Killen, L.A. Slinkard, and N. Macoby (1980). "Pilot study of smoking, alcohol, and drug abuse prevention." *American Journal of Public Health* 70:719–721.

McBride, D.C. and J.A. Schwartz (1990). "Drugs and violence in the age of crack cocaine." In Weisheit, R. (eds.), *Drugs, Crime and the Criminal Justice System*. Cincinnati, OH: Anderson Publishing Co.

McCleary, R., B.C. Nienstedt, and J.M. Erven (1982). "Uniform crime reports as organizational outcomes: three time series experiments." *Social Problems* 29:361–371.

McCold, P. And B. Wachtel (1998). *Restorative Policing Experiment: The Bethlehem, Pennsylvania, Police Family Group Conferencing Project*. Pipersville, PA: Community Service Foundation.

McCord, J. (1977). "A comparative study of two generations of native Americans." In Meier, R.F. (ed.), *Theory in Criminology: Contemporary Views*. Beverly Hills, CA: Sage.

_____(1979). "Some child-rearing antecedents of criminal behavior in adult men." *Journal of Personality and Social Psychology* 37:1477–1486.

McCoy., H.V., J.D. Wooldredge, F.T. Cullen, P.J. Dubeck, and S.L. Browning (1996). "Lifestyles of the old and not so fearful: Life situation and older persons' fear of crime." *Journal of Criminal Justice* 24:191–205.

McDevitt, J., S.H. Decker, N.K, Hipple, and E.F. McGarrell (2006). *Project Safe Neighborhoods: Strategic Interventions. Offender Notification Meetings: Case Study 2*. Washington, DC: National Institute of Justice.

McFarland, S.G. (1983). "Is capital punishment a short-term deterrent to homicide?: a study of the effects of four recent American executions." *Journal of Criminal Law and Criminology* 74:1014–1032.

McGahey, R.M. (1980). "Dr. Ehrlich's magic bullet: economic theory, econometrics, and the death penalty." *Crime and Delinquency* 26:485–502.

McGarrell, E.F., A.L. Giacomazzi, and Q.C. Thurman (1997). "Neighborhood disorder, integration, and the fear of crime." *Justice Quarterly* 14:479–500.

McGarrell, E.F., K. Olivares, K. Crawford, and N. Kroovand (2000). *Returning Justice to the Community: The Indianapolis Juvenile Restorative Justice Experiment.* Indianapolis, IN: Hudson Institute.

McGlothlin, W.H. and M.D. Anglin (1981). "Shutting off methadone: Costs and benefits." *Archives of General Psychiatry* 38:885–892.

Meehl, P.E. (1954). *Clinical vs. Actuarial Prediction.* Minneapolis: University of Minnesota Press.

Meier, R.F. and W.T. Johnson (1977). "Deterrence as social control: the legal and extralegal production of conformity." *American Sociological Review* 42:292–304.

Melton, G.B., S.P. Limber, P. Cunningham, D.W. Osgood, J. Chambers, V. Flerx, S. Henggeler, and M. Nation (1998). *Violence among Rural Youth: Final Report.* Washington, DC: Office of Juvenile Justice and Delinquency Prevention.

Menard, S. and H.C. Covey (1987). "Patterns of victimization, fear of crime, and crime precautions in nonmetropolitan New Mexico." *Journal of Crime and Justice* 10:71–100.

Merry, S.E. (1981). "Defensible space undefended: social factors in crime control through environmental design." *Urban Affairs Quarterly* 16:397–422.

Merton, R.K. (1968). *Social Theory and Social Structure.* New York, NY: Macmillan.

Metropolitan Life (1993). *Violence in America's Public Schools.* New York: Louis Harris and Assoc.

_____(1994). *Violence in America's Public Schools: The Family Perspective.* New York: Louis Harris and Assoc.

Miethe, T.D. (1991). "Citizen-based crime control activity and victimization risks: An examination of displacement and free-rider effects." *Criminology* 29:419–440.

Miethe, T.D., L. Hong, and E. Reese (2000). "Reintegrative shaming and recidivism risks in drug court: Explanations for some unexpected findings." *Crime and Delinquency* 46:522–541.

Millie, A. and M. Hough (2004). "Assessing the Impact of the Reducing Burglary Initiative in Southern England and Wales." *Home Office Online Report 42/04.* London, UK: Home Office.

Moffitt, T.E., A. Caspi, P. Fawcett, G.L. Brammer, M. Raleigh, A. Yuwiler, and P.A. Silva (1997). "Whole blood serotonin and family background relate to male violence." In Raine, A., P.A. Brennan, D.P. Farrington, and S.A. Mednick (eds.), *Biosocial Bases of Violence.* New York: Plenum.

Monahan, J. (1981). *The Clinical Prediction of Violent Behavior.* Washington, DC: U.S. Department of Health and Human Services.

Moore, D. and T. O'Connell (1994). "Family conferencing in Wagga Wagga: A communitarian model of justice." In C. Adler and J. Wundersitz (eds.), *Family Conferencing and Juvenile Justice: The Way Forward or Misplaced Optimism?* Canberra, AUS: Australian Institute of Criminology.

Moore, M.H. (1994). "Research synthesis and policy implications." In Rosenbaum, D.P. (ed.), *The Challenge of Community Policing: Testing the Promises.* Thousand Oaks, CA: Sage.

Morris, N. and M. Tonry (1990). *Between Prison and Probation: Intermediate Punishments in a Rational Sentencing System.* New York, NY: Oxford University Press.

Morrison, S.A. and I. O'Donnell (1996). "An analysis of the decision-making practices of armed robbers." In Homel, R. (ed.), *The Politics and Practice of Situational Crime Prevention.* Monsey, NY: Criminal Justice Press.

Mortimer, E. (2001). *Electronic Monitoring or Released Prisoners: An Evaluation of the Home Detention Curfew Scheme. Home Office Findings 139.* London, UK: Home Office.

Mustaine, E.E. and R. Tewksbury (1998). "Predicting risks of larceny theft victimization: A routine activity analysis using refined lifestyle measures." *Criminology* 36:829–858.

Nagin, D.S. (1998). "Criminal deterrence research at the outset of the twenty-first century." *Crime and Justice* 23:1–42.

Nair, G., J. Ditton, and S. Phillips (1993). "Environmental improvements and the fear of crime." *British Journal of Criminology* 33:555–561.

Nasar, J.L. and B.S. Fisher (1993). "'Hot spots' of fear and crime: A multi-method investigation." *Journal of Environmental Psychology* 13:187–206.

National Audit Office (2004). *Reducing Crime.* London: The Stationary Office.

National Crime Prevention Council (2009. http://www.ncpc.org/programs/

National Institute of Justice (1990). *Drugs and Crime: 1989 Drug Use Forecasting Report.* Washington, DC: author.

National Institute on Drug Abuse (1999) Principles of Drug Addiction Treatment: A Research-Based Guide. Washington, DC: National Institute on Drug Abuse.

National Law Enforcement and Corrections Technology Center (1999). *Keeping Track of Electronic Monitoring.* Washington, DC: National Institute of Justice.

Nee, C. and M. Taylor (1988). "Residential burglary in the Republic of Ireland: A situational perspective." *Howard Journal of Criminal Justice* 27:105–116.

Nelson, S. (1989). "Crime-time television." *FBI Law Enforcement Bulletin* 58:1–9.

New Jersey State Parole Board (2007). *Report on New Jersey's GPS Monitoring of Sex Offenders.* Trenton, NJ: author.

Newburn, T. (2002). "Community safety and policing: Some implications of the Crime and Disorder Act 1998." In G. Hughes, E. McLaughlin and J. Muncie (eds.), *Crime Prevention and Community Safety: New Directions.* Thousand Oaks, CA: Sage.

Newcomb, M.D. and P.M. Bentler (1988). *Consequences of Adolescent Drug Use.* Newbury Park, CA: Sage.

Newman, O. (1972). *Defensible Space.* New York: Macmillan.

_____ and K.A. Franck (1980). *Factors Influencing Crime and Instability in Urban Housing Developments.* Washington, DC: National Institute of Justice.

Newman, O. and F. Wayne (1974). *The Private Street System in St. Louis.* New York, NY: Institute for Community Design Analysis.

Nichols, W.W. (1980). "Mental maps, social characteristics, and criminal mobility." In Georges-Abeyie, D.E. and K.D. Harries (eds.), *Crime: A Spatial Perspective.* New York, NY: Columbia University Press.

Niederberger, W.V. and W.F. Wagner (1985). *Electronic Monitoring of Convicted Offenders: A Field Test Report.* Washington, DC: National Institute of Justice.

Normoyle, J.B. and J.M. Foley (1988). "The defensible space model of fear and elderly public housing residents." *Environment and Behavior* 20:50–74.

Nugent, W.R., M.S. Umbreit, L. Wiinamaki, and J. Paddock (1999). "Participation in victim-offender mediation and severity of subsequent delinquent behavior: Successful replications?" *Journal of Research in Social Work Practice* 11:5–23.

Nurco, D.N., T.W. Kinlock, T.E. Hanlon, and J.C. Ball (1988). "Nonnarcotic drug use over an addiction career- A study of heroin addicts in Baltimore and New York City." *Comprehensive Psychiatry* 29:450–459.

O'Brien, R.M. (1985). *Crime and Victimization Data*. Beverly Hills, CA: Sage.

Oc, T. and S. Tiesdell (1997). *Safer City Centres: Reviving the Public Realm*. London, UK: Paul Chapman.

Office of Community Oriented Policing Services (2006). http://www.cops.usdoj.gov.

Office of Justice Programs (2001). *Drug Court Clearinghouse and Technical Assistance Project*. Washington, DC: U.S. Department of Justice.

Office of Juvenile Justice and Delinquency Prevention (1999). *Violence after School*. Washington, DC: Office of Juvenile Justice and Delinquency Prevention.

Office of National Drug Control Policy (2009). *Drug Courts*. Accessed 12-12-09 from http://www.whitehousedrugpolicy.gov/enforce/drugcourt.html.

Ohio Commission on Dispute Resolution and Conflict Management (1993). *Conflict Management in Schools: Sowing Seeds for a Safer Society*. Columbus, OH: author.

O'Keefe, G.J. and H. Mendelsohn (1984). *"Taking a Bite Out of Crime": The Impact of a Mass Media Crime Prevention Campaign*. Washington, DC: National Institute of Justice.

O'Keefe, G.J., D.P. Rosenbaum, P.J. Lavrakas, K. Reid, and R.A. Botta (1996). *Taking a Bite Out of Crime: The Impact of the National Citizens' Crime Prevention Media Campaign*. Thousand Oaks, CA: Sage.

Oliver, M.B. (1994). "Portrayals of crime, race, and aggression in 'reality-based' police shows: A content analysis." *Journal of Broadcasting and Electronic Media* 38:179–192.

_____ and G.B. Armstrong (1998). "The color of crime: Perceptions of caucasians' and African-Americans' involvement in crime." In Fishman, M. and G. Cavender (eds.), *Entertaining Crime: Television Reality Programs*. New York: Aldine de Gruyter.

Oliver, W.M. (1998). *Community-Oriented Policing: A Systemic Approach to Policing*. Upper Saddle River, NJ: Prentice-Hall.

Olweus, D. (1993). "Victimization by peers: Antecedents and long-term outcomes." In K.H. Rubin and J.B. Asendorf (eds.), *Social Withdrawal, Inhibition, and Shyness*. Hillsdale, NJ: Erlbaum.

_____ (1994). "Bullying at school: Basic facts and effects of a school-based intervention program." *Journal of Child Psychology and Psychiatry and Allied Disciplines* 35:1171–1190.

_____ (1995). "Bullying or peer abuse at school: Facts and intervention." *Current Directions in Psychological Science* 4:196–200.

_____ and S. Limber (2000). *Bullying Prevention Program. Blueprints for Violence Prevention*. Boulder, CO: Institute of Behavioral Science.

Ortega, S.T. and J.L. Myles (1987). "Race and gender effects on fear of crime: An interactive model with age." *Criminology* 25:133–152.

Otto, H.A. (1962). "sex and violence on the American newsstand." *Journalism Quarterly* 40:19–26.

Padgett, K.G., W.D. Bailes, and T.G. Blomberg (2006). "Under surveillance: An empirical test of the effectiveness and consequences of electronic monitoring." *Criminology and Public Policy* 5:61–92.

Painter, K. (1993). "Street lighting as an environmental crime prevention strategy." In Zahm, D. and P. Cromwell (eds.), Proceedings of the International Seminar on Environmental Criminology and Crime Analysis. Coral Gables, FL: Florida Criminal Justice Executive Institute.

_____ and D.P. Farrington (1997). "The crime reducing effect of improved street lighting: The Dudley project." In R.V. Clarke (ed.), *Situational Crime Prevention: Successful Case Studies*, Second Edition. Gulderland, NY: Harrow and Heston.

Painter, K. and D.P. Farrington (1999a). "Improved street lighting: Crime reducing effects and cost-benefit analysis." *Security Journal* 12:17–32.

Painter, D. and D.P. Farrington (1999b). "Street lighting and crime: Diffusion of benefits in the Stoke-on-Trent project." In K. Painter and N. Tilley (eds.), *Surveillance of Public Space: CCTV, Street Lighting and Crime Prevention*. Monsey, NY: Criminal Justice Press.

Palm Beach County Sheriff's Department (1987). "Palm Beach County's in-house arrest work release program." In McCarthy, B.R. (ed.), *Intermediate Punishments: Intensive Supervision, Home Confinement and Electronic Surveillance*. Monsey, NY: Criminal Justice Press.

Palmer, T. (1975). "Martinson revisited." *Journal of Research in Crime and Delinquency* 12:133–152.

_____ (1983). "The effectiveness issue today: an overview." *Federal Probation* 46:3–10.

Papagiannis, G.J., R.N. Bickel, and R.H. Fuller (1983). "The social creation of school dropouts: accomplishing the reproduction of an underclass." *Youth and Society* 14:363–392.

Parker, K.D. (1988). "Black-white differences in perceptions of fear of crime." *Journal of Social Psychology* 128:487–494.

_____ and M.C. Ray (1990). "Fear of crime: An assessment of related factors." *Sociological Spectrum* 10:29–40.

Passell, P. (1975). "The deterrent effect of the death penalty: a statistical test." *Stanford Law Review* 28:61–80.

_____ and J.B. Taylor (1977). "The deterrent effect of capital punishment: another view." *American Economic Review* 65:445–451.

Pastore, A.L. and K. Maguire (2003). *Sourcebook of Criminal Justice Statistics* [Online]. Available at: http://www.albany.edu/sourcebook/[9/10/2003].

_____ (2006). *Sourcebook of Criminal Justice Statistics* [Online]. Washington, DC: Bureau of Justice Statistics. Available at: http://www.albany.edu/sourcebook.

_____ (2009). *Sourcebook of Criminal Justice Statistics* [Online]. Washington, DC: Bureau of Justice Statistics. Available at: http://www.albany.edu/sourcebook.

Pate, A., M. McPherson, and G. Silloway (1987). *The Minneapolis Community Crime Prevention Experiment*. Washington, DC: Police Foundation.

Paternoster, R. (1989a). "Decisions to participate in and desist from four types of common delinquency: Deterrence ad the rational choice perspective." *Law and Society Review* 23:7–40.

_____(1989b). "Absolute and restrictive deterrence in a panel of youth: Explaining the onset, persistence/desistance, and frequency of delinquent offending." *Social Problems* 36:289–309.

_____and A. Piquero (1995). "Reconceptualizing deterrence: An empirical test of personal and vicarious experiences." *Journal of Research in Crime and Delinquency* 32:251–286.

Paternoster, R., L.E. Saltzman, G.P. Waldo, and T.G. Chiricos (1982). "Causal ordering in deterrence research: an examination of the perceptions-behavior relationship." In Hagan, J. (ed.), *Deterrence Reconsidered: Methodological Innovations*. Beverly Hills, CA: Sage.

_____(1985). "Assessments of risk and behavioral experience: an exploratory study of change." *Criminology* 23:417–436.

Pawson, R. and N. Tilley (1997). *Realistic Evaluation*. London: Sage.

Pearson, F.S. (1985). "New Jersey's intensive supervision program: A progress report." *Crime and Delinquency* 31:393–410.

_____(1988). "Evaluation of New Jersey's intensive supervision program." *Crime and Delinquency* 34:437–448.

_____and A.G. Harper (1990). "Contingent intermediate sentences: New Jersey's intensive supervision program." *Crime and Delinquency* 36:75–86.

Pease, K. (1998). *Repeat Victimization: Taking Stock*. London, UK: Home Office Police Research Group.

_____(1999). "A review of street lighting evaluations: Crime reduction effects." In K. Painter and N. Tilley (eds.), *Surveillance of Public Space: CCTV, Street Lighting and Crime Prevention*. Monsey, NY: Criminal Justice Press.

Pennell, F.E. (1978). "Private vs. collective strategies for coping with crime: The consequences for citizen perceptions of crime, attitudes the police and neighborhood activity." *Journal of Voluntary Action Research* 7:59–74.

Pennell, S., C. Curtis, and J. Henderson (1986). *Guardian Angels: An Assessment of Citizen Response to Crime*. Washington, DC: National Institute of Justice.

Perkins, D.G. and R.B. Taylor (1996). "Ecological assessments of community disorder: Their relationship to fear of crime and theoretical implications." *American Journal of Community Psychology* 24:63–107.

Perry, K. (1984). "Measuring the effectiveness of neighborhood crime watch in Lakewood, Colorado." *Police Journal* 57:221–233.

Pestello, H.F. (1984). "Deterrence: a reconceptualization." *Crime and Delinquency* 30:593–609.

Petersilia, J. and P.W. Greenwood (1978). "Mandatory prison sentences: their projected effects on crime and prison populations." *Journal of Criminal Law and Criminology* 69:604–615.

Petersilia, J., P. Greenwood and M. Lavin (1978). *Criminal Careers of Habitual Felons*. Washington, DC: U.S. Department of Justice.

Petersilia, J. and S. Turner (1990). "Comparing intensive and regular supervision for high-risk probationers: Early results from an experiment in California." *Crime and Delinquency* 36:87–111.

_____(1993). "Intensive probation and parole." In Tonry, M. (ed.), *Crime and Justice*, vol. 17. Chicago: University of Chicago Press.

Peterson, M.A. and H.B. Braiker (1980). *Doing Crime: A Survey of California Prison Inmates*. Santa Monica, CA: Rand Corp.

Peterson, M.A., H.B. Braiker, and S.M. Polich (1981). *Who Commits Crimes?* Cambridge, MA: Oelgeschlager, Gunn and Hain.

Petrosino, A.J. and D. Brensilber (2003). "The motives, methods and decision making of convenience store robbers: Interviews with 28 incarcerated offenders in Massachusetts." In M.J. Smith and D.B. Cornish (eds.), *Theory for Practice in Situational Crime Prevention*. Monsey, NY: Criminal Justice Press.

Pfohl, S.J. (1978). *Predicting Dangerousness*. Lexington, MA.: Lexington Books.

Phillips, C. (1999). "A review of CCTV evaluations: Crime reduction effects and attitudes towards its use." In K. Painter and N. Tilley (eds.), *Surveillance of Public Space: CCTV, Street Lighting and Crime Prevention*. Monsey, NY: Criminal Justice Press.

Phillips, C. (2002). "From voluntary to statutory status: Reflecting on the experience of three partnerships established under the Crime and Disorder Act 1998." In G. Hughes, E. McLaughlin and J. Muncie (eds.), *Crime Prevention and Community Safety: New Directions*. Thousand Oaks, CA: Sage.

Phillips, D.P. (1980). "The deterrent effect of capital punishment." *American Journal of Sociology* 86:139–148.

_____(1982). "The impact of fictional television stories on US adult fatalities: new evidence on the effect of the mass media on violence." *American Journal of Sociology* 87:1340–1359.

_____(1983). "The impact of mass media violence on US homicides." *American Sociological Review* 48:560–568.

Phillips, J.C. and D.H. Kelly (1979). "School failure and delinquency: which causes which?" *Criminology* 17:194–207.

Phillips, L., S. Ray, and H.L. Votey (1984). "Forecasting highway casualties: the British Road Safety Act and a sense of deja vu." *Journal of Criminal Justice* 12:101–114.

Phillips, P.P. (1980). "Characteristics and typology of the journey to crime." In Georges-Abeyie, D.E. and K.D. Harries (eds.), *Crime: A Spatial Perspective*. New York, NY: Columbia University Press.

Piliavin, I., C. Thornton, R. Garten, and R.L. Matsueda (1986). "Crime, deterrence, and rational choice." *American Sociological Review* 51:101–119.

Piquero, A. and G.F. Rengert (1999). "Studying deterrence with active residential burglars: A research note." *Justice Quarterly* 16:451–472.

Piquero, A. and R. Paternoster (1998). "An application of Stafford and Warr's reconceptualization of deterrence to drunk driving." *Journal of Research in Crime and Delinquency* 35:3–39.

Podolefsky, A. and F. DuBow (1980). *The Reactions to Crime Papers: Vol. II: Strategies for Community Crime Prevention*. Evanston, IL: Northwestern University.

Police Foundation (1981). *The Newark Foot Patrol Experiment*. Washington, DC: author.

Polk, K., D. Frease, and L. Richmond (1974). "Social class, school experience, and delinquency." *Criminology* 12:84–96.

Polk, K. and D. Hafferty (1966). "School culture, adolescent commitments, and delinquency." *Journal of Research in Crime and Delinquency* 4:82–96.

Polk, K. and W.E. Schafer (1972). *Schools and Delinquency*. Englewood Cliffs, N.J.: Prentice-Hall.

Polvi, N., T. Looman, C. Humphries, and K. Pease (1990). "Repeat break and enter victimization: Time course and crime prevention opportunity." *Journal of Police Science and Administration* 17:8–11.

Popkin, S.J., V.E. Gwiasda, D.P. Rosenbaum, J.M. Amendolia, W.A. Johnson, and L.M. Olson (1999). "Combating crime in public housing: A qualitative and quantitative longitudinal analysis of the Chicago Housing Authority's anti-drug initiative." *Justice Quarterly* 16:519–558.

Popkin, S.J., L.M. Olson, A.J. Lurigio, V.E. Gwiasda, and R.G. Carter (1995). "Sweeping out drugs and crime: Residents' views of the Chicago Housing Authority's Public Housing drug elimination program." *Crime and Delinquency* 41:54–72.

Poyner, B. (1988). "Video cameras and bus vandalism." *Security Administration* 11:44–51.

____(1991). "Situational crime prevention in two parking facilities." *Security Journal* 2:96–101.

____(1994). "Lessons from Lisson Green: An evaluation of walkway demolition on a British housing estate." In Clarke, R.V. (ed.), *Crime Prevention Studies*, vol. 4. Monsey, NY: Criminal Justice Press.

____and B. Webb (1992). "Reducing theft from shopping bags in city center markets." In Clarke, R.V. (ed.), *Situational Crime Prevention: Successful Case Studies*. Albany, NY: Harrow and Heston.

Pratt, T.C., F.T. Cullen, K.R. Blevins, L.E. Daigle and T.D. Madensen (2008). "The empirical states of deterrence theory: A meta-analysis." In Cullen, F.T., J.P. Wright, and K.R. Blevins (eds.), *Take Stock: The Status of Criminological Theory*. New Brunswick, NJ: Transaction.

President's Commission on Law Enforcement and the Administration of Justice (1967). *Task Force Report: Juvenile Delinquency and Youth Crime*. Washington, DC: U.S. Government Printing Office.

Project Safe Neighborhoods (2003). *Fact Sheet, Project Safe Neighborhoods: America's Network Against Gun Violence*. Available at: http://psn.gov/crime.asp [2/7/03].

Pyle, G.F. (1974). *The Spatial Dynamics of Crime*. Chicago, IL: University of Chicago, Department of Geography Research Paper #159.

Raine, A. (1993). *The Psychopathology of Crime: Criminal Behavior as a Clinical Disorder*. San Diego, CA: Academic Press.

Rand, M.R. (2009). *Criminal Victimization, 2008*. Washington, DC: Bureau of Justice Statistics.

____, J.P. Lynch, and D. Cantor (1997). *Criminal Victimization, 1973–1995*. Washington, DC: Bureau of Justice Statistics.

Rasmussen, M., W. Muggli, and C.M. Crabill (1979). *Evaluation of the Minneapolis Community Crime Prevention Demonstration*. St. Paul: Crime Control Planning Board.

Ratcliffe, J. and M. McCullagh (1999). "Burglary, victimization and social deprivation." *Crime Prevention and Community Safety: An International Journal* 1:37–46.

Reichel, P. and C. Seyfrit (1984). "A peer jury in the juvenile court." *Crime and Delinquency* 30:423–438.

Reiner, R., S. Livingstone, and J. Allen (2000). "No more happy endings?: The media and popular concern about crime since the Second World War." In T. Hope and R. Sparks (eds.), *Crime, Risk and Insecurity*. New York: Routledge.

Reiss, A.J. and A.L. Rhodes (1959). *A Sociopsychological Study of Adolescent Conformity and Deviation*. Washington, DC: U.S. Office of Education.

_____ (1961). "The distribution of juvenile delinquency in the social class structure." *American Sociological Review* 26:720–732.

Reiss, A.J. and J.A. Roth (1993). *Understanding and Preventing Violence*. Washington, DC: National Academy Press.

Rengert, G.F. (1997). "Auto theft in central Philadelphia." In Homel, R. (ed.), *Policing for Prevention: Reducing Crime, Public Intoxication and Injury*. Monsey, NY: Criminal Justice Press.

_____ and J. Wasilchick (1985). *Suburban Burglary: A Time and a Place for Everything*. Springfield, IL: Thomas.

Rennison, C.M. and M.R. Rand (2003). *Criminal Victimization, 2002*. Washington, DC: Bureau of Justice Statistics.

Reppetto, T.A. (1976). "Crime prevention and the displacement phenomenon." *Crime and Delinquency* 22:166–177.

Rhodes, W., J. Norman and R. Kling (1997). *An Evaluation of the Effectiveness of Automobile Parts Marking on Preventing Theft*. Washington, DC: Abt Assoc.

Rhodes, W.M. and C. Conley (1981). "Crime and mobility: an empirical study." In Brantingham, P.J. and P.L. Brantingham (eds.), *Environmental Criminology*. Beverly Hills, CA: Sage.

Rich, T.F. (1995). "The use of computerized mapping in crime control and prevention programs." *NIJ Research in Action*. Washington, DC: U.S. Department of Justice.

Rifai, M.Y. (1982). "Methods of measuring the impact of criminal victimization through victimization surveys." In H.J. Schneider (ed.), *The Victim in International Perspective*. New York: de Gruyter.

Riger, S., M.T. Gordon, and R. LeBailly (1978). "Women's fear of crime: From blaming to restricting the victim." *Victimology* 3:274–284.

Riley, D. (1980). "An evaluation of a campaign to reduce car thefts." In Clarke, R.V.G. and P. Mayhew (eds.), *Designing Out Crime*. London: Her Majesty's Stationery Office.

_____ and P. Mayhew (1980). *Crime Prevention Publicity: An Assessment*. London, UK: Home Office.

Ringwalt, C.L., S.T. Ennett, and K.D. Holt (1991). "An outcome evaluation of project D.A.R.E." *Health Education Research: Theory and Practice* 6:327–337.

Ringwalt, C.L., P. Messerschmidt, L. Graham, and J. Collins (1992). *Youth's Victimization Experiences, Fear of Attack or Harm, and School Avoidance Behaviors. Final Report*. Washington, DC: National Institute of Justice.

Robinson, M. (1998). "Burglary revictimization: The time period of heightened risk." *British Journal of Criminology* 38:78–87.

Roehl, J.A. and R.F. Cook (1982). "The neighborhood justice centers field test." In Tomasic, R. and M.M. Feeley (eds.), *Neighborhood Justice: Assessment of an Emerging Idea*. New York, NY: Longman.

____(1984). *Evaluation of the Urban Crime Prevention Program: Executive Summary*. Washington, DC: National Institute of Justice.

Roehl, J.A., H. Wong, R. Huitt, and G.E. Capowich (1995). *A National Assessment of Community-based Anti-drug Initiatives: Final Report*. Pacific Grove, CA: Institute for Social Analysis.

Rogers, C. (2007). "Alley-gates: Theory and practice—A perspective from urban South Wales." *Crime Prevention and Community Safety* 9:179–200.

Rojek, D.G. and M.L. Erickson (1982). "Delinquent careers: a test of the career escalation model." *Criminology* 20:5–28.

Rosenbaum, D.P. (1987). "The theory and research behind neighborhood watch: Is it sound fear and crime reduction strategy?" *Crime and Delinquency* 33:103–134.

____(1988). "Community crime prevention: A review and synthesis of the literature." *Justice Quarterly* 5:323–396.

____(2002). "Evaluating multi-agency anti-crime partnerships: Theory, design and measurement issues." In N. Tilley (ed.), *Evaluation for Crime Prevention*. Monsey, NY: Criminal Justice Press.

____, R.L. Flewelling, S.L. Bailey, C.L. Ringwalt, and D.L. Wilkinson (1994). "Cops in the classroom: A longitudinal evaluation of Drug Abuse Resistance Education (DARE)." *Journal of Research in Crime and Delinquency* 31:3–31.

Rosenbaum, D.P. and G.S. Hanson (1998). "Assessing the effects of school-based drug education: A six-year multilevel analysis of project D.A.R.E." *Journal of Research in Crime and Delinquency* 35:381–412.

Rosenbaum, D.P. and S.L. Kaminska-Costello (1998). *Salt Lake City's Comprehensive Communities Program: A Case Study*. Washington, DC: BOTEK Analysis Corporation.

Rosenbaum, D.P., P.J. Lavrakas, D.L. Wilkinson, and D. Faggiani (1997). *Community Responses to Drug Abuse National Demonstration Program: An Impact Evaluation*. Washington, DC: National Institute of Justice.

Rosenbaum, D.P., D.A. Lewis, and J.A. Grant (1985). *The Impact of Community Crime Prevention Programs in Chicago: Can Neighborhood Organizations Make a Difference?* Evanston, IL: Northwestern University.

____(1986). "Neighborhood-based crime prevention: assessing the efficacy of community organizing in Chicago." In Rosenbaum, D.P. (ed.), *Community Crime Prevention: Does It Work?* Beverly Hills: Sage.

Rosenbaum, D.P., A.J. Lurigio, and P.J. Lavrakas (1989). "Enhancing citizen participation and solving serious crime: A national evaluation of Crime Stoppers programs." *Crime and Delinquency* 35:401–420.

Ross, H.L. (1982). "Interrupted time series studies of deterrence of drinking and driving." In Hagan, J. (ed.), *Deterrence Reconsidered: Methodological Innovations*. Beverly Hills, CA: Sage.

Roundtree, P.W. (1998). "A reexamination of the crime-fear linkage." *Journal of Research in Crime and Delinquency* 35:341–372.

Rubel, R.J. (1989). "Cooperative school system and police responses to high risk and disruptive youth." *Violence, Aggression and Terrorism* 3:295–325.

Rubenstein, H., C. Murray, T. Motoyama, and W.V. Wourse (1980). *The Link Between Crime and the Built Environment: The Current State of Knowledge*. Washington, DC: National Institute of Justice.

Sacco, V.F. and R.A. Silverman (1981). "Selling crime prevention: the evaluation of a mass media campaign." *Canadian Journal of Criminology* 23:191–202.

Sacco, V.F. and M. Trotman (1990). "Public information programming and family violence: Lessons from the mass media crime prevention experience." *Canadian Journal of Criminology* 32:91–105.

Sadd, S. and R. Grinc (1994). "Innovative neighborhood oriented policing: An evaluation of community policing programs in eight cities." In Rosenbaum, D.P. (ed.), *The Challenge of Community Policing: Testing the Promises*. Thousand Oaks, CA: Sage.

_____(1996). "Implementation challenges in community policing: Innovative neighborhood-oriented policing in eight cities." *NIJ Research in Brief*. Washington, DC: U.S. Department of Justice.

Saltzman, L., R. Paternoster, G.P. Waldo, and T.G. Chiricos (1982). "Deterrent and experiential effects: the problem of causal order in perceptual deterrence research." *Journal of Research in Crime and Delinquency* 19:172–189.

SAMHSA (2008). *Results from the 2008 National Survey on Drug Use and Health: Detailed Tables*. Washington, DC: U.S. Department of Health and Human Services. Accessed 12-1-09 from http://www.oas.samhsa.gov/nsduh/2K8NSDUH/tabs.

Samples, F. and L. Aber (1998). "Evaluations of school-based violence prevention programs." In Elliott, D.S., D.P. Farrington, and K.R. Williams (eds.), *Violence in American Schools*. Cambridge, UK: Cambridge University Press.

Sampson, R.J. (1986). "Crime in cities: the effects of formal and informal social control." In Reiss, A.J. and M. Tonry (eds.), *Communities and Crime. Crime and Justice*, vol. 8. Chicago, IL: University of Chicago Press.

_____and J. Lauritsen (1994). "Violent victimization and offending: Individual-, situational-, and community-level risk factors." In Reiss, A.J. and J.A. Roth (eds.), *Understanding and Preventing Violence: Vol. 3. Social Influences*. Washington, DC: National Academy Press.

Schafer, W.E. and K. Polk (1967). "Delinquency and the schools." In *President's Commission on Law Enforcement and the Administration of Justice. Task Force Report: Juvenile Delinquency and Youth Crime*. Washington, DC: U.S. Government Printing Office.

Schafer, W.E., C. Olexa, and K. Polk (1971). "Programmed for social class: tracking in high school." In Polk, K. and W.E. Schafer (eds.), *Schools and Delinquency*. Englewood Cliffs, NJ: Prentice-Hall.

Schaps, E., J.M. Moskowitz, J.H. Malvin, and G.A. Schaeffer (1986). "Evaluation of seven school-based prevention programs: A final report of the Napa project." *International Journal of the Addictions* 21:1081–1112.

Scheff, T.J. (1966). *Being Mentally Ill: A Sociological Theory*. Chicago: Aldine Press.

_____(1967). *Mental Illness and the Social Processes*. New York, NY: Harper and Row.

Scherdin, M.J. (1986). "The halo effect: Psychological deterrence of electronic security systems." *Information Technology and Libraries* (Sept.):232–235.

Schiff, A. (1999). "The impact of restorative interventions on juvenile offenders." In G. Bazemore and L. Walgrave (eds.), *Restorative Juvenile Justice: Repairing the Harm of Youth Crime*. Monsey, NY: Criminal Justice Press.

Schlossman, S. and M. Sedlak (1983). *The Chicago Area Project Revisited*. Santa Monica, CA: Rand.

Schmidt, A. (1986). "Electronic monitors." *Federal Probation* 50(2):56–59.

____(1989). "Electronic monitoring of offenders increases." *NIJ Reports No. 212*. Washington, DC: National Institute of Justice.

Schweinhart, L.J. (1987). "Can preschool programs help prevent delinquency?" In Wilson, J.Q. and G.C. Lowrey (eds.), *From Children to Citizens. Vol. 3. Families, Schools and Delinquency Prevention*. New York: Springer-Verlag.

____, H.V. Barnes, and D.P. Weikart (1993). *Significant Benefits*. Ypsilanti, MI: High/Scope Press.

Schweinhart, L.J. and D.P. Weikart (1989). "Early childhood experience and its effects." In Bond, L.A. and B.E. Compas (eds.), *Primary Prevention and Promotion in the Schools*. Newbury Park, CA: Sage.

Schweinhart, L.J. and Z. Xiang (2003). "Evidence that the High/Scope Perry Preschool program prevents adult crime." Paper presented at the American Society of Criminology Annual Meeting, Denver, CO.

Schwitzgebel, R.K., R.L. Schwitzgebel, W.N. Pahnke, and W.S. Hurd (1964). "A program of research in behavioral electronics." *Behavioral Science* 9:233–238.

Scott, M.S. (2006). "Implementing crime prevention: Lessons learned from problem-oriented policing projects." In Knutsson, J. and R.V. Clarke (eds.), *Putting Theory to Work: Implementing Situational Prevention and Problem-Oriented Policing*. Monsey, NY: Criminal Justice Press.

Seattle Law and Justice Planning Office (1975). *Evaluation Report: Target Hardening*. Washington, DC: Law Enforcement Assistance Administration.

Sechrest, L., S.O. White, and E.D. Brown (1979). *The Rehabilitation of Criminal Offenders: Problems and Prospects*. Washington, DC: National Academy Press.

Shadish, W., T. Cook and D. Campbell (2002). *Experimental and Quasi-experimental Designs for Generalized Causal Inference*. Boston: Houghton Mifflin.

Shah, S.A. and L.H. Roth (1974). "Biological and psychophysiological factors in criminality." In Glaser, D., (ed.), *Handbook of Criminology*. Chicago: Rand-McNally.

Shannon, L.W. (1982). *Assessing the Relationship of Adult Criminal Careers to Juvenile Careers*. Iowa City, Iowa: Iowa Urban Community Research Center.

____(1983). "The prediction problem as it applies to delinquency and crime control." Paper presented to the 1st National Symposium on Crime Control.

____(1991). *Changing Patterns of Delinquency and Crime: A Longitudinal Study in Racine*. Boulder, CO: Westview.

Shapland, J. (1988). "Policing with the public?" In T. Hope and M. Shaw (eds.), *Communities and Crime Reduction*. London: Her Majesty's Stationery Office.

Shaw, C.R. and H.D. McKay (1931). *Social Factors in Juvenile Delinquency. Vol. 2 No. 13.* Washington, DC: U.S. Government Printing Office.

_____(1942). *Juvenile Delinquency in Urban Areas.* Chicago, IL: University of Chicago Press.

Sheley, J.F., Z.T. McGee, and J.D. Wright (1995). *Weapon-related Victimization in Selected Inner-city High School Samples.* Washington, DC: National Institute of Justice.

Sheley, J.F. and J.D. Wright (1995). *In the Line of Fire: Youth, Guns and Violence in Urban America.* New York: Aldine de Gruyter.

Shepherd, J.M. (2004). "Murders of passion, execution delays and the deterrence of capital punishment." *Journal of Legal Studies* 33:283–322.

_____(2005). "Deterrence versus brutalization: Capital punishment's differing impacts among states." *Michigan Law Review* 104:203–255.

Sherizan, S. (1978). "Social creation of crime news: all the news fitted to print." In Winick, C. (ed.), *Deviance and Mass Media.* Beverly Hills: Sage.

Sherman, L.W. (1990). "Police crackdowns: Initial and residual deterrence." In Tonry, M. and N. Morris (eds.), *Crime and Justice*, vol. 12. Chicago, IL: University of Chicago Press.

_____(1995). "Hot spots of crime and criminal careers of places." In Eck, J.E. and D. Weisburd (eds.), *Crime and Place.* Monsey, NY: Criminal Justice Press.

_____and R.A. Berk (1984). "The specific deterrent effect of arrest for domestic assault." *American Sociological Review* 49:261–272.

Sherman, L.W., D.P. Farrington, B.C. Welsh, and D.L. MacKenzie (2002). *Evidence-Based Crime Prevention.* New York: Routledge.

Sherman, L.W., P.R. Garten, and M.E. Buerger (1989). "Hot spots of predatory crime: Routine activities and the criminology of place." *Criminology* 27:27–56.

Sherman, L.W., D.C. Gottfredson, D.L. MacKenzie, J. Eck, P. Reuter, and S.D. Bushway (1998). "Preventing Crime: What Works, What Doesn't, What's Promising." *Research in Brief.* Washington, DC: National Institute of Justice.

Sherman, L.W., D.C. Gottfredson, D.L. MacKenzie, J. Eck, P. Reuter, and S.D. Bushway (1997). *Preventing Crime: What Works, What Doesn't, What's Promising.* Washington, DC: National Institute of Justice.

Sherman, L.W. and D.P. Rogan (1995). "Effects of gun seizures on gun violence: "Hot spots" patrol in Kansas City." *Justice Quarterly* 12:673–694.

Sherman, L.W. and D. Weisburd (1995). "General deterrent effects of police patrol in crime "hot spots": A randomized, controlled trial." *Justice Quarterly* 12:625–648.

Shernock, S.K. (1986). "A profile of the citizen crime prevention activist." *Journal of Criminal Justice* 14:211–228.

Shinnar, R. and S. Shinnar (1975). "The effect of the criminal justice system on the control of crime: a quantitative approach." *Law and Society Review* 9:581–611.

Short, J.F. and F.L. Strodbeck (1965). *Group Process and Gang Delinquency.* Chicago, IL: University of Chicago Press.

Shover, N. (1991). "Burglary." In Tonry, M. (ed.), *Crime and Justice: A Review of Research*, vol. 14. Chicago: University of Chicago Press.

Sickmund, M. (2004). *Juveniles in Corrections: National Report Series Bulletin*. Washington, DC: Department of Justice.

Silloway, G. and M. McPherson (1985). "The limits to citizen participation in a government sponsored crime prevention program." Paper presented at the American Society of Criminology Annual Meeting, San Diego.

Simpson, D.D. and S.B. Sells (1981). *Highlights of the DARP Follow-up Research on the Evaluation of Drug Abuse Treatment Effectiveness*. Washington, DC: National Institute on Drug Abuse.

Skogan, W.G. (1981). "On attitudes and behaviors." In Lewis, D.P. (ed.), *Reactions to Crime*. Beverly Hills, CA: Sage.

_____(1987). "The impact of victimization on fear." *Crime and Delinquency* 33:135–154.

_____(1988). "Community organizations and crime." In M. Tonry and N. Morris (eds.), *Crime and Justice*, vol. 10. Chicago: University of Chicago Press.

_____(1989). "Communities, crime, and neighborhood organization." *Crime and Delinquency* 35:437–357.

_____(1990). *Disorder and Decline: Crime and the Spiral of Decay in American Neighborhoods*. New York: Free Press.

_____(1995). "Community policing in Chicago: Year two." *NIJ Research Preview*. Washington, DC: U.S. Department of Justice.

_____(1996). "The community's role in community policing." *NIJ Journal* 231:31–34.

_____and S.M. Hartnett (1997). *Community Policing: Chicago Style*. New York: Oxford University Press.

Skogan, W.G. and A.J. Lurigio (1992). "The correlates of community antidrug activism." *Crime and Delinquency* 38:510–521.

Skogan, W.G. and M.G. Maxfield (1981). *Coping with Crime: Individual and Neighborhood Reactions*. Beverly Hills, CA: Sage.

Skogan, W.G. and M.A. Wycoff (1986). "Storefront police offices: the Houston field test." In Rosenbaum, D.P. (ed.), *Community Crime Prevention: Does It Work?* Beverly Hills: Sage.

Skolnick, J.H. and D.H. Bayley (1988). "Theme and variation in community policing." In M. Tonry and M. Morris (eds.), *Crime and Justice,* vol. 10. Chicago, IL: University of Chicago Press.

Sloan-Howitt, M. and G. Kelling (1990). "Subway graffiti in New York City: "Gettin' up" vs. "meaning it and cleaning it"." *Security Journal* 1:131–136.

Smith, B.E. and R.C. Davis (1998). "What do landlords think about drug abatement laws?" In Mazerolle, L.G. and J. Roehl (eds.), *Civil Remedies and Crime Prevention*. Monsey, NY: Criminal Justice Press.

Smith, C. and T.P. Thornberry (1995). "The relationship between childhood maltreatment and adolescent involvement in delinquency." *Criminology* 33:451–481.

Smith, C.J. and G.E. Patterson (1980). "Cognitive mapping and the subjective geography of crime." In Georges-Abeyie, D.E. and K.D. Harries (eds.), *Crime: A Spatial Perspective*. New York: Columbia University Press.

Smith, D.R. and G.R. Jarjoura (1988). "Social structure and criminal victimization." *Journal of Research in Crime and Delinquency* 25:27–52.

Smith, G.B and S.P. Lab (1991). "Urban and rural attitudes toward participating in an auxiliary policing crime prevention program." *Criminal Justice and Behavior* 18:202–216.

Smith, M.J., R.V. Clarke, and K. Pease (2002). "Anticipatory benefits in crime prevention." In N. Tilley (ed.), *Analysis for Crime Prevention*. Monsey, NY: Criminal Justice Press.

Smith, W.R. and M. Torstensson (1997). "Gender differences in risk perception and neutralizing fear of crime: Toward resolving the paradoxes." *British Journal of Criminology* 37:608–634.

Social Psychiatry Research Associates (1968). *Public Knowledge of Criminal Penalties: A Research Report*. Washington, DC: author.

Sorenson, J., R. Wrinkle, V. Brewer, and J. Marquart (1999). "Capital punishment and deterrence: Examining the effect of executions on murder in Texas." *Crime and Delinquency* 45:481–493.

Sorenson, S.L. (1998). "Empowering capable guardians in high crime and low income settings." *Security Journal* 11:29–35.

Spelman, W. (1993). "Abandoned buildings: Magnets for crime?" *Journal of Criminal Justice* 21:481–296.

_____(1995). "Criminal careers of public places." In Eck, J.E. and D. Weisburd (eds.), *Crime and Place*. Monsey, NY: Criminal Justice Press.

Spergel, I.A., K.M. Wa, and R.V. Sosa (2001). *Evaluation of the Bloomington-Normal Comprehensive Gang Program. Final Report*. Washington, DC: Office of Juvenile Justice and Delinquency Prevention.

_____(2002). *Evaluation of the Mesa Gang Intervention Program (MGIP). Final Report*. Washington, DC: Office of Juvenile Justice and Delinquency Prevention.

_____(2003). *Evaluation of the Riverside Comprehensive Community-wide Approach to Gang Prevention, Intervention and Suppression. Final Report*. Washington, DC: Office of Juvenile Justice and Delinquency Prevention.

_____(2004a). *Evaluation of the Tucson Comprehensive Community-wide Approach to Gang Prevention, Intervention and Suppression. Final Report*. Washington, DC: Office of Juvenile Justice and Delinquency Prevention.

_____(2004b). *Evaluation of the San Antonio Comprehensive Community-wide Approach to Gang Prevention, Intervention and Suppression. Final Report*. Washington, DC: Office of Juvenile Justice and Delinquency Prevention.

Spohn, C., R.K. Piper, T. Martin, and E.D. Frenzel (2001). "Drug courts and recidivism: The results of an evaluation using two comparison groups and multiple indicators of recidivism." *Journal of Drug Issues* 31:149–176.

Stacey, T. (2006). "Electronic tagging of offenders: A global view." *International Review of Law Computers and Technology* 20:117–121.

Stafford, M. and M. Warr (1993). "A reconceptualization of general and specific deterrence." *Journal of Research in Crime and Delinquency* 30:123–135.

Stander, J., D.P. Farrington, G. Hill, and P.M.E. Altham (1989). "Markov chain analysis and specialization in criminal careers." *British Journal of Criminology* 29:317–335.

Stead, P.J. (1983). *The Police of France*. New York, NY: Macmillan.

Stempl, G. (1962). "Content patterns of small metropolitan dailies." *Public Opinion Quarterly* 39:88–90.

Stephens, R.C. (1987). *Mind-Altering Drugs: Use, Abuse, and Treatment*. Newbury Park, CA: Sage.

Stott, M. (1967). "A Content Comparison of Two Evening Network Television Programs with Four Morning Ohio Daily Newspapers". Master's thesis, The Ohio State University.

Stouthamer-Loeber, M. and R. Loeber (1989). "The use of prediction data in understanding delinquency." In Bond, L.A. and B.E. Compas (eds.), *Primary Prevention and Promotion in the Schools*. Newbury Park, CA: Sage.

Stuart, B. (1996). "Circle sentencing: Turning swords into ploughshares." In B. Galaway and J. Hudson (eds.), *Restorative Justice: International Perspectives*. Monsey, NY: Criminal Justice Press.

Surette, R.(1992). *Media, Crime and Criminal Justice: Images and Realities*. Pacific Grove, CA: Brooks/Cole.

_____(1998). *Media, Crime and Criminal Justice: Images and Realities*, Second Edition. Pacific Grove, CA: Brooks/Cole.

Sutton, M. (1996). *Implementing Crime Prevention Schemes in a Multi-agency Setting: Aspects of Process in the Safer Cities Programme*. London, UK: Home Office Research and Statistics Directorate.

Swadi, H. and H. Zeitlin (1987). "Drug education to school children: Does it really work?" *British Journal of Addiction* 82:741–746.

Swartz, J.A., A.J. Lurigio, and S.A. Slomka (1996). "The impact of IMPACT: An assessment of the effectiveness of a jail-based treatment program." *Crime and Delinquency* 42:553–573.

Taylor, D.G., R.P. Taub, and B.L. Peterson (1987). "Crime, community organization, and causes of neighborhood decline." In R.M. Figlio, S. Hakim and G.F. Rengert (eds.), *Metropolitan Crime Patterns*. Monsey, NY: Criminal Justice Press.

Taylor, M. and C. Nee (1988). "The role of cues in simulated residential burglary." *British Journal of Criminology* 28:396–407.

Taylor, R.B. (1988). *Human Territorial Functioning*. New York, NY: Cambridge University Press.

_____(1997). "Crime, grime and responses to crime: Relative impacts of neighborhood structure, crime, and physical deterioration on residents and business personnel in the twin cities." In Lab, S.P. (ed.), *Crime Prevention at a Crossroads*. Cincinnati: Anderson Publishing Co.

_____ and S. Gottfredson (1986). "Environmental design, crime, and prevention: An examination of community dynamics." In A.J. Reiss and M. Tonry (eds.), *Communities and Crime*. Chicago, IL: University of Chicago Press.

Taylor, R.B., B.A. Koons, E.M. Kurtz, J.R. Greene, and D.D. Perkins (1995). "Street blocks with more nonresidential land use have more physical deterioration: Evidence from Baltimore and Philadelphia." *Urban Affairs Review* 31:120–136.

Telch, M.J., J.D. Killen, A.L. McAlister, C.L. Perry, and N. Macoby (1982). "Long-term follow-up of a polit project on smoking prevention with adolescents." *Journal of Behavioral Medicine* 5:1–8.

Thistlethwaite, A., J. Wooldredge, and D. Gibbs (1998). "Severity of dispositions and domestic violence recidivism." *Crime and Delinquency* 44:388–398.

Thornberry, T.P. (1998). "Membership in youth gangs and involvement in serious and violent offending." In Loeber, R. and D.P. Farrington (eds.), *Serious and Violent Juvenile Offenders: Risk Factors and Successful Interventions*. Thousand Oaks, CA: Sage.

____, D. Huizinga, and R. Loeber (1995). "The prevention of serious delinquency and violence: Implications from the program of research on the causes and correlates of delinquency." In Howell, J.C., B. Krisberg, J.D. Hawkins, and J.J. Wilson (eds.), *Sourcebook on Serious, Violent, and Chronic Juvenile Offenders*. Thousand Oaks, CA: Sage.

Thornberry, T.P., M. Moore, and R.L. Christiansen (1985). "The effect of dropping out of high school on subsequent criminal behavior." *Criminology* 23:3–18.

Thornberry, T.P., M.D. Krohn, A.J. Lizotte, and D. Chard-Wierschem (1993). "The role of juvenile gangs in facilitating delinquent behavior." *Journal of Research in Crime and Delinquency* 30:55–87.

Tien, J.M., V.F. O'Donnell, A.I. Barnett, and P.B. Mirchondani (1977). *Street Lighting Projects: National Evaluation Program, Phase I Summary Report*. Washington, DC: National Institute of Law Enforcement and Criminal Justice.

Tien, J.M. and T.F. Rich (1994). "The Hartford COMPASS program: Experiences with a weed and seed-related program." In Rosenbaum, D.P. (ed.), *The Challenge of Community Policing: Testing the Promises*. Thousand Oaks, CA: Sage.

Tierney, J. (2001). "Audits of crime and disorder: Some lessons from research." *Crime Prevention and Community Safety: An International Journal* 3(2):7–18.

Tilley, N. (1992). "Safer cities and community safety strategies." *Crime Prevention Unit Paper 38*. London, UK: Home Office.

____(1993). *Understanding Car Parks, Crime and CCTV: Evaluation Lessons from Safer Cities*. London, UK: Home Office Police Research Group.

____(2002). "Introduction: Evaluation for crime prevention." In N. Tilley (ed.), *Analysis for Crime Prevention*. Monsey, NY: Criminal Justice Press.

____(2004). "Using crackdowns constructively." In Hopkins Burke, R. (ed.), *Hard Cop, Soft Cop*. Cullompton, Devon, UK: Willan Pub.

____(2005). "Introduction: Thinking realistically about crime prevention." In Tilley, N. (ed.), *Handbook of Crime Prevention and Community Safety*. Portland, OR: Willan Publishing.

____(2009) Crime Prevention. Cullompton, Devon, ENG: Willan Pub.

____and J. Webb (1994). *Burglary Reduction: Findings from Safer Cities Schemes*. London, UK: Home Office Police Research Group.

Tita, G.E., K. J. Riley, G. Ridgeway, and P.W. Greenwood (2005). *Reducing Gun Violence: Operation Ceasefire in Los Angeles*. Washington, DC: National Institute of Justice.

Tittle, C.R. (1969). "Crime rates and legal sanctions." *Social Problems* 16:408–423.

____(1977). "Sanction, fear and the maintenance of social order." *Social Forces* 55:579–596.

____and A.R. Rowe (1974). "Certainty of arrest and crime rates: a further test of the deterrence hypothesis." *Social Forces* 52:455–462.

Titus, R.M. (1984). "Residential burglary and the community response." In Clarke, R. and T. Hope (eds.), *Coping with Burglary: Research Perspectives on Policy*. Boston: Kluwer-Nijhoff.

Tobler, N.S. (1986). "Meta-analysis of 143 adolescent drug prevention programs: Quantitative outcome results of program participants compared to a control or comparison group." *Journal of Drug Issues* 16:537–567.

Tonglet, M. (1998). "Consumers' perceptions of shoplifting and shoplifting behavior." In Gill, M. (ed.), *Crime at Work: Increasing the Risk for Offenders*, Vol. 2. Leicester, UK: Perpetuity Press.

Tonry, M. (1990). "Stated and latent features of ISP." *Crime and Delinquency* 36:174–191.

_____(2008). "Learning from the limitations of deterrence research." In Tonry, M. (ed.), Crime and Justice: A Review of Research. Chicago: Univ. of Chicago Press.

Tonry, M. and M. Lynch (1996). "Intermediate sanctions." In Tonry, M. (ed.), *Crime and Justice*, vol. 20. Chicago, IL: University of Chicago Press.

Tontodonato, P. (1988). "Explaining rate changes in delinquency arrest transitions using event history analysis." *Criminology* 26:439–459.

Toseland, R.W. (1982). "Fear of crime: who is most vulnerable?" *Journal of Criminal Justice* 10:199–210.

Townsley, M. and K. Pease (2002). "Hot spots and cold comfort: The importance of having a working thermometer." In N. Tilley (ed.), *Analysis for Crime Prevention*. Monsey, NY: Criminal Justice Press.

Tremblay, P. (2008). "Convergence settings for non-predatory 'boy lovers'.". In Wortley, R. and S. Smallbone (eds.), Situational Prevention of Child Sexual Abuse. Monsey, NY: Criminal Justice Press.

Trojanowicz, R. (1983). *An Evaluation of the Neighborhood Foot Patrol Program in Flint, Michigan*. East Lansing, MI: Michigan State University.

_____and B. Bucqueroux (1989). *Community Policing: A Contemporary Perspective*. Cincinnati, OH: Anderson Publishing Co.

Troyer, R.J. and R.D. Wright (1985). "Community response to crime: two middle-class anti-crime patrols." *Journal of Criminal Justice* 13:227–242.

Tunnell, K.D. (1992). *Choosing Crime: The Criminal Calculus of Property Offenders*. Chicago: Nelson-Hall.

Turner, S., J. Petersilia, and E.P. Deschenes (1992). "Evaluating intensive supervision probation/parole (ISP). for drug offenders." *Crime and Delinquency* 38:539–556.

Umbreit, M.S. (1999). "Avoiding the marginalization and 'McDonaldization' of victim-offender mediation: A case study of moving toward the mainstream." In G. Bazemore and L. Walgrave (eds.), *Restorative Juvenile Justice: Repairing the Harm of Youth Crime*. Monsey, NY: Criminal Justice Press.

_____and R.B. Coates (1993). "Cross-site analysis of victim offender mediation in four states." *Crime and Delinquency* 39:565–585.

Umbreit, M.S., R.B. Coates, and B. Vos (2001). *Juvenile Victim Offender Mediation in Six Oregon Counties*. Salem, OR: Oregon Dispute Resolution Commission.

Umbreit, M.S., B. Vos, R.B. Coates, and K.A. Brown (2003). *Facing Violence: The Path of Restorative Justice and Dialogue*. Monsey, NY: Criminal Justice Press.

U.S. Attorney General's Commission on Pornography (1986). *Final Report*. Washington, DC: U.S. Government Printing Office.

van Andel, H. (1989). "Crime prevention that works: The care of public transport in the Netherlands." *British Journal of Criminology* 29:47–56.

van Dijk, J.M. (1978). "Public attitudes toward crime in the Netherlands." *Victimology* 3:265–273.

____and J. deWaard (1991). "A two-dimensional typology of crime prevention projects." *Criminal Justice Abstracts* 23:483–503.

van Dijk, J.M. and C.H.D. Steinmetz (1981). *Crime Prevention: An Evaluation of the National Publicity Campaigns.* The Hague: Netherlands Justice Ministry.

Van Dine, S., J.P. Conrad, and S. Dinitz (1979). *Restraining the Wicked: The Dangerous Offender Project.* Lexington, MA: Lexington Books.

van Kammen, W.B. and R. Loeber (1994). "Are fluctuations in delinquent activities related to the onset and offset in juvenile illegal drug use and drug dealing?" *Journal of Drug Issues* 24:9–24.

Van Ness, D.W. and K.H. Strong (2002). *Restorative Justice*, Second Edition. Cincinnati, OH: Anderson Publishing Co.

Vaughn, J.B. (1989). "A survey of juvenile electronic monitoring and home confinement programs." *Juvenile and Family Court Journal* 40:1–36

Veater, P. (1984). *Evaluation of Kingsdown Neighborhood Watch Project*, Bristol. Bristol, UK: Avon and Somerset Constabulary.

Vinter, R.D. and R.S. Sarri (1965). "Malperformance in the public school: a group work approach." *Social Work* 10:3–13.

Visher, C.A. (1986). "Incapacitation and crime control: Does a 'lock 'em up' strategy reduce crime?" *Justice Quarterly* 4:513–544.

____(1987). "The Rand inmate survey: A reanalysis." In Blumstein, A., J. Cohen, J.A. Roth and C.A. Visher (eds.), *Criminal Careers and "Career Criminals."* Washington, DC: National Academy Press.

____(1990). "Incorporating drug treatment in criminal sanctions." *NIJ Reports No. 221.* Washington, DC: National Institute of Justice.

von Hirsch, A. (2000). "The ethics of public television surveillance." In A. von Hirsch, D. Garland and A. Wakefield (eds.), *Ethical and Social Perspectives on Situational Crime Prevention.* Oxford, UK: Hart Pub.

____, D. Garland, and A. Wakefield (2000). *Ethical and Social Perspectives on Situational Crime Prevention.* Oxford, UK: Hart Pub.

Wachtel, T. (1995). "Family group conferencing: Restorative justice in practice." *Juvenile Justice Update* 1(4):1–2,13–14.

Walker, S. (1983). *The Police in America: An Introduction.* New York: McGraw-Hill.

____(1985). *Sense and Nonsense About Crime: A Policy Guide.* Monterey, CA: Brooks/ Cole Pub.

____(1999). *The Police in America: An Introduction*, Third Edition. Boston: McGraw-Hill.

Walklate, S. (1999). "Some questions for and about community safety partnerships and crime." *Crime Prevention and Community Safety: An International Journal* 1(3):7–16.

Waples, S. and M. Gill (2006). "The effectiveness of redeployable CCTV." *Crime Prevention and Community Safety* 8(1):1–16.

Warr, M. (1984). "Fear of victimization: Why are some women and the elderly more afraid?" *Social Science Quarterly* 65:681–702.

Watson, E.M., A.R. Stone, and S.M. DeLuca (1998). *Strategies for Community Policing.* Upper Saddle River, NJ: Prentice-Hall.

Webb, B. (1994). "Steering column locks and motor vehicle theft: Evaluations from three countries." In Clarke, R.V. (ed.), *Crime Prevention Studies*, vol. 3. Monsey, NY: Criminal Justice Press.

Weidner, R.R. (1996). "Target hardening at a New York City subway station: Decreased fare evasion—at what price?" In Clarke, R.V. (ed.), *Preventing Mass Transit Crime.* Monsey, NY: Criminal Justice Press.

Weis, J.G. (1973). "Delinquency Among the Well-to-do." Ph.D. Dissertation. University of California at Berkeley.

Weisburd, D. and L. Green (1995). "Measuring immediate spatial displacement: Methodological issues and problems." In Eck, J.E. and D. Weisburd (eds.), *Crime and Place.* Monsey, NY: Criminal Justice Press.

Weisburd, D., E. Waring, and E. Chayet (1995). "Specific deterrence in a sample of offenders convicted of white-collar crime." *Criminology* 33:587–607.

Weisburd, D., L.A. Wyckoff, J. Ready, J.E. Eck, J.C. Hinkle, and F. Gajewski (2006). "Does crime just move around the corner? A controlled study of spatial displacement and diffusion of crime control benefits." *Criminology* 44:549–592.

Weisel, D.L. (2005). *Analyzing Repeat Victimization. Problem Oriented Guides for Police.* Washington, DC: Office of Community-Oriented Policing Services.

_____and J.E. Eck (1994). "Toward a practical approach to organizational change: Community policing initiatives in six cities." In Rosenbaum, D.P. (ed.), *The Challenge of Community Policing: Testing the Promises.* Thousand Oaks, CA: Sage.

Weisheit, R.A. (1983). "The social context of alcohol and drug education: Implications for program evaluations." *Journal of Alcohol and Drug Education* 29:72–81.

Weitekamp, E.G.M. (1999). "The history of restorative justice." In G. Bazemore and L. Walgrave (eds.), *Restorative Juvenile Justice: Repairing the Harm of Youth Crime.* Monsey, NY: Criminal Justice Press.

Wells, L.E. and J.H. Rankin (1988). "Direct parental controls and delinquency." *Criminology* 26:263–285.

Welsh, B.C. and D.P. Farrington (2002). *Crime Prevention Effects of Closed Circuit Television: A Systematic Review.* London, UK: Home Office.

Wertleib, E.L. (1982). "Juvenile delinquency and the schools: a review of the literature." *Juvenile and Family Court Journal* 33:15–24.

West, D.J. (1973). *Who Becomes Delinquent?* London, UK: Heinemann.

_____and D.P. Farrington (1973). *The Delinquent Way of Life.* New York, NY: Crane Russack.

West, S.G., J.T. Hepworth, M.A. McCall, and J.W. Reich (1989). "An evaluation of Arizona's July 1982 drunk driving law: Effects on the city of Phoenix." *Journal of Applied Social Psychology* 19:1212–1237.

White, G.F. (1990). "Neighborhood permeability and burglary rates." *Justice Quarterly* 7:57–68.

White, H.R. (1990). "The drug use-delinquency connection in adolescence." In Weisheit, R. (ed.), *Drugs, Crime and the Criminal Justice System*. Cincinnati: Anderson Publishing Co.

_____, R.J. Pandina, and R.L. LaGrange (1987). "Longitudinal predictors of serious substance use and delinquency." *Criminology* 25:715–740.

White, R.C. (1932). "The relation of felonies to environmental factors in Indianapolis." *Social Forces* 10:498–509.

Whitehead, J.T. and S.P. Lab (1989). "A meta-analysis of juvenile correctional treatment." *Journal of Research in Crime and Delinquency* 26:276–295.

Whitney, I., I. Rivers, P. Smith, and S. Sharp (1994). "The Sheffield project: Methodology and findings." In P. Smith and S. Sharp (eds.), *School Bullying: Insights and Perspectives*. London, UK: Routledge.

Widom, C.S. (1989). "The cycle of violence." *Science* 244:160–166.

Wilbanks, W.L. (1985). "Predicting failure on parole." In Farrington, D.P. and R. Tarling (eds.), *Prediction in Criminology*. Albany, NY: SUNY Press.

Wilkinson, D.L. and D.P. Rosenbaum (1994). "The effects of organizational structure on community policing: A comparison of two cities." In Rosenbaum, D.P. (ed.), *The Challenge of Community Policing: Testing the Promises*. Thousand Oaks, CA: Sage.

Will, J.A. and J.H. McGrath (1995). "Crime, neighborhood perceptions, and the underclass: The relationship between fear of crime and class position." *Journal of Criminal Justice* 23:163–176.

Williams, F.P. (1983). "Deterrence and social control: rethinking the relationship." *Journal of Criminal Justice* 13:141–151.

Williams, H. and A.M. Pate (1987). "Returning to first principles: reducing fear of crime in Newark." *Crime and Delinquency* 33:53–70.

Williams, K.R. and R. Hawkins (1986). "Perceptual research on general deterrence: A critical review." *Law and Society Review* 20:545–572.

_____(1989). "The meaning of arrest for wife assault." *Criminology* 27:163–181.

Williams, P. and J. Dickinson (1993). "Fear of crime: Read all about it?" *British Journal of Criminology* 33:33–56.

Wilson, J.Q. (1968). *Varieties of Police Behavior*. New York, NY: Harvard University Press.

_____and G. Kelling (1982). "Broken windows." *Atlantic Monthly* (March):29–38.

Winge, S. and J. Knutsson (2003). "An evaluation of the CCTV scheme at Oslo central railway station." *Crime Prevention and Community Safety* 5(3):49–59.

Winkel, F.W. (1987). "Response generalization in crime prevention campaigns." *British Journal of Criminology* 27:155–173.

Witte, A.D. (1980). "Estimating the economic model of crime with individual data." *Quarterly Journal of Economics* 94:57–84.

Wolfer, L. (2001). "Strengthening communities: Neighborhood watch and the elderly in a Pennsylvania town." *Crime Prevention and Community Safety: An International Journal* 3(3):31–40.

Wolfgang, M.E., R.M. Figlio, and T. Sellin (1972). *Delinquency in a Birth Cohort*. Chicago, IL: University of Chicago Press.

Wortley, R. (1996). "Guilt, shame and situational crime prevention." In Homel, R. (ed.), *The Politics and Practice of Situational Crime Prevention*. Monsey, NY: Criminal Justice Press.

_____ (2001). "A classification of techniques for controlling situational precipitators of crime." *Security Journal* 14:63–82.

_____ , R. Kane and F. Gant (1998). "Public awareness and auto-theft prevention: Getting it right for the wrong reason." *Security Journal* 10:59–64.

Wortley, R. and S. Smallbone (2008). "Applying situational principles to sexual offenses against children." In Wortley, R. and S. Smallbone (eds.), *Situational Prevention of Child Sexual Abuse*. Monsey, NY: Criminal Justice Press.

Wright, R., M. Heilweil, P. Pelletier, and K. Dickinson (1974). "The impact of street lighting on street crime." Ann Arbor, MI: University of Michigan.

Wright, R.T. and S.H. Decker (1994). *Burglars on the Job: Streetlife and Residential Break-Ins*. Boston: Northeastern University Press.

Wright, W.E. and M.C. Dixon (1977). "Community prevention and treatment of juvenile delinquency." *Journal of Research in Crime and Delinquency* 14:35–67.

Wycoff, M.A. (1995). "Community policing strategies." *NIJ Research Preview*. Washington, DC: U.S. Department of Justice.

Wysong, E., R. Aniskiewicz, and D. Wright (1994). "Truth and DARE: Tracking drug education to graduation and as symbolic politics." *Social Problems* 41:448–472.

Yin, R.K., M.E. Vogel, J.M. Chaiken, and D.R. Both (1977). *Citizen Patrol Projects, National Evaluation Program, Phase I Summary Report*. Washington, DC: National Institute of Law Enforcement and Criminal Justice.

Yu, J. and A.E. Liska (1993). "The certainty of punishment: A reference group effect and its functional form." *Criminology* 31:447–464.

Zhao, J.S., M.C. Scheider, and Q. Thurman (2002). "Funding community policing to reduce crime: Have COPS grants made a difference?" *Criminology and Public Policy* 2:7–32.

Zhao, J.S., M.C. Scheider, and Q. Thurman (2003). "A national evaluation of the effect of COPS grants on police productivity (arrests). 1995–1999." *Police Quarterly* 6:387–409.

Zimmer, L. (1987). "Operation Pressure Point: The disruption of street-level drug trade on New York's lower east side." Occasional paper. New York, NY: New York University School of Law.

Zimring, F.E. and G.J. Hawkins (1973). *Deterrence: The Legal Threat in Crime Control*. Chicago, IL: University of Chicago Press.

Ziskin, J. (1970). *Coping with Psychiatric and Psychological Testimony*. Beverly Hills, CA: Sage.

NAME INDEX

Allatt, P., 124, 125
Allen, H.E., 93, 301
Andenaes, J., 150, 161
Anderson, D, 207
Anderson, D.A., 8–9
Andison, F.S., 133
Andrews, D.A., 296, 298
Anglin, M.D., 236, 241, 242
Aos, S., 37
Archer, D., 154
Armitage, R., 69, 123, 146–147
Atkins, S., 60

Babst, D.V., 276
Bailey, W.C., 158
Ball, J.C., 236, 289
Barclay, P., 123, 124
Barr, R., 108, 111–112, 316
Barrile, L.G., 132
Baumer, T.L., 287–288, 289
Beck, A., 62, 276
Belenko, S., 234
Bellis, D.J., 242
Belson, W.A., 132–133
Bennett, T., 64–65, 86, 87, 94, 116, 117, 193
Bentler, P.M., 237, 246
Berecochea, J.E., 276
Berg, A., 206
Berk, R.A., 278
Berrueta-Clement, J.R., 258
Bevis, C., 66
Bishop, D.M., 163
Bishop, Jesse, 157
Block, C.R., 183
Block, R.L., 183
Bolkcom, C.A., 88
Botvin, G.J., 245
Bowers, K.J., 123, 135, 147, 156, 157–158, 186, 187, 189
Braga, A.A., 123, 223
Braiker, H.B., 280

Braithwaite, J., 302
Brantingham, P.J., 118
Brantingham, P.L., 29, 118
Brennan, P.A., 180
Brodie, D.Q., 94
Brown, B., 62, 123, 146–147
Browning, K., 181
Buck, A.J., 64
Burgess, E.W., 173, 174
Bursik, R.J., 82, 102, 158–159

Capaldi, D.M., 178
Chaiken, J.M., 237
Chaiken, M.R., 237
Chamblin, M.B., 158
Chiricos, T.G., 14, 15, 17, 130, 135, 155
Clark, J.P., 164
Clark, R.D., 260
Clarke, R.V., 72, 108, 112, 113, 184, 188, 192, 195–199, 200–203, 280
Clayton, R.R., 246
Cloward, R., 250
Coates, R.B., 305
Cochran, J.K., 158
Cohen, A.L., 250
Cohen, J., 281
Cohen, L.E., 114, 116, 193
Collins, J.J., 236
Conklin, J.E., 3
Cook, R.F., 89, 94
Cooprider, K.W., 287
Cornish, D.B., 117, 198, 200
Covington, J., 17
Cox, S.M., 267
Crawford, A., 30, 86, 202, 225, 316
Cromwell, P.F., 117
Cullen, F.T., 299
Cusson, M., 192

D'Alessio, S.J., 159
Davis, R.C., 92, 94, 219, 278

Decker, S.H., 117, 157, 193
DeJong, W., 262
Deutschmann, P.J., 130
deWaard, J., 30
Dezhbakhsh, H., 159–160, 160
Dickinson, J., 15, 134–135
Dinkes, R., 255
Ditton, J., 62, 123
Dixon, M.C., 295
Dominick, J.R., 131
Donnelly, P., 66
Donohue, J.J., 157
Donovan, P., 145
Dowds, L., 83
Dunford, F.W., 278

Eck, J.E., 115, 125, 212, 215–216
Ehrlich, I., 153, 156
Ekblom, P., 26, 34, 47, 71
Elfers, H.D., 122
Ellingworth, D., 185, 186
Erez, E., 288
Erickson, M.L., 162
Erwin, D.E., 301
Esbensen, F., 264

Fabricant, R., 122
Fakouri, M.E., 251–252
Farrell, G.A., 184, 186, 187, 188
Farrington, D.P., 59–60, 63, 126–127, 174,
    205, 251–252
Faust, F.L., 29
Feld, B.C., 306
Felson, M., 108, 113, 114, 116, 125, 127,
    184, 193, 204
Ferraro, Kenneth F., 10–11, 14, 16, 17, 94
Fisher, B.S., 61
Fishman, M., 295
Foglia, W.D., 162
Foley, J.M., 67
Forrester, D.H., 90, 122–123
Fors, S.W., 233
Forst, B.E., 154
Franck, K.A., 67
Fraser, M., 154–155

Gabor, T., 124
Gaes, G.G., 296, 299
Garofalo, J., 83, 86, 135
Garrett, C.J., 296, 298
Geerken, M.R., 154
Gendreau, P., 299
Gensheimer, L.K., 295

Gerbner, G., 132
Gibbs, J.P., 275
Gill, M., 62, 63, 187
Gilling, D., 316
Gilmore, Gary, 157
Glaser, D., 275
Goetz, Bernard, 146
Gold, M., 251–252, 267
Goldstein, P.J., 236
Goss, Michael, 285
Gottfredson, Denise C., 257, 259–260,
    266, 276
Gove, W.R., 154
Graber, D., 130
Grasmick, H.G., 82, 102
Graziano, A.M., 295–296
Green, D.E., 123, 126, 134
Greenberg, D., 280
Greenberg, S.W., 67
Greenwood, Peter W., 173, 281, 282, 283
Gresham, P.J., 144

Hafferty, D., 251
Handford, M., 205
Hanson, D.J., 246
Hawkins, J.D., 164, 181, 266
Hearnden, I., 65
Heath, L., 134
Hesseling, R.P.B., 61, 124, 125
Hindelang, M., 194, 252–253
Hirschi, T., 180, 251, 252–253
Hoffman, P.B., 276
Hofstetter, C.R., 131
Hollinger, R.C., 164
Holt, T., 205–206
Homel, P., 197, 198, 200, 202
Hoover, L.T., 213–214
Hope, T., 98, 219–220
Hough, M., 15, 88
Howell, J.C., 181
Hser, Y., 236, 241, 242
Huba, G.J., 237
Hubbard, R.L., 242
Hughes, G., 224
Huizinga, D.H., 236
Hunt, D.E., 237
Hunter, A., 30

Inciardi, J.A., 237, 241

Jacobs, B.A., 163
Jaman, D.R., 276
James, D.J., 234

Jarjoura, G.R., 251
Jensen, G.F., 162–163
Jerse, F.W., 251
Johnson, B.D., 164, 236–237
Johnson, S.D., 123, 135, 147, 183, 187,
    189, 231
Johnston, L.D., 1989, 233
Judy, Steven, 157

Kandel, D.B., 237
Kaplan, H.M., 54
Katz, L., 157
Kelling, G.L., 203
Kelly, D.H., 181
Kelley, J., 145
Kennedy, D.M., 220
Kenney, D.J., 260–261
Kerby, J., 287
Kim, S., 246
Kimble, P.C., 66
Kleemans, E.R., 186
Klepper, S., 165
Knutsson, J., 62
Kohfeld, C.W., 157
Kurki, L., 302
Kushmuk, J., 54, 56, 68

Lab, S.P., 98, 175, 255, 260, 295, 296
LaGrange, R.L., 11
Lasley, J., 66
Latessa, E.J., 88, 93, 301
Lavrakas, P.J., 94, 98, 142, 147–148
Laycock, G., 30–31, 47, 125, 187
Lee, M., 10, 18
Letkemann, P., 125
Levi, M., 206
Lewis, D.A., 87, 98
Lichter, S.R., 132
Lilly, J.R., 289
Limber, S.P., 265
Lipsey, M.W., 296, 299–300
Lipton, D.R., 295
Liska, A.E., 154
Loeber, R., 178, 180, 181, 237
Logan, C.H., 155, 296
Love, Jack, 285
Loveday, K., 62
Lowenkamp, C.T., 296
Lumb, R.C., 14
Lurigio, A.J., 91–92, 94

Magill, C., 65
Maguin, E., 180

Maguire, K., 13
Mann, D., 251–25, 267
Marsh, H.L., 280
Martinson, R., 295, 298
Matthews, K.E., 88
Maxfield, M.G., 13–14, 102, 132,
    287–288, 289
Mayer, J.P., 296
Mayhew, P., 83, 204
Mazerolle, L.G., 219
McCleary, R., 5
McCold, P., 305
McCord, J., 178
McCoy, H.V., 16, 17
McCullagh, M., 187–188
McFarland, S.G., 157
McGarrell, E.F., 17, 305
McKay, H.D., 25, 82, 179
McLeod, M., 83, 86
Meier, R.F., 164
Melton, G.B., 265
Mendelsohn, H., 138
Merry, Sally E., 69
Merton, R.K., 250
Miethe, T.D., 124, 126
Millie, A., 88
Monahan, J., 172
Mooney, K., 295–296
Mustaine, E.E., 116

Nagin, D.S., 165
Nasar, J.L., 61
Nelson, S., 145
Newburn, T., 223
Newcomb, M.D., 246
Newman, Oscar, 52–56, 65, 67, 72, 74, 76
Norman, J., 154–155
Normoyle, J., 67
Nugent, W.R., 305
Nurco, D.N., 237
Nutter, J.B., 66

O'Brien, R,M., 5
Oc, T., 61
O'Keefe, G.J., 83, 86, 138
Oliver, M.B., 212
Olweus, D., 265
Osgood, D.W., 264

Painter, K.A., 59, 126–127
Palmer, T., 295
Passell, P., 155, 156
Pastore, A.L., 13

Paternoster, R., 163, 165
Patterson, G.E., 118, 178
Pawson, R., 46
Pease, F.S., 34, 47, 59, 108, 111–112, 183,
    186, 187, 188, 189, 207, 316
Pennell, F.E., 93
Perkins, D.G., 73
Perry, K., 87–88
Pestello, H.F., 164
Petersilia, J., 281
Peterson, M.A., 280
Phillips, C., 61, 133, 157, 158
Pierce, G.L., 156, 157–158
Piliavin, 1986, 162
Piquero, I., 163
Polk, K., 251
Polvi, N., 185
Popkin, S.J., 92
Poyner, B., 67, 203, 204

Rankin, J.H., 178
Ratcliffe, J., 187–188
Renger, G.F., 183
Rengert, G.F., 117
Reppetto, T.A., 64, 107, 116
Rhodes, A.L., 64
Rich, T.F., 220
Ringwalt, C.L., 246
Roehl, J.A., 89, 92, 94
Rogan, D.P., 123
Rojek, D.G., 233
Rosenbaum, D.P., 94, 101, 144, 212,
    225, 246
Ross, H.L., 158
Roundtree, P.W., 17
Rowe, A.R., 154
Rubenstein, H., 57–58

Sacco, V.F., 140
Sampson, R.J., 155
Sarri, R.S., 251
Schaps, E., 245
Scherdin, M.J., 205
Schweinhart, L.J., 258–259
Schweitzgebel, R.K., 285
Sechrest, L., 295
Sells, S.B., 242
Shaw, C.R., 25, 82, 179
Shepherd, J.M., 159–160
Sheppard, D.I., 94
Sherizan, S., 131
Sherman, L.W., 43, 46, 123, 159, 183,
    211, 278

Shinnar, R., 280–281
Shinnar, S., 280–281
Short, J.F., 62, 123
Simpson, D.D., 242
Singer, M., 280
Skogan, W.G., 13–14, 102, 132
Sloan-Howitt, M., 203
Smallbone, S., 207
Smith, B.E., 219
Smith, C. J., 118
Smith, M.J., 146
Smith, W.R., 16
Sorenson, J., 157
Sorenson, S.L., 61
Speckart, G., 236
Spelman, W., 73, 188, 215–216
Spencer, J., 205–206
Spenkelink, John, 157
Spriggs, A., 63
Stafford, M., 163
Stephens, R.C., 241
Stitt, B.G., 162–163
Stolzenberg, L., 159
Stouthamer-Lober, M., 178
Surette, R., 131
Sutton, M., 91
Swartz, J.A., 241

Taylor, J.B., 156
Taylor, R.B., 17, 73, 74, 95–96
Tewksbury, R., 116
Thistlethwaite, A., 278
Thomas, S.L., 134
Thornberry, T.P., 251
Tien, J.M., 59, 220
Tiesdell, S., 61
Tilley, N., 46, 62, 124
Tita, G.E., 223
Tittle, C.R., 154, 155
Tobler, N.S., 245, 246
Tonglet, M., 62
Torstensson, M., 16
Townsley, M., 183
Travis L.F., 88
Tremblay, P., 207
Trotman, M., 140
Troyer, R.J., 93
Tunnell, K.D., 117

Umbreit, M.S., 305

van Andel, H., 203
van Dijk, J.M., 30

Van Dine, S., 281
van Kammen, W.B., 237
Vaugh, J.B., 289
Vaughn, 1989, 288
Vinter, R.D., 251
Vishner, C.A., 283–284

Wachtel, T., 305
Waldo, G.P., 155
Walker, S., 281–282
Waples, S., 62
Warr, M., 163
Wasilchick, J., 117
Watson, E.M., 260–261
Wayne, F., 65
Webb, B., 124, 204, 205
Weidner, R.R., 203
Weisburd, D., 112, 123, 124, 159, 277
Weisel, D.L., 186, 212
Weitekamp, E.G.M., 302
Wells, L.E., 178
Welsh, B.C., 59–60, 63
West, S.G., 158, 251–252
White, G.F., 237
White, H.R., 235
Whitehead, J.T., 295, 296

Whitney, I., 265
Whittemore, J.T., 54, 56, 68
Widom, C.S., 178–179
Wilbanks, W.L., 174
Wilkinson, W.L., 212
Williams, K.R., 164
Williams, P., 15, 134–135
Willis, A., 62
Wilson, J.Q., 296
Winge, S., 62
Winkel, F.W., 146
Wolfers, J., 157
Wolfgang, M.E., 175
Wortley, R., 197, 198
Wright, R., 64–65, 116, 117
Wright, R.D., 93
Wright, R.T., 193
Wright, W.E., 295
Wycoff, M.A., 217

Xiang, Z., 259

Young, Arthur, 125
Yu, J., 154

Ziskin, J., 173

SUBJECT INDEX

Aboriginal tribes, restorative justice and, 302, 303
Access control
  crime prevention through, 55–56
  doors and locks, 65
Action, cognitive mapping and, 119
Active signaling systems, of electronic monitoring, 285
Activity support, environmental design and, 56
Actuarial predictions, 173–175
ADAM. *See* Arrestee Drug Abuse Monitoring program
Adolescence-limited, risk factors, 181
Advertising Council, 136
After-school programs, 268
Aggregate-level evaluation, 297–298
Aggressive behavior, mass media and, 132
Alarms, crime prevention and, 64
Alcohol abuse
  crime and, 231–233
  targeting, as tertiary crime prevention, 28, 29
Alcoholics Anonymous, 242
Alley gating, 66, 124
Alternative schools, 266–267
America's Most Wanted, 131, 135, 145
Analysis, of problems, 215–216
"An eye for an eye," 22
Anticipatory benefit, from publicity, 146
Apprehension, perceived certainty of, 162
Arrest, certainty, as deterrent, 154
Arrestee Drug Abuse Monitoring (ADAM) program, 234
Assessment
  of crime displacement, 110–111
  in problem solving, 216
  See also Evaluation
Assize of arms, 23
Association of Chief Police Officers (ACPO), 57

ATMs, reducing robberies around, 205–206
Australia, Crime Stoppers in, 144
Authority conflict, 181
Automobile. *See* Vehicle

Beat Health program, of Oakland, CA, 218–219
"Bedroom communities," increased crime and, 114
Behavior
  predicting future, 169–172, 284
  relation to perception and, 163
Benign displacement, 111–112
Bicycle patrols, auto theft reduction and, 204–205
Big Brother
  electronic monitoring as, 289
  situational crime prevention and, 201
Biological risk factors, of deviant behavior, 180–181
Block watch. *See* Neighborhood watch
Boost explanations, 187
Boundaries, in displacement, 109
British Crime Survey, 83, 89, 98, 185–186
British Home Office, 192
British Road Safety Act, 158
Brutalization effect, 158
Buildings, layout. *See* Environmental design
Bullying, efforts against in schools, 265
Burglary
  opportunity clues for, 117
  repeat victimization and, 186
  street layout and design and, 66
Burglary Reduction Initiative, 36
  territorial displacement and, 123

Cambridge Youth Study, 179
CAPS. *See* Chicago Alternative Policing Strategy
Career specialization, 175–176
Cars, crime and prevention (table), 72

CCP. *See* Comprehensive Communities Program

Celerity, in punishment for crime, 152

Center for Substance Abuse Prevention, Community Partnership Demonstration Program, 84

Certainty
of apprehension, 158–159, 165
of punishment, cross-sectional studies, 154–155
of punishment for crime, 152
perceived, 162–163

Charlotte School Safety Program, 259–260

Chicago Alternative Police Strategy (CAPS), 217–218

Chicago Area Project, 25

Chicago Public House Authority, Anti-Drug Initiative, 92, 94

Child sexual assault, situational crime prevention, studies on, 207

Circle Sentencing, as restorative justice, 303–304

Citizen participation, reality television shows and, 145–146

Citizen participation and support, of crime prevention measures, 96–99, 211–213
organizing, 99–102
who participates?, 97–99

Citizen patrols, for crime prevention, 84–85, 92–93

Citizen policing, 23–24

Civil abatement, efforts and assessment, 218–220

Clarke's 1992 Situational Prevention Techniques (table), 196

Clinical predictions, 172–173

Closed-circuit television
as crime prevention, 61–63, 201, 204–205
territorial displacement and, 123

"Cocoon neighborhood watch," 90, 206–207

Code of Hammurabi, 22

Cognitive-behavioral interventions, 299–300

Cognitive maps, 118–121
elements of (table), 119

Cognitive Thinking Skills Program (CTSP), as intervention, 299–300

Collective incapacitation, 279–282

College preparatory education, 253–254

Communities, cognitive mapping and, 118–121
multinuclei, with nodes and paths (figure), 120

Community
environmental design and, 56
successful intervention partnerships, 225–226

Community anti-drug (CAD) programs, 84, 91–92

Community-based intervention, Multi-Systemic Therapy (MST), 299

Community cohesion, neighborhood crime prevention and, 86–87

Community crime prevention, two examples of, 89–91

Community influences, on behavior, 179–180

Community-Oriented Policing, 85

Community Partnership Demonstration Program, 84, 92

Community policing
approach, to crime prevention, 29
community base, 214
community involvement, 213
defining, 211–212 (table)
efforts and assessment, 217–218
as partnership effort, 210
precursors to, 211
problem solving and, 213–214
redefined goals, 214
as secondary crime prevention, 28, 29

Community Resources Against Street Hoodlums (CRASH) program, Los Angeles, 239

Community Responses to Drug Abuse program, 92, 94

Community-Wide Approach to Gang Prevention, Intervention, and Suppression Program, 224–225

Comprehensive Communities Programs (CCP), 36, 221–222

Concealable items, product design, theft and, 70–73

Conflict management/resolution, 261–264

Consortium for Longitudinal Studies, 259

Constable, 23

Context
of evaluation, 47
of programs and interventions, 45–46

Continuous signaling system, of electronic monitoring, 285

Cooperative policing, by citizens, 23

Cost-benefit evaluation, of crime prevention programs, 37–38

Costs, of crime and victimization, 8–9

Covert behavior, 181

CPTED. *See* Crime Prevention Through Environmental Design
CRAVED, 70, 114, 184
    model for targets of theft (table), 114
Crime
    drug use and, 235–238
    fictional portrayals of, 131
    impact to society, 8–9
    as inelastic, 108
    level of reporting, 130–131
    measures of, 2–5
    media as cause of?, 132–134
    neighborhood prevention effects on official records, 87–88
    opportunity and, ten principles of (table), 113
    rates of, 3–5
    victimization, measuring, 6–7
Crime, fear of, 9–18
    group participation in prevention, 97
    lighting, impact of, on, 59
    neighborhood crime prevention and, 93–95
    See also Fear of crime
Crime and Disorder Act (CDA), 57, 223–224
Crime and Disorder projects, 36
Crime area analysis, as secondary crime prevention, 28, 29
Crime attractors, 120
Crime control, 26
Crime diffusion
    effects, 126–127
    implications of displacement and, 127
Crime displacement, 105–126
    assessing, 110–111
    benign or malign, 111–112
    crime pattern theory and, 118–121
    defined, 103
    diffusion and, 126–127
    diffusion of benefits, 112–113
    displacement effects, 121–125
        functional, 125
        tactical, 124
        target, 124–125
        temporal, 123–124
        territorial, 122–123
    forms of (table), 107
    implications or diffusion and, 127
    inelasticity and, 108
    mobility and, 108–109
    offender choice and mobility, 113
    opportunity and, 113–114
    race and, 108

rational choice theory and, 109, 116–118
    routine activities, 114–115
    summary, 125–126
    territorial, 107
Crime fuses, 112
Crime generators, 120
Crime pattern theory, 118–121, 194
    investigating patterns of activity, 175–176
Crime perceptions, classification and examples of (figure), 11
Crime prevention
    activities and (table), 99
    approaches (table), 28
    assessing rehabilitation and, 309–310
    as cause of displacement, 108
    citizen/police partnership initiatives for, 209–227
    defining, 26
    diffusion and displacement outcomes and, 127
    diversity in, 315–316
    early efforts, 22–25
    evaluation and, 33–36
    evidence of effectiveness, 312–314
    future of, 311–316
    improving knowledge of, 314–315
    mass media and, 129–148, 135–148
    micro, meso, and macro levels of, 30
    model
        primary, 27–28
        secondary, 29
    model of effects of (figure), 58
    models, alternate and crime science, 29–31
    predictions of participation in programs for (table), 100
    research, 95
    secondary extension of group activities, 97
    situational, 29
    tertiary, 29
    uses of media in (figure), 136
Crime Prevention Coalition of America, 136
Crime Prevention Through Environmental Design (CPTED), 52–54, 70–73
Crime science, and prevention, 30–31
Crime Stoppers, 135, 143
Crimewatch U.K., 145
Criminal code, 213
Criminal justice system, as primary crime prevention, 27–28
Criminal sanctions, deterrent effect of, 274–279

Criminal Victimization (2008, figure), 7
Cross-sectional studies, on crime deterrence
    certainty of punishment, 154–155
    combine severity and certainty, 155
    defined, 152–153
    severity of sanctions, 153–154
CTSP. *See* Cognitive Thinking Skills
    Program

D.A.R.E., Drug Abuse Resistance Education,
    245–247
DART. Drug Abatement Response Team, 219
Data. *See* Evaluation
Data collection, UCR as system of, 5
Death penalty
    impact of, 153–154
    panel studies on deterrence of, 159–160
Death penalty, certainty as deterrent
    in cross-sectional studies, 154
    in longitudinal studies, 156–158
Defensible space, 52–54
    challenge to, 69–70
    elements of (table), 53
Delinquency, relationship between school
    and, 250–257
    IQ and delinquency, 252–253
    prevention of, programs for, 257–269
    school practices, 253–254
Demographics
    fear and, 14–15
    media, fear and, 135
    of neighborhood crime prevention
        participation, 97
    punishment impact and, 155
Design
    of neighborhoods, 67–69
    street layout and, 66
    See also Environmental design
Designing Out Crime Association (U.K.), 57
Deterrence, effect of criminal sanctions,
    274–279
    domestic violence, for, 277–279
    future implications, 290–291
Deterrence, general, 149–166
    celerity, 152
    certainty of, 152
    chronic and first-time offenders and, 155
    defined, 150–151
    legal sanctions, deterrent effect of,
        152–161
        longitudinal research, 156–159
        cross-sectional analyses, 153–156
        panel studies, 159–160

perceptions and, 161–166
requirements for, 151–152
severity of, 151
specific, 150
Deterring crime, 22
    diffusion and, 112
Detoxification, as treatment for drug abuse,
    242
Deviant behavior
    family risk factors for, 178–179
    mass media and, 132–134
    in schools, 251–252
    societal response to, 24
Diffusion, effects of crime, 126–127
Diffusion of benefits, of crime displacement,
    112–113
Discipline, harsh as offender risk factor, 178
Disorder, incivility, crime and, 73–74
Displacement, of crime. *See* Crime
    displacement
Distance, territorial displacement and, 122
Distance decay, 122
Diversity
    in crime prevention, recognizing,
        315–316
    in fear-victimization relationship, 14–15
Domestic violence
    deterrent effect of arrest for, 277–279
    electronic monitoring and, 288
    repeat victimization and, 186–187
Doors, as crime prevention, 65, 124
Dropout rate, drug use and, 233
Drug Abatement Response Team
    (DART), 219
Drug Abuse Reporting Program
    (DARP), 242
Drug Abuse Resistance Education (D.A.R.E)
    programs, 245–246, 263
Drug courts, as rehabilitation, 306–309
Drug Free Communities Support Program, 84
Drug Market Analysis Program
    (DMAP), 184
Drugs
    programs fighting abuse of, 84, 92, 99
    relationship between crime and, 230–231
    weed and seed programs and, 220–221
Drug use
    among offenders, 233–234
    crime connection, 235–238
    drug use, self-reported (table), 232
    education/information/knowledge
        programs, 244–245
    interventions and prevention, 238–248

law enforcement efforts against, 238–239

prevention programs, 243–248. *See also* Prevention, drug use

relationship between (figure), 235

scope of, crime and, 231–248

self-reported, 231–233

targeting, as tertiary crime prevention, 28, 29

Drug Use Forecasting (DUF), 234

"Drug war," 238

Drunk driving, deterrent sanctions for, 158, 165

Early identification of problem individuals, 28, 29

Ecological fallacy, 174

Economic Costs to Victims of Crime (table), 9

Edges, cognitive mapping and, 120

Education

on drug use, programs for, 244–247

public, as primary crime prevention, 27–28

Educational institutions, as hot spots for crime, 183

Education/information/knowledge programs, on drug abuse, 244–245

Ego defense, 251

Elderly

crimes and physical injuries to, 16

perceived risk and harm of crime, 15–16

Electronic monitoring (EM)

active, continuous signaling systems, 285

benefits of, 286

as Big Brother, 289

domestic violence offenders and, 288

estimate of use in Europe (table), 286

global positioning system (GPS), 285–286

incapacitation and, 284–290

juveniles and, 288

as labor-intensive, 289

passive system, 285

pretrial supervision and, 287–288

programmed system, 285

Electronic security

reduces motor vehicle theft, 204

tagging of merchandise, 205–206

Electronic theft, situational prevention and, 206

EM. *See* Electronic monitoring

Emotional response, fear as, 10

Emotions, 11

England, early policing in, 23–24

Entertainment programs on television, crime information and, 131

Entrepreneurial policing, 23

Environmental backcloth, crime patterns and, 118–121

Environmental design, as crime prevention, 52–77

access control, 55–56

activity support, motivation reinforcement, 56

defensible space, challenge to, 69–70

implementation of, 56–58

incivility, disorder, and crime, 73–74

intervening factors, effects of

alarms, 64

lighting, 58–60

property identification, 63–64

survivability, 60–63

neighborhood, 67–69

as primary crime prevention, 27–28

product design, 70–73

street layout, 66

surveillance, 55–56

Environmental management, 195

Escape, 61

Euclidean distance, 122

Evaluation, crime prevention

about, 33–36

cost-benefit analysis, 37–38

experimental design, 42–46

follow-up periods, 41

impact, 34–36

intervening factors, effects of

locks and doors, 65

street layout and design, 65–66

lighting, surveillance, 62–63

neighborhoods

official records of, 87–88

physical design of, 67–69

process, 36–37

property identification programs, 64

realistic, 46–47

summary, 42

theory and measurement in, 38–41

Evaluation(s)

aggregate-level, of rehabilitation, 297–298

alternative schools, 267

anti-bullying programs, 265

burglary, 89–90

child sexual assault, 207

citizen patrols, 92–93

cognitive mapping and, 119

collective incapacitation, 280–281

community anti-drug programs, 91–92

Evaluation(s)—*cont'd*
   on community programs, 222
   conflict resolution programs, 264
   crime on transit systems, 202–204
   crime prevention, 314–315
   Crime Stoppers, 144–145
   defined, 34
   drug and alcohol abuse, 231–233
   drug court programs, 308–309
   drug treatment programs, 242–243
   drug use among arrestees., 233–234
   drug use and crime, 236–238
   education systems, 251–252
   electronic monitoring, 287, 290
   elementary and high school delinquency
      programs, 260
   fear crime, neighborhood crime
      prevention and, 94–95
   gang suppression programs, 224–225
   Guardian Angels, 93
   incapacitation, 279–280
   individual-level, rehabilitation, 297–298
   issues in neighborhood crime prevention
      programs, 95–96
   methadone maintenance programs, 240–241
   motor vehicle theft, 204–205
   neighborhood crime prevention, 85–86
   Operation Ceasefire, 223
   outcome myopia and, 39
   parole outcome, recidivism and, 276–277
   preschool delinquency program, 258–259
   process, prevention programs, 36–37
   rehabilitation, outcome measures of,
      296–297
   rehabilitation programs, 295–296, 298–310
   resistance skills programs for drug use, 246
   restorative justice programs, 304–305
   revictimization, 206–207
   Safer Cities Programs, 90–91
   Taking a Bite Out of Crime, 137
   theft offenses, 205–206
   two crime prevention programs, 89–91
   weed and seed programs, 220–221
Event dependency explanations, 187
Experiential effect, 162, 163
Experimental design, as evaluation method,
   42–46
External validity
   problems for, 45–46
   threats to, 44

False negative predictions, 170–172
   clinical, 172–173

False positive predictions, 170–172
   risk factors and, 181
False prediction, 171–172
Family factors, in risk of deviant behavior,
   178–179
Family-Group Conferencing (FGC), 303
Fare evasion, on public transport, 202–203
Fear of crime
   about, 9–18
   benefits of, 18
   common questions about (figure), 12
   crime and, 13–14
   defining, 10
   demographics and, 14–15
   discovery of, 10
   disorder and, 74
   factors influencing levels of, 17
   findings of study, explain divergent, 15–16
   group participation in prevention, 97
   incivility and, 16–17
   level of, 12–13
   measuring, 10–12
   media cause of?, 134–135
   methodological factors, 17
   neighborhood crime prevention and, 93–95
   neighborhood design, 67
   past victimization and, 14
   reduced via community programs, 222
   in schools, 254–256
   summary, 18–19
   vicarious victimization, 15–16
   worry about crime, (table), 13
Fearing subject, 18
Fear of Crime in America Survey, 12
Federal Bureau of Investigation, *Uniform
   Crime Reports*, 2–5
Feeble-minded, 252
FGC. *See* Family-Group Conferencing
Fictional television programs, crime
   information and, 131
Figgie International, 94
Figure
   Change in Property Crime Rate, 4
   Change in Violent Crime Rate, 4
   Classification and Examples of Crime
      Perceptions, 11
   Common "Fear" Questions, 12
   Crime Stoppers Facts and Figures, 2009
      (table), 143
   Criminal Victimization, 7
   Current McGruff Campaigns, 137
   Example of a City with a Geographically
      Bounded Neighborhood, 109

G.R.E.A.T. Middle School Curriculum, 263–264

Greenwood's Selective Incapacitation Prediction Scale, 283

Intersection of Domains for Crime Prevention Efficiency, 190

Model of Crime Prevention Effects, 58

Neighborhood-Based Crime Prevention Conceptual Framework, 81

NIDA's 13 Principles of Effective Prevention for Drug Abuse, 243–244

NIDA's 13 Principles of Effective Treatment of Drug Abuse, 240

Possible Relationships Between Drug Use and Crime, 235

A Problem-Solving Process, 216

Simplified View of a Multinuclei Community with Nodes and Paths, 120

Uses of Media/Publicity in Crime Prevention, 136

Flag explanation, 187

Follow-up periods, in evaluation measurement, 41

Fordbridge RBI project, evaluation of, 68

Functional displacement, of crime, 108, 125

Functional fear, 18

Functional surveillance, 61

Gallup poll, 14

Gang Resistance Education and Training (G.R.E.A.T.), 263–264

Gangs, drug use and sales, 239

Gang suppression programs, 224–225

Gatekeepers, police as, 3

Gender
crime deterrence and, 155
crime prevention attitudes and, 138

General deterrence, as primary crime prevention, 27–28, 150–166. *See also* Deterrence, general

Generalizability, of evaluation results, 44

General Social Survey, 12

Geographical crime. *See* Territorial displacement

Global positioning system (GPS), 285–286

"Gold standard" of evaluation methods, 43

Google Maps, 120–121

Google Maps Streetview, 120–121

"GOSSlink," 285

GPS. *See* Global positioning system

Graffiti, reducing, 203

G.R.E.A.T., Gang Resistance and Education Training, 263–264

Guardian Angels
evaluation of, 93
website of, 84

Guardians, of targets, 115

Guardianship, lack of, targets of crime and, 115

Gun Violence, 222–223

Handlers, of offenders, 115

Harris Poll, 12

Head Start program, 258

Hedonistic offenders, 151

Helmet laws, reduce motorcycle theft, 204

Here's Looking At You (HLAY), alcohol education, 246

Highwayman Act, 23

Home confinement, electronic monitoring and, 284–290

Homicide
as systemic factor of drug trade, 236
in schools, 255

Homicide rate
death penalty and, 157, 159–160
on television versus real life, 132

Hot products, 70, 114, 184

Hot spots for crime
analysis of, 215
defined, 183
predicting, 182–184

Hue and cry, 23

Hunting ground, node as a, 120

Identification and prediction, as secondary crime prevention, 28, 29

Identity theft, situational prevention and, 206

Image, defensible space and, 53

Immobilizers, electronic of vehicles, 204

Impact, direct, of physical design features, 57–66

Impact evaluation, of crime prevention, 34–36

Implementation, of environmental design, 56–58

Imprisonment. *See* Incarceration

Incapacitation, as tertiary crime prevention, 28, 279–290
collective, of imprisonment, 280–282
defined, 274
electronic monitoring and, 284–290
future implications, 290–291
level of change needed in imprisonment (table), 282
selective, of imprisonment, 282–284

Incarceration
  as deterrence for crime, 274–279
  reducing overcrowding, 288
  studies of imprisonment, 275–277
Incivility
  disorder, crime and, 73–74
  victimization and, 16–17
Individual-level evaluations, of rehabilitation, 297–298
Inelastic, crime as, 108
Inertia, weight and portability of item, 184
Information lines, media and, 143–145
Integrated Multi-Phasic Program Assessment and Comprehensive Treatment (IMPACT) program, 241
Intensive Supervision Probation
  defined, 298
  evaluations of, 300–301
Intensive supervision programs (ISP), 300–301
Internal validity
  defined, 42
  selected threats to (table), 43
International CPTED Association, 57
International Crime Victim Survey, 185–186
Internet, pedophiles and, 207
Intervening factors
  crime prevention and, 58–66. *See also* Crime prevention
  drug use, 238–248
  law enforcement efforts, 238–239
  lighting, 59–60
  Multi-Systemic Therapy (MST) as a, 299
  for schools. *See* Schools, crime prevention and treatment of users, 239–243
Interventions. *See* Crime prevention; Evaluation(s)
IQ, delinquency and, 252–253
ISP. *See* Intensive supervision programs

Journey to crime, 122
Judgments, of risks, 11
Jurisdictional boundaries, death penalty and, 153–154
"Just Say No" campaign against drug abuse, 245–246
Juvenile(s)
  adolescence-limited risk factors, 181–182
  conviction, as prediction of adult behavior, 176
  deterrence and, 155
  deterrent sanctions, 165

electronic monitoring of offending, 288
  lowered self-esteem and, 251
  perceived certainty of punishment, as deterrent, 162
  restorative justice in New Zealand, 303
  schools, crime, behavior and, 250–257
Juvenile court
  as early crime prevention approach, 24
  identifying at-risk youth and, 177–178

KEY program, prison-based drug abuse program, 241
Kirkholt Burglary Prevention project, 89–91, 188
  evaluation of burglary in, 89–90
  revictimization study and, 206–207
  target displacement and, 124
  territorial displacement and, 123

Learning disabilities, as risk factor, 180
Lex talionis, 22
Life-course persistent, risk factors, 181
Life Skills Training (LST), 245
Lifestyle perspective, 194
Lighting
  crime diffusion and, 126–127
  as crime prevention tool, 59–60
  temporal displacement and, 123–124
Locks, as crime prevention, 65
Long-distance telephone service, as target of theft, 206
Longitudinal analyses, on crime deterrence, 152–153, 156–159
  certainty of apprehension, 158–159
  drunk driving, 158
  severity of sanctions, 156–158

Macro-level crime prevention, 30
Malign displacement, 111–112
Managers, of places, 115
Manhattan distance, 122
Maori tribe, of New Zealand, restorative justice among, 303
Marijuana use, perceived severity and, 164
Maryland Scale of Scientific Methods, 43, 44 (table)
Mass media, crime prevention and, 129–148
  cause of crime and fear?, 132–135
  crime newsletters, 140–143
  crime prevention activities, 135–148
  crime-time television, 145–146
  information lines, 143–145
  level of reported crime, 130–131

McGruff campaign, 135–139
media accounts and actual crime, 131–132
other campaigns against crime, 139–140
potential for bias in court cases, 145
publicity and, 146–147
responsibility for, 147–148
McGruff campaign against crime, 135,
    136–139
current campaigns (figure), 137
evaluations of, 137–139
Measurement
measurement issues, 40–41
theory in evaluation, 38–41
two examples of crime prevention
    programs, 89–91
Measures
of crime, *Uniform Crime Reports* (UCR),
    2–5
of diffusion, 126
of fear, 10–12, 17
of victimization, 6–7, 88–89
See also Evaluation
Mechanism of evaluation, 47
Media
and crime. *See* Mass media, crime
    prevention and
as influence on fear of crime, 17
Merchant Police of England, 23
Meso-level crime prevention, 30
Meta-analysis, 267
Methadone maintenance, of opiate addicts,
    240–241
Metropolitan Police Act, 23–24
Micro-level crime prevention, 30
Milieu, defensible space and, 53
Military, as early police force, 22
Minneapolis Domestic Violence Experiment,
    277–278
Misdeeds and Security framework, 71
Mobility
as factor in crime displacement, 108–109
increased of population, 114
Monetary loss through crime, measures of,
    8–9
Monitoring the Future (MTF) Project, 231
Moral code, offenders and, 197
Motivation reinforcement, environmental
    design and, 56
Motorcycle theft, reducing, 204
Motor vehicle theft, evaluation of, 204–205
See also Vehicle theft
Multi-Systemic Therapy (MST), as
    community-based intervention, 299

Narcotics Anonymous, 242
National Academy of Sciences, 295
National Crime Prevention Council
    (NCPC), 136
National Crime Victimization Survey
    (NCVS), 6–7, 12, 185–186
impact of crime, 8–9
National Institute of Crime Prevention's
    CPTED Training (web site), 57
National Institute of Justice, 234
National Institute on Drug Abuse (NIDA),
    239–240
National Night Out, crime prevention
    program, 85
National Opinion Survey on Criminal
    Justice, 12
National Survey on Drug Use and
    Health, 231
National Youth Survey (NYS), 237
Natural surveillance, defensible space and, 53
NCVS. *See* National Crime Victimization
    Survey
Near-repeat, 189
Neighborhood(s)
defining for evaluation, 95
incivility and, 73
physical design of, 67–69
poor integration of, as risk factor, 179
Neighborhood crime prevention, 79–103
anti-drug programs, 84, 91–92
citizen participation and support, 96–99
citizen patrols, 84–85, 92–93
community cohesion, effects on, 86–87
conceptual framework for (figure), 81
cooperative participation (table), 83
effects on crime
    official records, 87–88
    victimization measures, 88–89
evaluation of, 85–86
evaluation issues in, 95–96
examples, 89–91
fear of crime and, 93–95
neighborhood/block watch, 82–84
organizing, 99–102
    problems with, 101–102
police-community involvement, 85
problems organizing watch groups
    (table), 101
summary of evidence on (table), 103
Neighborhood designs, access control and, 55
Neighborhood impact evaluations of crime
    prevention and, 35
Neighborhood incivility, fear and, 16–17

Neighborhood watch
   community policing and, 211–213
   as primary crime prevention, 27–28, 41,
      82–84
   problems organizing, 101
Netherlands, The, functional surveillance
   in, 61
Net-widening, effect of electronic
   monitoring, 287
Neurotransmitters, as biological factor, 180
New Jersey Intensive Supervision
   Program, 300
New Jersey State Parole Board (NJPB), 288
Newsletters, on crime, 140–143
   content areas (table), 141
New York Times, The, 147
Nodes, of activity in communities, 119
Northwest Neighborhood Federation, of
   Chicago, 89, 94

Obligatory action, by citizens, 23
Observations, predictions based on
   limited, 173
Offenders
   career specialization of, 175–176
   clinical predictions and, 172–173
   cognitive mapping and, 118–121
   drug testing of arrestees, 234
   drug use among, 233–234
   electronic monitoring and, 290
   juveniles, risk factors and, 176–182
   knowledge of legal statutes, 161
   lifestyle of, 194
   moral codes of, 197
   predicting future, 169–172
   repeat victimization and, 187
Office of Juvenile Justice and Delinquency
   Prevention (OJJDP), 224–225
Operation Ceasefire, 222–223
Operation Cul-de-Sac, of Los Angeles, 66
Operation Identification, 63–64, 83, 124
Operation Pressure Point, New York City, 239
Opportunity cues, for burglars, 117
Order-maintenance functions, police provide,
   210–211
OTREP, intermediate goals of (table), 54
Outcome evaluation, of crime prevention,
   34–36
Outcome intensity, 91
Outcome measures, of rehabilitation, 296–297
Outpatient drug-free programs, 242
Overt behavior, 181
Overview, of this book, 48

Panel design, 159
Panel studies, 159–160
Panel survey, 6
Parens patriae, 24–25
Parental supervision, poor, as risk factor for
   offending, 178
Paris, France, early policing in, 24
Parochial control, 102
Parochial police, 23
Parole outcome, recidivism and, 275–277
Part I Crimes, 3, 66, 155
Part II Crimes, 3
Partnership initiative, for crime prevention,
   209–225
   about, 209–210
   CCP, SACSI, PSN, 221–222
   community base, 214
   community involvement, 213
   community policing, 210–211
   crime and disorder partnership, 223–224
   defining community policing, 211–213
   efforts and assessment, 217–218
      civil abatement, 218–220
      community policing, 217–218
   gang suppression programs, 224–225
   gun violence, 222–223
   precursors to community policing, 211
   problem identification, 215–216
   problems and concerns, 225
   problem solving, 213–214
   redefined goals, 214
   successful partnerships, 225–226
      features of (table), 225
   weed and seed programs, 220–221
Passive electronic monitoring system, 285
Passive system, 285–286
PATHS. *See* Promoting Alternative Thinking
   Strategies
Paths, transit routes in communities, 119
Patterns, of crime. *See* Crime pattern theory
Pedophiles, the Internet and, 207
Peel, Sir Robert, 23–24
Peer factors, in deviant behavior, 179
Peer mediation, 261
Perceived incivilities, 74
Perception
   combined deterrent factors, 164–166
   of disorder, 74
   level of in crime, 11
   perceived certainty, 162–163
   perceived severity, 164
Permissibility, situational prevention and, 198
Perpetrator displacement, 108

Perry Preschool (High/Scope) program, 258–259

Personal crimes, territorial displacement and, 122

Personal identification numbers (PINs), as anti-theft aids, 206

Personality risk factors, of deviant behavior, 180

Physical and social signs, of disorder, 73–74

Physical attacks, in schools, 255–256

Physical design, impact of, 57–66
    summary of evidence of (table), 75
    See also Environmental design

Physical edges, cognitive mapping and, 120

Physical injury, measuring in crime, 15–16

Pittsburgh Youth Study, 181–182

Plea bargaining, 161

Police
    accessing impact of action of, 158–159
    community involvement in crime prevention, 85
    as community managers, 167, 214
    cooperative crime prevention, 209–227
    decentralization of in community policing, 214
    efforts against drug use, 238–239
    as gatekeepers, 3
    order-maintenance functions of, 210–211
    role of in community, 210

Policing
    by citizens, in early England, 23–24
    early attempts at formal, 23–25
    problem oriented, 213–214

Pornography, violence and, 133

Predicting future offending
    actuarial predictions, 173–175
    biological risk factors, 180–181
    Clarke's 12 techniques, 195–197
    clinical prediction, 172–173
    community influences, on behavior, 179–180
    criminal career research, 175–176
    expanding typology, 197–199
    family factors, 178–179
    hot spots for crime, 182–184
    implications for, 190
    peer factors, 179
    places and events, 182–184
    process of situational prevention, 194–195
    psychological/personality factors, 180
    repeat victimization, 184–189
    risk factors and, 176–178
    risk factors as predictors, 181–182

Predicting future offending, 169–172
    degree of accuracy in, 170
    potential outcomes of (table), 170
    variables, 170

Prediction
    cognitive mapping and, 119
    crime prevention and, 190
    problems, drug use as means of, 230–231

Pre-payment meters, removal of, 206–207

Preschool programs, for delinquency prevention, 257–258

President's Commission on Law Enforcement and Administration of Justice, 6–7, 10, 258

Pressures, situational prevention and, 198

Prevention
    of bullying in schools, 265
    of delinquency, 257–269
    primary, 50–166. *See also* Primary Prevention
    shift to situational, 313

Prevention of drug use, 238–248
    education/information/knowledge programs, 244–245
    effective prevention for (figure), 243–244
    law enforcement efforts, 238–239
    resistance skills training, 245–246
    summary of programs, 246–247
    treatment of users, 239–243

Primary crime prevention
    defined, 27–28
    displacement and diffusion, 105–127
    general deterrence, 149–166
    mass media and, 129–148
    neighborhood crime and, 79–103
    physical environment and crime, 51–77
    environmental design, 52–54

Prison. *See* Incarceration

Private control, 102

Private security, as primary crime prevention, 27–28

Problem-oriented policing, 213–214

Problem solving
    community policing and, 213
    Comprehensive Communities Programs, 221–222
    process (figure), 216
    SARA four-step process for, 215
    in school environment, 260–261
    school programs for, 262–263

Process evaluation, of crime prevention, 36–37

Product design, crime prevention and, 70–73, 114

Products, and misdeeds (table), 71
Programmed contact system, of electronic
     monitoring, 285
Project PATHE (Positive Action Through
     Holistic Education), 259–260
Project Safe Neighborhoods (PSN), 221–222
Promoting Alternative Thinking Strategies
     (PATHS), 262
Prompts, situational prevention and, 198
Property crime rate, change in (figure), 4
Property Identification Programs, 63–64
Property offenses, territorial displacement
     and, 122
Prospect, 60–61
Prospective mapping, 183
Provocation, situational prevention and, 198
PSN. *See* Project Safe Neighborhoods
Psychological risk factors, of deviant
     behavior, 180
Psychopharmacological reaction, of drugs,
     crime and, 236
Public control, 102
Public education, as primary crime
     prevention, 27–28
Publicity
     in crime prevention, (figure), 136
     mass media, crime prevention and,
          146–147
Public service announcements, exposure to
     crime prevention, 138
Public transportation, as target of offenses,
     202–204
Pulling levers, 223
Punishment, for crime, 151
     deterrent effect of, 274–279
     See also Deterrence, general

Race
     crime rates, deterrence and, 154
     as factor in crime displacement, 108
     fear and, 14–15
Radio Watch, crime prevention program, 85
Randomized control trial, 42, 44
Rational choice theory
     crime displacement and, 109, 116–118
     theoretical basis of, 193–194
RCCP. *See* Resolving Conflict Creatively
     Program
Realistic evaluation, 46–47
Reality television programs, crime
     information and, 131, 135, 145
Recidivism
     criminal sanctions and, 275–277

definitions of, 297
     outcome measures of, 296–297
     rate, intensive supervision and, 300–301
     sanctions, positive impact on treatment
          and, 296
Recidivistic activity, predicting, 169
Reciprocal relationship of crime and drugs,
     235–238
Recognition, cognitive mapping and,
     118–119
Reducing Burglary Initiative (RBI) of the
     U.K., 68, 88, 147
     target displacement and, 124–125
Reducing Conflict Creatively Program,
     (RCCP), 262–
Refuge, 60–61
Rehabilitation, as tertiary prevention
     assessing, crime prevention and, 309–310
     drug courts, 306–309
     evaluation, levels of, 297–298
     evaluation of programs for, 298–310
     intensive supervision, 300–301
     outcome measures, 296–297
     outcomes of treatment, 296
     restorative justice, 301–305
     subsequent analyses, 295–296
     treatment and, 28
     what works?, 294
Repeat victimization
     about, 184–189, 206–207
     effective and ineffective factors for repeat
          (table), 188
     explanations for, 187
     reduce crime by targeting, 188–189
     time frame for (table), 186
     typology of (table), 185
     virtual repeats, 189
Resistance skills training, drug abuse
     and, 245
Resolving Conflict Creatively Program
     (RCCP), 262
Responding in Peaceful and Positive Ways
     (RIPP), 262
Response generalization, 146
Responses, in problem solving, 216
Restitution, as form of restorative justice, 304
Restorative justice, as intervention, 301–305
     Circle Sentencing, 303–304
     Family-Group Conferencing (FGC), 303
     impact of, 304–305
     restitution as, 304
     Victim-Offender Mediation (VOM),
          302–303

Revictimization, situational crime prevention
and, 206–207
RIPP. *See* Responding in Peaceful and
Positive Ways
Risk
judgments of, 11
need, and response, evaluation of,
296–306
Risk, perceived
harm and, 15–16
neighborhood incivility and, 16–17
Risk factors, prediction and, 176–178
biological, 180–181
common factors found in research (table),
177–178
community factors, 179–180
family factors, 178–179
psychological/personality, 180
using as predictors, 181–182
Risk heterogeneity, 187
Rochester Youth Study, 179
Roman, Charles, 24
Roman Empire, early crime deterrence
and, 22
Routine activities perspective
crime displacement and, 114–115, 193
triangle (figure), 115

SACSI. *See* Strategic Approaches to
Community Safety Initiative
Safe and Drug Free Schools program,
267–269, 269
Safer Cities Program, 89–91, 90–91, 94
territorial displacement and, 123
Safe Schools/Healthy Children,
267–269, 269
Salient factor score
about, 173
example of items in (table), 174
SAMHSA. *See* Substance Abuse and Mental
Health Services Administration
Sanctions, deterrent effect of criminal,
274–279
SARA, four-step process for problem
solving, 215
Scanning, to identify problems, 215
School(s)
combined deterrence factors in, 164–166
as community factor in risk, 180
crime prevention and, 250–270
altering teaching and assessment,
265–266
alternative schools, 266–267

anti-bullying efforts, 265
conflict management/resolution,
261–264
delinquency prevention programs in,
257–269
educational factors, delinquency and,
252–254
fear, avoidance, carrying weapons, 255
future of programs for, 269–270
impact of school/education programs
(table), 270
other interventions, 267–269
school atmosphere, 259–260
theoretical views, 249–252
victimization and fear, 254–256
by selected characteristics
(table), 255
students miss school due to
(table), 255
crime prevention and, as secondary crime
prevention, 28, 29
drop out rate, drug use and, 233
importance of in developing behavior,
250–251
Seattle Community Crime Prevention
Program, 88–89
Seattle Law Planning Office, 65
Seattle Social Development Project, 266
Secondary crime prevention, 29
citizen/police partnerships for, 209–227
drugs, crime, and crime prevention,
229–248
prediction for, 168–190
school and, 249–270 *See also* Schools,
crime prevention in
situational, 191–207
Secured by Design (SBD), 57 (table), 69
Security guards, 61
Selective incapacitation
defined, 279
Greenwood's prediction scale
(figure), 283
of imprisonment, 282–284
Self-esteem, lowering in juveniles, 251
Severity, in punishment for crime
cross-sectional studies, 153–154,
155–156
death penalty across jurisdictions,
153–154
longitudinal research and, 156–158
Severity, perceived, 164
Shoplifting CCTV as deterrent to, 62
Silent alarms, crime prevention and, 64

Situational crime prevention
   child sexual assault, studies on, 207
   defined, 29, 192
   expanding typologies, 197–200
   growth of, 192
   issues and concerns with, 200–202
   misconceptions about (table), 201
   motor vehicle theft, studies of crime
      against, 204–205
   process of, 194–195
   revictimization, studies on, 206–207
   as secondary crime prevention, 28, 29
   theft offenses, studies on, 205–206
   theoretical basis, 193–194
   transit systems, studies of crimes against,
      202–204
   twenty-five techniques of (table), 199
Situational typologies, 195
Smart guns, 72
SMART teams, for civil abatement, 219
Social context, of process evaluations of
   crime prevention programs, 36
Social/crime template, 118–121
Social prevention, of crime. *See* Primary
   crime prevention
Society, problem of crime in
   measures of crime, 2–5
   victimization, measuring, 6–7
Socioeconomic status
   crime prevention attitudes and, 138
   education value and, 251
   fear of crime and, 14–15
   influence on deviant behavior and, 179
   school and, 253
Soft determinism, 116
South Asylum Hill, Hartford, Connecticut, 67
Spatial and Temporal Analysis of Crime
   (STAC) program, 184
Spatial displacement, of crime, 107
   cognitive maps and, 118–121
Specialization, in criminal career,
   175–176
Specialized Multi-Agency Response Team
   (SMART), 219
Specific deterrence
   criminal sanctions, 274–290. *See also*
      Deterrence, effect of
   defined, 150, 274
   as tertiary crime prevention, 28
Spurious, drug/crime connection, 235–236
Statutes, offender knowledge of, 161
Status offenses, 24–25
Statutes of Winchester, 23

Strategic Approaches to Community Safety
   Initiative (SACAI), 36, 221–222
Streetblock, 95–96
Street layout and design, crime prevention
   and, 65–66
Studies. *See* Evaluation(s)
Substance Abuse and Mental Health Services
   Administration (SAMHSA), 231–233
Substance abuse prevention and treatment, as
   secondary crime prevention, 28, 29
Suicide rate, mass media and, 133
Surveillability, as intervening factor, 60–63, 195
Surveillance
   cameras reduce motor vehicle theft, 204
   citizen patrols and, 92–
   closed-circuit television, intervening
      factor, 61–63, 201
   in early policing, 24
   environmental design and, 55–56
   impact of on levels of crime and fear, 96
   neighborhood watches and, 82–84
   temporal displacement and, 124
   vandalism, factor in reducing, 203
Surveys, as measures of victimization, 6–7.
   See also Evaluation
Swiftness, in punishment for crime, 152
Systemic violence, drug use and crime, 236

Tables
   Changes Made at Manufacture to Cars
      and Crimes Prevented, 72
   Clarke's 1992 Situational Prevention
      Techniques, 196
   Common Risk Factors Found in Research,
      177–178
   Cooperative Neighborhood Crime
      Prevention Participation, 83
   The CRAVED Model for Targets of
      Theft, 114
   Crime Prevention Approaches, 28
   Crime Prevention Domains and
      Activities, 99
   Definitions of Community Policing, 212
   Economic Costs to Victims of Crime, 9
   Effective and Ineffective Factors for
      Preventing Repeat Victimization, 188
   Elements of Cognitive Mapping, 119
   Elements of Defensible Space, 53
   Estimates of EM Use in Europe, 286
   Example of Salient Factor Score Items, 174
   Features of Successful Partnerships, 225
   Forms of Displacement, 107
   Intermediate Goals of CPTED, 54

Level of Change Needed in Imprisonment Necessary for Incapacitation, 282

Lifetime, Past Year, and Last 30 Days Drug Use, 232

Maryland Scale of Scientific Methods, 44

Newsletter Content Areas, 141

Potential Outcomes of Prediction, 170

Predictions of Participation in Different Crime Prevention Domains, 100

Problematic Assumptions Underlying Neighborhood Watch, 101

products and misdeeds, 71

Respondents Who Frequently Worry ... Victimization, 13

Secured by Design Core Principles, 57

Selected Threats to Internal Validity, 43

Seven Misconceptions of Situational Crime Prevention, 201

Students Avoiding School or Activities Due to Fear of Attack or Harm, 255

Student Victimization at School by Selected Characteristics, 255

Summary of the Evidence of Physical Design Impact on Crimes, 75

Summary of the Evidence of School/ Education Programs on Crimes, 270

Summary of the Evidence on Neighborhood Prevention Programs, 103

Teacher Reports of Victimization at School, 256

Ten Principles of Opportunity and Crime, 113

Threats to External Validity, 45

Time Frame for Repeat Victimization, 186

Twenty-Five Techniques of Situational Prevention, 199

Typology of Repeat Victimization, 185

Tactical displacement, of crime, 107, 124

Taking A Bite Out of Crime Campaign Evaluation, 12, 137–139

Target displacement, of crime, 107, 124–125

Target hardening
about, 55
as intervening factor, 195

Tautological presentation, 296

Television
crime information and, 131
See also Mass media

Temporal displacement of crime, 107, 123–124

Territorial displacement of crime, 107, 122

Territoriality, defensible space and, 53

Tertiary crime prevention
about, 29

defined, 271
rehabilitation as, 293–310
specific deterrence and incapacitation, 273–290

Theft offenses, evaluation of, 205–206

Theoretical views, of delinquent behavior and schools, 249–252

Theory
crime pattern, 118–121
measurements and in evaluation, 38–40
rational choice, 116–118
routine activities, 114–115
theoretical concerns, 38–40

Therapeutic communities, drug rehabilitation and, 241

Thief takers, 23

Threats to external validity, 44, 45 (table)

Three-strikes laws, 281–282

TimeZup, 222

Top Cops, 131, 145

Tourist attractions, as hot spots for crime, 183

Tracking, student needs, 253

Transit routes, between nodes, 119–120

Transit systems, studies on crimes against, 202–204

Treatment, of drug abuse, 239–243
detoxification, 242
effective treatment (figure), 240
focus of rehabilitation and, 296
forced in courts, 307–308
maintenance programs, 240–241
outpatient drug-free programs, 242
therapeutic communities, 241

Truancy reduction programs, 268

Typologies, expanding, 197–202

Uniform Crime Reports (UCR), 2–6
impact of crime, 8–9
problems with, 5

Union Avenue Corridor (UAC), of Portland, Oregon, 68

United Kingdom
ally gating in, 66
closed-circuit television in, 61–63
Crime Stoppers in, 144
data on fear from, 13
electronic monitoring data, 287
examples of community crime prevention programs, 89–91
impact of lighting, studies on, 59–60
property identification in, 64
Reducing Burglary Initiative of, 68

United States, early policing in, 24

Unsolved Mysteries, 145
U.S. Department of Education, 267–268, 268
U.S. Department of Justice, 254–255
U.S. Parole Commission's Salient Factor
    Score, 173

Vagrancy, reducing, 204
Value, of item, 184
Values, 11
Vandalism, reducing, 203
Variables, used in predicting future behavior,
    170–172
Vehicle identification tags, as theft
    prevention, 64
Vehicle theft
    prevention and, 72–73
    studies on, 204–205
    temporal displacement and, 124
Vicarious victimization, 15–16
Victimization
    about, 6–7
    costs of, 8–9
    incivility and, 16–17
    measures, effects of on crime, 88–89
    past, fear of crime and, 14
    rates of, 6
    repeat, 184–189
    surveys on, 6–7
    vicarious, 15–16
Victimization, fear and
    about, 16
    school, 254–256
    students avoiding school due to
        (table), 255
    student victimization at school (table)., 255
    teacher reports of at school (table), 256
Victim-Offender Mediation (VOM), as
    restorative justice, 302–303

Victim-Offender Reconciliation Programs
    (VORP), 302–303
Victim Risk Supplement (VRS), to National
    Crime Survey, 98
Victims
    of crime, fear and, 11
    lifestyle of, 194
Victim survey data
    impact of lighting, 59
    in measurement, 40–41, 68
Vigilante movement, 23
Violence, on television, crime and, 133
Violent crime, overrepresented in news
    media, 131
Violent Crime Control and Law Enforcement
    Act of 1994, 306
Violent crime rate, change in (figure), 4
Virtual repeats, 189
Visible, to offenders, 184
VIVA (Value, Inertia, Visibility and
    Accessibility), 184
Vocational education, 253–254
Voluntary bounty hunters, 23
VOM. *See* Victim-Offender Mediation
VORP. *See* Victim-Offender Reconciliation
    Programs

Watch and ward, 23, 24
Weapons, in school, as response to fear, 255
Weed and seed programs, 220–221
Whistle Stop, crime prevention program, 85
White House Office of National Drug
    Control Policy, Drug Free Communities
    Support Program, 84
Women, perceived risk and harm of crime,
    15–16

Youth in Transition project, 236–237